The Theory of Japan's National Polity and Pure Socialism

IKKI KITA

THE
THEORY OF
**JAPAN'S
NATIONAL
POLITY** AND

**PURE
SOCIALISM**

ANTELOPE HILL PUBLISHING

Translation Copyright © 2025 Antelope Hill Publishing.

The Theory of Japan's National Polity and Pure Socialism is a translation of 国体論及び純正社会主義, written and published in Japanese by 有斐閣, 1906.

All rights reserved.

First edition, first printing 2025.

Translated by J.S.

Cover art by Swifty.

Edited by Harko Sked.

Layout by Louis Condé.

Antelope Hill Publishing | antelopehillpublishing.com

Paperback ISBN-13: 979-8-89252-044-7

EPUB ISBN-13: 979-8-89252-045-4

Contents

Translator's Foreword ix

Author's Foreword xv

Volume 1: The Economic Justice of Socialism 1

    Chapter 1 1

    Chapter 2 21

    Chapter 3 49

Volume 2: The Ethical Ideal of Socialism 111

    Chapter 4 113

Volume 3: The Theory of Biological Evolution and Social Philosophy 155

    Chapter 5 157

    Chapter 6 203

    Chapter 7 231

    Chapter 8 269

Volume 4: The So-Called Theory of Japan's National Polity and Its Restorative Principle of Revolution 321

    Chapter 9 323

    Chapter 10 393

    Chapter 11 425

    Chapter 12 483

    Chapter 13 521

    Chapter 14 565

Volume 5: The Enlightenment Movement of Socialism 611

    Chapter 15 613

    Chapter 16 665

TRANSLATOR'S FOREWORD

Ikki Kita, real name Terujiro Kita, is often cited as a major influence in many current and historical Japanese ideologies, and his writings touched on a wide variety of different concepts and ideas ranging from politics to religion, egalitarianism, human rights, and other philosophical topics. This book is dedicated to his ideas around the Japanese theory of national polity of his time, but some of the ideas expressed here can be used to gain some insight, though partial and flawed, into his character and personal philosophy.

Indeed, *The Theory of Japan's National Polity and Pure Socialism* paints a picture of a man who had a nuanced understanding of not just his own nation, but a firm grasp on the inner goings-on in other nations as well. Especially considering the era in which he wrote this book, it is impressive just how educated he was on other nations. To that end, his ideas appear based on natural laws and science, rather than holding up or looking down on any particular nation.

First, his basic foundation seems based around the idea that natural laws are fundamental and lack any sort of errors or inefficiency.

Not only is he quoted several times in the book itself as saying a phrase similar to this, but many of his other ideas around biology, evolution, the theory of evolution itself, social evolution, and all those things seem to be formed around the concept of natural laws lacking any sort of error or inefficiency. In other words, if one thing happens now, everything before it was necessary in order for that to occur. One cannot skip any one step in a series, because natural laws deemed it necessary for that series of events to occur in order to lead up to the current climax. Perhaps "flawless" is not the best descriptor, because he doesn't go quite that far, but Kita certainly does seem to think that there's no waste or errors in natural laws, and if a long period of political turmoil occurs before a result, it was necessary in order to achieve that result due to the natural law of evolution. That theme seems to run through Kita's writing, though he is loathe to say that in such an explicit fashion.

Secondly, he did not like many of the academics of the time, especially his Japanese contemporaries.

Though he tries to be civil (perhaps only because he wants an open debate with these people), it becomes very clear throughout the book that he doesn't hold much respect for many of the lecturers and professors at Japanese universities of the time. He designates Kanai and Tajima to receive the brunt of his verbal blows, but any time he brings up university professors in a general sense, it's usually about what he considers that "academic" or "podium" socialism. It's surprising how blunt he is about it, especially for a Japanese person—the Japanese generally hate upsetting the status quo, which is both true back then and today.

It makes sense, considering the general consensus among academics of the time toward socialism was quite negative, and when he saw them using strawman arguments and not addressing what he considered genuine socialism, he was understandably upset. In contrast to this, he seems to treat most scientists with at least a modicum of respect. Perhaps this is untrue, but he seems to consider many scientists as one of the driving forces behind social evolution. Kita spends a chapter talking about how humans still needing to satisfy basic biological functions before engaging in the world of thoughts and ideas, and he seems to imply that breakthroughs in science could help us in evolving past these things.

Thirdly, he didn't have a high opinion on state socialism (or any other offshoot of socialism) at the time he wrote this book.

It is surprising how Kita expresses a fairly negative opinion on state socialism. Even the original Japanese translator noted it in one of the annotations, but how this ties into his later actions and views is fascinating.

Indeed, it appears he strongly disagreed with many of the top academics regarding state socialism, rather than the base premises of state socialism itself. This does make some sense, as some of the most (in Kita's mind) absurd criticism toward pure socialism came from Tajima and Kanai's critiques of socialism—especially the latter, who Kita seems to consider almost an enemy of socialism. Kita is very focused on breaking down the difference between state socialism (or the arguments of state socialists), and comparing it to his own "pure" brand of socialism and its arguments. Although it does seem like he isn't particularly keen on state socialism throughout this book, it more so appears that he doesn't want the views of many prominent state socialists of his time being conflated or interfering with his own views on pure socialism, rather than just an outright distaste for state socialism entirely.

Fourthly, he believes that humanity will eventually evolve into "godlike beings."

This point will likely seem particularly jarring to Western readers: that we will evolve past biological needs to eat, defecate, or perform most basic bodily functions. "Gods" (kami, 神) in Japanese are very different from what one would think of as "God" in monotheistic religions like Christianity. They bear more similarity to ancient Greek deities, though even then they are not quite identical. They can be a representation of concepts or elements, like greed or fire, or they can merely be humanoids to whom some of the laws of nature don't apply. Kita believes that humanity will eventually, through continued evolution, evolve into higher, self-sufficient beings, but not divine gods like one might think of them in the West.

Finally, despite what some modern academics might say, Kita appears ashamed of lingering ancient Japanese practices

This primarily refers to old Japanese religion where animals (tanuki, for example, come up a lot) or objects were worshiped. He mentions "barbaric" or "savage" people of the Orient many times, and this is unlikely to be him feigning humility for the sake of widening the appeal of his writing. No, his critique appears to stem from genuine belief, which stands out because contemporary sources paint Kita as something of a xenophobic Japanese nationalist, but his true beliefs are far more nuanced. While he clearly does love his country, especially Japanese history, he isn't blind to its flaws, nor does he see other nations as inferior. He wants the best for his country, but he doesn't exalt Japan—either as it having reached its potential, or relative to other nations. An extreme nationalist who ignores the flaws of his own country and the advancements of other countries, as Kita is sometimes depicted, would never write an entire volume, tens of thousands of words long, refuting the central point of his country's most popular ideology of the time like he did in volume four of this very book.

Kita's ideas of the near infallibility of natural laws, social evolution, and humanity's eventual evolution into some sort of godlike beings plays a large role in his ideology and thought processes—both in the book and later on in his life. However, the flip side is that, at least at the time he wrote *The Theory of Japan's National Polity and Pure Socialism,* he wasn't some surface-level jingoist who merely offered a few novel turns of phrase. He actually did have a nuanced understanding of both his own nation's history and the history of others. He understood the flaws of his nation, the flaws of other nations, what good ideas and advances he could take from other nations, and what bad ideas to discard from those nations.

Although he despised many capitalists, he didn't deny their validity entirely. He saw them as a natural and necessary process of social evolution, one that any society must go through to reach its next stage of evolution. Although he resented several of the foundational ideas which made up Japanese history and its historical interpretation in his own time, he didn't denounce them as evil, only that they needed to be discarded or reformed in his current era. He saw them as necessary parts of historical evolution as well. Kita's underlying assertion that natural laws have no waste or errors, and that even the most primitive or even violent society is merely in a necessary stage of social evolution as it works its way up simply doesn't seem to mesh at all with disparaging words that have been written about him.

Perhaps the main takeaway after reading Kita's writing is that, while he did hold contempt for many capitalists, Japanese academics, and Japanese political figures of his time, he saw most of them as simple barricades in a raging river—barricades that would be completely obliterated by the torrent of rushing water once Japanese society had advanced enough to understand and accept his arguments. He deeply wanted to raise the foundational level of Japanese society as a whole, and once his beloved home was elevated beyond a certain threshold, that would be enough for his arguments, and pure socialism in general, to gain foothold in Japan.

AUTHOR'S INTRODUCTION

What is most desired in modern times is not detailed research in various schools of learning, nor is it citation of data or abundance of facts. What is most desired is a complete and unified understanding of everything. Naturally, this powerless author cannot endure such a mission. In fact, one would say that such an endeavor is too good to be true. However, this effort of attempting to establish social democracy is built upon a unified knowledge of all social sciences. This includes but is not limited to the following: economics, ethics, sociology, history, jurisprudence, political science, biology, and philosophy.

The author admits that the parochial socialism from antiquity and the Middle Ages and the parochial individualism from after the revolution are in opposition to each other. Even so, the social democracy that has arrived today following their evolution does not ignore the demands of nationalism. The author also still believes that one shouldn't turn their back on the ideals posited by liberalism. Therefore, this book will not align with the reckless acts of many current socialists, which constantly refute the existence of the state, and will also not use scholars or theories of individualism as targets to attack or threaten. Specifically, this book directs most of its aim toward eliminating noncommittal or strange ideas such as so-called podium socialism or state socialism. In the first volume, *The Economic Justice of Socialism*, we've reduced the amount of time spent discussing individualism's old-style economics and instead focused on defeating the arguments of Mr. Kanai, Mr. Tajima, and others. In the second volume, *The Ethical Ideal of Socialism*, we easily refute individualism's idea of criminal jurisprudence and try to argue against the ideas on crime that Mr. Higuchi and others present. The individual makes up the society, so if they don't recognize its authority, socialism cannot exist. Unlike the West, Japan has not experienced the ideals of individualism nor a revolution under its banner. This means that it must first develop individualism as a prerequisite for socialism.

Volume three, *The Theory of Biological Evolution and Social Philosophy*, looks at social philosophy from the point of view of biological evolution. More specifically, it could be phrased as "a theory of social philosophy as one section of the theory of biological evolution." However, despite remarkable advancement in research on certain aspects of it after Darwin's time, the modern theory of biological evolution we have today is still quite chaotic and confusing. This is because it is lacking both "structure" and a "conclusion." Due to that, this book organizes the simple discovery of biological evolution and gives it structure, and, though most of the book's purpose and objective lies in the study of social philosophy, uses this structure as the basis for its outlook on social sciences in general. In addition, if this inference is tied to philosophical teleology and leaves an impact upon the future human race, though speculative, I can't contain my infinite joy at the idea that I will have been the first to speak of this "conclusion" of the theory of biological evolution. Of course, today's science does not provide enough evidence to infer the evolution of future mankind. It also should not need to be said that any results from me as a person will be heavily skewed in the direction of my biases, whatever they may be. Still, this area that cautious Western thinkers have still not attempted to tread could be considered a bold adventure for a scholar of an undeveloped country. We argue that the realization of social democracy is a spiritual belief that brings us one step closer to utopia. We call this the religion of social democracy, and it is knocking on a completely different door, one in an entirely different world, compared to Western socialists who are arguing over the conflict and harmony between socialism and Christianity. To begin with, Christianity, both in the present day and since the Holy Roman Empire, holds a grip over all of the Western thinking world. It is very similar to the idea of the theory of national polity here in Japan. As a Japanese socialist, we already suffer under heavy baggage from the problem of whether socialism conflicts with national polity or not. The West's problem is whether socialism conflicts with Christianity or not. Those socialists who want to add the latter's national polity to the former's, then find themselves conflicted on the subject, do not even realize the fact that these two situations are completely separate and different from each other. With all that said, I should not need to reiterate that the main theory of this book is not religious theory, nor is it an explanation of the theory of biological evolution. It is an explanation of how a biological species known as human society has responded to evolution. As I finish up this book during a time when the poor Benjamin Kidd[1] is celebrated as a wise man for trying to explain human society via the theory of evolution in his book, *Social Evolution*, I can't help but be a little proud of myself.

Volume four, *The So-Called Theory of Japan's National Polity and its Restorative Principle of Revolution,* includes a strong critique of Christianity in Japan. In other words, it could be said that this isn't a debate on whether socialism conflicts with national polity or not, but rather a scientific study on our very nation of Japan. The West's national polity was eradicated via small elements of knowledge combined after a long, arduous effort by Darwin and his successors. In the same vein, Christianity in Japan must take its last breath as logical scientific researchers progress the theory of social evolution. This is the volume I poured the most passion into. I completely reject the jurisprudence of all royalists and nationalists and make clear our modern national polity by interpreting it through a frame of both the Constitution and modern political science. I also give an explanation on how it evolved atop the backdrop of history. I secretly have faith. I believe that, if this book doesn't end up buried and forgotten in the annals of history, it will overturn the unchanging theories of history that all historians past and present cling to. This publication itself will be a historical revolution akin to the replacement of the geocentric model by the heliocentric one. Though this volume does exist

---

[1] A British sociologist.

alongside a unique theory of jurisprudence, it can be seen as writings on the philosophical history of Japan, somewhat divorced from socialism entirely.

Volume five, *The Enlightenment Movement of Socialism,* argues that the judgement of good and evil has followed a path of evolution, then goes on to pair with the explanation of social class conscience found in the second volume, *The Ethical Ideal of Socialism*. I proceed to then touch upon state competition, claiming that it is a prerequisite for imperialism and cosmopolitanism. A society built upon individuals who have no rights is merely a collection of slaves, not a social democracy. Similarly, this means that the socialist's world federation movement theory needs to establish ethical independence for the nations it is trying to unite. Much like a hundred rivers may flow into the sea, social democracy is only possible upon succession of so much evolution. Without the progress of individualism, there is no socialism. Without the progress of imperialism, there is no cosmopolitanism. Without the progress of private ownership, there is no communism. This is why social democracy should not see the current state of these things in the world and label them as enemies. It should instead accept them, and erect itself atop the pinnacle of evolution that these things will achieve. The old question of "Even if socialism's ideals are possible, can they really be achieved?" arose from thinking of current social democracy as an artificial, man-made construct, rather than as a natural result of historical evolution. This book, from beginning to end, explains that socialism accompanies historical evolution. I also base many arguments on logic and truths found in Japanese history itself. In fact, this is exactly why I explain in this volume the theory of the ideal nation found in Confucianism.

All social sciences are analyses based on experiments and research that can only be performed on real social phenomena, so one shouldn't think it prudent to dissertate on socialism based only on a single subject of research such as economics or ethics alone. This book was written without rules dividing it into precise, minute structures or singular detailed chapters, but rather with a focus on explaining the core of overarching arguments in detail. This will lead to many areas which, unless one has read the book in its entirety, may be difficult to understand completely. Naturally, this author understands that publishing a thousand-page book such as this,[2] then requesting such a herculean task of the reader is a sin in and of itself. It warrants an apology at the very least. However, it wouldn't be right to avoid some fair effort when dealing with this study of such a major controversy that stands before the entire world. I am not one of these so-called scholars that make advocacy and defense their life's calling, nor am I a revolutionary who has made it his sworn duty to repudiate and deny anything and everything. I am merely one who follows scientific principles and, in accordance with them, attempts to ensure that that which should be preserved is preserved and that which should be discarded is discarded. An academic's argument, unless forbidden by law, is free. Therefore, it is not my business, even in part, if this book is used as an excuse by the government for its own benefit to persecute the socialist party, nor if it serves as provocation for the socialist party to evoke feelings of loathing at their own less-than-favorable position. For instance, I have gone against the decisions of the Second International and approved the Russo-Japanese War.[3] I have also gone against the public opinion of nearly all Japanese citizens in repudiating the theory of Japan's national polity. A specific theory cannot be forced upon people, even via political power. Even with the large influence of the socialist party, they cannot use majority rule as an umbrella to belittle one's freedom of thought. I, the author of this book and a simple academic, have no use for things like government power or the influence of the socialist party outside of simple material for scientific study.

That means, of course, my socialism is not "Marxism," nor could the democracy I advocate be called "Rousseau's democracy." Naturally, I hold only

---

[2] This is the length of the original book.

[3] The original text uses the term "World Socialist Party Assembly" in place of what is commonly known as the "Second International."

my own views on social democracy. It does not even need to be said that, as an individual, I am far more average then either of the aforementioned men. However, looking at things from the view of social evolution, I am their great-grandfather, a balding old man with precious few tufts of white hair remaining; one who has lived many decades, a century even, longer than they have.

In order to assert a new idea, one must naturally take a stance of removal toward the previous way of thinking if they are in opposition. Deconstructing incorrect opinions and points of view is an essential step before discovering truth, which leads to my tone of aggressive arguments and confutation in this book. One goal of this book is to use such methods to subjugate what may be referred to as a social class of so-called modern academics.

I am a man who holds the most sympathy in the world for the current socialist party in modern Japan, struggling to fight under such enormous oppression. Be that as it may, whether I hold respect for their arguments is a completely separate matter. Most of them act on emotion and dogmatism, showing a pure and literal translation of these in their motives. Their thoughts and ideas are especially rooted in the individualism present around the time of the French Revolution. In other words, they should be recognized not as socialists, but as spearheads who were quite effective at arousing social issues. As I am a loyal servant of social democracy, I had no choice but to develop my arguments and ideals without any thoughts spared to sympathy. I must admit how unfortunate that is.

The only word I can use to accurately describe the academic social class that I proposed to subjugate earlier in this text is "adorable." If I may exhibit my frank virtues through a confession on the subject—though I do feel that it sullies through oversimplification of complicated matters that same pen which writes my arguments—many of these leaders in various theories and disciplines nest in university podiums and are appointed merely because they have power within the intelligentsia. I will, of course, take responsibility for my words here. However, leaving room for even a single word of defense from the current university professors in Japan would mean that I have been lax in my duty when writing this book. Their excuses or justifications themselves would disgrace the text. For those reasons, I have, of course, given due respect to certain academics such as Dr. Oka. However, with most academics featured in this book, especially those like Mr. Hozumi, I have attempted to butcher them in the most humiliating and derisive way possible. This is not because there are no laws to regulate academic wars in the same way as regular wars, but rather as revenge for the hubris and arrogance that modern academics have lauded and the cowardice they dare not display openly.

I have tried to make the writing itself simple in its explanation. However, there is one part in which I must beg your forgiveness and ask you to keep an open mind. That is, since scholars debating in this public and open space like to move their pens in such a baffling, unintelligible way, I too am bound by their same rules. Because of this, in my competition with this academic social class I have been constantly forced to give up seventy to eighty percent of the ring. When I have finally built up strength and am ready to throw a heavy punch, that same arm is tied behind my back and not allowed to move. In addition, those who are currently in positions as university professors speak of the sanctity of university while clinging to the seats of those in power, begging and crying for protection and backing. There is nothing I can do about this. Until those in power finally admonish this disgraceful behavior, independent thought will absolutely never be established there.

Following this paragraph, you will find my list of Japan's designated representative academics who use every opportunity to insult, disrespect, and set up social democracy to look bad, all while spouting their fantasies about Japan's National Polity. Because of this, I would say one should look at this text as not only an exhaustive discussion on social democracy, but also as a criticism on modern Japan's current trend of thought.

Mr. Noburu Kanai, *Socioeconomics*

Mr. Kinji Tajima, *Recent Economic Theory*[4]

Mr. Kanjiro Higuchi, *State Socialism's New Pedagogy* and *Main Discourse on State Socialism's Pedagogy*

Mr. Asajiro Oka, *Lectures on Evolutionary Theory*

Mr. Nagao Aruga, *Constitutional Law*

Mr. Yatsuka Hozumi, *The Essence of the Constitution* and his Imperial University lecture notes

Mr. Hisoka Inoue, records of lectures on the Constitution at Kyoto School of Law and Politics

Mr. Kitokuro Ichiki, Imperial University lecture notes

Mr. Tatsukichi Minobe, Waseda University lecture notes

Mr. Tetsujiro Inoue, various works

Mr. Aizan Yamaji and various State Socialists

Mr. Abe Isoo and various Socialist Party members

Spring of the year after the Russo-Japanese War

Ikki Kita

北 一輝

---

[4] The original text says *Newest Economic Theory*, but there is no book with that title in Tajima's bibliography. This was likely a mistake, and it has been corrected it to the appropriate title.

VOLUME 1: THE ECONOMIC JUSTICE OF SOCIALISM

壱

Socialism's profound, fundamental logic is a special philosophy and creed regarding humanity and the universe itself, built upon hard science as its base. It is not something for which one should take rash action based upon their own emotions and dogma. Still, the real-life, practical problem of being born in a society filled with poverty and crime, yet working to establish a new society through it, first requires us to completely eliminate poverty and crime as a logical prerequisite. Because of this, in this first volume, *The Economic Justice of Socialism,* we will explain the physical, material, practical happiness that socialism can bring. In the second volume, *The Ethical Ideal of Socialism,* we argue the mental and spiritual contentment and satisfaction of socialism. Then, in the third volume, *The Theory of Biological Evolution and Social Philosophy,* we argue the law and ideals of social evolution, explain our philosophy of socialism, and state the basic ideas of various social sciences. Following on from that we enter the fourth volume, *The So-Called Theory of Japan's National Polity and Its Restorative Principle of Revolution,* and attempt to remove the age-old fantasies that persist to modern times. This leads to our argument on the true nature of national polity, constitutional law, and Japanese history from the perspective of historical philosophy. Finally, we enter the fifth volume, *The Enlightenment Movement of Socialism,* and discuss how to implement what we've talked about leading up to this.

CHAPTER 1

Poverty and crime. If socialism would remove these two tragic and repulsive things from our society, one could liken said socialism to the discovery of a path that leads all the earth to heaven. Socialism would then, after this discovery, spread its wings of conquest over the entire world.

Look, though, at how the argument has been inverted. If anything, the modern government and academics persecute and mock socialism. They will, without fail, say things such as, "Socialism disrupts societal order" and "It harms the nation's public peace and well-being." However, these lies can only become truth if modern society already contains said order. They can only exist if the public peace and well-being they speak of actually exist in this nation. Socialism should retort with the following questions: "Is there enough order in modern society that one could even disrupt it?"; "Is there enough peace and well-being in our nation that it would be so abhorrent to harm it?" Today's scientific socialism is not satisfied through pointless, emotional wordplay. If the light of reason is not present in our current civilization and culture, then these questions are what should be coming out of every single person's mouth. If the use of police swords and soldiers' firearms to barely support a system of power and prosperity for certain social classes can be considered "order," then it is true that modern society does have order, albeit some complex version of it.

Without end, people lose their lives every day, and assets are mostly protected by those who have the physical power to do so. It is as if we are living in a village of barbarians. Despite this, we live under laws that say they will protect our assets and guarantee our safety. This is the peace and well-being that our nation bestows upon us. Socialism does not believe that this sort of order, peace, and well-being will last until the earth freezes over and no humans remain.

From this perspective, one might very well say that the government's persecution and academia's mudslinging come from honest and reasonable fears. Our modern nation can provide peace and well-being for the morbidly obese who wring the sweat and blood out from their fellow man. However, the order and structure of modern society, which must bear the burden of providing such offerings, is not such a wonderful thing to the class which must give up their sweat and blood; yet this is something which must not be disrupted at any cost.

A hell of unending starvation, inescapable from birth until death, exists right next to a heaven of wealth and plenty. In order to escape starvation in this realm of hunger, men become thieves and women become whores. The state then builds red brick prisons, bestows peace upon the thieves, and sends police to the red-light district to defend the whores, forcing well-being upon them. In order to foster prosperity, the government is furnished with the very money that these prostitutes, now forced to be safe and happy, make by plying their trade. They also, through an extensive code of law, limit the knowledge of scholars and academics and welcome the thieves, to whom they should be providing peace and order. The newspaper, which one could call a flower of culture, writes articles of theft and burglary and informs us of poisonings and bloodshed. It tells us of an old man hanging himself, a poverty-stricken woman jumping to her death, parents abandoning a baby, a beggar freezing and starving to death. These are the flowers of culture with which the paper decorates itself. We've become accustomed to this cruelty, so we forget the dots of blood speckling the front of the paper and the cries of anguish that leak from its pages. Instead, we wait for an even more miserable, cruel story, because the former misery is what we now consider normality. This societal order which results in eternal famine, this well-being and happiness which results in freezing to death, and this peace which results in bloodshed and casualties are not the sort of thing that a wealthy social class, one which receives nearly servile defense from academics, would want to lay a single finger on. However, under socialism, society and states would be forced to pursue true order, true peace, true happiness and well-being.

O poverty, O crime! Is it fate that you should pair with humanity forever? Christianity answers with the sophistry of "It is God's will." Buddhism answers with the falsehood that "We can eventually go to paradise." Too bad for the poor citizens, Malthus is already there and *An Essay on the Principle of Population* says they would be refused entry. The cruelty of making man and woman in your image, then forcing the man into thievery and the woman into prostitution merely to live should mean that we are incompatible with God's views. If anything, what I just described seems more demonic than holy.

That said, socialists should not get angry or feel resentment toward such obstacles, even in jest. In social evolution, it is completely normal for old ways of thinking to lie in front of new ideals and obstruct them. Though these old ways do lie down as obstacles, this means they have submitted to their duty of improving society. If one were to compare the birth of a new society to an egg hatching, these old ways of thinking would be the protective shell. It also follows that, upon facing the precipice of social evolution, the social class which holds power will attempt suppression. This is the right of those in power; it's impossible for socialism to avoid persecution in the name of both societal order as well as national peace and well-being. The reason socialism is sneered at by society and feared by the state is not because it is a baseless fantasy, nor because it is violent extremism. It only happens because the government persecutes it and the academics slander it. Socialism! How could it possibly be as they say?

What is socialism? In explaining this, one must first think about why, in modern society, the social class that makes up the vast majority of citizens is poor. Why? Why is the vast majority poor?

4 | The Theory of Japan's National Polity and Pure Socialism

Economists understand that poverty is the result of modern machine industry. We socialists believe this as well. However, things have truly become nonsensical if we are satisfied with such an answer.

It is said that our railways could circle the earth sixty times and are twice the length of the distance between the earth and the moon. However, most humans put down roots in their birthplace, as if they were a plant, and do not even have the luxury of free travel. Apparently, Waterbury pocket watches are manufactured in the span of only five minutes.[5] Despite that fact, if a farmer wants one of these necessities, he is told that it is a luxury. The manufacture of pins, which Adam Smith famously described using the division of labor, allowed ten people to create forty-eight thousand pins in a single day. This was considered a marvel at the time. Today, however, a single machine can create one hundred eighty pins in a minute. Adding to this, it only takes three supervisors to oversee seventy machines at once, easily allowing these machines to create seven and a half million pins in one day. Switching to farming, a mere eight horsepower steam thresher can allow rest for eighty farmers. A steam plough can, in a single day, till a field measuring five hundred to six hundred meters in length. Through wind, water, and steam power, a pump can, in a single hour, irrigate several tens of thousands of meters worth of fields. Things which eighty years ago would have taken five hundred well-built men an entire day to complete can now be done with a single machine and operator. Even old statistics from 1887 say that merely matching the amount of labor steam power from various countries can achieve would require nearly the entire human population. In other words, it matches the combined labor of over one billion people.

According to Ely, even during the golden age of Athens it was rare for one to be wealthy enough to have ten slaves in their home.[6] Now, however, we have

---

[5] This was a large maker of clocks and watches at the time.

[6] American economist Richard Theodore Ely (1854–1943).

invented machines that, in a single household, could produce labor equivalent to sixty slaves. What is the significance of this machine industry of modern culture? Well, there is absolutely no significance to these farm tools at all if we are still forced to live toiling in the mud, from the day of our birth to the day of our death. Isn't the point of these machines to allow all classes of people to enter mental and spiritual activity, using their minds as they please like the free people of Greece?

If we are to invent these machines, we must remove poverty from society as we do so. Instead, this modern machine industry is **causing** the majority to fall into poverty. This is exactly what one could call "one step forward, two steps back." It is the complete inverse of the correct answer. If machines are meant to take on the pain of labor, then the invention of these things should reduce the amount of time that a laborer must spend working. Instead, it is the number of jobs rather than the hours spent working that are being reduced, leading to massive and unending unemployment. Then, if one is lucky enough to acquire a job, they must spend twenty-four hours a day with a machine that needs neither sleep nor rest. It will turn them into a soulless automaton, automated only to work. These machines that were supposed to help support our life physically by supplying goods and materials are now instead taking the goods and materials that supported workers away from them. They do not give people the free time to form a coherent thought. They simply turn the workers around them into soulless animals. This is where the most likely source of poverty is. This is not a sin on the part of the machine industry. The cause exists within modern civilization, but said civilization is unaware of it. To put it simply, it is because modern culture consists of an economic aristocracy. It is because the rulers and aristocrats are plundering wealth in the name of order and regulation.

Today's so-called major capitalists and great landowners are not merely rich people. They turn a nation's source of economic income into their own private funds and have free power over life and death. In this respect they are true major and minor feudal lords. America's rich, for example, own large spaces of lands and treat tens of thousands of financial slaves however they please. Like Louis XIV, they are the true patriarchs and acting sovereigns. Just open one of these many "business magazines," as they call themselves, or one of these religious newsletters that are based upon the religion of money, and see what stares back at you from the opening page. Oil barons, mining magnates, ironwork rulers, bankers, coal kings—they are all lined up next to each other. I am absolutely not using these titles as allegory. I call them as such because these people actually do have the sanctity and power of kings. Rather, if one were to compare modern national sovereigns, who have become nothing more than institutions of the state, to the previously mentioned elite who use their power however they please, the former would hold little to no true power at all.

George Washington fought a war of independence to free the people from English tyranny, yet his own descendants now live and work as slaves under capitalist kings, who are no different from the sovereigns of old that owned public land and people as their own private property. All of Europe cried for freedom and equality as they stole back lands from the sovereigns and aristocrats during the French Revolution. Yet now these new kings and aristocrats are plundering all of their economic sources back and returning Europe to how it was before said revolution.

The situation is the very same in our own Japan. The old aristocrats have returned their land to the state, yet new minor and major feudal lords who steal the state's source of capital for themselves are being born. In today's Japan, not even the emperor has the right or power to steal the state's land and use the citizens as he pleases. The state's land is not the personal property of the royal lineage, nor are the citizens their slaves or private property. In other words, the country is not royal land belonging to landlords, nor are the citizens who live on state land mere retainers for capitalists. If one would believe that they need not pay heed to these economic sovereigns simply because they do not call themselves "king" or do not possess the title of "emperor," then one might as well believe the statement royals would often say of themselves: "Any king who does not call himself such is not truly royalty."

All types of political power come in the form of economic power. Look at the feudal lords back during the period of the shogunate, most of whom possessed both state land and the citizenry themselves. It was held by virtue of their economic power. Now look at the current nobility in Japan, in possession of mere public debt and government securities. One can clearly see how powerless they truly are, nothing more than relics of the past. Compare the sovereigns of various European countries, supported by limited civil lists, to the economic sovereigns who hold power over both land and goods. It's easy to envision what massive power the latter hold.

It is said that the Russian Tsar, who makes over fifteen million yen a year, is a despot who uses his economic power to bend the government to his will. However, it pales in comparison to the direct power over human life and livelihood held by John Rockefeller, who makes 286,000,000 yen a year. As another example, regardless of how much of a tyrant any sultan of the Middle East is, as long as they make less than twenty million yen per year, they will never hold more power than Carn the Conqueror—a wise leader who knew the power of the pen and wasn't afraid to use the sword if necessary—as he made over twice that twenty million figure.[7] Regardless of how much the German emperor declares imperialism in order to emulate the now insubstantial fame of the Holy Roman Emperor, as long as he makes less than one third of Sir Russel Sage's annual revenue of eighteen million yen, one can calculate that he will hold less than one third of the latter's power.[8]

---

[7] We assume this is the name of a historical captain of industry, but it is unclear. Is he talking about Carnegie?

[8] Sir Russel Sage was an American banker.

8 | The Theory of Japan's National Polity and Pure Socialism

The poverty of all society is caused by these economic lords, barons, and kings plundering wealth. These new landlords take the place of old major and minor feudal lords, becoming what these feudal lords were in all but name. The serfs toiling under these new feudal lords named "landlords" don't have many rights under the state, but rather an obligation of unlimited and total obedience. The landlords collect exorbitant annual tributes known as land taxes, and if one were to fall behind in these payments and defy their will, that person would have the land they live on taken from them; they would be forced out of their very home. These people act like the aristocratic government of the old shogunate, complete with the philosophy of "Govern the peasants so that they shall not die, but may not live."[9] The people are then forced to work like honey bees under these new aristocrats, and the honey they painstakingly produced is all taken from them via land taxes. Any independence from their landlords is lost, and they have no choice but to prostrate before them like serfs.

Osaka's major capitalists sit and occupy rural land while assigning the cruelest local governors that they possibly can. It is almost exactly the same as how lands under direct control of the shogunate were treated. In contrast to the land owners of the rural areas, who are often bound by old traditions when they make contracts, these new capitalists form contracts in accordance with the Ricardian theory of rent. They then wait for the increase in rent accompanying rises in value of the land, eventually resulting in the person's inability to pay what was agreed by the contract, thus allowing them to sweep the land right out from under the person's feet without any prior notice. People with this much power are not equal citizens of the state. They are not simple

---

[9] This quote has parts of the books *Honsaroku* and *Shouheiyawa*, both from the Edo period, mixed together. The former says, "The peasants should be governed with not too much yet not too little, wealth." The latter says, "The peasants must neither die nor live, so an appropriate tax should be..."

landlords. They are, without a doubt, sovereigns of an aristocratic country in all but name.

But no, that's not all! Those people aren't merely practically aristocrats, they also possess the honorary title of "Daimyo," or major feudal lord, and all the prestige and authority that brings. They are referred to by such respectful titles as "Lord" or "Nobleman." They build their residences, called "mansions," upon the remnants of old feudal lords' houses. These capitalists build castles, calling them factories or workshops, and assign scholars and politicians as their chief retainers. They assign their wage slaves as common foot soldiers and give orders to anyone they have power over, all in an attempt at a free-for-all war against other economic sovereigns. When these people drive down the street in carriages, they shoo away men and women of any age, just like daimyo once did. These feudal lords are absolutely the foolish daimyo of the modern day, and, due to a mixture of loyalty and self-serving maneuvering and scheming by their retainers, they maintain the same esteem and safety that their predecessors had.

These loyal retainers use taxes labeled interest and profit to make these foolish lords even stupider. These taxes accumulate, without the lord's knowledge, like a stream flowing into a lake, or soil piling into a mountain. These foolish lords continue to follow the opinion of those around them, thinking that their own "superior selves" must have bodies that are special. They feel that considering themselves the same kin as the citizenry somehow sullies their nobility. In the same way that old feudal lords would sometimes rule benevolently for their own amusement and pleasure, these new foolish lords have attempted to dupe their country and its people in the past using this pretense of charity. However, these lords of gold maintain power with the use of their money alone, so it's not a common occurrence. To them, if even a little bit of money is lost, their ability to fight the other feudal lords drops by exactly that amount.

Oh, the serfs and lowly townsmen! They are not people. They are seen as products, goods to be sold. They have market value. Much like fish, if these products aren't sold swiftly, they will rot. The market value of these products is controlled by the law of supply and demand. From the perspective of the law, they do not have human personality, but rather the status of goods. Much like the feudal lords of old could own the peasants and town commoners, these people are legal possessions of the capitalists; the latter able to do with the former whatever they please. They are not considered citizens of the state, with status as human beings and human rights. Because of this, as the law of supply and demand dictates, if too many of these goods collect together, the price of them will fall due to excess supply. The goods aren't even allowed the free time to think about their own conditions. If these goods end up dying a dog's death of starvation, not only does the supply decrease, but the total control the aristocrats have over them is reaffirmed, even in terms of when they die.

In other words, when the bankrupt, the unemployed, and those chased out of other lands come in front of the workhouse gates, under the effect of both oversupply and empty stomachs, it gives the feudal lords of this economic aristocracy an opportunity to use and show off their shocking authority and power. Their vassals and retainers then use that to encourage loyalty, and thus spread word of the lords' glorious deeds. Because this opportunity always exists and can pop up at any time, anyone whose feet are bound by this ball and chain in the guise of a "contract" continue to carry it to their grave. This is how a strict system of slavery has been revived.

Yes, a system of slavery! Such a system does not consist of only chains and whips. Legally, one can refer to a system that strips humans of their basic status as human beings and places them under the free control of other humans as a system of slavery. In other words, yes, the feudalism found during the Warring States period, where people and their land existed as possessions under the control of the wealthy, is a similar system of slavery. We don't know if slaves during the period of chains and whips, when each slave was worth three hundred dollars, were happy or not. However, we also can't believe that Roman slaves, chained and forced to work during the day and sleep in a dark cellar at night, and modern money slaves, forced to sleep like pigs—with child atop parent in a tiny rear tenement filled with viruses—then required to work for thirteen to fourteen hours a day chained to machines and without a moment's rest, are much better off. At the very least, Roman slaves never died of starvation. However, today's contract slaves and monetary slaves, due to any combination of bankruptcy, loss of work, economic slumps, or simple bad weather, can go without food for days or even weeks, and starvation because of this is not uncommon.

The law, which is supposed to represent justice, has clearly given freedom and equality to the average person, this is true. However, to a person that has fallen in the street from hunger, a piece of bread would be far more valuable than any whispers of freedom in their ear or demonstration of fair law in their eyes. Animals who can't subsist on freedom and equality alone will endure any amount of pain and shame for their love toward their wives and children, and, in doing so, won't even look at their own feet and question the iron chain fastened to them.

In the past, the children of slaves would be forced into slavery simply due to their lineage. Even in the early modern period of feudalism, peasants and common townsfolk would have no choice but for their children to become tenant farmers or day laborers depending on the parents' social class. Like prisoners of war would become the victors' slaves, or debtors would sell themselves into slavery for the creditors, the losers of this painful economic war, the debtors of this system of slavery, would have no path aside from living as a money slave.

Much like Russian serfs hang a piece of gold from their necks with their owner's name carved on it as they work, the money slaves who enter and exit the workplace like ants all wear uniforms branded with their master's symbol. Overwork makes them feral like wild animals. They take on an appearance similar to the Negro and regress back to the barbarian age, becoming much rougher and more violent. In the past the American South motioned to "Make as much profit as possible in the span of five years by working slaves to their absolute limits, then letting them die." This was met with thunderous applause as it was approved by the federal congress. Similarly to such motions, factory laws which prevent long hours of labor that shorten one's life, and laws which prevent women and children from working, for it harms human nature, have all disappeared in a haze from the Japanese Imperial Diet.

When Roman slaves fell ill, it is said that they were thrown into rivers to drown, their drowning cries ignored, because it was so much more profitable to simply buy a heartier slave than it was to nurse the sick slave back to health with food and medicine. Today's laborers are thrown away by their own employers even for wounds suffered not by disease or old age, but from their own labor. Not only this, but they are thrown away directly into the center of large cities. Often times one can see scenes of ignorant members of the public gathering around these people, who are writhing and screaming in pain from disease, the same way a curious boy might watch with pity and curiosity the body of a cat who was thrown into a river. Farmers and the like were often sold off with their land. They are what the Romans would consider "speaking farm tools," and were the medieval version of today's serfs. Those peoples' offspring were exported overseas as cheap yellow slaves. If that kind of emigration, created by the protection of national laws, is not a clear and complete example of a simple slave trade, then what else could it be? Poverty is not brought about by modern culture itself. It is not brought about by the machine industry. It exists exactly because of this economic aristocracy. (For information on the meaning of and historical context for things like the aristocracy, patriarchal sovereigns, and systems of slavery, see volume four, *The So-Called Theory of Japan's National Polity and its Restorative Principle of Revolution,* and volume five, *The Enlightenment Movement of Socialism.*)

Despite this, what is inexplicable to most is why individualism, which in the past defeated the aristocratic government and the system of slavery they employed, is now defending this new form of both, even working to sustain these new economic aristocracies. This is happening because one becomes blinded by the fancy garb, the surface level outfit of these dazzling nations. One then forgets that only ugliness is contained within. To put it simply, the fault lies in old style economics.

Of course, the foundational beliefs of socialism and individualism cannot coexist. However, when one thinks of how important individualism's ideals were in determining the course of cultural history, it is absolutely imperative that its noble significance is not ignored. When human history was about to fall off the precipice of evolution, the revolutions that resulted were all performed in the name of individualism. From when Martin Luther stood up and screamed freedom of ideals at the Roman pope, to when the French argued for inherent equality as they stormed the castle of Marseille, individualism has been the very origin of the ideals behind a revolution. There is a reason for this. When speaking as an explanative theory, individualism is nothing more than that, a single theory. However, when speaking of it as an ethical ideal, it possesses a certain nobility.

The structure and system of human society evolves if it makes freedom of living its ethical ideal, and human happiness is achieved through making human equality its ethical ideal. By contrast, no matter what the current savages do they can't escape some odd, cruel customs precisely because those customs have existed for hundreds of thousands of years. The average individual is born a victim of these strange customs and cruel superstitions. The custom of killing one's aged parents in order to hold a banquet, the superstition of getting a hold of an infant to offer it as sacrifice to a vicious beast—the specifics do not matter. Once they are considered old customs, the individual doesn't even think to question them. This is why those people, even after tens of thousands of years, still practice the barbaric custom of cannibalism today. They can't move forward.

Our history was the same; we had no choice in the matter. At the time, we were merely social animals that followed our social instincts in order to maintain the society that was already there, using it to fight other social groups for survival. Because we were so busy doing this, the individual had no choice but to become a victim of it. Even Egypt's shocking civilization was, from that perspective, nothing more than the futile civil engineering work done by the pharaohs and their priests. Not only that, but the individual had no space to wonder, even a little, why they must become victims, sacrifices for those pharaohs and priests. The flourishing of Babylon is the same. The prosperity of Assyria as well.

When we get to the final years of Greco-Roman history, the rights of the individual have been recognized somewhat, but even still, Socrates served them poison. This poison made the ignorant masses trample the concept of freedom of ideals and abandon their precious individuality, their personhood, in the name of society and state. The capital of Rome was known as a city of nobles and beggars, but the individual never questioned why they must become beggars. During the following millennium, known now as the Dark Ages, the Roman pope ignored the individual and individual rights completely. This continued until the previously barbarous German people began to evolve culturally. Everything—customs, actions, speech, thoughts, politics, law itself, even the act of sitting down, everything under the Sun—existed under the control of the pope. Priests breaking the commandments, the buying and selling of priesthood, indulgence in the church, all of it was accepted and believed in without a trace of doubt. This is not the despotism of a single pope alone, but rather the result of society's authority working through the pope to trample on individuals.

The evolution of history is based on the awakening and recognition of individuality and an individual's personhood. Through religious revolution, humanity learned of and understood the rights of the individual and obtained "freedom of belief." The awakening of the individual's personality evolved along with history, expanding ever larger. Through the French Revolution, humanity defeated both aristocrats and sovereigns to declare "freedom of government." They said, "Unnecessary aristocrats shall not make lands their personal possessions, nor shall they make citizens their personal slaves." They said, "The fate of citizens shall not be left in the hands of a single person who happened to be born lucky, even if he be King." Individualism's economics began here, chanted atop the winds of this revolution. (Read our arguments concerning polarized socialism and polarized individualism in volume three, *The Theory of Biological Evolution and Social Philosophy*.)

Individualism's old economics began in order to revolutionize the previous aristocratic economic systems, and it did so well enough. History must thank the economist Rousseau. Wasn't Adam Smith's *The Wealth of Nations* a revolution both in the face of the aristocratic system of economics and in explaining social contracts? Consider that all branches of science are main flow tributaries of the basic ideals of their time. In this case, the main currents of individualism became Luther's freedom of religion, Rousseau's freedom of government, and Adam Smith's freedom of occupation. This is how these things developed.

When looking at the economic system of the aristocracy during Smith's time, it becomes apparent that all the spider's nest of legalese, unorganized customs, and miscellaneous practices had to be destroyed; a revolution had to occur. At the time there was a law governing residence which could be used to remove foreign businesses when they couldn't help but irritate the state. Multiple people were not allowed to operate a business in that city because they didn't follow the law and join a union. For this very reason, James Watt was rejected from operating his business in Glasgow using his invention, the steam engine. Judicators, under the pretext of fairly distributing money, stood between capitalists and laborers in the name of "fairness." They were the cruel talons and fangs of the social classes who held authority. Professional duties would be carried out under the name of the state, but it was, in truth, despotism. Prices would be officially fixed according to nothing more than the whims of public officials, ones who held no knowledge of economics, no sincerity of mind, and no intent of fairness. The unions reached the climax of their authority and began placing limitations on everything from the appropriate age of one's apprentice, to which customs were and were not appropriate, the quality of manufactured goods, how large or small these goods were, and even what shape they may take. One couldn't take a single step without encountering these rules. There were also uncountable numbers of monopolies that were protected by the pointless aristocrats and national sovereigns. Looked at from the world of economics, the theory of the social contract was written in order to revolutionize the economic aspect of this aristocracy.

If any current individualist economist, one who follows the ideas of *The Wealth of Nations* and understands the significance of real individualism, exists right now and yet also defends the current economic aristocracy, then that person is a traitor to individualism. If any say that individuals are free in our current society, such freedom exists only on their lips during the moment they utter such things. For even on those lips, mere seconds after those words are spoken, freedom of speech and freedom of thought have already left. Luther fought a battle for freedom of religion, yet his protestant successors now sell their freedom of religion so as to offer massive donations towards the current monetary feudal lords. They then become pastors who serve these lords, reversing the modern social position back to the same one held by the old church of Luther's time. The blood-soaked Constitution that was finally achieved after Rousseau's freedom of government has become nothing more than stone used to carve out the thrones of modern aristocrats.

Where is Smith's freedom of occupation right now? The economic aristocrats use their connections and favor to monopolize sovereignty over jobs by keeping even those with great talent for state policy and administration toiling in dark mines for their entire lives, all for a meager pittance in payment.

Is the correct response here to let free competition have you replace them in the mines?

The student who is currently learning law and economics is exactly the same as someone in the feudal Tokugawa shogunate: someone who daydreams of marching forward victoriously with merely a single sword brandished against all authority and the world itself, as if he were in the Warring States era. To Yui Shosetsu and those like him, the Warring States period would be far more thrilling and fulfilling than the reality of prostrating themselves before foolish feudal lords.[10] If there had been someone who rebelled against Tokugawa feudalism with a single sword and replaced the barons and lords, then maybe the laborers who lived like apes, working with their hands rather than minds and words, could replace the economic sovereigns who make millions of yen worth of profits every hour doing nothing but sitting idly by. Or perhaps they would be like Yamada Nagamasa and sail to America, visiting Manchuria and Korea, in an attempt to become economic feudal lords.[11] But are foreign lands not already divided among the larger barons?

If today one wanted to gain a position as high as, say, Mitsui or Iwasaki, it would be akin to aiming for emperor of Japan. One would be seen as, if not a blasphemous man, then at least one who has gone completely insane. Free competition is an expression that only works if there is an opportunity to actually compete. If, in free competition, there exist people, fickle and elegant in appearance, whipping their obese horse and sneering at a passing young

---

[10] Yui Shosetsu was a Japanese military scholar in the early Edo period. He plotted to use the death of Iemitsu to overthrow the shogunate, but was uncovered and captured before he could act (Keian Uprising). As an aside, Yui Shosetsu visited Kishu several times, and it is postulated that Yorinobu Tokugawa (Ieyasu's tenth son) may have been involved in Yui's plot.

[11] Yamada Nagamasa sailed to Siam (modern day Thailand) during the early Edo period. He became the governor of the Nakhon Si Thammarat province there.

man—the latter filled with disappointment as he pulls a heavy cart up a hill, upon which are seated old and infirm parents, an anemic wife, and children crying of starvation—it would mean that hell exists in free competition.

Hunt down and spur on weak little girls and other very young children. Make them work under cacophonous machines for the rest of their lives. They will absolutely never, for as long as they live, have the opportunity to even see the face of the master of their workplace. Now, have the workers compete freely against the master! This is what free competition says. This is equivalent to saying a serf could compete with their feudal lord. It cruelly humiliates and ridicules people. These lords know that slaves, though technically free to do as they please, don't possess any weapons to fight with. Not only that, the lords don a sturdy armor of education and wealth, all the while protected by sneaky retainers. They then brandish their spears of capital and ask for a fair battle. This is not free competition. This is the torture of prisoners.

Smith didn't press the idea of free competition for the sake of free competition. He envisioned free competition to occur in a world with equal footing as a way to defeat the aristocracy. Now, however, an economic aristocracy has been rebuilt under the garb of law, which they named beautiful freedom and quality. Much like in Smith's time, society has built an impassable wall between the upper and lower class and separated the two. Freedom of occupation rings hollow, left as nothing more than ink on the pages of *The Wealth of Nations*. Look for yourself! We are prisoners, connected to the machines that surround us. The machines that were expected to alleviate humanity's labor have become the castle walls of the elite social class, standing atop society with their tumultuous sounds, allowing oppression of citizens in the same manner as eras past. Machines that were welcomed into society as objects to eliminate poverty now strangle and crucify the poor. Those lucky enough to escape strangulation and crucifixion still work under the anxiety and constant threat of losing their jobs. Yes, it's shocking how quickly the poor social class has expanded and people have lost their jobs, inversely proportional to machine development. What free competition could possibly be achieved in such a situation; a situation where greedy nobles are protected by an impregnable castle of machines, far sturdier than any watchtower built of stone walls and trenches?

Free competition has been separated into two categories by social class. One category is the cruel economic free-for-all between monetary nobles, a battle free to take its own course. The second is the struggle between wage slaves for a single scrap of bread so that they can avoid starving to death. Could this truly be why the esteemed individualist Smith wrote about free competition? The reason that *The Wealth of Nations* only referenced Newcomen's steam engine, which was closer to a children's toy at the time, in one particular section, and by coincidence nonetheless, is because Smith lived a century ago.[12] If he were alive today, he would make machines the main subject of economic study and discourse, relegating the rest to the appendix. Most problems in society today stem from machines. All social phenomena revolve around machines. In fact, the fundamental problem that most, if not all, social sciences build upon should be whether or not it should be possible for these feudal castles labeled "machines" to be monopolized by the wealthy social class.

I will explain later why individualism is a mistake with no foundation. If one was to advocate for it even under today's economic aristocracy, they would need to do it despite how flawed it is, as Smith did, in order to usher in a revolution. A person groveling before the economic nobles, becoming a money slave with no purpose and no hope just so he can work, could technically be considered freedom of occupation for the individual. However, Smith would roll in his grave if he heard such a thing. No, the logical conclusion of individualism is an anarchist statement that nations are "unavoidable evils." It is then a

---

[12] Thomas Newcomen was an English inventor. He invented the first practical steam engine in 1712.

natural conclusion that the advocacy of individualism as a theory would cause the appearance of people who, admiring the idea of absolute individual freedom, propose an anarchy. Some of those people resort to bombings and the like, and so they are currently suppressed by massive powers, but the people who, as individualists, are glorifying modern society's "unavoidable evil" are resorting to weaponized starvation on a far larger scale than mere bombs to achieve their ideas. They are essentially publicly approved anarchists. Whether through socialism or individualism, if modern society allows these economic aristocracies to exist, then one has no choice but to stand on the opposite side. Among those who consider all of Japan today to be socialist, there exist individualists who still chant the old mantra of dogmatic freedom and equality, yet admit that a revolution in modern society simply can't be avoided. These are people standing on the opposite side of modern society (and because of this, they can be classified under a wider definition of social revolutionaries; we will explain why later).

Chapter 2

Speaking of this economic aristocracy, unless one declares themselves a follower of aristocratism, all people must admit that such a thing must be broken down and abolished. This is why scientific socialism is built upon the foundations of all social sciences and why it advocates a fundamental revolution. To that end, socialism requires a knowledge of this economic aristocracy. What exactly happened so that, after feudalism was abolished via a revolution, this economic aristocracy was built atop the ruins, requiring yet another revolution?

This explanation depends on your interpretation of "capital" and "plot of land" or "region." Academics, brains made of fluff, are satisfied by explaining the aristocratic fortress known as capital as "the result of diligence, thrift, and savings." Such academics, born in poor households and thus believing in the Shinto sect known as Tenrikyo, spend their entire lives worshipping foxes and raccoons. That is just their pitiful nature. Because of this, they are left behind by the evolution of economic history, and their knowledge is limited to what people one century before them knew. Their knowledge is of the age of individual production and singular-scale industrial manufacture. Yet they try to explain and interpret modern social-scale production and large-scale industrial manufacture with that small-scale knowledge.

Still, those people have done their work. They have accomplished enough and deserve eternal peace and rest. We should not be whipping the dead bodies of those old economists.

Imagine, for a moment, if a large, wide river had a single part of its water stagnate and form a lake spanning tens of thousands of miles. Then a sly otter poked his small head out of the surface of the lake and said, "The reason this lake is overflowing with water is all because I put forth my utmost effort in scooping the water here from the riverside." The remaining economists who still believe in old economics would then say, "Exactly. This is a result of the otter's diligence, thrift, and savings." They would say and believe this, same as they say and believe the real-world equivalent. Economics should approach this problem not via the lake, not via the current of the river, but by going all the way back to the source of the water and investigating there.

The single hoe in a farmer's hand or the swinging axe owned by a carpenter is, of course, a result of their diligence, thrift, and savings. In the days when single families worked and lived happily ever after,[13] or when Adam and Eve were first cast out and ordered to perform labor, it was true that diligence, thrift, and savings were the source of capital. However, after machines were invented, this capital based on individual labor had little in common with the source of that massive current of water.

If a single bottle of fine liquor, distilled from the blood of hundreds of human beings, and glittering diamonds the size of chestnuts, created from the sweat and tears of tens of thousands of fellow people working south of the equator, isn't enough waste and extravagance to satisfy these economic nobles; if buying such things is so slow to deplete their capital that it makes them say "the pain of life is finding a way to spend enough," in response to said capital increasing at an exponential rate every year, yet this is still considered "the result of diligence, thrift, and savings," then every dictionary in the entire world needs to correct their definitions of these words. If one would call this wealth the result of the owner's individual labor, then these capitalists who have never labored in their lives must be able to create something from nothing. This isn't the diligence, thrift, and savings of the individual, small-scale manufacturing era. This is the accumulation of capitalists plundering and monopolizing the large-scale, society-wide manufacturing of today.

---

[13] Referring to many old folk tales and fables.

"Capital is the accumulation of robbery." This scientific conclusion is based on the fact that manufacturing is being done on a societal level, yet the results are being distributed among individuals. Meanwhile, the society that did the manufacturing receives nothing. Karl Marx's *Capital* was written using knowledge from the very distant past. Because of this, many of the smaller details are open to infinite criticism, but the key point—"capital is the accumulation of robbery"—is an immutable truth on par with the theory of gravity.

Marx created a value theory that says: "The value of goods is not determined by supply and demand, but set by the length of labor required to produce them."[14] He then used that as a base to form many different arguments. This means that a gem picked up on the side of the road, which only required a minute of labor, is many times less valuable than a desk which took hours of labor to make, right? Does it mean that natural products that took no labor to make have no value? Would one say that two identical pieces of coal could have different values if one was more difficult to mine, and thus required longer hours of labor to obtain? Could it be that a completely useless item that requires long hours of labor to manufacture holds a higher value than a very useful item that can be made quickly? Is the value of an hour that was spent catching a single fish equivalent to an hour of a clockmaker on the job or an hour of an author writing something? Because the original idea received these fair and reasonable criticisms, it was shaken to its very core. Unfortunately, the actual truth of "capital is the accumulation of robbery" was buried under the otherwise valid criticism.

It cannot be denied that, even today, among those who would call themselves socialists, there exist some who, much like many evolutionists would idolize Darwin, still worship Marx's *Capital* as gospel. These people are satisfied merely arguing that, "Value is calculated depending on the length of

---

[14] This is known as the Labor Theory of Value, developed from David Ricardo's theory.

labor spent." Even so, the truth that was found and honed through a long period of intense research not only modified and corrected his original theory of value, but also determined what makes up the fundamental base of an economic aristocracy—that being "capital is the accumulation of robbery." In other words, in the same way that the lands owned by nobles were completely reformed after the revolution because they were discovered to have been plundered, based on the historical interpretation of each country (Japan's historical interpretation is based on the *Theory of National Polity* during the Bakumatsu period),[15] Marx's *Capital* discovered by scientific induction that these economic aristocrats plundered their "capital" as well.

Thus, like the revolutionists who defeated the nobles of the past by showing, through historical descriptions and records, proof that the lands these nobles owned were in fact stolen, socialism, which believes that the economic aristocracy should be reformed, must now show through historical research the proof that capitalists have plundered all they possess.

Like Mitogaku's *Dai Nihonshi*, Marx's *Capital* makes clear the history that economic aristocrats have created and developed. The truth he arrived at after the correction of his mistaken theory of value is in the following simple sentence: The wages of the laborer are controlled by the laws of supply and demand. The increase in population has since caused an oversupply of laborers,

---

[15] The original says "Theory of Law and Obedience." "Law and Obedience" refers to the succession of the imperial throne and the arguments made regarding it. The "Theory of Law and Obedience" asks if the succession of the throne is legitimate or not. Neo-Confucianism makes this problem a focal point of intense study and debate, and this influence is what led Mitogaku to create the "Theory of the Southern Court's Legitimacy." In volume 1 of Jirou Kamishima's collection of literary works, he explained the Theory of Law and Obedience as the Theory of National Polity, so, in order to make all this as easy to understand as possible, we've translated it as "Theory of National Polity."

and the invention of machines (except in cases where it has caused a business to expand) has decreased the demand for those laborers. This has caused the market value of laborers themselves to fall below the value of the basic food they need. Capitalists sign contracts with these laborers that pay them just enough to feed themselves, then force them to work thirteen to fourteen hours a day. From what is produced during these long hours of labor (I would ask you to pay close attention here; we are valuing the laborer's time itself, and are not speaking of the value of what's obtained through these long hours of labor), the laborer receives currency equal to their food expenses, while the capitalist steals and pockets whatever remaining value is created through demand of the product. What's accumulated through this robbery becomes capital. This capital is then used to hire even more laborers, begetting robbery on an even larger scale, snowballing into more and more capital. This is akin to the budding of an aristocracy via creation of powerful local clans. The situation will gradually build into an era of economic war (such as in modern Japan), and will then proceed to, due to a stern and unmoving economic feudalism, an era where major capitalist giants merge together (such as with America's trusts).

The reason that minor capitalists, who are similar to the countless local clans, were able to become a small number of powerful lords who can stand on their own, and eventually develop into stern, authoritative economic lords, is because of the modern machine industry. That's why we call the machine industry the castles or citadels of these aristocracies. Like an object thrown in the air must fall to earth due to gravity's pull, historical evolution is also controlled by physical laws. Once we progressed into the nineteenth century, however, we saw development speed up at a pace so quick that it could give the steam locomotive, another of man's own inventions, a run for its money. Those who boarded this locomotive of trends quickly—or rather, those lucky few whose situation caused them to stumble aboard it without their own knowledge of the subject—are either the current economic nobles or their ancestors. Those who cleverly used machine production, or those lucky few again who happened to be in a position to use it, made use of their mechanized citadels to easily suppress and overpower independent craftsmen and artisans. Those independent craftsmen, still needing to feed themselves, could no longer afford to maintain their independence among such force. They instead became part of the winning army's forces, turning themselves into laborers. Thus was the bud of an economic aristocracy cultivated.

Independent craftsmen once had complete ownership over everything that resulted from their labor because they ran their own business. Today, the result of one's labor is stolen from him completely, besides the small amount necessary for him to buy food, and nobody thinks to even question this. Instead, they simply work more and more, nonstop underneath the capitalists, while the latter decree the sanctity of their possession of these stolen goods.

If one was even a single step too late in boarding that train, regardless of how fast he may run, he will never be able to catch up. Those who were lucky enough to board one step faster spend this accumulation of robbed value on new machines to overpower and suppress the smaller capitalists who can't afford those new machines. This leads to a cycle of increasing their wealth with these new machines, allowing them to switch to even newer machines, once again suppressing and overpowering any smaller capitalists who can't keep up. Overpowering others creates even more wealth for the conqueror, allowing him more power to overwhelm others further. At this point, the increase of capital isn't affected by whether the capitalist is diligent or lazy, intelligent or foolish. It progresses based on the development and invention of machinery with the certainty of a mathematical equation.

If any major capitalists cannot defend against the development of these new machines and thus fail, it means countless now-unemployed workmen gathering at their gates. The local clans of the economic aristocracy spread their wings of conquest here. These unemployed begin to compete with each other, making the market price of wages fall as low as they can bear, just enough of an amount sufficient for their survival as animals. Their empty stomachs and the cries of their wives and children transform them into ghouls as they are finally forced to fight for and seek out a slave's ball and chain. At first, there were at least attempts to keep a minimum wage that would allow a man to support his wife and children, but now, with machines which require no physical strength from their operators, the sanctity and happiness of the family is reduced to a matter for poets and moralists. At this point, mothers in their final month of pregnancy and innocent children are being captured and chained to the workhouse.

These lords of the economic Warring States era use their capital to invade other regions, turning them into plundered land as well. Naturally, the major landlords who perform this plundering of land use the land and capital they gain from such acts to enlarge the area which they control. This usury capital becomes the bullets used to maintain control over and occupy these territories. In Japan, much like the major landlords in Ireland or Europe before the revolution, the people who plundered land during the war were forced to give it back to the state during the Meiji Revolution. Those people are left as mere figureheads with no real power in the modern day. (This is why chanting socialism directly and with little nuance, declaring that "Any owned land is merely a good plundered during the war!" and advocating forfeiture, is akin to shooting a gun without taking aim at a target.)

In Japan, people who lived under the possession of these lords only had tenant rights. The state then gave those people human rights and the plots of land went into the possession of small independent farmers.[16] (This is why it

---

[16] The original uses the phrase "small agrarian farmland." We realize that the translation might be more vague or difficult to understand, but we had no choice but to translate it this way in order to keep the same meaning. This is because, while small farms were still common in the Meiji period, "agrarian farmland" makes it sound like an entire society and way of living, which didn't match the original meaning.

would be somewhat logical to say that the state is free to restore the rights that it gave by bearing the interest on the public debt.)[17]

Anyway, it's a fact that Japan's land has been wrestled from the plundering hands of those conquerors. However, a new thief is now beginning to use the power of capital to swallow up those lands again. In recent years, along with the progress of machine industry, capital has increased in demand infinitely, leading to it possessing infinite value. If one were to compare the profit on interest, profit that comes in every single year without fail—profits that are unparalleled in other countries—to the old and minutely detailed farming that occurs on paddy fields small enough to fit into a paper bag, one would find that the latter barely offers enough to survive on even if the entire family works hard, while the former is so much larger that the difference could stretch from here to the moon. Even the textile industry, which was often called an important source of extra income for farmers, has been completely stolen by capital.

The burden of land taxes to major landowners is like land rent, society's natural right toward a social product. To small independent farmers, however, it's a threat against their meager sliver of ownership. Most of them can't live a different life from the tenant farmers of the serf age, who worked like honey bees for their lords. The country bumpkins that city folk sneer at are valuable goods that are kept safely under lock and key, at least when they aren't being displayed for ridicule in Tokyo or celebrating some festival of a local deity. They live in thatched roof houses without even a straw mattress, wearing the same ripped, torn, muddy clothes every day. This is the average daily life of a small or even moderately sized independent farmer. If one of these farmers were to try to provide two or three children even a moderate education befitting of their station, they would need to go into debt. They continue this poor standard of

---

[17] In other words, "Because the state gave us these rights in the first place, they are free to take them back if they wish."

living, up to and including the education of their children, while maintaining the land that their ancestors considered sacred. As things like failed harvests and plagues assault these people, they fall deeper and deeper into debt. The usury capital entwines their lands like a snake, and they will never be able to pay off the exorbitantly high interest rate of this capital merely with the pittance their land makes them, regardless of how hard they labor or how much they lower their already poor standard of living. High interest thus begets high interest, and that sacred land of theirs is eventually absorbed, within a few years, by the metropolitan capitalists or major landlords who can use capital as they please.

In England, they performed a tragedy known as "The Industrial Revolution." Now, in this foolish Oriental England, machine industry, that which wiped out small independent farmers in an instant, is attempting another industrial revolution. Just look statistically at how quickly land is being absorbed here. The speed of it could make a grown man shudder.

We are absolutely not saying, "Don't let ignorant farmers know of the dazzling life civilization brings, don't let them educate their children well, merely bind them to their lands that they were born in." Rather, socialism advocates that, once it is adopted, Japan's underdeveloped methods of independent farming must be erased completely and reformed into machine farming using the methods of large-scale agriculture. However, let's touch upon the future of our fellow countrymen who have been driven off their land as much as possible in recent years, forcing them to wander aimlessly. Those who simply rejoice and say, "Things will naturally result in large-scale agriculture like in England," are forgetting one terrifying fact—that these people will meet the same fate as those in England's Industrial Revolution. Where will they go? These aging fathers and mothers can't bring themselves to leave the land of their ancestors' graves, so they stay in the plundered land and eventually reach the path of serfdom. The path young men and women reach is that of the wage slave, gathering in cities to work for food. Parents no longer live with their children, and brothers or even mother and child separate from one another.

Ah, Japan, made of those serfs and slaves! They simply do not know that they have no option but to become serfs and slaves, no matter where they wander under this economic aristocracy.

The rural laborers who were chased out of their own lands then congregate in cities, and, like a dog in a house where its owners lie deceased,[18] they loiter in front of an apprenticeship placement or employment agency. This is the same as when city laborers, in the same difficult situation as those rural laborers who were reduced to poverty, are swept out of the factory at which they worked. It's said that Roman slave traders would write the price, age, and basic abilities of a slave on his neck, then throw him into a small shed made for animals and wait for a buyer to come around. Today's placement agencies, though, don't even have enough sheds for the hundreds of peasants they see every day. Regardless of how much difficulty one endures, he has no choice but to work himself to the bone so he may eat—this is where the lords of this economic aristocracy brandish their economic sovereignty and increase their power even further. Competition between those who found employment and those still unemployed, competition between the unemployed themselves, and competition between the rural and city laborers. This ghoulish competition between these people within the starving wage slave social class is the epitome of an inhuman atrocity.

This starvation competition between wage slaves (which is free competition in full effect!), offset by the competition over land between capitalists, truly results in a stream of blood (this is what we meant when we

---

[18] The literal phrase, "A dog of a house where a funeral was held," is a phrase symbolizing the last years of Confucius. The basic idea comes from an anecdote of wanting to participate in national politics but never having an opportunity to do so. It can be found in *The School Sayings of Confucius*, in the section on oaths.

wrote earlier of free competition being split up into two distinctions, one for each of these two social classes).

Economic scholars see capitalists leading their chief retainer and those retainers under him, collecting wage slaves, and managing commerce and industry, then call this production. However, the truth is that much of this is not what it seems. They have not started an enterprise, business, company, or what have you, so that they can manufacture or produce anything. They are simply ordering labor in order to defeat the production of their rivals. I assure you, this is not a strange play on words. If anything, the ones writing texts full of unnecessary adjectives and wordplay are the economic scholars. They would say that the rival chiefs in the Warring States period would battle each other not for themselves, but for the benefit of the state and the happiness of its people. They would name this destructive cost, a cost that mostly revolves around the intent to destroy the production of others, as manufacturing expense—yes, this can very well be called a Warring States era of economics.

The sound of machines and hammers signal the attack in this war zone, one can call them the first battle cry before the charge. These rival chiefs forget about anything related to compassion, honor, refined pleasures, mental and spiritual development, and anything of this sort. All they do is embroil themselves in war, with nothing else on their minds.[19] As the bloodthirsty warlords of old hungered for gore, these new economic chiefs, hungering for money, don't even care if their own friends or family are caught in the resulting attacks and assassinations. Much like the Warring States chiefs would form alliances and easily gift their wives and daughters as property, or even abandon them completely, in order to obtain more information on their

---

[19] The original text uses an old form of "all," but with the same meaning "devotedly, single-mindedly, all one does," etc. The original word was often used in a compound meaning "devoted prayer," where one merely sits and prays constantly, with all their heart.

enemies, noble ladies and daughters are married off to form capitalist alliances, and divorced to force more market competition.

In order to remain moral, the barbarian moralist must first say that murder, larceny, and cannibalism are unavoidable. Similarly, in order to be a moralist for the capitalist class, one must possess a conscience capable of saying that all the acts they commit are "moral" acts. Even when sleeping in their beds, these capitalists can't help but think of how to steal customers, wonder how to defeat their rivals' workplaces, and plan ways to ruin someone else's entire family. Demons whisper to them in their dreams. To be an entrepreneur or business operator, same as them, means that you are their absolute enemy. You are a nemesis that must be beaten down to hell. If the entire family of the defeated were to fall as low as possible and separate, if their elderly father had to get a side job making matchboxes, if the young members of the family, ones who don't yet know of the harshness of the world, became the lowest ranked public servants with miserly salaries, if their beloved daughter was so poor that she couldn't afford even a single accessory to her name, it would make the victors the happiest and most satisfied they had ever been in their life. The victors then sneer, revealing their golden teeth, and clap along while singing victory songs.

Because of these battles, they possess a special conscience. Regardless of the conceit and arrogance present on their face, they will forgo any semblance of shame or honor in front of a customer, kneeling down on the ground before them. They will prostrate like a criminal at the foot of any government official who can offer them any type of profit. Boasts and big talk are the noblest morals to them. Their own honesty, their own diligence, their own shop's sincerity, and the excellence of their own goods are all falsehoods they use to slander, abuse, and reject others. They revere these inverted morals. Bribes, corruption, campaigning, advertising, the entire repulsive battle includes all manner of perverted "conscience" from these people. (Read our explanation on the conscience of social classes in volume two, *The Ethical Ideal of Socialism.*)

Of course, a war can't continue without war expenses. They rebrand these war expenses as "production costs," and make every working man in society bear their burden, as if the expenses were some kind of tax. Having lost their clarity due to these battles, they then produce more than is in demand. Then, when society in its entirety, already pillaged, uses up all its power to purchase these oversupplied products, a financial panic ensues. That's right, a financial panic. The mere phrase puts both the victors and the losers in their places as if it were an earthquake. Roscher said, "Only barbaric peoples can escape an economic panic. Still, even if they avoid such a thing, one can't call them blessed."[20] Ricardo also said, "To lament a financial panic is the same as mistakenly thinking that the wealthy, who don't want to sail in their ships filled with money lest they encounter a storm, are actually being cautious because they care about their people."

However, this thinking will lead to a tragic, horrible explosion, the magnitude of which even the savages cannot imagine. Unfortunately, very much like all of society boarding a ship only to wreck, several years' worth of accumulated wealth vanishes in no time at all. These large explosions come every ten years or so, without fail, with smaller ones occurring all the time, everywhere. Jevons claimed the blame lay with sunspots.[21] The ones who are forced to deal with this Warring States era catastrophe are the modern version of the peasants and common townsfolk who had to deal with similar wartime atrocities in the past, the laborers and all of society itself.

Despite this, when economists and economic scholars define these "industrialists," they will say, without fail, "Industrialists are people who use their own calculations and, under their own responsibility, hire laborers to

---

[20] The German historical economist Wilhelm G.F. Roscher.

[21] William Stanley Jevons, an English economist famous for his utility theory of value. He believed that business cycle patterns correlated with sunspot counts on the sun, in a cycle of around ten years.

manufacture and produce things for them." If "their own calculations" refers to completely empty miscalculations that are planned and executed only in the interest of their own profits, then that part has some truth to it. The part about laborers manufacturing and producing things for their employers is also, at least in part, not untrue. However, the part mentioning "under their own responsibility" is absolute, terrifying fraudulence. Have these industrialists ever even tried to accept responsibility? Yes, they will shoulder their own profits and call it their responsibility, but that's only because it benefits them to do so. It must be known, however, that when supply and demand expand to a global economic scale, the ones who must shoulder the failure, burden, disaster, and general difficulties that these people, ones who have only ever operated behind the scenes, have caused with their reckless "calculations," are the laborers and entirety of society.

The loss of capital, which in itself is merely the accumulation of plunder, is to these adventurers the same as returning to their real, penniless forms. It is merely returning them to what they always were. However, the closing down of their factories, plants, and other manufacturing houses causes the unemployment of their laborers. The danger, chaos, and "personal responsibility" this causes society is a completely different issue. Economics is nothing more than a systematic organization of stupidity and cruelty, and it will leave those who lost their jobs as nothing more than a throwaway statistic buried in the corner of a newspaper. However, if a single man loses his job, his elderly mother will hang herself, his wife will writhe in pain from malnutrition, and his daughter will end up a prostitute. The unemployed man will then end up in a situation of "possible criminality" as he wanders aimlessly, unable to find food. This will finally drive him to steal money, and eventually wind up as a possible thief by trade, or even a murderer.

Back in the actual Warring States period, every time one of the conquered had another child, it would only add another criminal to the lowest rung of society. Of course, the victims of these new criminals weren't the upper-class criminals with guard dogs and thick walls to protect them. Those were the criminals who engaged in things such as fraud, swindling, bribery, embezzlement, stockjobbing, and other various crimes against the government, as these very things let them build up defenses around their luxurious mansions. It is the middle-class manufacturers and laborers who have no defense against such things. The lower classes have all their production stolen from them by the upper-class criminals, and when they do buy goods for themselves, they are forced to pay war funds disguised as taxes, and the last little bit they have is under constant threat from the unemployed, born from those who are defeated in this economic competition. If these effects are the "responsibility" of a single industrialist, then it is not something that can so easily be erased by that single person losing everything.

This massacre between capitalists will stop in the near future. In the United States of America, for example, it is already nearing its end. After they defeat the minor entrepreneurs, followed by the major entrepreneurs, then move onto the even bigger industrialists, they will realize that they are essentially the same few dozen winners fighting among themselves. The economic Warring States period is a historical method for arriving at economic feudalism. Although capitalists may be lacking in moral conscience, they are extremely sensitive to what is advantageous or disadvantageous to them. These people say "money" or "currency" and whisper "economics" or "finances" all day long from the moment they wake to the moment they go to sleep. There is no way they would not recognize that people of similar power fighting each other will end in massive loss. Rather than tens of millions of yen spent on advertising and a decrease in the value of goods due to competition, it only makes economic sense for the few major capitalists who remain standing to join together. This is what one calls a trust. On the other hand, the laborers who are competing with one another form solid labor unions which results in both of these social classes ending the free competition within their respective classes.

Even in our Japan, still embroiled in this economic Warring States period, the voices of trusts sometimes grow to be heard. Within the next decade it's likely we will end up in financial feudalism like the United States of America. Historically, once capitalists reach this sort of feudalism, the big names join together and overpower the entire body of society. Because they're built on such strong foundations, they are then able to use their authority on society itself, creating a harsh collection of taxes and other resources. Because of this grand amalgamation they've formed, the capitalists now have money to spare and the freedom to adapt to new machines as they're invented. They buy basic resources at extremely cheap prices, and, because they now no longer need a massive budget to advertise against the other parties, they make even higher profits.

Consequently, the surplus from this is usually either distributed among the masses, or the prices of goods fall. Either of these is generally enough to bring society out of that economic war, this is true. That's exactly why we don't whine pointlessly about it, nor do we agree with those who argue shallow, first-stage opinions such as "Trusts raise prices!" Statistically, trusts clearly make prices fall and offer a happier and more well-to-do society when compared to any period where minor capitalists are fighting each other in a free-for-all. However, one must also look statistically at the harsh collection that trusts impose upon society. Why? Because that is a trust. Because that is economic feudalism. Though not as many atrocities are committed during feudalism when compared to wartime, the harsh collection of resources imposed during this period signifies that it in fact is feudalism.

If the financial lords were eternally wise, or at least were made up of only wise men, they would calculate society's purchasing power, then use the lowering of prices as an easy excuse to wring the sweat and blood out of laborers by having said people worship those lords as benevolent sovereigns. The nobles of yore used this extremely sly knowledge to their advantage. However, because most of them are foolish feudal lords, they grow arrogant and feebleminded over their absolute and limitless power. Trusts, which have extreme, almost exclusive, power in the economic world, don't bother considering how production is maintained by the purchasing power of society, and thus extreme inflation occurs. The overproduction that results from this—as Ely would put it—lack of spending, naturally causes chaos in the economic world. In fact, an example of this is currently happening if one simply looks at America.

In a financial aristocracy, the collapse of the lords through their own hubris and imbecility, and the resulting commoner uprising, is a completely natural phenomenon—and a trust is simply a feudal lord with complete and unrestricted power. They hold their control up against humanity's throat. To a trust, the private law known as contract of sale becomes a public law. If, as jurists put it, "public laws regulate relationships and connections of authority, while private laws regulate relationships and connections of fairness," and "relationships of authority are relationships between the will of the strong and the will of the weak, and are relationships of command and obedience," then would it not mean that trusts, who have complete and utter control over humanity's material livelihood, are rulers in the truest sense? Sales do not occur via the equal wills of both parties. The ruler decrees the price, and the buyer, society in this case, obeys. This is a clear relationship between ruler and subject. These are true economic nobles, financial lords who collect taxes from all of society itself under the false name of "buying and selling."

Still, much as aristocratic rule eventually led to a civic state with state sovereignty (see *The So-Called Theory of Japan's National Polity and its Restorative Principle of Revolution*), financial feudalism does not occupy the end of history. When these corporate trusts attempt a major joining together, they shut down useless or under-performing workplaces, and, like the Turks, destroy any cities that rely on them. They also use the unending torrent of new machines to force tens of thousands of laborers into unemployment, adding those to society as well. These unemployed are welcomed by philanthropists, eyes filled with contempt, yet grins still on their faces, and the iron bars of society's prisons await them with open arms like the gates of hell. This tension and urgency then stir the laborers up to revolt against their noble lords—much like the peasants would revolt during the age of feudalism. The laborers form large unions and, through strikes that can last over a month, they continue the peasant insurrection. Strike after strike, factory closure after factory closure. Anarchists then spring into action here and use the famine of the laborers to incite violence. This becomes an excuse for the police to act, and even for the army to get involved. Thus begins tragic urban warfare.

The current of a river simply flows to wherever the flow must arrive. Niagara Falls roars so that it may fall into Lake Ontario, and the body of society boils so that it may arrive at socialism. As strikes are born and fail again and again, the peasant revolt eventually appears, standing atop the political regime. When the people gather under the banner of "socialism," the financial aristocracy will be defeated and fall, flowing onward, from the precipice of the Meiji Revolution.

The spark that ignites a revolution is a change in the idea of rights. This is why socialism is built upon, from start to finish, a very thorough argument and theory of human rights, and cannot accept even a little compromise or reconciliation. If socialism were to show cowardice in the face of rights, not a single tear would be shed by any who share its principles if society and the state were to crucify it under the name of order, safety, and happiness of the population.

Individualism, wearing its golden crown made of "the sanctity of possession" is currently putting socialism on trial. But my dear individualism, socialism shows that the very golden crown you wear is nothing more than stolen goods. You must not undermine that golden crown. The right of possession is sacred, after all. However, calling the right to possession sacred is a mere empty phrase to begin with. This sacred right can be attributed to different places depending on the reason of ownership. In the fantasy socialism before Marx, if one were to recognize the capitalist social class's right of ownership and beg and cry to God for salvation, those strict rights would merely sneer in response. Scientific socialism, however, wears that golden crown itself, stands above all others, and passes judgment like God.

During the aristocratic period of the Middle Ages, the voice of rights said "I take the nation myself. If I wish to become king, I will. If I wish to become emperor, I will."[22] The Meiji Revolution did refute this retroactively via the rights of nationalism, but it has become known as the theory of possession now. An example of this point of view would be when Rome, an empire built by conquest and plunder, erected twelve copper pillars as the grounds for an argument for their possession.[23] This was a right that all citizens had during ancient and medieval times. Another example of this being when the ancestors of the Japanese people plundered this land and then set up a system of rights here. This is also the point of view of those who believe that ownership is determined by physical strength.

This ideal of possession and occupation continued for a long time. Until the French Revolution in Europe and the Meiji Revolution in Japan, the ownership of land by national sovereigns and nobles was considered sacred due to this theory of possession. However, the true possessor of land absolutely does not gain possession of the land as an individual, but rather as part of the

---

[22] "Voice of rights" is a phrase used in volume 4 of this text, attributed to Hideyoshi Toyotomi. It has been reused here.

[23] We believe this is referring to The Law of the Twelve Tables (because the twelves laws were scribed on copper tablets when made public). The Law of the Twelve Tables were the foundational laws for ancient Rome and regulated legal proceedings, familial relationships, inheritance and succession, contracts, property rights, crime, illegal activities, public law, and religious law. The world renowned Roman law used these twelves tables as its foundation, though Roman law had an underdeveloped jurisprudence.

discovery of that land by an entire group of people. Since ownership rights gained through possession cannot be possessed themselves, the reason for ownership is erased. A corpse cannot reach out from inside its grave and continue possession, so the concept of inheritance rights is also unsupportable by the theory of possession. Because of this, if one were to extol possession theory today, he would be assassinating both the wealth born of succession and the reason he tries to continue succession of that wealth.

Yes, this is exactly why the kings and aristocrats were struck down for land ownership rights and why, just around the time of the revolution, individualism's labor theory tried to explain ownership rights. The obvious reason that this theory asserts "Earnings made by labor become the property of the individual who performed the labor," is that, as we left the nomadic era and transitioned into farming (at the same time that ethnic groups began asserting the theory of possession against each other), it protected production from people within an ethnic group who tried to ignore earnings generated by individual labor. The demand for ownership rights from this theory of labor protected the craft and production of the townsmen against the pillaging of the feudal lords during the Middle Ages, and was then touted again in order to erase the kings' and nobles' ownership of land built on top of the possession theory.

Amid that huge explosion during the revolution, what brought down the lands and fortunes of said kings and nobles, all gained through plunder, was exactly this idea that "Earnings made by labor become the property of the individual who did the labor." It was accomplished by labor theory's rejection of the possession theory's plundering. Why does labor theory's individualism speak of ownership rights, dressing them with such adjectives as "sacred," merely so that social products such as land and rent capital are stolen under the pretense of "possession"? The days of considering the ownership rights of an individual, brought about through individual scale labor, as something sacred have been buried by history. Today, our labor is on a societal scale, and that means only the ownership rights of society are sacred. If anything, the phrase "sanctity of ownership rights" is a crown of gold to socialists, as they believe society's rights are sacred indeed.

Socialism speaks of the sanctity of society's ownership rights towards any earnings born of society's own labor. Yet how can one say that public ownership of machines is "ignoring the right of ownership"? If one were to say that my rights apply to an item I possess, despite being born from the labor of someone else, it would be an ideal of rights that reaches back to pre-modern ideas wherein ownership rights are determined by physical strength. It's the same as saying that humans are possessed with the use of chains and whips, so abolishing slavery means ignoring the right of ownership. If one would oppose socialism by espousing individualism, then he should rely on said individualism's arguments regarding rights, and the justice of ownership rights belonging to the one who labored for them is exactly what law under individualism wants. If, despite this, one wants to refute the public ownership of machines using individualism, which built itself upon labor theory, the only way he could assert his rights over such machines is if he were a descendant of famous inventors such as Watt. Capitalists, whose only labor is bodily excretion, only hold sacred rights to ownership of that unhygienic mess itself, as it was born by their own labor.

No, a machine itself isn't something to which you can define and credit, nor divide and attribute, a certain amount of labor. Watt's achievement as an individual regarding a single steam engine is not even one percent, or even one tenth of one percent, when compared to all the knowledge used in order to build that machine—this is why individualism is mistaken. Those who can assert towards these machines an amicable, true right of ownership under the ideal of law are not their original inventors, nor are they the capitalists of the social class that possess them. It is not the social class of laborers who currently operate the machines either. Only a historically continuous society made of humanity joined together as one can claim such a thing. Machines are crystals of human knowledge accumulated throughout history. The souls of deceased ancestors reside in machines, and the machines work so that those souls can be loved by their descendants, even if the majority of their beloved children are slaving away in hellish torment while a few of those wily kids assert their possession based on ideals of rights held during a more barbarous age. Let us say that, regarding capital produced on a societal scale of labor, justice today asserts public ownership under the sanctity of ownership rights.

Society's ownership rights towards earnings born of societal scale labor also apply towards land rent. Factually, the Ricardian theory of rent shows that land rent is both a result of population growth and a product of the increasing civility of society. Of course, as many scholars since Ricardo's time have pointed out, cultivation limits don't change as quickly as he claimed they do. Change could be obstructed by the likes of long-held beliefs or customs, and thus things such as rent paid by the tenant farmer is not something that rises or lowers according to the rules outlined in Ricardian theory. Reality may also fail to follow those rules in situations where new foreign lands must be cultivated, or rice is imported through foreign countries.[24] Because Ricardo was born in a pre-industrialized England,[25] he believed that land could only be cultivated in a set order, beginning from the most fertile regions. He likely did not consider the developing nation that cultivated its lands the exact opposite order.[26] Because of all this, one could say that in actuality the Ricardian law of rent had a weak base in regards to real-world practicality. In other words, he forgot about the impact of social conditions, and created the harmful

---

[24] At the time, Taiwan was growing rice and Japan would purchase it.

[25] The original text says "Old-world England," and we have taken that into consideration when translating it. We believe that Kita considered the world completely changed after the Industrial Revolution.

[26] The original text literally says "newly developing country." We believe it refers to America.

precedent of building academic economics on top of abstract arguments. This is plenty of reason for criticism.

However, even if his argument does have flaws, the average academic will not deny that one could only explain rent during his time from that exact perspective. Naturally, we socialists, as our name implies, realize that old-style economics, as a subject, contains countless errors. However, we also believe that one can think of land rent in a manner similar to Ricardo.

The market value of grains is decided based on the highest production cost. These differences in cost are created by the fertility of the land and difficulty of shipping.[27] The reason land with poor fertility is now being cultivated despite these increased costs is because the population has increased, and so the demand for grains has also increased. So even if one paid the landowner the entire difference in cost of production, then borrowed the land and cultivated it, one would make no more profit than what he would get simply cultivating infertile land. Because of this, all the difference in production cost becomes land rent. As the population continues to grow, we move on to even less fertile lands with even greater production cost, and the cultivation threshold lowers even more. The less one can cultivate there, the higher the difference in cost of production, and thus the higher the rent goes. As you can see, the reason current tenant farmers pay such massive rent to their landlords is because the increase in population makes them do so. What is, however, the relationship between the increasing population and the landlords, who don't even need to work to eat? In fact, land rent, the result of an increasing population, all being stolen by the landlords under the pretense of "sanctity of ownership" is hitching a ride on the back of individualism's ideal of rights.

---

[27] It might be slightly difficult to understand as "differences in cost," but what he means is "taking the difference between the revenue and production cost" and comparing that value for each different area of land.

Rent on city land is very clearly the product of the advancement of society. Setting up a railway station, thus increasing the rent of the land nearby, is not at all a reason to sanctify the landlord's ownership. When rent increases as a result of development of transportation or communication, the result should be attributed to electricity or steam power; it was not born of the labor of landlords, standing there screaming about eviction. The wealthy who bought land in Tokyo City,[28] after seeing that the value of such land would skyrocket in the future, do not have the right to steal whatever Tokyo City will someday make from its future advancements. Regardless of how landlords eat and defecate bits of land like worms, regardless of how they try and fill the rich Ginza district of Tokyo City, they do not possess digestive organs which can turn a bit of land into an equal bit of gold. The sanctity of ownership, a power from the days of the French Revolution, is something that society as a body should justly assert for itself, while landlords should be seen simply as thieves who use the right of possession to do their plundering.

Here, we do not intend to pointlessly harp on about the countless arguments excusing or defending rights regarding private property. We have already described why, through the theory of labor, machines should not be private property. We have also described previously why there is no reason for land to be owned through the theory of possession. However, even if land rent is a social product, the land itself is not currently possessed or occupied through plundering like it was with the aristocracy, so the above explanations do leave room to argue that the right of ownership itself shouldn't be ignored. In response to this, some retort by saying that there are countless trades made of stolen goods.[29]

---

[28] Tokyo was called this at the time.

[29] We're not sure what precisely this retort means. For now, we've translated it exactly as the original text said.

Others object to the invasion of the land by capitalists and their usury, which we also explained earlier, and attempt to defeat the argument that way. Those people are stopping at what could be called the cultivation theory and attempting a counter there. This theory uses as its base the idea that the long period of labor done to a piece of land has added value to what it is today. However, this argument has a weak base, and is forgetting that the only thing it's capable of cultivating are the tenant rights to a given piece of land, though the land is shared by an entire settlement.[30] Besides, this argument doesn't even realize that authors, who spend their entire life dedicating themselves to writing something will eventually lose their copyright after enough time has passed. Why can cultivating a single foot, a very minuscule amount overall, of a large piece of land determine the ownership rights stretching from heaven to the very axis of the earth? Is there also no time limit for this ownership? Will it continue for centuries or millennia to come? If some unskilled painter were to take a hanging scroll painted by the famous artist Okyo Maruyama and owned by a capitalist, smear it with some white paint, then claim, "I've worked on this!" would the capitalist abide by the artist's right to ownership? Earth was not made by landlords working miracles over a span of six days.

In contrast, we declare the following with absolute conviction. The aforementioned argument is the same as the baseless, speculative, and dogmatic rights argument from the era of individualism. Rights themselves are a social relationship. They determine the boundary lines when invoking the will or intent between multiple societies or between the people who make up said societies. The relationship between God and humanity is controlled by religion, and the relationship between people and other animals is controlled by biology. This is why, when attempting to explain rights, which are human social relationships, if one were to say that God descended from heaven and

---

[30] Legally, most of this sort of ownership is called "common ownership," and land owned in this way is called "common land."

gave man all his natural rights, or that humans are biological organisms and thus have a right to existence, though these things are similar to the ideals of socialism, one must understand that they are still absolutely part of the revolutionary theory from the age of individualism (and even today, there are still revolutionary individualists who use this very argument, mixed in with modern socialists).

To those who would defend the modern system using ideals of rights from the era of individual, small-scale production and manufacture, we should say the following. Though socialism may, as described above, show the path to overturning the foundations of the current economic aristocracy, and in that respect is similar to what the theories and arguments of individualism did to the aristocracy in the past, socialism should only speak and act on truth, and so should not try to set up societal rights of ownership using an incorrect argument about the natural rights of man from back in the individualist era.

In other words, both socialism and individualism occupy a position on the same side regarding the current economic aristocracy, but socialism is, in the end, socialism. It should not be considered the same as baseless individualism. In much the same way that individualist economics instruct that a revolution must occur again, and so anyone following individualism has no choice but to become a revolutionary, all one must understand regarding this problem of the rights argument is that individualism's jurisprudence will not offer a defense of the current financial aristocracy.

Socialism's rights argument does not even bother with these atomized individuals who only think of the theory as ideals on paper, but rather puts society as the subject to whom benefits are attributed. So if one doesn't think of the word "benefits" with crude connotations in mind, such as temporary treatment or immediate policies, the way State Socialists do,[31] but instead

---

[31] In multiple places, Ikki Kita holds a negative assessment of State Socialism. How this should be perceived in relation to the actions he took later on is a substantial question

thinks of it as a method that the organism known as "society" took in order to adapt to the goal of survival and evolution (see *The Theory of Biological Evolution and Social Philosophy*), then social relationships change and also become methods toward that goal—meaning that rights, which define relationships, also evolve according to that transition.

That means primitive equality and common ownership systems in villages were determined and set by social relationships that had adapted to that goal back during a peaceful, primitive society. This in turn means that equality and communism were the rights back then. Eventually the population increased and we transitioned into the nomadic period, where humans would wander and move around constantly. We then moved into an era of farming, but society still held the same goal of survival, and so adapted in such a way that it became just and correct to reject other settlements, and occupation and possession of other lands became the rights of that period. As the stronger villages forced weaker villages to accept their rights via physical strength, the people who lived in these settlements grazed cows and sheep and farmed the land through hard labor, and a system of private ownership was made for the rights to any earnings born of this. This means that possession of land by robbery and plundering was also a right of the time, and private ownership was considered justice in its own era as well. As society evolves, however, new concepts of justice erase the old rights and move forward. Ideals of the right to occupy land for possession were considered just in their day, but were defeated by labor theory as part of individualism's ideals of rights. At present, the ideal that the individual is the final goal has been denied by a new idea of justice: that society is the true bringer of benefits. Individualism's theory of rights was overcome by the foundational belief that socialism's theory of rights holds: that society is the source of benefits, and these benefits should be attributed to it.

---

and discussion throughout historical political thought.

It is said that socialism stands upon a thorough, complete argument for rights, but the idea of rights in socialism is not some dogmatic, idealistic admiration of justice which ignores the benefits of society. In fact, the benefits of society, the profits of society, and the advantages of society are themselves rights, and that is true justice. Perhaps, then, socialism, which asserts public ownership of land and industrial machines under the name of rights and justice, could itself be considered a benefit that has adapted to society's goal of survival and evolution.

Chapter 3

If socialism is to propose that land and industrialized machines are to be public property, then socialism must also be a benefit adapted toward society's goal. This is why the financial correctness and justice that we have discussed in this volume should be interpreted as the financial well-being and happiness that would occur if socialism was adopted. Anything that opposes justice can't be a benefit, and what does not bring benefits can't be justice. Socialism insists upon a just public ownership of land and industrialized machines because it means that, through an increase in benefits via public operation of these things, it will increase and advance the economic well-being of society as a whole. The economic Warring States era moves into a system of economic feudalism, which then advances to an economic civic state. Labor unions appearing, which are similar to conscriptions, are proof of this.

Of course, even today's manufacturing industry has labor unions that operate with a methodology similar to the military. Much like when the industrial revolution first began and people ceased to manufacture things individually, it became known that machines should be operated in large groups for efficiency purposes, and while using machines as such, labor unions came together to facilitate that method.

However, the military during the era of aristocracy (a figurative Warring States period), and the military of today's civic state are fundamentally different in two ways. The first is that warriors in the aristocratic era formed servile contracts with their lords, and thus engaged in battle following orders, while the troops in today's civic state are organizations that were conscripted as part of all citizens' duty and/or rights. The second difference is that the battles of the Warring States era held a goal of returning to the lords what benefits and profit they achieved, and the warriors and even citizens were no more than a method to do so. The battles of the current civic state exist for the benefit of the nation and the advancement towards its goals. The people are working together to fight the financial nobles in this modern economic Warring States era, and the relationship between capitalists and those under them is just like during the feudal period: it's comprised completely of wages and tributes.

The current morals, which advocate complete servile obedience, then make those people fight to increase the wealth of these financial nobles. Aristocrats in the past would dismiss their nearly servile retainers at will, and acted as if they had the right to massacre anyone as they pleased if they were angered. Economic aristocrats of today are similar in that it is considered their right to fire scholars and office workers, who have not even had a chance to work very long, however they please, and starve tens of thousands of laborers to death if it benefits them. Aristocrats in the past held the moral right to ignore the number of bodies buried in their pursuit of both profit—via expansion of their lands—and power to overwhelm any others.[32] Once again, today's modern financial nobles would sever the arms and legs of thousands of laborers using the blade known as machines, then slaughter them by forcing these people into unsafe mines to work, yet they still face no moral responsibility for such things. During the Warring States era, the various nobles defended their own regions and attacked others, causing chaos among the citizens, and, once again, something similar is happening today. Modern financial lords defend their own type of industry while attacking others, scorching the production and laborers of other lords in this economic free-for-all battle.

We must stop comparing the troops of socialism—laborers—against the military troops of the civic state. Why? Because there are, once again, two distinct and important differences between the two. The first difference is that

---

[32] Literally "Let a person's bones wither," a phrase which means to show no concern for sacrifices made.

the civic state's troops are used to expel and ostracize the rights and benefits of foreign countries, or at the very least to compete against them. They are recruited and trained for this very purpose. However, the troops of socialism, the laborers, manufacture and produce for the mutual benefit of the entire world. The second difference is based on organization. The civic state's army is made up of a commander who holds absolute authority, along with a rank of people who swear servile obedience to him. The rewards received by each are differentiated by that master-slave relationship as well. However, the troops, once again the laborers, of socialism are promised plenty of freedom and independence. In addition, laborers work on moral activities based on public duty and other encouraging motives, to the exclusion of any authoritative or commanding organization, and their material rewards are exactly the same regardless of how light or heavy their duties. To summarize, socialism's militaristic labor unions use requisitions to gather citizens, ranging from young adults to the middle-aged. The system is then based on the freedom and independence guaranteed to these people, along with their ability to choose the perfect occupation that fits them best. One can say, essentially, that this is a method of production which results in such orderly and grand united organizations.

This is precisely a large-scale economic revolution atop the stage of historical economic affairs. However, looking at political history from the era of provincial governors and local rulers, to the period of rivalry between local warlords, then progressing into the feudal system, until finally reaching the point where we have national military organizations through the rights and obligation of the civic state, one could ask the following question. After developing economic powers, experiencing the ups and downs of annexation during the Warring States era, then finally ending up at the economic feudalism knowns as "trusts," is there any way our flow of economic history could avoid the precipice of the Meiji Revolution and **not** end up as an economic civic state with a national labor army? The answer lies in humanity's most detestable flaw, the tendency to resign oneself to one's present fate and accept the bad conditions as inevitable. This is what made people think of feudalism as the final stage of humanity's social system and not want today's nation of free citizens. Like those people, there are some today who fearlessly follow the current of economic feudalism and drown in it. They shamelessly point their icy cold derision at socialism's ideals of these "conscripted labor organizations" and say things like,

> "If people aren't motivated by self-interest, won't they be lazy?"
> "Won't people hate physical labor?"
> "Will they really have the freedom to choose an occupation?"
> "How can the individual's freedom and independence be assured?"
> "Won't this usher in bureaucratic despotism?"
> "Isn't it unjust to try and make humans, unequal by nature, all equal?"
> "Won't it weaken manufacture and industry, thus plunging all of society into extreme poverty?"

These are by no means an exhaustive list of criticisms, either.

We will next reveal the response to this. The point of socialism is to fulfill all of these lofty requests. If socialism called itself socialism, yet lacked in even one of these noble areas, its final goal of social evolution would be nothing more than an empty ideal, a flawed diamond. Still, we earnestly hope that the people who ask these unending questions of socialism's proposals would take a moment to calm down before uttering them, and direct those same questions at the current society instead. Does current society not strain the peoples' motive of self-interest, and make society as a whole lazy? Does current society not cause people to hate physical labor? Does current society truly offer freedom to choose an occupation? Does current society assure an individual's freedom and independence? Does current society not suffer from awful bureaucratic despotism? Does current society really offer a fair and equal solution of unfairness? Is current society not plunging all of society into extreme poverty by ruining manufacture and industry via economic wars and harsh collections?

They will most likely say that there are other problems to resolve first. What they are really asking is whether or not the theory of evolution is false, and if human history will remain in the stage of economic aristocracy, unchanging until the very earth

In order to properly explain socialism and to answer the countless criticisms such as those listed above, we must designate some representative academics. These will be people who advocate academic socialism or state socialism.[33] The main reason is that we must expose the truth of these ideas called academic or state socialism and protect socialism from such fraud. Pure socialism absolutely cannot be tainted by that kind of deception.

Academic socialism is called such because it is asserted from college podiums, and state socialism is called such because of the government and ministry, but these two ideas don't even face the same vector as socialism. The nation is not the government, nor should the sanctity of the college podium be trampled on by the deception of the capitalist class. However, all governments and powerful classes use the term "nation" when it's convenient for them, and the capitalist class uses the intelligentsia for its own benefit.

Now these frauds, words filled with bent truths and actions brushing national rights aside, have stolen the sacred university podium and ethical system known as a nation for themselves. No, these people are not socialists at

---

[33] "Academic socialism" is defined as "A theory where capitalism is not reformed or revolutionized, but rather gradually improved via things such as social policy and social legislation." It is sometimes called "reformism." The term "academic socialism" was coined when a Marxian socialist cynically called reformism "A play on words that disconnected academics who don't understand reality spout off at university podiums."

all. They know that the current economic aristocracy shouldn't be maintained by strict individualism, so it's a simple matter of capitalism abusing the socialist flag and planning to violate international law by muddying the waters of their retreat.

Currently, socialism in our Japan is still in its infancy, and because our societal body is still in hibernation, capitalism holds absolute power here. Because of this, we will not call despicable the violations of international law which resulted from these people, who call themselves academic or state socialists in our country, compromising to the forces of socialism.[34] The average college professors, brains lacking in the power of comprehension, are closer to simple oral interpreters as they stand there translating and reporting the opinions and discussion of other people. So it makes sense that such brains are well suited to moderate stances and compromises. It also benefits them to be able to dodge the dislike that many people feel towards real socialism. Yet they abuse the flag of socialism to try and give an impression of strict fairness and equality. They use this to trick any socialists who haven't yet understood the truth and dupe real ideals of socialism to their side. In an attempt to give off the impression that they are the true exponents of socialism, they whisper to those socialists who still doubt themselves. This is especially effective against the average citizen, as these people are already likely to have a distaste for socialism, and so one should be extra cautious in that case. Academic socialism is not something that should be explained and lectured from the sacred university podium, but rather renamed "capitalist socialism," as it is asserted from impure podiums as a defense for capitalists. State socialism is also a

---

[34] It's not clear from the text, but it's likely he meant, "We won't say that academic socialism and the like are petty compromise plans from the capitalists who have been criticized by socialists." The reason is because the forces criticizing capitalists were extremely weak in Japan, so there would be no reason for capitalists to compromise at all.

misnomer, as it doesn't proclaim the right of benefit attribution toward the state; it is rather "government socialism," which attempts to use the government populated by the powerful social classes to maintain the authority of its bureaucrats. Pure socialism should not follow this same path of trickery and deceit.

State socialism does not understand the true nature nor the legal principles of a state, which will be explained further in *The So-Called Theory of Japan's National Polity and its Restorative Principle of Revolution* and *The Enlightenment Movement of Socialism*. Here, I will instead argue against two representative scholars, who assert state socialism despite not having an understanding of the correctness of socialism's stance on economics; in other words, a complete ignorance of the financial well-being that socialism asserts.

One representative is Tokyo Imperial University Law Professor Noburu Kanai, and the other is Kyoto Imperial University Law Professor Kinji Tajima. We can judge their main points based on the former's *Socioeconomics* and the latter's *Recent Economic Theory*. Something to keep in mind, though, is that *Recent Economic Theory* holds a deep sympathy towards socialism, but *Socioeconomics* is filled with a remarkable distaste for socialism, almost to the point of being anti-socialist. It's true that the latter asserts this ill-mannered sentiment: "the socialist party was formed with the goal of interpreting social problems, but the existence of the socialist party is now one of society's problems," but it isn't as hostile as the sentiment of *Socioeconomics*. *Socioeconomics* counts the benefits of economics, and starts with the following conclusion:

> We have the utility to correct a mistaken concept; one which knowingly and viciously provokes and possibly harms the public peace. This discipline exploits, no, abuses the dark facets of the world in general, and the memories of the horrible acts committed by its party members and adherents in Germany and elsewhere still exist fresh in

our minds. It is only possible to correct this by intense, accurate research in the field of economics.

The entire thing is written with an intense fear and hatred of socialism, so *Recent Economic Theory* can't even be compared to *Socioeconomics* on that front.

Still, the moderate attitude of *Recent Economic Theory*, which clearly hasn't lost its sympathy towards socialism, could actually result in a more favorable acceptance of the professor's errors. Meanwhile, even if one compares the impact of *Socioeconomics* to its clear goal of provoking discomfort towards socialism, the power that it gives to the public isn't any less. We must also remember that both of these men are major authors with over a dozen books written, and have implanted seeds of misunderstanding and distaste towards socialism along with the general concepts of economics in the minds of tens of thousands of public and private university students, in both the disciplines of law and economics. We firmly believe that, if the socialist party occupies power through an actual movement, while the state socialist party may accompany it, the only thing that will remain of state socialism in academia is the international violation of law of their abuse of the national flag; and this will remain as nothing more than the last point that the economic aristocracy can bring up as an enemy of socialism's truth, since pure capitalist economics cannot sustain itself today.

Firstly, we can gain an understanding of exactly how little Professor Kanai understands about the very foundations of socialism through an excerpt from *Socioeconomics*. In it, Professor Kanai writes the following:

> Those who argue for socialism sometimes say, "The source of capital is labor, so all profit made from industrial manufacture should be awarded to all the laborers." However, this is a very mistaken argument. Back before society had developed much at all, capital was

completely born from labor as the argument claims. At this point, one might conclude that the source of all capital is labor, but during such an undeveloped period, what could be called capital was consumed as soon as it was created. It wasn't yet true capital as we think of it today. Such primitive capital gradually evolved into what we could call capital today. That is a simple summary of the way capital increased. Now, if that is the case, then when capital increases, that which supports the increase is not only labor, but also the capital itself. One could say that the capital itself has the power to support its own increase. If no capital at all existed, then labor would be isolated completely, it would not be able to aid manufacture at all. In other words, labor only becomes useful when combined with capital, and capital finds a use in manufacture through labor. Because of this, the two hold an inseparable relationship like the wheels of a stagecoach. When adding the force of nature to these two, the truth that we understand regarding manufacture is similar to the way a coach needs ground to drive on and a force moving it forward in addition to its wheels. Assuming that the source of capital is labor, and if one could say all profits born of industry and manufacture should be awarded to the laborers, then one could use the same argument to say that, since capital is what allows such a thing to happen, all profits should be attributed to capital. If capital is only useful through labor while labor is simultaneously only useful if capital exists, then it means the two should each receive fitting rewards.

Even back during undeveloped times, labor was not the only source of capital. Labor should be considered the father of capital, but without the mother of capital, nature, it could never be born. It is only reasonable that the land owner who provides the land, a natural substance, should be justly rewarded as well. Though our economic society already distributes things unfairly, socialist arguers try to make things even more unfair. On top of all that, what is considered capital

58 | The Theory of Japan's National Polity and Pure Socialism

in today's society actually helps labor as capital, and much of that capital is put to use for manufacture as well. This is an age where capital creates more capital, and if that is true, it is obvious that capitalists should be rewarded as such. This should give an idea on how those who argue for socialism are mistaken.

This kind of misunderstanding is not limited to Professor Kanai at all. There are many other arguments that also assert a harmony between labor and capital, and one of the people with a similar misunderstanding is professor of literature Tongo Takebe, a man who lectures academic socialism from the position of sociology.[35] Though it's true that socialism is a deep subject that can't be easily researched, such an explanation of socialism, misrepresenting the fundamentals so thoroughly, can only stem from complete ignorance of the subject.

Professor Kanai was involved with the labor issue, so many average people think of him as a socialist. With great trepidation, he often makes excuses and defenses for himself regarding this belief, but the biggest proof that his excuses are true is the fact that he seemingly knows nothing about the foundations of socialism. We do find his socialism unpleasant, but we aren't trying to reciprocate with "an eye for an eye" mentality. That said, if one wants to criticize a different set of beliefs, then he must possess the ability to understand those beliefs. If this is extremely rude of us to demand, it is nonetheless something that a professor of law at an imperial university must possess.

When the professor attempts to understand socialism, he criticizes it by saying, "Those who argue for socialism sometimes say 'The source of capital is labor, so all profit made from industrial manufacture should be awarded to all

---

[35] Takebe was an academic during the Meiji and Taisho periods. He held the teacher's pointer at Tokyo University and became a pioneer of Japanese sociology.

the laborers.'," but socialism makes no such claim. Socialism does not demand that the current laboring individuals or social classes monopolize all the products that have been manufactured from existing capital, which is the accumulation of their ancestors' physical and mental labor. In order to deny the capitalist class its plundering of everything that has been produced via capital, which is, again, the accumulation of their ancestors' physical and mental labor, socialism does not endorse the idea that "It's the right of the laboring class to monopolize all results of past labor via their current labor." Socialism plans to eliminate classes all together.

Anyone who would put the capitalist class against the laboring class, then try to harmonize capital and labor must realize that their fundamental arguments, their basic ideas, are completely different from socialism. Trying to harmonize capital and labor means recognizing our current division of capitalist and labor classes as a never-ending, unstoppable system. It is merely a debate over which of the two classes will be able to plunder more of history's and society's production. Socialism wants to eliminate both these classes and give ownership rights of these products, which were born from social labor and the accumulation of knowledge throughout history, to "society" itself. This is why, if socialism was put into practice and the plundering classes, the monopolizing classes, were eliminated, there would be no more class robbing and monopolizing of society's products under the name of "harmony between capital and labor."

Once all products are owned by society, the remaining capitalists, children of landlords, frail women, young children, and those unable to work due to injury or incurable illness will obviously be able to request allocation from society as well. This is the reason we said earlier that the souls of our ancestors dwell in machines, and they work so that they can be loved by their descendants. This means that today's capitalist class cannot expect imbalanced favoritism from their ancestors. Similarly, it means that a burly man who can work hard cannot take more of their ancestors' soul and labor than what they deserve from their own work; they cannot take what would belong to a different descendant that their ancestors love, just because this other person has a weak body or mind through no fault of their own. Products produced in an era of societal-scale industry must not be allocated based on ideas from an era of individual-scale labor. That's all wrong! If capitalism can be loosely defined as ideas whose purpose is to assert that benefits be attributed to the capitalist class, then what Professor Kanai and any others who argue for harmony between labor and capital understand to be socialism are in fact ideals that put the benefits of the working class as their final goal. That should be reclassified as laborism or workerism. Of course, as workers are the main body of the current movement and in need of immediate relief, socialism does align itself with the laboring class. This shouldn't be mistaken as maintaining the laboring class. Socialism is merely trying to create an equal society without social classes at all. Socialism is called such because its final goal is the assertion that profits and benefits should be attributed to society itself. Anything that maintains the current standoff between social classes, or anything that maintains the position of the social class of thieves, is absolutely not socialism.

Professor Kanai's comprehension skills are lacking, so he interprets socialism, which aims to eliminate social classes, as the exact opposite, something which supports the laboring class and tries to reverse its position with the class of thieves. Not only that, but he is extremely confused about capital and capitalists, mixing them up completely. He says, "This is an age where capital creates more capital, and if that is true, it's obvious that capitalists should be rewarded accordingly." This confusion over the most important, the most fundamental ideal makes the over one thousand pages of *Socioeconomics* completely pointless. Professor Kanai needs to at least attempt to take a good look at himself and reflect on his ideas. Am I, Kanai, an economist, or am I economics? If the person known as Noburu Kanai is economics, it would mean that economics walks, talks, bows respectfully, and screams a salute to His Majesty the Emperor. Doesn't it seem impossible, however, for the discipline of economics to have such capacities?

Just like one would never confuse an economist for the actual field of economics, why then would one turn the subject from the benefits and utility of capital into talk of the plundering capitalists, then use that to give said capitalists the right to thievery? Socialism has only ever said that capitalists are useless, it has never said the same of capital itself. Socialism has only ever said that landlords are useless, it has never said the same of nature's bounty itself. Socialism has only ever said that laborers should be liberated, not that one should be able to live without working at all. The contradiction of saying that capital is useless, but then sacrificing oneself, fighting tooth and nail for the public ownership of that supposedly useless capital is nothing more than insanity. No human would ever say that, nor does socialism try to. Nature comes before landlords. If the latter disappeared, the former would still exist as the source of production. Socialism is not saying we should leave this planet and move to a different one.

The reason I have written in such an unintelligent way is to show exactly how Professor Kanai knows nothing about socialism. The reason socialism is called revolutionist is because it learned, through historical research of economics, about capitalist plundering, and because it discovered that the current financial aristocracy is engaging in similar robbery. The phrase "Capital is the accumulation of robbery" is precisely the fortress upon which socialism's banner wavers. If one wants to get a good attack on socialism, then he must target that phrase. Yet, take a look at Professor Kanai's explanation of capital. He says,

> during such an undeveloped period, what could be called capital was consumed as soon as it was created. It wasn't yet true capital as we think of it today. Such primitive capital gradually evolved into what we

could call capital today. That's a simple summary of the way capital increased.

As a major author, writing in a book that exceeds one thousand pages, that is far too much of a "simple summary." His opposition of socialism's firm, strict argument with his own—which is nothing more than a list of ideals on rights that have existed for millennia, many of which contradict and have even been used against one another—can only be described as shocking:

> An individual's right of private ownership finds its origin in the fundamental character of humanity, the ability to affix one's seal to wealth in the physical world, especially to one's assets. A social state then affirms this character trait through law in order to fully complete the idea.

This idea came about through the same possession and labor theories that caused the French Revolution. It's a completely overblown harmony, and only existed in mediocre minds where quarrels over rights didn't occur (for more on capital and labor, read *The Enlightenment Movement of Socialism*).

Looking at Professor Tajima's *Recent Economic Theory*, there is a section at the end where he attempts to outline Karl Marx's theories. Obviously, he doesn't make such grievous errors as thinking socialism is laborism or confusing capital with capitalists. However, because Professor Tajima is also a state socialist, it is impossible to overlook the many shallow views that such a system of ideals holds. A man who criticizes socialism from the perspective of human nature says the following:

> Extreme socialist scholars hope to convert selfishness, one of the main sources of economic activity, into moral sense. They want to have those citizens of their new social state pour their hearts and souls into

labor, then they would allocate the results completely fairly based on the amount of labor done by each individual. This is what they wish for. However, this concept wasn't created with the entirety of human nature in mind. Therefore, it should be obvious that the actual implementation of such an idea would be incredibly difficult.

In *Socioeconomics*, Professor Kanai also states the following:

> The idea of societal ownership of land capital, needed for any production, followed by the allocation of products to each individual based on how much work they did, is something that contradicts past states of cultural progress. If one were to completely eliminate human selfishness from the equation, and focus only on the desire to share, economic progress would cease completely. Much like societal progress as well, a standstill like that would, in practice, result in a decline. Any society built upon a system of communism will eventually fall into extreme poverty and hardship, or would be ruled by despotism the likes of which have never been seen before in all of human history.

We have seen this kind of old-style economics type of incorrect argument and erroneous understanding regarding human nature written in the first chapter of even academic texts on supposedly new-style economics. It is not limited at all to *Recent Economic Theory* or *Socioeconomics*. Of course, by this point, one wouldn't even need to know of the valuable rebuttal of new-style economics in order to refute the old-style economic theory of "humans are merely animals who desire money." It was already defeated by both socialists and those writers who sought to reexamine human spirituality long ago (such as Carlyle).[36]

---

[36] This "spirituality" could be referring to the mind or soul. We couldn't be sure so we left it as is.

It should be obvious that supposing humans are merely "animals who desire money" wouldn't explain any of the literature, art, history, or science, among other things, that human endeavors have achieved. Not only that, but it couldn't even interpret the very financial phenomena that are the focal point of economics as a discipline. If humans are selfish animals who only want money, giving to charity, circulating money through donations or political activities, honor, love, power and influence, and even the economic idea of bartering couldn't be explained at all.

We do praise new-style economics for discarding this prejudice and recognizing that humanity does have a public spirit—that a natural instinct towards society does exist, and that economic activities resulting from this public spirit are now part of their research. Still, the fact that they try to explain human selfishness by asserting that money can fulfill it completely, then moving the argument forward under that basis, is a good example of how they aren't that different from old-style economics in their understanding of human nature.

No, in terms of understanding the concept of economic activity by public spirit, new-style economics is not as egregious as old-style economics. Socialism expects that humanity will be able to manufacture via that public spirit that we've built up. If one knows that Japanese conscripts possess and act on public spirit much more so than Chinese mercenaries, it should be easy to imagine how much better results can be expected from socialism's conscripted laborer troops, born of their extreme public spirit and the financial activity it encourages, as opposed to today's mercenary-like laborers. It should be as obvious as the difference in morale between the Japanese troops and the Chinese in the First Sino-Japanese war. If we know that humans aren't built to die upon the order of a single person, then it makes sense that today's mercenary laborers will not work as hard as they can for the benefit of capitalist greed. The reason that mercenary laborers today will try to find ways to be lazy despite having countless supervisors watching over their every move is the same reason that Chinse mercenaries would break lines and run away from battle despite having the swords of their commanders pointed at their backs.

Professor Kanai and the like make the rash decision that socialism's laborer troops will require countless bureaucrats to supervise them and say that socialism will result in despotism the likes of which has never been seen before in human history. This is the same shallow vision and unfounded fear that others had immediately after the Meiji Revolution when it was thought that the cessation of military service by the feudal lords and beginning of the draft system in its place would mean that conscripted soldiers would not have the military might necessary to fight—this was decisively disproved by the Satsuma Rebellion.

Let us remove public spirit from the discussion entirely and proceed forward without it. What kind of superintendent would be needed? Even in terrible, despotic military forces, it is not rare for a battalion to continue fighting in war even after all of its commanders have been killed. All organisms have a desire to live, and yet even in the face of death, which is the one thing all humans want to avoid most, their public spirit will win out as motivation against all others. If these are the lengths to which people will go, yet one still claims that the mere four or five hours of physical labor per day that we do consciously for the sake of peace, pleasure, and society is actually our selfishness winning out over our public spirit, then that person's reasoning skill is lower than an infant's (for a little while we will continue using selfishness and public spirit the same way that these shallow minds do for the sake of argument. Read *The Theory of Biological Evolution and Social Philosophy*).

Actually, we crave four or five hours of labor per day as organisms. Organic bodies require organic activity. A scholar cannot read a book all day long without walking at all. A student cannot handle studying English or mathematics for long periods without moving around or playing somehow. A baby will move its arms and legs around in its crib almost like a machine. Regardless of how we talk about mental work or activities, humans are biological organisms that require a certain about of labor so that they do not become pained or bored. This is exactly why those in prison cannot deal with doing nothing, and instead often request some sort of prison industry.[37] (Bellamy writes about this very phenomenon in *Looking Backward*.[38]) Someone who is especially lazy would be forced to endure pain under these biological constraints if forced to live through clever words alone.

With that said, an organic being needs organic rest just as it needs activity. In order to easily explain why people must be lazy, we want the shallow-minded academics of today, who respond to seeing our wage slaves easily succumbing to laziness by saying that laziness is human nature, with the following hypothetical. Imagine, modern economics, if, from the day of your seventh birthday until you're a silver-haired old man, continuing even then until you are dead and buried, a life consisting of twelve or thirteen hours of work a day, three hundred sixty days a year. There is no rest, there is no hope, there is no change, and there is no interest in what you're doing. For example, perhaps reading through Fawcett's booklets on economics over and over again, with no rest, infinitely.[39] Think of this monotonous fate that would continue for your entire life. If this were the reality for these scholars, would they not think of giving up on economic research and live out their concept of laziness being human nature? This sort of supposition is generally not answerable by anyone who isn't completely devoid of common sense.[40]

---

[37] "Prison industry" here means forced labor for the inmates.

[38] Edward Bellamy was a nineteenth century American writer. In *Looking Backward*, he wrote of America in the year 2xxx as a socialist utopia. The book worked toward social change and influenced many societal and labor movements.

[39] We're not sure who he's talking about. Perhaps British economist Henry Fawcett?

[40] In this case, "supposition" refers to assuming something that has never happened did

Now imagine a university professor, a professor of law, forming such an argument using this lack of common sense, then using said argument to criticize socialism. Laborers, however, are actually living this nonsensical supposition. They labor from dawn to dusk next to machines which could rupture their eardrums, doing nothing more than repetitively making iron plates over and over. The worker repeats these unchanging days until their monotonous life ends. Laborers aren't stones inferior to biological organisms, nor are they gods superior to those organisms. Just as academics wish for organic activity in the form of walks, workers wish for rest as the organisms they are. The reason that this basic desire for rest is considered laziness is because workers are looked at as inorganic machines. Not only is that not the case, but laziness, with the way society is organized today, is a natural thing.

Humans do not operate with pain as their motive. The reason they can endure future pain or try to lessen physical pain and deal with it is because the prospect of future pleasure, be it physical or mental, wins out. Is it not obvious that today's wage slaves, who work meaninglessly to add to the wealth of someone above them—manufacturing, with only bleak darkness in front of them—would want to be lazy in order to avoid facing such anguish? If we consider this same situation in a socialist age, where the labor of the worker would advance the well-being and happiness of society in general, then even in specific cases where the physical pain during labor is significant, the self-serving idea of future mental pleasure should make them want to work anyway. Unfortunately, the mental and spiritual pleasure which could motivate a worker today is nonexistent, as labor is seen as a slave's job to be scorned and belittled (read *The Enlightenment Movement of Socialism*).

A certain connotation of contempt accompanies the word "labor." Why? Because it is a slave's job. Slaves are scorned while free men are respected. Though many believe military jobs to be sacred in modern society, back in the

occur.

days when they were considered the jobs of slaves, they were just as derided. By nature, calling an occupation "sacred" or "vulgar" depends completely on the state of society at the time, and has nothing to do with the job itself. That is why we, unlike the average socialist, will not be satisfied simply declaring, "War is a sin, while labor is sacred." If we lived in a perfect world, that would be true. Today, however, labor is absolutely not sacred. Today, it is a slave's job which should be scorned, while the only sacred thing is money. Whether the money comes from thievery, bribery, fraud, prostitution, or anything else, its value never changes.

"Sacred" is a term which can only be applied to that which has its own value and is not obstructed by outside influence. For example, lords, during the era where they held absolute power, also held the title of "sacred." The labor of today has its class and value decided by the relative kind of labor it is, so it is absolutely not sacred. The relative condition of whether the labor is physical or mental determines whether it should be derided or respected in the modern era. This fact shows that labor is not an absolute, nor is it sacred, and the reason that physical labor is scorned is because the existence of a slave is one that should be scorned. Slaves are scorned while free men are respected. This is exactly why most people desire mental labor and dislike physical labor. It is not because of the difficulty of the work, nor is it an issue of nobles versus plebeians, it is based on the ideals we hold about rights; people would rather be respected free men than be forced into obedient slavery.

Anyone bows before authority, and this applies to the sanctity of labor as well—this is where socialism, which wants to eliminate social classes, comes in. Mental labor shines as a background to the plundering class because it is a flower watered by that class's robbery, while physical labor is scorned because it represents those who have submitted, the slave class. Understanding this, the solution is simple. If the classes of free men and slaves were removed and, putting it differently, all of society was made up of citizens that held fair and equal rights and duties, and also worked based on their rights and duties, labor would no longer be classified based on those outside conditions, and it would turn into something absolute and sacred.

So why is socialism criticized with nonsense like "people hate labor" or "laziness will turn it into an autocracy of bureaucrats"? State socialism is what maintains the robbers known as the capitalist class and the slaves known as the laboring class, which is why labor is not sacred. Is state socialism not what's actually making people lazy and causing hate towards labor? Much like how a military troop went from being a position of ridicule to one of honor, let us change labor from being something subservient and despicable to a sacred thing that is part of no social class. Like the honor bestowed to military personnel, the sanctity of labor will take on the morale and public focus of a soldier during battle.

Yet Professor Tajima is still mistaken about something. Socialism does not assert that it will "immediately convert one of today's main motivations for economic activity, selfishness, into moral sense." We leave the word "immediately" out. This is because today's vigorous selfishness is something that humanity has built up since we entered the stage of private ownership, and it has turned into an instinct of ours. Once socialism has been implemented and three or four generations have passed, a moral sense that is adapted to communism will turn into our new instinct. There is plenty of foundation to support this idea based in social evolution. (See the section on morals becoming instinct in *The Theory of Biological Evolution and Social Philosophy*.)

Anyway, until social evolution reaches this point, it is an unquestionable truth that both public spirit and selfishness must coexist as the two pillars of societal activity. This is why socialism must not ignore selfishness as a motivation for financial actions. However, saying that we do not ignore self-interest does not mean that we think it can be satisfied by money. This is the reason that we said the understanding that new-style economics has of human nature is not so different from old-style economics. What they need to do is poke their heads out of the shell known as "economics" and try to analyze the elements within "money."

The body of money, gold, is a rare metal that shines and glimmers. It was considered precious because of this, and was thus used by barbarians. However, when gold is used as money today, it is not because it shines, nor is it used to represent other materials. What gold represents today is the value of human life itself. Inside a single piece of gold lies the prayer for a safe and peaceful life, the prayer for a quick recovery from disease, the prayer for the pleasures of home, the prayer for the raising and education of children, the prayer for rest and relaxation in old age, a boy's dignity, the sanctity of fidelity, the independence of conscience, the freedom of government, public activities, knowledge, character, authority, the origin of honor, and many other things significant to all people.

In spite of this, if one thinks that socialism would, upon its realization, stop the value of human life from being determined by gold, yet still keep gold the same meter as human nature,[41] then that person is sorely lacking in reasoning ability. Society is not a system of authority, so there is no authority that can be bought with gold. If the world becomes one where gold is not stolen in the name of government, then gold would not be required to become a politician, and politicians that buy off authority figures with money would cease to exist.

Regarding public activity, one person would not need to dedicate their entire life's worth of effort, but rather public machines would operate on public wealth. Wealth gifted to individuals as bribes would no longer be necessary, and the bureaucratic organizations that hold the power to give these bribes value and are tempted by tyranny and slavery would not exist either. Individuals would be physically protected by the state, so nobody would need

---

[41] We're not sure what "keep the same meter" means, but if it refers to "keeping the same distance," then it would mean "serving the same purpose" here.

to betray their own independent conscience. Moral actions would be performed instinctively and not be affected by economic threats or temptations. The shameful sight of a wise student or a devoted politician prostrating in front of a capitalist, an ignorant pig decorated with beautiful jewels, would never need to exist again. Adults would no longer cruelly take advantage of little girls simply to satisfy their animal urges. A child's education costs would be paid for by the state, and education would then become the state's role. If one falls ill, he has the option of choosing from public hospitals and doctors, and once he grows old, he will receive annual payments. Because money will be allocated fairly, households will be freed from submission and slavery towards finance and will instead be connected through clean and pure love for one's parents and kindness towards one's children. Today's uncertainty of life or death will no longer be seen even in one's dreams. Remove all of these elements that today exist in gold and think of what remains. Would money not be something that emits only a sparkle which shines of the future?

We will not, as other socialists have suggested, overlap two currencies so that paper bills represent currency and gold represents goods. Even if scraps of paper directly representing goods were used as currency, most of life's satisfaction would be filled by the greatly expanded public property, so it is unimaginable that those scraps of paper would be like today's currency, which holds as much value as human life and is a constant target to be fought over.

In other words, what those people who are called economists need is self-reflection; they need to look in on themselves. Do people want money merely because it is money? Is money something that actually glimmers? Can money give pleasure? Can money buy general pleasure? Is it the ego that receives pleasure? Is it in the realization of the ego? Or is it a means to reach another end, to reach a higher ego? Cheapness and decorum create one reason why money is sought. Fulfilling the necessities of life such as food and clothing would be another reason. The reason that money is infinitely pursued beyond those is because of its ability to buy honor and position.

The reason that such purchasing power is concentrated in a simple piece of metal is because our societal structure has built honor and position upon money. After socialism uses revolution and reform to change that societal structure, selfishness towards prestige and position will not be muddled by money. That selfishness will be directed at prestige and position itself, resulting in yet another motive for productive activity. If new-style economists could use their heads for even a moment, would they not acknowledge the fact that, with the disappearance of economic competition, warriors would, despite economic classes still existing, seek satisfaction for their selfishness through other civil and military pursuits, even going so far as to consider it immoral to touch gold with their hand fans? Yes, the conscript labor organization of socialism does greatly expect activity full of public spirit. However, until society evolves to that point, we do believe encouragement facilities are required to stimulate manufacture and activities born of selfish competition, which is itself motivated by selfishness towards honor and position.

Thus, one reason that socialism argues for fair distribution among the masses is, of course, to eliminate the extreme financial gap, which is one of the main sources of abuse of power. However, another reason is to ensure that the development of individuality is not hindered. If there is a man-made gradation in physical rewards, and it is possible to be graded as such, then the individual would not choose the path which gains them honor and position via development of their individuality itself, but would first choose a job that has greater physical rewards and thus allows them to reach honor and high positions faster. The development of their individuality would come second to this. This is why we have rejected the idea put forth today by socialism that there should be a gradation attached to any rewards from labor based upon relative performance. Those who criticize socialism will generally bring up arguments regarding unfairness and inequality here.

In *Recent Economic Theory*, Professor Tajima says the following:

Humans are naturally unequal. The various facets of society proceed to make humans even more unequal. Wishing for absolute financial equality is like wishing to have the exact same face as someone else, or to have the exact same lifespan.

Humans are naturally unequal. Intellectual power, moral strength, physical stamina, these things are even more obviously unequal than the previous example of one's facial structure. Because of this, when people create a system of society, there is no way to maintain an equal relationship; the wise will always lead the feebleminded. A sovereign will always use the little guy, and the strong will absolutely rule the weak. This is what creates the marital relationship where the husband says and the wife obeys. This is what creates the idea of humble peasants respecting their lord. This is what creates a divide between slaves and free men. This is what creates the disparity between the rich and the poor. If one looks at it like this, the unfairness in society is merely human nature, a natural result.

In *Socioeconomics*, Professor Kanai says the following:

"[Socialism] wishes to completely abolish the concept of an individual's private property and instead make the satisfaction of the people's desires and pleasure absolutely equal."

We will discuss distribution of resources under socialism later in this volume. However, there is one thing that must be addressed now. Equal distribution is not the same as absolute financial equality. Someone who grows ill often and thus requires treatment at a public hospital often is creating unfairness. One who has many children, which they send to public schools, is also creating unfairness. Travelers use public roads more often, students use libraries more often, artists and musicians use those public art museums and music halls more often. All of this creates financial inequality. These unequal people use public money unequally and any benefit or profit they make from it creates financial inequality. In other words, if the desire is to distribute rewards properly among these unequal individuals, socialism, which advocates a large expansion of public assets and wealth, could do that. Socialism does not forget about inequality between individuals.

Equal distribution simply means the private property that is allocated is equal. Someone like Professor Kanai, who would say that it means absolute equality in satisfaction of pleasure and one's desires, is approaching the matter with an flippant attitude unbefitting of an academic. Equality of distribution means distributing equal buying power. Unequal individuals using this equal purchasing power unequally to buy objects on the economic stage is certainly not absolute equality. It should be obvious that this is not the same as bestowing absolutely equal pleasure or absolutely equal satisfaction of desires. A book and a bottle of wine purchased for the same price do not, as financial products, give the same amount of pleasure. They are not equal. Nor do all people equally wish for both the book and the bottle of wine just because they cost the same.

Professor Kanai thinks it satisfactory to spread a fake explanation of a strict and firm set of principles. Sadly, even after studying the problems of society and becoming a professor of law, even after going so far as to become a professor at a university, Professor Kinji Tajima tries to deduce everything from the simple idea that humans are naturally unequal, as if spinning a yarn from that single thread. Of course, socialism does recognize inequality between individuals. However, this does not mean that we should hide behind the idea of individuality and be afraid to declare the idea of egalitarianism towards our fellow humans. Yes, egalitarianism!

Socialism is socialism in the end, and its final objective is the evolution and survival of society, but in order for that objective to be met, it demands a societal structure that secures equality and allows free competition on top of that. Thus, it clearly inherits the spirit of these freedom and equality arguments. However, these freedom and equality arguments are not advocated merely for the sake of freedom and equality, like they were during the time of individualism, complete with ideals born of the revolution. Neither do they assert that humans are naturally free and equal, so a society that makes them unfree and unequal must thus be defeated (via contracts, since this is an individualist line of thought). Why? Because if humans are naturally free and equal then there would be no purpose in setting up an unfree and unequal system of society. Freedom for the sake of freedom and equality for the sake of equality would have no effect at all, much as it is said that Ferri's work is nothing more than political self-satisfaction.[42]

Even so, socialism's arguments of freedom and equality can't allow the baseless speculation of "Humans are naturally unequal" which people such as Professor Tajima spout. This is because these scientific deductions were created for primitive societies, societies that functioned on instinctual sociability. Thus, primitive equality made these peaceful societies possible. In other words, socialism's arguments for equality do not include baseless conjecture on whether humans are inherently equal or unequal, and instead focus on society's existential evolution by eliminating the inequality of social classes and request a lifestyle of freedom where equality is secured.

So, when explaining equality, we will not resort to ideals that do not agree with biology, such as the unscientific: "We are unequal in height, build,

---

[42] Ferri refers to Enrico Ferri. He was a nineteenth century Italian criminologist and a proponent of what you might call a new school of criminal law. It is said that he influenced the ethics of the Soviet penal code. At the time of this text, his book, *Socialism and Modern Science*, had been translated.

strength, personality, hobbies, and the like, but we can think, reason, and possess logic, and in that regard are unlike other animals, and are thus equal in that one point." When we do recognize inequality in individuality, we will not dress up words such as "The relative merit between the lowest human and highest human is a difference higher than the relative merits between the highest animal and the lowest human," in a scientific coat and use that scientific austere to help form the basis for our arguments. The ability to do things such as reason and deduce is not limited to humanity, after all. To a certain extent, there are other higher intelligence animals who can do so too. This means that we cannot separate ourselves and create our own classification just for humans according to the foundations of the theory of evolution for the same reason that we do not classify similar species of animals within the same group as each other. We don't classify black dogs as cats, red dogs as foxes, large Western dogs as horses, or small Japanese dogs as sheep for this same reason. If we can only accept higher animals as humans or classify lower humans in with higher animals, then we cannot say that savages, who are closer to higher animals, are all that different from humans.

Thus, we will not assert that socialism's arguments on freedom and equality are just and correct because humans are naturally equal, nor will we criticize freedom and equality on the basis of humans being naturally unequal. Justice is a word that describes what adapts to society's goal of survival and evolution. It is a word that envelopes society from the outside and changes depending on the region and time period. When looked at from the perspective of society's survival and evolution, ancient feudalism was plenty just, and the argument for the all-mighty sovereign from the Middle Ages, and even aristocratic despotism, are known even by layman as something we should not criticize today.

However, the contents of justice must ebb and flow. If we know that the absolute and despotic justice of ancient feudalism, sovereigns, and aristocrats cannot be applied now, then how could someone like Professor Tajima say,

"Humans are naturally unfair," ignoring the historical evolution of justice with such firm dogmatism? He continues: "... when people create a system of society, there is no way to maintain an equal relationship; the wise will always lead the feebleminded. A sovereign will always use the little guy, and the strong will absolutely rule the weak." This assumption that the professor makes cannot be described as accurate one hundred percent of the time. However, that assumption leads to his conclusion:

> This is what creates the marital relationship where the husband says and the wife obeys. This is what creates the idea of humble peasants respecting their lord. This is what creates a divide between slaves and free men. This is what creates the disparity between the rich and the poor. If one looks at it like this, the unfairness in society is merely human nature, a natural result.

This is clear evidence that he is ignorant of societal evolution. In order to hold his premise and have no choice but to arrive as his conclusion, it would mean that state socialism asserts the following. Humans are naturally unequal. The history of society does not progress and evolve, and notions of justice are forever unchanging. Thus, we must reform civil law to the point before even Roman law,[43] where the head of the household had absolute power and the other members of the family were not even granted human personality. The emperor and his nobles will be appointed as sovereigns and given possession

---

[43] See note 23 in chapter 2 for more on the twelve Roman laws. Roman law developed most from the republic period until the imperial period, after which it declined. The book *Justinian Code* was written in the sixth century under Byzantine Emperor Justinian I, but was long forgotten. It was rediscovered under a church in the Middle Ages and greatly influenced all of Europe. Even modern Japanese civil law has much of its origins in Roman law.

of state land along with the people who reside there, and even the right to determine life or death. Prisoners of war and debtors would need to be chained up and worked as slaves. Since humans are inherently unequal, the massive gap between the rich and poor is part of human nature; it's a natural result.

Following this logic, harmony between capital and labor, laborer security, and even state socialism itself are all incompatible with the idea of inherent inequality, and thus are all empty arguments. Look at the traces of social evolution. Socialism responds to evolution and thus justice evolves as well. The river flows in the direction of the current, deep and wide. The massive river of history flowed harshly from the spring of instinctual society upon which primitive settlements were built, flowing strongly through development and recognition of society as a body—this is contemplation on the equality of all things. Limitations on the authority of family heads, the independence of women, liberation of slaves, and finally the cascade known as the French Revolution, which defeated the nation and its nobles—socialism is a major current that accepts this cascade and even tries to help it fall from such a great precipice through the use of social consciousness. Once it drops from Niagara Falls into Lake Ontario, splashing social consciousness into the clear face of the lake, equality of all things as it relates to humanity develops on a global scale—this is when the social evolution that socialism asserts and ideals of secured equality and free living that individualism holds can exist.

If we, who hold over six thousand years of history,[44] can't understand what floats atop this massive current, then we are below even the undeveloped barbarian settlements of the South Pacific, whose only history is oral tradition of their ancestors battling feral beasts. Untrue! Our undeveloped barbarian settlement of the Orient has used the concept of national polity to conceal the massive current,[45] which should have begun developing fundamental ideals on

---

[44] We don't know where he gets this "six thousand years of history" from.

[45] "Undeveloped barbarian settlement of the Orient" is a descriptor used to insult Japan.

equality for the past 2,500 years. We haven't developed any of those ideals of equality at all. If anything, what we have is much like those in the South Pacific, books that merely collect oral traditions such as *Kojiki* and *Nihon Shoki*. (Read *The So-Called Theory of Japan's National Polity and its Restorative Principle of Revolution*.) This is exactly why we assert arguments on freedom and equality as meaning such.

In other words, in order to achieve and implement socialism's ideals, society must continue to evolve, much like how it went from family patriarchy, to sovereigns ruling, and eventually to slavery. Society must continue to evolve until our sense of empathy grows very sensitive, then eliminate the unfairness that has become conventional justice. After this, the people who have banded together in equality can use the free lifestyle they've been given to continue the evolution of society.[46] The right to plunder through war and the private ownership of land via occupation were both considered justice that had adapted with the pace of society's evolution at the time. Much like that, the head of a household having absolute power, an aristocracy, slaves, all of it was plenty just for the progress of social evolution at the time.

Looking backwards at history from a perspective of freedom and equality, then criticizing it on its inequality is nothing more than a dogmatic, mistaken argument from the era of individualism. There are still some socialists that cling to this argument and continue it today, but that is only because those individuals have such a dogma, that is all. Individualism should not use socialism's truth as a shield for itself to hide behind.

However, resisting social evolution just because inequality was correct until society progressed to a certain point, and trying to downplay arguments

---

[46] The original text says "lifestyle of equal unity freedom," and we're not sure exactly what he means. We attempted to translate it with the closest meaning we could, but we're not sure if it's exactly the same as the original text. We think the wording will need to be reconsidered later.

on equality even as human empathy becomes more sensitive, to the point where we can no longer stand the horrible disparity between social classes, is absolutely worthless and trivial. State socialism holds not a single truth. We cannot go back and look at ideas of justice in history and decide what is right and wrong or defend our current arguments using those ideas. Conclusions such as humans being naturally equal or unequal are baseless and unscientific.

If one argues "humans are all naturally unequal," then one can retort with "from the start, humans were not unequal," using the theory of human monism. If one argues "humans are all naturally equal," then it would become a debate over how all life evolved from single-celled organisms, and thus all organisms are equal. In other words, it would merely shift the argument into the philosophical issue of disparity and quality. We simply assert and campaign for socialism. We simply take the methods that are best suited to the ideals of social evolution. Thus, we do not speak of whether things are naturally equal or unequal, and instead try to defeat this unequal society for the sake of social evolution's ideals, and try to create a new societal system based on equality and freedom. We will not argue over whether humanity is naturally equal or unequal, and instead require that, for sake of social evolution's ideals, material protection must be given equally and uniformly.

Understand clearly that socialism's arguments on freedom and equality are of this truth. If Professor Tajima and other state socialists would not misunderstand socialism's equality argument as "humanity is completely the same, with no differences at all," and instead realize that it is based on equality of material protection—which, if implemented even somewhat on today's laws, would guarantee equal material protection from dangers and threats towards the lives of all people, from beautiful women to ugly hags, from octogenarians to toddlers who died at only three years old—they would understand that the criticism of "wishing for absolute financial equality is like wishing to have the exact same face as someone else, or to have the exact same lifespan," is a misunderstanding so blatant that it could make one roar with laughter.

Socialism is egalitarianism. However, in order to not obstruct the development of individuality, it is an egalitarianism that only looks for implementation on a physical, material basis. (For more on equality arguments, read *The Enlightenment Movement of Socialism,* and *The Theory of Biological Evolution and Social Philosophy.*)

We are not here to intentionally and specifically harm Professor Tajima's intelligence. It just so happens that socialism is currently understood by many as an ochlocracy,[47] which has all of the poor, hobby-less individuals of the lower class melting together into one group labeled "equality." It also just so happens that, during certain periods of time, socialism was very much like that. Today's dogmatic argument of inequality using this understanding of socialism is now coming out of Professor Tajima's mouth, as he is a major influence in modern scholarly circles. A single scribe who once wrote a book directed towards Mr. Isoo Abe's *How to Solve Social Problems,* asking for an honorable debate, would drown among this sort of influence and power. The extent to which humans are unequal in their intelligence, morality, elegance, writing, and other fields, is shown by the writer himself with his own argument, so this could actually be used as an example to support arguments of inequality.

Capitalist-socialists persistently repeat this dogmatic inequality theory in order to maintain and support the financial aristocracy already mentioned. Read the following passage to see just how much Professor Tajima sullies *Recent Economic Theory* in order to defend such a thing:

> To begin with, the fact that modern workers do not need to face danger in the planning or management stage like proprietors do, and instead make definite wages is something that actually benefits them.

---

[47] Kita tries not to lower the standard of the capitalist class to that of the laboring class, but instead tries to raise the standard of the latter. It is generally regarded as—leaving aside whether this is correct or not—aristocracy.

I believe the following critique of wage systems made by French economist Mr. Émile Chevalier to be completely valid, "It is a unique type of association, where part of the association is outside of the dangers born from business, and the compensation they receive and the time when they receive it are scheduled in advance." We also have no choice but to agree with the implication of the following harsh words from Mr. Cernyski, "Reforming the wage system is wishing for the retrogression of society."[48] The categorization of people into managers and workers is a completely natural force. The theory which socialism posits of humans being equal simply is not compatible with reality at all. Try thinking about it for a moment. If the workers did unite and eliminate managers in order to create their own production organization, as long as there exists those among the workers with talent in management and those who are poor at it, yet those who are talented don't take charge and manage the group, how could it possibly compete and attain victory in the global free market? Even if, as they explain, the workers use their country's power to eliminate management only in that country, and all production and business in the nation are done by the previously mentioned worker association, other countries still have those talented managers and use their workers for labor. Compared to them, the former country without management will certainly be in a disadvantaged position. This is the same logic as to why a weak republic will, because of its military, end up disadvantaged during trade with a powerful despotic country. For those reasons, I cannot bring myself to agree with, as socialists argue, using one production organization for all manufacture and eliminating the current system of wages and management from our society. I must

---

[48] We believe Cernyski to be another French economist, but no more details could be found.

assign myself as a revolutionary, but not one for reforming the wage system.

If the above argument was written, like Professor Kanai's work was, to thoughtlessly spread sentiments of anti-socialism, then *Recent Economic Theory* would become, to us, a pitiful and foolish subject, serving only to show off a professor of law at a major imperial university whose writing power should be put into question immediately.

Of course, Professor Tajima is not a scholar of interpretation or translation, and his most objectionable habit is him citing "A scholar says this and we agree," so we believe that Émile Chevalier's words were employed in nothing more than an attempt at citing copious references.[49]

However, by calling today's wage system, contrarily, "a unique type of association," he holds responsibility for endorsing it. That is incredibly thoughtless. Production and manufacture through associations or unions is, to an extent, an expression of socialism, and is actually called the socialist production system. So if, as Chevalier says, the wage system is already a unique type of union production, then he is basically saying that modern society is already a socialist utopia. In that case, the world's socialist parties might as well disperse themselves, and *Recent Economic Theory*, which makes its main and most difficult problem out of how society should deal with the socialist party, could be burned and disposed of without issue.

Union production requires that the members of the union have a right to speak out, and the production itself requires a parliamentary system, much like a republic. In the current system, the economic aristocrats hear plans from their retainers, decide everything about production, and the laborers have no voice over anything aside from a small impact on how high or low their wages

---

[49] In other words, using many examples from a broad scope in an attempt to provide evidence and explanation for a claim.

are. How could anyone call that an association, union, or anything of the sort? A nation which can, for the benefit of a single person, take human life and steal their freedom of residence and occupation, can absolutely not be called a republic. Similarly, a country with despotic control over manufacturing and production, where capitalists have the authority to expel workers from the workplace and take any plans they had for tomorrow away from them, is not a productive republic. Another term is far more accurate, one used quite often today. It is a capitalist system. It is a wage system.

What must one suffer from in order to confuse words in a way that overturns the fundamental concepts of economics? Sovereignty is not the authority of the state, it's the authority of the ruler or sovereign. If one doesn't consider the period where any benefits were attributed to the government of these rulers and sovereigns to be a republic, then how could he say that what we have today, where production is attributed to the sovereignty of these financial lords, and the workers are treated as objects for the sake of the lords' benefit and goals, a production association or union under a productive republic? It should go without saying that socialism's production system is quite different from today's production union, but some people truly think that "Even without traveling the path of political revolution, we can arrive at socialism through a production cooperative."[50] With that in mind, all we can say when an academic points to one thing and calls it another, is that they have uttered the most thoughtless and imprudent words possible. A production association is a production association. A wage system is a wage system. Chevalier and Professor Tajima are people who don't speak any known human language.

It seems like the main reason that some people confuse a wage system with a production group or union is because they want to argue that profits from group production shouldn't be attributed to a single capitalist, and

---

[50] Perhaps the thoughts of gradualist socialists such as Bernstein.

instead be attributed to the workers such that they receive a higher wage. Of course, the old-style economic concept of wage-fund has no reason to exist in this world.[51] The argument that consumers of that fund (in other words, the laborers) have their wages fall and rise in accordance with the population does not hold water. Therefore, Lassalle's iron law of wages obviously needs to be revised as well, since it was built on the idea of wage-fund.[52]

The wages that entrepreneurs pay workers come from the future products, and are paid in advance for the laborer's work. This means that the explanation of wages being paid from products themselves is, in some circumstances, correct. We won't deny this, of course. However, that is only true in some circumstances, not all. If the entrepreneur fails to make a profit from those products, then the wage paid to the workers does not come from the products themselves. This means that such an explanation never leaves the realm of desk theory or hypothesis most of the time.

We will not quibble over such unimportant details. The real problem is not where wages are paid from, but the fact that wages are decided based on contracts. If an industrialist forms a wage contract with workers, they are, in the expectation that future profits from their products will allow them to pay wages, creating a "demand" for the worker's body, with the "supply" of these

---

[51] Based on the doctrine advocated by the British classical economist John Stuart Mill, the wage-fund theory regards the amount allocated to wages as a fund and believes that the total amount received is fixed. Therefore, it is necessary to limit the number of workers in order to raise wages.

[52] The "iron law of wages" is a concept introduced by Ferdinand Lassalle, which states that wages can only be earned to the extent necessary for the survival and reproduction of workers. However, in the earlier part of his article, Kita argues that the market price of wages declines as the number of workers increases, as if he is following Lassalle's "iron law of wages." There is some doubt as to whether the argument that the "iron law of wages" should be revised is really compatible with his own argument.

workers' bodies coming from laborers battling hunger and overpopulation on the free market. To put it simply, workers sell their bodies in accordance with the laws of supply and demand; a slave trade under the name of "selling labor." (Much like how prostitutes sell their own bodies but say they are only selling "sex.")

Not only that, but these slaves chained by contracts don't even have the right to ask for any of the profits from said products. Whether the wages are paid from money the entrepreneur already has, from what they believe to be an advance on the profits their products will make, or even if they make a lapse in judgement on future profits, become hard up for money, and so pay wages from the coffers of other capitalists, God only knows. It does not matter; the value of slaves is already determined by the market.

New-style economists like to selfishly decide that entrepreneurs expect to pay wages that exist from the profits of their products, and assume that no mistakes can occur there. They say, "a wage system is a certain convenient kind of cooperative production association where workers receive compensation in advance for their production work." That is nothing more than an abstract theory. It is not true! New-style economics calls itself scientific and practical, says that it is based on real world experience, but in this point alone, it is even more abstract and impractical than old-style economics:

> Part of the association members are outside of the dangers born from business and the compensation they receive and the time when they receive it are scheduled in advance... The fact that modern workers don't need to face danger in the planning or management stage like proprietors do, and instead make definite wages is something that actually benefits them.

Then unemployment must occur because those unemployed didn't bear the risks of the company and still received a scheduled fixed wage!

Professor Tajima's defense of the economic aristocracy lies in the previously mentioned dogmatic view of inequality. That is, the distinction between entrepreneurs and workers was born as a natural result of intrinsically unequal human nature and, even if a production union made up of workers manages things, those with managerial talent will end up as corporate managers while the others engage in physical work. Therefore, we can conclude that equal labor organization is impossible and entrepreneurs are immortal. That is the argument they're putting forth. However, if we reword this, one must call into question the writing ability of those who pen it.

Socialism, while excluding and criticizing today's entrepreneurs, does not entirely ignore those with entrepreneurial talents for the sake of some arbitrary egalitarianism. We do not absolutely deny the importance of the entrepreneur as the captain of industry like the excellent state socialist Dr. Illy does, but we also do not agree with the reasoning that the captain of industry must simultaneously own the metaphorical ship of industry as well.

Legally speaking, to say that today's entrepreneurs who operate enterprises for their own purposes are excluded does not mean that talented people who operate enterprises for the purposes of the state, for the interests attributed to the state, acting as agents of the state, are useless. Again, it could be said that the state itself is the owner of the ship of industry and the subject of its profits, while the people are agents of the state. Some use physical labor to benefit said state, while some use other talents for this purpose.

To reiterate further, our arguments says that the current economic aristocracy, which, much like the aristocratic lords of old, allows itself to be the main holder of rights, profits, and goals which only benefit itself, should be defeated. Then, managerial tasks should be assigned to those, as agents of the state, with the talent for them, just like today's central and local bureaucrats exist for the benefits, goals, and attribution of the state. In other words, even if a person with a talent for management were to engage in managerial work in a workers' production union, as the professor says, that manager would still be merely a certain kind of worker, an institution of the union completely different from the so-called entrepreneurs.

Just as there's no reason to say a person talented as a ruler must immediately become a lord and exercise a right to rule, there is no reason to say that a person gifted in management must necessarily become an entrepreneur and the subject of profit. In this respect, the professor must ask himself, like Professor Kanai, is the person known as Professor Kinji Tajima an economist, or the study of economics itself? Is it possible for those whose brains have been corroded by such a dogmatic theory of inequality to have their own wisdom covered and hidden from them?

Professor Tajima's defense of the economic aristocracy is unequivocal. He is not afraid to lay out the benefits of despotism at will. He says,

> Even if ... all production and business in the nation is done by the previously mentioned worker association, other countries still have those talented managers and use their workers for labor. Compared to them, the former country without management will certainly be in a disadvantaged position. This is the same logic as to why a weak republic will, because of its military, end up disadvantaged during trade with a powerful despotic country.

This is true. This means it is also true that domestic production unions, because they want to protect fair working hours and a decent living for workers, cannot compete on an open market with other capitalist organizations who would overwork wage slaves to mass produce cheap goods. Because of this, socialism appears atop a political administration, excludes the methods of a subset of production unions, and has the state absorb all industry under itself. However, since the presence of capitalist industry in foreign nations would be an obstacle to a nation that has implemented socialism, the socialist First International movement was held.

This is not something that a professor majoring in social issues should ignore. In fact, even Mr. Yano Fumio's *The New Society* gives major attention to this point, and one may consider it half-baked because of this.[53] However, despite how half-baked it may seem, Mr. Fumio's argument stating, "It is not absolutely impossible to implement socialism within a country, at least to a certain extent. It is also then possible to compete with more economically advanced countries by uniting capital and labor," more than cancels out the professor's baseless reasoning.

This is because the joint activity of large capital is far more potent than the divided competition of small capital, and it is a foundational principle of economics that ordered labor, through unity, will bring about greater production than counterbalanced, destructive labor. If we compete internationally in this way, it will be like when we united as a civic nation and defeated even the mighty Russia, in contrast to the various clans which were defeated by foreign nations during the end of the Edo period.[54] However, we must not overlook the phrase "powerful despotic country." These words betray the professor's underlying philosophy as praising the despotism of current production methods.

If the term "despotic country" means a form of government by state agents that exercises the right to rule tyrannically for the purpose and benefit of the state, then there is no doubt that the agility and secrecy that accompany despotism benefit the state in the extremely fierce competition of both war and

---

[53] Yano Fumio is the pen name of Ryukei Yano, a famous novelist and politician who wrote books such as *Keikoku Bidan (The Beautiful Story of Statesmanship)*. He participated in the formation of the Constitutional Reform Party and advocated the theory of civil rights. He later became president of the daily newspaper, *Osaka Mainichi Shinbun*.

[54] Likely meaning the reluctant opening of the country after being unable to resist extreme and mounting pressure.

diplomacy. However, if "despotic state" refers to lords using the power of rule for their own benefit, themselves the subject of any benefits, as they did back during the patriarchal era, then it is obvious that those benefits brought about from despotism go directly towards the lord, not the state. (See the portion of *The So-Called Theory of Japan's National Polity's Restorative Principle of Revolution* where nations are split into human personality versus status as an object.)

Therefore, in the current capitalist system, which is what Professor Tajima calls a strong despotic nation, if the capitalist, as an agent of production organizations, exercises the right of production for the benefit and purpose of the group, even if it is tyranny, if there are profits to be gained through said tyranny, the organization members who are responsible for that production should be allowed to enjoy those profits as their natural right. With that said, however, this is absolutely not the current state of affairs. Capitalists wield their right of production for their own purpose and profit like it is part of their right to rule, as if they are monarchs, and the collective members are their vassals and servants by virtue of their annual or monthly wages; they exist only as objects under the monarch's own personal goals.

Therefore, in this definition of a powerful despotic state, it is in the interest of the sovereign and the capitalists to have a powerful state or production organization, and it is in their interest as the main rights holders to lead a powerful state or productive organization to make the monarch and capitalists even more powerful. Whether or not these benefits and profit coincidentally trickle over onto others by pure happenstance is not part of the equation to begin with.

According to the statistics published in 1895 in England, out of the income of thirteen billion five hundred million yen,[55] up to eight billion five hundred

---

[55] The original text says "one hundred thirty-five quadrillion yen." If we take this literally, it results in a much higher level than currently understood for the time. At the

million yen belongs to the economic monarchs, who are only one-eighth of the entire population, and this is considered the right of a despot in their powerful, tyrannical state. The other seven-eighths of England exist only as starving objects under their sovereigns for the benefit of said sovereigns. This shows that England is not a powerful country.

The statisticians, enjoying cruel pranks as they do, calculate that the average population wealth of the American city of Chicago would amount to an income of ten thousand yen per person, or a family at the rate of fifty or sixty thousand yen, and so on. But America, filled with the unemployed and criminals, is a poor nation, and the only mighty ones to be found there number a few dozen despotic economic lords. The Golden Emperor Iwasaki climbed up on the high roof of his mansion and said, "I am rich, I am rich! Why are the people not rich?" The only powerful one in this was Emperor Iwasaki; the Empire of Japan, organized by wage slaves and serfs, was not powerful as a nation. Even if winning the Sino-Japanese War and the Russo-Japanese War, extending the line of interest,[56] and expanding the trade blocs may make the myriad economic lords even more powerful, whether the people and the nation are also made more powerful or not by this is a completely different question.

Behold the abomination of giants armed with an army of sixteen legions and a navy of hundreds of thousands of tons of battleships, starving like cattle, committing petty theft against the poor, and kneeling before the rich and powerful, weeping for the tax blessings they receive. The Empire of Japan has now been stripped of its personhood as the rights holder to which profits and

---

time Kita wrote this, however, the character for "ten thousand" could be added as a modifier for "million," so it's far more likely that the number should be read as "thirteen billion five hundred million." This is true for future values in this section as well.

[56] The "Line of Interest" refers to a nation's own sphere of influence. Until the Sino-Japanese War, it referred to the Korean Peninsula. After the Russo-Japanese War, it was broadened to include Manchuria.

other benefits should be attributed, and exists only as an object for the benefit of economic lords. Yes, these economic despots are powerful, surely. But does that make the Empire of Japan powerful?

It's likely that Professor Tajima did not use the term "strong despotic country" in this sense, but simply to contrast it with the term "weak republic" in reference to the socialist organization of production. O weak republic! Why must it be decided that a republic is weak? In fact, the term "weak" is a life-or-death problem for socialism. The completely false, ludicrous claim that "the realization of socialism will diminish production" is made not only by Professor Kanai, but also brazenly spoken by other scholars all the time. It is also found in Professor Kanai's *Socioeconomics*:

> If this were to be forced, it would inevitably require a very large number of bureaucrats to supervise not only production but also the education and support of the offspring of all those engaged in production, as well as supervising consumption in general. What is even more frightening is that the senior bureaucrats in charge of directing and supervising will have unlimited power and will be in a position to constantly exercise that power. Not only will society thus suffer from an oppression never before seen in human history, but the results of production will never be greater than under the present system, despite the endless interference and supervision. In fact, it will be less. We already know by experience, even in societies at the present time, anywhere in which there is either no or little activity motived by self-interest, production is bad, whether it's low in quality or amount of production. This is a general truth seen everywhere.

This would pose a dilemma to socialism. The two swords of "poverty for all society" or "state universalism" seem to leave no quarter for socialism, which insists on simultaneous individual freedom and the wealth of society as a whole. However, both of these swords are merely striking at air. Socialism is the certainty that society as a whole can be both astonishingly wealthy and protect the independence of the individual. We do not believe that the esteemed Professor Kanai is an interpretive scholar. However, those who misinterpret socialism as bureaucratic tyranny of state universalism and worship of the state, then fiercely assert individual authority, are presumably individualists. (Read *The Theory of Biological Evolution and Social Philosophy* for a discussion on the great significance of individualism).

However, this misinterpreted parochial socialism existed over a millennium ago,[57] before even Plato, but yes, the reach of bureaucratic interference is evident from the fact that it even allowed the supervision of women's chastity. Today's scientific socialism is by no means a restoration of antiquity, brainlessly connected to such rudimentary socialist ideals. It is an entirely separate ideal, newly built on a definite awareness of sociality and the individual, following the great awakening of individualism up to the nineteenth century. We go into further detail on this mentality in *The Theory of Biological Evolution and Social Philosophy*. We have also already explained how the argument of "productive activities will decline without bureaucratic oversight" is based on an unconscious dogma about human nature. However, this is not to say that a few supervisors are completely useless in a socialist world. Yet it is important to remember that those supervisors are a completely different breed from today's bureaucrats.

The important task of today's bureaucrats is to maintain the powerful class by suppressing the weaker classes, who are always trying to rebel against the powerful. They are placed under organizations that are easily corrupted by monetary temptations, and because of their class, they have the hubris of a tyrant and the servility of a slave. Thinking that such men will still exist after

---

[57] "Parochial" isn't generally used like this, but in the context of this work, it's probably fine to interpret it as "having a limited or narrow outlook or scope."

socialism is implemented would be like saying foxes will stay outside even when the sun rises. It is because society is enveloped in the darkness of this gross economic disparity and powerful classism that those who today are little more than servants on their knees before their bosses wield the power of sovereigns once they turn their focus to society.

The appointment of supervisors in a socialist republic is not like today's bureaucrats, which is based on wives' connections, examinations consisting of nothing but fluff, resumes with attached monthly bribes,[58] or political party fuss, including witch hunts against certain officers. They are voted for and elected fairly. And if that election is not like that of the late Roman emperor, who was elected from among the soldiers, but like Bellamy's proposal to elect suitable men in the laboring army from those who have completed their labor duties, where could tyranny possibly crop up? If the office of judge today has become an honored position for men of character, poised to watch for abuses of power and to protect individual liberty and independence, and the state's laboring soldiers, supervisors, and large national agents equivalent to today's entrepreneurs receive proper and equal payment, and are all in a similar financial position, how would it even be possible for a tyrannical and unfair bureaucratic class to arise?

For this reason, in Germany, where the ancient parochial socialism, or state universalism, cannot be completely overthrown by a revolution of individualism like in France, individual authority is asserted heavily in the name of democracy for the benefit of society, and "social democracy" is claimed in an attempt to expulse the ice floes carrying medieval baggage known as state universalism from their country. The reason democracy is being advocated along with socialism is because they demand that the authority of the individual should not be corrupted by the will of other individuals in the

---

[58] Money paid in order to attain and maintain a desired position.

name of society. So why would anyone think that today's bureaucrats could be put in charge of production? However, this isn't as it seems!

Is the so-called state socialism of Professor Kanai and others not the very thing which seeks to have production controlled or interfered with by the all-powerful bureaucratic tyranny of the modern state? The sword that Professor Kanai is using is only piercing deep into the heart of his own state socialism!

This brings the issue back to Professor Kanai's claim of diminishing production and Professor Tajima's remarks on a weak republic. These are absolute and complete falsehoods. Socialism is not about diminishing production, but about increasing it. It is not there to create a weak republic, but a strong industrial republic. Whenever we see this grossly incorrect misconception persistently maintained not only by these two gentlemen, but also by those who otherwise deserve full respect, we wonder why people with such a misunderstanding would make such an accusation. However, aside from the insensitive or thoughtless ideas which we have thoroughly repudiated, we have never found the reason for such accusations. Could it be that they are arguing against made-up socialists in their heads, or that they see some socialists focusing on the inequities of wealth and distribution and they think socialism will result in equal poverty because socialists won't care how much or how little is produced?

We will declare, however, that scientific socialism has never placed too much emphasis on theories or arguments over resource distribution. This may seem strange, but we are specifically trying to assert this. In the days of fantasy socialism, the rule of dogmatic egalitarianism was to simply reduce the upper classes to the lower classes, and that was it. However, since the motive that led to the discovery of socialism was the inequality and injustice of modern society's resource distribution, even socialists themselves cannot escape the impression that the theory of distribution is the main point of their argument.

The truth of socialism, though, is not in the theory of distribution, but rather the theory of production. In other words, the insistence on public ownership of land and productive institutions and their public management is at the heart of socialism. As a real-world example, the world's socialist parties have never been separated by the myriad different theories on distribution, but nor have they ever moved in unison around a theory of production.

Of course, the term "distribution" in general reeks of private property. If the resources to be distributed were given to all individuals as private property within their rights, the term would not be called unfair as such. But for those who know no other way of thinking except by the standards of modern society, the word distribution is immediately looked upon as an asocial observation of the private property system, without imagining that there is a far larger expansion of public property.

If we consider the current tiny amount of public resources today as nothing more than a small oasis in a desert, even the people who possess nothing more than asocial thoughts—such as it being natural for a library to have iron bars or a public park to have a metal fence—would still never insist on such distribution from a warship, or demand such from a barracks. This is because they don't think of military matters as the feudal lords of the past did, but rather understand that there are things which should be managed by the state. In the same way, if it came to be clearly understood that production should never be left to a single private individual, then there would no longer be this unreasonable idea of viewing factories larger than barracks or shipyards that build warships, as we do today, in terms of the distribution standards of the private property system.

This obviously means that the majority of social property should exist as common property, and the portion that is distributed would be the purchasing power necessary to satisfy individuals in accordance with daily life and the evolution of society, and would never be a distribution in the sense that is used today, which includes honor, power, life, and love. This is why socialists' proposals for resource distribution differ from one another. Saint-Simon and those who agree with him say, "grade the distribution in proportion to the labor force."[59] Louis Blanc and others hold the highest ideal: "produce according to ability and consume according to need."[60] While today's socialists say, "equal distribution for all."

Of course, Blanc's ideal of "produce according to ability and consume according to need" is our ideal, one that can be reached in the not-too-distant future. However, such an ideal communist society can only be realized with more and more production and a higher level of moral evolution. Therefore, scientific socialism will only provide "equal distribution for all" according to the current level of socialism while awaiting the next stage in our evolution. Yes, if we imagine that socialism is adopted in modern Japan immediately, like it is said in *The New Society*, implementing Simon's ideals would work, but in a country whose production and industry is as underdeveloped as Japan, it isn't realistic right now. (Read *The Enlightenment Movement of Socialism*).

Not only that, but it is not possible to define the extent of the personal labor of those engaged in production on the basis of a single product, nor can we know how much of the effect of cumulative historical knowledge is contained in it. Since a product of industry is an integral and indivisible social and historical thing, to attempt to establish individual grades of distribution in the present day would be like trying the distribution methods from the era of individual production, but in the modern age of societal scale production. This would be extremely contrary to what is considered just and fair today.

We take the view that distribution theory should evolve with the times. Resource distribution accompanies production. Even cannibals, whose production is the most lacking out of any group, still distribute the flesh of their fellow man among each other, and kill one another in order to assure

---

[59] A French socialist. Considered the ancestor of fantasy socialism. Famous as the mentor of Auguste Comte.

[60] A French socialist. Participated in the Révolution de Février of 1848, and later became a member of the provisional government.

society's survival. In the same way, the private property system of today is simply the distribution of plunder between classes, whether it be from war or law. In a primitive system of village communism based on simple, primitive equality, this can only take place when there is an abundance of those primitive products. This could be called primitive communism.

Future communal distribution will take place only after we achieve communal production through repeated invention, discovery, and advancement. In order to reach a stage of socialist distribution that can be equal for all, the amount of resources in society, including production and industry, must be so great and plentiful that the resources distributed to each individual will be enough that they will have no reason to want more financially. Mencius said,

> Without water and fire, human beings cannot survive a single day. However, if you knock on someone's door at nightfall and ask them for this precious water and fire, they will gladly give it to you because they have an abundance of it. When beans and grains are as plentiful as water and fire, the people will naturally be civilized, and how can there be anyone who is inhumane?[61]

This would have been true in the primitive village communal system of the Yao and Shun dynasties, when the population was small and the plains were

---

[61] Quotes from *Mencius* frequently turn up in this book. In translating them, we have referred to Kobayashi Katsuhito's translations of *Mencius (Jo)* [孟子（上）] (Iwanami Bunko, 1969) and *Mencius (Ge)* [孟子（下）] (Iwanami Bunko, 1972) [hereinafter only referred to as "Mencius (Ge) or (Jo)]. We should say beforehand that we have not modified them in any way to make them easier to read. The quote used here is from *Mencius [Ge]*, 7A.23

abundant.⁶² Upon entering the simple farming age, where we began using a system of private property, where classes of thieves formed like lords and aristocrats, and where wastelands were plowed by hand, such abundance became nothing more than fantasy. (We will explain Mencius' socialism later on in *The Enlightenment Movement of Socialism*.)

Today, however, machines are being invented one after another that can again produce far more than the population needs. If these machines are merely monopolized by the financial elite class, who do not increase production because they are too busy using them to destroy each other, then any theory of distribution can only be put forth with further evolution of production and industry in mind. We therefore hold the concept that society will evolve to reach a purely communist society, transcending class, with equal distribution for all, as a peaceful, harmonious ideal.

Today's socialists have removed themselves from the fantastical socialism of the past, such as Confucius' ideals of not worrying about less and instead focusing on what's unequal. Those who are focusing entirely on nationalizing methods of production do so because they know that everything can only be interpreted through achieving major production. The reason that socialism is called a "weak republic" in the modern day is because it is conflated with the previously mentioned fantasy socialism of history. It's interpreted as "Never try new things, simply indulge in the equality of poverty." Socialism doesn't claim to equalize distribution in poverty, but rather it idealizes bountiful public property, which can satisfy all through personalized use of it according to a person's individual talents and strengths. It does not reduce the upper class's standard of living to that of the lower class, but rather seeks for the lower class to evolve into the upper class. Calling those who condemn this "wrong" is almost too light of an accusation.

---

⁶² Yao and Shun are considered legendary emperors in China. They are held up as the ideal rulers.

How, then, can we produce so much that society as a whole will be able to enjoy the same kind of happy, fulfilled life as today's upper class? Let us answer in this way; we simply follow the course of historical progression.

As we said earlier about the history of economic aristocracies, from the era of economic local lords, to the era of economic Warring States, and then to economic feudalism, the tide of economic history is still flowing with great momentum, flowing right into the era of trusts. And just as those who suffered the wars of the Warring States period rejoiced in the aristocracy of the feudal system, today's economists are praising the great level of production of the trust era at every turn.

Of course, this is not surprising, for there is nothing to support a foolish belief that divided capital is more economical than united capital, nor is there a reason to believe that destructive labor forces pitted against each other can produce more than labor that works together. The lack of economic feuds and war that one would see in the feudal system is good for both the elite and society itself, and it certainly does raise the rate of production. This is an undeniable truth which has been practically proven before our eyes. No matter how hard American judges work to suppress trusts, no matter how much laborers and smaller capitalists fear their tyranny and do their utmost to thwart them, the great tide of history cannot be slowed by a wooden fence nor a block of stone. Trusts are now attempting to cover the entire world.

In North America, the competition for oil by oilmen was so destructive that the oil was wantonly thrown into warehouses, and many suffered extreme losses all across the land. However, when the Standard Oil Trust was organized in 1882, it reduced the cost of production by sixty percent, and the total dividend in recent years is said to be nearly six hundred trillion yen! Behold how the Carnegie Steel Trust, which was formed with a joint capital of four billion yen, has driven out the European capitalists, who have no such joint capital, from the Chinese market. The Glucose Sugar Company has united all of its competitors in the United States, the National Biscuit

Company has united ninety percent of the nation's large manufacturing companies, and in London even the greengrocers have become a trust organization.

Regardless of how tyrannical trusts may be, socialism does not wish to turn back the tides of historical progress and return to the last century, when small capital was divided. Rather, it seeks to inherit the progression of trusts and move forward into an even bigger union.

The great union of capitalists known as a trust, though it will end the destructive competition between capitalists, the enormous waste of advertising, and the waste of capital through their own destructive actions, is merely a large union among capitalists, nothing more. In fact, we do not even know how much capital and labor is wasted because trusts still do not stop the constant fight between themselves and the other great union, that being labor unions. This is why trusts are still an incomplete union regarding labor and capital, and why waste and hindered production are ongoing problems.

The great union of capitalists known as a trust is merely flying in the dark. It does have the advantage, however, of stopping the economic free-for-all and allowing us to look down on the relationship between supply and demand statistically and holistically, so we no longer have a depression every decade or so as we used to. In spite of this, because its management is based on the folly and arrogance associated with despotism, it will often obscure said supply and demand relationship, and because of the harsh collections of the lords, the purchasing power of society will deplete, and thus overproduction will occur. This results in a society not knowing how much capital and labor it is consuming. This is why trusts are still an imperfect union regarding consumption and production, and why this era still suffers from great expense and hindrance to production.

The great union of capitalists known as a trust does not need countless retailers, and rather than hire people to crush the competition or close down factories that are not making enough profit, it avoids the cost of labor by laying off workers. This brings large profits, but those profits cannot immediately be put to use in production. Thus, not only are the savings meaningless, but some of those laborers are then fed and clothed by society's charity, living in idleness until the next demand arises, while others threaten society and become criminals. We cannot know how much wasted labor society suffers from because of this. Socialism will transfer management of trusts over to society, so that they no longer engage in such massive waste of capital and labor.

Economic warfare led to economic feudalism, and economic feudalism will then lead to an economic civic state. Socialism does not use harsh taxation to exhaust the purchasing power of society through societal production. There is no overproduction, which results from the folly of tyranny. There is no unemployment resulting from irresponsible worker layoffs or factory closings. There is no waste of capital and labor resulting from the struggle between the two great classes, workers and capitalists. Finally, equal resource distribution will cause further free development and progress of individuality, resulting in vigorous activities of self-interest centered on attaining honor and prestige. This will result in stimulation of the sacred idea of public spirit, making the public think consciously how these benefits will be attributed to society, and how such benefits belong to said society.

Those called "economists" will praise the massive production that trusts can achieve until their pencil lead breaks and their tongues rot and fall from their mouths, yet they misunderstand socialism (which also wants to see trusts continue their massive amount of production) to be a "weak republic" which reduces production. Why? What causes this? If they think it such a wise system to let individual self-interest determine the economic sources of society, why do they not let factory owners of an artillery arsenal mix sand in with their cannonballs or stones in with their bullets, like a certain Kihachiro did?[63] If

---

[63] Okura Kihachiro was a successful arms dealer at the end of the Edo period and a businessman who founded the Okura Group after the Meiji Restoration. He established

they think that today's administration system, which allows the right of production, the lifeblood of a nation, to exist as an individual property right, is such a well-established economic organization, why not be like China or Korea, where the right to rule is treated as a property right, and so government offices are bought and sold for the benefit of the emperor?

Still, one must not misunderstand. The fact that the economic feudal system of the trust can turn around and eventually arrive at the economic civic state of socialism is a completely different matter from the fact that there is no room for small entrepreneurs and small capitalists in the age of trusts.

Statistics clearly show that trusts, a combination of large entrepreneurs, have swallowed and overwhelmed their small business peers, but they also show that small businesses who are helped by the blessings of trusts have arisen alongside them, and that other small craftsmen, such as art restorers who cannot produce on a large scale, exist outside of the trusts' sphere of influence. This is because both workers whose job requires more mental work rather than physical, who earn a monthly or annual salary, and physical laborers who earn wages can still buy stock in a trust and therefore become a small capitalist in some respect. We thus realize that it is complete and utter rash and dogmatic thinking to believe, as some cynical socialists do, that the power of trusts means that there is no longer room for any small businessmen, and that the great class disparities in society will grow worse as all of a trust's stock is monopolized by the golden aristocracy. That belief is pure dogmatism.

However, the existence of these small plunderers known as small entrepreneurs is possible because, just as the lack of widespread politics and punishment in feudal times allowed bandits to exist in the forests and grifters to exist in the streets, these small plunderers scurry away like moles, avoiding the eyes of the golden feudal lords. The fact that it is possible to become a small capitalist as a shareholder of a trust is just as if, in feudal times, there was a

---

the foundation of the Okura Zaibatsu.

social class above serfs and in between the aristocrats and warriors, who followed the aristocrats around and helped organize the aristocratic class.

If we understand that the political history of mankind did not end with feudalism, for even in feudal times there were bandits in the forests and grifters in the streets, and not only the aristocratic and serf classes, but also the plundering classes of samurai and foot soldiers in between, then we can say the following:

University podium socialists attempt to distress those socialist cynics by reasoning that small entrepreneurs and capitalists could exist even within this economic feudalism, but in doing so they make the mistake of themselves forgetting about historical evolution. What nonsense. There is not much criticism to be found from this point of view in Professor Kanai and Professor Tajima's books, but many behind the podium who call themselves socialists focus a lot on that point and attempt to resist pure socialism. Professor Kumazo Kuwata,[64] a professor of law at Kyoto Imperial University, and Mr. Hajime Kawakami, a bachelor of law who argued beautifully in the newspaper under the pen name "Senzan Mansuiro Shujin," and the other various authors who sought a debate against *Methods for Interpreting Social Problems* all fall under this category.

Socialism is not satisfied with the current state of minor thieves, known as small entrepreneurs, which exist outside the influence of the economic lords. Rather, it lets these small entrepreneurs exist for the coming era while asserting that they must not be allowed to plunder resources. We will not indulge in the present age in which mental and physical laborers get trust shares and exist as, in one aspect, the small plunderers known as minor

---

[64] A jurist and sociologist active in the Meiji era. He was involved in labor issues and participated in the formation of the Society for Social Policy Studies, as well as being an expert consulted in the Ministry of Agriculture and Commerce's survey of the artisan industry (later compiled in *Shokugyo Jijo*).

capitalists, still in servitude under the economic aristocracy. The fact that petty capitalists will still exist in the coming age is a simple reality. The fact that an economic classist state will eventually, resulting from the flow of historical progress, become an economic civic state is a completely separate reality and topic for discussion.

The previously mentioned lecturers, the podium socialists, fail to see the future as resulting from the progress of economic history. They instead base things on maintaining the economic aristocracy. Pure socialism follows the current of economic history and idealizes an economic democracy; today's rights ideology is not merely an assertion of ownership by a powerful force, nor is it about the justice of individual-scale resource distribution of individual-scale labor. To see that society is the producer and the sole owner of all wealth, one needs only look at how the state today is, under various laws, the "supreme owner." In these modern days, when the idea of rights has evolved to the point where the state is recognized as the supreme owner, and ideas of justice have improved, why is it that some use the existence of the small thieves known as minor entrepreneurs and minor capitalists to stifle an economic revolution? We mentioned this first consideration earlier. In other words, we're asking the following question: Is the theory of evolution a fallacy, and will the history of mankind stop at our current economic aristocracy, never changing until the earth freezes over?

The falsehoods about socialism that *Socioeconomics* and *Recent Economic Theory* spread are certainly not limited to those previously mentioned. The reason we singled out and struck down these two men is because we recognize that their titles, positions, and the prestige of their books lend credence to their thoughtless bad-mouthing. Because these two steal and wear the mask of socialism, as if they were mythical nue,[65] we believe it makes them much more harmful to society than pure capitalist economics.

---

[65] The nue is a mythical creature of antiquity said to have the head of a monkey, body of

In the above explanation, we have shown that there is not even the slightest socialist tendency in what they are complaining about, instead mostly "government socialism" or "capitalist socialism," and we believe that in refuting them, we have to some extent demonstrated the true meaning of pure socialism in the economic sphere.

Pure socialism does not try to switch the status of the plundering class, as the mistaken nue-socialism does. It intends to completely erase classes in general, and use society's rights to benefit society.

Pure socialism is not so ignorant of human nature as to defend modern society's oppression of the motives behind economic activity like nue-socialism does. Through vigorous stimulation of the peoples' public spirit paired with an unobstructed release of one's self-interests, we expect amazing economic activity.

Pure socialism does not maintain the current barriers between classes while disdaining labor like nue-socialism does. It places labor itself above any other external conditions and considers it absolutely sacred.

Pure socialism does not seek to go against the tide of history by maintaining today's class inequalities through dogmatic theories of inequality, as nue-socialism does. It responds to the acute sense of brotherhood that society displays as it evolves, but it doesn't obstruct the development of individuality for the sake of social evolution, and aims for equality of material protection.

Pure socialism does not glorify tyranny done for the sake of a single person's objectives like nue-socialism does, nor does it attempt to involve today's bureaucrats in production via state universalism. It accepts the awakening of individualism and, though few in number, makes fairly and wisely elected supervisors agents of society.

---

a tanuki, tail of a snake, arms and legs of a tiger, and a voice similar to that of a white's thrush. Therefore, any descriptions of it as "half bird, half bull" are not entirely accurate.

Pure socialism does not, as nue-socialism mistakenly believes, greatly reduce production and indulge in the equality of poverty. It does not place great important on resource distribution theories either. It knows that all things can be realized only through extensive production, and so it furthers the evolution of trusts, eliminates all wastefulness associated with these trusts, and turns the unions that were limited to capitalists into a greater union of society as a whole.

It also makes the personal right of production a public right for the benefit of the state, the result of which is great motivation through a combination of competitive individual development and strong public spirit, leading to astonishing wealth for the entire society. This affluence is without the obstacles of senseless selfish behavior, without crime, without blind enterprise, without class struggle, and without economic depression or bankruptcy.

Starting from an equal starting point, with freedom of competition, all economic temptation and unchecked widespread dissemination of knowledge eliminated, invention begets more invention, machines beget more machines, and capital that cannot help but accumulate more and more capital begets even more capital. It will move forward so quickly, accelerating faster and faster, at a pace so high that one could not even imagine it today. Pure socialism, which asserts the rights and benefits of society, takes this ideal of social evolution as its fundamental principle.

Those who defile the sanctity of the podium and the rights of the state for the benefit of the government and capitalists, screeching like nues as they do so, have nothing they could call socialism. For this nue-socialism, economic aristocracy will continue for the rest of human history, going on until the earth freezes over.

Pure socialism's reasoning in based on a firm foundation of science and tries its best to move forward with a clear understanding of the ideals of social evolution. It must never be confused with a mass of filth decorated with beautiful garments. However, since a sweeping victory in the class struggle against the capitalist class is not possible until our socialist utopia is achieved, it is another topic entirely whether the tracks of social evolution will travel through and manifest themselves via the path of state socialism or not. (Read *The Enlightenment Movement of Socialism*.)

VOLUME 2: THE ETHICAL IDEAL OF SOCIALISM

We have explained previously how economic evolution via the implementation of socialism will eliminate poverty. In this volume we will attempt to argue how socialism's moral evolution will eliminate crime as well.

Chapter 4

First, we must reject individualism's views on crime. Of course, there are crimes which criminal law scholars consider crimes of one's nature; crimes arising from an individual's pathology or physiology, crimes that occur from the inability to resist immoral temptations due to alcoholism, crimes resulting from the genes inherited from one's parents, and so on. In this case, the fault lies with the criminal, so there is still at least some reason for the idea of the individual being responsible for a crime, which you would find with individualist criminal jurisprudence.[66]

However, the era of looking at this small fraction of the population and assuming all criminals have some sort of inborn characteristics that make them criminal, focusing most research on such irrelevant aspects of criminality, has passed. Nowadays, crime is treated almost as an inevitable social phenomenon in any society. It is now understood that even a criminal with inborn criminal traits comes about from the inherited criminal tendencies of their parents or ancestors, who often fell under certain special circumstances or social oppression, resulting in the criminal tendencies which are then inherited genetically.

Of course, we do not ignore the responsibility of the conscious individual simply because crime is an inevitability in society. However, the fact that crime has increased dramatically since the turn of the nineteenth century leaves no

---

[66] Likely what's being brought up here is the doctrine of the new school (modern school) of criminal law (see note 72). The social defense theory of the new school of criminal law generally holds this view. However, it is not well supported by the current criminal law community.

question as to where responsibility lies: in the social organization itself changing via the revolution as part of the process of social evolution.

Those academics who have made defense and advocacy their vocation attribute this to different causes. Some say it is because of the increase in population, some attribute it to the increase in wealth, and some even say the cause lies with society becoming more meticulous in its detection of crime. However, such things as crime becoming more sophisticated in proportion to the development of judicial institutions and crime increasing in proportion to the increase in population and wealth are misunderstandings that result from not comprehending that modern society is running on a certain evolutionary slope, and the real reasons in most situations are that most of the wealth is being monopolized by a certain social class, which is protected by this more developed judicial system, and that the increased population is trying to avoid starvation by becoming more sophisticated in their crimes.

Man is a biological organism. Biological organisms have a desire for life. As long as we do not know the answer to the question "Why did we become living things?" we will never know why we desire life as organisms, but the fact that humans desire life as biological organisms is an absolute truth. One cannot be naked and starving if he wants to live. Man is compelled to commit crimes because his first desire as a living thing, this desire for life, overrides his second and third desires to live as a more advanced, noble creature. "Hunger equals crime" is not, as some cynical socialists believe, a complete explanation for crime, but it is precisely from this economic scarcity that nearly all criminals from the lower class of society emerge.

Untrue! They are the criminals of society because they try to be moralists regarding their families. Just like how in the animal world no single organism can be the pinnacle of the competition for survival (read the next volume, *The Theory of Biological Evolution and Social Philosophy*), the top position in the current society of a fierce economic fight for survival is the family. Look at how the crow goes mad like an eagle if a prankster steals its baby. Look how the cute pheasant battles as if in a cockfight when a weasel steals its eggs. Even man, born as the most delicate of herbivores, will turn into a wolf, a pure carnivore, for the love of his wife and child—yes, most of society's criminals exist because they are moralists when it comes to family. The ethical ideals of socialism do not endorse this, of course.

However, in these days when Machiavellianism, dressed in the guise of imperialism, asserts that the morality of the state entails, for its own benefit, ignoring human happiness and world peace, deceiving other nations through diplomacy, invading other nations through military force, and plundering them in the name of trade, what would we do if one of these criminals we mentioned were to say, "I have the honor of a minor imperialist, honor which is so often praised"?

Today, we steal air and do not fight each other over it. Yet, when a hundred Englishmen were taken captive in Calcutta by the cruel king of India long ago and put into a prison where they could barely breathe air through a small opening, the oppression of scarcity finally drove them to fight and kill each other in an attempt to breathe through that small opening, despite the fact that all of them were moral, principled men.

Why even mention ancient India? The same is happening right before our eyes this very day. As the cities spread out, they are sectioned off by walls like citadels so that, despite being surrounded by plant life and fresh air, countless numbers of children suffocate every day from the heat and stench of the rotten air in the small pig sties they call home, only nine feet wide, into which no fresh air blows. The statistics of child death in urban areas speak for themselves. If one could consider himself to be an individualist yet not demand the noose for the Englishmen in Calcutta who killed each other over air, then we ask for an explanation for the mass arrest of those lower-class citizens who steal a single coin amid this wealth, which is supposedly as abundant as air.[67]

---

[67] The original said, "bind them with tapestry," and we aren't sure of the meaning.

Does today's criminal law and criminal jurisprudence not recognize necessity as it relates to the law? In explanation of necessity in this context, we can use an example from Greece. If a ship is sinking and one of the persons grabs a floating log that someone else is holding onto, they will not be guilty of murder due to necessity even if the other person drowns. If this were allowed and extended to include saving one's direct family from drowning as well, then how could an individualist call a lower-class person a criminal for stealing a piece of wood from a battleship to avoid drowning due to the constant state of necessity that their own society's systems force them to live in? So these people, unable to maintain their homes, become fragments of destruction, and finally, out of desperation and despair, they commit a second or third crime, and the little bundles born of them become awful children as well, waiting to become the next generation of criminals.

Such is the case even with crimes of the upper class. Man, as a living creature, has a desire for life. However, as Plato said, man is an organism which desires not only to live, but also try to better itself and live in a noble fashion. However, this word, "noble," originally meant nothing. Today, it suggests nothing but gold. A doctor without a golden watch will lose his patients and an academic without golden glasses will be unable to keep any value in his theory. Even a rotten human who does nothing more than defecate will be called "Master" and worshipped if adorned with a golden halo. A woman who would only be considered beautiful in a poor Hottentot village can put on rings of gold and suddenly people will consider her a proper lady, following her large behind around with adoration.[68] Any philosophical meaning that Plato had in the word "noble" has been completely eliminated and replaced with "gold."

However, in the compounds used, words that could also mean "net" and "fabric" are used, so we think it means "round them all up and capture them."

[68] "Hottentot" is a common name for the Khoi people of Namibia, Africa.

In this day and age, just as the lower class try to obtain this gold by committing crimes, the upper class become criminals by trying to obtain this noble life. Whether they become criminals because of destitution or because they are surrounded by temptation, the criminals are the unfortunate victims, and society needs to reflect on its own responsibility of this as an inevitable phenomenon of society. If placed in a good environment, the lower class would not produce theft and robbery, nor would there be a reason for the upper class to perform crimes like fraud, bribery, or selling their integrity.

Scholars and academics sell truth for gold, and in order to live a nobler lifestyle, they corrupt that truth so that it sells for a higher value. Do government officials, who must live on the little gold they earn from their positions, not sell their positions for much more gold to live a more exalted life, taking bribes all the while? Even judges, whose livelihoods are protected by the Constitution and therefore have no threats to their lives in this regard, will eventually be unable to resist corruption in an attempt to live an even nobler life than they currently do. Just as a child raised in a brothel will have no understanding of chastity, there is no way to prevent bankers who live surrounded by gold from committing fraud and embezzlement if they do so in order to live a nobler life. When a politician of today cannot maintain himself by his education, his talent, his writings, his eloquence, etc., but must obtain a seat in the House of Delegates by buying votes with gold, then must decorate that seat with a chariot and massive villa, also bought with gold, and the free competition of capitalist economics which they so worship, through the principle of price decline, causes market prices to fall so low that it is laughable, Greek philosophers who believe that humans strive for a nobler life will pass it off as "inevitable." Individualist criminal jurisprudence unnecessarily dwells on individual responsibility, interjecting dogmatic assumptions of free will theory toward an impoverished lower class and an upper class surrounded by temptation.[69]

There is no need to explain again how the free will theory of individualism cannot withstand scientific criticism today. However, it is truly incomprehensible that a podium socialist, who is well aware of the lack of evidence for the theory of free will, should fail to understand the ethical effects of socialism. We will designate Mr. Kanjiro Higuchi as an example here, as he is a well-known podium socialist and pedagogue who has devoted much of his research to the ethical aspects of socialism. His writings, including *Educators and State Socialism, State Socialism's New Pedagogy,* and *Main Discussion on the Pedagogy of State Socialism,* argue a harsh, strict theoretical standpoint that this expectation, that socialism will completely eliminate crime, is a complete fantasy. We believe, also building upon a harsh, strict theoretical standpoint, that the implementation of socialism can be expected to cause a complete extinction of crime. We would like to quote his argument from *State Socialism's New Pedagogy:*

---

[69] In criminal law, there are two theories of punishment: free will and determinism. The old school (classical school) tends to adopt the free will theory, while the new school tends to adopt the determinism theory. Free will tends to be more compatible with individualism, while determinism tends to be more compatible with collectivism. The theory being referred to here likely belongs to the old school of criminal law, since Kita says, filled with sarcasm, "trying so hard to brandish free will theory." However, the argument at the beginning of this article, which refers to crimes of one's nature, is more like the argument of the new school, so it seems that Kita does not clearly distinguish between the old and new schools of criminal law. It is possible, however, that the difference between the old and new schools of criminal law was not recognized by the criminal law academics at the time, so Kita's vague distinction between the two cannot be unnecessarily criticized.

It is unreasonable to frivolously assert by simple deductive arguments whether social facts are pathological or not, given how complex and difficult they are to fully understand. It is for this reason that different people will argue that the same fact is pathological, while others argue that it is completely normal. It is difficult to distinguish between the two, which very often leads to endless debate.

For example, many criminal law experts say that a certain crime is obviously pathological, but Professor Durkheim argues that it is healthy (as long as it does not exceed a certain amount). He says, "Crime is not something that is only seen in certain types of society, but rather something that is seen, to some extent, across all societies. There is variation in how it takes form. However, there are actions treated as wrong and punished according to the law in every society. If society continues to climb the staircase of evolution and the proportion of population and crime decreases alongside this, we can say that, even if crime is normal now, our nature will gradually change like our religious beliefs do. However, we do not have a single piece of concrete evidence for this. In fact, there is more evidence for things heading in the opposite direction. We can observe by statistics the progression of crime since the beginning of the nineteenth century, and there is not a single country where the number of crimes has not increased. In France, crime has increased by about three hundred percent. Where on earth can we find a more universal truth than this? Not only is it universal, but is not the increase in crime also an inevitable result of crime's relationship with the other phenomena in society's organization? Saying that crime is a social disease is not to say that it is an incidental illness, but admitting that it occurs from the fundamental system of physiological phenomena.[70] This absolutely confuses physiological phenomena with

---

[70] Originally "living organism" is used here. In other words, "biological organism."

pathological phenomena. Of course, there will be times when crime shows itself in a different form, such as when crime is at an extreme high. It is no doubt that too much crime means society is not healthy. However, we must define approaching a designated number of criminals, yet not exceeding it, as normal. Only the society in question can designate what the appropriate number of criminals is, though.[71] Having said this, it is not like we cannot allow crimes to have different psychological or physiological appearances and display themselves in different ways. If we take individual criminals and look at them, crime is pathological. If crime appears up to a certain amount as a social phenomenon, it is not pathological."

Such a conclusion may seem odd at first glance, but upon a little reflection, one can see that crime is not only unavoidable as a defect of human life, but also an essential phenomenon for public health and one of the necessary conditions for a healthy society. First, since crime is something from which no society can escape, it must be considered normal. In previous chapters, we've made clear that crime on a moral level happens from violating society's public conscience. How can this be true only of crime from an ethical perspective? It is not; this is true of criminal law as well. Criminal law is the guardian of moral conscience. In order to completely eliminate crime from all society then, all members of any society must have the same conscience and willingness to submit to it. However, if current social conscience is to pry open a man's closed heart and enter it or make a jaded person feel strong emotions again, people must become stronger and more sensitive than before. For there to be no more murderers, the emotion of disgust

---

However, that phrase is sometimes used to emphasize the fact that it's a "living" or "biological phenomenon," so we went with "physiological phenomena."

[71] Basically, the proportion of criminals can only be decided by the state of each society.

at seeing blood must seep into the hearts of a society which already contains those who have murdered before. This can only happen if society as a whole gains more sentiment. Furthermore, the fewer murderers there are, the more the conscience of the public will become harsher and more austere in its view of murderers. This would also mean that the same sensitivities would be felt toward crimes that are not considered so serious today, giving the general public the same negative feelings that murderers gave them before. Both robbery and theft violate any sentiment of respect for the property of others. However, those who feel that robbery is vile might not feel as guilty about theft. However, it is reasonable to assume that the number of those who perceive theft as wrong will increase as the number of robberies decreases, as their feelings of wrongdoing towards other people's property become more and more sensitive. It would be a natural tendency for theft, which was at first treated as a minor crime, to become a more serious crime than it was before. Look at the society of barbarians. What we consider in our society to be grave crimes are not condemned or punished there. Even in the same society, as time passes lighter crimes are taken more seriously. Even within the same era, different classes and sub-societies have different consciences, and what is not a crime in a political society often becomes a crime in an education-oriented society. This is the reason why crime occurs in all societies.

To begin with, it is impossible to imagine people having exactly the same feelings because they have different genes, different constitutions, and grew up in different circumstances. If there are already some differences between these, it is inevitable that some will not follow a universal conscience, and if even the slightest offense gradually gives rise to strong feelings as greater crimes are reduced, there will never be a time when there are no more criminals.

Looking from that perspective, we can see that crime is inevitable in society. It has an inseparable relationship with all the circumstances of living in a society. Therefore, its manifestation in moderate amounts must be beneficial to society, just as a woman's menstruation is beneficial to her body.

Morality in human society evolves gradually, and this evolution is necessary for the evolution of society in general, but for this moral evolution to occur, the social conscience underlying morality must not be extremely strong. This is because if the social conscience is always so rigid that it oppresses even those who are slightly farther away from it, there will be no change, no transition among them, no evolution or progress. We have stated before that there are conservative forces in any organization which attempt to obstruct reform. Indeed, a harsh social conscience can lead only to inescapable stagnation. I would testify that a society with no room for even a single criminal is evidence of an extremely powerful social conscience, and nobody would agree to touch such a society of their own volition. This would eventually lead to a dead end on the road of society's evolution. For a society to progress, sacrifices of the individual must be demonstrated. For Socrates to appear in the moral world, for Galileo to appear in the physical world, for Rousseau to appear in the philosophical world, for Luther to appear in the religious world, there must be some "slack" in the society's knowledge. This "slack" is necessary to produce, on the one hand, above-average criminals who are the pioneers of progress, and at the same time it is an unavoidable consequence that this is accompanied by, on the other hand, below-average criminals who are the anchormen of progress.

We recognize as truth Durkheim's statement that crime is not an incidental social disease, but arises from the fundamental system of life and physiological phenomena—therefore, we see crime as an inevitable phenomenon accompanying the organization of modern society, and we plan to change it through socialism. This will be done via a revolution of this previously mentioned fundamental system of life and physiological phenomena.

However, we completely reject Mr. Higuchi's assertion that there will never come a time when crime will be extinct, which he deduced from Durkheim. We would assert that Durkheim suggests that if the proportion of crime within a population decreases as society advances to a higher stage, even if crime is considered normal now, its nature will change gradually along with societal progress, sort of like religious beliefs. So we expect in socialism that crimes based on economic competition today will disappear, just as crimes involving religious faith will disappear. This completely negates Higuchi's argument that universal conscience would be sharpened to the point that today's thieves would be treated with the same penalty as robbers.

Higuchi's argument that abhorrence at the sight of blood would have to seep into the hearts of a society which already has people who have committed murder in order for murderers to disappear is legitimate reasoning in the context of social evolution. However, the assertion that, in order to make universal conscience more sensitive to seeing blood, we must respond with blood to that which is not met with blood today, is speculation without a proper reason. Mr. Higuchi's statement that acts we consider major crimes in our society today are practiced in barbaric societies without reproach is, of course, true. But it should also be noted that some things that are not considered crimes in our society receive severe punishments in barbarian societies.

Mr. Higuchi's reference of crime being necessary for the health of society just as a woman's menstruation is necessary for the health of her body is nothing more than a worthless metaphor, but we are fully aware that outstanding people who aid in the evolution of society can be treated as evil by the general conscience. But the fact that men like Socrates, Galileo, and Luther, to whom he is referring, were condemned as criminals for turning their backs on the religious beliefs of their time, is because the universal conscience of the parochial socialism of the time allowed for the crushing of individuality. Today, after the awakening of individualism, society's conscience respects changes in the individual. We must think as Durkheim said, "We can say that, even if crime is normal now, its nature will gradually change, much like religious beliefs." Mr. Higuchi ignores the number and nature of crimes, ignores morality and law, and even ignores the evolution of the common conscience.

It is a gross disrespect to the honorable Mr. Higuchi, who is a specialist in moral phenomena, to say that he is ignoring these important points in the face of his wealth of knowledge and scholarship, but saying so is unavoidable. However, this is not in the least bit his fault; he merely made the mistake of falling prey to the seduction of podium socialism.

The banner which this podium socialism waves in opposition to pure socialism is encapsulated in the following statement: "Socialism is a fantasy that expects too much from the future." Oh yes, fantasy! The pervasiveness throughout society of this mistaken idea which claims that socialism is a fantasy is indeed the strongest enemy of us socialists, more so than government persecution or academic bad-mouthing. Podium socialism was born of the misdirection of this stereotype, and has made it its mission to pour oil on the fire of this mistaken idea—the reason that we consider podium socialism the immediate enemy of pure socialism, and intend to wipe it from the world of ideas and thought, is precisely because it operates under the banner of "socialism is a fantasy."

We must ask, if we treat the implementation of socialism on society the same as the discovery of the laws of gravity in the world of physics,[72] how could we forget the fact that we've made more progress in physics during the last century than we had for an entire millennium during the Dark Ages? A fetus

---

[72] It's sort of difficult to understand, but he means, "Just as the law of universal gravitation is recognized as an infallible natural law."

repeats the billion years of history of biological evolution within nine months,[73] and a twenty-year-old offspring of a civilized nation absorbs the fruits of six thousand years of civilization. But socialism does not leave all steering to the unconscious evolution of the past. Let us be clear. Socialism expects an astonishingly large number of things in the future, according to the very laws of social evolution, and the most immediate future expectation is, to begin with, the elimination of only two things from society: poverty and crime. Just as the economists who espouse podium socialism are misguided by it, and believe that poverty is something eternal within mankind, Mr. Higuchi, who espouses podium socialism, has his ethics misguided by podium socialism and understands crime as something eternal that will exist until the earth freezes over—this is why podium socialism, while decorating itself with a thin skin of scientific research, still bases its fundamental ideas in schools of thought from before evolutionary theory.

Look at the traces of social evolution through the idea of evolutionary theory. Crimes remain consistent in number, but many have waned in severity, law has gradually given way to morality, and the common conscience has evolved with the evolution of society. For example, in a time when society was organized around religious beliefs, religious crimes were the norm in those societies, as Durkheim states. To name an example, in barbaric societies today, false idols and disrespect towards extremely foolish rituals, things which would make us laugh in our own society, are still met with slaughter. More examples include the cases of Socrates, Galileo, and Luther, whom Higuchi mentions, who were considered criminals by the conscience of their respective societies.

Today, however, society is not organized according to religion, so religious crimes that arise from the fundamental, physiological system of life have all

---

[73] As before, this number has an extra four zeros on it, but we believe it to still be a modifier as mentioned in note 57.

but disappeared, as Durkheim said. Society's conscience towards religious faith has evolved so much that, except for pagan practices and pagan shrines considered guilty of (minor) offences against the law,[74] pagans and agnostics are now no longer (legally and morally) immediately recognized as criminals.

In fact, in an age when society was organized by the strength of the powerful, those powerful people were the source of all morality and law and it was a crime to go against their will. During the class state period, before the French or Meiji revolutions (for the significance of class states, read the later volume, *The So-Called Theory of Japan's National Polity and its Restorative Principle of Revolution*), going against the emperor or aristocrats' desires was considered a crime towards the prevailing social conscience and would result in punishments such as one's head on the prison gates,[75] beheading, hanging, or crucifixion. However, even though the aristocrats and lords of those days are now seen as vestiges of a completely different existence, and the emperors, who were the owners of the land and people, have been transformed into state institutions, in today's civic states, crimes and punishments of those who go against the will of the nobility and lords have completely disappeared.

Even the crime of impiety, which still exists under law, is now a system of protection by the state to safeguard the state's institutions and agents in order to benefit the state, rather than to maintain the authority of the sovereign. The German emperor is fortunate that the nation does not distinguish between modern emperors and medieval emperors. Because of this, he has bent state institutions to his own vanity, creating countless criminals of impiety year

---

[74] The term "offense against the law" was defined in the former Penal Code as one of the three categories of crimes (felonies, misdemeanors, and offences against the law). Specifically, it refers to crimes that result in detention and minor fees. This term is no longer used in the current Penal Code.

[75] Referring to beheadings where the head was then hung on the prison gate for all to see.

after year. In more advanced countries like the United States and France, crimes such as these, based around the power of the elite, do not exist. Is it not that the conscience of society has evolved to such a degree that those who go against the will of the powerful are never treated as criminals (legally and morally), except in certain circumstances?

If, as we've seen, every time we defeat one of the basic life or physiological systems with which some type of crime is inexorably linked as an inevitable result of said system, that crime itself changes, then, if socialism manages to defeat the foundational system of today's economic aristocracies, is there any way that the crimes of today, perpetrated due to economic circumstances, will not disappear? In *Reviewing Socialism*, Mr. Hajime Kawakami appraises current socialists as coming to a rash conclusion that a human's monetary desires have some sort of limit and criticizes socialism for expecting today's economic crimes to become extinct in the future, but this is a shallow viewpoint which does not consider the fact that humans are organisms which desire to live a nobler life, and that this desire is simply manifesting today in an economic direction because of economic competition.

Mr. Higuchi's reasoning still has room for improvement, which can be found in the following point. Even if today's economic crimes will disappear after the modern economic system is overthrown, since the nature of crimes change accompanying the revolution of society's systems, people do not all have the same conscience because they differ in heredity, constitution, tendencies, and circumstances. Since they are not all led by the same conscience, criminals will continue to exist forever, at least in terms of number rather than quality or nature of the criminals themselves. However, this ignores the idea of evolution of society's conscience.

For one in a position of parochial socialism—who does not know, like the scientific socialist does, that the authority of the individual should be respected and the spirit of the individualist revolution should be carried on—any individual who differs in genetics, constitution, tendencies, or circumstances, according to the conscience of a parochial socialist society, would be immediately treated as a criminal. The persecution of all previous great thinkers, whose individual authority was not recognized in the time of religious authority, is an example of this. Knowing that today the conscience of society towards religious faith has largely allowed individuals freedom of religion, can we imagine that in the coming age of socialism, the conscience of society will degenerate and revert to how it was at the height of the pope's power?

In particular, Mr. Higuchi has a misunderstanding relating to society's conscience becoming more acute. He says something akin to: "Crimes considered minor today will be punished more severely once society's conscience becomes more sensitive," and that those who disregard even today's less acute conscience of society "will be retaliated against with heavy penalties by this more sensitive conscience of society." (He's mixing the criminal law theory of retributivism in with his other thoughts.)[76] Even as a mere theory, this is highly contradictory. It even ignores the fact that society's conscience has grown so sensitive that even now it cannot stand punishing crime for the sake of it, and instead the law now merely attempts to separate criminals from the rest of society.

Taking the death penalty as an example, exactly as the criminal law scholars say, it used to be performed in any way one imagines a person could be killed. Some were fed to ravenous beasts, some were trampled to death by elephants, and there are even examples of some criminals being made to fight crocodiles to the death. Rome, for example, kept several species of tigers, wolves, and other beasts which criminals would be forced to fight. Moreover, this was considered the ultimate entertainment for the citizens.[77]

---

[76] The retributivist theory is what is known in the world of criminal law as the "retributive punishment theory."

[77] The Colosseum was the place to watch such things.

In Japan, there were hangings, beheadings where the head was then displayed to the public, and even a punishment where the head was sawed off. Other punishments include torture by fire or water, being pulled apart by two wagons or bulls, being stewed alive in kettles, and burning at the stake. Some were crucified upright, their hands and feet bound, while others were hanged upside down and beaten to death over a period of several days. Some were made to lie on a board, their limbs hammered with large nails, and their faces flayed until they died. Sometimes those who were sentenced to be burned at the stake were laid on their sides atop two bamboo shoots, while, if there were items around which could be burned, some were made to dance inside the fire, a form of punishment which Oda Nobunaga enjoyed, deeming it the "Dance of Azuma." There was also the brutal practice of setting the wives and children of the criminals on fire and using them as kindling.

Although such physical punishment does not exist today in any country except China and Turkey, brutal punishments such as gouging out the eyes, cutting off the ears, shaving off the nose, and cutting off the genitals were, until recently, common practice. A mere century ago in the Tokugawa period, criminals who failed to pay what they owed could be punished on a whim by drowning, being forced into a small bamboo basket,[78] made to sit on a wooden horse, or having their entire family, including elderly parents and infants, placed in a water prison during the bitter cold or made to stand knee-deep in cold water. These are only a few examples, but when we see that physical punishment was abolished, and that even in the case of capital punishment efforts were made to reduce pain considerably by changing the methods to hanging or electrocution, we can see that the reasoning of Higuchi and others who agree with him is precisely a reversal of cause and effect.

---

[78] The original says literally "basket curling." The basket refers specifically to a bamboo basket used to gather vegetables when farming. How this relates to "curling" we don't know. We've translated it as you see here for now.

In France, there were 150 kinds of crimes punishable by death in 1810, but today there are only twenty-two. In England, there were 270 kinds of crimes punishable by death in 1870, but today only the three most serious remain. Moreover, note the fact that almost all countries have ceased to carry out death sentences, implementing special pardons. Society now favors punishments which do not inflict external pain on the criminal, and even punishments which strip away their freedom or impose labor on the criminal are not done with the purpose of doing those things to the criminal, but rather are understood as the only ways to properly separate these people from society.[79]

The reason this is accepted by most today is because society's conscious has evolved massively. This is evidence that we are evolving from an era in which morality is encouraged by the external compulsion of law (i.e., the age of heteronomous morality) to a moral era in which the maintenance of morality is gradually changing to internal compulsion, or conscience (i.e., the age of autonomous morality). We are fully aware, along with Mr. Higuchi, that society's conscience will evolve and become more acute, but we should infer that this more sensitive conscience of society will become less able to bear the imposition of punishment on criminals.

The retributivist theory of criminal law, which calls for cruel punishments against criminals, inversely proportional to current sensitivities, has already been dismissed and would be inconceivable in the modern day. If one admits the evolution of society, admits the evolution of morality, then one must admit the evolution of ordinary conscience, a conscience that respects the differences between individuals. How can anyone use parochial socialism, the idea that asserts social tyranny, the idea which believes in the all-powerful state in the

---

[79] At the time, German scholars such as Liszt advocated a new school of criminal law, and the theory of social defense was a powerful argument. However, the old school of criminal law was still alive and well, so not all scholars were advocating this theory.

same way they did in the medieval period, to cast an arrow of criticism against the socialism which is to be realized in the twentieth century?

I merely designated Mr. Higuchi as a representative for debate because he seemed a good representative for podium socialism's ethical arguments, but this ideal is so outdated it is not even post-Darwinian, it comes from the philosophy of the era of Ishikawa Goemon,[80] who said, "Like sand on the beach, I will never come to an end." (Read *The Theory of Biological Evolution and Social Philosophy* for more on criminal law's thoughts regarding natural selection by the death penalty and arguments on the significance of the competition for survival.)

We believe that most crimes today are, in fact, a clash between the different consciences held by the different social classes, along with the consciences of those who hold nationalist or socialist ideals. Socialism exists for this reason, as it seeks to accomplish a fundamental revolution against class-based society.

From a legal perspective, countries after the French and Meiji revolutions are not class states as they were in medieval history. Even the emperor of Japan, as a member of the nation, has the same patriotic sentiment as the other members of the nation, and there is no class distinction in his patriotic conscience. From an economic standpoint, however, the content of the state is class-based, divided into economic classes of lords, warriors, and serfs. Thus, the conscience of each class is different and so they stand against each other.

Today, crimes are determined by the national society; in accordance with the conscience and perspectives of the various classes, that which is detrimental towards that national society, that which opposes the conscience of nationalism and socialism, is deemed criminal. In other words, all crimes based on economics perpetrated by both the upper and lower classes occur

---

[80] A famous bandit of the Azuchi-Momoyama period. The dialogue is probably from Kabuki or something similar.

because the state is a nation of economic social classes, and since each economic class has a different class conscience, they are treated as crimes by the laws and morals of the state society. For example, state law punishes robbery and theft by the poor class as a crime, but the class conscience of the poor class, like an educator of the poor saying, "I found a child who does not understand that stealing is a crime," does not consider it a crime against conscience. Again, while society's morals condemn the arrogance, extravagance, and greed of landowners and capitalists as going against moral principles, the class of the landowners and capitalists does not consider them atrocities which go against their conscience.

In the first place, conscience is simply the body that is conscious of moral decisions; it is otherwise empty of content aside from a few genetic tendencies. In other words, the consciousness which makes judgements is inborn, but how we make those decisions is completely acquired. The content of these judgments is formed by the moral teachings one receives from society, mostly imitation of one's parents' lifestyle, and by social customs and social knowledge that emerge through the home, neighborhood, school, social interaction, books, etc. In addition to individual mutations, all conscience is formed by the conscience of society, which exists in social circumstances that only affect the individual.

Although today's society and state are society and state only in terms of law, in terms of practical economic substance they are divided into countless classes, so that the individual exists as an individual within one class, and the class conscience within each class must be considered an overall "conscience." Therefore, even if there is a reason to execute a person from the point of view of the law, which prescribes nationalist and socialist ideals above all acts, from the point of view of morality, which only designates a crime if it violates one's conscience, a social class cannot be held morally responsible unless that crime violates their own conscience.

Therefore, from the perspective of the ethical ideals of nationalism and socialism, the almost humorous luxury and grossly unreasonable oppression that the German emperor is engaging in under the guise of "I am the emperor, I rule all" is treason against the state and a crime which is detrimental to the interests of society. But if he is an heir by inertia to the conscience of the medieval era of the class state, we cannot hold him morally responsible for his conscience, no matter what his actions may be. Why? Because in his conscience, from birth nothing more than a void, there is no patriotic sentiment that suggests "the emperor exists for the benefit of the nation," but instead a medieval view that "the nation exists as a means to satisfy the self-interest of the emperor alone," and a sovereign view that "I am a sacred person granted eminent subjects by God and heaven.[81] I am superior to those normal human beings who must defecate." This attitude is also facilitated by the "long live the emperor" sentiment that emanates from a social conscience which is engrained with skillful pandering towards the emperor. This comes in the form of customs of the court and other slave-like customs, and from the sycophantic judges who approach the emperor like eunuchs. For example, Seydel teaches that "The state is its land and people, and the sovereign dangles in the air outside that state,"[82] while Bornhak teaches that "The state is another name for the sovereign, and its land and people do not exist on this earth."[83] Because this conscience is formed of these medieval ideas, looking at him from the point of view of the modern social state would mean criminalizing actions which do not violate his conscience.

---

[81] The original text said "verdant." However, "verdant" seemed strange in that context, so we used "eminent" in order to show what we think is the original meaning, "blessed with talented subjects."

[82] Max von Seydel, a nineteenth century German (Bavarian) public law scholar.

[83] Konrad Bornhak, a nineteenth century German public law scholar.

Capitalist and economic aristocrats of the land-owning class are the same. Just as the nobles of medieval history considered all land and people to exist only for their benefit and so used harsh collections however they pleased, economic aristocrats think of laborers and peasants as creatures lower than humans, born into the world to build the prosperity of the golden feudal lords. Therefore, they do not care if people die of starvation lying in the streets, but continue to plunder as much as they wish. In addition, politicians, clerks, and others of their ilk who could be considered the economic warrior class, swear an oath of allegiance respectfully, so that they stand above the general class in an extremely arrogant manner as aristocrats, much like the way aristocrats in the past considered serfs as less than human. So we must understand that, although cruel from the standpoint of a state or society, if we judge from a moral responsibility standpoint, based on their conscience, their actions are not immoral.

Just as people are born physically naked before being clothed in the various garb known as social classes, the conscience, which is equally naked, is clothed in different garments according to different social classes. The German emperor's physical body, born naked, is adorned with ludicrous metal toys such as a stupid, foot high crown and medals akin to children's playthings, and so is his conscience tattooed, like a barbarian, with medieval era privileges. These include such things as a photo of someone with a Kaiser mustache being an object worthy of worship,[84] or that certain things cannot be said during speeches on naval expansion.[85] As the naked bodies of the nobles are adorned

---

[84] At the time, German Emperor Wilhelm II had a distinctive upward-pointing mustache. The name "Kaiser" (German for "emperor") was used to describe this upward-pointing mustache.

[85] Specifically, words that signaled approval when said at a prewar congress (which can sometimes, rarely, mean de-escalation as well), or words that signaled disapproval all the same. In other words, whether it was approval or disapproval, it was disrespectful

with beautiful garments woven by the sweat and tears of the laborers, so their conscience, born equally naked, is like the heart of a ravenous beast, hungry for the blood and bones of the laborers.

Now look at the general rabble! As those tens of millions of laborers and peasants have their naked bodies clothed in rags, so are their consciences, also born naked, clothed in all kinds of ugly and dirty customs. Families whose parents are cruel, neighbors who starve to death like dogs, solicitation into prostitution, induction to crime, dirty, brutal, and violent thoughts; they are clothed in all the dirty, tattered rags of the world. This is what makes up the final form of their conscience. The fortunate are born in well-developed circumstances, taught and nurtured in the bosom of a warm mother and by the hands of a dignified father, and the contents of their conscience are formed by accumulated ancient and modern knowledge and the spirit of our world, while the general lower class is instead born like a pig in a crowd of filthy, coarse animals. Even when they cry from illness, they are restrained by the beating of their mother, who is busy just trying to get by, and the father, who never sees them except in the evening, returns home desperate from the toil of the day and the despair of the road ahead, a raging alcoholic, drunk off some cheap liquor. They have no knowledge; they have no world.

We maintain as a complete truth that poverty, in this sense, means crime. It stands to reason that a person who is placed in an environment of economic well-being and who has a developed conscience, or whose conscience has been developed by approaching an already developed conscience, will not become a criminal, even if he falls into a state of economic scarcity. So it would be unscientific to push the "hunger causes crime" argument in this case, like many of the more cynical socialists do. It is an arbitrary, dogmatic decision to espouse the honored ideals of nationalism and socialism towards someone, then call something a "crime" without measuring it against the conscience of

---

for the subject to say anything toward an imperial rescript.

the social class a person is born into, an economically disadvantaged social class with no developed conscience and no chance to develop one's own conscience by approaching an already developed conscience.

From a legal standpoint, today's nation is a fine nation and society in its own right, and criminal law can demand the same behavior from the people of the nation and the members of society because of their nationalist or socialist conscience. However, from a moral standpoint, the people and members of society cannot be criticized using the same nationalist and socialist conscience because they are acting according to their own class conscience. If we know that it is not immoral in the Negro community to abandon Negro babies, if we know that cannibalism is not immoral in the cannibal community, if we know that slave-like subjugation in aristocratic times was not immoral then, if we know that independent actions are not immoral in today's democratic countries, if we know that morality varies from region to region (e.g., vertically) and era to era (e.g., horizontally),[86] it obviously makes no sense to try and rule all of modern society, which is extremely chaotic due to the impending major revolution, by the same moral judgements for everyone.

On the one hand, we have a poor social class with a similar conscience to the Negro, while on the other hand, we have a capitalist social class with a similar conscience to the cannibals. On the one hand, there is a conscience that still considers the slave-like obedience of the aristocratic period as its moral obligation, while on the other hand, there is a conscience that tries to act with a strong awareness of the democratic state in the modern era. It is as if we have mixed several ethnic groups from different regions and eras, and some ancestors from centuries ago, within a single nation and society.

---

[86] The original text said "vertically" and "horizontally," with a (sic) next to it. We think that Kita believed in a relationship between moral concepts where region or location is vertical and time period is horizontal.

The crimes of today are not so much a defiance of conscience in the original sense of the term, but rather a sign that the vastly different class consciences have been struck by a conscience whose ideal is to serve the interests of the overall state and society. Some criminals may be committing evil against the orders of their own conscience, but what their conscience deems slightly immoral is considered a grave evil by other consciences, and they may believe that they have done right according to their conscience, yet this might be considered a crime by other consciences. This is why socialism becomes revolutionary. It seeks to overthrow the present economic class state, to make it one nation and society equal in economic terms, and thereby to sweep away the present class conscience underneath a conscience based on the moral ideal of national and societal interests.

This general conscience unified by sweeping away any class consciences will evolve as a conscience that most respects the freedom and independence of the individual as well as the interests of society and the nation, and not as a biased conscience that suppresses the development of individuality, as was the case in the era of parochial socialism. In a socialist world where any class consciences have been done away with and replaced by a unified common conscience, and where that common conscience has evolved to respect the development of individuality, is it really a fantasy to believe in the extinction of sin? (The explanation of class conscience is essential to the explanation of class conflict. This is because conflict between social classes is not merely conflict between interests or sentiment between the classes, but rather about the clash between class consciences.)

Bergemann said, "Humans can only become human with the existence of society."[87] This one sentence is precisely where socialism hopes to realize its ethical ideals by revolutionizing social institutions. Bergemann's social

---

[87] Paul Bergemann was a nineteenth-century German pedagogue. He advocated social pedagogy and influenced the Japanese pedagogical community of his time.

pedagogy has three translations in Japan alone and is the basis of Mr. Higuchi's pedagogy, but the fundamental principle of today's scientific ethics and pedagogy also relies on this concept that "Humans can only become human with the existence of society." Just as a lotus grows and blossoms in a swamp, or a rose gives off a pleasant scent in the sunlight, or a butterfly dances in a flower garden, or a lion roars in a desert, all living things are placed in different circumstances, and the principles of evolution, which establish these species, require ethical circumstances that are suited to the survival of them as ethical organisms.

Mr. Higuchi, who was misguided by podium socialism, seems to have little understanding of the ethical effects of socialism, yet in his *State Socialism's New Pedagogy*, he presents a startling fact, showing how the individual is created by society. He states,

> In the Natural History Annual Report of 1850, Sir Roderick Murchison reported five facts from Colonel Sleeman,[88] who had found a child among a pack of wolves in the Sultanpur region of the Oude Kingdom.[89] According to him, there were many wild dogs and wolves in the Kabul and Lucknow regions, and they often took away infants. Of course, many of them were eaten alive, but on rare occasions they fed and nurtured them. On one occasion, as the military police were proceeding from Oude to the shore of the Gomti River, three animals came to drink. They rushed to the waterhole and caught the animals, but how could they have known that they were two human infants and a toddler? When they tried to catch the three, they were so angry that they bit the military police, then scratched them as well when the police

---

[88] A British soldier and administrator in British India

[89] Region of present-day Uttar Pradesh

tried to take the three away with them. Moreover, they knew no language, and their comprehension resembled that of a puppy. [90]

This is not limited to India alone. Tennyson's poem based on the tales of King Arthur says,

> And ever and anon the wolf would steal,
> The children and devour, but now and then,
> Her own brood lost or dead, lent her fierce teat,
> To human sucklings; and the children, house,
> In her foul den, there at their meat would growl,
> And mock their foster mother on four feet,
> Till, straightened, they grew up to wolf-like men,
> Worse than the wolves. [91]

As we can see, this has not been rare even since ancient times.

This fact that humans possess a nature where, if a human is left in a feral environment, they will devolve into an animal after only one generation, does not allow us to reason that "humans possess a nature where, if a human is left in a sacred environment, they will evolve into a godlike being, though it will not happen after only one generation." Obviously, one must not neglect the fact of heredity. The customs of ancient cannibals still appear through atavism, and if we speak of someone being guilty of murder, it is not inconceivable that the infinite number of sins we are currently committing manifest themselves in the form of heredity due to a particular environment. However, in today's

---

[90] The following quotation is from Kanjiro Higuchi, *State Socialism's New Pedagogy* (Tokyo: Dobunkan, 1904), 11.

[91] Alfred Lord Tennyson, "The Coming of Arthur," in *Idylls of the King*, lines 26–33. Tennyson's work was influential in Japan as well.

criminal law, this kind of thing has already been placed outside of crime as a pathological phenomenon. Moreover, since heredity is something that only manifests itself in an environment which caters to it, it is not likely that the criminal heredity of today's individualistic age would have many opportunities to manifest itself in a socialist environment. (Also, read our argument about morality becoming instinctual in *The Theory of Biological Evolution and Social Philosophy*.)

Just as the son of man, nurtured in a society of wolves, became a half-beast, half-man monster by imitating the walking of a beast, we are nurtured by human society, and it is only by imitating how our parents walk that we can attain a human form. We have said since ancient times that a man is a creature with ideals and an organism that responds and conforms to tendencies. Today's scientific research has also confirmed that man has a nature of mimicry, of imitation. Because of this mimetic nature, we move our lips in the shape of a circle from the time we are held in our mother's lap, as if we are trying to figure out how to pronounce the same words as our mother, imitating her lip movements. When we can barely pronounce a word, we imitate the pronunciation as well as the idea itself contained in the pronunciation, without considering its meaning or whether the idea contained within is good or bad.

As children mature and begin to play with each other, they imitate the language and behavior of their neighborhood peers without making a conscience choice. As they enter school, they imitate the speech of their teachers and friends and the language of ancient and modern figures written in books. During this time, their intelligence develops, and they gain the ability to judge what they want to imitate. The result of choice after choice is that they find something greater to imitate. Once they succeed in imitating that goal, they then move on to imitating something greater. Once they succeed in imitating that, they then move onto imitating something even greater, and the cycle repeats itself.

In this way, the initial target of imitation is the mother, the family, the neighborhood, etc., which gradually becomes the school, society, books, ancient and modern figures, and the world's ideas. When these previous ideals are no longer sufficient, and when people begin to seek an even greater target, they begin to conceive, according to their own individual characteristics, of this greater target based on the materials they have already imitated, and strive to reach that greater object by imitating the ideal they conceived. If their ability to conceive and the conceived ideal are noble and great, then that person becomes a hero.

Therefore, it must be said that the heroes who have left their mark on history have possessed great and noble qualities, but they have also been fortunate in their social environment to have been supplied with the basic materials that enabled them to display these qualities. All the legends of heroes, ancient and modern, attest to this. For example, a hero of war sleeps in a cradle covered with bloodstains, and a hero of revolution is born in the darkest circumstances right before the winds of revolution blow. The poet Saigyo was born through a leisurely journey along a mountain river, and *The Tale of Genji* was written as the author gazed at the moon over Ishiyama Temple. In a non-partisan cabinet and a congress that blindly follows it, eloquence like Gladstone's would never be born.[92] Jefferson's Declaration of Independence was not written to assemble material for some theory of national polity.

Humans can only become human with the existence of society. Today, we are barbarians because we're unable to escape the uncivilized social system of

---

[92] William Ewart Gladstone was an English politician. He served as prime minister four times and was famous for his liberal reforms. The phrase "an extraordinary cabinet and a blindly obedient parliament" clearly refers to the cabinet and Diet of Japan at the time. He was making fun of Japan's current situation by comparing it to England, the founder of constitutional government.

today's barbaric villages. Do we not realize that the majority of people in society are, much like the infants found in the German forest, fed and clothed by beasts in the middle of large cities, complete with steam power and electricity? Look at the society of landowners and capitalist social class. The first object of imitation before the eyes of a newborn babe, born as a human being capable of sacred development, is the father, cruel as a wolf and as drunken and ill-behaved as a baboon, and the mother, called a noble "lady" by others, who has become nothing but a pig dressed in silk because of the sycophancy of her neighbors. The only objects of imitation when the children play are their nannies, who try cleverly to appease the children for their own benefit; vulgar and lecherous servants and maids; and the other children who are merely obeying the orders of their elders out of fear and intimidation. How is it surprising at all that these people, who have become human in the most unfortunate environment possible, are made into humans with consciences similar to cannibals, even though they are humans like any other?

When it comes to the lower, poorer classes, they are completely fed and raised by wolves, as wolves. They are not taught to crawl on all fours, but they behave completely like beasts. They do not learn to claw or bite with their fangs, but it is true that fights between children are often welcomed by their wolf parents.[93] When the blank, unspoiled hearts of these children are influenced by seeing the "wife" starving and desperate, and the drunken husband, alcohol still on his breath, yelling epithets at others,[94] an image hammered into the gray matter of their brains, which are still unformed like a newt's clenched fist, is there any room to question how they grow up with a conscience like the Negro? Neither today's upper nor lower classes develop

---

[93] In the old days, it's likely that the common folk thought "it's a good thing if they're healthy enough to fight."

[94] The "epithet" specifically mentioned here is "beranmee," which is a word yelled at other townsfolk as an insult.

within themselves a conscience which makes them try and benefit the state and society, which is what the law and morals desire. In this sense, not only does hunger mean crime, but gorging means crime just as well.

Humans can only become human with the existence of society. Socialism has discovered that an ethical organism can become an ethical organism only in ethical institutions, and therefore attempts to lower the hand of revolution onto our society's systems.

However, one must not misunderstand. Socialism does not dissolve the individual within society. It is necessary for an ethical organism to become an ethical organism by means of ethical institutions, and to have the responsibility to strive for the further evolution of said ethical institutions. This happens by being enveloped by a social conscience which respects equal material protection and freedom of individuality. This is what is meant by socialism's theory of freedom and equality. (The significance of the theory of equality was explained in the previous volume, *The Economic Justice of Socialism*.)

The social conscience in the era of parochial socialism was very narrow in scope and did not allow for the free development of individuality, so much so that the individual was completely at the mercy of socially powerful men of the time. Socrates, Luther, and Galileo were all treated as criminals, thus greatly slowing the evolution of society. One should not arbitrarily decide, like parochial socialism did up until the French revolution, that the atomic individual who thinks only based on ideals is the final goal, and that society is simply mechanically created and exists for the sole purpose of the individual's freedom and equality. An individual's freedom absolutely does not exist in thought or faith alone. Freedom exists because of a free social conscience which respects the freedom of an individual's faith and thoughts. This is why, in a time when the conscience of society did not allow freedom of thought and faith, Socrates, Galileo, and Luther were all criminals.

Science, which has shown that conscience is socially created, has concluded that, except in rare cases where individual idiosyncrasies develop, both thought and faith are completely inherited from ideas and beliefs already existing in society, from which individual ideas and beliefs are created. Unlike what parochial socialism says, ideas and beliefs are never free from the start.

The conscience of society during the time of parochial socialism and social tyranny, which has the ideas and beliefs that see the state as all-powerful, does not recognize the independence of thought and freedom of faith while building up the conscience of the individual. The conscience of society in the age of parochial individualism, which views society as a machine, creates an individual conscience with the ideas and faith that states that independence of thought and freedom of faith must not be violated, even if it interferes with the interests of society—so when our pure socialism says to respect individual freedom for the sake of society's evolution, it does not mean that thought and faith already exist independently and freely before the emergence of the atomic individual. It means that we should allow independence of thought and freedom of faith according to the conscience of society, which respects individual freedom for the evolution of society. Whatever the social conscience includes in order to aid society's evolution must not be parochial. The evolution of society should be the ultimate goal, and the free development of individuality should not be impeded in order to achieve this goal. Pure socialism clearly inherits the purity of individualism in this respect.

Individualism! Parochial individualism, along with parochial socialism up to the medieval era, are exactly the two pillars upon which pure socialism is built. It is precisely for this individual freedom and equality that pure socialism seeks to turn public the modern economic aristocracy's monopoly of economic sources (e.g., land and capital), just as individualism refused the medieval aristocracy's occupation of land (which was, at that time, the source of all economy) and called for freedom and equality. Without economic freedom and equality, one cannot be free and equal in all other respects. Just as we said earlier that equal distribution of resources allows for the development of individual freedoms via the equal protection of materials, the individualist French Revolution tried to secure economic freedom for the sake of individual freedom by establishing private property and barring the aristocratic classes from possessing all sources of economy.

Pure socialism also clearly inherits the evolution of the private property system in this regard. Whoever is economically independent is politically and morally independent, and whoever is economically subordinate is politically and morally subordinate. In the time periods when a sovereign owned the land and the people (as economic property), the people did not have property rights, but were in a relationship of economic subordination to the monarch. In other words, the people were politically and morally subordinate, while only the monarch was economically independent, and so the monarch was politically and morally independent too. (The time period before the Kamakura shogunate in Japan is an example of this.) Then, when the aristocratic class plundered the land and became economically independent, they became politically and morally independent in opposition to the sovereign, not recognizing his right to rule and rejecting the obligation to fulfill their loyalty to him. (In Japan, this was the case in the aristocratic period before the Meiji Revolution.) The common social class, as serfs, were the property of the nobility along with the land, rather than people with status as human beings and property rights, and were therefore subject to unlimited political and moral subordination due to economic relations. The warriors, for example, wielded immense authority over the lower classes, but because of their economic subordination, they were never politically or morally independent of the aristocracy. (Read the later volume, *The So-Called Theory of Japan's National Polity and its Restorative Principle of Revolution*.) Nevertheless, the ideals of individualism, in the name of the French Revolution and through the labor of all the people, placed land that had been monopolized by the aristocracy under a system of private property. This great wave of revolution eventually spread to the Orient, causing democracy to emerge in the economy through the Meiji Revolution, and establishing a private land ownership system.

Despite this progress, where are we now? We seem to be reversing history, and the world is once again in an era of economic aristocracy. No, if we think about it logically and calmly, we are passing through the economic aristocracy as part of the progression of economic history in a process leading up to the economic civic state. The economic sources, land and capital, have become the feudal citadel of the economic aristocracy. Only the economic aristocracy has unlimited political and moral freedom, while the people have lost all independence and have become subjugated like slaves.

The podium socialist Professor Tajima praises the relationship between capitalists and workers, likening it to that of sovereign and vassal, and that's true. Both the mental worker, subordinated by his annual or monthly salary, and the physical worker, subordinated by his wages, are completely dependent on a tyrannical power, like the warriors or serfs of old. They recognize this power's right to rule, and, as slaves, fulfill their duty to obey it faithfully and obediently. Even though the warrior class of the aristocratic state period was as powerful as a tiger against the lower classes, they would kneel or even prostrate themselves before the foolish lords. They considered themselves the property of the lords for the sake of economic subordination and never once questioned why they had to obey even when ordered to commit seppuku or when they were cut down by their own lords. In the same way, the current class of economic warriors such as clerks, political contractors, etc., which are now enslaved to the lords of gold, are extremely oppressive and insulting towards the lower classes, but are not politically and morally independent at all due to their economically subordinate relationship of receiving annual and monthly salaries. Therefore, no matter how arrogantly they are greeted when seen by the foolish lords, they remain on their knees and show the meekness of a cat, not thinking that their control over the lower classes keeps them on the throne of the lords, but rather believing that they survive by the grace of the foolish lords above them, and even if they are reduced in salary or dismissed, they do not question nor even think hard about it. When it comes to the common class of laborers and peasants, they are pure slaves and serfs.

Without political freedom, there can be no moral independence. The system of private property, which is the basis of individualism, now, for the majority of society, only means that they can live off the private property of the economic aristocracy, just as the lower classes did in the days of the actual aristocracy. Why should we doubt that there is such a lack of political freedom and moral independence now, just like it was before the revolution, when we were economically enslaved under the aristocracy, that it is necessary to repeat said revolution of individualism again?

We said at the beginning of this book that those who seek to defend modern society by individualism are traitors to individualism precisely because the majority of society has lost their individual private property. Socialism, of course, has the ultimate goal of the evolution of society and does not, like parochial individualism, treat society as a means to be used by an individual, as a machine for accomplishing that end. However, it still contains the basis of individualism in that it makes the freedom and independence of the individual the sole means to achieve its goal of social evolution. In socialism, individuals are not in a relationship of economic subordination among themselves. No one individual is oppressed in his political freedom or insulted in his moral independence because of another individual. Since society would not be hierarchical and individuals would not be economically subordinate to individuals who are in the upper class, there would be no political obligation to blindly submit to the power of individuals in the upper class and no moral obligation to strive for the well-being of individuals in the upper class. No individual would have a relationship of economic subordination to any other individual, he would merely be under the protection of the economic equality of society. Therefore, no individual's freedom would be violated by any other individual, and the extensive conscience of society, which respects the freedom of the individual, will make the individual responsible for political and moral obligations aimed at the well-being and evolution of society.

Before the Meiji Revolution, when society was economically subordinated to the aristocracy, there was a political obligation to submit to their rule, which served the interests of the aristocrats, and a moral obligation to strive for their well-being. Contrary to the individual responsibility of "loyalty," today, because the people are legally and economically subordinate to the land and capital of the state (because the state has the supreme right of ownership to absorb all individual property for the benefit of the state), they have a political obligation to submit to the rule of the state for the benefit of the state, and a moral obligation to strive for the well-being of the state—in other words, it seems that "patriotism" has become an individual responsibility.

No, socialism does not stop at a mere ideal, like today's law, but in fact seeks to make the interests of the state and society the conscious responsibility of the individual. Socialism does not hold individuals responsible for themselves for the sake of the individual, but rather demands individual responsibility for society and the state for the sake of society and the state. Consider what we said earlier, that the state and society must obtain true order and peaceful happiness through socialism. This is because the state (and society), exercising the supreme ownership it holds as a legal ideal, exists to all its citizens and members as the main body of all economic sources, and thereby expects all its citizens and members to be individuals responsible to the state and society, politically and morally.

To condemn our socialism with a theory of individual responsibility is to equate our present socialism with the era of parochial socialism before individualism, when the individual was subordinate to the upper class and not the subject of responsibility.

There is another reason why socialism rejects podium socialism, which seeks to maintain buying and selling relationships between individuals by means of labor—labor like a conscripted military organization. Of course, one can think of this as a simple economic theory, but it shouldn't be thought of as such. In this situation, there are countless stores, merchants, clerks, middlemen, exchanges, and so on investing useless capital and useless labor, wasting large sums of money by attacking each other, not moving immediately from production to consumption, passing through the battlefield of exchange, resulting in much of their produce being destroyed, being forced to bear military expenses, and coming into the hands of consumers at double the cost of production is a folly that humanity should naturally abandon.

However, the reason why pure socialism insists on the production method of a conscript labor organization in particular is that it seeks to directly connect society and the individual in a relationship of economic subordination. That is specifically a system in which all the goods produced by conscript labor belong to society. Then society distributes pieces of paper displaying equal purchasing power over society's goods, which makes the individual aware, through an obvious responsibility, of his existence for the sake of society. (See the previous volume, *The Economic Justice of Socialism*, where we discussed the economic activity of the public spirit.)

The warrior class, the Bushido spirit, has died out, and the townspeople's morality, centering on vile self-interest, exists today because of the following reasons. Bushido is a noble moral code of devotion to the lord to whom one is economically subordinate, even though it includes an element of self-contempt for one's own slave-like obedience towards the aristocratic class. However, the morality of the simple townsman is self-centered and despicable because the townsman is sustained by his own economic efforts.

Today as well, it is believed that all individuals are not in an economic relationship subordinate to the social state, and that they maintain themselves through their own economic efforts. Because of this, the individualism of those simple townsmen is found more suitable, and has been inherited today. Individualism is precious and noble under socialism. This is so because the individual under socialism has a conscience which strives for the well-being and evolution of society itself, and they act accordingly. The existence of the individual's freedom and independence for the sake of the freedom and independence of the individual has no value. An individual's freedom and independence are noble and precious when they exist for the sake of society's well-being and evolution. Just as the warriors of the aristocratic era, within their Bushido or chivalry, had a moral code of devotion towards the aristocrats to whom they were economically subordinate, when the economic aristocracy is overthrown and the nation and society become one economically, all the citizens and members of society will realize the ethical ideals of nationalism and socialism, including a moral code of devotion to the state and society to whom they are economically subordinate.

Pure socialism is not an individualist revolutionary theory that demands individual freedom for the sake of the individual itself and seeks to ignore the well-being and evolution of the social state. It seeks to overthrow, by revolution, the systems of individualism which ignore the well-being and evolution of the social state, and to realize and implement the economic fact that society is the body of all economic sources. It also seeks to realize the ideals held by today's laws, which make the state the supreme owner of these economic sources, and thereby make the individual the subject of moral obligations and responsibilities to act freely for the benefit of the social state. (We explain in greater detail the relationship between economics, morality, and the law in the later volume, *The So-Called Theory of Japan's National Polity and its Revived Principle of Revolution*.)

Among those who call themselves socialists, in advocating individual freedom, they will say, "Since each member of society desires free development, it is necessary that individual freedom in politics be as great as possible and the power of society be as small as possible. In other words, the power of society should not exceed what is necessary for the survival and development of society and to guarantee the freedom of its members." Others say, "The complete freedom of thought and belief, which others or society cannot do anything about, must stand outside all social norms of artistic, religious, scientific, and political expression and practice. This is, without a doubt, a fundamental principle." A hypothesis such as these merely resemble socialism in their conclusions, but have completely inherited the dogma of individualism. We should not use this to lay blame on socialism itself.

One example is when Mr. Kanjiro Higuchi, a self-proclaimed advanced critic of socialism, is attacking this very individualism in his *Main Discussion on the Pedagogy of State Socialism* while mistakenly calling it the freedom and equality theory of socialism. Thus, even in his condemnation of the ideals of social evolution, he is actually arguing against a purely individualist scholar. He says,

> A society in which each member's life and property are protected by, as Rousseau calls it, a common power,[95] yet they continue to follow this power's orders of their own volition, is nothing more than a kind of utopia. An individualist society which runs perfectly, without any exterior oppression, in addition to Spencer's distant ideal of self-will, should add the adverb "infinitely" to the original "distant," creating the phrase "infinitely distant." This obviously means an ideal that's incredibly difficult to realize. This new society that Mr. Yano imagines, in which there are almost no lawsuits, almost no crime, or, taking this to the extreme, no lawsuits or litigation at all, is nothing more than a dream. Indeed, *New Society* was written as an unfulfilled dream, and it is clear from what he said in *The Complete Works of Socialism* that he was describing his own socialism in terms of a dream. If that is the case, is not it true that he is also maintaining fantasy socialism in the most literal sense?

---

[95] Likely means "a common will."

Through this, one can see the strange phenomenon of how socialism and individualism, antithetic to each other, are confused and conflated by both socialists and non-socialists.

At any rate, genuine socialism does not look for paradise or heaven in the afterlife, as in conventional philosophies and religions, but looks forward to a future in which society has evolved. Human society evolves like an organism. Therefore, social philosophy must be discussed as a theory of social evolution, a subsection of the theory of biological evolution.

Volume 3: The Theory of Biological Evolution and Social Philosophy

Today's criticism against socialism from a fundamental philosophical perspective is that, since socialism attempts to eliminate the biological competition for survival, it is a fantasy that goes against the fundamental principles of the theory of evolution. This is a massive problem.

CHAPTER 5

If the basis of all philosophy and science is the theory of biological evolution, and if the fundamental principle of biological evolution is the theory of competition for survival, it goes without saying that even socialism is not exempt from this. However, today's theory of biological evolution has merely discovered the fact that biological species were born through evolution. The theory of competition for survival, which is taken as the reason for the fallacy of mankind's position in the animal kingdom, is an extremely incoherent theory, to the point where such incoherency is unparalleled in history, and is also interpreted through individualism. For this reason, biological evolutionists invoke this theory of competition for survival to denounce socialism as fantasy, unscientific, and a scheme to accomplish the impossible task of stopping social progress. Many socialists also try to circumvent the theory of biological evolution or build weak arguments to try and counter said theory, such as that socialism destroys competition for survival, yet there is still other competition such as honor, morality, etc. We believe if socialism does truly contradict the theory of competition for survival, socialism is nothing more than an unscientific fantasy, and any attempts to label itself as "scientific socialism" is meant only in economics, moral philosophy, history, and other subjects similar to these. On the basis of social philosophy, which underlies the aforementioned subjects, it is nothing more than a type of utopia.

Socialism is based on the ideal of the evolution of the biological society of the human species, and so it obviously is not exempt from the competition of survival, which is the foundation of the theory of biological evolution and includes all biological organisms, with humans being no exception. If we were to simply hurl insults at science itself without any solid foundation to criticize the theory of competition for survival specifically, it wouldn't matter what we said, it would be impossible for socialism to not be unscientific—scientific socialism must be built atop a sincere theory of science. However, the pseudo-theory of biological evolution of today's scientists is nothing more than a theory that is so contradictory and confusing that we must step up to the plate and intrude into biology's territory in order to systematize it. This contradiction and confusion exists in two points: the interpretation of the facts of biological evolution according to the dogmatic ideas of individualism, and the inclusion of mankind's place in the biological world among the other species of animals. This is why we must discuss the theory of biological evolution.

Here, we will take up Dr. Asajiro Oka,[96] a professor at Tokyo Higher Normal School and a doctor of science,[97] as the Japanese representative on the biological theory of evolution, and designate his *Lectures on Evolution Theory*, which is a criticism on socialism, as the subject of our arguments. We deeply regret that socialism has been condemned by a scholar such as Dr. Oka, who argues for the truth itself, but this is by no means his fault. Darwin himself has turned the theory of biological evolution into a type of animalism, and has interpreted and communicated the theory of competition for survival through individualism. As someone who simply brought the theory of evolution to the public, Dr. Oka advertised its fallacies as well.

We have singled him out specifically because of the power present on the last dark page of the great book, *Lectures on Evolution Theory*, which was written for the purpose of popularizing the theory of biological evolution to the

---

[96] Asajiro Oka was a zoologist active in the Meiji and Taisho periods. He contributed to the popularization of the theory of evolution through his research on leeches, ascidians, and moss beetles, as well as by writing a general book on the theory of evolution, as discussed in this text.

[97] The original says "Imperial University," and is later referenced as "Tokyo Higher Norm"; we're certain this was a mistake, and it's supposed to be "Tokyo Higher Normal School."

general public. Its last page impedes the promotion of social evolution and spreads lies about socialism with astonishing force. And because in all of its blind pages, the animalist theory of biological evolution and the individualist interpretation of the competition for survival theory are on full display. There is a theory of criminal law that advocates natural selection, or culling, by the death penalty. There is the ideology of social cycles, which ignores historical evolution and fails to understand the significance of the revolution. There is an aggressive theory of reverence for the emperor and foreigner expulsion, which advocates a race war between the human races to kill each other. There is an individualist theory of competition for survival, which holds that the development of a race and the strength of a nation is based solely on competition among individuals within the race and within the nation. There is a population theory that fails to understand that reproduction is what sustains a race. There is an immature theory of the state that says that wars between different races and nations will never disappear, and that the future of social evolution, in which the world will become one single society, is a fantasy. This is not so!

Throughout all of *Lectures on Evolution Theory*, Dr. Oka fails to define any denomination of competition for survival, which is the ancestor of the still chaotic, unorganized theory of biological evolution, fails to understand the purpose of the competition for survival, misunderstands the opponents in competition for survival, fails to know the evolution of the contents of the competition for survival according to the classes of biological species, pays no mind to the status of competition for food and competition between the sexes in the theory of biological evolution, and does not speculate about the current status and future evolution of the human species. Thus, let us display his criticism of socialism in the following passage:[98]

---

[98] *Lectures on Evolution Theory* is written in an antiquated fashion, so we've changed some of the text into more modern language.

We all must admit that the current social system is not perfect, but when discussing the question of how to improve it, we must always think soundly on the basis of evolutionary theory, or we will not gain any benefit. The reason why social reformers, however many they may be, always talk about foolish dreams, is because of two things. Firstly, they do not fully consider what human beings are, mistakenly thinking they are some noble existence. Secondly, they do not realize that competition is the only source of progress and that competition is inevitable during life, even in the most desperate of circumstances. We have explained before that the result of competition among different races equates to the rise or fall of each race, while the result of competition among the same race is the improvement and progress of that race.

This is completely true if we look at it in human history, showing that competition for survival between different races leads to the rise and fall of the competing races, while competition within the same race leads to evolution among that race. Therefore, as long as there are many races existing relative to each other, not only is competition among different races inevitable, but neither can competition among individuals within the same race be eliminated. A biological species with a large area of distribution and a large number of individuals will always divide into several varieties, which will later fight against each other. Humans are in this state right now, and so fighting with other races in some form is inevitable. However, in human competition, a race which progresses slowly can never hope to win, so each race must strive for its own improvement and progress, and this requires competition among individuals within that race. There are many examples in history of people who were not satisfied with the state of society and started great revolutions, but they attributed all sins only to the social system, forgetting what human beings are like and thinking that simply changing the system would lead to a perfect world. After the revolution ends, they simply look at the fallen state of the former tyrants, who once wielded the power of subjugation, and feel happy for a while, but nothing else of note would happen. The world is still in a state of degeneration,[99] as ever, and competition is just as intense as it was in the past. Today's advocates of socialism often preach outlandish reforms, but if we were to look at them in this light, we would see the same results as above. As long as human beings live and reproduce, they are not exempt from competition, and when there is competition, life every day will be as hard as any other day. As we have already explained, the purpose of education is the maintenance and prosperity of one's own race, and from the perspective of evolutionary theory, the purpose of social improvement should also be the maintenance and prosperity of one's own race.

Some people in the world want to abolish all wars, or have the idea that if civilization advances, the whole world will become one nation, but these are biologically impossible, and as long as groups with conflicting interests exist side by side, a war of some kind between them can never be avoided. It is clear that no human being in the world can be in a position where there are no conflicts of interest. As the saying goes, "Without enemies and foreign interests, a nation would quickly perish," and because there are always enemies and foreign interests, a nation is united. Even if one race were to prevail over all others and take over the world, if the interests differ from place to place, conflicts would quickly arise and the nation would be divided into several smaller nations. Even small groups of elected representatives from different parts of a prefecture can be seen to be engaged in violent conflicts due

---

[99] The original text used a word meaning "an age of declining virtues, where human emotion and sentiment have become cold-hearted."

to clashes of local interests, so it is obvious that there is no hope for the world to become one nation or to cease warfare. As long as there are a few races living side by side, each race must strive to maintain itself and prosper, but it cannot hope to maintain itself and prosper unless it advances as fast as other races, and the only way to advance this quickly is through competition among individuals. If this is the case, then the people who are alive today must be prepared to constantly progress through competition among allies in order not to be destroyed by the enemy race, and if they are unwilling to compete with their allies, they will lose to the enemy race because they will not be able to progress as a whole. There are many aspects of today's social systems that need improvement, but no matter how they are improved, competition is an unavoidable part of them.

If only one race existed, confined to a place where there is no interaction with other human beings, that race would not be subject to intense competition, but would instead progress so slowly that if they came into race with other humans later, they would be quickly destroyed like moa in New Zealand. In the eyes of the world, the suffering of living is based on competition, and competition is caused by population growth. Because of this, some people think that it is necessary to limit the number of children born, but this is not a good idea, according to our previous explanation. What is needed today is not to stop competition, but rather to change our systems which currently stifle natural selection. From the standpoint of racial survival, it is necessary to reduce as much as possible any system that places a heavier burden on the race as a whole by artificially allowing those of inferior ability and health to survive while perfecting as much as possible any system that allows those of superior ability and health to work as the mainstay in any field, so that the entire race may progress rapidly as a result of competition among individuals. In such a world as ours, we who have been born into it have no other choice but to try to win this competition to the best of our ability, knowing that it will be a competition for survival. Often, mistaken theories based on empty arguments written only on paper are put forth, such as advocating humanity, respect for human rights, and respect for the individual. For example, the abolition of the death penalty is not only a completely baseless theory from the viewpoint of race maintenance, but is, in fact, clearly harmful. Just as the flowers in a garden will wither and die if the weeds are not cut out, the removal of harmful molecules is necessary for racial improvement, and if this is not done, there can be no improvement at all. In the interest of racial preservation, it would be far more beneficial to further increase the use of the death penalty, and to eliminate without mercy those wicked people who will not change their minds even after repeated punishment.

Such demonic rhetoric is, of course, based on a lack of knowledge about jurisprudence, history, national science, and sociology, but ultimately it is because the theory of biological evolution itself has not yet been systematized—it first puts the human position in the biological kingdom on the same class as other animals. In the first edition of *On the Origin of Species*, Darwin avoided explaining the status of humankind because of the profound discrepancy with Christian beliefs. In the same way, today's biological evolutionists are in such a hurry to break the dogma that Christianity holds, "mankind is the son of God," that they have not had time to precisely define mankind's position, but have passed the point where the pendulum's law of motion should stop them, and are running to the opposite extreme, the other dogmatic idea, "mankind is a beast." The pendulum is not in perpetual motion. We must bring this pendulum to a halt where it should stop.

If our God, a creature far more evolved than mankind, inhabits other planets, as is assumed by scholars today, and if this planet we inhabit is evolving like other planets, and if evolution has no pinnacle and mankind is not the pinnacle of evolution, then we humans are transitional creatures, somewhere between the God whom we will evolve into in the future and the beasts whom we have evolved from in the past. Today, if we excavate the fossils of our ancestors from the time when we humans differentiated from being apes, and find what we name apes, or anthropoid apes, just as we humans have gone extinct as apes, archeologists of the deities who have differentiated from humans today, after our extinction as humans, will excavate us as true "anthropoids," half gods and half beasts (this is explained in detail in *The Ideal of Social Evolution*).

They say that humans evolved from apes, apes evolved from four-legged beasts, four-legged beasts differentiated from reptiles, which together with birds had an amazing morphology, reptiles evolved from fish, which have a completely different morphology today, and that humans experience a billion years of evolution from fish in the first nine months of their lives in the womb. It is a laughable phenomenon, then, that they supposedly reason about the past but their reasoning is completely halted by the future progress of human evolution.

The theory of biological evolution to date has been organized around the dogma of human evolution as if humans were the endpoint of evolution. Since Darwin's time, the theory of biological evolution has sought to overthrow the Christian belief that humans are the children of God, created by God, by comparing skeletal, muscular, organ, cerebral, and developmental conditions to other sciences to prove that humans are entirely animal. Thereby there is no fault in arguing that Christian doctrine is nothing but dogma that cannot stand up to scientific criticism.

Needless to say, we do not deny that it is unscientific to place mankind in a heavenly realm, separate from other creatures, as being entirely the children of God. However, those who dogmatically state that we are exactly the same as other beasts, even though our skeleton, muscles, organs, and brain are not exactly the same as theirs, are no more careful in their scientific research than are Christians, whom they call "intolerant of scientific criticism."

If it is unscientific to say that we are fully God's children, it is equally unscientific to say that we are completely like beasts. Humanity is a species of animal. However, just as beasts are in a different class from birds or fish in the animal family, so are we in a completely different class from beasts. We are animals of the species "humanity." The first fallacy of today's biological evolutionary theory is that it places mankind in the same class as the beasts. If Christianity, which collapsed under their blows, was a superstitious religion, then this theory of biological evolution is clearly a superstitious animalism. And much as the superstition of God, which was the core of society until it evolved to a certain point, has killed countless scientists and impeded the evolution of society, so too biological evolution, which contributed to the evolution of society by overthrowing the superstitious God, has finally become a superstition of animalism, impeding the evolution of society today. The very same animalist biological evolutionists exist today as pure Roman priests in ideology and in society.[100] Just as Darwin and others were condemned by the superstitious believers in God, so it is inevitable that the philosophical religion of socialism is persecuted by the superstitious believers in animalism. This is the norm for social evolution.

Because the human race is included in the ranks of the other species, the beasts, the current theory of biological evolution sees no difference between the competition for survival among humans and among beasts, and deduces no distinction between the fittest of the beasts and the fittest of the humans. This is where we get the dogmatic and horrifying phrase "law of the jungle." If the so-called "law of the jungle," usually meaning that the strong feed on the weak,

---

[100] The original word was "monks," but that generally makes on think of Buddhism, so we changed it to "priests." Because the "Roman" probably means Roman Catholic, there shouldn't be any need to be overly considerate of Protestants.

means that cows are weak because they are bitten by mosquitoes yet people are strong because they are fed on by fleas, then it is true enough as a biological fact, despite its outlandish use of words. But for those who use these words, much of the standard measure of strength and weakness lies in claws and fangs.

Needless to say, phrases such as "survival of the fittest" or "the law of the jungle" are empty words that only envelop already existing phenomena. In other words, it merely means that "those who are suited to the environment of their species will survive as the superior ones," but the content of this statement, who is suited, who is "stronger," varies according to the environment in which they are placed. The environment differs according to the different classes of each species. Han Yu's singing, "If even a Koryu rises from the water to the land,[101] he will be humiliated by ants and crickets," in one of his poems is perhaps the clearest illustration of how the most superior, the fittest, and the strongest species differ depending on their environment.

The lion is the fittest and survives as the superior animal only in the tropical desert environment, while the docile reindeer is far more fit and survives as the stronger animal in the Arctic ice and snow, where the environment is different. The eagle is fittest and strongest in the open sky, but if we bring the eagle to the edge of the roof, between the wall and the eaves, it is no better than the swallow or the sparrow; it is the loser, the weakest. For digging in the dirt, the horse is inferior to the mole, and for hiding in the mud, the sea bream is far less fit than the loach. When it comes to burrowing in decaying filth, the earthworm is better adapted to its environment than the socialist, and the maggot survives better than the biologist in the manure pit. How can any current biological evolutionist, knowing this, dare to make an

---

[101] A "Koryu" is a "Mizuchi" (snake-like animal which hasn't matured fully into a dragon). It's a mythological animal. It is also used as a metaphor for heroes whose time hasn't quite come yet.

analogy between the superiority of beasts to the fitness of mankind in a completely different environment?

If we must lose our normal state of mind to say that we should throw a sea bream into the mud to suffocate because a loach is superior in the mud, or that we should bury a horse alive in a pit because a mole is superior under the earth, or that humanity can only become the fittest, the most superior, and the strongest by seeking conditions like earthworms and maggots, then any argument which conflates humans with beasts, and doesn't consider the completely different environment of the beasts, who live with claws and fangs, is nothing more than a self-defeating argument.[102] If the survivors in a quadruped's environment were to be compared to humans, as in biological evolution, the moralists would be the losers in the race for survival because they have no fangs, the intellectuals because have no claws. The most brutal and tyrannical would be the fittest, the best, and the strongest. And Dr. Oka's theory of culling by death penalty would be like a horse coming out of a gourd.[103]

Humanity's competition for survival, much like culling the immoral using the death penalty, means both complete moral superiority and moral strength. To begin with, let us first note that the current theory of biological evolution does not define the unit of competition for survival.

---

[102] The original text reads "If we lose our common mentality and say that a loach is so superior in the mud that a bream should be thrown into the mud to suffocate, or a mole is so superior in the earth that a horse should be buried alive in a hole, and that mankind must seek conditions similar to those of earthworms and maggots to become fit, superior and strong, what kind of logic is it to confuse mankind and animals, who live under completely different conditions, together with quadrupeds with claws and fangs?" The rest of the sentence after "if" is a rhetorical question, but it doesn't quite make sense this way, so we tried a liberal translation of it.

[103] This is an old phrase that means "something not reasonably possible."

We believe that the current theory of biological evolution defines the unit of competition for survival by the dogmatic preconception of individualism. We seek the truth of the species unit of the competition for survival discovered by the theory of biological evolution, or, in other words, the truth of the competition for survival by the social unit for the purpose of the survival and evolution of society. This explanation requires that the definition of the individual, the unit of competition for survival, be established, and we are inclined to believe in the definition adopted by biologists. That is the definition of "classes of individuals" as taught by Haeckel and those who agree with him.[104] (Haeckel is a biologist who most strongly argued for the contradiction between biological evolution and socialism, and whose address to the Munich Great Convention of Biologists forms the basis of the arguments of Dr. Oka and others in their critique of socialism.)

Before the invention of the microscope, the term "individual" could only be defined as "something discrete, with space in between itself and that which is not itself" or as "something grown from a single egg." Under these definitions, an amoeba, for example, which results from the division of a single cell, does not grow from a single egg, and some plant organisms that gemmate form a close-knit group of individual organisms that reproduce by forming a tree-like shape, thus having no space in between.[105] It is impossible to determine whether they are one individual, a fragment of one individual, a collection of individuals, or none of the above. Due to this, that definition becomes an extremely unclear concept. To put it plainly, since the invention of the microscope, the idea of an intermediate space or a single egg as the basis of an

---

[104] Ernst Haeckel was a German zoologist.

[105] "Gemmate" means to reproduce by budding. Budding refers to the formation of small protrusions on a portion of a cell, which gradually grow and separate from the mother to form a new individual. Hydra, for example, reproduce in this manner.

individual has come to be disregarded as a completely unsustainable hypothesis.

According to the explanation of "classes of individuals," each of the many unicellular organisms that divide from an individual unicellular organism can be thought of as many individuals. At the same time, we can think of all the unicellular organisms that arose from the division as still being part of the first individual, as component molecules of the original unicellular organism. In other words, the unicellular organism which was produced by division is, from the fact that it is a unicellular organism, an individual, and the original unicellular organism which produced the second one can be thought of as an individual, but in a larger sense. As for organisms which gemmate, each molecule that is connected to the larger individual without becoming separated by space is an individual organism, while the first organism has simply grown larger as an individual organism, just as a tree grows larger.

Higher organisms, such as human beings, are divided into two sexes of yin and yang for the purpose of reproduction,[106] so they are each one individual as male or female; parent, child, or sibling; and are each also one individual which divided off the large individual known as society, which is separated with space in between. The theories of social organisms and national organisms, which are spoken as truths today, originated from this point of view. (This explanation is important for the discussion of state-personality existence theory found in volume 4, *The So-Called Theory of Japan's National Polity and its Revived Principle of Revolution*.)

It is understandable that Dr. Oka attacks socialism with the theory of biological evolution in his *Lectures on Evolution Theory*, since he doesn't even explain the fundamental unit of competition for survival, the individual. However, it is bizarre that Haeckel, who taught the concept of the class of

---

[106] In the Chinese study of divination, yin represents woman and yang represents man. In other words, yin and yang here refers to female and male.

individuals, argued in his speech at the Great Convention of Biologists that "socialism is unsustainable if it follows the theory of competition for survival."

Throughout the biological world, the unit of competition for survival is not just a small class of individuals as they interpret it through individualism. A single organism (in the case of humankind, an individual person) is a unit of competition for survival as an individual, but a species or family of organisms (in the case of humankind, a society) is also a unit of competition for survival as an individual. And an individual has a conscience as an individual. When an individual is conscious of itself as an individual, we call that something like egoism, or individuality. When a society is conscious of itself as an individual, it is called public-spiritedness or sociality. This is because the individual is a molecule of society separated by space between itself and another, and society is an individual of which the previously mentioned individual is a molecule, so the individual and society are one and the same.

By virtue of the classes of individuals, an individual is conscious of themselves as an individual person, but they're also conscious of themselves as an individual of society, as a molecule of society. In other words, when our consciousness works as an individual person, it takes the unit of the individual as a person, and when it works as a society, it takes the unit of the individual as the society, and this is why we have the public spirit along with egoism, and sociality along with individuality. In other words, public-spiritedness or sociability is when the self-interest of a large individual called society is made conscious by an individual person as a molecule of society, and the self-interest of an individual person, when he or she is conscious as a small individual relative to society, is also the self-interest of society because that small individual is a molecule of society. In fact, this also means there is no reason for antithetical terms like "altruistic" or "selfish," when in fact terms such as "large ego" or "small ego" are much more fitting.[107]

---

[107] In philosophical usage, "large ego" refers to the one and only absolute spirit as the

If such scientific knowledge of the individual is not lacking in the current biological evolutionists, then how could they recognize only the self-interest of the individual person and forget about the larger self-interest of society, then make both the fact of competition for survival between individual people and society's competition for survival the result of the individual person's self-interest? It is difficult to understand how they forget all about the large ego, about society's self-interest, the fact of the competition for survival among societies, and the existence of sociality and the public spirit, which is the social self-interest that conducts the competition for survival among societies.

Both of these individual human and social self-interests are equal, and there should not be any relative weight to either of them. However, one self-interest is personal, while the other belongs to society. Because humans have been able to surpass other animals through social cohesion, and even use social cohesion as a unit in order to compete with other cohesive social groups, it is society's self-interests which are more necessary. This phenomenon has been given special names, such as public spirit, sociality, moral instinct, and divine mind, among others, and is in a position of relative importance. Most solitary creatures, such as carnivores, maintain their status through competition for survival based on their self-interest as a single animal, while those living in groups, such as herbivores, improve their status through competition for survival with society as a unit, based on social self-interest. Hobbes and Spinoza, writing at a time when biology was not advanced at all, should not be blamed for embracing dogmatic individualism based on vague ideas such as

---

main body of the universe, and "small ego" refers to the corresponding ego of oneself (i.e., the distinction between Brahman and Atman in Upanishadic philosophy), so the question is how to interpret the "big ego" and "small ego" here. Here, Kita is talking about the self-interest of society and the self-interest of the individual, and does not seem to be giving such a philosophical meaning to the term. He may simply be using the terms "big ego" and "small ego" in that same sense..

the previously mentioned space between subjects and whether they came from a single egg, since they could not consider the individual through a microscope. But how should we consider the biologist himself, who even now accepts this dogma as if still ignorant of the definition of the individual, insisting only on the competition for survival between individual people, completely forgetting about the competition for survival based on sociality?

Current biologists are holding a gem, thinking that it is garbage. Do they not realize that the revelations biological evolution has given mankind is beyond any theories on morality or any religion we have ever known? The theory of competition for survival, whispered like a demon by Darwin himself, led to Kropotkin discovering the organization theory of mutual aid.[108] This was a competition for survival based on society, a higher class of individuals, as a unit, and it gave a clear scientific basis to the ancient, vague moral consciousness. Ancient people recognized this by speculative reflection and intuitive recognition of social instincts. For example, Aristotle said, "Man is a political animal. A man who lives alone is either a Beast or a God."[109] Since society is always found in the form of a political organization, Aristotle defined man as an animal that creates a political organization by his nature and exists by living together with others, and on this basis he discussed the state. His conclusion that "A man who lives alone is either a Beast or a God" was the first written conclusion in the history of philosophy that humans can only be human

---

[108] Peter Kropotkin was a Russian aristocrat and anarchist. It is well known that Tatuso Morito, who studied him during the Taisho era, was forced to take a leave of absence because of it.

[109] This is from Aristotle's *Politics*. "From these things therefore it is clear that the city-state is a natural growth, and that man is by nature a political animal, and a man that is by nature and not merely by fortune city-less is either low in the scale of humanity or above it . . ." Aristotle, *Politics*, Book 1, 1253a. In the same section, Aristotle also says, "For the whole must necessarily be prior to the part . . ."

if they have a society, which is the same conclusion of modern science. Cicero wrote,

> And again, as swarms of bees do not gather for the sake of making honeycomb but make the honeycomb because they are gregarious by nature, so human beings—and to a much higher degree—exercise their skill together in action and thought because they are naturally gregarious.

This is a principle explained by Kropotkin in biology, but it already lived as an axiom long before in Roman times. This social self-interest was most sought after in ancient times, when social competition was most intense, and the equally important individual person's self-interest was completely suppressed. So, as soon as social competition subsided, self-interest of the individual person rose to the top. This is why individualism emerged in the later years of Greek and Roman history, and as the competition among social units ceased under the medieval Christian unification, freedom of thought and faith was realized, as was political and economic independence. Individual freedom and independence were finally demanded parochially, and the idea of individualism became a vast river that washed over the lands of Europe; the aftermath of this great wave continued to surge until the middle of the nineteenth century.

Since this is so, it is not the least bit strange that the students of Hobbes and Rousseau, floating and flowing in this great river of individualism, did not understand that humanity is a social entity. Some imagined a state of nature called pre-contract, saying "the struggle of all against all,"[110] and others saying that "each person has divine freedom and independence,"[111] and building their

---

[110] This is referring to Hobbes.

[111] Since he's talking about Hobbes and Rousseau, it stands to reason that this other

social contract theory upon it. So how strange is it that biologists themselves, who through their own discipline have taught that humans, as well as many other animals, live not individually but exist in social groups, are still drowning in the current of individualism, clinging to the legs of the drowned?

Darwin's *On the Origin of Species*, written in the mid-nineteenth century during the aftermath of parochial individualism, placed the unit of competition for survival as the individual person or individual animal, and thus ran contrary to the moral demands of the theory of competition for survival. However, as the practical discoverer of the fact of biological evolution, his haste to break the concurrent theory of conventional creationism made it so that he wasn't required to arrive at any conclusive theory through interpretation of that fact.

Individualism has become totally unsustainable today because of the following reasons. First of all, the theory itself is based on fundamental ideals which are terribly inconsistent. Hobbes, for example, contradicts himself by saying that "man is, by nature, a deceiver of others," while also asserting that "society was organized by the contract." Rousseau said, "man naturally has the sovereignty of freedom and independence," while still positing that an oppressive and irrational society was "organized by the contract." Not only that, but biological research has shown that people did not exist individually as a matter of fact. Today's political science, economics, and other social sciences hold that man never created society by any means similar to a contract. Moreover, the discovery by biology that human societies existed from the beginning, since humans are social animals, just as other animals exist in social groups, has awakened the sciences from their traditional speculative dogmatism and rebuilt their structure from the ground up.

The fact that mankind has, from the beginning, not been struggling all against all, and that each person is not a free and independent being like God,

---

person is the latter. This assertion probably refers to the natural state as peaceful.

but a social being which exists as a social animal, combined with the evolutionary explanation that social cohesion is greater and stronger, and that survival of the strong in a large individual unit through mutual support allows that unit, in this case society, to win any competition against other singular units, has made the sciences of individualism increasingly worthless.

In other words, in response to both economics, which argues—based on the assumption that people are individually independent and that there is only individual, personal self-interest in society—that "it is far more productive for each to destroy and crush one another than for capital and labor to work together," and political science, which—based on their determination that free and independent individuals existed before the contract—teaches that "union and cohesion, like the state and society, are unavoidable evils," we can say the following. All of that has been overturned by the biological discovery that "it is in its social self-interest as a social organism, e.g., mutual aid, that mankind has achieved the status of a winner over many things." It is a principle throughout biology that unity is a powerful force.

Herbivores, which compete for survival as units made up of high-level individuals through mutual support, have prevailed over carnivores, each of which is a unit made up of independent lower-level individuals. If the current evolutionists, not limited to Dr. Oka, understand competition for survival as only between individual people or between individual organisms, they will not understand how herbivores, which are individually much weaker than carnivores, were able to defeat carnivores in this competition, nor will they understand many other natural phenomena, such as how a herd of horses, all herbivores, will not lose a single individual horse to predators as long as their group is not split up.

If these biologists are correct, does it not make sense that humans, organisms with no fangs or claws, would have disappeared long ago in the proto-human era? But they did not! The flesh that cannibal savages eat is also not obtained through the battles of individual people, but rather through a community which works together for, at the very least, battle. This is their unit in the competition for survival. Even the most uncooperative carnivores, regardless of their unit in the competition for survival, can at least be said to understand mutual support, such as when a female cuddles with its baby to keep both of them warm.

As the organisms become more advanced, the classes of their individuals become higher, and in the case of birds, beasts, and other higher organisms, they are found almost entirely in the form of vast and strong social bonds, as we see in human societies, and they compete for survival as units of these classes, which have higher degrees of social unity. This competition for survival which uses individuals of the higher classes as its unit is only conducted by the self-interest of the individuals, which is social self-interest, or, in other words, mutual support among the molecules in a society, the individuals themselves, and the organisms with the largest individuals and the strongest mutual support remain the winners in the world of competition for survival. Humans are the most remarkable example of these winners.

Biologists need to reflect on their own high value. The gospel of the competition for survival of social units or the fact that mutual aid can decide victory or defeat is a gospel far nobler than that of Christ or the Buddha. Because biological evolution has held up this gospel and overthrown all demonic knowledge, the golden crown of "socialism" has been placed not merely over political science and economics, but also over ethics, pedagogy, and psychology, and the history of human thought has begun to flow toward an entirely new and enlightened world. Biological evolution was indeed a revolution of unprecedented proportions in philosophical history. We build socialism atop the theory of biological evolution and proclaim ourselves as great a revolutionary force as the theory of evolution because we are trying to do in the real world what biologists have already accomplished in the world of ideals. We are those who cannot help but rejoice to see that the facts of biological evolution can only be explained by waiting for socialism, even if we are insulted by biologists who interpret biological evolution with the dogmatic assumptions of individualism as the basis of their ideology.

Let us dispel the doubts held by Dr. Oka and lead him down the correct path. We do not necessarily believe that Dr. Oka, seeing that he often speaks of racial or national competition, has failed to consider the existence of some higher unit of competition for survival than the individual person. However, since he was so careless as to fail to even define the individual as the fundamental point for determining the unit of competition for survival, it is as if he did not understand at all that the unit of competition expands as the species evolves. In other words, he does not understand that the unit of competition for survival in lower animals is the lowest class of individuals, e.g., individual competition for survival, but as one advances to higher animals, the unit of competition, which is the class of individuals, becomes higher and evolves into competition for survival based on mutual support among molecules which make up the larger individual, with the ultimate goal of a large individual called society. Similarly, he does not seem to have the slightest idea of the "theory of social evolution," which says that this "individual unit" will expand alongside the evolution of society, especially in the human species (over the course of human history). Thus, he has become an ignorant and brutal eulogist of imperialism, casting insensitive sneers upon historical revolutions and belittling the world federalism that will result from the coming revolution.

The public will not demand historical knowledge from a biologist like Dr. Oka. However, we are suspicious that he, a biological evolutionist, would disregard historical evolution as if it was a matter of the theory of cosmic cycles. Aren't the cyclic theory and the theory of evolution incompatible? If Dr. Oka believes in the theory of biological evolution, but he also believes in the theory of social evolution, which states that the history of mankind is the path of the evolution of a single species, then to speak of historical revolutions as merely the repetition of disturbances resulting from a kind of dreaming is thinking purely from the perspective of cyclic theory, which is unbecoming of an evolutionist. And if we take the present geographically limited society, the nation, as the unit of perpetual competition for existence, and determine the racial differences that have emerged in the course of evolution as if they are the competitors of eternally opposing units, we are thinking of everything in static terms, as things which exist and will not change, which is even more inconsistent with evolutionary theory.

From the original villages of the primitive people who formed small groups of tens or hundreds of people on mountainsides, swamps, and streams and survived by fighting or simply not interacting with each other, we progressed, through annexation or merging of these small groups, into small city-states,[112] which then progressed through conquest, division, and so much more, into the huge nations we have today, with populations in the tens or even hundreds of millions. If Dr. Oka looks on this history, looks at the current state of today's massive nations, and understands the principle of evolution behind them, then he should be able to deduce that we will continue to evolve into even larger nations in the future. To look at national competition using the units that exist in the present and racial competition based on discrimination today and to immediately try to counter socialism, which is striving to anticipate future evolution, with these arguments is evidence of a failure to understand the theory of biological evolution.

We will discuss imperialist national competition later. However, we are very sorry to see the attitude of Dr. Oka, who has become an endorser of imperialism from the standpoint of his own biology. We are sorry to see that a scientist who should be teaching and guiding the world has instead become another follower of the zeitgeist. Of course, as Dr. Oka says, it is a fact of biology that we have competition for survival among taxonomical variants,[113]

---

[112] In Japan, this most likely refers to the Yayoi period of small "states."

[113] Organisms are classified into species, subspecies, and variants. Here, the term refers to a class of organisms.

and we do not deny that much of that competition is resolved through fighting. However, this comes from a failure to understand that, as I said earlier, as the classes of biological species evolve, the content of that competition evolves. The fact that beasts compete for survival with their fangs and claws is one thing, but the idea that they must compete in the same way with other species, such as the human race, is another. Even if competition for survival among different races and nations has been conducted through combat in the past and during the present of mankind, this was only the case in the beginning, and it is a separate issue whether the content of human competition for survival will further evolve with the evolution of mankind and whether it will be determined by other methods.

Socialism's theory of war extinction says that, because the unit for competition expands accompanying the evolution of a biological species, the human race will be the complete winner over other biological species as a unit of competition for survival, thus rendering war superfluous. Along with that (as I will explain later), we seek to have national competition determined by congressional argument of the world federation for the reason that a biological species will evolve the content of competition as they evolve until the human unit reaches that point. If we, unlike Dr. Oka, do not immediately equate conflicts of interest to the immortality of war and create vague reasoning which likens the debate between some group of bumpkins in the prefectural assemblies to the mountains of corpses and rivers of blood caused by international war, if we infer that just as conflicts of interest between provinces have progressed from the stage where they were decided by war to being decided by majority vote of the prefectural assembly, and thus infer that conflicts of interest between nations will be decided by resolution of the federal assembly, not by war as today, then we will not make the blunder of excluding socialism when speaking of the theory of biological evolution.

Dr. Oka ignores historical evolution and mixes socialism and imperialism, which are totally incompatible, just as he mixes evolutionary and cyclical theory, which are equally incompatible. Socialism's theory of war extinction expects this conclusion through the creation of a world federation, while imperialism dreams of an endgame of peace in which one nation, dominated by one race, will be able to annex and oppress other races and other nations so that they cannot compete.[114] This is what has been done by peoples led by many heroes in history, and what was once dreamed of by a certain arrogant German emperor (the German emperor has reportedly now abandoned imperialism in his attempt to unify the world because of the might of other nations and the power of the socialist party at home).[115] And yet, a man named Dr. Oka condemns the socialist ideal of universal peace, saying, "Even if one race were to prevail over another and take over the world, it would be quickly divided into several nations, each with different interests in different places." What could this mean? This is the assertion of imperialism, a fantasy which socialism is using all its power to try and eliminate.

Of course, history does not literally repeat itself, as Dr. Oka, a cyclic thinker, would have it. Even if nations are unified by conflict, then divided into smaller groups afterward, they are still opposing each other in larger units than before they were unified, or they may even divide into yet smaller units in order to combine and become a larger unit. Nothing in history is insignificant. In this respect, it is true that the national competition that has taken place to date has evolved society through a form of conquest and annexation—that is to say, it has raised the class of individuals through what sociologists call assimilation and evolved them into the great states that they are today. Therefore, we very much recognize imperialism as the most powerful

---

[114] In short, socialism and imperialism both seek peace, but under very different circumstances. Note that Kita doesn't repudiate imperialism as a means to an end (this will be discussed in volume 5).

[115] This "might of other nations" probably refers to England.

path of social evolution in history. However, along with assimilation comes differentiation.

The evolution of national competition, which had no choice but to assimilate through external coercion, was a very slow evolution of society, as the assimilation was inhibited by differentiation, which was another type of evolution, and the differentiation was also pressured by the external coercion of assimilation. The world federation that socialism advocates is an attempt to facilitate global assimilation on the basis of the differentiated development of nations and races. Therefore, it repels those who threaten a nation's own independence and does not tolerate aggression aimed at forcing its own assimilation onto other nations—in this respect, socialism recognizes the state and thus recognizes national competition.

Although we respect the greatness of Darwin, who advocated biological evolution, and Marx,[116] who taught social evolution, we do not take their words as pure articles of faith because we are modern people more evolved than they were. We are people who recognize national competition as well as class competition as facts. This is because classes are a latitudinal society, while nations are a longitudinal society.[117] However one mustn't overlook that, as assimilation gradually wipes out the significant disparities between classes, and as the rivalry between small nations disappears through historical evolution—that is, as it evolves by raising the class of individuals, the unit of competition—it further evolves the content of that competition.

---

[116] Perhaps this refers to Marx's assertion that the transition from a capitalist to a socialist system would eventually lead to the establishment of a communist society. However, it's unclear whether Marx spoke of this in the same nuance as the theory of social evolution.

[117] We're not quite sure what this means. Perhaps, when representing society, classes would be on a horizontal axis, while states would be on a vertical one? For now, we've translated this literally.

Socialism's world federation theory seeks to evolve this unit of competition into a worldwide unit, as well as to evolve the content of national competition into a vote of the federal parliament. The class struggle, which has always been carried out by way of revolt and assassination to determine competition, has evolved today to a system of voting to determine competition. In the same way, since there is still no political body to determine competition, the current competition among nations, which is still being conducted by diplomatic maneuvering and the slaughter of nations in war, will be determined by vote in the future, just as class competition is today—such is the world federation theory.

One cannot imagine that, once socialism is realized, interests within the federal congress would be totally united, even if assimilation were to take place between nations as it does between classes, or that, after further evolution, competition between nations in the federation would become totally extinct as class warfare would become extinct, so that mankind would reach the golden age of a single nation and evolve society through the differentiation of individuality, which would develop without hindrance along with assimilation and make all mankind fellow citizens. Socialism is not a utopian fantasy of world unification, as imperialism is. If Dr. Oka wishes to compare the heated debates of the prefectural assembly members to something, he should never apply them to international war, but to the speeches, the questions and answers, of the representatives of various countries within this federal assembly. If one wishes to immediately attribute the conflict of interests to the immortality of war theory, one must first assume that shots were fired and swords drawn in the prefectural assembly. In the first place, it is strictly forbidden for a scientist to play with words using metaphors like this.

Come to think of it, many of those who cruelly and ignorantly assert the race-competition argument are those who have the preconceived notion that civilized people and savages are inherently different. If Dr. Oka is one with this preconceived notion, it is a very unfortunate situation indeed. It would mean that he subscribes to the creationist theory which Darwin had already defeated. As we will explain later, many of today's biological evolutionists still unconsciously inherit the creationist theory, placing it at the center of their thoughts. Civilized people have not been civilized since the formation of the earth. Savages were not created to end their lives as savages until the earth freezes over. Even a barbarian, if brought up breathing the air of a civilized country, will be as fully developed as a civilized man, and even one who is called civilized will stagnate as a complete barbarian if taken as a child and placed in a barbarian village. "Humans can only become human with the existence of society." As we said in the ethical discussion in the previous chapter, one can be a wolf depending on one's circumstances.

If this is so, it is easy to imagine that the social environment by which we are surrounded makes us civilized. When we are in a civilized society, we are civilized, and we are savages when we are in a savage society. We are raised in a civilized society, and we absorb and acquire knowledge that has been gathered over a long period of time—calculated to be one hundred thousand years from the barbaric period of primitive man to the present day—until we are, at twenty years old, finally becoming a civilized human being. Surrounded by a social environment that is either still in a primitive state or has evolved in a different direction from ours, a savage is constantly repeating a life of savagery because there is no knowledge for him to absorb throughout his life.

We do not know how long it took our distant ancestors, the proto-humans, to discover fire, and as we hold our mother's breast in our mouths, we watch the amazing ignition of petroleum and the incredible glow of electricity. We do not even know exactly when in history the decimal system was invented, nor how much it helped organize human knowledge later on, yet by the age of five or six, we know more advanced math than that. It was only five or six hundred years ago, which is nearly 99,500 years after the beginning of the proto-human era, that we learned that the earth, on which we live, orbits the sun while rotating on its own axis. Yet now, we learn the precise reason for this in elementary school. The theory of biological evolution was discovered because a great steamboat, loaded with social and historical knowledge, with a captain named Columbus and a first mate named Watt, set sail with Darwin on a journey around the world. And, finally, I am using this brush in my hand to discuss all this amazing knowledge right this moment.

We civilized people are not made civilized people by our physical bodies at birth, but by being placed in a society that has inherited this historical knowledge, and by accepting that knowledge we are made civilized people. See the countless examples of how a child from a barbaric village, raised under a civilized education, can develop knowledge and morals to the point where he is almost on par with civilized people, as cited even in *Social Evolution* by Benjamin Kidd, who is considered the leading scholar on the individualistic interpretation of evolutionary theory.

We are not trying to downplay the differences in heredity due to racial differentiation and development, which have divided the races to the extent that they are today, we are simply abiding by the belief that "Humans can only become human with the existence of a society." However, if anyone tries to attribute everything to physical heredity, forgetting social heredity, in other words, the accumulation of knowledge through history, and says, "Some South Seas natives get headaches when they try to count beyond ten," we will, with all due respect, respond with the following. That is only because the central nervous system deteriorates with age. It is the same as saying, "Even if a knowledgeable barbarian elder is told how mistaken the animalist competition for survival is, he doesn't have an opportunity to understand that knowledge before his death." They're incorrect! Heredity itself is the instinct to pass on tribal knowledge through biological evolutionary theory.

It goes without saying, however, that savages as they exist now will not exist as scientific material of interest to scientists forever. We, as socialists, through the theory of human monism, possess knowledge which is based on the idea of the brotherhood of mankind and the fact that humans are all brethren. However, we do recognize the differences between races as simple fact. One mustn't misunderstand. We argue for the extinction of the lower races, not by racial competition in the conventional form of extermination or slaughter, but by their own extinction as barbarians by advancing to a state of civilization, or by their inability to maintain their present status as barbarians by the laws of ruthless competition for survival.

We preach socialism according to the laws and ideals of social evolution, not according to crying humanitarianism. Part of evolution is the competition for survival. Just as the process of social evolution eliminates countless inferior individual persons who lack the morality of mutual aid, it is inevitable that races that cannot advance in parallel with the progress of civilization will perish. The great society of mankind is one large individual that transcends above any geographical small society. Just as the evolution of the small society was obtained by the culling of individual persons inferior in truth, goodness, and beauty,[118] so in the evolution of the great society it is inevitable that the races inferior in truth, goodness, and beauty will be eliminated—however, it is one thing to say that those barbarians who cannot advance to civilization will be culled as barbarians, and quite another to say that civilized people have the right to oppress and eliminate these barbarians.

The content of the struggle for survival evolves as the human race evolves, just as it evolves with the evolution of the classes of biological species. Just as individual people without the morality of mutual aid were once eliminated by the death penalty, and are now being eliminated by other methods of competition that have evolved since then, so competition for survival among the races will be conducted in a manner consistent with today's ideals of justice, without relying on methods such as extermination or slaughter.

---

[118] As human ideals, three values are considered universally valid: cognitive truth, ethical goodness, and aesthetic beauty. This is what this refers to.

Do not tremble at the mention of extinction. If those individual persons or human races that lack sociality are not culled, how will the "anthropoid" evolve to a higher level? If a race or a nation is counted as an individual like a small society may be, then even if individual persons who are unfit as smaller molecules of this individual society are eliminated, as long as individual persons, themselves also molecules of this society, are evolving fittingly, from the perspective of the individual society that has them as its molecules, this is evolution, not extinction. In the same way, the extinction of a race that is unable to keep up with evolution is not destruction but a joyous evolution as long as other races evolve and enter sacred territory.

To those who advocate the humanitarian theory of individualism, such an affirmation will sound ruthless. Yes, it is ruthless. The cruel laws of survival ruthlessly cull those losers who are unfit for their environment as "anthropoids," those who have no truth, no goodness, and no beauty. When it comes down to it, socialism buries the corpses of inferior people and races in worship of "God," the same way the crusades did in the name of Christ. However, as we explain later, individuals do not die. The great individual, monistic humanity, weeds out its disqualified molecules, but it lives by other molecules and thereby evolves towards an infinite heaven. A molecule that has gained truth, goodness, and beauty through its own evolution causes those who are unable to gain truth, goodness, and beauty to disappear, and any molecules which can never gain truth, goodness, or beauty will live on in the evolution of the molecules which do gain truth, goodness, and beauty.

In order to immediately dismiss this competition for survival as mutual slaughter, a criminal law theory advocating selection by death, such as Dr. Oka's, emerges, and the competition for survival becomes an ignorant and brutal theory of racial competition. Mankind has evolved the content of the struggle for survival, and thereby the meaning of justice, since the beginning of recorded history. If there are academics who, in spite of the concept of justice evolving so far and today's social consciousness becoming so acute that it can no longer bear the impoverishment of its fellow man, still wield the ignorant and brutal theory of racial competition to oppress the unfortunate, we would ask of them the following. During the nine months that babies are in the womb, mankind experiences the age of fish, the age of beasts, and finally becomes human once born. Even then, while children, they simply repeat the age of savages, the era of proto-humans. So, since abortion and things of the like could be considered the same as reeling in a fish, or shooting a beast, wouldn't it escape the criminal law theory advocating culling by the death penalty? And rather than using warships to go to the distant tropics, why do you not first lay the hand of slaughter to the savages you give birth to and place under your lap? This is true of even the most extreme savages. Why, then, do we slaughter each other simply because we have different skin colors?

In fact, there is much of the criminal law theory, which advocates culling by the death penalty, that can be more closely examined. If we argue, like Dr. Oka and other criminal law scholars who interpret the state's penal power in terms of the competition for survival do, that those who cannot be reformed should be put to death for the betterment of the race, then by that logic, the state's criminal law cannot punish those who poison and kill their elderly parents who have no hope of recovery from an illness. If we argue that the death penalty should be more widely used to kill repeat offenders and third-time offenders for the sake of racial betterment and progress, then by that logic, we must attempt to install guillotines in hospitals that house patients with lung diseases,[119] as that is the greatest obstacle to racial betterment and progress. In that case, for the sake of racial improvement and progress, not only ugly women and foolish men must be put to death without any leniency,[120]

---

[119] Pulmonary tuberculosis, otherwise known as consumption.

[120] The original text used a word that can mean "foolish man," but also "pervert," as it's now more often used. Either way could be correct, but when considering the previous "ugly women," we think it's more likely to be the former.

but also scholars and others who are detrimental to racial improvement and progress must be hitched up like donkeys and sent to the executioner's pen.

It goes without saying that the improvement and progress of the race is, in part, carried out by the competition for survival, but there is no reason why this competition for survival must necessarily be carried out by means of the death penalty. During the era of parochial socialism, it was the general conscience that the molecules, sometimes groups of molecules, within the larger individual known as society, would slaughter each other, but that doesn't hold up as justice today. Two examples of a great molecule being criminalized and put to death by other molecules or groups of molecules are Christ and Socrates. As mentioned in the previous chapter, a crime is a violation of the general conscience. The prevailing conscience of one age is not necessarily the prevailing conscience of the next age. The general conscience of the coming age is often created by a special molecule with excellent foresight that was criminalized by the general conscience of the earlier age. The assertion that the conscience of today's parochial socialist age entitles one molecule to be slaughtered by another molecule or collection of molecules is precisely an attempt to revive the pope's right to punish scholars and scholasticism. Let Darwin be born in that era instead of Galileo. Let *Lectures on Evolution Theory* be written in medieval Italy. Biological evolutionists must go to the gallows by their own logic. Dr. Oka likely does not have extensive knowledge of criminal law. However, should we not question whether the supreme authority over the evolution of all things can be held in the hands of one special person?

At any rate, the competition for survival of the human species is one that has some moral content, just as the criminal law theory of culling by death has morals which remain today. It isn't limited to humans alone. It is a competition that applies to all living creatures, including herbivores that survive in groups and compete for survival as a social unit. The unit of competition for survival of lower forms of animals is the absolute bottom class of individuals, and the content of them is the simple individual self-interest, but as we advance to higher animal stages, the unit expands into a higher class of individual and competition for survival becomes about societal self-interest, in other words, a competition of morality based on sociality. Therefore, while fangs and claws determine the superiority or inferiority of carnivores based on individual self-interest, in general herbivores that form social groups, those with well-developed sociality, are superior and stronger, and those who harm social unity motivated only by their small egos are eliminated as inferior in the competition for survival. Elephants, for example, will expel from the herd those who harm the peace of their society, and in ape society, adultery is punished with the most severe penalties. Everyone is familiar with moral selection in ant and bee societies.[121] Humans are the moral organisms which have formed the largest societies, and so the moral competition for survival is so intense that culling via the death penalty has been employed.

Indeed, humans have been moral organisms since the distant proto-human age. We are inclined to assert this. Such falsehoods as the fantasy spouted by the individualism era scholars that, before the contract, it was a struggle of all against all, or the presumption that the proto-humans were pure cannibals who were solely engaged in killing, are now unfounded hypotheses to be discarded. Even if we imagine the original proto-human condition as fishing and hunting, and infer that they learned cannibalism from killing fish and birds, that's something that came much later. We believe it is much more reasonable to infer that mankind lived peacefully, harvesting resources from the never-ending fertility of the land until they evolved enough to invent the tools necessary for fishing and hunting. If the proto-humans were cannibals, then a child, which repeats that proto-human period in a short period of years, must surely at one time express a cruel character, just as a child sits with the

---

[121] We are unfamiliar with this. Kita may mean that those who don't work are run out of society.

soles of its feet together as a beast does when it sits down. However, the truth is the exact opposite. Isn't the period of childhood the most peaceful, timid time in a person's life, so much so that it is often given the title of God's laughter? This peace and timidity of the child can be seen as explaining the peaceful life and cowardice of the proto-humans, who had innumerable fears of thunderstorms, wind and rain, fierce beasts, demons and gods, darkness, etc.

We believe that it is a fundamental fallacy to immediately name today's savages as primitive and to infer our primitive times by the actions of today's savages. Conflict and cannibalism are limited only to starving peoples and those whose character has been made violent by their climate. It is incorrect for those who recognize the differentiated development of the races today to infer the primitive era of today's civilized peoples, who developed in a different, much more fortunate environment, from the customs of conflict and cannibalism of today's savages. Humans today eat meat occasionally, but that is also something that began much later. When primitive man, along with the monkeys we know today, first differentiated from anthropoid apes, they would have survived as pure herbivores in social herds on the rich plains. Because it is a biological fact that herbivores in social groups outcompeted carnivores living in isolation and spread across the earth as they do today, unless you believe that humans today are closer to felines than monkeys, it is a completely unfounded fantasy to think that proto-humans killed each other like tigers rather than grouping together peacefully like apes.

No, even tigers do not kill each other unnecessarily, and as I will later explain about food competition, their conscious opponent in the competition for survival is the herbivore; the tiger's competition for survival is a competition between different species: the species that will become food and the species that will feed on it. For there is no such thing as indirect, unconscious, individual competition that occurs between members of the same species for the same food, except when overlapping desires clash because of the scarcity of food. If this is true, that even carnivores with fangs and claws such as tigers do not fight each other when food is plentiful, it is inconceivable that primitive man, presumably placed in the midst of abundant natural products, would have been an asocial creature that exclusively fought and ate people when food was plentiful.

The period of emperors Yao and Shun refers to just such a primitive age. Nevertheless, as the population multiplied and the rich and fertile land became scarcer, some entered an era of fishing and hunting while others became nomadic hunter-gatherers, thus starting a fierce competition for survival in search of fishing grounds and pastures. This competition was a village-based competition for survival, in other words, a competition for the survival of a small social unit, and mutual aid was strongly demanded of each member of the village. The independence and freedom of each member was completely disregarded and the competition for the survival of the village became the ultimate goal of life in their naive minds. Perhaps this thought process is the result of the unconscious and instinctive social nature of primitive man— "Leave nature as it is and you will be influenced by nature,"[122]—being awakened as a moral consciousness as a result of social evolution caused by the competition for survival.

To look at the deadly struggles of the fishing, hunting, and nomadic eras and quickly dismiss them as "a situation without morality" is an extremely childish idea, for it is because of these struggles between villages that we first became aware of our social existence. This was the ancient era of parochial socialism, when individual freedom and independence were completely trampled upon for the sake of the survival of the social unit and anyone found to be immoral by the general conscience of the time, by the will of one molecule

---

[122] In the original text, the phrase is "to do nothing and become." Lao Tzu, *Tao Te Ching*, 57.

or a collection of molecules of society,[123] in the name of society, was culled by the death penalty in a truly brutal manner.

In that parochial socialist era, Louis XIV said, "I am the State,"[124] because the emperor himself was not only a molecule of society, but all of society.[125] Only that one molecule, the emperor, is the state, and all other molecules in the state exist for the benefit of the state, the emperor. The existence of the emperor made the moral obligation to loyally obey him coincide with the patriotic obligation to treat those who were disloyal to him as traitors to the state.

This moral selection by parochial socialism continued from the time of the proto-humans until the end of recorded medieval history, and is still taking place before our eyes today. flourished. As a democratic state, the collective will of the molecules was the will of the state, rather than one molecule being the state itself, such as with Louis XIV; this collective will even led them to poison Socrates, who disturbed the cohesion of the state.[126] Because of the intense competition for survival in the feudal quarters during the Dark Ages of the medieval period, those who went against the will of the molecules that organized the aristocracy were weeded out as traitors to society by the most thoughtless and brutal method of execution, and the only ones who remained free and independent were the sovereigns or the aristocratic class, as they

---

[123] Perhaps a molecule refers to a monarch, and a collection of molecules to a council of nobles.

[124] This quote is frequently attributed to Louis XIV, but in fact he never said this; it's merely an anecdote.

[125] This understanding is carried over into the theory of government systems developed in volume 4.

[126] In the original text, it says "(and he even poisoned Socrates)," and this isn't linked to the rest of the text. It's likely that, since it was in parenthesis, Kita simply forgot to link the sentence, so we fixed it.

could express the will of society. Individual persons in the lower class had no recognized rights at all.

The simple historical philosophy that "without an enemy or foreign threat, any nation would perish," indicates that throughout antiquity and the Middle Ages, the competition for survival was based on ethnic groups or small, geographically divided societies, and that the individual person existed for the sake of the nation, which was the unit of that competition for survival (more accurately, they existed for the sake of a molecule or group of molecules of society, which is where the spirit of the nation resided). Interpreting the competition for survival according to the dogmatic assumptions of individualism around the time of the French Revolution cannot explain the history of the human race, or social evolution, at all. (This explanation is important when discussing the nature and will of the state later. See *The So-Called Theory of Japan's National Polity and its Revived Principle of Revolution*.)

Still, social evolution depends on assimilation and differentiation. Societies were divided into small social groups as units for the competition for survival, and the clashes and competition between them via conquest and annexation resulted in the unit of society expanding by means of assimilation, which then divided the units even smaller, into individual persons. These individuals then competed for survival amongst each other, ushering in the era of individualism in human history. The reason why there were signs of individualism in the last years of Greek and Roman history is that the social unit expanded through assimilation by conquest and annexation, and at the same time, the competition for survival among societies as units quieted down. This awakened demand for the differentiation and development of competition, but it was destroyed by the Germanic tribes, who happened to also be competing for survival as social units at the time, and it did not blossom during parochial socialism in the Dark Ages of medieval history.

However, when the competition for survival among small social units according to feudal divisions was assimilated under the power of the Roman Catholic Church, the seeds of this competition sprouted into a major trend of individualism, leading to an era in which society evolved through the differentiation of individual persons. As the law of social evolution continued its march in waves, as it still does, the theory of biological evolution said that humanity was bestial, opposing the theory of creation which asserted humans as children of God.

In the same way, the value of the individual person was recognized as the ultimate goal in order to overthrow the class state in which the individual person, one molecule of society, was sacrificed to the king and nobility, other molecules of society, and to make the social state a mechanical, human-made artifact that was organized for individual freedom and independence of a single person. It was in the spirit of individualism that said "the individual should be the end, not the means."[127] It was in the aftermath of this parochial individualism that Darwin insisted that competition for survival consisted entirely of the individual person as a unit, and Dr. Oka and biological evolutionists in general should know that the struggle for survival that he claims today is that of a much later historical process.[128]

This competition for the survival of society as a unit and the individual person as a unit was built on the two pillars of social evolution theory: parochial socialism and parochial individualism. Social evolution, which has been supported by these two pillars, which sometimes lengthen and sometimes shorten, will evolve at a steady and rapid pace for the first time with the ideal of social democracy, which is built in parallel with these two pillars.

---

[127] Kant is reported to have said, "We must not treat man only as a means to an end." Kita may be referring to this expression.

[128] The meaning of the sentence is not clear. Could it be, "We should recognize that Darwin's theory of evolution is transitional"?

Social democracy has as its ultimate goal the interests of society, while at the same time asserting the authority of the individual. The individual person is one of the molecules of society, and society is that molecule itself, so the individual person is, in other words, society. If this is interpreted as the mechanical view of society in the era of parochial individualism, in which only the individual is real and society is a relationship or state created by the aggregation of these individuals, the phrase "the individual should be the end, not the means" is meaningless; but if the individual person is a molecule of society, and thus is society itself, the goal of an individual person should be the goal of society as well. Socialism succeeds individualism in this sense. However, the molecule known as an individual person perishes completely with its death. Therefore, when the ultimate goal is this molecule known as a single person, the goal will come to an end after fifty years and will be meaningless.[129] Therefore, individual freedom and independence only have gravity under the ultimate goal of social evolution.

Moreover, if, as is the case in parochial socialism, the freedom and independence of the individual, a molecule of society, is trampled under another molecule or group of molecules, it is impossible to enrich the conscience of society by the competition for survival among individual persons, which is carried out through the differentiating action of individuals, because the intent of the powerful classes, such as the sovereign or the aristocracy, is absolutely inviolable. So, even if society's existence is placed as the ultimate goal, only a very slow social evolution can be expected. Thus, society cannot bring happiness and evolution to all the molecules of society, and only a certain class of society's molecules will gain freedom and independence, while the lower classes will only be the foundation upon which to build the prosperity and happiness of those higher-class molecules.

---

[129] The average life expectancy in Japan at the time was around fifty years old.

The evolution of society depends on differentiation as well as assimilation. When the freedom and independence of the individual person, which are necessary for the complete differentiation process, were limited to the sovereign (in the era of lords) or to a few members of the aristocracy (in the era of aristocracies), it was inevitable that evolution during those eras was not rapid. It is also natural that, in today's democracy and the upcoming future democracies, society is evolving and will continue to evolve at an alarming rate, since it was recognized that all citizens are free and independent, and that differentiation is carried out by the majority. Socialism cannot be considered noble without individualism. It is the development of individualism for which we should be grateful.

One would hope that today's individualists and nationalists would be united on the state of modern society. Economic aristocrats occupy each region (if they are landowners) and each profession (if they are capitalists) like lords of a herd, plundering the economic resources of the nation, treating the nation as if it were a means to an end, forgetting that they are obligated to work for the well-being of the state as one of its molecules—how can nationalists be so complacent about the current status quo?

Only the economic aristocracy is economically independent and claims individual freedom as it pleases, while the economic warrior class and the economic serf class are obedient to them to the point of slavery, their authority as individual persons driven down to the ground as it was before the French Revolution—do the individualists not question this state of affairs?

We do not preach socialism with wails and tears, but only theorize on the basis of scientific fatalism. As such, we do not participate in the fallacy of considering the period of economic aristocracy to be an evil. As a natural course of social evolution, it is recognized that since all molecules of society cannot be happy, only a certain class of molecules first gained economic independence and political and moral freedom. However, this is merely a process, and not something that will last forever. In the past, the aristocracy built its authority at the expense of other molecules by force of arms, but as society evolved, the lower classes, who were once the sacrificial molecules, gained freedom and independence, and then spread legal political and moral freedom and equality to all the molecules of society. We are in a similar situation now, as only the current economic aristocracy has been subject to economic evolution as part of the ongoing process of economic history. However, with the economic evolution of public ownership of land and capital, the lower classes, the economic warriors and serfs, who today are the victims, will gain political and moral independence through economic freedom and equality—why do the individualists not repeat the French Revolution? Why do the nationalists not repeat the Meiji Revolution?

One must strictly understand that the present age is an economic class state with an aristocratic government. The nationalism of the Meiji Revolution, which defeated the classist state and returned the capital and land to the nation from the "ultimate ownership" of the aristocrats, and the individualism of the French Revolution, which swept aside the aristocratic government and gave people democratic legislature, must scream for freedom and independence once again, changing the despotism of the economic aristocracy's production into a democratic system of government.

Why is our pure socialism persecuted in the name of the state or the individual person? It is precisely through socialism that nationalism and individualism can realize their ideals completely. The state contains the molecules of the individual person and becomes one individual itself, and the world contains the state and becomes the molecule of that individual. Therefore, just as the individual fulfills its noblest moral obligation to the state and society when it does best for itself, so the state has a moral obligation to do what is best for itself because it contains both individual persons and the world at large as its molecules. In fulfilling this duty, the state becomes, as Luther said, an ethical institution.

Yet, just as it is a crime from the perspective of the state's big ego if an individual person harms the interests of the state with their small ego set as their ultimate goal, if the state also—no, not so! It is precisely the crime of the state to, as imperialists extol, ignore its function as an ethical institution, forgetting the world's big ego and centering all its actions around the small ego of the state, as it does today. Just as individual freedom has significance for the big ego of others, national independence exists with grave significance for the world's big ego. Therefore, treating the state as a means to the benefit of the individual person, as in parochial individualism, is immoral in terms of the great ego of the state. In the same way, to ignore the differentiated development of all nations and peoples of the world with the state's small ego as the ultimate goal, as in the case of parochial socialism, is unacceptably immoral in the eyes of the world's big ego.

Just as the freedom of an individual person is a crime if abused, the independence of the state can cause terrible crimes if abused—this is why socialism is cosmopolitanism. It respects the independence of the state as it recognizes the freedom of the individual, but excludes the forgetting of the national ego for the sake of individual freedom, and the forgetting of the greater ego of the world for the sake of national independence. No! The state in the era of parochial socialism, with small societies as its unit, tramples on individual freedom for the sake of national competition, and the state, with its individual freedom trampled on, has nothing to contribute to the differentiation of the world, and it is therefore inferior in the national competition for survival. Thus, the independence of the state as an ethical institution will be realized by a socialist world federation, and the full freedom of the individual will be realized by a socialist universal peace without localized social competition among small societies.

Even though the individualist French Revolution occurred in order to realize the theory of liberty and equality, when it finally started a competition for survival against the surrounding allied forces using the nation as its unit, individual freedom was completely trampled upon, sending Madame Roland to the guillotine,[130] depriving the royalists of all their freedom, and slaughtering them. In the same way, we can see how the ideal of individualism is only a dream under the conditions of national competition, as we saw that, at the time of the Russo-Japanese War, those who advocated against war were deprived of all freedom by the parochial socialism of "national unity"; so we see that the socialist ideal of universal peace must be asserted, because this ideal overlaps with the individualist ideal.

Equating modern socialism with the parochial socialism of the age of the universal state, where competition was measured in small social units, and to argue that it dissolves the individual person into the larger society is indeed shallow thinking. With the realization of universal peace, national competition would take place on the congressional podium without fear of death or destruction, becoming an ethical institution for the world's cultures, and individual freedom would fulfill its moral obligations to the world's cultures via the state, or possibly even transcending it. Likewise, the class warfare fought today from the podium in the House of Representatives will be completely extinguished and we will have a society without horizontal disparities. Then the national competition fought within the congress will be completely extinguished and we will have a single nation without vertical barriers—oh, this is a golden land. The assimilation of grand society, which uses the world as its unit, and the unimpeded differentiation of individuality will cause "anthropoids" to evolve even wings. Nationalism and individualism can fully realize their ideals only when they are encompassed by social democracy.

Let us return to the explanation of the theory of competition for survival. As explained above, the human race's struggle for survival was, as in the case

---

[130] The wife of Roland, who belonged to the Gironde faction during the French Revolution and served as Minister of the Interior.

of all living species, one with units comprised of both society and individual organisms. As a transitional organism on its way to evolving into a higher form of life, the human species gradually transformed itself from a small society into a larger one through assimilation. Moreover, through differentiation, what was first differentiated into larger individual units, such as villages or family groups, was further differentiated into smaller and smaller units, finally arriving at the individual as the unit of competition, and became more and more finely differentiated.

However, along with the assimilation and differentiation of the units of competition for survival, the competition for survival of social units, which has expanded through assimilation, and the competition for survival of individual units, which has become finer through differentiation, have evolved the content of their competition as well. In other words, from the time of fishing, hunting, and nomadism, the competition for survival among social units and individual units was conducted entirely by combat. Thus, of the nations with superior military powers and individual persons with superior military prowess, some became chiefs (in the age of fishing, hunting, and nomadism) and others (from the beginning of recorded history into medieval times) became kings, nobles, and warriors, rising up as victors of this competition for survival.

Today, the competition for survival utilizing military force is limited only to competition between societies as units, so the military class is only a winner in that limited scope.[131] In the competition for survival among individuals within a nation, however, men who are merely physically strong are no longer recognized, as was the case with the aristocrats and warriors before the Middle Ages, as if the cutthroat robbery practiced by the warriors had been eliminated by the death penalty and other serious punishments.[132]

---

[131] This is clearly talking about war.

[132] "Cutthroat robbery" might have been practiced by samurai, much like how they would sometimes attack a passerby just to test their skill or sword.

The competition for survival within the country has completely changed since the French Revolution (in Japan, since the Meiji Revolution), and the winner is now the one who is superior in economic activities. However, just as the most powerful people were better off economically before the revolution, even among the upper class, as power was the basis of all ownership rights, today those who are the most competent in economic activities have their rights perfectly encapsulated by the labor theory of individualism.

Nonetheless, the winners of economic warfare inherited the ancient ideology of the occupancy theory and are committed to becoming an economic aristocracy.[133] If the labor theory of the French Revolution, which overthrew the monopolization performed by the armed classes, had taken place in a world of individual competition between persons based on equality, where steam power and electricity had never been invented, the individual person who labored best would have indeed been the winner in the competition for survival. However, this was nothing more than an ideal. When the economic aristocracy is holed up in the feudal citadel of the machine, the best of the best in the race for survival are the babies born inside that citadel, as if the eggs of flies laid on their filth triumph as well, the winners of the flies—oh, praiseworthy victors!

Such concepts as "survival of the fittest," "winner-takes-all," "the weak and the strong," and so on, only appear valid when viewed from the outside. This is what is meant when it is said that "What is the fittest, the best, and the strongest differs according to the environment that the species lives in." Born into such an environment of economic aristocracy, any philosopher, any scientist, any poet is a loser in the competition for survival, scolded before the chariot of the aristocrats. Just as in the era of the economic Warring States, the most twisted, clever, and brutal Mr. Kihachiro Hiranuma was the winner,

---

[133] For more on labor theory and occupancy theory, refer to volume 1.

so in the era of economic feudalism of trusts, the pure, foolish feudal lords are the fittest, the best, and the strongest. Repeat such praise.

The government and scholars persecute socialism in order to maintain this world of competition for survival. In this age of economic aristocracy, the great government clerks and scholars who make up the economic warrior class consider the human heart to be like those of Masashige or the santayu,[134] who took absolute vows of slavery to their masters. Within the economic serfs, an entire class of losers, the winners are those who have at least avoided unemployment and have food and clothes. They are slaves in the truest sense of the word, with no spirit left, and not even an understanding of what rights are.

In the age of socialism, these best, fittest, and strongest will naturally be culled, and could thus be called the losers in the competition for survival.

---

[134] Masahige Kusunoki was active during the Nanbokucho period.
A "santayu" is a person in charge of the household chores, accounting, etc., of a noble or wealthy family. An all-encompassing term meaning the family orderly, the family assistant, and the family butler.

Chapter 6

A question naturally arises here. In a socialist world, there is no culling by death penalty, no culling by force of arms, no selection by economic competition, nor any selection by war between nations or races. How, then, can there be a loser which is culled by the competition for survival? Indeed, a fair question.

Socialism seeks to put the authority for the evolution of everything in the hands of the individual person, an element of society, and to eliminate any kind of competition for survival that hinders the evolution of society—such as culling by the death penalty, which severely impedes on the authority of other persons, who are also elements of society. It seeks to eliminate the barbaric and brutal competition for survival which humans, as transitional organisms striving to realize lofty ideals, engage in, beating and biting each other in competition for food. Though we are all elements of one large individual, all of us originally coming from the same human species, a competition for survival consisting of murder and slaughter simply because groups may be from different nations or races still occurs, and we plan to eliminate it with the implementation of the world federation. But is there not still social competition between large units, or individual competition between small units?

We will begin by explaining the competition for survival where the unit is defined as individual persons.

The reason that such a question would arise is because the idea of the individual is the same as it was before the invention of the microscope. In other words, because the asker doesn't understand the individual, nor how it extends—competition for survival with the individual as the unit will occur during the socialist age as competition over that extension—in other words, it will be a competition for sex.[135]

From the point of view of the horizontal expansion of the individual, all human beings living today are one large individual. If looked at from the point of view of vertical extension, the 100,000 years of history from primitive man to the modern day is a record that tells of the longevity of this one large individual. Just as siblings, viewed from a horizontal perspective, are not separate individuals, so parents and offspring, considered from a vertical perspective, are not separate individuals.[136] The former is only one that has grown larger and the latter is only one that has grown longer. The parents divide a part of themselves and hold it in their arms, naming it a child, just as an amoeba divides infinitely to reproduce. Just as the myriad amoebas that split from a single amoeba can be viewed as each being a single amoeba and at the same time as the first amoeba growing larger as elements separated by space, so the parent and child that split from a single individual can be considered each being a single individual and at the same time the life of the parent being lengthened.

We know that Weismann's hypothesis that reproductive cells are immortal could not be maintained in the face of many harsh criticisms, so we dare not cite his theory.[137] Such a view depends simply on the fact that the cells of the parent are transmitted to the child, the child's cells to the grandchild, the grandchild's cells to the great-grandchild, and that these cells are part of the body of the parent who transmitted them. The phrase "We have eternal life," means, in this context, that the body itself will exist forever, never dying. If an amoeba divides, and even if the original part that divided dies, the other part

---

[135] Competition for sex is intense competition for reproduction.

[136] A vertical perspective refers to direct lineage, while a horizontal perspective refers to collateral lineage.

[137] August Weismann was a German evolutionist and geneticist.

continues to live, divide, and reproduce, the original amoeba will obviously remain immortal because of the amoeba that reproduced. Similarly, if the parent, the old portion which divided out a child, and the child, the new portion, then reproduces by dividing out a grandchild, the original parent clearly exists as the reproduced offspring itself, immortal both physically and spiritually. In other words, the supposedly dead parent is merely removing itself from the child as an unnecessary part which is no longer needed to live, just as one's fingernails fall off, hair falls out, and dead skin sheds—science thus becomes monism and returns to religion. The immortality of spirit, the demand of mentalism,[138] is satisfied by the immortality of matter, the explanation of materialism.[139] Matter and spirit are, of course, monistic, and man is immortal in both physical and spiritual terms. To define the unit of competition for survival in this way, it is necessary to know both the expansion and extension of the individual.

Survival through competition for sex can only be understood if we understand this extension of the individual. An organism survives because it has the desire to survive. Organisms must compete for survival because of this desire to survive. No organism can escape this competition for survival. Therefore, organisms must compete for survival for the sake of surviving in the present, but most compete even more intensely to survive eternally—one could say that the competition for food and competition for sex are the two pillars of competition for survival throughout the living world. This competition for sex for the purpose of reproduction doesn't exist in some other organisms, such as amoebas who can reproduce asexually through division, aphids, who can

---

[138] Mentalism is the position that the main body of the world is spiritual. The Buddhist Avatamsaka sutra takes this view.

[139] Materialism is the opposite of mentalism. It does not recognize a spirit, mind, or consciousness separate from matter. Marx was a typical materialist, and his view of history is well known as "materialist history."

reproduce countless times with only females,[140] or leeches, who possess both male and female reproductive organs, and so can reproduce through contact with any other leech with no need to take male or female into account.

Competition is evolution. All evolution is the result of competition. When we get to the more evolved higher organisms, as the competition for survival between species—food competition—becomes more intense, the competition for survival within species—sex competition—becomes even more intense; the latter being the competition for survival that has evolved organisms even more so than the former. This is a fact shown countless times even in Darwin's chaotic and unorganized theory of biological evolution, and I think of food competition and sex competition in the struggle for survival in the following way. Food competition is species against species, and competition between individuals of the same species against individuals of another species is indirect and unconscious. On the other hand, sex competition is individuals competing among members of the same species, and is a direct and conscious competition for survival in which individuals of the same species participate as competitors, independent of other species.

In all that can be called "the beauty of heaven and earth," there is nothing that is not the result of competition for survival for the continuation of life. The protective coloration that makes some insects beautiful, for example, is an evolutionary result of species-on-species competition for food against birds that seek to feed on them. The lion's fangs, the eagle's beak, the ox's horns, the horse's legs, all evolved through competition for food, but none of these are quite comparable to the direct and conscious competition for survival, individual against individual, called sex competition.

---

[140] Aphids reproduce by monogenesis in the summer and distinguish between male and female aphids in the fall. Strictly speaking, aphids do not propagate solely by monogenesis, as they lay eggs after distinguishing between male and female aphids.

The first cry of the warbler, waiting atop a snowy mountain, evolved through sex competition to attract the female. The love song of the cuckoo, which drops its faint chirp into the window of the poet's house and disappears into the clouds, evolved through selection in the struggle for the continuity of life. The white winged dance of the meek little dove is also an evolutionary result of sex competition, and the indomitable rooster's fight with its kick claws and crest is also a result of culling during competition for the continuation of life.[141] The beauty of the male mandarin duck and the beauty of the male peacock, though they differ in that one is monogamous while the other is polygamous, are both the result of sex competition to attract the love of females.[142]

Yes, beasts are the same. The lion's long, fluffy mane is absolutely not for catching food. The horns of the stag, which are for the sake of displaying their majesty and thus attracting females, yet inconvenient for the purpose of obtaining food, are also the result of the evolution of fierce sex competition and culling. The beautiful colors and sounds of insects, with the exception of a few colors which are used to scare predators, are all the result of this evolutionary process of sex competition. Without the spring dancer, which we have named the butterfly, who has mastered the art of decorating itself, the fresh green fields of spring would be nothing more than a desert. Without the autumn musicians known as the bell and pine crickets, playing their haunting, sad music, a full autumn's moon floating in the sky would be nothing more than a lump of copper. It is precisely because of these endearing competitors that spring dances and autumn sings of love.

This isn't true of only animals, either. Entomophilous flowers are those plants which pollinate by means of insects touching their stamen and pistils.

---

[141] A "kick claw" is a slightly sturdier sharp protrusion that grows on the back of the feet of a chicken or other animal. It's a weapon for fighting.

[142] Male mandarin ducks have beautiful winter plumage.

Look at how these flowers bloom beautiful faces in order to attract these messengers of love.[143] This is also the reason why cherry blossoms bloom and why tree peonies are so bewitching and beautiful. It's also why spring grass is elegant and autumn flowers are graceful, and why there is not a single beautiful flower which did not evolve through sexual competition.

And yet, when the current followers of animalism lecture on biological evolution, they always hurl a spray of mockery and cursing at the poet. "The poet sings emphatically about the beauty of heaven and earth, but the universe is not what they think it is. The sparrows target the butterflies as the butterflies dance, the eagles watch the sparrows as they do so, and the hunters try to shoot the eagles in turn. The poet who sings of the joys of heaven and earth is a mere fool." In reality, however, poets intuitively perceive the beauty of heaven and earth, and we have confirmed this intuition through scientific research. The beauty of the universe was created by love. Everything created by love is the beauty of the universe. It is no wonder that these animalists, who don't understand the place of sex competition within the theory of biological evolution, instead merely echoing Darwin's theory without any reflection, nor conceive of heaven's great divine providence as anything more than an appendix, do not understand the poet either. They go too far in attempting to hold up the theory of biological evolution, disparaging others as much they please. We declare with great force: the only direct, conscious, individual-on-individual competition for survival between members of the same species is this sex competition, and it is this direct, conscious, individual-on-individual competition that is the most beneficial and powerful aspect of biological evolution. This assertion demands a restructuring of the organization of current biological evolutionary theory.

---

[143] In fact, it's said that insects don't see the bright colors of those flowers, but are lured by the honey and fragrance.

The competition for survival in the socialist era between individual persons as the unit of measurement is a competition for the opposite sex in order to continue living. Since there would be no competition among individual persons for food to sustain life as it exists today, the competition for sex will be remarkably vigorous and will evolve society at an astonishing rate. In other words, the great authority for the evolution of everything will not be left in the hands of a special individual, but will be left to free competition by all members of society, and while all the members compete in free love, those who do not obtain truth, possess no virtue, and lack beauty will be weeded out as losers in love.

Nature causes pain because it is in contrast to pleasure. Some of those who badmouth socialism today fire arrows of criticism which call it a fantasy that wants to remove pain from life completely. If anything, this is merely praising the effects of socialism. These critics must listen to some of the socialists who are already propounding the free love theory today.[144]

This free love theory says that one is free to invoke selection by sex, and that socialism can do nothing about those who are culled as losers in love by this facet of competition for survival. This is deplorable when viewed with the dogmatic humanitarianism of the individualistic age, but the principles of social evolution cannot be obstructed with tears. Humanity is a living species. Socialism, which strives for the evolution of humankind as a living species, cannot naturally be outside all the laws of biological evolution, as the theory of social evolution is one of the final chapters in the theory of biological evolution. Socialism asserts as its first principle that, although humans are creatures which strive for a more noble existence, we must recognize that, as living organisms, there is still competition for food (we will explain the true significance of the competition for food later) because we must obtain these

---

[144] It seems that socialists of the time also considered love as a subject of socialist discussion. Naoe Kinoshita also wrote an article on love.

physical resources in order to survive. We also argue that human society was the first to reach the highest level of evolution, but because it is a living organism, like other organisms, it must evolve its society through competition for sex, which is a significant natural law of biological evolution. That competition for survival pertaining to sex, as if it were a food competition, differs in content from the different classes of biological species, much as the competition for food differs between insects and birds, or between birds and mammals. In the same way, the content of the human competition for sex, which differs from that of beasts, is one of love between "anthropoids."

Even so, "love comes after a full stomach." Throughout all living species, the competition for sex is overpowered by the competition for food, with the condition that the winner of the sex competition is determined from the winner of the food competition. Our ideal is a higher reality that will eventually be reached in the future after satisfying certain conditions in the present reality. Since the sex competition is fought for the continuation of life in the future, the superior one, the winner, is sought by comparison with the ideal. Since the food competition is fought for the continuation of life in the present, the superior one, the winner, is satisfied when obtaining its prize in the present. The ideal is the reality that will come after the present reality.

Therefore, in a biological species that has no choice but to maintain its survival in the present reality against other species, there is no sex competition to realize the ideal in the continued life of its offspring, and the lower organisms such as leeches, aphids, etc., to which I drew comparisons earlier, remain in a mere gradual survival competition between species. Even for higher organisms it is difficult to compete for food with a species that feeds on them, or any species that feeds on a species that feeds on them, so the only urgency they feel is towards maintaining their own lives in the present reality. Therefore, it isn't too severe to expect the realization of the ideal in the descendent, the continuation of life from competition for sex. A striking example of this is that the winner of the sex competition among carnivores is often the winner of the food competition as well, and many people know that roosters lead a large number of hens after winning a battle.

Even the human race is not exempt from this example. It is a fact that from the beginning of history to the present day, in order to maintain an organism's present life, food competition has either overpowered or been a condition for the competition for sex, which is the continuation of life in order to realize the ideal. From the era of fishing, hunting, and nomadism, when food competitions were held in villages and decided by battles, to the medieval era, when food competitions (land disputes) were held in feudal plots and decided by military force, the chiefs, kings, and nobles were the winners of the competition for food, and they also used said military force to win the competition for sex.

Today, in the international struggle for dominance via land disputes in the competition for food, which are settled by military force, the military class has become the winner of the sex competition because it is first the winner of the food competition. In this sense, one may say that we who call ourselves civilized today are not so different from the Sioux of Iowa who, after taking a man's head for the first time, are entitled to put a feather atop their own heads and demand marriage.[145] Not true! Today's civilized people limit their barbaric methods of food competition to international competition and have come to idealize the individualistic labor theory in domestic food competition. However, as we have explained several times before, this too has remained merely an ideal.

Since the invention of machines made the country a pure economic aristocracy, and the theory of possession of the armed age still prevails, the competition for sex was completely overwhelmed by the economic winners of

---

[145] The Sioux are one of the indigenous tribes of North America. They are also known as the Dakota. We are not certain whether the men of the Sioux tribe were unable to marry if they did not win in battle.

the competition for food (as the lower classes were sold to become wives and concubines of the upper classes), and becoming the economic winner in the food competition became a condition for competing for sex (for example, the amount of property one has being a condition for marriage). In this sense, today's civilized people are not at all different from the natives of Churaderuhiigo who pay property or labor to the parents of girls to buy those girls as wives.[146] Reality over the ideal. The competition for food comes before the competition for sex.

The labor theory of individualism says that it is labor for a prostitute to sell her chastity. We recognize this respectable labor theory and would never say that boys are paying money to rape prostitutes, or that a "traveling prostitute" is merely a gang rape in which the positions are switched.[147] This is because of the remarkable fact that the competition for sex was overwhelmed by the competition for food. We also can't help but recognize that, for the upper class, the amount of wealth one possesses is a condition for marriage, which goes perfectly with the fact that one must be a winner in the competition for food in order to win in the competition for sex. These ladylike prostitutes, who will stay for life with a simple hairstyle and promise to pay for their livelihoods,[148] are much cheaper than the lower-class ones, who require fifty coins for a single night, complete with liquor and snacks.

Some ladies will say, "My husband's position is under my bottom." This is absolutely not a joke to be laughed at, but rather someone stating a well-

---

[146] Since the Sioux tribe came up earlier, we suspect this is somewhere in America, but we aren't sure. It may be a reference to Philadelphia, but since it is too far removed from the original language and there is no evidence to confirm it, we will leave it as is.

[147] We're not sure how to translate this. Could it be a prostitute who travels around plying her trade to various men?

[148] Specifically, the "simple hairstyle" refers to the way a bride would do her hair from the Edo period to the Meiji period. It is said to have been oval-shaped and slightly flat.

asserted right. Of course, one can't know the secrets held by those who are called "husband" by one of these ladies, whether that be political secrets or otherwise, but the phrase "under my bottom" is an insult which shows that most of the male class today has lost their right to choose a member of the opposite sex. We are socialists. However, we are also men. We must reflect on our own pathetic, ugly situation rather than overstep our bounds by interfering with the female class.

It goes without saying that a prostitute is a whore, and the lady who looks down at the honorable poor housewife who tries her best to help her husband while living in poverty, is nothing more than a high-class whore, both of which deserve nothing more than scorn and derision. However, how many male prostitutes, known as politicians and academics, who drive horse-drawn carriages through the streets and scold passersby while smiling arrogantly, are there? There are parents who sell their daughters, and parents who buy their sons-in-law. The reason why girls all over the world are decked out in face powder and silk, wearing reddish-brown hakama, and gilded with a diploma from a girl's school, is so that they can sell themselves for the price of a diamond ring. Similarly, the reason why most men today wear high-collared clothes, apply liquid face powder,[149] study political science or economics, or require themselves to have a degree from Waseda or Imperial University, is to increase the dowry of a young lady.

We must ask—how many men today can declare they have stripped all decorations, including social class, from a woman, held her naked body in their hands, and said, "I have looked directly at your beauty and will exchange vows with you so we can create a second generation"? Women are passive and men are active. Thus, the lower class passively become criminals in order to live, while the upper class actively become criminals in order to lead a more noble life. In the same way, female prostitution, with the exception of the class of

---

[149] Also known as a form of "oshiroi."

noble ladies, is mostly done passively as a means to make a living, while the men prostitute themselves actively in order to seek a nobler life. Not so! As we noted a bit in the previous volume, those who are not economically independent have no political or moral freedom. In the past, men and women did not have equal rights—women could not be the holders of property, but were instead property that men could gift as they pleased—so it is indeed a scientific law that the male class, which today embrace their rights but have no real property, is oppressed under the bottoms of ladies for the sake of the upper-class women. Those who can't assert their rights are slaves. Because of this, while admitting that countless women are prostitute slaves, we can't defend all the politicians and academics as free people of character when their right to love has been stripped away. (If anything, they are slaves—with the will of the slaves being considered the will of the nation, and us being made to breathe under it.)

If it is more honorable to be a freeman than a slave, then a lady who buys an actor or a young noblewoman who asserts her right to sit her bottom atop her husband are far more honorable than the male prostitute slaves they purportedly serve. This is a right recognized as far back as the distant days of Roman law. Rather than a politician who bows his head to the wife his superior bought him, trying to defend himself for staying out too late at night; rather than a rising businessman who holds back his desire to go to his concubine's house, as if a loose woman with a male lover is serving her husband properly; rather than a scholar who bends his knee in an attempt to please his incredibly ugly wife, people such as Mr. Hirobumi Ito, who left his name in history with his Fukuhara statue, or Mr. Taro Katsura, who is famous for the geisha Okoi, are, from the perspective of ancient Athens, much more free people.[150]

---

[150] Hirobumi Ito was the first governor of Hyogo Prefecture, and the statue was erected in honor of his achievements during the Sino-Japanese War. Okoi was a geisha who was a favorite of Taro Katsura.

Freemen and slaves are separated on an economic basis. People like Mr. Ito and Mr. Katsura have the right to play with women—yes, we call this a right—as they please in the same way that women of the capitalist class have the complete freedom to boldly enter machiai spots as they please and treat the male class as victims of pleasure.[151] There is nothing immoral about buying a prostitute to be your wife. It is an extremely contemptable sin to point out that men are bought and sold, even including their chastity. There are parents who sell their daughters and parents who buy their sons-in-law. Girls who are sold by their parents become prostitutes, while boys who are bought by their in-laws become politicians and scholars. The time when the theory of equal rights for men and women was necessary and significant has passed with the establishment of the private property system through the revolution of individualism. And yet, now that we live in a world of economic aristocracy, where the majority of society has no property as a basis for rights, the right to love is granted to those men and politicians who can afford a lady wife or concubine, and to those women who can afford a scholar or actor, while the other classes of men and women are completely enslaved, as women were in the past. It is a disaster, just as it was a disaster for women who were slaves, without any rights, in a time when only men retained their economic independence. Having lost their economic independence, men are now slaves to the women of the upper class. Yes, this is merely the theory of equal rights for both the rich and poor, but anyone still asserting the meaningless theory of equal rights between men and women are simply trying to translate and parrot foreign theories in Japan.[152]

---

[151] "Machiai" is an abbreviation for "waiting teahouse" (machiai jaya). The word "waiting teahouse" refers to a teahouse that rented out seats for meeting people, and nowadays, it refers to a teahouse that invites geisha to entertain. In modern terms, it's probably best to think of it as a host club.

[152] In other words, simply bringing foreign theories into Japan as they are.

This is exactly how it is today. Neither men nor women have the right to choose in the competition for sex. To clarify, we aren't speaking of love for the realized ideal via the continuation of life, but rather the center point of the law of competition for sex shifting depending on where the most brilliant substances pass by or accumulate. In other words, the so-called "marriage of the sexes" is no longer determined by a republic council based on the public opinion of the Izumo gods,[153] but by the tyrannical dictatorship of the Fukugami god, who has become the god of relationships. An image or statue of the Fukugami must be placed on the wedding floor. Socialism has been trying to exterminate this image for the ideal of social evolution, and has come to advocate the theory of free love.

Higher animals have become divided into male and female, evolving from the asexual means of reproduction of the amoeba, or the parthenogenesis of the aphid,[154] and compete with each other. Their evolution to higher stages has been almost entirely due to this competition, and they have received a special blessing from the laws of evolution as such. The realization of the ideal depends on competition for sex. Because of this competition for sex, organisms desire to select and obtain the best and most beautiful of the opposite sex. And in order to achieve this desire, an effort is made to overcome the other competitors of the same sex by making oneself the best and the most beautiful among them. Because of this effort, each member of the opposite sex makes its own self more virtuous and more beautiful, and each new child born becomes more virtuous and more beautiful through heredity and post-natal education.

It is as if the universe itself follows this competition for sex in order to make cherry blossoms and peonies bloom, butterflies dance, crickets chirp in

---

[153] The Shinto deity of marriage.

[154] Though parthenogenesis is also a form of asexual reproduction, it is distinct from that of the amoeba, the former creating an egg cell which does not need to be fertilized by a partner, the latter splitting one cell into two.

the fall, and birds sing, striving to realize an incomprehensible, absolute ideal. The "anthropoid" is charged with realizing at least some part of this ideal—that is, evolving towards the ideal relative to our understanding of human evolution. Because humans are at the forefront of that evolution, they receive the greatest number of special blessings from the laws of evolution that are not given to other higher organisms. That is, humans have relatively equal numbers of men and women, as opposed to a very large number of males compared to females as seen in other animals. So, contrary to the fact that in many other organisms it is only the males that have evolved (except for evolution due to food competition), both human men and women have evolved, and the beauty of human women is particularly remarkable.

Most species have a markedly different relative number of males to females—to the extent that one could say one hundred male butterflies compete for one female butterfly—and even the ones where the relative numbers are similar to each other, because of the polygamist nature of one male and many females, females do not need to compete as much as males, and are allowed the freedom to choose a male partner from many different males. Plus, due to food competition, in which laying eggs, beautiful colors, noticeable vocalization, and other such things are dangerous because they easily attract the attention of other animals, females cannot evolve in parallel with the evolution of the males and remain in a lower class with a marked disparity in everything. Thus, the females among these organisms stand outside the laws of the sex competition, remaining on the sidelines and adopting a passive attitude; in other words, they have been excluded from the benefits of the laws of evolution, and are instead its stepchildren.

Yet, when it comes to the human race, which is at the forefront of evolution, since there are equal numbers of men and women in every case, they are both blessed to be carried in the bosom of this compassionate Mother, and to run with her. The equal number of men and women means that women evolved their enticing laughs and grace through the competition between women, and men evolved their dignity and knowledge through the competition between men.

Even so, what a state of affairs we're in now. Her enticing smile, designed for love, now has within it a financial desire, placing a burden on her graceful shoulders. The wrinkled forehead and spectacles of the old spinster are by no means the picture of a girl's beauty, and a girl with arms of iron and buttocks like a millstone would be called ugly even by barbarians, except the natives of Somalia. No matter how men cover up with silk hats, the increasing number of parasites that have no more than a flat lump of material in their skulls can never be "the evolution of boys, those who have developed knowledge." Politicians and scholars, who are elements of the same society, yet are forced to kneel before economic sovereigns and aristocrats in dutiful slave-like obedience, can never be said to possess the dignity of evolved men, no matter how grand of beards they grow or how they adorn themselves with coaches, no matter the medals or the great ceremonial dress they wear, not even if they become ministers.

Today's competition for food is not at all done on the level of simple individual persons as units. In fact, we would say that it is a family affair, from the time when humans try to ensure that their offspring, who are the continuation of life, are not losers in the food competition. In other words, whether we call it a food competition or a sex competition, one is an effort to maintain the present self and the other is an effort to maintain one's continued life; both are economic competitions to obtain the material resources to sustain life. Today's sex competition is not so much about each man and woman making themselves better and more beautiful to evolve their offspring, who are the continuation of life, as it is about making sure that one's children can maintain their own lives, which is the aforementioned continuation of life, and choosing the perfect man or woman as their partner is secondary to this. So the offspring can't be more evolved than their parents, and the offspring, the realization of their ideal, merely becomes the heir to reality instead.

Today, the economic superiors are the ideal men or women. So, as we said, the ideal certainly is filled with a dazzling substance. That substance being gold, and the men and women who possess it are yearned for as the ideal lover. There is nothing irrational about the evolution of society. In the early days, when human races competed for survival via physical strength for the maintenance and evolution of their race, those with superior strength were the winners of the sex competition because they brought the most benefit to the maintenance and evolution of society. The women of that era fell in love with the strongest and most skillful fighters as their ideal, and those ideal men also selected the ideal women of the time, resulting in the most ideal union of the sexes in society. Their offspring inherited the most ideal genes from the most ideal bond between the ideal man and ideal woman, and became strong and skillful fighters, thus realizing and advancing the ideals of society.

Today, economic warfare is not fought with brute strength, but with labor or knowledge. Those who plunder other economic goods by force of arms are criminally liable and become the losers in the competition for sex, to the extent that their actions become grounds for divorce claims. The content of that ideal has completely changed, with those who have become economically superior through labor or knowledge becoming the ideal object of love. Social evolution is economic evolution. So, the ideal of sex competition for those who are economically superior in labor or knowledge is that which will weed out the lazy, foolish, or dull elements, so those who labor best and have the most knowledge will be blessed with offspring, and their offspring will inherit the most ideal knowledge in the society, and will thus become those who labor best and know the most.

One must not misunderstand, though. Social evolution cannot be classified in simple stages. Today's economic winners, understood through labor and knowledge, still inherit the ideas of the era in which competition for survival was determined by physical force. Their labor and knowledge are not directed toward the economic resources of other races, but are used in the struggle between members of their race, that is, between their own people. The economic Warring States period we mentioned in volume 1, *The Economic Justice of Socialism*, refers to this. The knowledge used by the upper classes and the exploited labor of the lower classes are merely used to counteract the knowledge and labor of the others. In this brutal and ugly economic warring age, just as the winner of the food competition, the competition for survival that sustains the individual, is a brutal and ugly person, the winner of the sex competition, the competition for survival in which offspring evolve, must also be a truly brutal and ugly person.

Just as the rooster who wins a cockfight leads dozens of hens, the lucky winner of the golden feudal class must feed countless hens in his concubine's house while the monogamist glares at him. Even as the bard sings a song of lost love, filled with what sounds like cries of blood from a lesser cuckoo, human females, whose competition differs from a bird's, decorate themselves with gold, snicker at those who declare love as holy and sacred, and flock together in front of the aging lechers. Just as the undeveloped people of Borneo bring back human heads to show their eligibility for marriage, would these supposedly developed people not feel that they lack the qualifications for marriage if they did not present a diamond ring that shines and is coated in the blood of their brethren? No different from the barbarian who must prove himself the most ferocious and brutal to win the women of his village, the barbarians who live in villages with steam and electricity will only get women if they are the most ferocious and brutal in the war for gold. Those without gold cannot make a home, and the homes that are made are destroyed.

The family is the only sacred place in social evolution where the ideal man and woman, obtained through the competition for sex, seek to realize their ideals in their children through heredity and education. And yet, still maintaining today's economic warfare (which, of course, we should not maintain, but even so), consider that this kind of competition for sex will continue for several generations. In what direction will humanity really change? The sultry laughter and grace of women are not maintained by masculinized learning and masculine labor, nor are the dignity and knowledge of men evolved by the slave-like subjugation of the economic warrior, serf, and parasite classes.[155]

The sacrifice of mundane reality for a lofty reality (the ideal) exists in all higher organisms. The beautiful colors and beautiful sounds of some insects attract the attention of the birds that prey upon them, making them extremely unsuitable for maintenance and survival as individual insects, and yet the males, far outnumbering the females, make many sacrifices because they are so devoted to evolving the beauty of their music and the garb in which they dance. It is not enough for a living organism to simply maintain its species. They will compete with each other for sex in order to evolve as a species, and, in order to evolve the competition for sex, they will easily make countless sacrifices during the competition for food.

Since humans reign as the predominant winners above all other biological species in food competition (although they still cannot completely outcompete species like microorganisms),[156] they are much less worried than other biological species about being obstructed by food competition when it comes to the competition for sex. Female humans—unlike the female insects, who do not compete in the competition for sex because they are too scared of being eaten by other species in competition for food—will never fall behind in evolution. Men and women are similar in number, and so the competition for sex between women is evolving them at a rate just as fast as the men. The laws of evolution, which produce equal numbers of males and females and show a biased favor only to mankind, are threatening to take sex competition's right of selection out of the hands of all men and women and place them under the

---

[155] "Parasite classes" refers to the capitalist classes.

[156] This still holds up well, as we have been plagued in recent years by resistant bacteria, although we have gained the upper hand since the invention of antibiotics.

absolute, infinite, unlimited right of selection of the ignorant and cold-blooded Fukugami. Even in the aboriginal villages, people put their lives at risk for love affairs; likewise, in today's era of economic warfare, the fact that knowledgeable, morally upright, and good-looking men and women are still considered the ideal of love, shows that the demand of all the elements of society is realizing the ideal of social evolution for their descendants, and it is here that the free love theory of socialism takes on significance.

In a world where socialism's free love theory becomes a reality, food competition will not be based on individuals, families, economic groups, or nations as it is today, nor will the same species compete among themselves—in other words, when socialism is implemented on the economic front is when humanity as the unit of measurement must enter the competition for food with other species. It is also significant, of course, that the theory of free love is advocated in the sense of eliminating the oppression of the parents, who hold old ways of thinking, so that the new self breaks away from the old part of itself for the interests of the new self. This is a clash between the old and new elements of society, and society evolves as the new elements replace the old (through the death of the old elements, or through them being displaced by the new).

However, man isn't free from the beginning. We explained in the previous volume that the state of freedom is achieved because of the conscience of society, which recognizes one's freedom, and that one is free within the limits of that conscience. In the same way, even the freedom of love cannot be said to be congenitally free, outside the scope of the conscience of the parents. When a child's conscience evolves to the point where it is no longer satisfied with the conscience created by the parents, it means that it can act according to its now-evolved conscience. While the child is under the will of the parents, and while their conscience is still being formed, the parents have the power to forbid love with their own conscience. There is no freedom to love until the children recognize that their own conscience deserves to exclude the conscience of their parents.

Socialism's theory of free love has additional immediate significance as well. If free love simply means eliminating the old ideas of the parents, one does not have to wait for socialism to find their own way—simply embrace each other and whisper sweet nothings under the moon. Socialism's theory of free love, however, is advocated in order to overthrow modern society. "While politicians argue, hunger and love rule the world."[157] Socialists preserve the poet's intuition by scientific evidence, and during a time when the upper classes are now forming governments, creating parliaments, and debating daily, the socialists are wielding these two hammers of "hunger" and "love" to rebuild the organization known as society from the ground up. What organisms demand in reality is food, and what they demand as an ideal is love. A society in which this solemn demand of life—the demand for the maintenance and evolution of society—is ignored and oppressed is a society that stands on a shaky foundation which could be overturned with a single blow.

Two striking examples of societies where this demand is only satisfied for a portion of society, and the other elements simply exist as complete and pure sacrifices, are those of ants and bees. (Upper-class academics strive to liken the societies of ants and bees to human society, using the fact that bees have a queen to justify the existence of the now-pointless late Queen of England or the current Queen of the Netherlands,[158] or the fact that only male ants exist

---

[157] The original text uses "abundance" (instead of "hunger"), something that still doesn't exist much in the world today. In the collection of Kita's writings, the word "hunger" is pointed out here, and, judging from the following text, that is the correct translation, so that's what we used.

[158] The "late Queen of England" is Queen Victoria (who died in 1901). The Queen of the Netherlands at that time was Wilhelmina Helena Maria van Oranje-Nassau. She reigned from 1890 to 1948.

without working to grant rights to the poor behavior of the aristocrats. However, if we compare humanity to bees in that the worker bees will gather around a queen who is no longer useful after reproduction and tear her to pieces, we would instead call it "disturbing the order.")[159]

However, as mankind is the most advanced creature, all men and women have ideals, and the realization of these ideals is obtained through the competition of all the elements of society. Once an ideal is realized, an even higher ideal soon emerges. As mankind evolves, that is, as it realizes more and more of its ideals, it becomes more idealistic and its romantic demands become accordingly bolder and more splendid. Let Ariwara no Narihira be born in the German royal court of today.[160] Humans will greatly evolve in terms of beauty, and the ugly Kaiser beard will be culled out of mankind. Let the girl who said, "There is no above or below in love" (we are ashamed to say we forgot the name of this bold egalitarian hero) stand beside the German crown prince. That beautifully adorned toad will be the loser in the competition for sex, and mankind will greatly evolve in beauty.

Ah, "hunger" and "beauty!" Why do the hungry not even have a scrap of bread? Why do those in love have the man or woman they love taken from them? The moment when the answer to these questions will be given to the hands of all elements of society—yes, that moment is when the economic aristocracy crashes to the ground as if from a massive earthquake! Let us get back on topic.

Oh, you lovely, sheepish family theorist. As long as you have only one beloved wife and one beloved child, even a meager monthly salary can be enough to fortify your home as if its walls were those of a citadel. However,

---

[159] In other words, he's saying that the shallowness of these people lies in their penchant to only imitate what's convenient for them.

[160] Ariwara no Narihira was a poet of the early Heian period. He is said to be the hero of *Ise Monogatari* and was famous for his beauty.

once you have two or three beloved children, you will have colluders in your castle. When the adventures of the capitalists to whom you cling do not go well, when society goes bankrupt, or your husband is dismissed, and he can no longer use his worn-out shoes and the contents of his lunchbox expires, how long will your rations sustain you? To maintain this small fortress and store up provisions, the masters of the household, who by nature were like sheep, have become wolves while fighting against the world. They have lost their hopeful and dazzling vigor and are as weak as old men at only thirty years old. Though their smiles were once full beneath their thin beards, they now have only dark lips closed like stones. The little girl who wore a maroon hakama, smiled like a flower in full bloom, and chirped like a little bird, was gone in an instant, her plump cheeks emaciated by the hardships of life, never to be lifted in a smile again. The child's small hands, full of the light of love, search for the mother's breasts as if attempting to further chip away at the bones of her skinny chest. Isn't the family theory one of a smile made from the falling tears of misery? Open the window of the home and see from where the tidal waves are rushing forward, accompanied by monstrous noise.

When Professor Kanai's *Socioeconomics* denounces socialism and says, "The abolition of the system of private property will damage and destroy the sanctity of the family, which is essential for moral and economic good," he is really expressing a will that is not in tune with humanity. O family theorist, the sanctity of the family became a theoretic fact only with the individualist revolution. In other words, it is not the same as it was in the days when only the aristocracy owned land and the common people only had rights as mere peasants, nor is it the same as when only men were the subjects of ownership and women had no economic basis for maintaining their independence. In this day and age, women, surrounded by economic well-being, are actually so free that they can play around with men. What we have to thank the system of private property for is the democracy it has established and this liberation of women.

At first glance, it would seem as if socialism, which cries out for the destruction of the private property system, is the enemy of those who create theories of the family by advocating things such as the sanctity of love and monogamy. Take a closer look, however. Private property, which is essential for the maintenance of the family and the independence of men and women, is, like property used to be, reserved for the economic aristocracy. The peasant serf, the laborer living in a back-street tenement, and even the cute family theorist, have no more private property than they are given at the end of the month to pay the miso shop. If a monthly wage that is available today but gone tomorrow, or a wage that is earned in the morning but gone by evening, is a system of private property, then socialist private property, which is distributed as equal purchasing power with a fixed term of one year, should be called hereditary property.

A world in which one can speak of family theory, a peaceful world in which men can enjoy themselves, exists only in the distant future. Just as men bore the greatest burden of combat in the military age, forgetting the differentiated development of the sexes has caused men, who are able to bear the burden of battle the most, to be quietly isolated in their own small world while children and women play about. Let the women be placed beyond the reach of the cruel battle cries of archers,[161] and instead take upon themselves the task of making laurel wreaths.[162] To seize their delicate hands during the revolutionary war and throw them vigorously into the fray is something only to be thought of directly before the fall of one's castle. Socialism is not so hopeless as to look to Gozen Tomoe to fight for it.[163] The free love theory of socialism has nothing to

---

[161] This battle cry is known as an "arrow cry," and it is when an archer shouts when shooting their bow. In other words, it's a cry only heard on the battlefield.

[162] The laurel wreath was a symbol of praise in ancient Greece, worn by the winner of various competitions.

[163] Gozen Tomoe was a woman who married Yoshinaka Kiso. She was renowned as a

do with the issue of women's rights in the age of individualism. Those who have created a theory of the family and are now the very onlookers of society deserve sympathy for their sheepishness, but they are merely passive egoists who try to do in poverty what the economic aristocrats are doing on a large scale. What the world should scorn instead is the fad of the family theory.

It is exactly as we have said. The theory of equal rights for men and women that accompanies the theory of free love is not based on dogmatism, as was the case with the theory of equal rights for men and women in the individualist era, which compares individual men and individual women while ignoring reality and saying that they have the same capacity for mental and physical activity (this is a common fault of those who inherited the dogmatism of individualism but call themselves socialists). Understand our theory to mean that men and women should be given equal rights to choose partners in order to allow the competition for sex, the most powerful force in biological evolution, and thus complete freedom for the evolution of society.

The theory of freedom and equality must be advocated in the interest of social evolution to all intents and purposes. Women use enormous amounts of energy due to the great sacrifices of menstruation, pregnancy, childbirth, and breastfeeding. Therefore, unless they are unusually masculine, hermaphrodites, or spinsters (many of these lose their feminine qualities later in life), they will never be able to stand on equal footing with men in mental and physical competition. The dogmatic individualist theory of equality, which posits an atomic individual who can only think in terms of ideas rather than reality, and which bases its theory of equal rights on a comparison of all individual persons with each other, is not unlike comparing an individual adult with a child and saying that they are the same in mental and physical capacity. Socialism recognizes that just as adults and children differ on a scientific basis,

---

beautiful woman with outstanding military prowess. It's said that she followed Yoshinaka Kiso as a military commander until his death.

men and women, who have undergone evolutionary differentiation, are not the same. However, free competition between the old elements and new elements of society based on a scientific foundation—in other words, free competition between the current old elements who have realized the ideals of the previous generation and seek to maintain them and the new elements who work to realize modern ideals and reach new stages of evolution in the future—is how society evolves. In the same way, we assert that society can evolve only when the male and female elements of society each seek to realize their ideals (ideals that are largely the ideals of the society of their time, but which are further specified by their individuality) in their offspring, who are the continuation of life, and when the men and women who have best mastered the social ideals of their time are the center of the competition for sex. In other words, the theory of equal rights for men and women is a theory of freedom and equality in the area of love.

The freedom and equality of all individuals can only be realized if they stand on a plane of equality, free from economic subordination. Because our modern age is one where women don't even have the right to possession and are subservient to men economically, or are otherwise less able than men in terms of economic activity anyway—actually, there are many men who are subordinate to financially powerful women today in the process of social evolution—the theory of freedom of love for men and women is nothing more than a distant ideal. (In this point, as with all others, economic independence is an all-encompassing independence. So, by plundering the land, the economically independent aristocrats rejected their duty of loyalty to the sovereign and gained independence in all things. Much like that, the long period of peace preceding and during the Genroku period allowed the common class to set up an economic foundation, reject their loyalty to the aristocrats, and set up a democracy through the Meiji Revolution. In the same way, what is now called the degradation of female students is evidence of their rejection of slave-like submission to men through economic independence [that is, the former obligation of fidelity to "serve none but your lord" for men, and the former obligation of chastity to "show chastity by never remarrying"[164] for women], and of the bright signs of freedom and equality. Much as the old lords would call the aristocrats of the time "rebellious subjects,"[165] so too were those who believed in democracy called the same during the Meiji Revolution. In the same way, the male class calling it "depraved" when they see girls love as freely as boys do, is no different from savages saying that the world is coming to an end when history, which is the traces of social evolution, evolves to the point where a new non-discriminative manner of thought emerges and expands. Be depraved. As long as the men are depraved, be parallels and be as depraved as they are. The degradation of the female student is actually an evolution, and it is a thing to be praised. Let us praise it.)

As explained above, the competition for survival between individual persons as units, which holds the key to their evolution, will, during the age of socialism, be placed in the hands of all the elements of society, and the one path by which we can make ideals a reality, the competition for sex, will occur both equally and freely.

---

[164] "Show" means demonstrating her service toward her husband.

[165] "Rebellious subjects," or "Ranshin Zokushi" (乱臣賊子) (lit. rebellious subjects, bandit sons), were subjects who disrupted the state and/or children who turned their backs on their parents.

Chapter 7

There is an issue here which arises without fail. Yes, the theory of population. The Malthusian theory of population explains what should be done about the increase in population, which would be necessary if free love between men and women were left to its own devices.[166] We have thus arrived at this opportunity to explain in the socialist era the competition for food, which is a competition for survival using society as its unit.

This is true to a certain extent if, as the individualist economist Mill interpreted it,[167] Malthusian population theory does not mean an iron wall lying in the path of society, but rather a net laid under the present society. This is because both are individualists who interpret society as the relationships or status between groups of individual persons. So instead of understanding society as evolving for its own purposes and exhibiting a multitude of phenomena as part of that process, they simply attribute the reason for the poverty of the poor classes to the moral responsibility of the poor individual people themselves and say, "You had too many children, so you deserve what you get." To put it bluntly, they are saying the capitalist class's indulgence in lascivious and decadent play is the right of rich persons, and the

---

[166] Thomas Robert Malthus was an English economist. In his impactful *An Essay on the Principle of Population*, he argued that population increases geometrically (at the rate of a geometric sequence), but food supply increases only arithmetically (at the rate of an arithmetic sequence), and so poverty arises as a natural phenomenon.

[167] John Stuart Mill was an English thinker and economist. He revised Bentham's utilitarianism from quantitative to qualitative. He's also famous for his books *On Liberty* and *Considerations on Representative Government*.

poverty of the poor is merely the result of them forgetting their personal obligation to curb their reproductive acts, which those in poverty must do.

We do not deny that many of today's working class treat the act of reproduction as a pastime, because they have no other noble or spiritual pleasures, and because they have been placed in an environment where their carnal desires are provoked from an early age. There is also the Lamarckian theory of evolution to consider, so we do not deny that the repeated act of reproduction itself heightens one's desire for reproduction.[168] However, if we make them, who have been made miserable by their unfortunate circumstances, bear all the responsibility for poverty, we must stop being so lenient that we overlook the careless, undisciplined lives of the capitalist class, who have also been made miserable by their unfortunate circumstances. Plunder creates the right to a lifestyle of careless slack, while poverty takes away something that is the essential duty of any living creature—is that a stance that someone with an ounce of humanity could support?

The statistics show things clearly. They show that because of an increased population we began to control more machinery, which allowed us to cultivate more newly discovered land, and thereby create today's capitalist class of increased wealth. The economic aristocracy of today is maintained because of the intense desire of the poor to reproduce. How can you be a monk, yet meddle in another's bedchamber?

However, as theorists, we must avoid any shameful emotionalism. There are some self-proclaimed socialists who look at people like Malthus from the age of individualism and get upset, even hurling insults, but those people are merely interpreting his population theory through his own individualism. Socialism itself has a different basis for argument entirely. Simply standing

---

[168] Jean-Baptiste Lamarck was a French natural historian. Until Darwin's theory of evolution, Lamarck's theory of use and disuse was said to be the prevailing theory.

alongside Malthus and viewing population theory from that same individualist angle is nothing more than worthless dogmatism itself.

The Malthusian theory of population begins its deduction from a single dogmatic point, leads with a preconception from that dogmatism, interprets statistics which support that dogmatism, and then returns to that initial dogmatic point with the idea that such a recursion is the peak of scientific study. The mirage of population theory is dreamed up from two phrases: "arithmetic progression" and "geometric progression."[169] These are, in fact, baseless dogmatism. Malthus dogmatically stated that food is an arithmetic progression which increases at a rate of one, two, three, four, while population is a geometric progression which increases at a rate of two, four, eight, sixteen, and that this means poverty is an inevitable fate that will exist forever. It is impossible to understand how this dogmatism, more incredible than even a dream, could form the entire basis of population theory, or how the academic class doesn't doubt said dogmatism at all, instead worshipping him as an authority on the matter.

He does provide statistics with his argument, of course. However, in his average mind, the dogmatism of arithmetic progression and geometric progression already exist as solid ideas before any induction is done from the statistics, so any sort of processing of said statistics will always be through that dogmatism. One example is his conclusion that the population doubles every twenty-five years while food increases are much smaller; he compared different categories which are not at all comparable. The statistical calculation on which he bases the idea that "the population doubles every twenty-five years" refers to the undeveloped period in the United States. He does not take

---

[169] An arithmetic sequence would be an=a+(n-1)d where "a" is the initial term and "d" is the common tolerance. A geometric sequence would be an=a·rn-1 where "a" is the initial term and "r" is the common ratio. Numbers increase much faster in the latter than the former.

into account the fact that, in the United States at that time, food was increasing, as a natural phenomenon, at the same rate, in the same geometric progression, as the population. Yet he does not compare the geometric progression of food in the United States with the geometric progression of the population, but rather takes the population of the United States, flies over the ocean with it, and places it squarely beside Europe's food. He then pointed to a completely different set of statistics, saying, "Behold, population increases at the rate of a geometric sequence, but food increases at the rate of an arithmetic sequence."

Even if there are traces of some induction in the treatments of these statistics, how much evidence does it really add to the underlying idea of geometric versus arithmetic sequences? To begin with, neither food nor population grow based on arithmetic progression. Neither do they grow by geometric progression. The plants and animals that are eaten as food by humans today are a biological species, and the humans who take them as food are also a biological species. The academics of today should be ashamed of themselves! Even if one grain of rice doesn't multiply ten thousand times, is there any law which dictates that a stalk which produced one grain of rice must then increase to exactly two grains, as per the arithmetic sequence? It is said that rats are born in a geometric progression. However, this is merely the rate at which they're born. Most of the rats will meet with physical hazards—some are outcompeted for survival with other organisms such as cats or the plague germs—and will die before they can produce more offspring in another geometric progression. Thus, even when increasing, such a geometric progression can never be maintained. The current economists who put their hands together in worship of Malthus must be making a mountain of geometric sequences on their desks as their rats reproduce at a rate where, in one year, a single mother can give birth to eight thousand rats.

Needless to say, Malthus is a mediocre person. The lower biological species that are considered food for mankind bear dozens of times more offspring, bear hundreds of times more fruit, and lay tens of thousands of times more eggs than the humans that feed on these species. So, even if an average person were to make a mistake and dogmatically think "food increases in a geometric sequence, while population increases in an arithmetic sequence," they would never arrive at the exact opposite conclusion from that at which Malthus arrived.

It is true, of course, that in Malthus' time there was a reaction against the mercantile system (mercantilism), which excessively encouraged population growth for the sake of national competition. It is also true that he was unable to maintain his sober judgment because of the Industrial Revolution in England, which had begun and showed increasingly disastrous consequences. Moreover, since it was the beginning of the Industrial Revolution and the era of powerful economic local lords, just as the vestiges of the lords' plundering were only discovered near the end of the Edo period, no matter how many people tried, nobody could become Karl Marx at the time due to the current degree of social evolution.

However, the use of the geometric and arithmetic sequences, in which one's understanding of the concept of numbers is even more inaccurate than that of a barbarian's, is truly the work of an inferior mind—yet, for the next hundred long years, it was carried on by countless scholars and became a kind of scripture. After it was adopted by the powerful, it came to be used as a means of brutal and unreasonable oppression and abuse of the lower classes. Mankind's spirit is truly a dubious thing. However, our spiritual knowledge has increased at the rate of a geometric sequence since the days of Malthus,[170] and Professor Kanai, who has access to all of this knowledge would say, "Even if we cultivate the entire earth, humanity will simply build three or five story

---

[170] In this context, "spiritual knowledge" means knowledge of **mysterious**, yet precious things.

houses,[171] increasing into the sky, and so an increase in population is inevitable." Humanity certainly has vastly increased its spiritual knowledge.

However, regardless of how mediocre an academic may be, one shouldn't simply deride him, then continue on their way. Rather than speaking the truth, these lowly scholars are simply following behind the prevailing force of the time, echoing that force's prevailing opinion. If it is the main force of the time, that is enough for them to dispel any doubt, regardless of how worthless the idea is. And when we see that the noble Professor Kanai, who is not a mediocre man, still makes the Malthusian theory of population his last stand against socialism, we cannot overlook the fact that the theory of population is certainly that prevailing opinion. Kanai says, "If the starving underclass is eliminated, isn't it logical that this would lead to an increase in population throughout society, resulting in starvation of the entire society?" This is not to interpret Malthusian population theory as a net laid under modern society, as in Mill's interpretation, but as an iron wall that stands in front of social evolution.

Socialism requires a solemn knowledge of the future of social evolution, since the very basis of socialism resides in the theory of social evolution. Therefore, if one builds economics on social philosophy to oppose socialism, that person could be considered a staunch denouncer of socialism. However, if one imagines that "houses built with three or four floors could reach from the North Pole to the South Pole," which even a child would not dare to say, and then goes on to celebrate Malthus, who claimed that such nonsense was the proportion of geometric progression at work, we can only call the entire situation unseemly.

Many of these scholars, in an attempt to distinguish themselves from socialists, are self-proclaimed patriots, believing that one must be able to see a

---

[171] We don't know why it says "three or five" and doesn't mention four. Kita does say "three or four" in the criticism that follows, so it's obviously inconsistent. Did Kita misquote? We'll leave it as is.

thousand years into the future. For this reason, along with the larger question of what to do with the Great Japanese Empire after the earth freezes over, this issue of the population one thousand years in the future is an urgent one that must be discussed at all times, unless one is starving to death on the street, and socialists are always demanded to lecture about this in front of these scholars. We declare the following publicly: the best answer to these scholars is silence filled with derision.

Since economics discusses the material basis of society, it requires knowledge of sociology, and since sociology studies the laws of survival and evolution of one living social organism, the human race, it is a chapter of biology that studies the survival and evolution of all living species. Yet the population theory, which economists today, shut off in a very narrow shell, study blindly and passively, does not approach things with any knowledge of biology at all. Arguing for the new society via sociology or discussing the new society's population via biology with today's economists, whose brains are littered with preconceived notions and organized around the leftover sake lees that existed before the birth of biology or sociology, would have as little effect as talking to a stone statue.

Oh, but that's not true! They talk about infinite food, which is the subject of economics today. They say that if the plains of the United States alone were cultivated, they could still feed 35 billion people. They say that two thirds of the earth is covered by farmland they call oceans. They have such a rich poetic imagination that they could cultivate the entire earth and still build three or five story houses on all of its surface. Because that's how they are, it makes sense they will, without fail, use their wisdom to look one thousand years into the future and be at a loss, wondering what to do when the population increases by ten or even one hundred billion. If they say that the food of the future will be obtained by chemical formulation, unless they can show us a dose of these pills, we will reply that that's not empirical science. We cannot be such sticklers for courtesy. We should declare now that volume 5, *The Theory*

238 | The Theory of Japan's National Polity and Pure Socialism

of Biological Evolution and Social Philosophy, is not speaking to today's academic class, whose pitiful minds are on full display.

Since the Malthusian theory of population is a problem of population versus food supply, rather than thoroughly discussing "population" in terms of biology, we will first think about "food" in the context of the current scope of economics, and interpret his theory as a wall in front of future social evolution, believing there to be no reason to fear it.

Are economists unaware of the evolution of food? They do not know that the types of food and methods of food production have evolved and will continue to evolve with the evolution of society—they do not understand that today's rice, wheat, fish, poultry, and other types of food, along with other methods of production which haven't changed much since ancient times, such as boiling and baking,[172] will evolve further—and so their brains, already conforming to the dogmatism known as the geometric sequence, immediately interpret this as population growth. They then create a laughable dilemma that either the situation will result in starvation for all of society, or that any other result is merely a socialist pipe dream.

If today's economists are to accept the theory of evolution and see today's society as something other than stagnant or cyclical, we must first turn our heads back and reflect on the economic evolution of the types of food and methods of production that have evolved to what they are today. It goes without saying that this is still a miniscule amount. It should be noted, however, that as society evolved from fishing and hunting to farming and agriculture, different types of food evolved. Mr. Inazo Nitobe,[173] a respected

---

[172] "... other methods of production which haven't changed much since ancient times, such as boiling and baking..." is a slightly difficult to understand example, but Kita interprets methods of cooking as "methods of production." (See his later examples.)

[173] Nitobe was a graduate of Sapporo Agricultural College and served as Deputy Secretary General of the League of Nations. He is also famous for writing *Bushido*. It

professor of agriculture, quotes the opinion of Frenchman Foissac in his *Discourse on Agriculture,* saying that there is between a twenty- to thirty-fold difference in the amount of people that can be fed by agriculture compared to livestock-farming, and another twenty-fold difference between live-stock farming and fishing.[174] In the opinion of Settegast,[175] a space of between five tan[176] and one chobu can support a single person via agriculture, while livestock-farming would require a space of between fifty to seventy chobu to support that same person. He then gives examples of how livestock-farming requires a lot of land, saying that in Russia it takes between eighty and one hundred hectares of grazing land to feed one man, and in Queensland, Australia, it takes one square mile for each sheep.

During the fishing and hunting era, when the main types of food were the purely primitive products of wild fish and birds, it was not possible to use for production any part of the earth other than that where primitive food existed, and this, along with the small number of human beings, was the reason for the scarcity of food. As society evolved, a little human intelligence emerged on the subject of production and began to artificially breed cattle and sheep, which

---

was during his time as principal of Ichiko High School that Kenjiro Tokutomi, who criticized the court decision in the High Treason Incident, gave a lecture at the school. He also published *Main Theory of Agriculture.*

[174] Inazo Nitobe, *Discourse on Agriculture* (1898), 175.

[175] Original text says "Zeottegast," but "Settegast" is correct. We think he was an agronomist, but details are unclear.

[176] The "tan" (反) and "chobu," [町歩] (sometimes just "cho" [町]) are measurements of land area. In the past, one "bu" (歩) was defined as six "shaku" (尺) and three "sun" (寸) (about 190 centimeters). Thirty "bu" equals one "se" (畝), ten "se" equals one "tan," and ten "tan" equals one "cho." (However, this was after Toyotomi Hideyoshi's nationwide land survey of 1582.) The area per one tan (dan, 段) equals approximately 991.7 meters squared. Therefore, the area per chobu is about 991.7 meters squared, or one hectare.

already existed primitively. As this happened, the parts of the earth used for production were expanded by human wisdom, resulting in an increase of food as the population grew. Furthermore, as society evolved and the variety of food increased, and rice and wheat were grown, humans were able to produce even more because plants reproduce much faster than animals, and that, along with further expanding the area used for production, resulted in an increase of food along with an increase in population. Does Professor Nitobe's dissertation not demonstrate this? There was no "Malthusian theory of fish and birds" in the fishing and hunting era,[177] and there was no "Malthusian theory of cattle and sheep" in the cattle-raising era. Why, then, did the "Malthusian theory of rice and wheat" emerge only once humanity evolved into the agricultural era, and why did so many people believe in this superstition?

As the food available to a society evolves, that society further evolves its methods of food production. The evolution of production methods is the breeding of biological species (such as cattle and sheep in the era of livestock, rice and wheat in the agricultural era), which were initially left to their own devices in a primitive manner, but which gradually became food through the wisdom of man. To give an agricultural example, Delbrück says that they have quadrupled production over the course of one century thanks to advances in German agronomy,[178] almost in direct proportion to the statistics Malthus brings up from American, where "the population has doubled in twenty-five years." The Malthusians are stuck in the theory that "the amount of arable land is limited," but the agronomists—just as land and sea armies expand their territory by seizing foreign land—have used science to invade domestic land and expand it by three or four times.

---

[177] The original just says "Malthus' fish and birds," but that makes it somewhat unclear, so we've supplemented the translation.

[178] Perhaps the German economist, Delbrück, but we are not certain of this translation.

During the time when the types of human food evolved into rice and wheat in the agricultural age, the methods of rice and wheat production evolved equally. However, the word "production," which we use here to mean the various forms of food production methods, is an academic term used in economics. The word "production" means both a method of production for reproduction of the biological species that humans consume, and also the economic activity aided by human wisdom that occurs during the time in which those biological species are brought to human mouths. In other words, using wisdom to breed sheep in order to obtain wool is an act of production, and adding wisdom to wool to make textiles is equally an act of production. In the same way, using wisdom to breed pine and oak trees in order to build a house is an act of production, and adding wisdom to pine and oak trees to cut them down is equally an act of production. In addition, agriculture and livestock farming, which use wisdom to breed species that will become food, are acts of production, and "boiling" and "baking," which add wisdom to plants and animals, are acts of production in the economic sense. We must doubt the economists who have forgotten this meaning, this fact that the production methods of foods evolve.

It is an economic fact that all production evolves from primitive production to industrial production. In the primitive age of society, resources were used for food, clothing, and shelter in their primitive state; as society evolves, those resources are used for food, clothing, and shelter after changing state or being transformed completely by human wisdom. However, since we still use food in its primitive form, which is not much different from that of primitive man, most of the food we consume today cannot be digested and is excreted out of the body. We are more industrially productive than primitive man in that we know a little about cooking and eating, but we know only how to bake bread from wheat, cook raw rice into edible rice, and boil or roast the meat of fish, fowl, and beasts. We do not have the same precise knowledge like we do regarding making clothes or dwellings, but only know of methods which make food to suit our palates, almost entirely according to our instinctive tastes.

Primitive dwellings were built on trees and dug into the mountainside. However, the use of wood and stone, as they existed in their primitive state, led to the addition of the meager industrial production practices to build huts, and then, as today, to the industrial production practices of five- or ten-story buildings in large cities. This is why today's economists have developed the Malthusian theory of dwellings, which says, "Everyone, abstain from reproduction. The world's treetops and mountain caves are limited, and we will have no choice but to live in nests or holes in the ground.[179] Mankind will surely drown in plain floods. (It was said that humans in China lived in nests and holes in the ground until Yu the Great's flood control was implemented.)"

Primitive clothing required a single sheep with a square mile of pasture just to make one garment. Today, however, the era of primitive garment-making as in the days of livestock-farming are gone, and we have evolved to the industrial production of spinning, which harvests wool every single year. Yet you do not hear today's economists developing a "Malthusian theory of garments," which says, "Everyone, stop reproducing. The number of pastures in the world is limited. Soon you will freeze to death." The evolution of housing production methods has prevented us from drowning due to a lack of housing, and the evolution of clothing production methods has prevented us from freezing to death due to lack of clothing. Why, then, do they think that food production methods will continue to exist in their present primitive forms and never evolve? Why does only the Malthusian theory relating to food remain, ranting about starvation from a lack of food supply?

The reason we have progressed from the proto-human age, when we chewed raw grains and ate raw meat, to boiling and baking our food is because

---

[179] In the chronicles of Emperor Jinmu in *Nihon Shoki*, he states in one of his rescripts, "The people's hearts are simple. They live in nests and holes."

a few industrial acts of production, such as the use of fire and knives, became available for use in food. Even if this act of industrial production is only slight, and even if it is nothing more than a blind act, it still means that a person now can digest more from the same amount of food compared to a primitive barbarian who would eat food raw, even if much of it travels through the mouth and is excreted as a nasty substance. (Funny story, even the German emperor isn't exempt from this as an organism who has undergone this evolution.)

Imagine if today's primitive food were to undergo an industrial production process that could allow man to digest and absorb all the nutrients observed by scientific analysis. Imagine that what is considered food today would immediately become mere raw materials, capable of sustaining a population dozens or even hundreds of times larger than today's. Let us repeat. We are not speaking to the feebleminded academic class. We are simply convinced that the laws that have evolved to this day are the laws that will lead to further evolution in the future, and that the principle of economics that all production proceeds from primitive to industrial production ensures that the food that remains in primitive production today will likewise enter the industrial age of production. It is precisely because we are convinced that this industrial food age is coming that we bow and listen to the prophecies of scientists who occasionally open their laboratory windows today and tell us that the time will come when mankind will obtain food through chemical formulation.

One could say that the nutrients needed to maintain mankind's survival and evolution have evolved from being produced in the factory known as the stomach from the primitive organisms which were eaten, to production in the large stomach equipped with steam power and electricity of the industrial digestion age, until finally the time comes when those nutrients will no longer require primitive organisms at all, and will eventually be obtained artificially.

The poet points to heaven, the scientist builds a ladder that leads to heaven. Science becomes monism, the distinction between inorganic and organic matter disappears, and the conclusion from experiments that everything is a living species leads mankind to create organic matter from inorganic matter that was previously considered nonliving. For example, in 1854, the chemist Berthelot was able to synthesize fatty oil, not at all different from natural substances, from glycerin and acid, and even more easily from hydrocarbons.[180] Today, sugars are also synthesized in the chemist's laboratory, leaving only proteins left to synthesize. In one extreme example—though this has yet to be accurately reported—an academic is said to have created an entire living organism in his laboratory. This gets rid of the duplication and brutality of inorganic matter eaten by organic matter, the plants eaten by animals, and then the animals and plants eaten by mankind, and instead has humans seeking food on the foundation of inorganic and organic matter (which is actually just an indiscriminate collection of chemical elements).

Though this reasoning does run into the shockingly distant future, if one imagines the age of "divine beings," which will come after the extinction of "anthropoids," it can be viewed as a philosophical speculation after all (see where we explain the ideal of social evolution later). We must remember that Malthus is not an old school economist being mocked by the new school economists, but indeed lived one hundred years ago, fifty years before Darwin's *On the Origin of Species* was published. We would rather follow the careful experiments of scientists, considering past evolutionary traces of history, than stubbornly believe in the theories of this mediocre old man and preach the coming of Noah's Flood in the world of economics.

---

[180] Nineteenth century French chemist Marcellin Berthelot. The original text says "Bettereau," but this is just a typo.

"Hydrocarbons" is a general term for compounds consisting only of carbon and hydrogen. Typical examples are benzene and naphthalene.

We must now explain "population" based on a foundation of science. This is to solidify our position biologically in the competition for food, which is part of the species against species competition for survival.

By Darwin's own admission, his theory of the competition for survival was conceived from Malthus's theory of population, and its current state seems to confirm Malthus's theory in biology. It is precisely because of this egregious carelessness in Darwin's work that his *On the Origin of Species* simply fails to provide any theory beyond the discovery that "biological races are not created by God, as told in the creation theory, but come about by evolution." Malthus said that people, who are born at the rate of a geometric sequence, compete over food, which increases at the rate of an arithmetic sequence, and Darwin expanded that idea over all living species and made it the reason for his theory of competition for survival.[181] Just as Malthus lived by the air of individualism at the end of the eighteenth century and failed to understand the profound natural laws of population growth, Darwin, while understanding the facts of biological evolution, which should have been the scientific basis of socialism, was still carried along by the aftermath of individualism, and thus fell into a regrettable error regarding the place of food competition in the theory of biological evolution. For him, it is merely that individuals within the same species clash over competition for the same food as part of the competition for survival, and the winner of that clash continues living.

This truly is regrettable. If only Darwin had been swept up in the winds of socialism, winds advanced enough that Karl Marx had come forward on them—at the very least, if he had been able to shake off that individualist dogma, surely he would not have made the mistake of understanding the competition for survival as merely a competition between individual members of the same species. The most accurate understanding of the time comes from

---

[181] In other words, he came up with the theory that there would be an absolute shortage of food, which would lead to culling within the species.

his contemporary, Huxley.[182] He clarified that the competition for survival between the same species is indirect and unconscious, while the competition for survival between different species, such as between those who feed and those who are consumed, is direct and conscious. Of course, Huxley's "indirect and unconscious competition for survival between members of the same species" refers to the food competition in a narrow sense. It excludes survival competition in the broad sense we have used, that is, the most direct and conscious competition for sex in order to achieve an ideal via the continuation of life. It should also be obvious that, though he says that the competition for food is a competition for survival between members of different species, he has not clearly specified the unit of competition as we did. We know this because, while food competition, which is a competition for survival between species, is direct and conscious when occurring between different species, it is also a direct and conscious competition for survival when the same species competes as a certain unit over the same organisms as food (this unit could be a village during the nomadic era, a nation or social class as it is now, or even a simple family or individual in the case of famine).

However, direct and conscious competition for food among the same species is nothing more than the elimination of other members of that species in order to become the winner of the direct and conscious competition for survival against the different species that serve as food. In a place where the other species that serve as food are so abundant that there is no need to eliminate other members of the same species (for humans, an example would be the primitive age of emperors Yao and Shun), or when the effort put toward eliminating other members of the same species is instead used to cooperate, unify, form one large unit, and become a complete winner above all other

---

[182] Thomas Henry Huxley was an English zoologist. He served as a military doctor and became famous for his research on marine animals. He also defended Darwin's theory of evolution.

biological species (for example, in the era when socialism's ideal is realized), the direct and conscious competition for food becomes species against species.

If, like Darwin, who interpreted the facts of biological evolution from the standpoint of individualism, we interpret, through the competition for survival, the Malthusian theory of population as taking place in all living species—that is, the competition for survival between individual organisms of the same species against other individual organisms of that species—then how could one explain some of the most easily understood facts, such as the protective vibrant colors of certain insects? Everyone knows that this protective color mimics poisonous plants in order for the insect to survive by avoiding the attacks of birds which catch them for food by making these predators think the insect is poisonous, and is not there to scare or to trick and steal the food of other members of the same species.

Although examples such as the protective colors of caterpillars clearly show that the competition for survival is with another species, dogs often fight each other and cats bite each other before the eyes of those who hold cynical views, so they make the rash judgement that carnivores and the like compete with each other individually.[183] However, carnivores are simply asocial creatures who do not cooperate. Their fangs and claws are never honed for the flesh of their own kind, but to rend the flesh of other species who will become prey, thus winning in the competition for survival.[184] If individual creatures are to exist as competitors against individuals of the same species, they must compete directly and consciously for food, even when other species are not scarce and their hunger doesn't overlap with each other, and the very flesh of their own species must fall under the claws and fangs of the victors of the

---

[183] Basically, it's a rash judgment to think that lions, tigers, and the like are fighting each other among their own kind in a competition.

[184] In other words, they become the winners in the competition for survival by taking other species of animals as prey.

competition. Not to mention the phenomenon of carnivores such as wolves existing in packs of thousands in the Siberian wilderness, where other species are abundant. This could only be dismissed as nonsensical. The flesh of thousands of wolves can absolutely never be the food of thousands of wolves. But we cannot dismiss this as nonsense! If the biological evolutionists who idolize Darwin today still want to maintain the individualistic competition for survival, we must ask this very question. Do amoebas survive by eating amoebas? Do budding organisms eat budding organisms to make coral? Do cows eat cows, horses eat horses, swallows eat swallows, pigeons eat pigeons, and butterflies eat butterflies to compete for survival? Do rice plants eat rice plants, potatoes eat potatoes, and pine trees eat pine trees to compete for survival?

We must reiterate here the significance of the most skilled, the fittest, and the strongest in the competition for survival. In other words, the so-called winner of the competition for survival is the one who has the most points of superiority among their peers in the competition for survival against other species, and is able to maintain that superiority for survival. This significance in peer competition is different from the significance this would pose in an opponent. To repeat, the most skilled, fittest, and strongest among their own kind do not compete for survival against the unskilled, unfit, and weak among their own kind, but against other species. The survival of those of the same species who are the most skilled, fittest, and strongest against the others species is the result of the competition for survival.

For example, let us assume that each of us leads one army corps in war. What remains after the war, as a result of the war, are the most skilled, fittest, and strongest in our corps, but the opponent of the war is, of course, the enemy's corps, and the significance of the most skilled, fittest, and strongest is not determined by the battles that each member of our corps wages against the other members of our corps. The significance of the competition for survival is the same. The horse's evolved four legs are not for kicking members of their own kind, but are the result of a superior being able to escape from competitors who are of another species. The canine teeth of cats, tigers, and other members of the feline family are not there to allow them to bite each other, but are the result of a superior being able to overcome a competitor of another species. The needles that hairy caterpillars or hedgehogs have are not there so that members of those species can stab each other. The stinky fart that a mustelid might emit when running away is the result of the fittest member of their species being able to fight off opponents of other species in the competition for survival.

Even though the result of competition for survival and the different opponents are this easy to understand, the fact that, in very specific circumstances, members of the same species will engage in direct and conscious fighting is given as a reason to believe that the winner of the competition for survival is the one who fights other individuals among its own species. It is a unique and extreme situation when a starving tribe of cannibals eats the flesh of another village, and expanding this into a law which extends to the entire biological world is nothing more than irresponsible nonsense.

It is exactly as it seems. The competition for food in the biological world is a competition for survival between the species that seeks to obtain food and the species that is being used as food. It is a competition for survival with the species as a unit, or in the broadest sense, society as a unit. Socialism takes the unit of society in the broadest sense as the entire human race and seeks to make the human race the winner of the competition for survival above all other species. Therefore, in the age of socialism, there will be competition for the realization of the ideals discussed previously, namely, the competition for sex, done with individual persons as the unit, as well as a competition with society as the unit in order to maintain reality, this being the competition for food against other species. How, then, should we think about population theory as it relates to the competition for food in the socialist era?

We see here biology in a very noble light, and we look up to see Darwin's greatness stretching high over the clouds. He says, "A biological species will bear only as many offspring as is necessary for the survival and evolution of that species." From the beginning of the history of philosophy, the existence of a purpose to the universe has required that it be interpreted by speculation. Biology, which Darwin helped significantly in its development, explains the existence of a purpose for everything in the universe as a corollary of scientific research. Does the warbler have a beautiful call because it wants to chirp, or does it want to chirp because it has a beautiful call? Does a butterfly have beautiful wings because it wants to dance, or does it want to dance because it has beautiful wings? Does the lion have fangs because it wants to eat meat, or does it want to eat meat because it has fangs? Such questions are and always have been philosophical subjects. Those who hold either the creationist view or the old-fashioned materialist view, which holds that there is no purpose to the universe, argue that the warbler chirps because of its beautiful voice, the butterfly dances because of its beautiful wings, and the lion is brave and valiant because of its fangs. Yet biology, by induction from solemn facts, has overturned the theory of creation, broken through old-fashioned materialism, and established a theory of cosmic purpose in which everything evolves.

Everything in the universe is attributed to the result of evolutionary desire for survival, from a single wild flower on a roadside, to pines and oaks soaring toward the clouds, insects fluttering above the ground, small birds flying among flowers, whales wailing in the ocean waves, snakes, lizards, dogs, cats, horses, and monkeys wandering across open valleys, to humans waiting for scientists to invent wings to fly like birds, enraptured by the eastern sky dyed red at dawn. The universe has an eternal purpose that mankind, a transient creature, cannot comprehend, an absolute ideal that mankind, a relative being, cannot conceive. It is precisely because of this purpose and ideal that all living things reach their respective goals and try to realize their respective ideals. Those who have the purpose of singing evolve beautiful voices to sing, and those who have the ideal of dancing evolve beautiful wings to dance. The conclusion to this dispute between the two schools of thought, a dispute which has lasted throughout the history of philosophy, has been examined in evidence and unequivocally decided by the solemn and fair judges of biology (it is a pity that many biologists today are not these gold-crowned judges, but rather are content with the lowly profession of executioner).

Population theory is also understood by the biology of cosmic teleology. That is, all living species evolve into their own unique species, each taking the necessary forms in an attempt to adapt to their environment (including other competing species) in order to maintain their existence or evolve. In the same way, each bear as many offspring as necessary for the purpose of survival and evolution. Assuming that the competition for food puts individual organisms against other individuals in the same species, or that the unit for competition is the individual when different species compete against each other, is an error brought about by the dogmatic ideas and speculation of parochial individualism, but using Darwin's greatness to cover and conceal a point sticking up on the horizon of Malthus and his like is not the right way to know genius.[185] Rather, the way to know genius is to know the underlying scientific foundation of socialism, which is that biological species will only bear as many offspring as necessary for their survival and evolution. (So it is an inconsequential and foolish delusion when some at the Munich Convention of Biologists were so fearful that the theory of biological evolution would lead to socialism that they actually sought to eliminate and attack it right there, but

---

[185] We're not sure what the second half means. Does it mean "Darwin's doctrine should not be used to cover up the flaws in Malthus's population theory"? Or does it mean that "it is wrong to use Darwin's doctrine to say things like 'it is okay because some will be culled' when the population exceeds Malthus's limit"? It's difficult to choose, so we translated the text literally.

we can say that some were able to surmise from yet uncertain ideas that the theory of biological evolution would indeed arrive at socialism.)

We ask that those who would study Darwin keep two points in mind. The first is that Darwin is a great man in these two respects: that he confirmed the fact of biological evolution and opened the door to the theory of competition for survival, even if he did not give a deep explanation of it. The second point is that Darwin should be immortalized for his induction of cosmic teleology, and for the solemn fact that all living species evolve into their own specific species in their own forms for the purpose of survival and evolution, and that they bear only what offspring are necessary for that purpose.

Population theory can only be understood on the basis of the conclusions given by Darwin, and the many words of today's economists, who are content to inherit the knowledge of the past before the theory of biological evolution even existed, are but the croaking of frogs without any value whatsoever. According to Darwin, the number of offspring required for a species' survival and evolution decreases as one progresses from the lower classes of biological species to the higher classes of biological species. For example, the rat's birthrate, used when talking about the Malthusian geometric sequence and other less scientific calculations, is a rate of eight thousand rats from one mother born over the course of one year. A bee gives birth to fifty or sixty thousand offspring in a year, and a fly lays two hundred thousand eggs at a time, which will be fully grown in fifteen days—a rate that is said to increase population by one million-fold each week. A single cod has ten million eggs in its abdominal pouch, and the tapeworm has one hundred million eggs in a single node, and moreover, its entire body has 150 nodes. Aphids increase at such a rate that they could cover the entire earth in a few years, and Huxley calculates that almost all plants produce seeds at a rate that would envelope the entire earth in eight or nine years. Yet, as we progress to the higher classes of living species, their numbers decrease, and when we come to birds or beasts, etc., as we all know, they are very few in number.

Darwin concluded from these numbers that "all living species produce as many offspring as are necessary for their survival and evolution." In other words, all living species produce the necessary number of children for the survival and evolution of the species (in the case of humans, the survival and evolution of human society), and if the species needs an enormous number of births, yet these births do not occur enough, the species will quickly perish, just like many lower species. It is not that two hundred thousand flies each compete with two hundred thousand of their own kind for survival, or that fifteen billion tapeworms each produce such huge numbers to compete with fifteen billion of their own kind for survival. Plants with the greatest number of seeds produce enough seeds that they could cover the entire planet because they must maintain their species by the few lucky ones whose seeds are accidentally carried by wind, insects, or birds, and who happen to be spared from becoming food for other organisms. Some tapeworms, which have 150 nodes and hold one hundred million eggs, accidentally enter the water and happen to be eaten by a particular fish they meet. Then, by chance, it enters the fish's body, and by chance, the meat of the fish is eaten by a person, who must also happen to eat it raw. Only then can they enter the intestines of humans, and only then can they sustain their species, thus necessitating such a huge number of eggs.

In the competition for food, the goal is the maintenance of the species, the unit is the species, and the opponent is another species. Thus, a lower species which will produce many more losers in the species-on-species competition will give birth to more offspring in order to maintain their species—in fact, they will often give birth to more losers as sacrifices so that enough molecules will survive in order to maintain their species. As organisms advance through the higher classes, the number of offspring decreases dramatically because they have evolved to the point where there are not so many losers in competition with other species for the survival of their own species; meaning the number of offspring decreases because they do not need as many to maintain the species. Of all the biological species, the human species has the fewest children because it is the biological species that has evolved to the extent that it has the least need to have many children.

Darwin, completely misguided by Malthus, sought to prove in his experiments how intense the competition for survival is throughout the biological world. One example of this was an experiment in which he prevented the invasion of other biological races and experimented with plants reproducing at an alarming rate. Because of this experiment, the competition for survival was interpreted to mean a competition among numerous elements of the same species to exclude others of the same species for their own survival purposes, as if Darwin had extended Malthus' population theory to all species and confirmed it in terms of evolution. In other words, this is individualism, in which each individual person has their own purpose. Thus the Malthusian theory of population, as confirmed by Darwin, is, for the slightly more knowledgeable among economists, the most solid fortress against socialism, and the Malthusian theory of population has today almost extended itself atop the theory of social evolution. The brilliance of a great revolutionary in the history of ideals, however, is not obscured by petty clouds. The biological evolutionists who are now milling about cannot see him in his full glory, but the light that is cast through the clouds is clearly shining in their eyes.

We do not know exactly why Dr. Oka limited himself specifically to "human race," because if the state exists as a unit, then so does the group of peoples within it; in the past there were strong and united religious groups, today there are social classes created by the grand alliance, and there is a single entity known as society formed by humanity against other species. The fact that an ignorant, cruel, and irrational argument was deduced from the authority "for the biological evolution of human races," shows that it is by no means an exception to Darwin's guiding theory of cosmological teleology. If economists, recognizing that biological species have the purpose of survival and evolution as a species, still consider population theory to lie right in front of social evolution, then they can only be called barbaric.

Human beings, which were forced to become losers for the purpose of the survival and evolution of their species, have many children today. However, once socialism is realized, the competition for food will produce fewer losers (we do not say "no losers," the reason for which will be explained later). Yet, they would still say that the number of children required for the continuation of the species, in other words, the population, will grow in a geometric sequence, to the point where three- or four-story buildings would need to be built, causing starvation for all of society, and turning what was once activities which would maintain the survival of the species into that which will actually destroy humanity instead. What a wild, rough conclusion! Truly, those called "professor" or "doctor" are all nothing more than American Indians who have put on some Groucho glasses.

We repeat this declaration: today's astonishing population comes from the fact that the evolution of human races is still in a low state, resulting in a constant stream of losers in competition with other species, which is a natural law necessary for the survival of the species. We understand how an economist who lived before modern biology could do such a thing, but how could a biologist, someone shouldered with the most important duty of giving a foundation to all social sciences—O, Dr. Oka!—allow such a great man as Darwin to be trampled underfoot by the mediocre Malthus, and not find shame in this at all?

Consider that when Malthus said that three-quarters of all children born either die as babies or die after only a quarter of their normal lifespan, it is precisely because human evolution is not yet complete and only one quarter of the human race has evolved to survive, forcing us to constantly produce three-quarters of our species as losers in the competition for survival. The barbarians, whose survival is most difficult because of the material scarcity of natural resources or because of the abandonment, neglect, etc., of their mothers (as is the case with many animals), bear the most children, and today's lower classes, which have the most difficulty surviving under the oppression of the plundering classes, must have many children due to their poverty.

Everything is a law of nature. Thus the lower classes are able to obtain from the fortunate few among their many children the continuation of their own existence (in other words, maintaining reality) and evolution (in other words, the realization of their ideal by the continuation of life). Many others, as Malthus said, up to three-quarters, die as babies in back alleys, malnourished and with lungs full of putrid air. Even those who survive there, due to excessive labor and low degrees of living, die of starvation at one quarter of their normal lifespan, as Lassalle said. We see the so-called overpopulation of the poor as a necessity for the poor themselves. If they did not have so many children, their continued lives would have been ended long ago, perishing as complete losers in the competition for survival. However, the laws of evolution have heightened their reproductive desires astonishingly high, with equal love, so that they have just barely been able to survive and evolve, despite the many losers they produce.

One mustn't express the scorn of a sovereign towards the words "love is the heightened desire to reproduce." The beginning of a vigorous reproductive desire is by no means only found in the unfortunate working class of today. Consider that we Japanese had such a vigorous lust for reproduction that, until the time of Emperor Yuryaku,[186] a shocking number of reproductive relations between humans and fowl or beast had to be forbidden by strict punishment, or even exorcised, accompanied with apologies to the gods.[187] This included not

---

[186] Emperor in the latter half of the 5th century. The "military man" who sent a tribute messenger to China in 478 is seen to be this Emperor Yuryaku. Note that this particular reference is found in the section on Emperor Chuai in the *Kojiki*, and referencing it to Emperor Yuryaku is incorrect. The same example is cited again in volume 4.

[187] Specifically, rituals in Shinto performed in order to remove sins or prevent natural

only human relations, such as between mother and child and brother and sister, but also between human and horse, chicken, and dog. This does not apply exclusively to Japan. Simply look at the Law of Moses—"Whoever lies with an animal shall be put to death"—where it was forbidden under the most grave of punishments.

Such things are unimaginable to our evolved senses now, but in ancient times, when the survival of a species was most difficult and they were forced to produce many losers, it was an essential and vital desire for the survival and evolution of human society. This is nothing mistaken or superfluous in the laws of nature. Let us say that today's vigorous desire to reproduce is God's command to do so for the greater good of the evolution of the universe. If this is true then how can we, once we reach the age of socialism, look back on the raunchiness, disorder, and desolation of today's society and not see the same thing as we see today when we look back at the Law of Moses or the exorcism of the fallen Emperor Yuryaku? What authority does Malthus's skeleton have when laid horizontally directly in front of the theory of social evolution? Socialism removes poverty, which is the main reason for those losers of livelihood, and renders unnecessary the multitude of births that sustain the survival of offspring, which is what lower lifeform must do to survive.

Another reason for the overpopulation of the lower classes is that in addition to poverty, the losers in wars are all from the lower classes. In other words, they are always the losers in the vertical national competition, just as they are forced to make many sacrifices in the horizontal class competition. Just as poverty leads to unavoidable procreation, so too does war lead to overpopulation as a necessary consequence. For example, France today has a population right on the average, and because of this it cannot handle national competition, and, exactly the opposite of what Malthusians would say, it has

---

disasters. Offerings to the spirits were sometimes given.

been said that "too small of a population will destroy a country."[188] This is a fear pervasive among all, not just the imperialists. However, during the period of repeated invasions under Louis XIV and the Napoleonic warfare that engulfed all of Europe, the proliferation of the population was astonishing.

The same was true in the Warring States period of medieval history, when the mercantile system (mercantilism), out of necessity, made population increase its primary objective both in ideological circles and in actual, real-world policy. This increased population became the losers of warfare, and the lower classes were maintained by the few survivors among them. The population, which is increasing at the rate of 500,000 per year in Japan today, is the result of the end of the period of plunder under the Tokugawa aristocracy—that is, the end of the long line of wars and poverty since the beginning of the medieval Warring States period—at least, that's what one might think. In reality, this period of poverty continued under the economic aristocracy, and the unending wars continued with the wars of the Meiji Revolution, the Ten Years' War,[189] the Sino-Japanese War, and the Russo-Japanese War. These wars were not a result of the population seeking refuge in Manchuria or Korea, but a result of the need to maintain the survival of the Japanese people. Because of the nationalistic ideology that demanded the national competition of an uncivilized age, and because of the losers that war and the poverty accompanying war created, the population increased as a result. It is similar to what I explained earlier; a warbler does not sing because it has a beautiful call, just as a butterfly does not dance because it has beautiful wings. The beautiful chirps and beautiful wings were born because there was a purpose to chirp and an ideal to dance. In the same way, the overpopulation

---

[188] In fact, France in the late nineteenth century was suffering from a population shortage and was trying to increase its population through strictly punishing abortion.

[189] The "Ten Years' War" probably refers to the frequent uprisings that occurred during the decade leading up to the end of the Satsuma Rebellion.

of Japan today, according to the theory of cosmic teleology of biological evolution, is not the result of wars being created because of overpopulation, but the result of the proliferation of a nation with a medieval ideology that aims for war, a nation with barbaric ideals that seeks to be victorious through war. The law of nature has given poison to the snake whose purpose is to bite, and fangs to the wolf whose purpose is to eat. As long as the people and the nation do not break free from this snake-like purpose and wolf-like ideal, the Japanese people will forever be subjected to the natural law of lower life forms and suffer from overpopulation. And, transcending class sentiments, the upper classes now stand on this low evolutionary path as much as those in the lower classes.

Thus, socialism seeks to remove the tyrannical institutions that tend to lead to international wars, to overthrow the industrial tyranny that is causing the capitalist trade wars, and to renew the people and the nation even more profoundly in their aims and ideals. Just as the laws of evolution do not give poison to the warbler or fangs to the butterfly, how can overpopulation exist in an ideal socialist age, with the goal of universal peace under a world federation? (We find it unfortunate that those self-proclaimed imperialists who argued for war during the Russo-Japanese War under the pretext of needing more outlets because of overpopulation, and those socialists who argued against war [understanding that the war was fought for the sake of two or three capitalists who, despite their vigor, were not yet a major force], both ended up as worthless, cynical explanations.)

As pure socialists, we must move past emotions regarding social classes, and must absolutely not sully the attitude and manner of scientific research. In other words, just as it is a fallacy to interpret population theory from the side of the capitalist class through individualism and to place the burden of moral responsibility on the poor as individuals, so is rejecting population theory through individualism from the side of the lower classes and arguing that the capitalists are poor because they are greedy and immoral; both of these are dogmatic arguments which have no contact with socialism whatsoever.

Clearly, the large population of the lower classes is a social evolutionary process at the disposal of the upper classes. More specifically, for the sake of one general's success, many bones wither,[190] and for the sake of one man's prosperity, thousands of peasants and laborers pass away in poverty and collapse from hypothermia and hunger, to the point that a large population is needed. This is what we meant when we first turned the moral discretion of the lower classes, Malthus's so-called restraint, upside down and declared that "without the vigorous reproductive desires of the lower classes, there would be no wealthy classes today."

As the reproductive desires of the poor are despicable when viewed through the lens of individualist ideology, it goes without saying that our assertion resonates as a disregard for the rights of the lower classes as individuals. A socialist cannot be an individualist no matter what. If there are philanthropists who, in the name of socialism, say that all we have to do is to insist on the well-being of the poor as individuals, we should despise these philanthropists for trying to be faithful servants of socialism, which draws all its theories from cold, hard science. Guided by their own discontent, those who have gathered under the great umbrella of socialism, or those who have inherited the individualism of the French Revolution a hundred years ago, yet remain silent about its dogmatism, blame the current poverty of the lower classes on the sins of the upper classes and regard all those in the upper classes as criminals. There is no irrationality in the laws of evolution known as the laws of nature. Yet, because they have built their banner of socialism on such dogmatic reasoning, despite some impassioned arguments based on noble character, they are always rebuffed with the question, "Then is God biased,

---

[190] In one of the Chinese classical texts, there is a passage which laments the sacrifices made by ordinary citizens as a result of war in this same way, "For the sake of one general's success, many bones wither." (Specifically, this is found in "Two Poems Written in the Year of Ji Hai" by Cao Song.)

and His abilities imperfect and lacking?" This has led to the misrepresentation of socialism as a nest of traders with a solid mass of jealousy who bemoan social injustice.

Human society is a single, unified entity. The poor and the rich are each part of a single entity called society. In other words, the individual person is the society, and the poor are sacrificed today not because of the sins of the rich, but because of the sins of the other individual persons. For society to evolve, it must first evolve certain parts of itself, at the expense of other parts of itself. Therefore, the rich, who today are placed in a happy environment, are also part of the body of the poor. The poor who are sacrificed are part of the body of the rich, the German emperor is part of the beggar on the street, and the whore who prostitutes herself in the shade of a willow tree is part of the Dutch queen. The pitiful Malthus is part of us, and the laughable professors and doctors, and even the Buddha, are part of Christ.

Mankind did not exist individually before the contract came about or before conquest and consummation, as was hypothesized in the age of individualism. As the scientific basis of biological evolution proves, we are merely parts of a single individual that originally split off like an amoeba from a single humanity. Individuals have a purpose of evolution and survival as individuals. In order to achieve this purpose, each takes a form that is adapted to that purpose. The single organism of human society—the single organism which is an element of humanity separated by space—takes on forms over the course of its evolutionary process that are each adapted to its survival and evolutionary purposes.

For the purpose of this explanation, we will do a little comparison of this large individual, the human species, to an individual of a lower life form. Of course, we should not understand society as a single body with a neck, legs, torso, and stomach, as in the old explanation of society as an organic life form, an explanation which existed before biology and was little more than playing with metaphors (this will be explained later in *The So-Called Theory of Japan's*

National Polity and its Restorative Principle of Revolution). However, the reason we treat the lower classes as sacrifices in human society today is entirely because the degree of evolution of this large individual is the same as that of a pure lower organism.

The lower organisms, because of the difficulty of survival due to material dangers or other species, always sacrifice a part of their body to escape. The sacrificed part is then quickly replaced and they return to their original form to achieve their purpose of survival as an organism. Worms, leeches, and other organisms that cannot run away quickly regain their original form even if a part of their body is cut off. A crab can lose its pincers, but soon grows small pincers to compensate for the loss. Even if a newt loses all four legs or a lizard escapes with its tail cut off, they will quickly make up for the loss and return to their original form, because all of them have no other choice but to sacrifice parts of themselves in order to achieve their purpose of survival, and how they function is built upon that necessity of sacrifice. Even in the great human society, at today's level of evolution, we have no choice but to make the same sacrifices to survive as the lower forms of life.

With that said, we are gradually learning how to avoid material dangers such as earthquakes, floods, winds, harsh waves, etc., and we are also gradually advancing to the position of victors in the competition for survival against other living species, such as plants, animals, and the microorganisms that feed on us. However, smaller political units—that is, nations—or smaller economic units—that is, companies and trusts—are in fierce competition for survival, and each unit, as a unit, must constantly compensate for the deficient parts of the individuals living within it to maintain its individual survival. To elaborate, the lower classes of the nation—that is, the classes that are doomed to wither and die as skeletons—compensate these deficiencies of the nation via the means of overpopulation, and the lower classes of companies and trusts—that is, the laborer class, who is plundered and wails in poverty—compensate for deficiencies economically or in companies via the means of overpopulation.

Population growth is not something to be feared, for without it poverty and war would have wiped humanity off the face of the earth long ago. That is true. Population growth is not something to be feared. What is to be feared is that the lower classes have begun to question why they are needlessly giving birth to so many children who will only die—and, not waiting for scientists to prepare answers to their question, have begun waving their manes around in anger, like caged lions, and rejecting their duty of sacrifice. O wonderful laws of nature! They were once used like pigs, giving birth only for most of their children to be used as slaves, landowners taxing them viciously, able to do nothing more than shed tears and hope to be saved in the afterlife, never even knowing they were being used as sacrifices.

Even today, not knowing this, the peasants and wage slaves bear many children, carry them on their backs, pat their heads and sigh, "My children, how can you make it in this wayward world?" The evolution of society is the deepening and broadening of a sense of brotherhood. In ancient times, the sense of brotherhood among siblings was shallow; to them, not only other village nations, but even their own chiefs and sovereigns were incomprehensible, and their sense of brotherhood was narrow in this respect. Yet, as society evolved, the sense of brotherhood spread widely throughout nations and the world, and at the same time, it made people deeply love their parents, children, and siblings as much as or more than themselves. It is to seek the satisfaction of this love that the interpretation of population theory was demanded.

It is not that the population only increased once we entered the era of Malthus. Japan's birthrate did not reach 550,000 per year only once economics started being lectured on. The proportion of population was much higher in the Middle Ages than during the modern age, and was much higher in ancient times than during the Middle Ages. People simply had shallow and narrow sympathies, so they did not feel much pain for the death of children, nor did they have any doubt about the freely growing upper class. Natural law, however, does not stagnate.

The deep and broad brotherhood consciousness of our time is by no means that of a time when people were content to allow sacrifice in the form of slaves and serfs. Thus, this brotherhood consciousness put mankind on the rails of human evolution and brought about the French Revolution, which overthrew the king and the aristocracy with cries for bread and a constitution. This bread, however, was not given, and the new nobility, born on a thrown constitution, began stealing the bread once again. Mothers and fathers cried tears of love, thicker than drops of oil, onto the faces of their innocent, sleeping babies, lamenting that life was still so difficult.

Malthus shakes the sleeves of his priest's garb and ruthlessly holds the poor morally accountable. However, although natural law takes knowledge from their hands, art from their eyes, and music from their ears, it also pulls on their sleeves and lures them to the city of carnal lust, opens their lips and pours cheap liquor within, and even takes their bedding and makes them sleep with their spouses on a daily basis, provoking their lust to reproduce as much as it can, almost like a prostitute trying to intoxicate her customer. This is how children are born. The children are then nuzzled in the parents' laps. Where is the distinction between the Virgin Mary and our own mothers when it comes to their love for their children? For the love of its child, even a pheasant, crying in a burnt plain, will turn into a hawk and chase down a weasel.

Remember that the first of the troops that stormed the castle of Marseilles was a very delicate little girl—revolution happens to satisfy love. Go to heaven, where Malthus said the deceived poor go, and argue the population theory that the number of ascendants who get there is too high. This is the time for parents with a deepened sense of brotherhood to look at their many children sleeping on their knees and raise their eyes to look at the upper classes, worried about their future! Here is where the broadened sense of brotherhood, with the force of a flood, overturns carriages, sends diamonds flying, climbs over laden tables, breaks through the glass windows of the ballroom, and becomes a revolution—overpopulation is based on social necessity, and the upper class should fear it in that sense. Only in this case, though. In a world where the red flag of socialism, torn with arrows and bullets, is placed in a museum and becomes the story of a people enjoying peace and equality, there is no reason to think that population growth is a fearful prospect (we will explain more about population in a socialist world later).

Humanity, being the most evolved of all other living species, has the fewest number of losers to sacrifice. Thus, it is also the biological species with the fewest number of births. Finally, as a transitional organism evolving into a higher species, it is the species that will sacrifice even fewer inferiors and therefore give birth to even fewer children in the future. To think that, even after today's humanity evolves further and realizes socialism, thus lowering the rate of losers even further which also results in a lower birth rate, somehow the population will still increase in a geometric progression, and thus all of humanity will starve to death (or this implemented socialism will be destroyed, and society will cycle back to the beginning, as was the school of thought before evolution)—it is the same as looking at a newt who has lost all four of its limbs, seeing it regrow those lost limbs, and applying that to humanity. When humanity has evolved to the point of no longer needing to sacrifice its limbs like that, they still say, "Humanity isn't losing any of its limbs at all, so eventually we will grow eight limbs, then sixteen limbs, then thirty-two limbs, and so on in a geometric sequence." It completely ignores reality—open your hands and look at them. It is unimaginable that even university professors in this newt society would draw such inferences.

Of course, the Japanese scholars who exist as mere translators are not the responsible actors in these matters,[191] rather the responsible actor is our

---

[191] Meant to be bitter cynicism against scholars who merely bring Western theories to Japan literally and directly, without any other thought.

Darwin. He took Malthus's dogmatism as a guide, so while he provided the basis for socialism with his induction of the fact that "a biological species will only bear enough offspring to ensure its survival and evolution," he counteracted this with the individualist stance that "human evolution is by competition with each other based around excessive fertility." These words were adopted by Benjamin Kidd and became *Social Evolution*, which is heralded as the greatest book since *On the Origin of Species*, and furthermore, it resonated with the current academic class, who cannot even understand it, thinking of it as a theory of social degradation or extinction. Humanity's excessive reproductive capacity is not due to competition. It is for the survival of the species in a competition for survival against other species.

If one thinks that an individual who merely has high fertility intensifies the individual-on-individual competition for survival and best evolves a biological species—their reasoning power is so low it is worthy of derision! Flies, for example, lay two hundred thousand eggs and have such excessive reproductive capacity that their numbers grow to one hundred million every week, so they must have evolved two hundred thousand times, in fact one hundred million times more than human civilization, and must be building their own civilization by hovering like a black mountain over our decaying corpses. Since tapeworms have the excessive reproductive capacity to lay fifteen billion eggs, they must have evolved fifteen billion times higher than mankind. The present world must be the twentieth century of the tapeworm; an age where the little tapeworm Kidd authored his book on tapeworm evolution, attracting the adoration of the fly-like academic class. To the scholars of today who worship Malthus with hands clasped together in prayer, Kidd and others like him must seem like people with brains radiating golden light. To us, they are merely three-foot-tall children who deserve to be teased and scorned with a few words.

Let us not forget about *Lectures on Evolutionary Theory* by Dr. Asajiro Oka, who we designated as a representative scholar of Japan although he wrote in the language of Westerners. He says this:

> Some people believe that the suffering of life is based on competition, and that the reason for the competition is the increase in population, and that it is therefore necessary to limit the number of children born, but, as we explained earlier, this cannot be said to be a good countermeasure.

Needless to say, we know, as does Dr. Oka, that the neo-Malthusians' social reform measures were blind and purposeless. However, the whole of *Lectures on Evolutionary Theory,* on which Dr. Oka looked back in his conclusion and said, "as we explained earlier," is complete chaos, a mere list of facts and not a single theory created from them. What *is* explained therein is that, since all biological species evolve via the competition for survival between individual members of the same species, the evolution of humanity, with its excessive reproductive abilities, follows the Malthusian theory of population. However, this error is equally the fault of the lack of organization in the current theory of biological evolution itself. We have specifically singled out Dr. Oka, who has been faithful to his research, because he is a leading scholar in Japan, and not because he alone is to be blamed:

Socialism is not an attempt to stifle, discourage, or slow down the competition for survival, which leaks out of evolutionary theory, as explained above. It still accommodates the competition for food in order to maintain the reality of the whole human race as a large social unit against other species. It also accommodates the competition for sex between individuals among their own species to realize the ideal, which we discussed earlier.

Chapter 8

We will now explain how human beings are transitional organisms who will most likely go extinct. Yes, this is a conclusion of the theory of biological evolution. Until today, the theory of biological evolution had no conclusion.

According to the knowledge that mankind has attained to date, everything across the entire earth is evolving, and all evolution is a competition for survival. The desire to survive as a living being is the very essence of evolution, even in the lower animals, birds, insects, fish, and shellfish, which, like our species, are not considered to be making a clear conscious effort to evolve. That consciousness is the difference between different degrees of evolution, and the desire for survival—this evolutionary consciousness—is the absolute consciousness of the universe. We should not be overly concerned with philosophical speculation. At any rate, if we as a species have a desire to survive as living beings, and if there is a competition for survival because of that desire, then this is sufficient to affirm that we are a transitional organism that will evolve further, unless one is skeptical of evolution itself.

First, we must continue our discussion of population from earlier. Upon entering the age of socialism, what will happen to the competition for survival with society as the unit, the human race as a large individual against other species, and the human race with individuals as a unit against other individual human beings?

Two inferences can be drawn. One is that socialism will result in fewer losers in the competition for survival, and that the number of births and deaths will balance out. It is one's own choice to infer this, and of course it fits perfectly with the facts and theories of biology. Of course, it is possible that this situation will come about immediately after the realization of socialism, when the production mechanisms of steam and electricity will allow mankind to be a complete winner in the competition for survival against the species it feeds on, just as the fangs are the production mechanism for the tiger and the wing is the production mechanism for the warbler. However, we are still not a perfect winner against those species that seek to feed on us, such as microorganisms. Thus, it is clear that the uninterrupted survival and evolution of the human species will require a large population, even at the expense of those who die from disease. There are also material dangers such as earthquakes, volcanoes, floods, wind, and tides. Still, as we evolved from the savages who were forced to compete for survival against the beasts of prey, building houses on lakes or sleeping in trees to shelter ourselves, today we have achieved complete victory over those beasts. Similarly, there is no doubt that medical progress will lead to a complete victory over microorganisms, though microorganisms are certainly more difficult adversaries than beasts. Thus, the time when a high population is needed to compensate for the deficiencies caused by disease will be over, and the need for that population will diminish.

The class of scholars who call themselves empirical would probably scoff at such reasoning by calling it a "fantasy," were it not for the fact that they see before them the condition of the modern savage, as they see before them the excavated remains of primitive man. But if they are capable of looking at the ancient remains and the modern savage's condition and deducing the principles that have caused the evolution of our civilization of today, it only makes sense that the same level of reasoning can be used to describe the conditions that are most likely to evolve from today onward. The inference that there will be no more deaths from disease (today often due to social causes) is possible if one understands the evolution that has taken place so far, in which today's civilized people are no longer eaten by beasts, and applies that continued evolution to the future as well. Just as a house on a lake or a nest-like house in a tree excavated today would not be strange in primitive times when people were struggling for survival against beasts, so a hospital, which is not considered strange at all today, would be of great interest to "the deities" if its buildings were excavated with the remains of "anthropoids," as it shows they were struggling for survival against microbes during the age when the ruins were preserved. The material dangers that are slowly being eliminated today will also be removed with evolution, and so the inference that the number of births and deaths will balance out is justified.

Another inference, we would argue, is that the population will grow even more. The human population has been increasing as it advances to a position of victory in the competition for survival against other species, despite the fact that since the time of the proto-humans, there have been countless losers in the competition for survival against other species. Therefore, the inference is that we will see continued population growth as we advance further to the top through the realization of socialism. This is why we said earlier that population growth is not something to be feared in the age of socialism, and thus left room to discuss it from different perspectives. Of course, it goes without saying that natural law is not something to be feared by anyone. Today's population growth is feared only from the point of view of the class interests of the upper classes, but from the point of view of the survival and evolution of society, it is an indispensable design from heaven.

We believe with infinite joy that we are entering an era of socialism and that the population will grow even more massively—but upon hearing this, economics will interject with: "If true, then the competition for survival will grow intense once again." We are not speaking to these little ostriches with their heads buried in the sand. All living species not only strive for the goal of maintaining the survival of their species, but they also work with even greater intensity toward the ideal of evolving their species. We know, as Darwin experimented with plants, that all living species reproduce endlessly when other species, their enemies, are eliminated, because their methods of survival, which had produced countless losers against the other enemy species, develop without hindrance. It is a biological fact, however, that all living species seek to reproduce and evolve even further than they are able to sustain themselves.

The human species, which has reproduced from the original one to today's billion, has reproduced in large numbers to compensate for the deficiency of all the losers in the survival of it as a species. In addition to this, our own evolution has eliminated other species, as Darwin showed with plants, either by eliminating our enemies, such as beasts of prey or microorganisms, or by conquering or subjugating other species, such as plants and animals, by means of livestock-farming or agriculture, thereby increasing their population to what it is today, and thus reaching the level of evolution we see today.

Therefore, population growth can be considered to have two designs. One is to maintain the status quo by compensating for the loss of the losers in the competition for survival with other species. The other is the result of species evolution with the goal of realizing the ideal, which can be seen since there are fewer and fewer losers in the competition with other species for survival. From this we would like to go beyond the first inference that the number of births and deaths will balance out as we enter the age of socialism, and infer that the population will increase even more significantly.

Regarding this, there is a pessimistic viewpoint which assumes that all living species have no purpose other than the mere survival of their species. There is also an optimistic viewpoint which holds that all living species seek to achieve the goal of species survival as well as to realize the ideal of further species evolution. If one believes that a race is simply about survival, then what is first and foremost incomprehensible is the evolution from the original human being to billions of individuals. Specifically, it is as follows. In the ancient days of the monarchies, all members of society were obliged to be loyal to the monarch and sacrifice for the survival of the species in order for the monarch, a molecule of the society, to survive. Then, during the aristocratic period of the Middle Ages, in order for a small minority of society, the aristocracy, to survive, many members of the warrior and commoner classes assumed the obligation of loyalty and sacrificed themselves for the survival of their race. Now, in modern democracies, all the molecules of society have evolved to the point where they all survive individually and seek the survival of the species. The inference that the only purpose of a species is to maintain survival ignores this fact of social evolution. The progression from the survival of a species by one person alone, to the survival of a species by a few classes alone, and then to the ideal of the survival of a species by the entire population without any classes at all is an expression in the ideal of law, which shows that the existing population increases with each victory in the competition for survival. (The ideal of law is the ideal of society. Justice, which is the ideal of law, has evolved from monarchies to aristocracies, then to democracies, because the ideal of the organism known as human society has evolved. It is the height of ignorance to interpret the law as if it were created for the plundering classes to do evil,[192] as some cynical socialists do.) If we accept this past social evolution, it is not difficult to infer that the realization of socialism will lead to a great increase in population in the sense of evolution of the human species, as the species of humanity advances to a more victorious position in the competition for survival against other species.

The fact that population growth today is feared comes from the fact that the lower classes have evolved to the point where their deep and thick sense of brotherhood means they cannot bear to mourn their children dying as sacrifices, this evolution being the evolution of society, and that the upper classes now fear a revolution, which is a method of social evolution. So, even though the population is increasing in the sense of species evolution more than in the sense of species survival, the increase in population in the socialist era is not an increase in a frightening sense, but in the sense of social evolution. It is similar to how an increase in the population of the upper class would not be a target of fear, but rather a target of joy for them.

---

[192] This interpretation is the conception of "law is a tool of the ruling class," which Marx stated.

Socialism becomes monarchism in the biological world when human society is viewed as an individual, and aristocracy in the biological world when humanity is separated and viewed as separate classes. The current monarchs and aristocrats have become the greatest winners in the race for survival that sustains the status quo, and so they have many children in order to evolve further, and every child itself survives and evolves. If the realization of socialism leads to the entire society becoming a monarch, an aristocrat, and a complete champion over the biological world, the population will multiply with infinite joy to realize its ideal and will survive completely. (This is what we meant when we said, "Socialism is not something which drags the upper class into the lower class. It is social evolution which seeks to erase all classes by lifting the lower class into the upper class," back in volume 1, *The Economic Justice of Socialism*, and so it should be obvious that socialism is not "egalitarian democracy" as it is commonly referred to.)

Yes, we would like to believe from this inference that the population will increase. Social evolution will then use this form of increased population as an intense competition to develop individuality, and the greater the population grows, the more outstanding this individuality will be, and so the speed at which it will develop is unimaginable to us right now. The decisive factor in this competition will be the competition for sex between all molecules of society. All men and women, all molecules of society, will compete with each other to obtain the ideal man or woman, and through the union of the ideal man and woman, society will evolve by realizing the ideal of that society through the offspring of this ideal couple, and that offspring will be the continuation of life. We believe that human society will become a complete victor in competition for food and that the population will continue to increase because humans are a transitional organism which will continue to evolve further based on the theory of biological evolution. Likewise, we believe that just as the rate of evolution is much faster today with a billion competing males and females than it was in the time of Adam and Eve, when there was no competition at all, so too will the competition between an even larger population of males and females be much faster than today with a smaller population of one billion.

Therefore, even in a socialist world, it is inevitable that there will be many lost loves. Although there is no competition for food, the lack of which creates a true, physical pain in reality, the pain experienced by the losers in the competition for sex who look towards the ideal but are unable to realize it is simply a result of the natural laws of social evolution. We socialists cannot prevent it, nor do we dream of doing so. The pain felt in reality of looking towards a higher ideal, yet being unable to reach, it must grow larger. We must have intense competition for sex in order for "anthropoids" to evolve into "deities."

It goes without saying, however, that we should not imagine the losers in love from the era of socialism to come from the competition for sex which exists in today's society (see the previous explanation). All love affairs today are hindered by social classes. And not only is class the obstacle to romance between mutual love, but because of class segregation, many are subjected to the most devastating arrows of love, the so-called unrequited love. In the socialist age, however, love between those in mutual love is not obstructed, and the losers in love are those who have unrequited love. This is because the men and women who have the most truth, the most goodness, and the most beauty, in other words, personalities closest to the "deities," are the focal point of love in society as a whole, and, therefore, to get close to these deities requires someone who is both close to a deity themselves and also the opposite sex of their partner deity, and so many who are not these things will have to suffer the pain of unrequited love.

However, the inadequate truth, goodness, and beauty of today's losers in love have been created by their unfortunate social class, and so they don't have the virtue, knowledge, or looks required to attain their ideal member of the opposite sex. To put it simply, the lower classes despair at ever having an unrequited love at all, let alone the agony of wanting and not being able to have it with the opposite sex of the upper classes. Society first gradually realizes its ideal at the expense of many of its molecules and then exerts its realized effect on all its molecules (some sociologists call this "assimilation by imitation.")[193]

The general fact is that the knowledge, morals, and appearance of the upper class are the ideals of that class, as well as of society as a whole, in that they are what society as a whole tries to imitate and attain. Therefore, even a dull country girl cannot fail to fall in love with the mind of a philosopher. A prostitute who sells her chastity for a living cannot fail to fall in love with the beard and cheekbones of a handsome moralist. A chauffeur who drives a wagon around in the dust cannot help but fall in love with the sound of a koto leaking from deep within his living room.[194] The only reason they have no unrequited love is because they have already despaired of it. They think of it as "out of their league," and although they have already fallen in love, they despair that it will not bear fruit, and so they will not move their hearts to love—what a tragedy!

Not only is free competition limited to within the same classes, economically speaking (see where we explained the two categories of free competition in the first volume, *The Economic Justice of Socialism*), but free competition of love is limited to the narrow confines of society within the castle walls of a class. It is a lowly and tepid competition consigned to the ideal within that class. Beggars love beggars, laborers love laborers, peasants love peasants, prostitutes love players, foolish noble ladies love potato-faced young masters, the husband loves his wife, the male thief or arsonist loves a female

---

[193] Considering what is mentioned later in 8-5, we believe the sociologist alluded to is Gabriel Tarde.

[194] A koto is a Japanese zither instrument.

thief or pickpocket. What kind of social evolution is there today, limited to such a small society and satisfied with such a low ideal of the opposite sex?

When socialism is realized, when the present lower classes advance to the upper classes, when all mankind become monarchs and aristocrats standing above all things in heaven and earth, the world of love will no longer be limited to a small bedroom or a meet-up club. The ideal object of love will not be a prostitute, not a potato-face, not a diamond, but the love between the Buddha and Mary, which has a large audience of all mankind. The ideal of love is the ideal of society. When men and women, the molecules of society, fall in love with the ideal of society, society realizes that ideal through its offspring, the continuation of life, and thereby evolves. Ask today's men and women about the ideal. True, good, and beautiful like Buddha and Christ, and true, good, and beautiful like Mary will surely be the ideal of love.[195] This is the ideal that society should realize.

Yet today, society has not evolved to that level, and because of the class divide, all knowledge, all morality, all appearance of a class remains true, good, and beautiful within that class, class-created by class ideals. As we also said in the previous volume, *The Ethical Ideal of Socialism*, conscience today is goodness based around class, and much of knowledge is also truth based around class. Similarly to how much of knowledge is only class-truth, much of the faith of the lower classes is carried out by sardine heads,[196] and their

---

[195] The original text says "Mary Avalokiteshvara." This may be referring to the practice of Japanese Christians disguising the Virgin Mary as a Buddhist deity (usually the Bodhisattva Kannon) when Christianity was heavily persecuted in Japan. Kita may also be trying to make a point about a synthesis between Christian and Buddhist ideals in the Virgin Mary.

[196] We don't know about other events, but there is still a custom of attaching holly to sardine heads during Setsubun to drive away demons. It is probably with this custom in mind that Kita uses the sardine head as an example to explain folk beliefs. According to

philosophy is also destined to involve many foxes and raccoon-dogs (just as the knowledge of the upper scholarly classes, which we have now been fortunate enough to transcend, is also class-generated and pathetic). In other words, because all people are socially created, moral and intellectual judgments are created by that person's social class, and thus become class-goodness and class-truth.

It is the same with appearance. What we have today is nothing more than class-beauty. As the saying goes, "the apple doesn't fall far from the tree." Today's beautiful and ugly women are, with the exception of the slightest variation in individuality, completely class-created and stereotyped. And the "same blood" is merely the inheritance of a class formula. That famous criminal anthropologist who did not know that social class produced looks, saw that the criminal class had a stereotypical look, and concluded that criminals were all born that way.[197]

In the same way (to begin with, the only reason there is such a thing as innate is because the criminal classes are "of the same blood" in that they inherit what is socially created by that criminal class), the looks of the upper classes and the looks of the lower classes are all socially created by their upbringing and inherited from the same blood, their socially created ancestors. The reason such cruel, cold laughs escape the lips of the capitalist class is because, much like those poor who are resigned to live in honorable poverty cannot be honest or frank, the capitalists are forced to be cunning and conniving by the social situation they are in. The reason they have their hair done to show off and their noses pointed towards the sky is because they don't know how to equally respect others or be humble regarding themselves, and

---

Kita, these beliefs were created by the class conscience of the lower classes.

[197] No name was mentioned, but Kita is likely referring to the Italian Casare Lombroso. Lombroso was well-known as the founder of criminal anthropology and expressed the sentiments that Kita references here.

are instead placed in the social situation of being surrounded by those constantly trying to suck up to one another. A young master of an estate has the interesting byname "potato" because of his class conventions from the time he foolishly plowed the fields, and a noble lady has a conformist appearance with no respectability or attractiveness because she is confined to the inner parlor of the estate. It is absolutely not funny when a noble lady is actually the loser in the competition for sex compared to a prostitute.

Just as we, who were originally separated from a single human race, have become several races according to the geographical environment (climate, etc.) and dozens of ethnic groups according to the historical environment (each of which has its own formulation), so too does the class environment have its own formulation. The same is true of the workers' ugly faces, crude limbs, and demeanor. These are born from the socially created class patterns of the present generation along with the inherited socially created class patterns of our ancestors. Because of the difficulties of life, they do not have the wealthy appearance of those who have risen to power and call themselves "businessmen," nor do they have the razor-sharp beards of the politicians who are favored by fate. They are pure savages, skeletal, their skin becoming like the Negro's after being exposed to the summer heat, the wind, and the snow, and they have no knowledge, no hobbies, and no high morals; they are controlled and driven like a machine. It is no wonder that they do not even fall in love with the upper classes whose figures are slender, fingers like silk, and cheeks like white roses. If an English princess, or one similar station, met a passerby, the passerby would not even be able to flatter her, but would flee in fear after being unnecessarily scolded by a policeman. If the German emperor were to visit Japan and his carriage were to enter a city with hilly roads,[198] one would not be able to invite him over with a simple "Can you spare a moment?"

---

[198] Kita may be referring to Nagasaki specifically, which is known for its hilly terrain and exotic atmosphere

Beautiful women and men are in love with the younger generation of all societies. But the reason why these lower-class men and women do not feel the pain of love when they see a beautiful upper-class person is precisely because of despair, just as the average laborer does not feel the pain of wanting to be a member of Mitsui or Iwasaki. They may not be aware of this despair, just as they are not moved by love. Similarly, though, there is a passive awareness of "Why are we so hungry?" and an active awareness of "Why are they so rich?" Along with the negative awareness of wondering why the men and women we fall in love with have been sold or bought by their parents, and thus have lost so many opportunities for love, comes the positive awareness of wondering why they are so beautiful and we, who are so ugly, cannot fall in love with them.

This is when the revolution will appear on the horizon with bold and brilliant steps, and with the fulfillment of the revolution there will be no despair of love in this sense. Not daring to limit oneself to the aspect of beauty, all the members of society, with equal material protection and free spiritual development, will have complete freedom: those who love knowledge will fall in love with those who are broad in knowledge, those who adore morality will fall in love with those who are high in morality, those who love beauty will fall in love with beautiful women or beautiful men. And because of the freedom allowed and high number of competitors, men will evolve their truth, goodness, and beauty through competition with men, and women will do the same with women. The one who has the most truth, goodness, and beauty in his or her evolution will acquire the opposite sex who has truth, goodness, and beauty, and will pass on that truth, goodness, and beauty to his or her offspring, thereby realizing the ideals of society. This is the world of geniuses in the broad sense of the word. The individual who has acquired the truth of heaven, the goodness of heaven, and the beauty of heaven will become the center of love and will be revered by society as a whole—and once it reaches this form, it will be the perfection of socialism, which also happens to coincide with the ideal of individualism.

The great tide of individualism began to flow by eliminating the absolute and unlimited rights of the pope and invoking freedom of thought. It goes without saying that the pope, who is only one member of society, has no right to determine what is true and what is good for all members of society, and it also goes without saying that the "theory of national polity," a school of thought, has no right to reign as pope over the world of thought, oppressing the free development of individuality and enforcing what it holds to be true and good. Nor is anyone allowed the power to pass judgment on beauty, as the "Fukugami," or god of fortune, reaches out his ugly hand to separate and unite men and women.

All evolution is a competition for survival. The deciding authority in the competition for survival is the great authority possessed by all evolution, and even Christ must not have it. The truth, goodness, and beauty approved by a majority vote in one age are only the truth, goodness, and beauty of that age. However, in the next age, the majority vote of that age will determine their own truth, goodness, and beauty. And the majority vote, the most numerous and true vote, is not based on parliamentary debate, nor on public opinion in the press, nor on direct legislation, but on the ideal of men and women from among all molecules of society.

However, since today's society is hierarchical and class-based, the ideal of love has become the husband, the potato, the prostitute, and the lady with her nose pointed at the sky, which is a very low-class ideal. As the ideal evolves with society and classes are removed entirely, that ideal will broaden and elevate itself. When equal material protection and free spiritual development are extended to all members of society, that is when the clasped hands of young men and women will have absolutely unlimited power, like that of the pope. This is the world in which the individual is absolutely free.

Individualism, which was sparked by anger at the will of the pope or emperor to determine what is true, good, and beautiful, would actually have its ideal be realized by the realization of socialism. Therefore, we do not exclude individualists, nor do we exclude many of today's social revolutionaries who call themselves socialists though they have inherited individualist ideas. An individual person and society stand on different ground when viewed as a small individual compared to a large individual. Socialism's final destination asserts the ideal that the will of all members of society, men and women, will have the absolute freedom to decide all truth, goodness, and beauty just as the pope and emperor did in the past. As Plato put it, "The part does not precede the whole, and the whole does not precede the part."[199] The individual person is part of society, and society is the totality of the individual person. However, those who can be called "podium socialists" do not understand the evolution of society and do not have any ideals (Mr. Higuchi's description of Mr. Yano's ideals as "fantasies" in the previous section is an example of this). Put simply, they are just a blind bunch of activists.

It can be said that the demands of individualism are satisfied under socialism. However, socialism is only socialism, and the ultimate goal is the survival and evolution of society. How, then, will society evolve through the realization of socialism?

Still, though I may speak of this future of social evolution, my own deductive capabilities are quite poor, and my pen just as weak. I sometimes feel a full-body shudder with a kind of religious exultation. But please let me have the most conventional scientist's attitude and imagine the society of the near future—first of all, poverty and crime will disappear. Then there will be no more suffering of life, no more brutal conscience or ugly countenances created by our bitter struggle. The evolution of material civilization will spread equally throughout society, and the spiritual development of society as a whole, also spreading equally, will raise the degree of knowledge and art to a much higher level. Economic marriage and slave morality will disappear, all

---

[199] This may be a reference to Parmenides, wherein Plato discusses the part and the whole.

members of society will gain godlike independence, and the development of individuality will be almost absolutely free. The demands of the ego become a social evolution with their own moral significance, and the development of sociality becomes an unnecessary morality as there are no more conflicts between unethical social organization and moral obligations. The whole society develops the ability to understand the individuality of a genius by raising their standard, and men and women who embody the truth, goodness, and beauty of heaven become objects of veneration by the older members of society, and are rewarded with love by the younger members of society. Boys, in order to obtain girls who possess the ideal of truth, goodness, and beauty, will increasingly improve their own truth, goodness, and beauty, and girls, in order to obtain boys who possess the ideal of truth, goodness, and beauty, will increase their own truth, goodness, and beauty. In society, the most outstanding individuals in terms of truth, goodness, and beauty flourish through heredity, engaging in competition for sex to pass on even greater truth, goodness, and beauty to their children. The superior individuality, truth, goodness, and beauty of those children with the added truth, goodness, and beauty through heredity will also add more truth, goodness, and beauty through their own sex competition and will further pass this on to the next generation.

Ah, what will the "anthropoids" evolve into after accumulating all this hereditary truth, goodness, and beauty? According to biology, instinct is the accumulation of heredity, and it is precisely the accumulation of heredity that has evolved organisms from a single-celled organism into countless species, each with its own instincts. Therefore, when the time comes when the ideal "anthropoid" of today can be realized through the accumulation of heredity by the perfect competition of love between men and women, the human race will cease to exist and a world of "deities" will be established. And just as humans differ from monkeys in their species and instincts, the deities, whose instincts differ from those of humans, will be regarded by the biologists of the deities as "the most evolved creature, different from the human species."

The first imaginable instinctive change will affect the concept of "good." In other words, morality will become instinctive within a couple of generations (i.e., within a century) after the realization of socialism. According to some ethicists, moral conduct is in the spirit of "self-mastery,"[200] and acts that follow instinct or are guided by pleasure are, at the very least, unethical. Of course, there is no better explanation for the ethics of individualism than this, but it is a worthless explanation because it fails to understand that humanity is a social entity, a large individual which divided like an amoeba. If we do any act guided by discomfort or for the purpose of disadvantaging ourselves, then we are a strange animal unlike any other from the biological world. This is an argument that cannot be understood unless we adopt the creationist assumption that we are children of God, distinct from other living creatures.

Moral action is an initiation of sociality required for the survival and evolution of society. Before the development of biology, when the concept of an individual was nothing more than a vague idea, such as an animal separated by space from other animals or an organism grown from one egg, this "little self" was considered an individual in itself. Therefore, when the individual self-interest of the small individual was overpowered by the social self-interest of the large individual, of which that initial individual was but one molecule, they looked at only the pain and disadvantage felt by the small molecule and did not understand that their actions were in fact more pleasurable than painful and more beneficial than disadvantageous due to the social gratification that overcame the pain and disadvantage.

If it is only through efforts to conquer oneself that one can have a moral evaluation, then loving one's wife and loving one's community and nation would not be worthy of being considered a moral act. Moreover, there is no reason for a mother to love her children more than herself, since this love is not due to pain, nor is it due to self-control, nor is it due to effort. The idea of

---

[200] Literally "to overcome oneself."

the wise man that "at the age of seventy, one can do as one pleases and not deviate from the rules,"[201] for example, should cause the moral value of a habitual moral act to hold lesser value than a moral act in an age when it is non-habitual, since there is no pain, no effort, and no self-denial. It must be argued that the actions of those who have inherited their moral tendencies through ancestral heredity, for example, have no value in the marketplace because there is no effort at all. However, like Marx's fallacy of value, just as we pay a price for the value of even natural products, shouldn't the so-called naturally extraordinary figures be the most respected? Yet, even the most valuable thing has no value if it exists as abundantly as air. The rare things that are of little value but cannot meet the demand are valued more than their original value. Today, "morality" represents infinite value because there is so much demand for it, yet there are fewer natural products, in this case natural saints, than diamonds, and in unethical social organizations there is so much meaningless effort that no man-made gems can be obtained.

From the standpoint of the individual, humans have self-interest, and from the standpoint of society, they have social self-interest. Therefore, the theories of free will and determinism are not controversial at all, considering the scientific basis of the individual since the invention of the microscope. Free will agrees with determinism in that freedom of will is the strongest inner necessity, and determinism agrees with free will in that the necessity of will is due to the strongest inner freedom. In other words, we do moral acts because we are driven by our strongest inner necessity, and we commit sin because we follow our strongest inner freedom. Humans have both sociability and individuality in their innermost soul. When sociality is most active in one's mind and works to suppress the other side, individuality, we are driven by the necessity of our sociality to practice morality. That sociality here feels free and becomes free will. However, when individuality is oppressed, it loses its

---

[201] Confucius, *The Analects*, 2:4.

freedom, and in this sense it becomes deterministic. Similarly, when individuality is most active in one's mind and appears by suppressing the other side, sociality, the person is overcome by the strongest freedom of individuality, and sociality feels inevitable and becomes deterministic. However, the overpowering individuality gains freedom, and in this sense it becomes free will.

Needless to say, it is wrong to advocate determinism as the fatalism of ancient religions, where it meant "to aspire according to the will of God, who exists above mankind," and free will as the dogma of individualism that emerged after Luther,[202] where it meant "man has an inherently free will." This sociality and individuality are not only innately different for each individual in their degree of strength and weakness, but under today's social system, which contains a great amount of variety, they also vary greatly according to class rank. Those who have an inherently stronger sociality, who have inherited a sociality that was made stronger by the social environment of their ancestors, or who have acquired a sociality that is made active by being in an educated class, easily commit moral acts by the freedom of will, which is driven by the necessity of that active sociality.

Today, however, such examples are scarcer than stars in the sky just before daybreak. On the contrary, since the majority of society is congenitally raised into classes, each of which has a terribly weak social nature inherited from the social environment of its ancestors and is exclusively engaged in fighting for self-interest, only one of the two parts, individuality, is strong enough to overpower the other, and such a powerful freedom of individuality overwhelms the person, inevitably leading them to become a criminal. Those who do not are gradually able to resist, and with great effort maintain their

---

[202] Luther himself, however, denied free will. He famously argued with Giovanni Pico della Mirandola, who accepted free will.

surviving sociality, but only to the extent that they become common passive good guys who believe all they need to do is not commit many crimes.

Morality is how sociality requires us to act as molecules of society for society's survival and evolution. So it is a sufficiently moral act that we strive to elevate ourselves as a member of society (not for the sake of the small ego). Along with that, many are called upon to perform more moral acts, to abandon their small ego for the sake of the big ego, in other words for the sake of other molecules or future molecules. This is why not only is the act of seeking the honor and glory of the small ego without regard to the survival and evolution of the big ego considered immoral, but also why an act aimed at the benefit of the small ego itself (not as a member of society) is generally not considered a moral act, even if it happens to benefit society.

Indeed, modern society is, even in law, socialist in ideal. Yet the reality of society is that individualism and its underlying system of private property have made it a de facto economic aristocracy, with no private property owned by individual persons, thus leading individualism to the verge of extinction. Yet, we are in a situation where all of a person's individual effort goes towards acquiring much private property, and freedom is desired only for the purpose of benefitting the individual person. Our Japan, for example, has not, as in the great European revolutions, broken with the parochial socialism of the state and social tyranny in one fell swoop, and has not demanded absolute individual authority. The Meiji Revolution was not so thorough in comparison, and the mechanical view of society, which considers the state and society as a means to individual freedom and independence, was not stipulated above all laws and morals as in Europe. Thus, both what the state enforces by law and what society demands by morality—even though it is unacceptable for socialism to ignore individual authority in favor of continuing parochial socialism—are yet dim hopes for the socialist ideal in that they make sociality the supreme authority. (In the West, advocating public ownership of land and capital is potentially disruptive from the perspective of laws established by individualism, but from the perspective of Japanese law, which is the successor to the parochial socialism of universal state ownership, there is no reason to punish such advocacy as being contrary to the law. This also means that Japanese law has the right to punish a purported socialist advocate of individualist freedom and equality who professes a denial of the state itself, while Western law has no reason to oppress him on the grounds that he is disruptive.) However, even though Japanese law inherits parochial socialism, it merely expresses in its legal ideals that the state is the supreme owner, while in reality it adopts a private property system that in effect gives birth to individualism.

Of course, even in the West, where individualism has been advocated to the extreme, theory cannot dictate fact. It goes without saying that society and the state cannot exist even for a day without sociality, just as celestial order cannot be maintained without gravitational force. In Japan, the individual became the subject of private property rights with the Meiji Revolution, and, in the Land Tax Ordinance of 1873, the right to own land under the supreme ownership of the state was further acquired, thus laying the foundation for individualism. Despite this, there are still invocations of the medieval and barbaric spirit of sociality within the voices of "patriotism." However, that sociality is very minor. It has been destroyed by the individualistic social systems of the private property system, which only breathes the individualist air surrounding it, raised in a class with individualist ideas. This has caused it to plant roots so deep and grow into such a massive tree that it cannot be pulled out. Under such a social system, where only individuality grows and the seeds of sociality are quickly nipped in the bud, it goes without saying that we—those of us whose sociality has been nipped and only our individuality allowed to flourish—either commit crimes driven by the necessity of our individuality, or have no choice but to be satisfied with becoming passive good guys who just barely avoid committing crimes through great effort and self-control.

This would not be the case in a world where the current legal and moral ideals have been realized through socialism. Moral fulfillment requires neither effort nor self-control. Every man follows his social freedom and morality as a matter of course. Therefore, if moral conduct can be achieved without self-control and effort, there will be no moralists in a socialist world, and people will feel that morality has as little value as air, even though it is the most necessary thing. In this way, it is not wrong to call the socialist world a moral world, but it is more correct to call it a world of non-morality. Even today, for thieves and the poor, "not to kill" and "not to steal" are moral principles that can only be attained through great effort and self-discipline, but for those with a certain income and an unwavering heart, they are simply ordinary, unconscious behaviors that are not considered extra precious at all.

In today's social systems of gold and power, it is precisely by doing even the most passive moral acts, which are no more than not being stingy, not taking bribes, not being bought off, or not abusing one's power, that one is considered a tolerant and mature businessman, a clean bureaucrat, an honorable legislator, or a wise minister. But this applies only to the few personalities who are able to resist immorality through great effort and self-discipline, and they are like diamonds, in such high demand but with such little supply that their sparkle seems so extraordinary.

However, in a socialist world where social organizations built on gold and power have disappeared, the morality of "not killing" and "not stealing," which thieves and the poor finally achieve through great effort and self-discipline, becomes something banal, of little value entirely. Because all individual persons are in economic subordination to society, they will be conscious of their position as a molecule of the big ego, and thus a devotional morality will be born. (See the where we explained the relationship between economics, morality, and the law in volume 2, *The Ethical Ideal of Socialism*.)

Society organizes all its institutions for the benefit of itself so that sociality can operate freely, and so sociality is not overpowered by individuality, nor does it feel that it has been deprived of a freedom. The freedom of individuality is respected for the development of both individuality itself and for the individual person as a molecule of society, and the development of the personal ego itself has moral significance. If this is the case, then free will and determinism are useless arguments, and what each person does, whatever they please, is itself a moral act.

Furthermore, sociality, fostered by social organizations that nurture sociality, is accumulated and inherited through the competition for sex and becomes an even stronger social instinct. Instincts are the accumulation of heredity. The sociality that has been strengthened by an acquired social environment will then pass on that strength acquired from that social environment, and will eventually become a congenitally strong sociality; in other words, innate. If anyone denies morality becoming instinctual in this way, he is a believer in creationism, not someone who lives in the post-Darwin age, because it is impossible to claim today that instinct is fixed unless one believes that from the beginning of the heavens and the earth there have been distinct and separated categories of biological species.

To put it differently, the fact that each species has different instincts and forms its own class is due to the genetic accumulation of experiences in the environment of each species, and the fact that human instincts are as they are today is due to the genetic accumulation of experiences after humans became distinct from apes. The current biological evolutionist, who cannot even imagine the future evolution of the human species, will find it difficult to infer how our instincts will change in the future. However, this should not lead one to equate evolutionists with those who believe that "the heavens and the earth were created in a fixed manner from the beginning." Likewise, to think that today's instincts are fixed is pure creationism. It is not so! The countless materials supplied by the theory of biological evolution lead us to assert that morality will be instinctual in two or three generations after the realization of socialism!

The reason that artificial culling would create a completely different species in two or three generations is precisely because this sort of change in instincts is easy to achieve. A good example is the creation of the Eurasian duck. When we created them from wild ducks, they maintained the instincts of the wild duck for two or three generations, trying to fly away, but eventually, from the influence of their environment, the Eurasian duck we created had completely different instincts. If we can observe this obvious fact in a species, why should we doubt that the instincts of another biological species, the human race, can be transformed into socially active instincts after a few generations in a socialist environment? We believe. We believe it is that same changing of instincts that gives us the strong self-interest of the small ego that we have today, and that the ninety-five thousand years from the dawn of proto-humans to the days of the private property system, during the moral world of emperors Yao and Shun, where "people were governed as nature dictated," would have had a thriving sociality.

Let us give other species as examples of this. For example, pigs are raised by people as livestock and have lost the instincts of wild boars, but after two or three generations in the wild, they will gain the instinct to adapt to the wild environment and become wild boars again. Indeed, we believe this with infinite joy. Today's thriving egoistic instincts are a process of human evolution, and if we evolve into a socialist world, we will have a thriving social instinct to adapt to our environment, just as wild ducks become ducks and pigs become wild boars again. That age will be the age of the deities, when the bud of sociality present in the age of Yao and Shun will bloom as full as cherry blossoms.

Surely, we will evolve in regards to "truth" as well. Here we must further defeat the dogmatic inequality theory via biology and silence its breathing altogether. We have often quoted Bergemann's statement that "humans only become human through the existence of society," and in *The Ethical Ideal of Socialism* we have explained why goodness in the lower classes remain a very low-grade goodness. We also explained in this volume why the savage is made a savage. We will go further than that and affirm: "Mankind are marsupials like the kangaroo."[203] This is absolutely not a metaphor. The solemn biological fact is that mankind is indeed a marsupial, no different from a kangaroo.

As everyone knows, a baby kangaroo is just over three centimeters in size, and they enter their mother's pouch about one week after being born. Then they are raised in their mother's pouch for the next nine months, and only then do they become fully independent kangaroos. Meanwhile, viviparous animals have this pouch as part of the internal structure of the mother, with babies only emerging from the mother's body after nine months in the womb. The dogmatic inequality theory compares the three-centimeter kangaroo with a nine-month-old kangaroo, and argues that kangaroos are unequal in nature— a newborn human baby is a kangaroo only three centimeters large and sent out into the world after one week. It is only after being educated in a pouch known as society until at least twenty years of age that one can stand in the world as an independent kangaroo. Behold the noble lesson of biology. That lesson is that education is part of reproduction (not just a compensation for a deficiency, but an actual part of it). Just as for the kangaroo, whose nine months of reproduction are completed outside the body as opposed to inside the body like other mammals, the period of education until the age of twenty for humans is part of the reproductive process that must be nurtured in the external pouch of the mother, society.

For the lower class of organisms, the reproductive process is completed at the time of delivery, and after delivery they become independent as a complete organism without any education at all. On the other hand, the reproductive

---

[203] Mammals are generally referred to as viviparous animals and are raised in the womb until sufficiently grown before they are born, whereas marsupials are raised outside the body without being raised in the womb. Therefore, they're weaker than viviparous animals. For this reason, it's believed that marsupials were once found in many regions, but disappeared in other regions as they were being displaced by viviparous animals.

process is not completed by birth alone in higher organisms, as education is a core part of it. Cats, for example, teach their young to catch mice by constantly wagging their tails in a quick motion, which the kittens become accustomed to. The same is true of tigers, which teach their young to catch their prey by having their young put small teeth marks on the heads of animals their parents have chewed to death. It is, then, an essential and vital part of the imperfect reproductive process that the highest class, mankind, requires the longest, most thorough, and most elaborate education. To compare the present, largely uneducated lower classes with the upper classes, raised in a pouch filled with six thousand years of knowledge, is as nonsensical as comparing a young fetus, barely even in the shape of a humanoid yet, with a freshly born child.

In the nine months leading up to delivery, humans experience the evolutionary history that led to humanity, and in the period between delivery and age twenty, they experience another one hundred thousand years of evolutionary history, from the proto-human age until modernity. If we compare a fetus and a child and do not forget that one is in the era of the beast and the other is in the era of mankind, there can be no proper comparison. So how can you compare the barbaric age of the primitive man with the civilized age of a hundred thousand years later and preach inequality? The very fact that today's lower classes are still at the intellectual level of hundreds or thousands of years ago has led the pitiful scholars to say that "humans are naturally unequal." Such a theory of inequality ignores all the time and places the children of the twentieth century experience, with their understanding of steam power and electricity, which sends that theory of inequality back a distant six thousand years.

Obviously children should not be left at birth, but should be educated. However, in addition to the purpose of obtaining food, like kittens learning to catch mice, if a person does not enter the pouch of accumulated knowledge, which has been built up in the ten thousand years of human civilization, it cannot be said that such a person has had a complete birth as a civilized human being. It must also be remembered that the difference in the degree of reproductive perfection between a person with enough knowledge to barely read a story about the saga of Musashi Miyamoto (though not to say he has received no education at all), and a person who has been brought up to the age of thirty with the accumulated knowledge of both ancient and modern humanity, is like comparing a kangaroo who has been brought out of its pouch in three weeks versus nine months. (Therefore, all knowledge is true regarding the class in which it exists in the present time, when there is class inequality. The ignorant class that still inherits the dogmatic egalitarianism of the French Revolution, and the academic class that has been brought up with false knowledge because of the class divide and thus is dogmatically unequal and disrespectful of others, are both varieties of kangaroos from different pouches.)

For those who treat reproduction as a recreational activity, it is difficult to understand that education is part of reproductive activity. However, from the point of view of biological philosophy, reproductive activity is a way of inheriting tribal experience and knowledge—e.g., instincts—in the physical body. Education, on the other hand, is a way to pass on six thousand years of socially inherited experience and knowledge, on top of instinct, in the spirit and mind. Therefore, the dimly lit bedroom is a podium from which a hundred thousand years of lessons are taught in a single night, and the teachings of the celibate Christ,[204] preached as he stands in a field, is also a great reproductive act that has produced countless children, as his descendants for 1,900 years have looked up to him as their father. The home is also a school. The library is a bedroom. *The Analects* of Confucius are the words of love. A letter written with a red brush is scripture.[205] All of society is a woman's bed at childbirth.

---

[204] Likely referring to *Sermon on the Mount*.

[205] A red brush is a brush made for women, thus making this a love letter.

Socialism demands, first and foremost, that all members of society leave their tiny rooms and the lecterns, which are like meeting houses for vice, and give birth to the *Analects* and the Bible as words of love or even love letters in the beds of society's nursing mothers. This is consistent with individualism, which absolutely recognizes the authority of the individual person in terms of the equal need of this for all individual persons, who are all molecules of society.

Because socialism is currently understood as a lower class equality of stagnation and honorable poverty, and because many socialists do simply think of defeating the emperor and aristocrats, then pulling down the upper class into the commoner class, to the point where it has even been christened "egalitarian democracy," it has been mistakenly thought of as ignoring the authority of individuality wielded by ancient great emperors or virile nobles, which in turn makes others perceive socialists as merely losers in the competitions mentioned earlier, crying out for help. If this is what socialism is, then I will break the pen I'm currently writing with and say that I would rather advocate monarchism and aristocracy. The authority of the individual should not be violated simply due to the majority. Socialism is not "the greatest happiness for the greatest number."[206] What kind of socialism is there without "individual freedom" to the extent that an emperor with absolute and unlimited power, sacred and inviolable, oppresses the majority, the entire society, by the authority of his personality? The evolution of society does not immediately extend to all the molecules in all things. Therefore, individual freedom first evolved only in one component, the emperor, to become a monarchy, and then extended this evolution to a minority of the population to become an aristocracy, granting aristocrats individual freedom as well. The nobles had absolute freedom as sovereigns over the warriors and serfs (they were as much sovereigns as the emperor in this respect), and when their

---

[206] This is the famous formula of utilitarian philosopher Jeremy Bentham.

authority clashed with that of countless other free sovereigns, the decision was made by force. (We will show examples of exactly how the individual person's freedom was determined by their power later in *The So-Called Theory of Japan's National Polity and its Restorative Principle of Revolution*.)

From the beginning of recorded history, the Japanese emperors, by their mighty power, have expressed absolute freedom in their personal authority. Many sovereigns of the aristocratic classes of rulers also determined any conflict of liberty by their equally mighty power, and when their mighty power overpowered other powers, they wielded absolute and unlimited freedom, their blades gleaming over the heads of many other sovereigns (with the imperial family among these sovereign). Thus, the principle of liberalism, which asserts that "for the sake of personal authority, one must boldly stand up to the enemy, no matter how numerous," is precisely what society has held up as an ideal since the days of the monarchies. When socialism is advocated in defiance of the laws of social evolution, it is quickly suppressed in the real world as civil unrest, while in the world of ideas it dies in battle under the flurry of arrows labeling it "fantasy." When a segment of society intimidates the majority of society with its shining eyes under a golden crown is when the ideal of individual authority as absolute and unlimited power is first realized by a segment of society.

Social evolution is the imitation of the lower classes in their attempt to reach the upper classes as an ideal. (Tarde's theory of imitation explains this same thing in the field of ethics, where there is agreement on several points, and all of them are correct.)[207] And, as Tarde said, the result of imitation is to gain equality. The nobility, the lords, with their equality on their bloodstained blades, began to imitate the rulers in order to gain the same individual and absolute freedom. The ideal of ruling with supreme authority was not for the

---

[207] Gabriel Tarde was a French sociologist who sought the driving force of society within imitation.

sake of wealth or prestige, but only to assert personal authority by suppressing all those who would interfere with one's freedom! In one age, the ruler who was powerful enough to realize that ideal became Emperor Go-Daigo and destroyed the other rulers, the Hojo clan. In another age, those powerful rulers became the Tokugawa clan, oppressing many other rulers, both emperors and lords, and thereby wielding their personal authority over society as a whole. The less powerful rulers of the lord classes expressed their freedom absolutely toward the lower classes, the warriors, and the serfs.

The evolution of society was an expansion of how equality was viewed. Authority of the individual person was initially realized by only one molecule of society, but eventually spread to a small number of molecules via the expansion of views on equality. After that, views on equality were expanded to all molecules of society, and that's when both the French and Meiji revolutions occurred, ushering in a world of democracy which asserted that "individual liberty cannot be violated by another person, no matter who they are." Thus, the current laws represent social democracy. With a democracy in which no individual should be sacrificed for the benefit of another, when that individual is sacrificed, it is in the interest of society. Those who demand sacrifice are individuals (military chiefs, judges, etc.), but they do so not as individuals, but as representatives of the state, asserting the interests of the state. So the very ideal of law is social democracy. However, as an economic aristocracy, humanity has yet to become a sovereign or aristocrat atop the biological world because of poverty and casualties in war in the competition for survival with other species and competition for survival where society as a whole is the unit.

We repeat and affirm. Socialism is not "egalitarian democracy" that overthrows the monarchs, breaks up the aristocracy, and dissolves the upper classes into lower-class equality. It is an attempt to realize for all members of society the absolute authority of the individual that was realized by one member of the former monarchy, the monarch himself. Look at the laws of today. There were no commoners in the Tokugawa period, no nobles in the

Warring States period, and no monarchs in the reigns of emperors Yuryaku and Nintoku. There is only the state and the people (the emperor is also a citizen in the broad sense of the word). The state embodies socialism because it is seen as a large individual. The people embody democracy because they are thought of from the viewpoint of small individuals. (Once again, see *The So-Called Theory of Japan's National Polity and its Restorative Principle of Revolution.*)

If one understands this explanation, it will be clear to see that there is no reason for the accusation that socialism will result in the majority of the foolish masses oppressing the genius, as the citizens of Athens did to Socrates. Socialism is a principle of genius. Moreover, it is genius which encompasses all of society. (This is why we hope to change what some current socialists have named "The Plebeian Society" to "The Genius Society." Our pioneers were absolutely not ordinary "plebeians.")

A genius is an individual person with authority who has been able to overcome the oppression of the foolish masses and demonstrate the mutation in his individuality. Throughout history, many geniuses ignored the foolish populace and approached the great willed monarchs and aristocrats who wielded personal authority. However, in the past, in order to demonstrate the mutation of their individuality, geniuses fought against the narrow social conscious which ignored the authority of the individual person, and their great will and great minds were more consumed by the effort to free that demonstration of their individuality than by the demonstration of their individuality itself. But that will not happen in the world of socialism. The absolutely unlimited freedom of the individual, to an extent that, in ancient monarchies, was only realized by a single molecule, is extended to all the molecules of society, so that geniuses do not have to strive for freedom itself, and instead all their efforts are devoted to the exercise of their given individuality.

The seeds of genius have fallen to the ground in abundance. But until now, the world has not been a fertile ground where genius could be nurtured freely, and so many have decayed into anonymity. If not infertile, then the soil would be sown into different classes of different quality, and many geniuses would be warped, only able to exercise a given or altered part of their genius. Socialism is a genius system in that it is a fertile ground where genius is free to develop, and can also be called a genius system in that it supplies abundant fertilizer to nurture and raise geniuses. Seeds must not be hindered from developing freely, and they need fertilizer to develop.

Genius is a flower that absorbs fertilizer from society, blooms, and releases a pleasant fragrance. Even a great poet, stuck in a barbaric village, has only as little language as a child of ten years old. What can he possibly sing with such language? The roots of thought take their material from the society that already exists, and the eyes that see the heavens and the earth are opened by the hand of the mother, of society. If the great Buddha were not born in India, where there is no lack of food and clothing, and where exists the philosophy of the Brahmins, but spent his life working hard under ice and snow in an Eskimo village, where there is no philosophy, he would be but a small founder of an idolatrous religion. The reason that Christ still had no global insight, but only dealt with scholars and Pharisees, was that he had no footprints outside of Judea. Christianity first flooded the world when Paul, with the ideas of Christ, entered Rome, which had wings over the world. Yoshitsune was merely a warlord in Hinodorigoe because he was in an island nation where he had no other environment in which to express his individuality,[208] while Hannibal's crossing of the Alps became world-famous because it took place on a continent. The reason the German emperor, who laughably calls himself a ruler, dreams

---

[208] This is a difficult spot where Yoshitsune proceeded to attack the Heike during the Battle of Ichi-no-tani. It's extremely famous that Yoshitsune ran down from the cliff and attacked the Heike after passing through the Hinodorigoe.

of taking over the entire world is because he lived during the nineteenth century. However great Caesar might be, he could only be satisfied with conquering the Mediterranean coast and saying that was where the world ended.[209] When Columbus stated that the earth was round, the scholars of the time quickly dismissed his argument, saying, "If that were the case, then the world beneath our feet would be upside down, and mankind, birds, and beasts would all fall into the abyss." However, this is because they were born in an age where the theory of gravity didn't yet exist, and, regardless of how outstanding their individualities may have been, they were still no better than elementary school children today.

Great construction requires many materials. Even a genius can only show their architecture, that is, their individuality, if they first obtain materials by absorbing the ideas of society. For grand architecture, it is necessary to look to the building techniques of our predecessors. The South Pacific aboriginal villages do not have twenty-story houses. Greek and Roman architecture, medieval Christian churches, and Buddhist monasteries in Indochina show that historical development exists. Today's astronomy did not come from a primitive village without a decimal system. Aristotle's deductive method was not the only reason for the emergence of today's scientific research. A genius is a person who once inhales the social genetic knowledge, or social spirit, up to his or her era, uses their unique, singular power of composition to create a unique model of themselves from the inhaled material, and radiates it onto society as the social spirit of the future generation. This is the reason why all

---

[209] Caesar came into conflict with the Senate, and after his expedition to Gaul, he had an all-out confrontation with Pompey, who had been appointed dictator by the Senate (Caesar's Civil War). After Pompey was defeated by Caesar, the Pompeians fled the Italian peninsula and tried to rebuild their power in the cities along the Mediterranean coast, resulting in the two factions fighting over the Mediterranean coast. Caesar was ultimately victorious.

geniuses have a coloration in their thoughts and ideas that is limited by the times in which they lived. This is also the reason why the history of philosophy is organized by a chain of systems of thought.

It is not completely true that genius is a social organism, but it is an undeniable fact that genius is a flower nurtured by the soil and fertilizer of society. Yet, what about the history of mankind up to the present day? The seeds of genius fell into the human world as though blown in by the wind, but they did not sprout because the land was stony and barren, with no freedom, and the few that did sprout were trampled by the horses known as rulers and aristocrats. And even if a few seeds fell into the upper classes, who had finally received their freedom, or were transferred by them to free lands and planted, the flowers that bloomed were little more than wildflowers because of poor fertilizer in less-evolved societies. In such cases, it goes without saying that the geniuses of history hope that their ideas will be accepted a hundred generations from now, but their light fades and fades with each passing generation.

When people of the past and people of today leave their mother's body, they are the same primitive people. Genius is also a mutation of the individual, and they become a primitive genius in a primitive village. However, in the bedroom of society, through the reproductive process of inheriting socially accumulated knowledge, the man of the past becomes the man of the past and the man of the present becomes the man of the present. Christ pointed beyond the distant stars to show heaven. Yet, we, who know more than he did, are moving forward today, acknowledging that there will be a paradise on earth in the near future. The Buddha practiced Zen meditation, but he could not go beyond the theory of cosmic cycles. However, we today, who have studied more than he did, can clearly see that the universe and life are evolving. Aristotle was a wise man. However, from our point of view, he was a child prodigy, never venturing further than that. Darwin seems to have been the great architect of biological evolution. However, we, inheriting his ideas, know more at twenty-three than he did at the old age where he had a full white beard.[210] Ah, this is the truth of the "anthropoid," who accumulates and passes on knowledge with no limit!

Individuality is what makes the social spirit unique, and society receives this spirit of individuality that has become unique, makes it universal, and passes it on as the spirit of society to future generations. And when individuality absorbs the spirit of society in order to make it unique, it absorbs the spirit of countless individuals created by previous generations, which society has made universally present through heredity. Society and an individual person are simply different standpoints, the big ego and the small ego. Why, then, do we understand socialism, with its absolute respect for individual freedom, as a set of principles that sees the foolish masses as almighty?

The reason why socialism requires the spread of spiritual development as well as equality in material protection is that any individual genius's special spirit will grow poor if the level of society is too low, and they will not be able to receive their unique spirit and turn it into a social spirit to be passed on to future generations, thus causing the genius to decay in obscurity and social evolution to be slow. That which must be most clearly understood is the agreement in the ideals of socialism and individualism. The freedom and equality developed by all the historical and social knowledge of all the molecules of society (i.e., all individual persons) makes every molecule and every individual person shine like a genius themselves. It also makes universal the spirit of the most brilliant and greatest genius among them all, makes the social spirit great, and gives this foundation to the greater geniuses of future generations. This greater genius, standing on the foundation of the previous greater genius, will make the greater social spirit into something special by their own greater hand, and radiate it to society. The greater social spirit takes

---

[210] Kita was twenty-three at the time of writing.

this greater spirit and makes it universal, so that the greater genius of future generations may use it as the basis for even greater genius.

Having reached this point, humans will change their instincts regarding "truth." In other words, just as humans, having diverged from apes, have evolved a brain and nervous system through social reproduction that cannot be compared with those of other species, the anthropoids evolving into the "deities" will acquire instincts of astonishing mental clarity.

We have used the word "deity" to distinguish it from the idea of "god" that many traditional religions have used. Let us now further imagine how humanity will evolve in terms of "beauty." Since all truth, goodness, and beauty evolve, and what is considered true or good in one time period or region cannot be inferred as true or good in all times and regions, so it goes without saying that beauty also differs from period to period and from region to region.

In some regions, a barbarian's head is considered beautiful if it is extremely cone-shaped, and those with flat noses, thick lips, and tattoos are the most admired. White men and women are considered ugly by many Blacks, and many are unable to find spouses within that community. The buttocks of Somali beauties, which Darwin's boldly described, are considered the height of beauty in their villages. The Chinese consider women with flat faces, round foreheads, thin eyebrows, and small feet to be beautiful.[211] In Europe, a person with a broad chest, tall stature, and a well-defined face is considered beautiful, while in Japan, a person with small hips, dark hair, and egg-like facial features is considered beautiful.

The same is true of time periods. The ideal of beauty evolves as society and ideals evolve. At one time, prostitutes idealized valiant men on horseback with

---

[211] Until the Qing Dynasty, women used to "bind" their feet, wrapping them with cloth to prevent them from getting bigger. A woman with "small feet" was a woman who bound them like that. Incidentally, Emperor Kangxi issued a ban on this practice, but it was so widespread that the ban was ineffective.

inked eyebrows, and so Tanjiro of Genroku became the ideal.[212] From there, chests decorated with medals, the orator's beard, the novelist's thin face, and the square hats Japanese university students wear all became the ideal at one point or another, eventually giving way to the ideal of people wearing maroon hakamas. Thus, the ideal in one age continues to flow and change. It goes without saying, then, that today's ideal of beauty, which is only one part of an evolutionary process, cannot forever be the rule.

The figures that are today held up as ideals and the objective of our efforts are, for men, Christ and Buddha, and for women, Mary. These are the perfect faces that embody truth, goodness, and beauty, and are the pinnacle of beauty that we aspire to, even though we have given up on them because we cannot find them in this world. However, it is clear from what we have already said that this is an ideal of beauty that will no doubt be realized in a couple of generations after socialism is realized.

Unfortunately, the beauty of the ideals that mankind looks up to as God and Buddha (not the real people who actually existed)[213] has no excretory function, while we do perform this very disgusting and unbecoming act. All ideals are to be realized. If we maintain this ugliness, we can never reach God's beauty. We are convinced that the philosophy of teleology and the facts of biological evolution will enable mankind to break free from this excretory action.

We still retain our scientific foundation. According to the theory of biological evolution, all living organisms have evolved some organs and degenerated others in response to their environment for the purpose of survival and evolution and their ideals, resulting in the myriad species that we see

---

[212] "Tanjiro" is the main character of Shunsui Tamenaga's *Shunshoku Umego Yomi*. (春色梅児誉美). He's portrayed as a meek and good-looking man. "Genroku" refers to a kimono, and is named as such because it originated during the Genroku period.

[213] As in the ideal image of these figures, not the actual people Jesus and Buddha.

today. Even among reptiles, birds have amazingly evolved forefeet that became wings and feathers. Those that split off into four-legged beasts but then went into the water degenerated their legs into half-tails, as in the dolphins, or into full tails, as in the whales.

The same is true of humankind. The goal of human survival and adaptation to the environment, the ideal of evolution, has led to significant evolution of some organs and significant degeneration of others. The fingers and toes of the forelimbs, necessary for all industrial production, were allowed to move freely (in other monkeys, the thumb has no specialized function; in others animals, it is merely used for walking). The unparalleled development of the brain, nervous system, and the like (this is why humans must be classified in a separate category from the other monkey genera) are examples of how organs have evolved. The loss of hair all over the body (in other genera of monkeys, only the area around the eyes and the red part of the buttocks loses its hair, and many other beasts have evolved to be quite hairy), the inability to move one's ears (many other genera of monkeys can move their ears freely, and animals like rabbits have evolved massive ears), the reduction in number and size of teeth (other genera of monkeys have a higher number and larger size of teeth, and the teeth of most carnivores have evolved much further), and the tail bone shrinking back into the body after birth (all other genera of monkeys have tails, and many other beasts have much more highly evolved tails) are all examples of organs degenerating.

If we do not adopt the old-fashioned materialism or creationism, and therefore do not believe that from the creation of the earth by God, or perhaps for no reason at all, some animals have fangs, some have wings, and some walk upright, that spines, tails, hair, etc., all existed on certain animals, then we have no reason to reject the reasoning that mankind is evolving or degenerating organs according to their ideal by the philosophy of teleology and the theory of biological evolution. That is not wrong! Just look at how the digestive organs of mankind have degenerated to date. The mouth has degenerated significantly. The cleft lip common to beasts have degenerated to such an extent that in mankind they are found only in deformed children by pure accident. The number of teeth has also degenerated from that of apes, and the number of teeth of civilized man have degenerated even more than the barbarians. The third molar is completely absent, and city people among civilized society are so degenerated that their upper incisors drop out earlier than those of country people. The gastrointestinal tract, although longer than that of pure carnivores because of our vegetarian diet, is remarkably more degenerated than that of other pure herbivores, and the belly of the civilized man is even smaller and more degenerated than that of the savage. The appendix, which is attached to the end of the large intestine and which in other animals acts as a digestive organ, has degenerated so much in mankind that it has ceased to be a necessity of life and can be cut off in cases of disease.

The fact that the digestive organs degenerate is an illustration of Lamarckism in that the organs which aren't used gradually degenerate. Species such as cattle have four stomachs and intestines that are very long in order to feed on the most difficult to digest foods. The reason why birds have stomach walls that are hard as stone, and why they put stones into their stomachs, is so that when they swallow food whole, the stomach and stones act as a mortar and pestle to digest the food. The reason why the teeth of the barbarian are more numerous than those of the civilized man, and why the teeth of those who live in the country are much healthier than those who live in the city, is because they put food into their mouth without cutting it up, and so need some sort of cutting implement in the mouth. The reason the savage has a longer gut than the civilized man is that he does not know how to prepare food for digestion as we do—to boil or bake it—so he has pots and pans in his bulging belly.

Why cannot human beings remove the knives in our mouths just as we have no mortar and pestle in our stomachs? Can we not take out all the pots and pans of the digestive system, as we have done with the appendix? Cannot we make having an anus a deformity, just as having a cleft lip is a deformity for mankind? We state this on the honor of scientific research. Just as the reasoning of biological evolutionists attributing the degeneration of mankind's digestive organs to food evolution to date is the reasoning of scientists, so we follow the reasoning of scientists that the future evolution of mankind will be, also by biological evolutionary theory, a complete degeneration of mankind's digestive organs.

Of course, the evolution of food is to be expected, unless you are an economist with your hands on the rotting bones of a century-old Malthus. In the near future, when primitive food, which is not much different from what is eaten by today's savages, will be industrially produced and digested by a large digestive apparatus with steam and electricity instead of by the pots, pans, and umbilical cord in the small belly of a human being as it is today, the digestive organs will gradually begin to degenerate in accordance with Lamarck's theory. And if, in the more distant future, we enter an age in which food will be prepared by chemical means, as the chemists of today predict from their laboratory windows, then this will be the so-called elixir, the ideal envisaged since ancient times. Here humans will degenerate (or leave traces of) all their digestive organs, dropping them like the cleft lip, the tailbone, and most body hair. This is when kitchen duty, once served by the stomach, will be transferred to a big factory, and the intestinal aqueducts will no longer drain the sewage. This is when the anus of the maid, whose hands are stained with the dregs of sewage, will become a lady wearing a kimono with a chrysanthemum flower pattern, with a chemist as her servant. This is when excretory actions are no longer needed, and when the ideal of "beauty" is thus perfected.

The ideal is a higher reality that will eventually come. Evolution is a series of ideals and realities. Have we ever imagined God, the highest ideal we have held up since the beginning of human history, the reality to come as a result of our long evolutionary process, defecating or farting? Today, we long for the ideal of love and lend it names like "my lover, my heavenly nymph." However, the nymph is an ideal, and the reality of the lover is that he or she is secretly dropping about one kan of potatoes.[214] The German emperor himself considers himself the ideal of all his people and says, "I am the all-powerful God." However, the scent of a pungent fart from under his decorated garments would not express the dignity of God. No physician would look at the swirling, yellow, snake-shaped substance on the scale and say, "Ah, look at the beauty of the emperor." (As the maid servants who cleaned chamber pots in the past would say, "You act so proudly as generals, but look at what drips out of you." In this respect, communal latrines are jointly liable, so we should be grateful for them.)

If this work were written in German, the German emperor would have lodged a protest with the Japanese government as a violation of his dignity. The question, however, is why farting is not in harmony with the dignity of the Kaiser mustache. Prime Minister Bülow's name is so similar to the sound of a fart in Japanese that one could expand the theory of ministerial responsibility and hold the prime minister responsible for farts, as well as for diplomatic blunders.[215] The question is, however, why would the German emperor himself avoid assuming that responsibility and wield his inalienable right towards it? And when this book comes into the hands of ladies, it will be attacked as trampling on women's rights, even by socialists. The problem, however, lies with the reason that female students who constantly assert women's rights are not afraid to walk around alleys and side streets to buy baked potatoes they will shove in their mouths, yet they walk down the street as if not knowing what the little potatoes for which they will later raise their hakamas and let drop from their bodies even are. It is said that, in the West, it must be a secret

---

[214] A "kan" is a unit of measurement in the old Japanese system of measurements. One kan equals about 3.75 kilograms.

[215] Bernhard von Bülow. He served as the chancellor of the German Empire from 1900 to 1909.

when noble ladies use the latrine, even from their parents and siblings. The problem is why it must be kept a secret.

We write about these issues because they are no more shameful as scientific studies than a medical doctor stirring feces and urine with his fingertips. The question, however, is the reality of why mankind considers feces and urine shameful. The degree of shame is stronger in adults than in children, and the emotional evolution is stronger in civilized people than in barbarians. We declare that this is a feeling of inadequacy of reality in relation to the ideal—that is, the desire for a higher reality but the inability to break free from a lower one. The philosophy of teleology and the theory of biological evolution provide an explanation for this feeling. Humanity is an evolving organism. It is a manifestation of a universe that is constantly striving to break free from reality for the purpose of reaching an ideal. If the universe has no evolutionary purpose and mankind is not an evolving organism, then there is no reason to idealize a God or a heavenly nymph who never excretes. Thus, there is no reason to be ashamed of anything that demonstrates the stark departure between the ideal and the reality—defecating or farting.

The feeling of shame is dissatisfaction with reality as opposed to the ideal. We feel immeasurable shame about our morality and infinite shame about our knowledge. In other words, we feel shame for not being good, shame for not being true, because we are ashamed of the reality of our lack of goodness and knowledge, which is far less than the ideal of morality or knowledge. When we idealize Socrates, we are ashamed of the reality that we have fallen far short of the truth that makes up the wellspring of his philosophical history, and of the good he taught about the immortality of the soul. When we think of Washington and Lincoln, we are ashamed of the reality that we have not reached the ideal of their goodness, and when we think of Marx and Rousseau, we are ashamed of the reality that we have not reached the ideal of their truths.

310 | The Theory of Japan's National Polity and Pure Socialism

This matter is no different. When we look in the mirror at the barber shop, we think of the beauty of Byron and Goethe, and are ashamed of our own ugliness. Even though the mirrors most girls look at themselves in are small western mirrors with mercury added to the glass in order to make the viewer look more beautiful than they really are (please forgive me!),[216] they still think of the plump cheeks of Sotoorihime,[217] whose beauty was said to be visible even in the dark, or the beautiful eyes of Cleopatra, dewy as they were, and are ashamed of their flat noses and broad foreheads which aren't fully covered by their hisashi-gami hairstyles.[218]

Shame towards excreting is a sign that we have evolved to the point where we strive to attain the ideal of God, the ultimate source of beauty. The lower beings, for whom the ideal is rarely recognized, or even very low organisms with no ideal at all, have no or very little shame of reality in regards to truth and goodness. Likewise, the lower beings have no feelings towards feces or urine because their ideal of beauty is so low it is barely different from reality. For example, cows and horses sleep and wake in feces and urine, and are not afraid of getting feces and urine on themselves. Some dogs, cats, and other animals of a higher class than cows and horses know how to bury their own feces with their hind legs,[219] and monkeys are even more averse to excrement, though not comparable to the lofty ideal held by humanity.

---

[216] Otherwise known as "unubore kagami" in Japanese, a small mirror from the Edo period with mercury added, as the text says.

[217] The queen of Emperor Ingyo. It's said that the color of her beautiful skin shone through her robe.

[218] The "hisashi-gami" is a hairstyle where the front and sides of the hair are tied forward. It's said to have been popular among female students from the middle of Meiji year 35.

[219] It's true that cats will bury their feces, but this is to prevent enemies from noticing their location, not out of shame.

As a human being progresses from child to adult, from barbarian to civilized, it gradually becomes more and more averse to excrement. Children, for example, are so much a part of the primitive life that they do not think twice about excrement sticking to their sleeves, and the barbarians pile it up in heaps in front of their thatched houses. We can see from this theory of biological evolution (and thus social evolution) that the inability of Western ladies to say, "Oh, excuse me," and fart, or to be so impartial as to say, "Farts and birth defects come out without notice," as those called *ebicha shikibu* would,[220] is evidence that they are far more evolved.

We have often said that the principle of social evolution is first realized by a member of society, the emperor. Though we do find the German emperor such a notable exception to this rule that it is almost praiseworthy, he still nonsensically tries to make himself the ideal to which his people should aspire, and that alone gives him reason to try and pass responsibility for farts onto Prime Ministers Bülow. While a husband may drink cheap liquor, bend over, and unleash a vigorous fart, it would not be appropriate for the head of a federal state to do so. Even if that smell were to waft through the court, it would not be done at one's own discretion for the sole purpose of immense satisfaction, as if he were a skunk.

In summary, we humans feel a lot of shame toward the good and toward the beautiful because we are ashamed of the reality of not reaching the ideal that we hold as an evolving species. When we strive to make this reality which has not attained the ideal attain that ideal, and when we find a way to make that ideal a reality, we call that "evolution." That is why we say the following: evolution is a succession of ideals and realities. The way to realize ideals of goodness in the future is through social democracy. The way to realize ideals of truth in the future is through social democracy. The way to realize ideals of

---

[220] This is a name for female students. Apparently they were called this throughout Meiji years 30-39.

beauty in the future is also through social democracy. There is nothing useless or fallible in natural law. Whether in the age of monarchies, aristocracies, democracies, the capitalist system today—the private property system—poverty, crime, greed, brutality, everything under the sun is an effort toward the ideal of social evolution. The inheritance of the ideas of dualism long ago, the abuse toward science, the abuse toward material civilization, etc., is done because those people do not understand that one aspect of the religious desire of God's beauty can be realized by the chemical preparation of food. Matter and spirit are one thing, not two. All things in heaven and earth are one.

Humanity will eventually abolish sexual intercourse as well. The inexpressible shame of sexual intercourse is greater than the shame of excretion. Everything is the philosophy of teleology; everything is the theory of biological evolution. Separating love and lust into two categories, leaving one in the light of God and discarding the other as animalistic and carnal is an ideal which stems from the fact that humanity, which desires such, is an evolving organism—even if that interpretation cannot escape the realm of dualism. Mankind has come to this point, and we can say that we have finally touched the throne of God with our fingertips. O Lord, who is visible right before us!

Unfortunately, today's science has not yet provided us with an adequate foundation. We must not forget the attitude of the scientific researcher and unnecessarily reach out to pull on the sleeves of God's image, which we see through the clouds. Even if the distinction between organic and inorganic matter, which forms the basis of dualism, disappears through scientific evolution, and even if some scientists create organic matter out of inorganic matter or even create a fully living organism, we do not assert that the time has come when the myth that God took one rib and made man will soon become a fact. But we wait for such a time to come.

Keeping our reasoning within the confines of biology, see how different the methods of reproduction are. The ugly method in which the two sexes embrace each other is not the reproductive act of all creatures. Many fish (with some exceptions) reproduce by sprinkling the male sperm on the female's eggs. Why do humans have to spray our sperm inside the body of the opposite sex? Why must mankind spend nine months in the mother's body? Today, medical science has advanced to the point where a baby can be removed at seven or eight months for the benefit of the mother. Why does mankind bind women to the venture of childbirth and make them wait for nine long months? Does not the bulging belly of the pregnant woman itself defy the ideal of beauty and provoke the violent behavior of men? Does not the delivery itself remind us of the shame of sexual intercourse, and is not the innocent child taught that it came from the mother's umbilical cord?

Amoebas, for example, reproduce countless times simply by division. How come mankind cannot take one of its ribs and infuse it with spirit? Does the lack of distinction between inorganic and organic matter not tell us that there is spirit within that rib? How can one deny the inference that a tiny creature created in a chemist's laboratory was made to resemble a human being, as in the ideal of God's creation? To immediately conclude that a woman of low status who dreamed of a dragon snuggling on her belly and gave birth to Liu Bang,[221] or Mary who dreamed of God and conceived Christ,[222] were committing adultery, after biology had discovered that aphids reproduce countless times without males, is no better than imagining a beast with a horn on its forehead.[223] This is simply because aphids and humans have evolved at

---

[221] Liu Bang, the first emperor of the Han Dynasty. This story is found in Sima Qian, "Annals of Gao Zu" in *Shiji*.

[222] The famous *Annunciation* story. To be precise, the Bible says that the angel Gabriel announced the conception of Christ to Mary. Therefore, Jesus is not related by blood to his father Joseph.

[223] Likely referring to a unicorn.

different levels, and when it comes down to the main body, aphid and human origins start from the same thing, a single cell.

Everything is an evolutionary process. Just as the division of an amoeba is a process of evolution, the parthenogenesis of an aphid is also a process of evolution. Just as the seasonal sexual reproduction between male and female beasts is a process of evolution, the sexual reproduction between male and female humans, not limited to any specific time of year, is also a process of evolution. When the time comes that humans no longer need the evolutionary process of the competition for sex—what is there to be afraid of? We declare that sexual reproduction will die out. In such a time, romantic love becomes slight and the name of the competition for survival becomes crude. The small ego becomes the big ego, and the big ego becomes anatman, or "non-self."

The theory of biological evolution is attributed to the philosophy and religion of the great Buddha. The demand for love that transcends carnal desires will thus be realized, and the entire world will realize Platonic love.[224] We must not put down the wings of the ideal and flee from the narrow society of biological evolution.

We said earlier that reproduction is the way to realize the ideal and that romantic love is very noble. On the other hand, however, we have also said that the realization of the ideal of Christ is a vast and everlasting love affair, a love affair so great that it is impossible to know how many offspring it will produce. The celibate saint, who often realizes his ideal, reproduces more than the average person who has dozens of children, and it is the gray-haired Leo Tolstoy who reproduces with the whole world as his bedroom, not the young man who indulges his debauched pleasures. Reproduction in the form of a man and a woman making love to each other only allows the inheriting of a reality that dates back to the proto-human age, but the Buddha's love affair, in which

---

[224] "Platonic love" means idealistic love. It derives from the fact that Plato was an idealist.

he abandoned Yasodhara,[225] brought all the men and women of the world to sleep together, inheriting what is considered the ideal of the last four thousand years.

The explanation of physical inheritance and social inheritance needs to be reiterated even more strongly. Rather than society being a large individual with all of humanity as its molecules separated with space in between them, its space is filled with matter and spirit, or in philosophical terms, a close-knit individual with absolutely no space at all. Therefore, both reproduction in the belly of a small individual and education in the belly of a large individual are themselves both reproduction and education. The education by social heredity is reproduction in the belly of a large individual, and the education by physical heredity is education in the belly of a small individual. We left our mother's belly and we entered Christ's belly, we entered the Buddha's belly. Not so! We are still in the belly of society, and Christ, Buddha, and society as a whole are in our belly. What is monogamy when we have come this far? What is the sanctity of love? It is the love of the big ego, the love of the non-self, absolute love.

"Humanity" will go extinct and the age of "deities" will come.

Are there those who feel fear when we say "extinction of humanity?" The extinction of the human race that we speak of here is not an unrealistic and pessimistic inference, such as "when the earth freezes over, the human race will go extinct." It is a joyous thought that the spread of the deities will be the end of humanity. If our ancestors, which we shared with apes, had not perished forever and given birth to us, we would still be half-human, half-ape creatures today, and if our even more ancient ancestors, reptiles, hadn't gone extinct after giving birth to us so long ago, we would certainly have no choice but to be shocking half-reptile, half-human creatures today. What else would it be but a

---

[225] Wife of Gautama-Siddhartha (Buddha). She was a cousin of the Buddha. She was later ordained together with the Buddha's adoptive mother.

thrilling joy for us to see the swift destruction of mankind with its foolish knowledge, its despicable morality, its hideous appearance, its behavior of excretion and intercourse, and witness the coming of the deities? Besides, all creatures are immortal. Just as we are descended from reptiles and apes, the deities are the descendants of our life, which they inherit and continue to evolve. This is the philosophy and religion of socialism—the traditional philosophy and religion of the little individual seeking the afterlife, believing that ideals remain in one's own heart and cannot be realized, is the same as the philosophy of polytheism and the religion of ancestor worship, and should be discarded as the old philosophy and religion of individualism. The universe evolves as one, and we evolve as eternally immortal. Happiness after death does not exist in another world. Every ideal is realized. Heaven or paradise is the earth of the deities, a race of beings which have evolved from humans.

This is the very philosophy and religion of socialism. We will make it our scientific religion until the great philosophers and saints of the future emerge, and we will leave our minds at rest and our bodies to their natural destinies. However, one thing we absolutely must understand is that the ideal is gradually realized, and that evolution never exceeds a set degree. Anatman and absolute love occur in the world of deities, they are not the reality of humankind. Mankind is not a deity in any respect, just as we are not reptiles or apes today. How is it possible, then, to preach the non-self and absolute love, which can be realized only in the world of the deities, to humanity, which is in the process of evolving today? This is the same unreasonable demand as saying, "live like a reptile, live like an ape," to the human race, which has already evolved to the present day.

Therefore, the philosophy and religion of social democracy excludes Christianity and retains Buddhism,[226] but will stand only as the philosophy

---

[226] The original text reads, "The philosophical religion of social democracy excludes Christianity and adds Buddhism..." and has a (sic) by it. Literally interpreted, this

and religion of social democracy. Today's human beings cannot survive without food and clothing—so we assert socialism. Without love, we cannot be immortal—so we assert democracy. Social democracy is the only great bridge between mankind and deities. As long as humanity cannot break free from the shameful reality of excretion and copulation, it will not be able to break free from the unpleasant reality of competition for food on a species-by-species basis and for sex on an individual basis.

There are no errors in the natural law known as the law of evolution. Without the competition to develop the small ego, it is impossible to attain the big ego, and even more impossible to attain selfless love or absolute love. Christ preached absolute love. However, he commanded monogamy. This means the exclusion of love outside of the couple, which is not absolute love. This is the love of the small ego. Buddha preached selfless love. However, he broke the flesh of his loins and gave it to the wolf. This is an acknowledgment of the wolf's small ego, not absolute love. We do not speak of Buddha defecating or Christ farting, as we said of the German emperor earlier. However, these two people, still forced to perform such excretory acts, do not have the beauty of God or the Buddha as a sacred concept. One could say that they are similar to us regarding beauty, goodness, and truth in that they are elements of human society who idealize the world of deities which will be reached in humanity's distant future. The ideal of the deities is the ideal of all humankind, not just a few of them. However, social democracy has its own path from reality toward the ideal. The two eyes of social democracy look up to the sky and recognize the world of God. However, its feet step out far and walk, but do not leave earth.

---

means that Christianity is excluded, but Buddhism is not. However, if this is the case, the consistency of the statement that the Buddha preached "non-self" is questionable. Since Kita is saying that non-self love or absolute love can only be realized after evolving into the divine, it should be necessary to also exclude Buddhism, which preaches this non-self love. We can only assume that Kita made an error in his argument.

Social democracy's gate to heaven is not Amen. The road to paradise is not Sukhavati. It is in the class struggle, in the development of individuality, in the enlightenment according to one's ability, in free love, and in science.

Needless to say, we are not so arrogant as to say that we have found even the guidance of scientific religion that the whole world is demanding. I have only stopped my hammer, one of a single laborer, for a moment, pointed to the other side of the river, and told you the purpose for which the social democrats work, that they are trying to build an iron bridge connecting mankind and deities. We merely confess that our thankless work, our arduous job of constructing this iron bridge, does not cause us any pain at all when we see the light on the other side of the river bank, rather, it fills us with uncontainable joy from our religious convictions. We are definitely not on the side of Christians who preach absolute love, Buddhists who preach selfless love, and especially those who, in recent years, have proclaimed themselves prophets and saviors. They demand that mankind immediately become deities and ridicule the bridge construction projects of social democracy, abusing the people truly trying to reach that goal. We respect the sincerity of their passion, provided, of course, that they are harmless madmen who do not tell humanity to live like "apes" or "reptiles." In this respect, we should most regret the loss of such a man as Mr. Hajime Kawakami, who abandoned the pen of *Review of Socialism* to preach anatman love.

Given what we've said above, the conclusion is as follows.

All current theories of biological evolution are based on the preconceived notions of creationism—which biological evolution has used all its power to refute—and interpret the facts of biological evolution through this creationist understanding. In other words, the conception of individuals is based on the individualistic idea that human beings existed as individuals from the beginning of the world, and does not understand the competition for survival which uses society as its unit, which is a large individual that divided like an amoeba from a single entity. Therefore, it is impossible to determine the status of the competition for survival with the individual person as the unit, the competition for sex, and the version of competition for food which uses the individual person as its unit in the theory of biological evolution. They think of humankind as something that will exist until the end of the world, and they do not understand the place of humankind in the hierarchy of biological species. Therefore, they are unable to infer the future evolution of the earth in which the ideal will be realized and a higher level of creatures will take the place of humankind.

The reason we do not arrive at the scientific religion, which says the future evolution of humankind will bring heaven to earth, is also due to the preconception of the religious belief of creationism. Since social philosophy discusses the laws and ideals of the evolution and survival of the living species known as human society, it must naturally be discussed as a theory of social evolution in a chapter at the end of the volume about the theory of biological evolution. The philosophy of cosmic teleology and the science of biological evolution are in agreement for the first time here, and become a scientific religion through mutual induction and deduction. However, since we humans are a species of relative beings, the universe as viewed by humans and the purpose of the universe as conceived by humans are only relative ideals in terms of the size of the universe. As long as we exist as humans, the deities are the absolute ideal. Therefore, we maintain that the theory of biological evolution has no conclusion without the single word "anthropoid."

Of course, deities should take up the pen in the next section.

Volume 4: The So-Called Theory of Japan's National Polity and Its Restorative Principle of Revolution

肆

Chapter 9

In the previous three volumes, we have reviewed the serious badmouthing of socialism and given a compendium of what constitutes the fundamental theory of socialism. This is how the study of socialism should be conducted, and it should be sufficient to describe socialism generally. However, when socialism is advocated in this land named Japan, there remains something bizarre that must be interpreted in a special way. That is the so-called "theory of national polity," or "kokutairon" in Japanese, and the dreaded question of whether or not socialism is in conflict with national polity. This question is not limited to socialism, but is asked whenever any new ideology is introduced.

Touching upon this "theory of national polity" results in an immediate strangulation of thought and ideas. Because of this, even political commentators have their free tongues bound, like slaves or serfs under tyrannical rule. It is also because of this that newspaper reporters are not ashamed to skillfully use extremely ugly words for the purpose of flattery, listing off these words like drummers following a beat. This theory of national polity has hurt all ethical and moral theory, from university professors to elementary school teachers, makes both Christianity and Buddhism into corrupt and idolatrous religions, and then insults and denounces every other idea or school of thought as "dangerous to national polity," eliminating them. If this is the case, it is not at all surprising that socialism is today persecuted by scholars and the government as being "in conflict with national polity."

It is only to be lamented that a socialist would not stand before this pope and give a rigorous defense. At the very least, if one believes that there is a conflict with national polity, the way to avoid the danger of public statements is indeed to remain silent. Yet, there are those who would say, "they are not in conflict," or, worse, try and run away from the conflict with the argument that socialism is "in line with national polity," which is an insincerity that can only be found in Japan. In particular, those who advocate state socialism, for example, are rather assassins of socialism in this respect, as they attempt this abomination of trying to build socialism on top of the "theory of national polity." We will argue forever in the name of pure socialism: one's spirit must be infused before the physical body is created.

For Western socialists, the first revolution is over, and next is the current mission of defeating economic disparity. For the socialists in Japan, still in the midst of the industrial revolution, it is more urgent to seek independence of conscience by exterminating delusion than to worry about economic disparity, which is relatively less extreme here. Yes, for the people of this nation, a clear understanding of the current system of government and national polity is especially important when advocating socialism as a practical matter. If we remain on our knees like dogs under the threat of "national polity," no matter how much we cry for public ownership of land and capital, such materialistic blindness alone will leave socialism as nothing but a rotting corpse whose spirit has left.

What about today, however? Like the Nanto battle monks rushing forward carrying their mikoshi,[227] or portable Shinto shrine, the only way for the cowardly academics and despicable politicians to attack is to hide behind "the theory of national polity" while wielding their blades of persecution and

---

[227] Refers to the famous direct petitions by the battle monks, where they would display the power and authority of Buddha and the gods, and thus demand and request things of the imperial court. It was performed by the battle monks of Kofuku-ji and Enryaku-ji temples. "Nanto" refers to Kofuku-ji (Enryaku-ji is referred to as "Hokurei.") The Kofuku-ji battle monks often brought sakaki, a species of evergreen sacred to Shinto, from Kasuga Taisha Shrine to the court, and since the Fujiwara clan's god is worshipped at Kasuga Taish Shrine, it was difficult for the regents to blindly refuse them, causing said regents much grief and worry.

shooting arrows of insults. And just as the warriors guarding the imperial court would bow respectfully to the mikoshi of the battle monks of Enryaku-ji Temple, calm their hearts, and admonish them, so too do all principles and theories simply evade in the face of the mikoshi known as "national polity."

So, some who see us now stooping before this mikoshi and attempting to take a shot at it would say that it is a risky venture. However, we will submit to this task, this mission, peacefully. For, just as there has never yet been a true god who inflicts divine punishment in the mikoshi of the priests, so those who are enshrined in the mikoshi of "national polity," and claim that "anyone who touches me is impious," are not actually the emperor, but "dogū," or clay figures created by the superstitions of these battle monks. In other words, the emperor in "the theory of national polity" is not the emperor of Japan in today's constitutional state, but a clay figure in a village of savages, fabricated by slave morality, Shinto superstition, ignorance of the nature of the state and its laws, and inverted and false historical interpretation.

The dogū of the savage village, whether it lies as an enemy in the front of socialism or rolls to the back of the political camp, is of no use to the socialist world and movement. Fear of dogū is a practice in the villages of the undeveloped South Pacific—though even in the villages of the undeveloped people of the Orient, people are fighting each other for these dogū, trying to make a profit for themselves. Socialism needs only stride forward under the banner of truth.

We will start by stating the conclusion of this volume. What is commonly called "the theory of national polity" is absolutely not today's national polity, nor does it refer to the past history of the Japanese people. We will refer to it as "restorative revolutionism," something which is clearly trying to destroy today's national polity. We are not making up something self-serving as a means to avoid persecution because we believe it is dangerous to stand against such public opinion—in other words, against an ancient, established theory. We say this because the history of the Japanese people and the current national polity are not compatible with "the theory of national polity" in the slightest. Oh, even though it has been thirty-nine years since this nation's great revolution, there are still only a few such as us who are trying to defeat the so-called theory of national polity. Why is this happening in the first place? It is because there is such an egregious corruption of the sanctity of academia everywhere in the world. We do not say this as singular socialists. We are doing it precisely for the sake of the sanctity of academia. It is absolutely not for socialism! It is for national polity itself! It is for the history of Japan itself!

First, we will discuss the current national polity. Then, in accordance with most academics who classify the national polity according to the location of sovereignty, we must explain the national studies and constitutional jurisprudence as to whether the state or the emperor is the main body of sovereignty.[228]

Truth is truth above all things. Socialism is not merely truth about economics, ethics, sociology, history, and philosophy; it is also truth about jurisprudence. It is, in other words, an assertion of the sovereignty of a geographically limited society: the state. The jurisprudence of socialism is statist. So, to speak of monarchism or democracy based on the jurisprudence of the individualist era is clearly in error. When we speak of monarchism in the conventional sense, it is based on the principle that the sovereign is the target to which benefits are attributed, and when we speak of democracy, it is based on the argument that the ultimate goal is for the citizens to be the target to which benefits are attributed. They are individualist in that they have the fundamental idea that rights exist in the location where benefits are attributed and purpose exists. Socialism—or nationalism in legal terms—is the idea that the state is the object and subject of the rights to which the interests belong, and argues that sovereignty resides in the state. Individualism posits that in

---

[228] This refers to the theory of the emperor as the sovereign versus the theory of the emperor as a state institution.

primitive times, individuals existed without cohesion, so if we look at social cohesion today from the standpoint of individualism, we naturally have no choice but to explain it by the social contract theory. However, since it is a biological fact that human beings have been social beings since primitive times, the fallacy of the social contract theory is obvious and there is no reason to argue about monarchism or democracy over the location of sovereignty.

So, if we advocate monarchism or democracy on the basis of the jurisprudence of the age of individualism, we take issue with the following. Since this social state is determined to be organized for the freedom and independence of individuals (in other words, for the purpose and benefit of individual persons), and since it is imagined that sovereignty existed in each of the people before it was organized (peacefully in the case of Rousseau, or in a constant state of struggle of all against all in the case of Hobbes), the question is where sovereignty, which was assumed to exist individually before organization, will exist after organization. However, since that method of organization was conceived because there was nothing better in the thoughts of the time than the social contract theory, today, when the social contract theory has been discarded, the individualist theory of the location of sovereignty has become a meaningless theory that disputes the conclusion without having a premise itself.

Of course, just as the theory of national polity was of great significance at the end of the Edo period, the theory of the social contract was once the basis of all discussions. Until the French Revolution, classes did not live under equal laws as they do today, and the laws themselves indicated a class state. Even in parliament, each class had its own objectives and interests, which resulted in different resolutions, and the laws were never made as a unified state, as is the case today. They were of a treaty-like nature, based on the contract of each class. So the social contract theory was adopted in the mindset of individualism—although it's only an unfounded hypothesis that this mindset influenced the origin of the state and primitive society—and it was, unavoidably, the only conclusion of the explanation and interpretation of the law of the state at that time. Without this hypothesis, no social phenomena could be interpreted.

But that is not the case today. Even if the development of the capitalists has led to the institutions of the state being monopolized by one class, and the classes of society have come to confront each other in great divisions, this is something for economics to deal with, and from the standpoint of jurisprudence, the Japanese nation is without doubt a unified state. Even if the clan government has the emperor to enact laws that benefit its own class, and the congress is completely a pawn of the capitalists and cooperates with the goals of that class to pass laws, once they become law, jurisprudence should naturally look at them as the laws of Japan that transcend class, without regard to the circumstances under which they were passed. So, while the nature of constitutions made according to the medieval theory of social contract was that of a treaty between the monarch and the nobility or the people, today's constitutions are by no means contracts. The monarch and the people are not two classes that are opposed to each other in their relationship of rights and obligations by virtue of the execution of a contract known as the constitution. It is not because of an obligation of the monarch to restrain himself before the rights of the people that his actions are restricted, nor are the people made to bear obligations in an attempt to satisfy the monarch's rights under the monarch's demands. In other words, the duties the people must bear are the rights demanded by the state, and the rights claimed by the monarch are the duties the state must bear.

The Japanese people and the Japanese emperor are not two classes opposed by a contract of rights and obligations, and their rights and obligations are not rights and obligations that these two classes can directly assume and demand by contract. In summary, the rights and obligations that the Japanese emperor and the Japanese people have are not rights and obligations that are in direct conflict with each other, but with the Empire of Japan. For example, the Japanese people have an obligation not to ignore the emperor's government, not because the emperor has the right to demand it directly from the people, but because the state has the right to demand it and the people have an obligation before that state. The reason why the Japanese emperor is obligated not to issue laws and orders without regard to the will of the Diet is not because the people have the right to demand it directly from the emperor, but because the state has the right to demand it, and the emperor is obligated by the state to do so—this is what separates the medieval class state from the modern civic state. (For more on the medieval class state history, read the later section on interpreting history.)

Of course, this is not to say that even today there are no traces of class states, such as monarchs, aristocrats, and the general public, in the law itself. Nor is it to say that the place to which the law confers benefits is not, in some views (especially those of political science), limited to monarchs or aristocrats alone. This is because the state is an evolving organism (read where we define "individual" in *The Theory of Biological Evolution and Social Philosophy*), and its polity and system of government evolves in accordance with the growth of the organism, so it is not possible to artificially distinguish a clear evolutionary process. However, the legal theory that the state of today should not be viewed as the class state of the medieval period is based on the fact that monarchs and nobles do not exist as entities that receive benefits that should belong to the state, as was the case in the medieval period, and that the state has become a system in which monarchs and nobles are maintained as benefits belonging to the state for the purpose of the state. For example, the benefit of the emperor holding no responsibility could be understood from a certain perspective as benefitting the emperor, but from a legal perspective, it is derived from laws and regulations that exist for the purpose and benefit of the state, and the benefit belongs to the state. In addition, the fact that only the nobility and a limited number of persons are entitled to become members of the House of Peers is also seen as if it benefits their class, but since this is also derived from laws that exist for the purpose and benefit of the state, it is inevitable from a legal perspective that the benefit is attributed to the state. Needless to say, other categories such as sovereigns, nobles, and citizens are subjects of rights because they are independent and have their own purposes and interests that belong to them, according to their status. However, such rights are what is called political power, and in the case of monarchs, it is the right to assume the imperial throne, which is a position of great authority. For the nobility, it is the right to be a member of the House of Lords or to hold elections with special powers, and for most citizens, it is the right to hold elective positions,[229] which are important when elections are being held.

However, the right to the throne and the right to be an elector are never sovereignty, but the right to a position where one can exercise sovereignty. Therefore, in a modern civic state, the monarch and the people are never the body of sovereignty, even in any despotic monarchy or in the largest democracies that can legislate directly. The body of sovereignty is the state, and the sovereignty of the state is exercised by the monarch or the people for the purpose of the state itself, which lives independently. Therefore, the rights and duties of the sovereign and the people are not a direct contractual conflict, as in a class state, but are rights and duties toward the state. It follows naturally, then, that the state has a legal personality and status as the entity to which rights and duties are attributed,[230] and it is also a natural logical consequence that the sovereign and the people become the agents of the state for the purpose of the survival and evolution of this personality.

Therefore, unless one maintains the social contract theory of the class-state era and the assumption of individualism, there is no reason to interpret the present Constitution as placing the sovereign and the people in conflict in

---

[229] Most likely this includes both the right to vote and the right to be elected.

[230] This is the theory where the state or nation has personhood, or personality.

terms of rights and duties, nor to determine that the ruler or the people are the body of sovereignty.

However, while the state existed from the beginning on the basis of social cohesion and its members slept under the purpose of the state in a primitive, unconscious state (see where we explained the primitive age in *The Theory of Biological Evolution and Social Philosophy*), that social cohesion became the property of the monarch along with the land during the evolutionary process up to the Middle Ages, and the legal status of the state became that of an object during this time. The state was not a subject of sovereignty to realize its own goals and interests, but an object of property subject to the disposition of its owners, such as marriage, inheritance, and cession, for the benefit and purposes of the sovereign.

In this period, the sovereign ruled the state for his own purposes and interests, so that the place where those purposes existed and benefits were attributed became the subject of rights and the ruler was the body of sovereignty. The state was the object of governance. Let's name this period when the state did not have personality but was instead a thing, an object, the "patriarchal state," and we will say it continued like this until the Middle Ages. Today, even if we call it a democratic country or a monarchy, it is not like the Middle Ages when the monarch inherited the land and the people as his property, gave them as gifts, or killed them as he pleased. The state is a legal personality, it has personality, and even the monarch is included as a member of the state. Thus, it is clear that the ruler is not a sovereign who stands outside the state and owns it, as in the Middle Ages, but an agent of the state as a member of the state. In other words, the state has come to govern for its own purposes and interests with an obvious consciousness, rather than primitively and unconsciously, and the state has become the body of sovereignty as the place where purposes exist and benefits are attributed. Let us name this the "civic state," and place it as our national polity today.

Because they do not categorize the state in evolutionary terms and because they do not define the issue as to whether the state is a person or a thing, both those who argue sovereignty of the ruler and those who argue sovereignty of the state today are guilty of countless contradictions and meaningless arguments. In the first place, they are fundamentally mistaken in their method of jurisprudence. A national polity or system of government should never be interpreted in terms of a formal number, such as Aristotle's number of rulers.[231] Today's jurisprudence does not indulge in static speculation as in ancient Greece.[232] National polity and systems of government should be studied kinetically, as an evolving, or historically progressive, social phenomenon.

If today's constitutional scholars took this attitude, there would be no such controversy as whether the right to govern the German Empire, as it has evolved today, belongs to the federal states or to the Empire,[233] and there would be no debate as to whether Great Britain is a monarchy or a democracy. In particular, there would be no egregious fallacies, which both those who argue ruler sovereignty and those who argue state sovereignty have fallen into, with respect to the majority of what today would be called constitutional monarchies. If we do not study legal phenomena in a dynamic way, if we do not consider the state or polity as evolving, then the ancient state and polity and the medieval state and polity are completely outside the study of jurisprudence. If we do so, we will also not be able to explain the modern national polity and system of government that have inherited the evolution of

---

[231] In his *Politics*, Aristotle divides the systems of government into monarchy, aristocracy, and democracy (with corresponding worse forms being tyranny, oligarchy, and ochlocracy). The term "number of rulers" probably refers to this division.

[232] "Static" means an analysis of economic phenomena without taking into account time factors or cause/effect relationships. The opposite is "kinetic."

[233] Germany is a federal republic consisting of "Länder" (states).

the ancient and medieval national polity and system of government. This is why Japan has the superstition it calls "the theory of national polity."

So, despite their countless different interpretations, these theorists are united in their inability to explain today's national polity and system of government due to the lack of evolutionary consideration of the nation of Japan. Look at the nation from an evolutionary perspective using the principles of national studies. Then the national polity and system of government of today will be clear, and the various theories of academic classification will be found to be of no value at all. Because of their lack of understanding of this point, people such as Mr. Yatsuka Hozumi have finally thrown up their hands and insisted that neither national polity nor the system of government can be classified and dealt with separately.[234]

University writings say the following:

> The national polity is the result of history and is not the same in every country. Therefore, there is no such thing as a universal national polity. Nor can scholars exhaustively enumerate the different types of

---

[234] A constitutional scholar of the Meiji and Taisho periods, Yatsuka Hozumi is the younger brother of civil law scholar Nobushige Hozumi. He is a typical example of a constitutional scholar who stands on the theory of emperor sovereignty. He is also famous for his criticism of the Civil Code drafted by Boissonade, which he wrote as *Minpo Idete Chuko Horobu* (*The Civil Code Defeated by Loyalty and Filial Piety*). However, in *The Conscious Development of Japanese Jurisprudence* (Yuhikaku, 1942), Ono Seiichiro, a criminal law scholar, clarified the distinction between national polity and system of government, stating that "the former refers to the state system according to where the sovereignty resides, while the latter refers to the form of government behavior, and our national polity is characterized by its being a 'pure' monarchy," (pages 85-86). So, it is not quite correct to say that Hozumi doesn't differentiate between national polity and government systems at all.

national polities. The location of sovereignty in the past and in the future is the result of history and can vary from country to country. Therefore, I believe that the discussion of national polity is a discussion of a specific country and time period, and that it is impossible to enumerate the categories of national polity in a general and abstract manner. In explaining our constitution, we can only explain the national polity defined by the history of our country.

Even if Mr. Yatsuka Hozumi and others say that history defines the national polity, this is not a kinetic study, but merely a way to argue that because history is different in all countries, the national polity is different in all countries. Even if the so-called "particular nation" refers to a particular Japan, nothing is heard about the so-called "particular period." One moment they might say, "It is a characteristic of our national polity that the sovereignty of the government of the nation has remained unchanged under the throne of all generations," and the next, "The revolution of the Meiji Restoration restored the sovereignty of the nation." As such, one could not expect a dynamic explanation of our national polity, which is apparently "determined by history," from someone who lacks any such historical knowledge. What is very strange, however, is that Mr. Nagao Aruga,[235] a jurist and monarchical sovereignty theorist who is recognized as one of the foremost historians of sovereignty, is not, similarly to Mr. Hozumi, conducting evolutionary research. Mr. Aruga, like Mr. Hozumi, is an authority on monarchical sovereignty, and like Mr.

---

[235] A jurist and sociologist of the Meiji period. He served as Secretary of the Privy Council and Director General of the Patent Bureau of the Ministry of Agriculture and Commerce, and lectured at the Tokyo Senmon Gakko (the predecessor of Waseda University) and the Military Academy, where he discussed national jurisprudence, but he turned to international law after the Sino-Japanese War. His academic style is said to have been sociological positivism.

Hozumi, he maintains that sovereignty is determined by history. Very much in accordance with this, his books, such as *Constitutional Law*, devote no small number of pages to the historical description of the Japanese people versus the imperial household.

We believe that the whereabouts of sovereignty is determined by history, and that national polity and government systems can be understood only through dynamic study. Mr. Aruga used that historical knowledge significantly to reveal the following truth:

> A popular theory that is nothing more than that, and which does not consider history whatsoever, is to assume that the Japanese people are all descendants of the god Amaterasu, and to base the sovereignty of the emperor on this fact alone.

Seeing that someone who argues monarchical sovereignty like Mr. Hozumi had become completely worthless in front of Mr. Aruga, we expected *Constitutional Law* would become something that gives some historical foundation to the theory of monarchical sovereignty. It's likely that Mr. Aruga expected this as well.

However, when we see that the words "governing power," "reign," and "emperor" in today's sense have remained the same for 2,500 years, or rather, are discussed in a way that reverses the historical course, we are forced to assert that no one in Japan has yet conducted an evolutionary study of the nation.

Of course, we absolutely do not deny that some of the oldest written works in Japan such as *Kojiki* and *Nihon Shoki* are important and sacred books. However, to rely on a text written in the fourteenth century after the Jinmu era,[236] as Mr. Aruga does, and to use a single phrase from said text:

---

[236] Jinmu era in this context refers to the year of the accession of the first Emperor Jinmu

That Toyoashihara's land of Mizuhonokuni[237] marks the land wherein mine descendants shall be crowned kings, and mine descendants shall rule as offspring of Amaterasu, where the ascension of the imperial throne should be unparalleled, harmonious with heaven and earth,[238] as the basis for your ideas and theory is a clear dogmatism of incredible imprudence.

Even if the characters for "king" or "rule" are written in the script of the fourteenth century after Jinmu, can we truly apply the similarity in form and pronunciation of the characters for the "right to rule" of today and connect the ancient past with the present day, so many centuries later? The long fourteen centuries before the *Kojiki* and *Nihon Shoki* were written—at the very least, there were no written characters at all during the ten centuries until Japan made contact with foreign culture—was a time of primitive life, when it is said that people would tie ropes in order to remember the deeds and words of their predecessors. Suppose the following. There are no written characters at all for

---

in the Chronicles of Japan as the first year of that era. In other words, year ten would be the tenth year after the ascension of Emperor Jinmu. In the Western calendar, this would equate to 660 BC. *Kojiki* was finished in year 712, and *Nihon Shoki* was finished in 720, so approximately fourteen hundred years had passed between the first year of Jinmu and the completion of those classic texts. The expressions in the text are based on this.

[237] A term of beauty for Japan.

[238] These words are said to have been uttered by Amaterasu when Amaterasu sent Amatsuhiko Hononinigi-no-Mikoto to Ashihara no Nakatsukuni (Japan) (the so-called "descent of Amaterasu"), and are found in the *Nihon Shoki*, volume 2, under the Jindai period (however, these words are not in the text of the *Shoki* but in an attached volume called the Issho). The modern translation is as follows. "Mizuhonokuni of Toyoashihara is the land where my descendants will be kings. You of the imperial line will be kings and rule over the land. There will be no limit to the prosperity and development of the imperial throne, along with heaven and earth."

ten centuries after today. Then, through Martian communication, Meiji history is written fourteen centuries from now in their Martian characters. Would it really be possible to express the relationship and system of the Meiji government in this *Kojiki* and *Nihon Shoki* fourteen centuries later written in the Martian language equivalents of "king" or "rule"? Even if we today keep records by tying rope, and even if the rope is of a metal that will not corrode for ten centuries, and even if our brains have evolved to such an extent that the words and deeds of our predecessors over the past ten centuries can be transmitted by language from the mouth of the grandfather to the ears of the grandchild without error, the letters of Mars will represent the ideas of Mars, and an evolved people fourteen centuries from now will use the letters of Mars written with the ideas and concepts that exist fourteen centuries from now.

Mr. Aruga, then, has argued dogmatically that because the old word "king" is like the "king" who is the ruler of a kingdom, and the old word "rule" is similar to today's "govern," that the ideas contained within, from the ancient age with no writing, through the days of contact with Chinese civilization when Japan learned writing, and now to the days of European civilization with writing, have not changed or evolved in any manner. His total lack of care whether the ideas of today's government relationships can be traced back thousands of years to a primitive era when the written word didn't even exist yet already shows a complete lack of qualifications as a historian.

We assert that the characters for "king" and "rule" are characters and ideas imported from China, and whether for a thousand years of primitive life people used phonetic, hieroglyphic, or even no characters at all is not clear. Therefore, it is only clear that Emperor Jinmu was not called "emperor" in today's script or manner of thinking,[239] and that his rights over the people should not be inferred from the rights or authority of the emperor today. (We

---

[239] It was Emperor Tenmu who first began using the title "emperor." Before that, they were known as "great king."

assert that the thousands of years making up the era of primitive life in which written words did not exist should be excluded from political history. Read the later section on the interpretation of history.)

Mr. Aruga is a historian who says that if the form and pronunciation of a character are the same, its content is the same now as in the past. Therefore, ignoring the rights of emperors from back then who owned lands and people as their patriarchs, historians will use the rights of the present emperor to criticize the actions of past emperors, such as Emperor Yuryaku taking his subjects' wives based on his own property rights;[240] Emperor Buretsu killing his own people, which were his property, as he pleased; and Emperor Go-Shirakawa giving his land to warriors, then taking it away to give to his favorite concubine.[241] They would then go on to call it tyrannical and irrational, inhuman and illegal. The emperor at that time owned the entire nation, a different meaning of "emperor" from that of today, and the people had no status as human beings, but were his possessions, along with the land, as his "great treasures."[242]

However, some of these historians, like Mr. Aruga, do not make such retroactive criticisms, and do recognize the rights of the emperor of the time, but on the contrary, they argue that the rights of the emperor of the time are attached to the emperor of today, as if he were still the patriarch who can treat the land and people as he pleases. Today's emperor is a privileged class of the state, a completely different meaning from in those days. He can't cede the

---

[240] There are many stories about Emperor Yuryaku obliterating his political enemies (including assassinations), and there are stories about Emperor Buretsu's cruelty as well. According to *Nihon Shoki*, Emperor Buretsu would have people climb trees only to cut the trees down or shoot the person climbing with arrows. There's also a story of having a pregnant woman's stomach cut open in order for him to see the baby.

[241] Reffering to Takashina no Eishi. Her name comes up in stories such as *Tokushi Yoron*.

[242] Refers to "the emperor's people."

state through marriage to a foreign ruler. He can't divide the state between two or three princes. He can't usurp and violate the property rights of the people. He can't injure or destroy the lives of the people as "great treasures." These very people, who have rights and obligations only to the state, can obtain relief from the state or exercise the right of self-defense against the emperor's blade. Even though the form and pronunciation of the word "emperor" is the same, today's emperor is one of the state agents that operate under the purpose and interests of the state as a privileged class of the state.

To be more precise, the emperor before the Meiji Revolution was not the governing body of the Japanese empire as he is after the revolution. Though he may have identified himself as such in ideals only, in legal fact he was a patriarchal monarch who was able to dispose of the people he owned as objects, not people. Therefore, when the emperor was at his most powerful (as in the period leading up to rule of the Fujiwara clan) or at his weakest (as in the period after Yoritomo),[243] the land and people within his sphere of influence existed under his purposes and interests, and he was the subject of the right to rule where his purposes existed and where his interests were attributed. The Japanese national polity has not remained the same over a period of thousands of years. The Japanese emperor has not remained the same, unchanging from past to present. Why are there people who, in spite of this, will advocate the idea of "I am the state," which Louis XIV claimed as part of his natural rights during the medieval patriarchal period, and say that it applies to the current national polity as long as it's prefaced by the phrase "Regarding our national polity," telling us that "It's unjust in the West, but not in our national polity"? The words of Louis XIV weren't unjust in the West in the national polity of those days. They weren't unjust in our national polity until the Middle Ages either. However, if they were to be invoked today,

---

[243] "rule of the Fujiwara clan" refers to the Heian period, and "after Yoritomo" refers to the Kamakura period and later.

whether in the West or in Japan, they would not only be unjust, they would clearly indicate treason against the state. Do they not know that national polity is different not only on the horizontal plane, but also on the vertical one?[244]

If they argue that there is a difference between Japan and a foreign country, the latter of which can be traveled to in a matter of ten days, do they not realize that there is no reason to believe that the past and the present, separated by thousands of years, are the same when it comes to national polity? If they believe that, even though the word "emperor" is the same, a Russian emperor, Turkish emperor, and Belgian emperor are all different, do they not also think that, despite all being called "emperor," Jimmu, Go-Daigo, and Meiji are all just as different? As long as they are pronounced the same, they would interpret the English word "miserable," which translates to "hisan" (悲惨) in Japanese, as being the same as "mizore buru," (みぞれ降る) meaning "falling sleet" in Japanese, because they sound similar. Or what about interpreting the English word "soldier," which would be "heishi" (兵士) in Japanese, sounding the same as "sou ja," (そうじゃ) meaning "in agreement" in Japanese, because they sound similar as well? Just because the character for "shimobe," (僕) meaning a servant or slave during the Kamakura period, is the same as the character in the phrase "kimi boku shikkei" (君僕失敬),[245] doesn't mean they have the same meaning, and anyone who thinks they do probably also thinks that a lack of manners between friends would be a crime of disrespect, punishable by five years of heavy imprisonment.[246]

---

[244] The terms "vertical" and "horizontal" have been used before, with different meanings attributed to these axes. Here, horizontal seems to refer to space/region and vertical to time.

[245] We're not sure what this phrase means. From the later "lack of manners between friends," it probably refers to people close to each other not using stiff formalities.

[246] In the days of the old penal code, imprisonment was divided into two types: light

In the first place, the most important task of jurisprudence is to determine the content of written characters. This is very different between natural sciences and social sciences, where the latter focuses on research determining the content of academic terms, since terms in natural sciences such as oxygen and hydrogen, stomach and heart, do not change geographically or with time. In particular, among the social sciences, the final goal of jurisprudence especially is determining the content of a script, since it inherits and uses the same forms and pronunciations despite the evolution of society and differences in social phenomena. Some historical research of law needs to be incredibly strict on this point. Now, then, if we forget that the content of the word "emperor" has changed endlessly over thousands of years, we must know that any discussion of the Constitution involving such, no matter how historically based, would result in nothing more than highly exaggerated advocacy. This is why Mr. Hozumi understands the modern emperor as from an era in which the emperor owned the land and the people, while Mr. Aruga thinks of Emperor Jinmu, who lived in a time without written characters, as an emperor who owned the right of governance as his property right.

Here lies the crux of our argument for classifying nations according to their evolution.

However, this is not to say that today's constitutional scholars do not classify Western states according to their historical evolution and their time period. So, for what reason do they always ignore the distinction between the ancient and the modern when discussing our Japan, and why do they always use the special preface "in our national polity" from their introduction to their conclusion when arguing over our Constitution? It's because there is such a thing here as "one eternal imperial lineage." Because of this phrase indicating

---

imprisonment and heavy imprisonment, with prison work being imposed for heavy imprisonment. This is a penalty not found in the current penal code. Note there's also a pun between two Japanese spellings of "the crime of disrespect."

that all the emperors share one unbroken bloodline, Japanese people believe that while the national and political systems of Western countries have evolved in accordance with the evolution of history, the national and political system of the Japanese people is outside the laws of evolution, sitting still and not evolving at all. Therefore, when Japanese constitutional scholars discuss the national polity in their constitutional theory, they say that we must determine what kind of national polity we have, that is, where sovereignty resides, but they are always consistent in their interpretation that "in our national polity or eternal lineage, sovereignty resides with the emperor."

This is not an interpretation at all. It is an argument that sovereignty resides with the emperor because sovereignty exists in the unbroken lineage of the emperor. It is the same circular answer as when A was asked his age, he answered "the same as B," and when B was asked his age, he answered "the same as A." It is not only jurists who should laugh. Ethicists and philosophers, too, have been hit in the side of the skull with the single phrase "one eternal lineage," and have all become braindead. This is why there is no classification in Japan according to the evolution of the nation.

I will clearly explain one eternal imperial lineage in a later historical discussion. Here, we only need point to Mr. Yatsuka Hozumi, whose constitutional jurisprudence makes this single phrase, "one eternal lineage," the basis of all deductions. Mr. Hozumi's brain has become profoundly foolish after pitiably being hit by this phrase. So everything related to the Constitution has no cohesion or organization, and he will mention something, then erase it, making assertions only to defeat them himself later on. He will seem to preach Takamagahara and the Shinto theory of the gathering of the gods only to then immediately fall from Takamagahara and become a scientific researcher of mythology.[247]

---

[247] "Takamagahara" refers to the country in heaven where the gods reside. Amaterasu rules over it.

In one particularly egregious case, he completely abandons his position as a monarchist and turns into a nationalist in his theory of the nature of sovereignty, and in what appears to be a theory of history, he seems to advocate the sovereignty of the emperor or the sovereignty of the shogunate. This volume's arguments have been influenced the most by Mr. Hozumi because he is the chief spokesman of the theory of national polity. Because I need to study his theories as closely as possible, I have read all the books he has published, almost all of his articles in various journals, and his written lectures at universities and other private universities, where he says the same thing year after year. However, it goes without saying that it is impossible to find coherent thought in a string of contradictory language, and no psychiatrist could extract any meaning from a mind struck by the phrase "one eternal lineage." In fact, in his very conception of the state, he takes a national sovereignty view of the state.

I dare say that this point is not limited to Mr. Hozumi. All those who advocate the theory of monarchical sovereignty, in their definition of the state, steal the definition of the modern state and remain unaware of it. Mr. Hozumi and all monarchical sovereignty theorists, when organizing their constitutional studies, divide the subject of governance and the object of governance. The subject of governance is made to be the emperor, and the object of governance is made to be the land and the people. If they say—as we said earlier that in the medieval state the land and people were objects that existed for the purpose and benefit of the sovereign—that the state exists of two elements, the land and the people, and the emperor exists as a ruler of the state outside the state itself, then the Great Empire of Japan is a medieval-era state made of the two elements, land and people, with said land and people as objects, since Article I of the Japanese Constitution states, "The Great Empire of Japan shall be ruled by the emperor of one eternal lineage." If we take the theory of monarchical sovereignty and divide it into a subject and an object of governance, then the Empire of Japan must be a state composed of the two elements of the Middle Ages. Yet, Mr. Hozumi and all the current monarchists, standing completely on the modern view of the state, reject this interpretation. Mr. Hozumi says, "A state is a human society formed on a certain land and organized by a ruler and the people," and, "The state, subjectively speaking, is the subject of the right to govern."

Isn't the idea that the state, subjectively speaking, is the subject of the right to govern the very core of state sovereignty? The idea that the state consists of three elements, the ruler, the people, and the land, is an idea of the state that did not exist in the Middle Ages, when the sovereign gave or inherited the state as his property, and is instead the idea of the modern state within the theory of state sovereignty. If the state consists of these three elements, then the monarch himself is also included, and thus a monarch's gift or inheritance of the state is a contradiction of his own gift or inheritance at the same time. In the medieval idea of the sovereign as the owner of the state, when they spoke of "my state" as the absolute owner and ruler, the state was composed of two elements.

In other words, in the Middle Ages, the monarch was placed outside the state in legal theory as the subject that governed the state, and the state was the object to be governed by the monarch, but in the modern philosophy adopted by Mr. Hozumi and those who agree with him, the monarch is included as part of the state, as a member and part of the organization of the state. If outside the state, a monarch can own that state. Thus, the state was the property of the monarch and the object of his governance. If within the state, he could not own the state, as an element contained within the state could not be a subject of governance that could claim ownership over the state which contained him as an element. Therefore, if we are to argue for monarchical sovereignty by dividing governance into a subject and an object of governance, that Article I of the Constitution says that the Great Empire of Japan must be made up of two elements, the nation and the people, which are classified as medieval objects. If, on the other hand, the state is considered to have personality and is the main body of sovereignty, then the Empire of Japan in Article I is the main body of sovereignty with three elements, and must be interpreted as follows: "In the Great Empire of Japan, a modern state and the main body of sovereignty, said sovereignty is exercised by the emperor of one eternal lineage."

Not only that. If the Great Empire of Japan is to be a modern state with three elements, with the emperor as the subject of governance, Article I must be corrected and rewritten as, "The land and people of Japan, which is not a nation, shall be governed by the emperor of one eternal lineage." This is because, if one takes the modern conception of the state, which consists of three elements, then the Great Empire of Japan includes the emperor, whom Mr. Hozumi calls the ruler of the people, and that emperor is the subject of governance, which would place one of the three elements outside of the state. This would mean that the Great Empire of Japan, as stated in the Constitution, is not a unified state, but merely consists of the land and people, two elements of a state. If a nation is composed of three elements, including the ruler, it would be incomprehensible that the emperor, who is also the ruler, would rule the Great Empire of Japan, including its ruler. An empire, whose Article I states, "The Great Empire of Japan shall be ruled by the emperor of one eternal lineage," would then have an empire and an emperor who both govern and are governed by each other, making each one have their own elements of governance.[248] To summarize, Mr. Hozumi, and all other monarchical sovereignty theorists are in a dilemma. This dilemma is whether to adopt the medieval view of the state as consisting of two elements, the land and the people, or to adopt the modern view of the state as consisting of three elements, and to believe that one element of governance is the emperor of one

---

[248] This sentence is unclear. It may mean that mixing a medieval-like view of the emperor with a modern theory of the state would result in a contradiction, since both the state and the emperor would be the subject and object of governance.

eternal lineage and that the Great Empire of Japan in Article 1 of the Constitution refers not to the state but to the land and people.[249]

However, against Mr. Hozumi alone, this dilemma doesn't work. This is because when he says that "from a subjective point of view, a nation is the body of sovereignty," he isn't referring to the Great Empire of Japan, which is a nation made up of three elements, but to a certain part, one of the elements—the emperor. It does not refer to the state, which is clearly defined as the Great Empire of Japan in Article 1 of the Constitution, as the main body of governing power, but to the emperor of Japan, who is of one eternal lineage, as the main body of governing power. Therefore, Mr. Hozumi's argument is unique because it names the emperor as the state.

However, this confused use of terms is contrary to the purpose of a definition, which is to be a method of arranging ideas in an orderly fashion. Moreover, it would only unnecessarily disturb jurisprudence, because it would confuse the very foundations of thoughts on the matter. When the Constitution, a product of the modern state, speaks of an "empire," it refers to the unified state present in modern thought, which consists of three elements, as defined by various academics, and when it speaks of the "emperor of one eternal lineage," is speaks precisely of an emperor of one constant, unbroken bloodline. If, however one asserts that, as Mr. Hozumi asserts in his view of the state, "The state is, from a sovereign perspective, the subject of governing

---

[249] Let us summarize this. According to Kita, since Hozumi's thought includes the modern way of thinking, the emperor, although absolute, is included in the state, and the view of the emperor is slightly different from that of the emperor as in the Middle Ages. Therefore, the theory of emperor sovereignty emphasizes the "absoluteness" found in medieval emperors **while grafting them with the modern concept of monarch.** Kita sees a crucial difference between medieval and modern monarchs, who either stand outside the state or not, as incompatible with each other. On this basis, he criticizes Hozumi's theory as inconsistent.

power," then names that subject of governing power, the emperor, as the state however he pleases, it means that the Russo-Japanese war was not a national war, but a war waged by the emperor alone. This means that one must also argue that the sixty thousand people who died were all the emperor of one eternal lineage.

Because of this use of the written word, even today's state sovereignty theorists have no choice but to favor Mr. Hozumi as a man of superior and unfading wisdom.[250] When we hear the idea of a nation today, in any nation's languages, it is always the idea of a nation in modern thought; a society of human beings united politically over a certain territory. Just as when Americans hear the word "nation" they don't think of Congress, nor do the French think of voters when they hear it, does anyone in Japan think of the imperial throne or even the emperor himself when they hear the word "nation" or "state," as Mr. Hozumi does?

If one says, like Mr. Hozumi does, that the imperial throne is a state, it would mean they think nothing of fields and cows existing on the imperial throne, citizens living on it, and even all different types of buildings being built on it. This is like an elementary school child thinking of Japan's imperial throne as a thousand-mile-long dragon, much like the Kingdom of Italy is thought of as a giant boot. And if we say, as Mr. Hozumi does, that the emperor is a nation, then we can say that there are states consisting of beautiful men, that some nations have potato faces, that there are times when the nation has a sniveling look, and that there are nations whose heads are gradually balding. A nation called Germany will have an extremely foolish looking mustache and

---

[250] The original text says "one whose wisdom does not shift." It's difficult to understand, but in *The Analects*, there's the phrase "High wisdom and low foolishness are not interchangeable," which means, "The most knowledgeable person and the most foolish person aren't interchangeable regardless of how much one cultivates them." We've taken the meaning from this.

make grandiose speeches, and a nation called England may marry and kiss a single woman. When the monarch is hurt, the nation will cry out in pain; when the monarch walks, the nation will walk, and when the monarch wanders off to other countries, the nation will move about the earth, collide with other nations, and slide along the surface of other nations. The words of Frederick III, "if a monarch's foot is amputated during surgery, it means that the nation loses its foot,"[251] will become an authority that Mr. Hozumi must remember to cite in his constitutional studies.

In particular, in order to prove the words of Louis XIV, the greatest authority of all, "I am the State," he must provide evidence from ancient texts written in Latin that a person close to Louis XIV, equivalent to Ranmaru Mori,[252] followed the state around as it defecated, and was given a dagger for protection to carry in his pocket for his services in counting the state's farts. Nobody could understand how a medical scientist could say that the stomach, subjectively, is the heart, or that, objectively, it could be named the bladder. Likewise, the terms subjective and objective should not be used for completely different things, as Mr. Hozumi uses them. How confusing is it that the state seen subjectively is the same as the emperor seen objectively? The phrase "The state, seen objectively, is the subject of governance" is a theory of state sovereignty which subjectively dictates that the state is the main body of sovereignty. It is not a phrase intended to be adopted by monarchical sovereignty theorists who claim that the objective emperor is the body of sovereignty, and then attempt to name him as the state.[253]

---

[251] Perhaps Holy Roman Emperor Friedrick III (reigned 1452-1493), whose leg amputation was one of the best-documented surgical procedures of the Middle Ages.

[252] "Ranmaru Mori" was a samurai who was a close assistant to Nobunaga.

[253] This is difficult to understand, so we'll supplement it. The phrase "subject of governing power" is supposed to refer to a subjective evaluation of the state. By "the emperor viewed objectively," Hozumi probably means "absoluteness based on the idea of one

However, in actuality Mr. Hozumi says that the imperial throne is the body of sovereignty, but all state sovereignty theorists and some monarchist sovereignty theorists—for example, Professor Hisoka Inoue,[254] a professor of law at Kyoto Imperial University—have sufficiently disproven the idea that the imperial throne is a state institution. Today, it seems that they assert that the physical body of the emperor has the right of governance. State sovereignty theorists will argue, "If that were the case, wouldn't the nation perish with the death of the emperor?" Mr. Hozumi gives a very clever response. He says, "The emperor is not a mortal being. The emperor does not die. It is the life of Amaterasu itself, which has been continuously extended through one eternal lineage."

It is very clever to claim that the extension of life has scientific significance, thereby avoiding the criticism of state sovereignty theorists. The individual is prolonged and never dies. The life of Amaterasu is eternal, immortal, and thus is still alive today (see our discussion on the extension of the individual in *The Theory of Biological Evolution Theory and Social Philosophy*). So, we do not question whether or not Amaterasu had sovereignty as Mr. Hozumi says.

If the sovereignty of today's emperor itself exists, as Mr. Hozumi states, it would not be severed as long as the imperial lineage is eternally unbroken. Therefore, we can fully recognize that his nation will not die out. However,

---

eternal lineage." He also says that subjectivity and objectivity are mutually incompatible and should not be used for different things. In short, Kita is probably trying to say that there is a logical inconsistency in the fact that the theory of the sovereignty of the emperor mixes subjective and objective evaluations, which should be incompatible, in order to justify its claims.

[254] Constitutional law scholar of the Meiji era. He taught at Kyoto Hosei Gakko (now Ritsumeikan University) and also lectured on constitutional law courses at Kyoto Imperial University.

individuals extend infinitely and reproduce countless times, and this is a serious problem for Mr. Hozumi and those who agree with him. The current emperors, the ex-emperors who became monks, and the retired emperors are all individuals who will increase through reproduction, and as long as they are all alive, there will be three entities, each with complete authority to rule, and they will be in conflict with each other. And as soon as they fall, their right to rule remains in their body, and is carried off with them to the grave. Since Mr. Hozumi says that the emperor's body itself is the body of governance and the state itself, modern Japan would be three states at that time. The emperors exiled to distant islands were also the subjects of governance and the nation itself,[255] which means that the nation was exiled to the island and died. The ordained emperor, then, would have entered the temple, wrapped in vestments, as the subject of governance, and as the shaved head of the Empire of Japan, he would have struck a wooden fish while chanting a Buddhist prayer.

It must be said that Mr. Hozumi is right. His so-called extension of life is an escape route found in the difficulty of maintaining the theory of imperial throne sovereignty because it cannot be argued that the emperor ceases to be the subject of governing power by virtue of his abdication of the throne. Also, since it is not known whether the life of the emperor is extended by the eldest son or by the second or third imperial princes, and if the right to rule passes only to the life of the crown prince and not to the other princes, then when the crown prince is deposed or dies young, there will be no life with extended right to rule, no emperor, and the body of authority will disappear and the nation will cease to exist as a result. Therefore, the right to rule must be extended to every prince as a physical part of his body, and since Emperor Keiko had

---

[255] These emperors include Sutoku, Go-Toba, Juntoku, Tsuchimikado, and Go-Daigo. Incidentally, Emperor Juntoku was exiled to Sado, Kita's birthplace.

seventy-two sons,[256] there are seventy-two subjects of ruling authority and a state whose life has been extended. Thus, the seventy-two princes who settled in the provinces, became local rulers and heroes, flourished and waned, and later became feudal aristocrats could all be considered as having reproduced and extended the emperor's right to rule.

Mr. Hozumi has no choice but to reply that this is true. If we deny this, then the right to rule of someone other than the imperial family, such as Emperess Suiko, who was the empress of Emperor Bidatsu and was sired by Soga no Iname,[257] must be explained by the right to rule of Emperor Kogen, who extended his life to Taknoeuchi no Sukune,[258] the ancestor of the Soga clan, since Emperor Suiko's life was not extended from the imperial family but from Iname's life. Even from today onward, the Imperial House Law stipulates that when there is no direct lineage, the lineage shall be inherited by a collateral lineage, and the "one eternal lineage" to this day is by no means a narrow one that maintains a strictly direct lineage. It is a very broad line that has leapt from countless collateral lines to countless collateral lines, so that the right to rule as well as their lives have been transmitted to the emperor's brothers, to his nephews and nieces, to their brothers' brothers, and to the

---

[256] A legendary emperor from the *Kojiki*. He was the twelfth emperor, the father of Yamato Takeru. According to *Kojiki* and *Nihon Shoki*, he had eighty children in total, and twenty-seven of them were sent to the provinces.

[257] Soga no Iname was a minister during the reign of Emperor Kinmei and was at odds with Monobe no Okoshi over the introduction of Buddhism. Empress Suiko is the granddaughter of Soga no Iname (the way it's written in the original text may make it seem like she's his daughter, but that's not the case).

[258] Takeuchi's name is spelled differently in the text (竹内), but we've used the modern spelling of it here (武内). Takeuchi no Sukune is said to have been active during the early years of the Yamato Imperial Court. He was the great-grandson (some say grandson) of Emperor Kogen (the eighth).

nephews and nieces of their nephews and nieces. Thus, the right to rule extended and reproduced with the life of Emperor Keitai,[259] who was hiding in the countryside, and to Emperor Koko, who went under the Minamoto clan.[260] In the same way, the Minamoto clan, descendants of Emperor Seiwa, and the Taira clan, descendants of Emperor Kanmu, are not the disrupters of the state that Mr. Hozumi thinks they are. It must be argued that they are legitimate rulers who have received an extension of the emperor's life. Furthermore, according to the so-called "one family of ruler and ruled" theory of the emperor's descent from Amaterasu, it must be argued that all forty-five million Japanese citizens are the body of sovereignty, since they are the extension of Amaterasu's life without death—is this not democracy? Is this not the very idea of "the same peoples lead to democracy"? (This reasoning is absolutely not meant to play with or insult Mr. Hozumi. Contrast this with our later historical interpretation where we trace lineage and discuss the historical expansion of the bud of political power.)

If this is the case, then even Mr. Hozumi must reply, "Yes, that's true," and follow this line of reasoning, and if not wanting to be led to the world of democracy, must then stop and stagnate at a certain spot. The first thing that must be done is to limit the ruling power to those whose lives are propagated and prolonged by Amaterasu, especially those who ascend to the throne of the emperor. This, however, abandons the claim of sovereignty in the physical body of the emperor and returns to the theory of sovereignty in the imperial throne, from which it fled earlier, and the fact that the theory of the sovereignty of the

---

[259] Emperor Keitai is considered to be the twenty-sixth emperor. After Emperor Buretsu, he was received by Otomo no Kanamura from Echizen and ascended to the throne.

[260] We have seen no record of Emperor Koko being under the Minamoto clan. However, there was a period of time when Emperor Uda was under them, so this is probably an error and Kita meant Emperor Uda.

throne cannot be sustained by the refutation of the national sovereignty theorists is evident from his own abandonment of it. He says the following:

> The throne is an institution of the state, and only when one ascends this throne through this state institution can one exercise the right to rule. The right to ascend to the throne, moreover, is a right limited by the state institution to be held by a certain limited line of people, and the right to the throne is a state right exercised by the state for the purpose and benefit of the state.

Not only that. If we say, as Mr. Hozumi does, that the right to rule resides in the emperor himself and that he never dies through the extension of the individual, then it could be said that not only our country, which is a nation of one eternal lineage, but also dynasties that died in three generations had their right to rule extended with life during the three generations. Even in England and Germany, the throne is the subject of governance as long as the royal lineage does not go extinct, and so, unlike when arguing that the emperor himself is the state, it isn't necessary in this case to dedicate a lifetime of effort into arguing that "We're discussing our national polity, which can't be compared to other countries," or "We're discussing the Japanese Constitution, which has been defined by Japanese history," or "Comparisons and analogies are pointless."[261]

To begin with, the root of this fallacy is the belief that Japan alone is controlled by a special, unique statecraft and historical philosophy. Needless to say, being different in race and ethnicity is a special mutation in a special environment, and obviously different racial and ethnic groups have their own special political forms and different degrees and directions of evolution.

---

[261] In other words, what Hozumi asserts applies not just to Japan only, but also to Germany and England, so the way he argues about only Japan is strange.

However, just as it was thought that people of different races and ethnicities were not human beings during the period of national isolation, it is an extremely uncivilized view of the nation to think that Japan will not evolve historically like other countries simply because it has a slightly different political form. It is a shameful knowledge of the people of Japan that they still try to make the Constitution consistent from its initial argument to its conclusion by talking about this idea of "revere the king, expel the barbarians."

All monarchical sovereignty theorists, even though their view of the state is a modern idea that follows the progress of society, still build their theory of monarchical sovereignty on the fundamental idea of state sovereignty because of the phrase "one eternal lineage." In particular, Mr. Hozumi, a leading scholar of the theory, indiscriminately conflates the emperor, the throne, and the state. Let us look at Article I of the Constitution as organized according to his thought. It would be as bizarre as the following: "The land and people of the Great Japan, which is not a nation, (if this is untrue, then it would be the medieval Great Empire of Japan, complete with the two elements of state land and people, neither of which have personality) are personal property and slaves which exist for the purposes and benefits of the sovereign. The one eternal lineage of the Great Empire of Japan will rule this. The throne or perhaps the emperor is the Great Empire of Japan."

All monarchical sovereignty theorists today must either throw away the current idea of the modern state that they use and replace it with the idea of the state from the Middle Ages, or correct Article I of the Constitution.

Make no mistake, however. We do not set up this dilemma by thinking of constitutional doctrine as being defined by the particular writing used in laws and ordinances. Thus, it is of course within the scholar's freedom to correct the phrase "the Empire of Japan" in Article I of the Constitution and change it to "not a nation, but merely land and people," as all monarchical sovereignty theorists do today. This is because no constitution can be interpreted only in terms of the exact writing of its law and ordinance, and the interpretation of a constitution is to determine the meaning of the letter of the law through a clean consideration of its fundamental thought and the many written characters that express it. So, Mr. Hozumi is free to interpret the phrase "the emperor of one eternal lineage" as "the Empire of Japan of one eternal lineage." Likewise, just as all current constitutional scholars, with the exception of Mr. Hozumi, have discarded the words "The emperor is sacred and must not be violated" as meaningless and historically-implemented,[262] we must also be free to fiercely debate Article IV of the Constitution through freedom of academic study. This is the article which states that the emperor is the head of state, that he is in control of the governing power, and that he exercises his governing power according to the provisions of the Constitution.[263]

The problem comes down to the single phrase, "head of state." If the phrase "head of state" is simply a trace of historical practice, like the word "sacred," scholars may pass it by without paying it any heed. This is because, much like the way Article I states, "The Great Empire of Japan, with his cherry blossoms in full bloom, shall be ruled by the emperor of one eternal lineage, furnished with heavenly knowledge and virtue, and adept in matters of both literature and battle," phrases and expressions such as "cherry blossoms in full bloom," or "furnished with heavenly knowledge and virtue, and adept in matter of both literature and battle," are meaningless to jurisprudence. It is not as if a nation without cherry blossoms lacks an element of the state, or that one can't ascend

---

[262] The original text has two characters in the compound for "following history" switched, with a (sic) mark. The correct version of the term is used later, so this is definitely a typo. However, even "following history" is vague. What we think "meaningless and historically-implemented" means is, "expressing the emperor's character based on following history, but has no meaning in terms of law."

[263] Article IV of the Imperial Constitution states, "The emperor is the head of the Empire, combining in himself the rights of sovereignty, and exercises them, according to the provisions of the present constitution."

to the imperial throne if they lack this knowledge and virtue, so it only makes sense that jurists would want to remove these phrases. Is the phrase "head of state" one of these kinds of phrases? We believe it is.

Yet, all constitutional scholars in Japan today organize their discussions around this single phrase as the center of their thought. Mr. Hozumi, for example, takes it as an authority, while Mr. Inoue, another monarchical sovereignty theorist, says that it is "the place where national consciousness resides" and that this phrase is the only argument for defining Japan's national polity and for placing sovereignty in the hands of the emperor. Even state sovereignty theorists argue that the emperor is the supreme authority of the state because of the phrase "head of state." In contrast to Mr. Hozumi, a leading scholar of the theory of state sovereignty, Professor Kitokuro Ichiki,[264] a professor of law at Tokyo Imperial University, argued that this is the basis for the classification of government systems, that the state is the body of sovereignty, and that the Japanese system of government is a monarchical one. Yes, the single phrase "head of state" has become the foundation of thought of today's constitutional scholars.

The issue, however, is not to dispute the literal meaning of the single phrase "head of state." Rather, the question is whether or not there is a head of state. Does a nation have a head of state? And what is this head of state? In this respect, we do not agree with Professor Inoue's adoption of organic state theory as the basis of his argument.[265] Of course, we do advocate organic state theory. However, if we equate today's organic state theory with Dr. Inoue's

---

[264] Kitokuro Ichiki was a constitutional scholar of the same era as Hozumi. He was the founder of the theory of the emperor as a state institution. However, Ichiki's theory doesn't seem to be oriented toward limiting the power of the emperor, and it was Tatsukichi Minobe who gave such a direction to it.

[265] In short, he's trying to say that "the place where the national divine consciousness resides" spoken of by Inoue corresponds to the brain of the nation.

adoption of organic state theory at the time when the term "head of state" was used, it would be akin to confusing the alchemy of the Arabic priests with nineteenth century chemistry.[266]

As we stated in *The Theory of Biological Evolution and Social Philosophy*, the state is a large individual, with humanity as its elements, which are separated by space. In other words, it is an organism that exists and evolves with its own purpose. The authentic organic state theory advocated today is a truth that could not have been discovered at all in the time when the words "head of state" were used. The old organic state theory was merely another dogma—comparing the state to a living organism, and thereby naming it the "organic state theory," in order to say that the state is not merely a mechanical thing, but a thing with life (a reaction against the consequences of the parochial individualism, which held dogmatic view of the state or society as if it were a machine-like, artificially created thing)—advocated up to the time of the French Revolution. This metaphor was nothing more significant than a child's joke. A similar example would be if we said "the territory is the skeleton and the people are the muscles," "the mail and telegraph are the nervous system, and the railroads and ships are the arteries and veins," and "soldiers are like claws and fangs, and musicians and orators are like tongues."[267]

The metaphoric organic state theory was appreciated by the emperor and the government, which were likened to the head and neck, while the working class as the limbs were the most unfortunate. The mechanistic statecraft of parochial individualism is dogmatic, yes, and it goes without saying that such dogmatic metaphors should not be allowed to exist in academia, even if it is a reaction against an individualistic view of the state. If we use the metaphor of a single creature with a neck, legs, body, and belly instead of the organic state theory as a truth today, we must say that an orator becoming a soldier is a

---

[266] "Arabic priests" refers to Islamic scholars.

[267] Herbert Spencer's social organism theory actually does raise examples such as these.

tongue turning into claws, and that the working class, as limbs beheading Louis XVI, are still living without a head somehow—very bizarre creatures indeed. The analogy to an octopus eating its own limbs is quite a bit more apt, since useless foreign monarchs live lives of extreme luxury, wasting thirty million yen or fifty million dollars a year on court expenses. However, this interpretation would lead to the inference that the emperor is an octopus, and while Professor Inoue could argue this about foreign countries, Japanese law does not allow it about Japan. (Read the section later where we explain how considering the current Japanese emperor the same as rulers of foreign countries isn't allowed.)

Some might liken it to Hobbes' Leviathan, since today's nations are guarded externally by land and sea forces. Certainly, the skin is similar to a crocodile, but one must also consider that the German crocodile would also be a bizarre creature with a handlebar mustache on its neck. If we liken it to a horse, we would say that a nation has no tail; if we liken it to an ox, we would have to argue that the emperor has horns. We must ask all current constitutional scholars, some of whom argue for monarchical sovereignty and others for state agency, to reflect on the fact that they all revolve around the single phrase "head of state."

To what kind of animal should a nation be compared? To which animal head should we compare the head of state? The Japanese Constitution was drafted by Mr. Hirobumi Ito, who returned to Japan without any originality, merely imitating the work of Stein,[268] so is he saying, as Stein did, that the nation is a higher form of humanity? But while Louis XVI was beheaded on the guillotine and left behind only the head of the noble human race, the Japanese emperor is not only a head of humanity, but a full human being without any defects. The man who took the metaphorical national organism to its extreme

---

[268] A German jurist.

was Bluntschli,[269] who compared the church to a woman and the state to a man. If today's constitutional scholars do not abandon the term "head of state," they are endorsing the figurative organic state theory. And since no creature with a head can reproduce asexually like an amoeba, it must always be stipulated that the state has some gender, as Bluntschli suggested.

Let us ask the following question: Is the creature called Japan male or female? If we follow Bluntschli, we would answer that it's male. What about the Netherlands, then? A male nation with a female head of state. Look further than that. In England, a male state, recently had a female head of state, Victoria, who was replaced by a male head of state with the accession of the current king.[270] This makes England a very strange creature. And such a creature, however advanced, is a monster that can't be found among the human race. In the same way, when we look back at Japan's history, we cannot escape the fact that Japan, too, is a bizarre creature. As such, the nation is not an ox, a horse, a crocodile, a sexual organism, or a noble human being. The "head of state" is not the head of humanity in its entirety, not the head of a bearded crocodile, nor the shaven head of a monk. In short, the head of state is nobody in particular, an entity that means nothing, merely a short phrase of meaningless characters that combine to form nothing. It is completely unjustifiable that the current crop of constitutional scholars, while treating the word "sacred" as a historically-mired adjective, take the phrase "head of state," a vestige of some dogmatic metaphor which has become equally meaningless,

---

[269] Johann Kasper Bluntschli was a German public law scholar. He was a liberal who advocated the organic state theory. His theories were supported by Hiroyuki Kato and others and became a theoretical pillar of the Meiji government. On the other hand, he also influenced the journalist Katsunan Kuga (Kuga's arguments influenced the constitutional scholar Soichi Sasaki), and it seems that he also influenced liberal thought generally.

[270] The King of England at that time was King Edward VII.

with extreme emphasis, to the point where it becomes the focus of their arguments.

In particular, these words contain the nature of scientific and scholastic principles. The state regulates the external lifestyle, and it is a principle of the modern state that it does not enter into the interior of thought. In other words, just as it is not for the state to establish medical truths or chemical laws by law or decree, it is not for the Great Empire of Japan to attempt to enforce an old theory of statecraft, the metaphorical organic state theory, in interpreting the articles of the Constitution. It is merely that certain ideas that had major backing at the time of the Constitution's enactment happened to have left their mark on the text. So, for example, just as the provision that "the Great Empire of Japan is a triangular globe, revolving around the moon according to the articles of this Constitution" would not compel an astronomer, so too is a constitutional scholar free to think independently outside of the nature of scientific and scholiast principles of statecraft that these words contain.

By this assertion, we believe that the emperor is not the head of state. Furthermore, in accordance with the spirit of the Constitution and other articles, we would argue that the emperor is not the controller of governing power. This assertion makes us absolutely reject the classification of systems of government made by all the current national sovereignty theorists.

Current state sovereignty theorists categorize the government system according to its supreme authority institution, dividing it into two types: monarchical and republican. However, this classification obviously doesn't do justice to the current constitutional monarchy. If the supreme authority is the institution which holds the highest authority, then the supreme authority of what we call the constitutional monarchy of a modern state is the combined body of the monarch and parliament. This is neither a monarchy, nor a republic. Constitutional monarchies do not fall into the two classifications they make. Government systems should be reclassified into strictly three categories—we would put great force behind this particular assertion.

Look at the text of the Constitution. Article V reads, "The emperor shall exercise legislative power through the approval of the Imperial Diet." Article LXXIII states, "If it becomes necessary in the future to revise any provision of this Constitution, the proposal shall be submitted to the Imperial Diet by imperial decree." We are surprised that, in spite of these clear and unambiguous sentences, the ideology of the class-state era interprets the monarch and the Diet as if they were in direct and contractual opposition, and that they are fighting over interpretation as they see fit. The problem is solved by defining and interpreting the meaning of "supreme authority." Constitutional scholars today, while repudiating the class state of the social contract era, still consider the sovereign and the people of today to be in direct conflict in terms of rights and duties. In the same way, they hold that the emperor is the one supreme authority because their minds are still held prisoner by Montesquieu's theory of the separation of powers, which they supposedly discarded as an unsustainable fallacy.

Of course, they do not see the monarch as merely the head of administration, as in Montesquieu's theory of the separation of powers, in which the three institutions are clearly independent. However, unless we consider the monarch or the Diet as a single independent institution, there is no reason to regard the monarch as a complete supreme authority. It is clear that the emperor in Japan is the head of the administration, and when he heads the army and navy, he is the head of each of those institutions. This is because an institution can only be a complete singular institution when it engages in punctuated activities with clear boundaries, and the emperor engages in activities with clear boundaries and definitions when he is the head of the administration or when he heads the army or navy. However, in Japan, unlike in the United States, the three bodies are not clearly independent, and while the emperor is a full institution as the head of the administration, the Diet is not a full legislative body by itself. It is an element of the legislative body together with the emperor. Because of this, just as Congress is merely an element and not a complete institution, the emperor, who is also an element of the legislative institution, cannot be a complete legislative institution with total control of the governing power. In other words, a legislative body can act as a distinct singular body only when it is organized by the emperor and the Diet. The emperor, under Article IV of the Constitution, exercises legislative power with the support of the Imperial Diet, and without the support of the Diet, the emperor cannot be a legislative institution that exercises legislative power because he lacks the elements of a legislative institution. Nevertheless, some scholars argue that since Congress determines laws and the emperor is the one who orders them, Congress is merely a background institution operating behind the scenes.

Of course, it is clear that Congress, the organizing element of the legislative institution, is not itself a legislative institution because it does not have the power to actually order said laws.[271] But the emperor, who cannot order a law before its content is determined, is equally not a legislative institution. In the first place, such a division of law into content and enforcement is an egregious example of meaningless academic falsehood. A law is not a law if its contents have been determined but it isn't actually enforceable. A law is not a law if its contents have not been determined, since it's impossible to enforce nothing. A legislative body that only has the power to

---

[271] The power to "order laws" used here seems to be different from the power to "execute laws." "Power to order laws" makes it seem like laws issued toward the people. Perhaps this phraseology was influenced by the doctrine of John Austin (an English jurist), who regarded law as "the command of the sovereign." Henry Taylor Terry, who was teaching at the University of Tokyo at the time, was in agreement with Austin, and thus influenced the Japanese legal community with Austin's doctrine. Kita may have seen this from behind the scenes and considered it a requirement for a sovereign "to be qualified to issue commands of the law."

mandate something with zero content is a legislative body that has nothing to mandate, which means that it isn't a legislative body.

Other scholars say the following: "The supreme authority of the state is the emperor, and the Diet is the second institution following him." The reason for this interpretation by these scholars is that the formation of the Diet must be ordered solely by the emperor. This, however, is an absurd interpretation of the common man, who sees the opening of the Diet by the Speaker and the opening of debate, and assumes that the Speaker alone is the Imperial Diet and that the other members are mere additions to it. The emperor assumes the duty of convening the Diet within one year and shall be the organizer of the legislative body together with the Imperial Diet. "Supreme authority" means the institution which holds the highest authority. This means specifically the institution which holds the authority to amend the Constitution.[272] In some other countries, the institution that amends the Constitution is organized outside of the regular legislative body, but in Japan, it is simply a designated procedure, and it's done by the regular legislative body. Just as the normal legislative procedure is complete only through the joint action of the emperor and the Diet, the supreme legislative act of amending the Constitution can only be done when there is an emperor who has the power to initiate constitutional amendments and a cooperative Diet with at least two-thirds of the members

---

[272] This approach to the search for the location of sovereignty based on the location of the right to amend the Constitution is similar to the view that the person with the power to establish the Constitution is the sovereign (the theory of the power to establish the Constitution). The theory of the power to establish the Constitution was originally proposed by the French Revolutionary thinker Sieyes in his book *What is the Third Estate?* It took until after World War I that this theory gained traction and was argued for in Germany. Considering this, one could say Kita's thoughts on this matter were very forward-thinking.

present, and a majority vote of two-thirds of those members.[273] So the emperor and the Imperial Diet are the supreme authorities that can amend the Constitution.

Therefore, if we call the institution in which the will of the nation is expressed sovereign and ruler, then the emperor is not a sovereign and the Congress is not a ruler. We should say that the institution in which these elements are combined is the sovereign and the ruler. If this is the case, then the so-called constitutional monarchy that exists today should not be regarded as a variant of monarchies, one of the two types of government systems, as scholars now classify them. Rather, it is a democratic form of government with an equal majority and a single, privileged ruler. In other words, those who believe that the supreme authority is composed of a single person, such as state institution theorists, are merely a slight variant of the theory of monarchical sovereignty. In particular, it is obvious that one of the most prominent state institution theorists, Professor Tatsukichi Minobe,[274] who asserts that "the sovereign is not the one who controls the right to rule," is contradicting himself when he says that the sovereign of a constitutional state is still supreme authority composed of one person, just as there is absolutely no good reason to name English national polity as a monarchy. (Regarding the democratic system of government that Japan has today, see the later section on our

---

[273] Article LXXIII, paragraph 2 of the Imperial Constitution stipulates, "In the above case, neither house shall open the debate, unless not less than two thirds of the whole number of the members are present, and no amendment shall be passed, unless a majority of not less than two thirds of the members present is obtained."

[274] Constitutional law scholar at the University of Tokyo. He is more famous for his theory of the emperor as a state institution than its founder, Kitokuro Ichiki. The criticism of his theory from the right wing in 1935 is well-known as the "Emperor Institution Theory Incident." He's also the mentor of Toshiyoshi Miyazawa, who led the academic world of constitutional law after the war.

historical interpretation in which we argue that the true significance of the Meiji Revolution was the development of egalitarianism.)

We agree with Professor Minobe's assertion that "the emperor is not the controller of the right to rule." This is because the view that the emperor is the general supervisor of the right to rule is deduced from "head of state," a phrase based on the metaphorical organic state theory of statecraft, and is inconsistent with all other articles in the Constitution and contradictory to the spirit of the Constitution. We have no basis on which to imagine whether or not Professor Minobe would have rejected the words "controls the right to rule," as he clearly believes that today's Japanese Constitution bears the traces of the metaphorical organic state theory. However, given that he says that he himself rejects the organic state theory, we are inclined to believe that he was speaking from a position one step higher than other theorists of national sovereignty.

For example, Professor Ichiki says the following:

> If we assume that the sovereign is the subject of sovereignty, we cannot understand many various relationships. The sovereign is the ultimate authority of the state, and is the general overseer of the right to govern. The general overseer is neither the subject of the right to govern nor the institution that exercises it. In other words, the institution that controls the exercise of the right to govern has the power to expand and contract its own authority. The one who has the right to expand or contract his authority is the one who has the right to change the Constitution. Therefore, the general overseer of the right to govern is the ultimate authority of the state and has the power to change the Constitution.

Professor Ichiki makes it sound as if the emperor can amend or change the Constitution as he pleases without the support of the Diet, while arguing that the general overseer can't be an institution of the state unless also a subject of sovereignty, making for an uninterpretable set of ideas. Professor Minobe does not have these kind of muddled, mixed-up thoughts.[275]

Nor does he do what another national sovereignty theorist, Mr. Giichi Soejima,[276] does. Mr. Soejima argues as follows:

> The emperor is the supreme authority among all state institutions. Therefore, it is appropriate that the position of emperor should be the head of state. The emperor's control of the right to govern is, in other words, a substantive reason for his being the head of state. Because the emperor controls the right to govern the nation, all of the right to govern the nation has remained in the hands of the emperor. In our country, where the emperor himself exercises the right to govern, or creates other institutions, gives them authority, and they act on his behalf, he is the sole ruler of the nation.

This, however, only encourages arguments of wording with other monarchical sovereignty theorists in a dispute over statecraft based on that metaphorical organic state theory. Professor Minobe doesn't run blindly ahead like this either.

However, it should be affirmed based on the other article[277] and the spirit of the Constitution that "the emperor is not the general overseer of the right to rule" and that the emperor alone cannot organize the supreme organ and amend or change the Constitution, which is the supreme legislation. If, like

---

[275] Since Minobe doesn't regard the emperor as the subject of all-powerful sovereignty, he doesn't give the indecipherable explanation that the emperor is neither subject nor institution, which is what Ichiki says.

[276] A prewar constitutional scholar (1867-1947).

[277] Article LXXIII

Professor Minobe, one were to interpret the Japanese national polity as a monarchy with a supreme authority composed of a single person, there would be no basis for such affirmation, not to mention the obvious contradiction in ideas. We believe that it is this lack of care and attention toward the nature of the state that keeps all the state institution theorists wandering in the deep fog of tyranny and leads Professor Minobe and others into such contradictions.

We have our thoughts on the matter. The idea of sovereignty theory should not be understood only in the words of jurisprudence, but the basis of knowledge must be sought in statecraft. Of course, constitutional theory is not statecraft. The essence of sovereignty is a matter of statecraft, but it should be obvious that the location of sovereignty should depend on the clear text and spirit of the Constitution, and not on an interpretation of the Constitution that transcends existing law, especially with regard to the purpose and ideals of the state.

It is also clear, however, that the current Constitution itself is influenced by the statecraft prevalent at the time of its enactment. For example, the fact that the term "head of state" is based on the statecraft of the period of reaction to the French Revolutionary, and therefore can only be understood according to the metaphorical organic state theory,[278] is an indication of this sort of influence from a certain period. Sovereignty is an idea that can only be understood according to the theory of state essence. Dr. Inoue's attitude of interpreting today's nation based on the metaphorical organic state theory as the basis of his thought, and his assertion that the term "head of state" is "the place where national consciousness resides," is a reasonable order of thought—

---

[278] The idea that the concept of head of state arose in connection with the organic state theory is shared by current constitutional law scholars. "Originally, the head of state was called such because it was the institution that served as the brain according to the theory that compared the state to the human body, linked to the organic state theory." (Miyoko Tsujimura, *Genpo* [Nihon Hyoronsha, 2004] p. 83)

even if it is based on a theory which has been completely erased by the modern day—as he first holds a certain belief about the essence of the nation and then goes on to interpret the Constitution, which is the basic law of the nation, according to that belief. The fact that Mr. Hozumi, for example, builds his mirage-like theistic constitutional theory on the very old theory of the state in which the state is a further developed, inflated version of a single family is of course not enough to even make it worth a subject of discussion, but it is legitimate enough as a method of research.

Yet, the current state sovereignty theorists are all too often devoid of such an attitude, reversing the starting point and the end of their research. Professor Ichiki's profoundly inexplicable, expert interpretation of the head of state as "neither the main body nor an institution of sovereignty," is a fine example of this. Professor Minobe's "interpretation of the state in jurisprudence regards how we should think of the state in order to interpret the existing laws without contradiction," shows a view of the nation that is very ad hoc, and is another good example. It is an undeniable fact that the idea of deriving the essence of the state from something that is constantly changing, such as "existing laws," and of thinking of the nation simply as a condition that makes existing laws consistent, is extremely ad hoc, even if it is unavoidable because one has abandoned the mechanical view of the state held by individualism and the dogma of the metaphorical organic state theory, and thus has no statecraft to base one's ideas and thoughts on. In particular, the attempt to abstract a jurisprudential idea of "the state" without contradiction from the artificial existing laws, which have been fraught with contradictions and conflicts from the beginning and naturally exist with contradictions and conflicts due to the evolution of the times, is an attempt to perform a miracle.

How can we interpret the current Constitution's provisions, such as the word "sacred" and the words "head of state," without contradiction, and what kind of state idea can we derive from these contradictory provisions? If we take the word "sacred" in its original meaning, we may come up with the theory of the divine right of the emperor, or we may derive the idea of a state in high heaven, as Mr. Hozumi does. The state that can be deduced from the literal meaning of the phrase "head of state" would have to be an animal with a head, legs, torso, and belly, as in the metaphorical organic state theory. The state, the body of sovereignty, is not, as Professor Minobe and others claim, an idea that can be drawn without contradiction from the articles of the current Constitution. If the state in jurisprudence is merely an induction to the existing laws so that they are consistent with each other, then Professor Minobe has no basis upon which to utter such authoritative words:

> The monarch is not the controller of the right to govern. The constitutional provision that the monarch controls the right to govern holds the nature of a doctrine, and the state does not have the right to establish official doctrines. Scholars are free to revise and study the words of the Constitution.

This is clearly inconsistent with Article IV of the current Constitution, because the conception of the state, which is supposed to be obtained by interpreting the current law without contradiction, does not have the power to tell us to study the contradictory text anew.

We believe the fact that the state has no right to set an official doctrine means that it cannot enforce a metaphorical organic state theory, a doctrine of statecraft, just as it cannot order people to believe in geocentric theory, and the fact that scholars are free to consider the text of the Constitution is because they have the independence of thought to decide which of the conflicting articles to discard in accordance with the spirit of the Constitution. So, when there is a conflict between Article IV of the Constitution and other important articles like V and LXXIII, we are free to discard them according to what each finds to be the spirit of the Constitution—we think this is the essence of the state. Then, those who embrace the metaphorical organic state theory or theistic beliefs of the state can choose Article IV, and ignore the other articles as they wish, while we are free to pay attention to articles V and LXXIII and discard Article IV. This is because the letters and words of laws and ordinances hold no legal force with respect to the spirit of the Constitution and statecraft. Unlike what Professor Minobe believes, "controls the right to govern" by no means holds the nature of a doctrine or scholarly principle. In the absence of the other two articles, Article V and Article LXXIII, it is only natural that the interpretation of the law must infer that the emperor is the sole supreme authority to control the right to govern, in accordance with Article IV. The spirit of the Constitution and the principles of statecraft are judges who are called upon to make decisions in cases where there is a conflict between legal texts, and Professor Minobe's view of the state, obtained by considering the so-called existing laws without contradiction, cannot be a judge with such solemn power. Moreover, the view that interprets the Japanese Constitution and names it a monarchical state with a single supreme authority can only be interpreted as finding no contradiction at all in all the text of the law, and in that case, insisting on a free study of Article IV is a demand without a reason. To carry through with Professor Minobe's argument, it is necessary, with a clear and certain view of the state, to say that the Japanese system of government is a democratic one with a supreme authority organized by a single privileged person and an equal majority (see the later historical interpretation for more about the spirit of the Constitution).

We argue for three types of government systems in order to interpret today's civic state without being unduly limited by the two types created by the traditionalists of state sovereignty theory. The first is a system in which the supreme authority is organized by a privileged member of the state (e.g., Russia after the emancipation of the serfs and Japan until twenty-three years after the Meiji Revolution).[279] The second is a system in which the supreme

---

[279] In Russia, the Emancipation Manifesto which proclaimed the emancipation of the

authority is organized by an equal majority and a privileged member of the state (e.g., England, Germany, and Japan twenty-three years after the Meiji Revolution). The third is a system in which the supreme authority is composed of an equal majority (e.g., France, the United States of America, etc.).

We do not seek to maintain the distinction between "kokutai," national polity, and "seitai," national systems of government, in the same manner as the monarchical sovereignty theorists. However, we do not agree with conflating the two, as the current state sovereignty theorists do. This is because seitai, the government system in this context, is the form in which the right to govern is invoked, and the main body of the right to govern can, for its own purposes and benefits (such as according to the interests of the monarch in the case of a state in the era of monarchical sovereignty, or according to the purposes of the state in the era of state sovereignty), amend or abolish the institutions of the state (or the monarch's institutions in the case of monarchical sovereignty) by a legal procedure established by the state (or by the monarch). On the other hand, kokutai, national polity, determines the essence of the state, whether it is the subject of the right to govern or the object to be governed by sovereignty. Yet current state sovereignty theorists, inattentive to the science of the state and not attempting to classify the state according to its evolution, still only apply the word "supreme authority" to the formal number of Aristotle's "number of rulers." Some say there is only a distinction between national polities, but not between government systems. Others say vice versa. For example, Professor Ichiki makes only the distinction between monarchical and republican systems of government, while Professor Minobe makes only the distinction between monarchical and republican national polities. In other words, kokutai, national polity, and seitai, system of

---

serfs was issued in 1861 (the emperor at that time was Alexander II of Russia). The phrase "twenty-three years after the Meiji Revolution" refers to the period between the great decree restoring the monarchy and the promulgation of the Imperial Constitution.

government, are now considered by modern state sovereignty theorists to be merely different names for the same supreme authority.

However, this still does not explain all states today. In states such as China and Korea, the monarch is never the supreme authority existing for the purpose and benefit of the state, and the right to rule is not a state right. Based on the monarch's property rights, government offices are bought and sold for his own benefit, and the land and people exist for his purposes. This is a different kind of national polity, one that has evolved to a completely different degree. In particular, this confusion on national polity and systems of government not only prevents us from describing all states today, but also leaves out the ancient and medieval states altogether. Even if we were to study only what we call civilized nations today and assume that today there is only one civic state, today's civic states have the same national polity as ancient states such as Greece, but different systems of government, while some medieval states have very similar systems of government to today's civic states, but completely different national polities.

In the ancient Greek state, the cohesive power of the state, the main body of sovereignty, was invoked naked and did not undergo any political formatting or formality, and so it stood above the individual with a pressure that had no order or regularity. Seitai, or the system of government, which guarantees the freedom of the individual against this cohesive power, did not exist in ancient times, to the point that the minority and criminals were treated indistinguishably, leading to the so-called age of tyranny of the majority. An era of tyranny of the majority always suddenly bore a dictator, and was always followed by a sudden change to an era of dictatorship, an era of sole tyranny, and then another sudden change to an era of tyranny of the majority again. From tyranny to tyranny, individual freedom was completely ignored in the name of the state. Although the kokutai, the national polity, was the same as today, a civic state, the seitai, or system of government, was what one would call tyrannical, completely different from today's system where the form of governing power is fixed under the influence of the theory of separation of powers,

Although tyranny ceased with the emergence of class assemblies in the Middle Ages, monarchs and nobles (in Japan, shogun, lords, and emperors) each had their own purposes and interests, and their lands and people existed as possessions for these purposes and interests. This is a completely different national polity, the "patriarchal state." In other words, a monarchical national polity where the state was not the subject of the right to rule, but the object to be ruled—a sovereign state in which the two elements, land and people, existed for the purpose and benefit of the state's owners.

So, if we say, as Professor Ichiki does, that there is only a distinction between government systems and not national polities, then despite the fact that the Middle Ages consisted of the aforementioned patriarchal state, completely different to today, their government systems did have some similarities to that of today, so one would need to equate the contract between social classes of then with today's constitutional monarchy, consider the medieval rulers and nobles as state institutions, then divide them into the same classification of national polity that we have today.

On the other hand, if we say, as Professor Minobe does, that there is only a distinction between national polities and not government systems, we must either take the medieval national polity of the patriarchal state, which he himself recognizes, outside the classification of national polity, or line it up alongside the currently existing monarchy national polity and republic national polity. This view of national polity and system of government as the same is precisely what happens when one doesn't study the evolution of the state.

This is why we reject such a groundless and confused theory of state sovereignty and instead advocate the theory of state sovereignty on the basis of the theory of actual state personality. Of course, jurisprudence determines whether or not the state is the subject of rights based on the recognition of law, regardless of whether it is an actual, existing personality or a personality based on legal fiction.[280] It goes without saying that even if the state is a real personality, it cannot be considered the body of sovereignty while its personality is not yet legally recognized.

However, those who study law according to its evolution should never confuse the recognition of a real personality by law with the moment that something without personality is given personality through legal fiction. The evolution of law is in the recognition of real personality as legal personality. In the patriarchal state period, the state, despite its real personality—as if that real personality were a slave—was a legal object that existed for the benefit of those who owned it. Therefore, in the Middle Ages, no demand was ever made "for the state," for the state's own independent existence, but always "for the sovereign," for the purposes and benefits of those who owned the state. However, even though the slave was not a legal personality, it was from the beginning a real personality. Similarly, the state finally acquired legal personality after a long evolution, but in being a real personality, it has been unmovable since the time of the patriarchal state, since the time of primitive equality—or, for that matter, since the time of our differentiation from the ancestors we shared with apes.

The question of whether the great personality of the state is of the mechanical finesse known as legal fiction or a real personality is an important matter which deals with the evolution, origin, purpose, ideals, etc., of the state,

---

[280] A real person is called a natural person, and a legal person is one whose personality is recognized by law. A typical example of a legal person is a company. A legal person is considered "legal fiction" because the legal fiction theory was strongest. Postwar discussion made the legal existence theory, which emphasized the actual existence of legal personalities socially, so there's no need to stick to only the "legal fiction." Incidentally, the theory of state personality is also called the "state legal personality theory."

and is not limited to statecraft. It is a fundamental idea that jurisprudence must not neglect. If the state is a personality by legal fiction, it can be dissolved and extinguished by the force of law, and if it is a real, existing personality, it can never be extinguished by any artificial legislation.[281] Even though the French Revolution of individualism dissolved the state, the state still exists in the form of social cohesion. It is the rotten skin that has been destroyed, not the skeleton of the nation, which has never been damaged. The state, as a real personality, even under the patriarchs, sometimes broke their laws for its own benefit and acted for its own purposes and interests. As it evolved and acquired a legal personality, it would amend or repeal laws that were contrary to its purposes and interests as it saw fit, and it would create the basis for all its laws.

Because they have little knowledge of this fundamental point, today's national sovereignty theorists understand the state as an association. This view of the state as an association-like personality of legal fiction is precisely based on the parochial individualistic view of the state that dates back to the French Revolution, and this is the reason why Mr. Hozumi still persistently resists and claims that the origin of society is in the family system. If we advocate the theory of state sovereignty as the truth, we must not make the mistake of criticizing based on the old hypothesis of social origins, as Mr. Hozumi and others have done. Socialism is a truth in jurisprudence as well. The personality of the state is based on the fact that society is an organism, as we have already explained in *The Theory of Biological Evolution and Social Philosophy*. In other words, it is based on the fact that it is a large individual with humanity, separated by space, as its elements. All social sciences are grounded in biology.

---

[281] In other words, a critical difference arises depending on whether one interprets it as something real or something created by legal fiction.

In the Roman period of the distant past,[282] the term "individual" seemed to be limited to just one individual person, and it was thought that the individual person was the only real personality and all others were legal fiction. This belief was unavoidable because biology had not yet been developed. Today, there are monarchical sovereignty theorists who hold the contradictory view that the state is a legal personality and at the same time that the sovereign is the body of sovereignty, and state sovereignty theorists who argue that the state is merely a convenient thing for ideas and speculation and then put forth the slight counter-argument that if the personality of the state is legal fiction, the sovereign's personality is also legal fiction. They make such claims perhaps because of their exposure to Roman law during their studies of jurisprudence and a resulting preoccupation with the Roman conception of the individual as the basis for their judgments. So, however detailed the argument may be, both sides are equally engaged in a backroom battle of hypotheticals. If scholars say that the existence in reality of a national personality is the same as the existence in reality of a slave personality, it would be a consistent attitude for scholars who deal only with legal phenomena if they argue that the Great Empire of Japan is merely a de facto entity that is not yet recognized in today's law and is merely ruled as an object for the benefit and purpose of the emperor. We must debate the words and spirit of the Constitution and its history to determine whether today's nation is a civic nation with a legal personality, or whether it remains as a patriarchal state in its national polity and has no personality at all.

However, not only the monarchical sovereignty theorists, but also all state sovereignty theorists, struggle in the dark and not only fail to see the state as an evolutionary entity, but also inherit the popular conception of the individual as the basis of personality from the Roman era, before the invention of the microscope. Thus, it's impossible not only for the opposition, the monarchical

---

[282] Probably referring to treatment under Roman law.

sovereignty theorists, to say that the state has no personality and is the property of a monarch, but also for the state sovereignty theorists, who seem to be similar in form to what we argue, to say that the state is a real lifeform with an existing personality recognized by law. Thus, they are forced to be content with arguing that the state is nothing more than a mechanical contrivance or a personality of legal fiction.

Indeed, the state is not a mechanical thing created by legal fiction; the state is a real personality with its own purpose from the beginning. This personality acts for its own purposes and interests. Of course, when the theory of human monism becomes an accepted theory and socialism is realized around the entire world, the highest class of individuals will be one personality with the purpose of survival and evolution: the whole human race. Then, as an ideal for the distant future, we can look forward to the realization of a global state of all humanity by this highest class of individual, this personality. At the present level of evolution, however, the nation has the purpose of an individual personality in the form of a certain class of individuals limited to an ethnic or racial group, a geographical division, and so on. The civic state of today has gradually increased its class of individuals, from the city-states of antiquity and the feudal states of the Middle Ages, to become the state with a large personality that it is today. This real personality has been recognized as a legal personality in certain periods or in certain regions, or has existed as an object of governance in the interests of its owners. But today all civic nations clearly recognize the actual personality of the state as a legal personality, either by the words of the law or by the legal beliefs of the people—so today, people say "for the sake of the state," and the state is considered to be the place where interests are vested, where purpose resides, and the national belief in the sovereignty of the state is expressed in the belief of the people.

In the Middle Ages, however, when the state was the property of the monarch and was an object under the monarch's purpose and interests, there was no such thing as "for the sake of the state," but rather "for the sake of the monarch," an expression of the sovereignty of the monarch. Even in that period, though, saints and sages of both the East and West with lofty ideals asserted the interests of the state for the sake of its own personality, as opposed to the demands of the legal sovereign (see the section in *The Enlightenment Movement of Socialism* where we discuss the Confucian theory of state sovereignty).

If the personality of the state is interpreted as nothing more than legal fiction, then it would be incomprehensible that saints and sages abandoned their own wellbeing for the sake of the state long ago, when there were no laws that provided for such a legal fiction. It would also be difficult to understand how even today, human beings are shedding blood to fight for the maintenance of legal fiction. It is said that today's international wars are not fought in the name of a monarch for the benefit of the monarch, as in the Middle Ages, but in the name of the nation. This is because a sense of brotherhood has not yet developed, and a geographically limited class of individuals, the nation, as an individual personality, demands allegiance in law and in national conviction, using the single phrase "for the nation," for its own purposes and interests. If it is to be argued that this real personality cannot be recognized as a legal personality in the degree of evolution that Japan has undergone today, then one must think as follows. The obligation of military service is not an obligation borne by the elements of a nation to satisfy the purposes of that nation, but the people are to be interpreted as slaves owned by the sovereign and subject to the dispositions of their owners, and that the Russo-Japanese War was fought not for the purposes of the Great Japanese Empire but for the interests of the emperor. Needless to say, this is a misinterpretation of the Constitution and contradicts the prevailing belief of the majority of the people.

Therefore, we study the state according to its evolution on the basis of the theory of real state personality, and on that basis, we reject all monarchical sovereignty theorists and state sovereignty theorists who continue to engage in meaningless debates without the slightest grounding in fact. It's an obvious fallacy of the highest contradiction to build a theory of sovereignty on today's modern view of the state, as monarchical sovereignty theorists do. Nor is it correct that the sovereignty of the state was given personality by legal fiction, as the state sovereignty theorists interpret it. In the national polity of the patriarchal state era the owner of the state had sovereignty, and although the state had a real personality, it was still considered an object legally. In the civic state, the state is both a real personality as the body of sovereignty and a legal personality. The phrase "for the sake of the lord" was spoken in the age of fealty to one's monarch and in the Middle Ages of monarchical sovereignty. The phrase "for the sake of the state" is spoken in the age of patriotism, which is the modern age of state sovereignty (also, read the later sections where we discuss historical interpretation and the moral relationship between the emperor and the people).

Today's organic state theory, which interprets humanity as a large individual with elements separated by space, has driven out of academia the metaphorical organic state theory that leads to interpretations such as Professor Inoue's, where the "head of state" is the residence of the national consciousness. We want to be clear in our assertion that in no ancient age of patriarchal despotism, no age of absolute imperial power, has national consciousness ever resided in the brain of a single person, leaving the rest of mankind as mindless limbs. Simply put, there is no reason why there should be any unity, subjugation, politics, or laws between people who do not share the same consciousness. Mr. Hozumi, for example, always says that a nation is united by the sovereign's inherent power. However, if, unlike Mr. Hozumi, we don't change the meaning of words as we please, and we assume that "inherent" would mean that the sovereign is born with it in his body, then power and authority are never inherent in the sovereign. Rather, it is the unifying power of society. In other words, the reason why a monarch is seen as having power is because this unifying power pushes up the monarch from behind, and if he is separated from this unifying power, even a person like Emperor Go-Daigo, who has outstanding personal power, cannot do much.

It is true, of course, that the people in a time when the monarch wielded absolute and unlimited power were terrified not of his power directly, but of their conception of his power, which was in fact greater than the personal power of the monarch—just as a lover might not be in love with the beauty which exists in reality, but rather with the idea of beauty they have in their own mind, which is thousands of times more beautiful than the real beauty. However, the innate power of any individual hero is limited, and much of what is seen as the power of the Japanese emperor is the collective power of the state in combination with one's own personal vision of it. In other words, despite countless revolutionaries like Mr. Hozumi with his stubborn ideology of restoring the nation to the national polity of the patriarchal state era, the evolution of the nation finally realized the ideal of a civic state as indicated by the Taika Revolution, and the Japanese emperor fully demonstrated the unifying power of the nation as an important institution of the Great Empire of Japan. Even the monarchs of the patriarchal state period, who are described by detractors as "tyrannical and oppressive towards the people," could not do anything against the will of the multitude, which was tens of millions of times greater, by the coercive power of a single person alone. The reason things were the way they were was because the people either accepted the monarch's right to dispose of the people or tolerated it based on inertia.

The most despotic ruler was the one who was both priest and monarch in the age of unity between politics and religion, but the people submitted to his tyrannical rule only because they were united by a strong religious faith, not because the national consciousness resided in the brain of one person who was mechanically obeyed by others. Tyrannical power cannot be maintained if it is not united by a social consciousness of the same religion, or if it is not accepted with the belief that it represents the will of the ancestral spirits or the village gods. It could not be more obvious that there is no such thing as inherent sovereign power. So, even if we try to argue, as in that social contract theory, that the monarch's power is lent by the people, there is no contract on which to base the lending, and even if we try to argue that the lender has the right to take it back, this must be mistaken since it comes from individualist revolutionary theory that the sovereign power to lend is innate in each person before the contract. But since the essence of power is that of a united and powerful force, it is clear that no individual is born with such power inherent in them.

The patriarchs who wielded despotic power in the East all prospered or perished depending on how much of this united and powerful force they possessed. The Greek dictators also held their despotic power by virtue of this united and powerful force. The unity that was the source of this power was bound together by social instinct and, as time went on, by a definite social consciousness. In primitive times, it was not a clearly conscious awareness, but a dormant instinctive sociality—not a contract based on the idea of self-interest, as individualism says, nor a union or submission forced by fear of power, as Mr. Hozumi and others have argued. As social creatures, human beings existed in unity from the beginning without relying on force, just as they had language without a contract, and unity itself was force (also see *The Theory of Biological Evolution and Social Philosophy*). Professor Inoue's view of national consciousness as residing in the head of state is insignificant because it is based on a dogmatic and metaphorical organic state theory. Mr. Hozumi's assertion of unification under the authority of the monarch is as worthless a hypothesis as the social contract theory of individualism, which he is so fond of debunking, and it is a fallacy in premise and conclusion. It is not the case that only monarchs are state-conscious and the rest of us are mechanically submissive. Depending on the awakening of national consciousness and the degree of its evolution, institutions arise or disappear. Rather than uniting under the power, the unity itself exists as the body of power.

However, for this national consciousness to be recognized by law and awakened as a political power, it would have to be gradually extended through historical evolution. The most primitive proto-human communities were republican and egalitarian, but they were completely united by social instincts and were peaceful, without political institutions, so that no one had political power.

However, after a long period of evolutionary expansion, when villages began to rely on the spirits of their ancestors to maintain them (something that all peoples have experienced at least once), the patriarchs, as representatives of the will of the ancestors, first awakened to political power. Furthermore, as competition with other villages led to systems of slavery and land disputes, the state with a real, existing personality came to exist as the property of the monarch for the monarch's benefit—just as the land and slaves existed as property of the monarch. These were the buds of the patriarchal and monarchical state, and if we do not think of them in terms of Aristotle's three types of states as based on formal mathematical figures, but see them dynamically and according to evolution, the monarchical state belongs to the first stage of evolution. Aristocracies are limited to a small class, but can be evaluated as an extension of this awakening to political power, and democracies are those in which this awakening is further extended to the majority, and should be considered as the third stage of evolution.

The nation of Japan is equally a state, and since it has evolved according to historical trends since ancient times, it is not specifically alone and separate from the principles of statecraft, no matter how isolated from other nations it may have been or how quickly or slowly its evolution has moved. The Japanese people experienced a republican and egalitarian primitive period in other lands, and migrated with a family-based national polity that had already evolved into an agricultural era.[283] Obviously the master of that national polity

---

[283] It's said that there was a land bridge between Japan and the mainland during the Ice

was not an emperor in the manner that we conceive of an emperor,[284] but it is quite imaginable, unless we interpret all the oldest records as meaningless, that they came with the bud of a patriarchal state and monarchical government. As the population grew, however, the family system, which was the backbone of social organization at the time, was disrupted, and the great clans that developed in parallel with the imperial family forced families and slaves to unite and compete with the other great clan, the imperial family. Here, a fanciful plan—a plan that was often attempted in emerging countries on the basis of fantasy socialism—to realize an ideal state was formulated by knowledgeable revolutionaries among the royal family,[285] with the goal of forming a national polity of a sovereign civic state with an institution of monarchical rule as its government system.

However, it goes without saying that in such an undeveloped age, the ideal state was merely an ideal, and that ideal was finally achieved in the far later Meiji Revolution. What was in fact constructed at that time was a patriarchal state of sovereignty, and all emperors during the long period until the end of the Middle Ages were emperors as patriarchal monarchs. There were countless other patriarchal monarchs, named "heroes" and called "lords" and "shogun," who competed with each other. Until the end of the Fujiwara rule, however, the emperor existed as a patriarchal monarch who owned all of Japan and all of its people as his "great treasures." There was no legal doubt that the emperor was the sole sovereign and sole authority, even if regents and the main advisor were in fact tyrannical, and even if the de facto governing power was exercised

---

Age.

[284] In other words, he wasn't an existence that would be viewed like Emperor Jimmu and others in the *Kojiki* or *Nihon Shoki*.

[285] Referring to Emperor Tenji. Kita talks about his evaluation of Emperor Tenji in volume 5.

only in a small area of the Kinki region. This was the first stage in the evolution of political power, awakened in one person.

The development of the native priests and local rulers led to the emergence of many more patriarchal monarchs during the Middle Ages, carrying the medieval period through up to the civic state of the Meiji Revolution. In the medieval history of Europe, the pope, the Holy Roman Emperor, kings, and nobles overlapped and intermingled, vying for supreme governing power, or sovereignty, which is of course neither governing nor political power in today's sense. However, the emperor, king, and nobles each had the right to rule as the owner of the land and the people, and each of them became the subject of the right to rule by treating the state as an object of ownership, expanding and contracting the right to rule through inheritance, gift, and marriage, each of them awakening to political power. In the same way in Japan, the imperial family had the right to rule as the "pope of Shinto" based on Shinto beliefs, and the "Holy Roman Emperor of Kamakura," who was called the barbarian general after being crowned by the pope, had the right to rule along with the "king" and "nobles" under the feudal system in the Warring States period. Each of them disposed of the land and people as their property, and each of them competed for sovereignty—that is, the supreme right to rule.

The period in which those in power were at the same time the subjects of the right to govern was the patriarchal state, which is different from today's civic state, showing that the emperors, kings, and aristocrats from that time can't be equated with those in power today. However, the fact that each of these patriarchs came to have the right to rule is the evolution of the second stage, when the awakening of political power was extended to the class of lords, e.g., the nobility. This second phase lasts a very long time in any nation. This includes Japan, in which it lasted until the Meiji Revolution. The revolution repudiated the aristocratic monopoly of power through countless peasant revolts and the so-called theory of national polity of the low-ranking warriors, and extended the awakening to power to the majority. "Politics follows public opinion,"[286] democracy was achieved, and thus we entered the third phase of evolution. The personality of the nation, awakened by the competition of nation against nation, broke away from its position as the object of governance, which it had long enjoyed, under the Edo-era principle of excluding foreigners, using the words "Great Empire of Japan" and "for the nation" to assert that the nation had a purpose and that the nation was the subject of rights to which its interests belonged. The national polity of this civic state and democratic form of government, with the state as the main body of sovereignty, was maintained by the legal beliefs of the people and the political morality of the emperor until twenty-three years after the Meiji Revolution. The Meiji Revolution came to an end when the Imperial Constitution explicitly codified the sovereignty of the state as the main body of law, thus giving legal recognition to the present national polity and the present system of government (see the later sections in our historical interpretation, and also *The Theory of Biological Evolution and Social Philosophy*, where we discuss the historical philosophy of the theory of social evolution).

Thus, we reasoned from Mr. Hozumi's argument, in which "the emperor himself has the right to rule and that this right is transmitted through one eternal lineage via the extension of individuals," that it also spreads to all people in the form of individual reproduction, leading to democracy. Professor Inoue is the most clear-cut monarchical sovereignty theorist, teaching that the emperor himself has the right to rule, pointing out that the theory of sovereignty of the imperial throne, which Mr. Hozumi had initially advocated, could not be sustained. State sovereignty theorists laid forth the criticism that "if the emperor himself did have the right to govern, it would mean that the state would perish upon the emperor's death." In response to this, Professor

---

[286] The original text says "It shall be decided by public opinions on all occasions." This is derived from the phrase in the Charter Oath, "A wide-ranging conference shall be held to decide on all matters by public opinion."

Inoue didn't leap up to high heaven and begin arguing nonsense such as that the one eternal lineage can never die and will continue forever, as Mr. Hozumi did. Instead, he opposed them using the most scholarly explanation possible. He said the following:

> The subject of the right to rule is the emperor, but the right to rule does not cease with the death of the emperor and the nation does not perish. The subject of the right to rule simply renews. If the renewal of the subject of the right to rule means the extinction of said right to rule, then the argument that the nation is sovereign cannot be sustained by its own logic, since all the people living today will die eventually.

This is more than enough to repel the arguments offered by the mechanical view of the state, which has no basis in the current theory of state sovereignty. This simultaneously reveals the fact that Professor Inoue, modern state sovereignty theorists, and monarchical sovereignty theorists are all equally preoccupied with a jurisprudence based on the individualism from the time of the French Revolution.

The truth lies in socialism. We maintain through socialism that the right to rule, which is the right of the state, does not exist in the elements of the state, being the emperor and the people. Those who are terminated with the renewal of the elements are those in power, not the subject of the right to rule. The emperor, who is an element of the state, is not the subject to whom the benefits of the exercise of the right of governance are attributed. Nor are the people the subjects of the right to exercise the right to govern—they are not its ultimate goal. In the modern state, the state is recognized as the subject of rights to which the purpose of survival and evolution and corresponding interests are attributed, and the supreme authority is organized by one element with special privileges, or many equal elements, or one element with special privileges and many equal elements, and that institution is not the subject of rights but exercises the right to rule the state for the purpose and benefit of the state. The historical continuity of human society, the state, does not cease to exist in legal terms. Elements are renewed, but the state itself is not renewed. In other words, the state is the subject of the right to govern. (So one mustn't misunderstand. "Social democracy" accepts an awakening of individualism, with the ideal of spreading political power to all the molecules of the state—it does not dogmatically dictate that sovereignty resides in the people, as in the mistaken revolutionary theory of individualism. As the name socialism suggests, it asserts that sovereignty resides in the state, and it seeks to maintain or acquire a democratic system of government in which all molecules of the state have political power and are elements of the supreme authority, in order to maintain the sovereignty of the state, fulfill its objectives, and perfect the interests belonging to the state.)

The above can be summarized as follows. Today's kokutai, or national polity, is not the same polity of the era when the state existed as the property of the monarch for the monarch's benefit. Today's national polity is a civic state in which the actual, real personality of the state is recognized as a legal personality. The emperor is not the emperor of an era when the nation consisted of two elements, the land and the people. As Professor Minobe included in the broad sense of the word "nation," the emperor is a member of the nation and has great privileges in that he is an institution of the nation equally with other members of the nation. The people are not the same as the possessions that existed as "great treasures" under the ownership of the emperor. They are subjects of the state in the sense that they have rights and obligations to the state as molecules of the state. The seitai, or system of government, is not a monarchy in the sense of a government by a single privileged citizen, nor is it a pure republic with equal citizens as a given. In other words, the system of government is what is often called a united government of monarchy and citizenry, and is organized by a privileged single member of the state who holds supreme authority along with other equal molecules of the state. Thus, the ruler is neither the monarch alone nor the people alone. The supreme authority is the one who operates the governing power of the state for the benefit of the state as the ruler. This is the current national polity and system of government as indicated by law. It is socialism in the sense that the state has sovereignty, and democracy in the sense that the people (in the broadest sense) have political power.

In this light, there is no reason to accuse socialism of being "in conflict with the state" just because it is revolutionary. It calls itself revolutionary because it seeks to overthrow the patriarchal monarchy in the economic sphere and to make the economic resources that are the lifeblood of the nation into benefits belonging to the nation, for the purpose of the nation's survival and evolution. To deprive and enslave even individuals of their real personality is an impossible restoration in this day and age. Ignoring the legal personality of the state, which is a great entity that has evolved over a long period of time, and to instead consider it an object that exists for the benefit of the monarch, is nothing short of the restorative revolutionism of the so-called theory of national polity. We socialists must rather be the defenders of the present national polity today and in the future.

Why would anyone seek to defeat our national polity? Since the system of government is an institution that exercises the right to rule, the state will evolve that system according to its purposes and interests. How it will evolve, however, is not known. Will it remain the democratic form of government it is today, or will it become a monarchy organized by a single privileged person, or will it become a pure republic? Or will society evolve to such an astonishing degree that all forms of government will be rendered irrelevant and a heaven on earth will be established? These are questions which have nothing to do with national polity. We can follow Mr. Hozumi, who says, "The theory of national polity is a theory of sovereignty," and determine where sovereignty resides. We also understand Mr. Hozumi's modesty in not daring to publish his university lecture transcripts for fear of the Publication Law, which stipulates that "anyone who publishes a book that plans to change the political system shall be punished with two years of light imprisonment,"[287] because it contains a plan to overturn the current state sovereignty of the national polity, make the land and people the emperor's private property and slaves, return the state to the object of the emperor's property rights as a thing without personality, destroy the current democratic system of government, and make the system of government an absolutely limitless patriarchal government.

Let us by all means go where the logic of state sovereignty leads us! The Constitution, anticipating that the state would take measures compatible with the aims of survival and evolution, stipulates in Article LXXIII the procedure to be followed in the case of the revision or abolition of state institutions. Of course, this is the procedure that should be followed in most cases. However, in times of monarchical sovereignty, it was the legitimate right of the monarch to break the laws established by his own sovereignty with other laws made by his own sovereignty as well. In the same way (just as Mr. Hozumi, who holds that today is a national polity of monarchical sovereignty, follows through with an argument that the emperor has the right to freely issue laws inconsistent with the articles of the Constitution, or to amend or repeal the Constitution as he desires),[288] today and in the future, that is the invocation of the state's

---

[287] Article XXVI of the Publication Law stipules, "If an author, publisher, or printer publishes any document or drawing that desecrates the dignity of the imperial household, disturbs the political system, or disrupts the national constitution, he shall be punished with light imprisonment of not less than two months and not more than two years, and a fine of not less than twenty yen and not more than two hundred yen."

[288] The original text reads, "Therefore, Mr. Hozumi, who today considers the national polity to be one of monarchical sovereignty, argues that the emperor has the right to promulgate laws that are inconsistent with the text of the Constitution or to amend or repeal the Constitution without following the procedures of Article LXXIII, and that the emperor is free to do so without following the procedures of Article LXXIII." However,

sovereignty, which is a state's right, and it applies even if that procedure is inconsistent or conflicts with the provisions already set forth, or if it is significant legislation that conflicts with the articles of the Constitution without following the prescribed procedures. The state has complete freedom to create, alter, or abolish the institutions of the state in accordance with its own purposes and interests. This is because, among laws that are also invocations of state sovereignty, Article LXXIII alone carries a special weight over other currently existing articles, but it is not so powerful as to cancel or invalidate many other laws that may be issued in the future.[289] Just as laws, ministerial ordinances, etc., that ignore the spirit of the Constitution today strip people of their freedom of speech, assembly, and association without following the procedures of Article LXXIII,[290] and effectively amend the Constitution, so too, when other laws establish significant state institutions outside the constitutional state institutions, this is equally an exercise of state sovereignty and occurs because the laws have no weight. (This is why the currently baseless state sovereignty theorists can't be as consistent in their arguments in this regard as monarchical sovereignty theorists. They haven't penetrated into the ideas of sovereignty enough, and so they have no choice but to lament over it.)

Do not mistake us for those who advocate state universalism. That refers to a period when the state was allowed to enter the internal lifestyle of the people, their very thoughts and beliefs. Socialist jurisprudence is statist only so far as it asserts that the state is a sovereign body with complete freedom to regulate the external lifestyle of its citizens. However, the factual theory of

---

the "and that the emperor is free to do so without following the procedures of Article LXXIII" is merely repeating what he already said, so we took it out.

[289] This is difficult to understand. Basically, he's saying "because laws can't be repealed or invalidated, contradictions can't be avoided unless they can be freely amended."

[290] This probably refers to Security Police laws.

what constitutes the exercise of sovereignty compatible with the purposes and interests of the state is of course a separate issue from legal principles, and is merely the will of those in power who are in a position to exercise the sovereignty of the state. In other words, whether or not the will of those in power in fact exercises power for the purposes and interests of the state is beyond the reach of legal theory—this is why we say constitutional law theory is decided by a powerful force (look at where we discussed class conscience in *The Ethical Ideal of Socialism* and where we argue over the class war in *The Enlightenment Movement of Socialism*).

Even if there are those who call themselves socialists and who insist on dismantling the state into atomic individuals and reorganizing society anew, this is the individualism of the French Revolutionary era and must not be confused with socialism. Socialists are clearly aware that the present state has a national polity of state sovereignty, which only becomes the will of the strong through a long time and a great effort. Why should we say that we are going to overthrow and renew the current national polity? Under the will of the strong, as it is today, we have a duty to be persecuted in the name of state sovereignty (read where we discuss the right of persecution in *The Enlightenment Movement of Socialism*).

Chapter 10

As noted above, we have clarified the "current national polity" by means of state studies and constitutional law, and argued that the so-called theory of national polity is a "restorative revolutionism" that seeks to overthrow the current national polity. However, it is not from the study of statecraft and constitutional law that all current scholars who deal with the nature of the state and constitutional law fall into this kind of restorative revolutionary ideology. It is because there is already a so-called theory of national polity which tempts both statecraft and constitutional law. If this is the case, then discussing the nature of the state, as we did above, explaining the legal principles of the Constitution, and thereby talking about the sovereignty of the state, will not provide any stimulus to the savage villages of the Orient. The theory of national polity is something which drives savages to join their hands and worship on their knees, reigning like a barbaric god above all state studies and constitutional theory. What we should be discussing, then, is not statecraft and constitutional studies, but the very theory of national polity that tempts them. What exactly is the theory of national polity?

First, there is the inertia of theistic superstition as the basis for the argument that the nation today is a patriarchal state. "In our unparalleled national polity, the people are the children of one family, and the emperor is the patriarch, the father and mother of his people." This is the argument, and it comes under different names such as the theory of one family of master and servants, the theory of familial piety union, and the theory of loyalty and patriotic union, among others. This is the actual force that forms the basis of the people's moral judgment, and it is the source of the view of the state, as well as of the legal theory that Mr. Hozumi's and many other monarchical sovereignty theorists promote.

Second is a completely inverted interpretation of history within the theory of national polity itself, which leads one to believe that the emperor is a sovereign body or a single supreme authority. In other words, "The Japanese people are all loyal and filial, and have supported the eternal imperial lineage." This argument is also the basis for the idea that Japan's national polity is unparalleled and can't be compared to any other country. For a period of 2,500 years, not a single one of the forty-five million citizens have doubted this idea. All ethical and moral theories have been twisted by this argument, and it is the authority that made Mr. Aruga and all the monarchical sovereignty theorists argue that the basis of sovereignty is determined by history.

The little clay figures known as dogū that are found in the theory of national polity are fabricated based on this delusion. The dogū are simply taken out of the mikoshi and crushed.

Let us begin with the first point—the point which Mr. Hozumi and other stand on. The inertia of theistic superstitions which say that today's Japan is a patriarchal state must be eliminated.

If possible, we would prefer not to get involved in such trivialities and contaminate the pen of debate. What should we say to superstitious people with the titles of dean of a law school, professor at an imperial university, and doctor of law? If common sense and science can awaken those old men, who worship foxes and raccoons, from their superstition, then we can convert Mr. Hozumi from the many gods of Shintoism. When it comes to faith, the foxes and raccoons of old men and women, as well as Dr. Hozumi's true gods, are of a different world that borders on another realm in the vein of religions such as Christianity and Buddhism. Therefore, we have all due respect for Mr. Hozumi's religious beliefs. At the same time, we and anyone with an independent conscience must be free from his faith. To a true Buddhist, Mr. Hozumi's faith is meaningless if stripped of the doctrine of manifestation theory,[291] and to a Christian, who believes in one God, his religion will be seen as the polytheism of a barbaric age. And to those of us who regard the Shinto record as an ancient, bygone religion and treat it scientifically as a myth when we look at it today, his idle talk is no different from a priest's eboshi and noshi.[292] Does he believe that the many deities are not religious beings but historical figures? If so, we are very much free to discuss this as a historical argument. For freedom of religion and independence of thought can't be threatened by the power of the Great Empire of Japan while it remains in one's internal life, nor even when it is manifested in action, except in certain cases. By "certain cases," we mean cases of disobedience to the obligations of being a subject of the state.

We said earlier that the obligations of subjects are not obligations owed directly to the emperor in contractual opposition to the emperor, but are obligations owed to the nation as a member of the nation. We said that subjects are not slaves who exist under the ownership of the emperor and are forced into unlimited obedience, nor are they in contractual conflict with the emperor in the relationship of rights and duties, but the people of the state are state subjects. Therefore, the article of the Constitution that says, "Subjects shall have freedom of religion so far as they do not disobey their duties as subjects," does not mean that subjects can maintain their freedom of religion regardless of their sovereign's faith, as in the contractual constitution of the medieval class state. Today's emperor is not an emperor who owns the state and stands outside of said state. As Professor Minobe included among the broad sense of the word citizen, he is an emperor in the sense of a privileged authority as a

---

[291] The manifestation theory, or "honji suijaku" is the theory that Japanese gods are reincarnations of Buddha. Amaterasu is thought to be the reincarnation of Vairocana. The inverse of this is the "shinpon butsujaku."

[292] "Eboshi" is a long, black hat worn on the head by aristocrats. "Noshi" is the daily wear of the aristocrats in the Heian period.

member of the Japanese empire, as a molecule of humanity which is separated by space from the single organic body known as the nation of Japan.

This privileged molecule is never in contractual opposition to the other molecules. So, just as all other rights and obligations are not directly demanded or borne, so the obligation prefixed to the freedom of faith "so far as they do not disobey their duties as subjects"[293] is never owed by the state molecules to the other molecule, the privileged one. Basically, "so far as they do not disobey their duties as subjects" indicates that it excludes, for example, Quakers who refuse military service,[294] which is one of their duties to the state. If, then, a person who believes in Shinto superstitions comparable to those of Mr. Hozumi were to assume the imperial throne and, like Mr. Hozumi, interpret the subjects of the state as subjects owned by the sovereign, and take up the matter of not believing in Shinto as "disobeying one's duty as a subject," this is of course a demand not acceptable to the national polity and system of government of the Empire of Japan (in fact, the current emperor seems to have embraced Christianity as well).

Moreover, even if a fervent follower of Buddhism such as Emperor Shomu emerged and demanded Buddhist faith from his subjects, Mr. Hozumi would not have to abandon his precious Shinto faith due to the right of freedom of religion that the people have before the Empire of Japan. And even if a future emperor were to embrace Christianity, priests throughout Japan who observe the solemn precepts of the faith would have no reason to attack Buddhists as traitors, as they do today against Christians. We do not know what beliefs the

---

[293] The Constitution says ". . . not antagonistic to their duties as subjects" (Article XXVIII)

[294] Quakers are a Christian Protestant sect. Because of their position of absolute pacifism, they refuse military service, as stated in the text. This is still a point of contention in constitutional law as an issue of "conscientious objection to military service."

imperial family holds. However, what right does someone preaching the theory of national polity today, who seems to worship some clay doll idol, have to call others outlaws because they differ from his superstition? It is our duty to defend the sovereignty of the nation against restorative revolutionary ideology, and such battle monks calling us outlaws, even if it comes in waves, is not the least bit disruptive of solemn debate. The Empire of Japan and its institutions were never built on a religious foundation. The time when the patriarchal state was built on Shinto beliefs and faith was placed above it in the sense that the emperor was the head of the priesthood is buried in the very distant past.

The battle monks at National Polity Temple can't see today's national polity or system of government because of their superstitions. They are relying on the people to be asleep in their superstition, as the battle monks of old once did, to force the people to break through the law, subvert the Constitution, and worship the mikoshi before the emperor and all the people. In the days when the people were afraid of superstition, the mikoshi of the priests and soldiers made the samurai guards take off their helmets.[295] Today, we only draw the sharp sword of science in the name of defending the state. By all means, let us quickly awaken the people from their superstition and burn down the National Polity Temple.

Mr Yatsuka Hozumi is indeed the head of the National Polity Temple,[296] the general in charge of the battle monks. He says the following:

> Our people share the same ancestor. Some say that the worship of the imperial family as a religious family is in fact false, but this does

---

[295] In other words, they made even the samurai warriors pay respect.

[296] This "head" refers to the highest-ranking priest of the temple. It is known as "zasu" (座主) in Japanese. The head of Enryaku-ji Temple is known as "tendai zasu," and has historically been followed by such famous people as Jien (Fujiwara-no-Kanezane's younger brother) and Prince Moriyoshi (Emperor Go-Daigo's son).

not go far enough to disprove my theory. Behold, Christians are united by their belief in God. And the argument about whether God exists or not cannot repudiate this unity. Faith is first and knowledge second. One does not investigate every cause and take every action. They are moved by faith. So it is with the people. They will always be united by faith.

This is a quote from his university transcripts, but needless to say, it is not to be sniffed at that he expresses a novel theory of faith based on his dignity as the head of National Polity Temple. His entire constitutional theory is built on this faith. He also says the following: "The emperor, who now resides on the throne, rules this people on the throne of his ancestor, Amaterasu. On behalf of Amaterasu, he takes the power of Amaterasu and protects the descendants of Amaterasu." He continues thusly:

Our national polity was developed from the unique tribal system of our people. Therefore, by inference, the imperial throne is an idea that connects the ancestor Amaterasu, who held the imperial throne in the past, the present emperor, and the future sovereign. Just as the position of the patriarch of a family is the same as of the ancestor of the emperor, so the imperial throne is the throne of the emperor, and his descendants ascend to this position and represent the authority of Amaterasu to the people.

Notably, he always uses the same words but their meanings fluctuate, at one point referring to Amaterasu or the ancestors of the emperor as gods in faith, and at another referring to them as historical figures. Therefore, when we discuss "Amaterasu" with him, we are almost always at a loss as to whether we should consider it from a religious point of view or as a subject for scientific consideration.

Therefore, Mr. Hozumi's attitude, when studying the antiquity of the Japanese people, makes him seem less like a scientific researcher and more like a superstitious Shinto believer who uses *Kojiki* and *Nihon Shoki* as his bibles. Even as a scientific researcher, in fact, he appears to be a superstitious person, because of his stubborn single-mindedness about the high heavens. Indeed, he is someone who stands on a university lectern wearing an eboshi and noshi, but with the high collar of an academic. Yet, if you are a believer in Shinto, you may believe in Shinto as a religion. To interpret ancestor worship as the worship of power, for example, is not only an erroneous theory of jurisprudence, it is the attitude of a scientist in defiance of the Shinto faith. If we look at Amaterasu from the viewpoint of faith, we must worship in the morning and evening, as she exists in the sun.

Today's sociology interprets that matrilineal lineage as "one in which the father is not known because the marital relationship is not fixed, although not due to complete promiscuity,"[297] and argues that it belongs to a very uncivilized age in which people were aware of their lineage by their mothers. Referring to Amaterasu as a matrilineal deity is a two-headed monster with the head of a scientist and the head of a Shinto believer on its shoulders. Of course, he is only implicitly instructing the university not to publish his lecture transcripts, perhaps out of some sense of caution, for fear of the punishment which befalls those who attempt to change the national system of government, but see the following words of Mr. Hozumi in his contribution to the *Journal of the National Society*, No. 60:

---

[297] This hypothesis of the most primitive form of marriage was postulated by the American sociologist Morgan. However, it's based on erroneous observations and has no ethnographic basis. The term "today's sociology" here probably refers to Morgan's theories.

400 | The Theory of Japan's National Polity and Pure Socialism

There are those who argue that the development of the male lineage took place after the development of society, and that the female lineage is the universal old form across the world. I cannot firmly assert this, but it seems to me that female lineages are probably found everywhere. As for the history of Japan and China, I dare not assert it. Japan's national constitution, for example, defines it as a male lineage, but if one were to say that it was a female lineage prior to the beginning of recorded history, that would be a major problem.

Regarding whether this is a valid theory, of course there are those who disagree. However, if Mr. Hozumi himself is so convinced, there is no need to play with such cautious language. The laws of the state will protect his independence of thought against the insults and disrespect thrown at him by the unwise, even if he clearly asserts it. What is truly strange is that the two monstrous heads on his shoulders do not wrestle with each other, but remain at peace.

Consequently, we do not know which of these heads to question. However, if one of them says, "Scientific reflection is the approach of the jurist," then we have found the right speaker—in other words, the origin of the state is absolutely not merely the expansion of a single family. It is true, of course, that the old theories of a certain era ascribed the origin of the nation to a single family. However, it was much later in evolution that we became aware of lineages and the creation of families, and the matrilineal lineage, as Mr. Hozumi describes it, did not exist. The matrilineal lineage, which is very undeveloped from today's point of view, only emerged after the evolution of the mother-child connection reached a point of permanence through an awakened consciousness. The patrilineal lineage is only possible when this awareness is further extended to the father, and a permanent marital relationship and contact between father and son is created. Society and the state, which Mr. Hozumi believes to be a family system, already existed before. Society existed as a social organism by instinctive sociality, even without a contract and without the power of the father, as he claims.

Neither did the roots of public law arise, as he seems to believe, only after the family system was introduced and people began to fear the power of the patriarch. It is more natural to infer that the moral sanctions and customs of the village, which existed in primitive societies even in the distant past, are the roots of public law. This is because even higher social creatures without family systems or patriarchs have simple sanctions to maintain their societies. If Mr. Hozumi, in his attack on the mechanical view of the state, which is based on a highly parochial individualism, whips the corpse of the social contract theory and places the foundation of the state and society on sociality, naming it patriotism or public spirit—though this would contradict his other words about unity through fear of the patriarch's power—he would not infer, as Hobbes did, that the primitive age of society and the state existed in a state of struggle of all against all.

In other words, if he understands the theory of biological evolution and knows that humans have been social creatures since the time of their differentiation from apes, he would know that it would go beyond biological evolution to believe that such things as maternal or paternal lineages existed in a familial sense from proto-human societies. The conclusion of science that proto-humans, who differentiated from apes as social creatures, continued their social existence in the form of instinctive bonding, has displaced the theory of social origins with unity based on the power of the father. He who does not know the beginning does not know the present, nor does he know the end. The entry into class-based societies, such as the family system and social classes of the same bloodline, is merely a situation in which society is in the process of great evolution. It is essentially a manifestation of the degree of our current evolution, the fact that our social consciousness has only awakened to creating bonds among our immediate bloodlines. It's absolutely nothing primitive, only the current situation that we are in. Nor is it, of course, something that will continue forever (see *The Theory of Biological Evolution and Social Philosophy*).

If one is so inclined to discuss the roots of public law and to study the origins of society, look at everything according to its evolution. Even if we can conclude that the family system developed in primitive societies and that the root of public law was the power of the patriarchs, what kind of an imitation is it to regulate the present and the future based on the idea of past patriarchal power and states, now that society and laws have evolved? Mr. Hozumi's argument is like saying that, since the primordial humans shared ancestors with apes, the world's humans are and will remain apes, and since the animal species to which apes belong, along with birds, differentiated from reptiles, Mr. Hozumi and all the rest of us are really still reptiles.

Mr. Hozumi is not inferring and studying the origins of Japanese society based on Shinto. He is making up whatever he likes using the unsustainable hypotheses of sociology, which were abandoned long ago. Is it not laughable? We can do nothing but hold our noses up at his faithful assertion to "Believe in Shinto and place knowledge second." Even the old men and women who still believe in the Tenri sect of Shinto would laugh at him, as he advocates using knowledge yet believes in the old knowledge which makes up the theory of social origins, and in such destroys his Shinto faith, which is supposed to be put before knowledge. Behold, how can Shintoism claim that the nation of Japan is an outgrowth of a single being, Amaterasu? Shinto only says that Izanagi and Izanami were the beginning of mankind. And this is only a general theory of human origins as far as ancient thought is concerned, the same as how Jewish people say that Adam and Eve were the ancestors of human beings.

So, if one believes in this theory of human origins, does one try to make Shinto a world religion like Christianity, just as Christ advocated a cosmopolitanism of fellow human beings based on this theory? Or, as it is said that only the Jews are the children of God, descendants of Adam and Eve,[298] should it be that only the Japanese are the people of God, descendants of Izanagi and Izanami, and that Shinto should be developed in the same way as Judaism with its exclusionary ideology? It must be one or the other.

If we imagine the text as written in the fourteenth century after the Jinmu, we can say that Amaterasu was the direct ancestor of the conquerors we call the Jinmu family.[299] The Japanese peoples who migrated before and after Jinmu, the many peoples who already referred to Amaterasu as many gods, and the descendants of the countless naturalizations and conquests throughout history that have bred and left behind other peoples, known as today's Japanese peoples, have nothing to do with Amaterasu. To put it differently, all we can say upon looking at Takamagahara is that the same people live there as here. Nowhere is there any record which says that the people divided off from Amaterasu are the one large global family known as Takamagahara.

If Mr. Hozumi sees Amaterasu as a real person—and if he doesn't, his reason for monarchical sovereignty, in which an ideologically created god extended her life and gave the right to rule to the emperor himself, is void—how could Amaterasu reproduce a population of so many as only one woman? Is Susanoo-no-mikoto,[300] mentioned in the classics, not of the same collateral bloodline as Amaterasu, but a child Amaterasu bore through a virgin birth? When Susanoo-no-mikoto entered Izumo, the population was large enough to

---

[298] Judaism is a religion with an idea of being a chosen people, reflecting the situation of the Jewish people, who have been persecuted since ancient times.

[299] Emperor Jinmu entered Kumano from the Land of Hyuga (around present-day Miyazaki Prefecture) via the Seto Inland Sea and conquered the Kinki region. He is said to have ascended the throne at Kashihara Jingu in the Land of Yamato.

[300] The younger brother of Amaterasu.

be eaten by the giant serpent, Yamata-no-orochi,[301] but did the grandfather and grandmother of the young lady eaten by the Yamata-no-orochi come from the belly of Amaterasu, who was probably younger than them? If one believes in Shintoism, then he must hold that Izanagi and Izanami learned how to reproduce by watching wagtails mate and thereby gave birth to the human race.[302] In this way, rather than through the Jewish myth of God creating Adam and Eve in his own image, Christianity would have given birth to the noble ideal of the fellowship of mankind. Amaterasu, who did not give birth to the millions of gods, is not the so-called "ancestor" of the majority of the people, many of whom are probably descended from one of those deities. However, it goes without saying that this precious cosmopolitanism is too far outside the beliefs of those who advocate a so-called theory of national polity. Therefore, he must argue that the Japanese people alone are the descendants of a special deity born of two persons, Izanagi and Izanami, just as some say that the Jewish people alone are the descendants of Adam and Eve, the children of a special deity. However, this would cancel his earlier argument that Amaterasu alone is the ancestor of the Japanese people, and that the Japanese people were bred through the virgin births of Amaterasu, and move on to a completely new argument. Still, it would be beneficial to his argument if the Japanese nation developed from the expansion of a single family, such as in the "master and servant family" theory. One's argument must be interpreted in the best sense possible.

---

[301] It is said that Susanoo-no-mikoto vanquished Yamata-no-orochi, at which time the Kusanagi-no-tsurugi sword came out of its tail.

[302] The "wagtail" is a generic name for birds belonging to the family of the wagtails of the order Sparidae. In *Nihon Shoki* (not in the main book, but in the addition known as the Issho) it is said that once one sees the wagtail move its head and tail, one understands. It's also known as the "teaching bird" for this reason.

Therefore, we will do our best to show Mr. Hozumi the words of the late Professor Mayori Kurokawa.[303] If he is unable to finish reading the following words and accidentally begins laughing, then our good intentions have been rejected. At that time, he must either become like Christ in Shintoism, advocating a cosmopolitanism of brotherhood, or else he must give up his Jewish-like ideas of Shintoism.

Professor Kurokawa says the following:

The robe is made to fit the body; the robe is for the upper body and the hakama is for the lower body. We live our lives wearing these garments. Nowadays, however, people think as follows. "People in the past didn't use clothing. Man was originally an animal, and that animal was a monkey. After living for a while, the monkey gradually lost the hair on its body and became a man. As the hair fell, they began to feel cold, so they began to make clothes from the bark of trees and plants." This is a foreign theory. There are those who say that foreign theories are worthy of belief, but they are merely people who haven't studied the classics of our country following the foreign theories.

Foreign peoples may have evolved from apes, but not the people of our country. In our country, people are people and apes are apes. Apes did not evolve into man. In the words of Izanami-no-mikoto in *Kojiki*, "My beloved darling. If you would do such a thing, I would twist the necks of one thousand of your people on earth." "Ah, my beloved dear. If you would do such a thing, I would bear one thousand five hundred people a day."[304] If they were referring to monkeys, it would have to say

---

[303] A scholar of ancient Japanese literature and culture and a professor at Tokyo University. He died the year this book was written (1906).

[304] The original text took this from *Kojiki*, but since it was different from what's actually in the real *Kojiki*, we've used the reading from Nihon Shiso Taikei's publication of *Kojiki*.

"monkeys on earth" instead. In fact, there would be no need to erect houses at all just for monkeys to have babies. In this light, it is clear that the Japanese people did not originate from monkeys.

We do not use these quotations as fodder for ridiculing the deceased. We only quote them with the good intention of giving Mr. Hozumi the benefit of the doubt when he chooses to address the Shinto Adam and Eve from the standpoint of Christian cosmopolitanism, or from the standpoint of Jewish exclusivism.

The modern translation is as follows. "'My beloved darling. If you would do such a thing, I would twist the necks of one thousand of your people on earth.' To this, Izanagi-no-mikoto said, 'Ah, my beloved dear. If you would do such a thing, I would bear one thousand five hundred people a day.'" This conversation took place when Izanagi went to Yomi. Izanami was seriously wounded when she gave birth to the god of fire, and passed away from her wounds. After her death, Izanagi went Yomi, the land of the dead, in an attempt to bring her back. Izanami responded to Izanagi's call by consulting with the gods of Yomi on whether she could return, but said she couldn't reveal herself during that time. Izanami went to the consultation but didn't return for quite a while, and Izanagi, unable to contain himself, went deep into Yomi. He broke the teeth of a comb to light the way, and once he made it inside, he illuminated Izanami's figure, but the illuminated Izanami was a ghastly sight to behold. Her body was covered in maggots, and pus was oozing out of her body. Frightened by Izanami's appearance, Izanagi hurriedly fled, but Izanami, angry that her ugly body had been seen, ordered the goddesses of Yomi to pursue him. Izanagi managed to fend off the pursuit of the goddesses, flee back to the border of earth, and sealed the entrance to Yomi with a large rock. After the goddesses failed to catch Izanagi, Izanami returned to the border with the earth in pursuit of Izanagi. Izanagi offered to void their promise, but Izanami grew angry at this and said the quote used in this text.

Mr. Hozumi does not understand the theory of biological evolution to such an extent that he still follows the old hypothesis that the origin of society is the family unit. This is comparable to Professor Kurokawa's opposition of biological evolution by quoting classical scripture. The degree of conviction to which Professor Kurokawa asserts, "Foreign peoples may have evolved from apes, but not the people of our country," and "In this light, it is clear that the Japanese people did not originate from monkeys," along with the coherence of his argument, to the point where he's trying to pull a heavy sack of coins with a single hair, is far above Mr. Hozumi.[305] If Mr. Hozumi's faith in the Jewish Shinto religion is so firm that he demands others to follow the Shinto religion, and if he himself sincerely believes in the theory of "master and servant family" or "unity of loyalty and filial piety," then he would not fail in his honor as the head of the National Polity Temple.

It should be noted, however, that the National Polity Temple has no more followers than the decaying Hongan-ji. Otherwise, wouldn't it be more reasonable to hear holy words or chants of "Takamagahara"[306] all across Japan, drowning out the Buddhist prayers of other old men and women in the street? And it would be an incomprehensible phenomenon to find that, among those who call themselves new intellectuals, few get down on their knees at shrines, but many more go to churches. What kind of revolutionaries would replace the Empire of Japan and one of its most important institutions, the emperor, with a Shinto foundation in these days when Shinto beliefs have become practically extinct? Perhaps even the head of National Polity Temple

---

[305] This compound in the original text is misspelled. The correct phrase is "pulling one thousand pounds with a single hair," and it comes from Han Yu's writings (*Ye Meng Shangshushu [与孟尚書書]*). It basically means "to do something very dangerous."

[306] The words are slightly different from the original. The actual celebrants (words used when performing rituals) are slightly different. The chants used during these are usually something which means "to stay as a god," or "to sit as a god in Takamagahara."

himself, whose scientific research has undermined Shinto doctrine, is merely advocating such an argument for the sake of revolutionary expediency, and deep down inside does not have even the slightest faith in it.

We know that we should be careful not to go into the depths of other people's beliefs without reason, and to refrain from imagining things that we do not know. However, Mr. Hozumi's argument is clearly revolutionary in the context of today's nationalist state polity. Is it not an attempt to ground the civic state, which was envisioned as an ideal long before the Taika Revolution and finally realized in the Meiji Revolution, and the emperor, who was placed on the foundation of the state as its national institution, on the basis of Shinto beliefs that he doesn't even hold? A faith in which neither he nor the common people believe is a dead faith, and that means it would place the emperor on something empty. This means that it is not placed above anything else, but turned upside down—meanwhile, fact rests upon history.

The reason why the Taika Revolution was intended to create a Confucian ideal state was because the emperor was in danger of not being able to maintain his position according to the ancestral religion. For the Soga, who were followers of Buddhism, an emperor who believed in a different religion was not a respectable existence![307] To the foreigner pawns, the Ayauji,[308] Emperor Sushun was not the "father and mother of the people" of the master-servant family theory. Because of this, did not a bold and daring idealist within the imperial family dream of a civic state, even if it was only a pipe dream?

---

[307] To begin with, it is said that Prince Shotoku of the imperial family was so devoted to Buddhism that he wrote *Sangyo Gisho*, and that the imperial family at the time also valued Buddhism.

[308] The Ayauji are said to be descendants of Achi no omi, who came to Japan during the reign of Emperor Ojin. In the chronicle of Emperor Sushun in volume 21 of *Nihon Shoki*, there's an article that says Umako Soga had Emperor Soshun assassinated by Yamato no Aya no Ataikoma

What do we call Mr. Hozumi if we do not call him a restorative revolutionary, since he is overturning the national polity of today, in which that ideal was finally realized, and allowing the Soga clan and its pawns to try and assert their rights today?

Since the nation has the purpose of independence and survival, and the emperor is a national institution that maintains the nation as a benefit to the nation, the emperor should not be violated as a duty to the nation. If we say that the people of Japanese nationality are precious because they are "the emperor's children" and the emperor, as their patriarch, is "the father and mother of the people," then Italian anarchists who do not form a family of sovereigns, but who have entered Japanese nationality, would be claiming the right to use bombs based on Mr. Hozumi's constitutional theory. "The unity of Christians does not depend on whether or not God exists. The people are united by their faith." This theory of faith technically gives permission for the disciples of Nicolas II to unite in Russia and rebel against their nation—but surely Mr. Hozumi would say "that's different" in response to such revolutionary theory.[309] Then the infidels must be slaughtered and the foreigners strangled and crucified. But this is a revolution in the same regard.

If Mr. Hozumi stubbornly advocates a patriarchal state, the master and slave family theory, and unity of loyalty and filial piety, and builds all jurisprudence and ethical theories on this basis, we ask him the following. What if your chauffeur asks, "Who are your relatives, master?" Would you answer, "My relatives are the exalted emperors," or not? If he does answer that,

---

[309] The Czar of Russia at the time was Nicholas II. Nicholas II visited Japan in 1891 when he was still the crown prince, and is known to have been seriously wounded by a police officer (Sanzo Tsuda) who cut him down in Otsu. Incidentally, the attack and defense between the Grand Chamber of Inquiry and the Cabinet over the punishment of Tsuda, the perpetrator of this incident (the Otsu Incident), shook Japan at the time.

the chauffeur will say he is an impious fellow, and we will admire his bold egalitarianism. And if he says, "The holy emperors and I are blood brothers," any nearby police would take out their notebooks and question him. If he says, "I've had a child. Inform my relatives, the heavenly emperors," then the noble lady sleeping next to him in bed would be shocked and upset. If he were to walk down a main street and say, "The Hozumi family is a branch of the imperial family," a little rascal would surely run after him yelling, "You fool!" Do not misinterpret this as playing with a pathetic and foolish man. Look at the later section on historical interpretation where we trace bloodlines and see how egalitarianism expanded and developed through history. Now, if that is the case, it means that even the strongest advocate of the master—slave family theory would not consider the imperial family and the Hozumi family to be kin in an equal relationship. If the blood relationship is so weak and estranged that one would be considered insane if one were to speak of kinship, what an inferior intellect it must be to use this as the basis to endorse the emperor and as chains that bind the nation together.

If Mr. Hozumi were a Shinto missionary and not a jurist, there is no reason why he should not interpret the present Civil Code, which has not yet completely removed the legacy of the patriarchal system, as limiting patriarchal rights to two or three privileges,[310] and the law of kinship as setting a limit to a certain number of equal relatives. At the funerals of rich people, even those who have no more relationship than caring for their cats show up claiming to be their relatives. If the imperial family were not so generous, it would say exactly the following: "O Yatsuka and the forty-five million slaves who are taking advantage of our good words. You would say that the foul

---

[310] It is said that the Meiji Civil Code retained some pre-modernity in kinship law, but even so, the privileges were more limited than those of the patriarchal system of the early Meiji period (referenced from Fukushima Masao, *The Development of Japanese Capitalism and Private Law* [University of Tokyo Press, 1988]).

Hozumi family is a branch family of myself, the ruler of all, even down to the beggar and all? The imperial family is not a relative with the same ancestors as your lowly race. When the ancestors of the imperial family fell into ruin, you watched on, as if looking at people on the street, or throwing stones at them, but now that they are prosperous, you suck up to them.[311] And you presumptuously call those who are over three thousand years old, distant, and of unknown lineage, your relatives, your head family, and act as if you are trying to realize your own ulterior motives. What flattery you give from behind your mask. The imperial family did not branch off of the same ancestor. It is an imposing conqueror who oppressed the people with its mighty power."

We declare that not only does Mr. Hozumi not believe in the patriarchal state of the master-servant family, but if you look deep into his heart, you will find that there is not a shadow of a Shinto belief. If he does believe in Shinto, it is merely an outward embellishment, like the wicked mother-in-law chanting a Buddhist prayer or the lazy students saying "Amen" when they go to church. We take back everything we have said about Mr. Hozumi's constitutional theory as being based on Shinto beliefs. He does not believe in Shinto, and his so-called faith is an old-fashioned theory of social origins. The spinal cord of the so-called theory of national polity of his and others is the sociological superstition that the ancestral religion and its accompanying patriarchal system, which every nation at one time or another has taken as an evolutionary step, is the origin of the nation and that it will continue until the extinction of the human race.

How can we say that the patriarchal system and ancestral religion are unique to the Japanese people and that Japan is the only nation with a national polity unmatched by any other nation? All European countries have experienced this at one time or another. Not only is this an indisputable fact, but it is also the only option, because no advanced nation evolves by leaps and

---

[311] Refer to chapter 13.

bounds. Therefore, even in Europe, there was a time when the patriarchal system and patriarchal authority were the dominant explanation for the origin of kingship or public law. Perhaps Mr. Hozumi and others, not being naturally superior, tried to explain Japan by imitating them and became revolutionaries by mistake. Nevertheless, if Mr. Hozumi insists, "My Shinto faith is primary and my knowledge of social origins is secondary," we should not show any leniency when stripping away these falsehoods.

Let us ask Mr. Hozumi this—the ancestral religion is polytheism, is he a believer in polytheism? It's likely that Mr. Hozumi will respond proudly, "Yes. I believe in the many deities of Shintoism." Of course, it's possible to respond like that. However, there are many other deities to be worshipped in the polytheism of ancestral religion. In India, where religious freedom is at its most extreme, there are still polytheistic religions that worship ancestral spirits,[312] including serpents, trees, stones, birds, beasts, and even genitalia. Similarly, before the spread of Christianity, Europeans worshipped various animals, strange stones, and strange trees along with the spirits of their ancestors. Japan's ancestral religion of many deities is similar to these, and in its polytheism, it worships countless laughable things.

Does Mr. Hozumi dismiss the explanation of fire as a compound of oxygen and carbon and believe in the fire deity Kagutsuchi instead?[313] Does he fear storms caused by changes in atmospheric pressure because he believes the wind deity Shinatobe-no-kami gets angry and knocks down large trees? Or does he fear that sea tides are the work of the sea deity Watatsumi? Are locusts the work of Toshigami?[314] Is agriculture a pagan religion of Shinto that harms national polity? Does Mr. Hozumi put offerings in the hearth and latrine to

---

[312] Referencing Hinduism. The worship of the elephant god Ganesha is a typical example.

[313] "Kagutsuchi" refers to the fire god born of Izanagi no Mikoto and Izanami no Mikoto. He was cut down by Izanagi no Mikoto for burning Izanami no Mikoto to death.

[314] "Toshigami" is the deity who can bring good harvest.

worship the deities of the hearth and latrine? Does he insist that a serpent from the zoo be worshipped at the shrine, or does he join his hands in worship in front of genitalia carved from wood every morning and evening? Because of the existence of shrines dedicated to these pagan gods and paganism, the Imperial Constitution was prefaced with the phrase "so far as it does not disturb peace and order."

Ancestor worship and polytheism are the buds of religions and philosophies that sprang from the same root. Of course, many of them are laughable in retrospect, and even now, in savage countries, or in civilized countries in the countryside, far from the cities, these superstitions seem to persist among foolish couples and are the subject of pathetic laughter. But this is the first stage in evolution that no people can avoid. That is, mankind first begins the development of spiritual wisdom and acquires philosophy through polytheism (this does not refer to pantheism), which holds that all things in heaven and earth are divine. Humans put their minds at ease and entrusted themselves to heavenly destiny through ancestral religion, which believes that people do not die at all, but remain as souls on rooftops, in graves, and in the sky (this is not the same as immortality as an "extension of the individual," which we discussed earlier regarding scientific religion).

There is this religion, there is this philosophy, and without this philosophy this religion doesn't exist. If, then, Mr. Hozumi makes an escape route by saying, "I believe in Amaterasu and the many other gods, but I do not worship snakes, latrines, or genitalia," then he must possess a tongue capable of saying the words "correct" and "incorrect" at the exact same time. Therefore, we have no choice but to think of Mr. Hozumi in one of the following three ways, and he must choose one of them. Is Mr. Yatsuka Hozumi a philosopher on par with Aristotle and Bacon who has invented a new logic that can affirm one thing and deny another at the same time?[315] Is he a professor of law, legal scholar,

---

[315] The English philosopher Francis Bacon. He wrote *Novum Organum* and argued for a

and professor at an imperial university, who affirms polytheism and clasps his hands together in prayer in front of wooden genitalia? Or will he deny his patriarchal doctrine, deny his constitutional law, deny his theory of master-servant family, and thereby deny the so-called theory of national polity?

In the so-called theory of national polity, the theory of the coincidence of loyalty and filial piety is further derived from the previously mentioned theory of master-servant family. It is, of course, absurd to put such an outrageous theory on the theoretical pen, but what is truly horrifying is that simple and sincere educators, unaccustomed to questioning, are still being deceived by the little clay idols of battle monks and infusing them into their young minds as the basis for moral judgment. This sort of disorder is normal, however, for the countrymen whose heads have been slammed by the hammer of "one eternal lineage."

Even if today's Japanese people are a family of masters and servants bred from a single emperor, as Dr. Hozumi and others have argued, how can this be deduced into the theory of loyalty and filial piety coincidence? If, like some, we separate the theory of loyalty and filial piety coincidence from that of a family of sovereigns and simply say, "If you are loyal to the sovereign, you will make a name for yourself and your family will prosper, so loyalty and filial piety coincide," this would be highly logical. Cromwell made his name and his house prosperous through the revolution, so filial piety and killing the sovereign coincide; with Washington, filial piety and independence coincide; in Watt and Johnson, filial piety and steam and electricity coincide. For Taira no Shigemori who, "cannot achieve filial piety if attempting loyalty, and cannot achieve loyalty if attempting filial piety," it means he is an idiotic man who can't understand the theory of unity, loyalty, and filial piety.[316] In addition,

---

philosophy of empiricism as opposed to scholastic philosophy.

[316] The eldest son of Taira no Kiyomori. He is said to have been mild-mannered and deeply loyal to his father. In *Heike Monogatari*, volume 2, "Hoka no Sata" there is a

Yasutoki, who exiled the three emperors for his filial devotion to his father Yoshitoki,[317] was a loyal subject of the three emperors in line with his filial duty, and was respected as a sovereign by the ancestors of the people, and so it is completely reasonable to argue that he was a sovereign who was furnished with both loyalty and filial piety.

However, those who advocate the theory of master-servant family are led to argue that "since the masters and servants are one family, loyalty and filial piety coincide." This is exactly what one would expect from an undeveloped village in the Orient. Even if all forty-five million people reproduced by Amaterasu's monogenesis, the theory of loyalty and filial piety coincidence could only be held to be true toward Amaterasu herself. How could the right and obligation of loyalty arise between offspring? A savage could establish grades among offspring and sacrifice one child for the sake of the other through slavish morality. If you look up to Amaterasu in faith and call her your parent or ancestor, then you should see all people as equals and give them benevolence. Or, since we are a branch family of hers, should we omit equality and instead say how much loyalty we must give to our main family? According to the order of moral performance taught in the Imperial Rescript on Education,[318] in an emergency one should be loyal to the head family, which

---

section that reads, "If I should do my duty for the sake of the sovereign, I would forget my father's kindness, which is greater than the eighty thousand mountain peaks. And if I think to flee my sin of disobedience to my filial duty, it would mean I have become a disloyal traitor for the sake of my lord." *Heike Monogatari (Jo)* (Tokyo: Iwanami Shoten, 1991), 99.

[317] Emperor Go-Toba, Emperor Juntoku, and Emperor Tsuchimikado were the emperors he exiled.

[318] The Imperial Rescript on Education says, "the people should show filial duty toward their parents, friendship toward their brothers, harmony with their spouse, and mutual trust with their friends."

was divided in the parent's generation, before helping the destiny of the eternal emperor, who is the head of a distant family that existed three thousand years ago, and one should show even more loyalty to the branch family that was divided in the elder brother's generation.

But those who know the law, such as Mr. Hozumi, will argue for the termination of kinship by limitation of kinship, and will argue that there is no duty of loyalty.[319] Even if this is called disrespectful or disloyal, a stern judge, standing with the sovereignty of the nation on his shoulders, will protect those who have observed the lovely Imperial Rescript on Education. If we look at this theory of loyalty and filial piety coincidence based on the Imperial Rescript on Education, it is simply egalitarianism at its core. We seek an explanation for those who advocate the principle of loyalty and filial piety coincidence based on the theory of "master-servant family." Are the old fathers of the branch families shedding their blood for the children of the head family? Are the adult members of the branch families dying for the children of the head family? Does each member of a branch family prepare a beautiful meal for the head family? Do the eldest brothers of the branch families avoid the road for their younger brother of the main family, run away in fear at the shouts of the police, and bow respectfully while reciting the national anthem? If the so-called theory of national polity advocates do not owe this duty to the head family, then to make a distinction between the equal relationship of the head and branch families and apply it to the relationship between the imperial household and the people is a radical revolutionism that should not be tolerated by the state today.

Japan's national polity is not one family of masters and servants but an imposing state. The emperor is not a member of the main family or a branch of the main family, but the emperor acting as an institution of the state.

---

[319] In other words, "We're so far removed from the blood of the imperial family that, since our kinship is now limited in scope, we have no familial relationship with the imperial family, and thus do not need to be loyal to it."

Imperial expenses are not a plunder of the branch families by the head family, but a right of the imperial family against the state. Military service is not the killing of branch family members for the benefit of the head family, but the duty of the people to the state. The reason that the emperor has a massive right of honor so grave that it can't be compared to anyone else and that the people can't make equal demands is because that is the system designed to maintain the state for the benefit of the state. Thus, the state can't be allowed to ignore the emperor's privileges. In other words, the Great Empire of Japan is not a nation created by the delusions of a family of masters and servants, but an actual nation. The emperor is not the head of a family with equal kinship to the people, but a member of the state who has grave privileges against the state for the benefit of the state. In other words, it can be said that those who advocate the theory of loyalty and filial piety coincidence are committing treason against the state by using the master-servant family theory as reason (for more on the patriarchal system and the principle of loyalty and filial piety, please see the later discussion of Japanese ethical history).

The theory of national polity which says "the nation of Japan is a patriarchal country with one extended family, the people are the emperor's children, and the emperor is the father of the people," has fallen into a dilemma by the idea that foreigners can walk around, live, and work anywhere they like in Japan. Today's law provides that any foreigner, upon acquiring Japanese nationality, has no grade of obligation as a subject of the nation. For red-bearded, blue-eyed Europeans, acquisition of Japanese nationality merely means that they have entered the Japanese nationality. They wouldn't recognize that they are "the emperor's children," but they are full-fledged subjects of the Japanese nation. Even if the emperor were to allow Blacks to acquire Japanese nationality and become subjects of the Japanese nation, he would not be pleased if they were to regard him as "the father of the Blacks." For what reason do national polity theorists, such as Mr. Hozumi, who hold the emperor to be the patriarch and demand fidelity according to the master-slave family theory, demand duty from naturalized citizens? There are two paths that those who advocate the theory of national polity can take. One, as mentioned before, is to give rights to the Italian anarchists (who became naturalized in Japan) who performed assassinations and pagans who rebelled, and argue that naturalized foreign citizens are exempt from obligations as subjects of the state. The other option is to eliminate the law mentioned earlier which allows foreign people to live, walk, work, etc., anywhere in Japan.

It is true that even the savage national polity theorists opposed this as much as possible, since they knew that such a law was a serious life-and-death issue that would clearly wipe out the patriarchal claims of the nation. However, not only did the restorative revolution of the theory of national polity not succeed, but now that the evolution of history has so overwhelmed them, and we are currently living under the law they so opposed, shouldn't the real question now be what they will do in the future? No! Threats against the so-called national polity theorists have existed since the beginning of history. Mr. Hozumi, are you saying that Empress Jingu,[320] who graces Japanese history as a hero, is a destroyer of the national polity because she is a descendant of a naturalized ancient Korean? Is the mixed-race child Sakanoue-no-Tamuramaro,[321] who most delights elementary school children, a national pirate who has damaged the national polity? Do you say that the descendants of Achi no omi,[322] who led the people of Agata and was naturalized at the time

---

[320] Empress of Emperor Chuai, and mother of Emperor Ojin. It is said that she went with the emperor to conquer Kumaso, then conquered Silla as well. This is what is known as the "conquest of ancient Korea."

[321] A warrior in the early Heian period. As a grand shogun, he fought the Emishi and won. He was from a family of the Yamato-no-Ayauji.

[322] The original text says "Achiki," but it's Achi no omi. He was a migrant who arrived in Japan during the reign of Emperor Ojin. Among all the migrant clans, he held the most power.

of Emperor Ojin,[323] and the descendants of all the naturalized people who imported the Chinese civilization of the time, are not subjects of the emperor, and that the emperor is not their sovereign? Does the concentration of blood of the surprisingly large number of slaves brought back as prisoners of war for the purpose of increasing the population during the conquest of ancient Korea, mixed with the blood of naturalized lowly people of the conquered areas, grade the rights, duties, and moral relations of the emperor and his people? The answer is no.

We present to you now the dreaded destroyer of the theory of national polity.

Who is it? Shockingly enough, it is the exalted emperor of Japan himself! Do not fear, though, national polity theorists. We do not mean that you should carry the real emperor on your mikoshi and try to take a shot at our theory of national polity, as we are now doing toward your dogū. However, just as the Nanto battle monks could do little more than use the mikoshi to threaten to send the then-emperor to hell, and all we can do is stand by and watch as the current emperor is called "impious" for acting in a manner inconsistent with the theory of national polity of these dogū, it is still a fact that the nation has a solemn criminal law. That law states that it is the emperor's right to include foreign nations in Japan's territory. The inclusion of the Chinese in the Sino-Japanese War was already a precursor to the destruction of both theories of master-slave family and loyalty and filial piety coincidence.[324] The Russo-Japanese War's incorporation of ethnic Russians into Japan's nationality was a crushing blow to the mikoshi of the battle monks.[325] It was His Imperial Majesty the Emperor of Japan who excluded the stubborn national polity

---

[323] "Agata" refers to the territory directly under the ancient Yamato Imperial Court.

[324] Refers to the colonization of Taiwan.

[325] Refers to the acquisition of Sakhalin by the Treaty of Portsmouth.

theorist savages and concluded the treaty which allowed for foreigners to live freely in Japan.

Not quite true! It goes without saying that the Japanese people are not a family of masters and servants, nor have they ever been the children of the emperor, nor has the emperor ever been their father. From the time of the founding of the nation, the Japanese people have not been the expansion of a single family. And what do they do with the fact that it is a common theory that the Japanese people themselves have already existed since prehistoric times as a mixed race? We are not experts in such matters, so we cannot decide whether or not to accept the countless theories of the Japanese race, but the location of the traditional Japanese heaven, Takamagahara, is being considered on maps, as if it were not high in space. Therefore, the one thing that's certain is that nobody is claiming the Japanese were specially bred from the gods Izanagi and Izanami, and that only foreigners descended from monkeys. This alone is a certainty, which means that the fundamental idea of the theory of national polity, that the Japanese nation is the expansion of a single family, is certainly false. Since we dare not despise Blacks nor worship Whites, we are not necessarily pleased with the interpretation that the ancestors of the Japanese people "are Phoenicians who came to the South Pacific via India, followed the tides from there until landing at Hyuga, then mixed with the Chinese who had already settled there."[326] However, it is certain that those who interpret it in this way are not offering such an

---

[326] This Phoenician civilization origin theory is presented in Yosaburo Takekoshi's *Two Thousand Five Hundred Year History* (1896), 316. Kita dropped out of junior high school due to an eye disease and did not receive a satisfactory English education. (In a debate with Gisaku Hayahsi, he said "I don't understand 'a' from 'b', so I do not know the details of Nietzsche." ["Mizuochisei to Rinko" *Sado Shinbun*]) Because of this, he seems to have had a complex towards the English language and perhaps others, so when he says "nor worship Whites," this is probably indicative of his true feelings.

explanation merely to explain the master-servant family theory. Also, as the Hayashi family explains, "Tai Bo of Wu disappeared into Chuxi."[327] Although this, along with the fact that almost all of our culture comes from China and ancient Korea, at least since the start of recorded history, does influence the opinion that our ancestors emigrated from China and Korea at every turn, we do not say this, nor do we say that the view of Japanese people being purely of Chinese descent is necessarily worthy of belief.

However, the fact that this theory has been in force since before the emergence of the so-called classical scripture school of thought certainly does not provide material for the validity of the theory of loyalty and filial piety

---

[327] Refers to the Hayashi family of Confucian scholars of the Edo period. Here it refers specifically to Razan Hayashi.

Tai Bo (written both 泰伯 and 太伯 in Chinese) was a Chinese figure from the 12th to 11th centuries BC. He was the uncle of Ji Chang (King Wen), who established the Zhou Dynasty. He and his younger brother, Yu Zhong, ran away to Chuxi in order to allow Ji Chang to succeed him. The Zhou people came to bring them back, but the two, both with their hair cut and tattoos all over their bodies, refused, saying that they were not fit to return to the palace. The relationship between this anecdote and the origin of the Japanese is due to the similarity of customs. The custom of cutting hair and getting tattoos was seen in ancient times among people who dived to catch fish. The same custom is also mentioned in the history books about Japan. Because of the similarities between the customs of the Wu region and Japan, it has been suggested that the Japanese are descended from Tai Bo. Razan Hayashi supported this theory in his book, *Honcho Tsugan*, or *Comprehensive Mirror of Japan*. The story of Tai Bo is quoted in old Japanese literature in Kukai's *Sango Shikki* (Kato Seiitsu, *Sango Shikki*, trans. Kato Sumitaka [Tokyo: Kadokawa Bunko, 2007], 132). Chikafusa Kitabatake also wrote, in his *Jinno Shotoki*, "It is written in a book of a different dynasty that 'Japan will be the descendants of Tai Bo of Wu.'" (*Jinno Shotoki* [Tokyo: Iwanami Bunko, 1975], 60). However, he later denies that this is true.

coincidence. Of course, we have no right to say whether or not the Japanese people are a mixture of Malay, Yezo, and Han Chinese, even if most scientific researchers determine that they are a mixture of Malay, Yezo, and Han Chinese from the standpoints of linguistics, anatomy, and racial studies. However, in these days of scientific research on everything, it is only natural that we should follow the research results of scientists whose explanations are generally accepted, rather than listen to the empty theories of Confucian scholars and academics of statecraft. And since not a single scholar has yet claimed that the Japanese are a special race of people who have inhabited this land from the beginning, the view that they are a hybrid, coming from one place and mixing with another, at any rate, is unassailable. Now then, no matter how poorly organized one's brain matter may be, in the same way that the public pays attention to Mr. Hozumi's constitutional law theory, even if Japan's racial studies today are unsophisticated and infantile, one would think it better to listen to the opinions of leaders in that field. What does it mean that a professor of jurisprudence at an imperial university, in lecturing on constitutional law, the basic law of the nation, should derive everything from the primitive religion of the primitive age, which neither he nor anyone else believes in, and make it the fundamental thought of constitutional law? From the viewpoint of restorative revolutionism, does it mean that the study of race in Japan is detrimental to the construction of a theocratic patriarchal state? This is not something that should be said of today's national polity. It should be said of the time when the restorative revolution of the theory of national polity succeeds, destroys the present civic state, overthrows the emperor as the institution of the state, and the dogū idol reigns supreme. We cite here again the words of the late Mr. Chisou Naito to guide Mr. Hozumi in the path he should take.[328] This is precisely because he was an idealistic national polity

---

[328] Chiso Naito was a Mito clan official and historian of the late Edo and Meiji periods. He authored a number of historical books, including *Ansei Kiji, (or Ansei History)*.

theorist, and his attempt to have those with the imperial court's authority suppress racial research was a consistent stance that Mr. Hozumi and others could not possibly match. He said the following:

> The people of Shinshu are a race of people who were originally born in this divine land, not those who migrated from other countries. They are the descendants of a special kind of god who was born in this country since the beginning of the world. At this time, there are some unscrupulous people who would like to think that our holy people were born of some other race that migrated to this country. These people use this interpretation to flatter Western scholars. While these motivations are despicable to say the least, and not at all worth arguing, it is still true that some people believe these lies. Those who make such speculations and defile our sacred court are truly treasonous and incompatible with the gods. Therefore, they must be punished. In the days of Emperor Kanmu, a clear decree had already been issued to warn against such unscrupulous people. Why, then, does the court not punish them today?

The very idea that the national polity of Japan today is a patriarchal state is such a Shinto superstition that has no basis in fact. If the theory of "master-slave family" or the theory of "loyalty and filial piety coincidence" were advocated at a time when the patriarch or the head of the family had absolute and unlimited power over the family and its branches, there would be a reason for such a claim, regardless of the facts. However, advocating this in this day and age, when the principle of equality of kinship is the rule, is clearly a suicidal argument. Therefore, such terms as "parents of the people" and "children of the emperor" are merely historical emulation, and are as meaningless as the word "sacred" in the Constitution.

Chapter 11

As discussed above, such concepts as "one family" and "coincidence" are nothing but fabrications of superstitious people, but the "lineage principle," which is the fundamental idea on which the theory of "one master-servant family" is based, and the "loyalty and filial piety principle," on which the theory of "loyalty and filial piety coincidence" is based, should not be lightly dismissed.

Of course, not only the with Japanese, but with any other ethnic group as well, before the awakening of social consciousness is extended to all races and all humankind, it must be expanded step by step—there is no other way to achieve this but to trace a group's lineage. As such, social consciousness is limited by blood relations, resulting in the lineage principle, and thus, naturally, in patriarchal nations, which arise in the process of evolution, the principle of loyalty and filial piety is born. There is no nation under heaven that has not experienced both the principles of lineage and loyalty and filial piety. However, the Japanese people did not follow the same path as the Germanic peoples in Western history, who were able to look back to the Latin democracies that existed in ancient times as they completed the medieval history of the patriarchal states. Since the Japanese were isolated by the ocean, they were not able to escape medieval history as quickly as the Europeans. In other words, because the Meiji Revolution happened later than the French Revolution, despite national sovereignty being established, the old inertia still resulted in superstitions such as the "single master-servant family" theory and the "loyalty and filial piety coincidence" theory.

Under these circumstances, the principles of lineage and loyalty and filial piety have developed remarkably in Japan without any obstacles. So, while it is clearly a restorative revolutionism to advocate those principles of lineage and loyalty and filial piety today, now national sovereignty has been established, when looking at the history of the ancient and medieval periods, which is said to have lasted for over 2,500 years, they can't be opened without this key. For this reason, the so-called national polity theorists would say the following: "As the Japanese people are extremely loyal and pious toward their parents, so do they assist the imperial throne of one eternal lineage, and have created a national polity unparalleled in other nations." This is a false premise and conclusion, since both the principles of loyalty and filial piety and lineage were adopted in the savage villages of the Orient—in fact, because the Japanese people honor family lineage through this principle of lineage, they actually persecuted the imperial family. They have also attacked the imperial family because they considered loyalty and filial piety as the ultimate good. We are not rebelling against what has been established in the past on weak grounds. Political and ethical history make it impossible for us to avoid this judgment. The assumption of this principle of lineage, of a pedigreed people, has been true for all peoples of the world throughout antiquity and the Middle Ages. However, it is a total fallacy to conclude that Japan's history is dedicated to the imperial family of one eternal lineage. The assumption that Japan was a nation of loyalty and filial piety is true, but it is also true throughout the ancient and medieval periods of all peoples of the world. However, it is obviously false to conclude the history of Japan by assuming that the Japanese people had been nothing but loyal to the imperial family for over 2,500 years.

This is political history that decides the question of jurisprudence: sovereignty of the monarch or sovereignty of the state. It is also ethical history that determines the ethical question of loyalty to the ruler or patriotism toward the state. It is a theory of social evolution which applies to everything; in other words, it is Japanese history viewed through historical philosophy. Regarding only the point of not considering their own history, there is no distinction between the South Pacific and the Far East. They are both undeveloped villages unaware of their own history.

First, let us consider political history. History is a solemn judge. And yet, the Japanese people today, standing before this judge, hide all the facts, twist interpretations, and make false statements. The so-called theory of national polity is one example of this. They say, "All Japanese are loyal subjects and righteous warriors, and any rebellious subjects are exceptions." And the fact that no one questions this theory of national polity is similar to the unquestioning belief that the sun once turned from the east to the west of the world.[329] But we affirm—much like how it has become clear that the sun does not turn from the east to the west of the world after the heliocentric theory emerged—the actual exceptions are those loyal subjects and righteous warriors. The vast majority of Japanese people are all rebels toward the imperial family. Those who are shocked at these words are the same as the geocentric Roman papacy who grew angry at Galileo's words. They want to use the historical interpretation of the theory of national polity much like the pope's authority was used in the past. "Why does the imperial court not punish them today?" The restorative revolutionist who said this would cite, "You subjects have been faithful, you have expressed filial piety, have united your many spirits as one, and you have aided the everlasting destiny of the emperor," in order to persecute even our meager words, not at all reaching the heights of Galileo.

Of course, the Japanese emperor is not the Roman pope. The emperor is not a state institution that establishes academic doctrine. Therefore, just as an imperial decree by a police officer is invalid, it is also ineffective for the emperor to issue a law commanding medical doctors to follow a certain principle of microbiology or force the use of one chemical equation on a university of science. It is unforgivable to confuse the dogū clay figures of national polity theory with the lucid emperor. The emperor has shown remarkable genius in composing poetry, but he has never thrown a new school of poets who sang of

---

[329] Referring to the geocentric model.

stars and violets in jail for violating the Poetry Composition Law. In the same way, however much the emperor clearly espouses the views of a certain school of historical philosophy regarding his knowledge of ethics, we can be independent outside the Imperial Rescript on Education by virtue of the rights we have before the state.

The idea that the emperor has the authority to establish ethical theories and is the institution that defines the official philosophy of history is something that does not exist in the Great Empire of Japan, and we should not erroneously assume that this phantom of the emperor created by delusions is the real emperor. Therefore, the Imperial Rescript on Education's statement, "Amaterasu and her descendants, the emperors of the past, are deeply virtuous," isn't compatible with the opinions of the current restorative revolutionists who desire the tyranny of Louis XIV, and those people are equally free to think of the ancient emperors as tyrants like Louis XIV. We will argue our own opinion—that is, many of the emperor's ancestors were gentle, elegant, poetically gifted, and that they were expected to act in the interests and for the purposes of the nation based on Confucian ideals of political morality—but will not yell, "what a blasphemous man who violates the Imperial Rescript on Education" while doing so, nor do we or the emperor have the right to persecute such a man.

So, even if the emperor's view that "his subjects displayed the virtues of loyalty and filial piety well and served the imperial bloodline of one eternal lineage" doesn't align with our views at all, it is no different from how the emperor's poetry might differ from the songs of another poet. What is there to be afraid of in asserting, by our freedom of scholarship, that although the imperial family has always been gentle and graceful, the people's ancestors have always persecuted and attacked the imperial family, and that the "eternal lineage" has not been damaged only because the imperial family has protected it by its own power?

The strange practice of covering up one's own abominations by quoting the views of the politically privileged in matters of scholarship is not to be found outside of the savage villages of the Orient. From another perspective, the words in the Imperial Rescript on Education can simply be seen as the emperor's praise of the people. Whenever the emperor praised the Japanese people for their victories in numerous wars, they would simply decline the praise by saying, "This is all due to the authority of His Majesty the Emperor," as if they were following a set pattern. Why is it that there are traces of people trying to ingratiate themselves with the imperial family by interpreting the lineage that the family itself has protected as if it is thanks to the people's respect for the emperor and loyalty to the sovereign? If anyone were to say, as we do, that the ancestors of our people were all disloyal and unjust to the imperial family, he would probably be called a "blasphemous bastard." Such a lunatic would be hard for any psychologist to diagnose.

The criminal law of the nation, as a system established for the benefit of the nation, does not tolerate those who have disrespected the emperor and the imperial family. When the people are held up to the mirror of history and their past deeds and conscience are described, if they protect themselves by the crime of lèse-majesté, this is an act of intrusion by forty-five million people into the iron railings of the emperor. Mr. Hozumi is an example of such an intruder when he says in his book, *Constitutional Synopsis*, "He who says the Japanese people are lacking in the concept of loyalty and filial piety is someone who insults the Japanese people." Let history insult the Japanese people enough.

In Japan, historical facts have been recorded, but there isn't yet a single shred of historical philosophy. The significance of history is to understand the process of social evolution. In other words, the philosophy of history is the theory of social evolution included in social philosophy. Yet, the Japanese people, whose intelligence is inferior because they have been hit on the skull with the hammer of the "one eternal lineage" idea, have never attempted to study Japanese history according to evolution, and their political and ethical history has placed only the Japanese people outside the laws of evolution—laws which they then criticize using the theory of national polity.

Mr. Nagao Aruga, mentioned earlier in this volume, who is recognized as one of the only political historians in Japan, is an example of this. He builds a mirage around the word "emperor" and believes that the Japanese people revolve around it and do not evolve in the slightest. Contemporary ethical histories argue that today the same relationship exists between the Japanese people and the imperial family as the relationship that existed when they first migrated to Japan, and that today's relationship is the same as that of the time of emperors Yuryaku and Nintoku. Contemporary authors write a history of ethics based on the belief that the Japanese people have been loyal and filial, and have observed the Imperial Rescript on Education, since the time when they lived in caves. Woe to the undeveloped villages of the Orient. If railroads and electricity are all it takes for a country to be civilized, then the interior of Africa is civilized too.

Political forms have not circulated on the same track for 2,500 years. Moral content has also evolved without interruption since the beginning of the world. Yet to imagine an ancient age in terms of a later political system and to evaluate ancient morality according to today's norms, what could one call this but a village of uncivilized people? So, we will try to describe the political and ethical history of Japan according to its evolution, to see the traces of the evolution of political forms and moral contents. What we can't do anything about, however, is the covering up of the historical facts through the so-called theory of national polity—the retroactive criticism of history. Therefore, as an unavoidable measure, we must take an exclusionary attitude and, first and foremost, eradicate this theory of national polity.

The theory of national polity refers to the delusion that the Japanese people are all loyal subjects of the imperial court and righteous warriors, with the exception of any rebellious subjects. Because of this retrospective approach, the Japanese people understand Emperor Jinmu as if he were an emperor of a later era. The use of the same characters in form and pronunciation not only makes us forget the difference between the medieval and modern periods, but also leads us to consider the primitive life of the emperor, who was only given his name as a gift later on, as the same as that of the present emperor. If the relationship between the imperial family and the people was the same in the time of the so-called Emperor Jinmu as it was in later generations, how are such things as the marriage of Emperor Jinmu to be understood? If he had the same prerogatives as the emperor we see in today's "otori,"[330] he would not have stood by the side of the road and asked seven young girls to marry him with his own lips.[331] Also, if he was the honored emperor we hear of in *Imperial Celebrations* he would not go to a girl's house himself and sing, "In a rough hut in Ashihara, I laid out tatami mats woven from sedge, and we two slept together."[332]

While it is true that there is no hierarchy in love, there is nothing more class-divided than love. Today, it is unimaginable for a sovereign of any country, even when he is out of his normal state of mind, to stand by the side of the road and talk about love, or to go to some thatched hut to make love. Needless to say, since Emperor Jinmu was a man who lived several thousand years ago, we should not make inferences based on today's level of knowledge, but we would like to believe that he was not so ignorant that he would corrupt his political and moral position for the sake of love, since he is considered the founder of Japan. Do historians who do retrospective studies which do not

---

[330] This refers to having an audience with someone of very high status.

[331] Written about in The Emperor Jinmu Chronicles within *Kojiki*.

[332] This is a song by Emperor Jinmu from the middle volume of the *Kojiki*. The original text reads, "In a dirty hut in Ashihara, I laid out the sedge tatami mats and we two slept." The original quote has what seems like a misspelling of "dirty" or "rough," and is fixed in the version of *Kojiki* that the translator is using, so we believe it's supposed to be "rough" or "dirty." Incidentally, the woman he's referring to here is Princess Isukeyori.

recognize the evolution of politics and morality believe that from the very first page of Japanese history, "emperors" and "empresses" were able to corrupt the throne and become the so-called fathers and mothers of the nation? For the emperor of the time, roadside courtship and going to a dirty hut were not acts so separated from his position that they could damage it.

The mother of Emperor Suizei,[333] who is said to have ascended to the throne after Emperor Jinmu, for example, remarried to Jinmu's son, Tagishimimi,[334] even though she was Jinmu's empress, and when Tagishimimi tried to kill Emperor Suizei, Suizei fought back and took his place.[335] This shows how different today's evolved morality is from that of that time. Not only that, when Tagishimimi was killed, despite the fact that he was an imperial prince, he was living in a cave.[336] One can only imagine from this how the status of the imperial family should not be based on the standards of later generations. How could such an immoral person, however powerful, rule over the unity of the people?

The content of conscience is not the same in ancient and modern times, just as it is different in the East and West. Today, now we have reached our current stage of evolution, we have today's conscience. In an uncivilized age when people lived in caves, there was the conscience of the cave age. In an age when there was no class gap between the imperial family and the people, Emperor Jinmu's love did not tarnish the political status of the imperial family. In primitive times, when marital relations were weak, marriage between a

---

[333] Referring to Princess Isukeyori.

[334] According to *Nihon Shoki*, Tagishimimi-no-mikoto (written as 「手研耳」) was the child of Princess Ahiratsu, and was not related to Princess Isukeyori by blood.

[335] Written about near the end of the Emperor Jinmu Chronicles.

[336] In the Emperor Suizei Chronicles in *Nihon Shoki*, when Emperor Suizei and his brother (Kanyaimimi-no-mikoto) went to attack Tagishimimi-no-mikoto, the latter was lying alone in a cave.

mother and her half-brother was not an immoral affair that would have brought disgrace to the imperial family. In summary, there is no reason to assume that in primitive times only the ancestors of the imperial family had the same political privileges and moral obligations as in later times.

It was a purely primitive life. Pottery was simply clay hardened with water and baked over a fire, and food was served on a bed of green leaves. Desks did exist, but as there were no nails yet, they were merely one board atop four legs of wood, tied together with vines. There was no such thing as a scale or ruler, of course, and people simply used their fingers or hands to measure the approximate length of a piece of wood, using words like "ata," "tsuka," and "hiro" to measure things.[337] It was not until the reign of Yamatotakeru-no-Mikoto, eight hundred years later (after the reign of Emperor Jinmu), that flint was finally used to ignite fire.[338] Until then, fire had been ignited by the friction of cypress wood, as is used today at the Grand Shrine of Ise and Izumo Taisha, which are the inheritors of this tradition. There were no dyes, but rather, like today's American Indians, grass, plant leaves, or colored clay was applied to

---

[337] For some reason, the readings on these three words are noted in the original text. We kept them in our Japanese translation, assuming there was some meaning to this. "Ata" refers to the distance between the bottom of the palm to the top of the middle finger. "Tsuka" refers to the width of the four fingers when one grips their hand. "Hiro" refers to the distance between the tips of one's fingers when both hands are extended horizontally. In fact, the term "eight-handed mirror" refers to this "ata," and means a mirror eight times the size of one's hand.

[338] Yamatotakeru-no-Mikoto was a prince of Emperor Keiko. By order of the emperor, he defeated Kumaso and later pacified the eastern provinces. In the Emperor Keiko Chronicles in *Nihon Shoki*, there is a record of him being caught in a bush fire in Suruga-no-kuni, but he managed to escape by using flint to start a bonfire (some accounts say he used the sword Kusanagi no Tsurugi [Amenomurakumo no Tsurugi] to knock out the flames).

cloth, and this cloth was worn only by the upper class. Moreover, that cloth was sewn together via barbaric methods such as shoving cocoons in one's mouth and using the heat of the spittle to make threads. Yes, it is completely natural to exclude from political history this primitive time period before we imported the written word from cultural exchange with China.

If we believe in the *Kojiki* and *Nihon Shoki*, which were written 1,400 years later, only four hundred years after we first imported our written language, then, in accordance with the Martian script hypothesis we discussed earlier, we can accept that the one thousand years during which there was no script as simply a legend. For it is no different from the pre-migration tales of Takamagahara, the heavenly realm, which is treated simply as a legend even by today's historians. We firmly believe that, just as today's South Pacific primitives have no historical awareness beyond a few legends of their ancestors' battles with monstrous birds and beasts of prey, despite the fact that tens of thousands of years have passed, so too do we lack enough awareness of our so-called thousand years of primitive history to record any of it via the written word.

We are conscious of history only during those time periods when civilized peoples or the civilization of those peoples were advanced enough. This can be seen in the time of Emperor Jinmu, which is calculated to be long before the era when today's European civilization still existed as barbaric people in primitive, republican, and equal villages in the forests of Germany, during which time the Japanese culture was so purely primitive and without historical consciousness that only a few legends of later generations (or perhaps complete fabrications and fantasies of later generations) could be used to try and estimate the empress' presence, the location of the imperial palace, and so on. One example of this are the four hundred years after Emperor Jinmu. These were known as the ages of Emperor Annei, Emperor Itoku, Emperor Kousho, Emperor Koan, Emperor Korei, Emperor Kogen, and Emperor Kaika, but all these are names gifted far later in the future, and absolutely no historical facts were written of these emperors at the time.[339]

Some historians today argue that the Jinmu era is much later than 2,500 years ago. The basis for this argument is of course weak, but it goes without saying that the *Kojiki* and *Nihon Shoki*, which were written 1,400 years after Jinmu and are collections of legends from when there were no written records, are no more certain than the legends themselves. In other words, calculating that Emperor Jinmu's migration happened 2,500 years before today based on the legends in *Kojiki* and *Nihon Shoki* is like each saying, based on legends, "his lifespan is eighteen thousand years." This is because an imprecise concept of time—in other words, the inability to count things accurately—is something common of primitive life. In fact, even the "civilization" of today's civilized society is only the closest approximation of modernity.

Now, if that is the case, then these primitive times without written words—whether they be a thousand years or a hundred thousand years—are not the subject of political history, and therefore are merely transitions of years of no value in terms of political history. Even if something happened between the ancestors of the imperial family and the ancestors of the people during that period, primitive times should be evaluated according to primitive morality, and history should not be retroactively criticized according to a later theory of national polity. This legendary period, which is counted as a thousand years in which there were no written records, should rightly be deleted from political history. It is a great disgrace to claim that the history of Japan is "2,500 years' time," just as it would be a great disgrace for Chinese historians to claim that the history of China reaches back tens of thousands of years, calculating that each of the imperial princes had a life span of eighteen thousand years.[340]

---

[339] From Emperor Annei to Emperor Kaika, there are essentially only genealogical descriptions in the *Kojiki* and *Nihon Shoki,* and that's all.

[340] In China, there's a legend that Pangu, the god of creation, ruled for eighteen thousand

It is especially important to note that many of the ancestors of the forty-five million people who make up today's population were primitive people from villages in other regions that had nothing to do with the war victors, who were then confined to the Kinki region. It was imagined by later classics that by the side of Emperor Jinmu, there was no place under heaven that was not his royal land, and even to the farthest shores of the earth there was no one who was not his subject, but this is no different from the pope in Columbus' time. Despite being the supposed owner of the still-undiscovered world, China, Japan, and India were never his lands, nor were they subjects, but were each independent of the pope. The land that is inside the retrospective criticism of the theory of national polity is really only a small section of the Kinki region. The Emperor Sujin,[341] who for the first time levied taxes—rather than bearskins and deer horns to pay for rituals, etc.—said, "The wild people in distant lands still do not subject themselves to my rule."[342] This is, of course, a

---

years. In *Jinno Shotoki*, it's written that "In the beginning of Zhendan . . . Pangu, the first sovereign, reigned for eighteen thousand years." (Chifusa Kitabakabe, *Jinno Shotoki* [Tokyo: Iwanami Bunko, 1975], 42.) The description seems to be based on that legend.

[341] According to *Nihon Shoki*, the country was in disorder during the reign of Emperor Sujin, so he decided to worship the many gods and built shrines to them. He established the Kobe system during that worship. (Kobe refers to the people who are associated with a shrine and support it. These people paid taxes in order to pay for the shrines' building and upkeep, and to prepare offerings to the gods.) This is what Kita is referring to.

[342] The original text reads "Serve mine almanac," where "almanac" refers to "calendar." It's an expression that means "submit to rule." It comes from the fact that, in ancient China, whenever a new dynasty came to power they would change the calendar, and serving the calendar meant submitting to rule. This expression is also found in *Nihon Shoki*, volume 5, Emperor Sujin Chronicles. Emperor Sujin sent out four shogun in order to subjugate various regions (Oohiko-no-mikoto to Hokuriku, Takenunakawawake-no-

retroactive statement from the classics, based on the same idea as the pope's ownership of the world. But what it means is that the emperor's right to rule was rejected, and the independent peoples of mixed blood in the Northeast and the Chinese vassals or independent villages in Kyushu were defending themselves against other invasions. Therefore, the claim that from the beginning of the nation the Japanese emperor was the sovereign of the ancestors of the people scattered all over the map, and that all the ancestors of the people and all the lands of today were his subjects or kingdoms, is something asserted only by those who ignore history.

For the Roman pope known as the theory of national polity, *Kojiki* and *Nihon Shoki* are bibles, but the clay figures are not omnipotent in the realm of historical philosophy, nor are they sacred and inviolable as far as filling in the gaps in the legends is concerned. And even though the emperor did exist in the Kinki region, the extent of his holdings was greatest at first, but as other large families developed, their holdings and their subjects became more and more powerful, until finally they were able to keep up even with the imperial family. The lands and people outside the emperor's domain were the property of other clans and peoples, unrelated to the emperor. The vast majority of the nation that was not subject to the emperor's rule and was independent, as well as the majority of the people who were the possessions of other chiefs, had nothing to do with the imperial household. So, naturally, all of this is a separate issue from the theory of national polity.[343] In other words, the primitive period known as the first thousand years after Jinmu had an uncertain conception of years (to the point where some will say that his lifespan lasted over eighteen thousand years), no historical awareness, and no writing to record the

---

mikoto to Tokai, Kibitsuhiko-no-mikoto to Nishi no Michi, and Tanihanomichinushi-no-mikoto to Tamba).

[343] It's not exactly clear, but what he means is, "the error of the theory of national polity is obvious."

historical facts. Therefore, the period should be removed from the political and ethical history, and naturally from "the theory of national polity" as well. The word "emperor" should be determined to mean a strong man of the primitive age.

Not so! Until four hundred years later, when historical records were finally compiled, we still inherited a primitive way of life with no historical awareness to the extent that we did not need historical records. If there were no historical records for the next four centuries from today, do you think we and our descendants of the next four hundred years would be satisfied? Look at the extent of the culture of that time factually. When Emperor Yuryaku died, his bereaved family sat in fear and humility in hinkyu and gathered offerings from all over the country to seek forgiveness for various sins,[344] such as the fresh skinning of beasts, reverse skinning of beasts from the buttocks upward, having sexual intercourse with one's child, having sexual intercourse with one's mother, having sexual intercourse with mother and child, marrying a horse, marrying a cow, marrying a chicken, marrying a dog,[345] and so on, by conducting a large nationwide purifying ritual to apologize to the gods.[346] This

---

[344] "Hinkyu" is a term used to honor the first word in the compound, "hin" (殯), which refers to a place where a coffin, body inside, is temporary placed in order to show respect before a noble person is properly buried.
The original text says something with the same reading as "nusa," which means that "country" here refers to Tsukushi.

[345] "Fresh skinning of beasts" means to skin while the animal is still alive. "Reverse skinning" means killing an animal and skinning it from the buttocks upward. Sexual intercourse with a family member means incest, and the rest refers to bestiality.

[346] There was a mistake in the original text regarding one of the characters, but it should be "great purifying ritual." This refers specifically to a ceremony in Shinto on the final day of the sixth and twelfth month of each year where the sins and impurities of the people are purified. This anecdote is found in the middle section of the *Kojiki*, in the

shows that the morality of the time was purely primitive. They did not enter into familial marriages in which married couples lived together, and many were only temporary reproductive relationships. Because of polygamy, siblings did not know each other and half-sibling marriages were freely practiced even after the arrival of Confucian formal morality. Even two hundred years after the arrival of Confucianism, no one could read the Korean written reports except for one naturalized citizen, Shinni Ou,[347] and so it can be understood that we still communicated our thoughts and feelings using primitive pronunciations and manners. The upper classes were always the object of ridicule by the emissaries of ancient Korea, and it was not until the Emperor Nintoku learned about civilized agriculture and built an embankment in

---

section on Emperor Chuai. It's the story of when the emperor entered the Land of Tsukushi (Kyushu) to conquer Kumaso, and a ceremony was conducted to hear divine messages. According to the *Kojiki*, the god took over Empress Jingu's body and told her to subjugate the Western Lands (Korea). Emperor Chuai then stopped the ceremony, saying the god was false, and that "I cannot see any lands to the West." The god then grew furious and took Emperor Chuai's life. Fearful that the god was angry enough to take the emperor's life, they held a purification ceremony, repented of their sins, such as incest and bestiality, and asked for the god's forgiveness.

[347] "Shinni Ou" was a Korean immigrant. According to *Nihon Shoki*, volume 20, Emperor Bidatsu Chronicles, when an envoy from Korea presented a letter to the emperor, the emperor asked his historians (naturalized Japanese who were in charge of records, etc.) to decipher it, but no one could, except for Shinni Ou. From this, Kita probably surmises that many Japanese couldn't yet read written words. However, the story continues. According to the story, this text was written on the wings of a crow, and since the wings and ink were both black, no one noticed the writing (probably a kind of encryption). Only Shinni Ou noticed this, and was able to read the words by steaming the wings on paper, thus copying the letters. Thus, the story should be viewed as an anecdote of an inability to decipher encryption rather than strictly speaking an inability to read the characters.

Mattagun to prepare for drought that he realized how primitive production was at that time and how primitive people lived like monkeys, merely shoveling food from their hands to their mouths. Until the minting of coins in the Wado period, the government had to grant peerage to people to encourage the use of the few foreign coins that were imported.[348] This economic condition is what scholars call the age of barter, and is considered proof of primitive life. As for the life of the emperors, only Buddhist temples were built in a foreign style until Emperess Saimei built her palace with tiled roofs some 1,300 years after Jinmu.[349] The greatest and most powerful of the people lived in houses similar to those found in the South Pacific today, with wisteria and kudzu tied to dugout poles and thatched roofs protected from the wind by katsuogi.[350]

Not exactly! The four hundred years after the introduction of Chinese characters is, in this sense, also a legend of an unrecorded period. So, it's not as if we mean to put national polity theorists in a difficult position by tracing today's political ideals and moral judgments back to these times. Contact with foreign civilizations caused western Japan to reject strictly the right to rule by imperial ancestors and to act freely, and the evolving philosophical religions of Confucianism and Buddhism began to exterminate the uncivilized ideas of polytheism and ancestral religion, beginning with the upper classes. It must be noted here that the foundations of the imperial family were swept away and

---

[348] Coins made in the first year of Wado (708) are called "Wado kaichin." However, coins called "fuhonsen" existed in the era of Emperor Tenmu, so Wado kaichin weren't the first coins to ever exist. Granting titles was also practiced after the circulation of Wado kaichin (the Chikusen Joi order is an example of this).

[349] An attempt to tile the imperial palace is found in *Nihon Shoki*, volume 26, Empress Saimei Chronicles. Although Empress Saimei and Empress Kogyoku are the same person, strictly speaking, Empress Saimei is correct.

[350] "Katsuogi" is a decorative tree laid horizontally atop ridge beams of a shrine or other holy structure.

various large tribes began to appear in turn as what were called "rebellious subjects." This insult to the theory of national polity has been present since the first chapter of the first volume of historical writings after entering recorded history. The so-called tyranny of the Soga clan is a striking example of a large imperial family losing its position of strength and being overwhelmed by various other large tribes. The expansion and development of the tribes into a force that could compete with the other chiefs, the emperors, began precisely at the end of the primitive period. The history of Japan during the first 1,500 years of its existence, excluding the so-called "primitive thousand years," undermines what could be called the papacy of the national polity theory.

Those who believe that the Imperial Rescript on Education is a direct eulogy for the nation, and that "all the people of Japan have united their spirits in loyalty and filial piety, and have demonstrated their virtues from generation to generation, thereby upholding the imperial eternal lineage," should reflect on the history of the nation over the last 1,500 years since the primitive era was abolished. That 1,500 years is the entire history of Japan, and we should look back on that entire history. We do not criticize the actions of our children by the moral standards of adulthood. In the same way, we do not retroactively evaluate the long period of 1,500 years according to the conscience of the era of the theory of "reverence for the king" and dare to make illogical statements such as "loyal retainer," "righteous warrior," or "rebellious subject."

However, not only is the attitude of retroactive criticism of national polity theory already inverted as an attitude of historical theory, but the very criticism so retroactively obtained also ignores historical facts and is completely inverted in its induction. It is inevitable, then, that we will be writing for some time with the same attitude as their retroactive criticisms, so that we can indicate that their inductions are inverted. This is the only way to break down the old theory in order to formulate a new view. Much like geocentric theory in comparison to heliocentric theory, the historical understanding that national polity theorists have of Japan, which says that the rebellious subjects towards the imperial family are few in number and are generally exceptions to the rule, and that almost all Japanese people are loyal subjects and righteous warriors, is the exact opposite of the truth. Since recorded history, Japanese people have almost all been rebellious subjects towards the imperial family, with the exceptions being the few loyal retainers and righteous warriors. Therefore, in order to overthrow the theory of national polity itself, it is best to point out these facts, which are the most likely stimuli to awaken people from their superstitions.

It's true that the exception is the slight and singular, and if we speak of the majority of the general public as the norm, then rebellious subjects are the norm, and the loyal subjects of the imperial family and the righteous are the slight and singular exception. And yet, because of the complete opposite interpretation, which has been the established theory from the past to the present, there is no other history in the world that is as laughably enigmatic as that written by Japanese historians. Facts are facts, and history is history. Facts are honest and cannot be falsified, no matter how they are assembled or written by those of lesser intelligence who have been hit on the skull with the hammer of "one eternal lineage." History is impartial and exact, and it can't be covered up. As long as the dreams of national polity theorists are not realized, Qin Shi Huang does not take the throne and these ancient records are not burned, said records will continue to exist and help defeat the theory of national polity, which they don't get along with at all. Behold.

Strictly speaking, the period in which the history of the Japanese people came to be written was about one thousand years after the compilation of the *Kojiki* and *Nihon Shoki*. However, let us define the period when those two records were believed and history was being written as the 1,500 years since we began communication with ancient Korea, minus the one-thousand-year primitive period when we had no writing. Of course, the imperial family was the most powerful of the various great tribes at the time of the conquest of ancient Korea. Some monarchs, such as emperors Ojin and Nintoku, adhered strictly to Confucian political morality, while others, such as emperors Yuryaku and Buretsu, exercised their patriarchal rights to the utmost, thereby exercising sovereignty over the other great tribes.

As society developed and the population grew, various large tribes came and went, prospering and perishing in turn. However, when the Soga clan finally became powerful, it overpowered and subjugated the other tribes and began to compete with the imperial family for the rights of the powerful. Like the leaders of the imperial family, they named the tombs of their chiefs "big tombs" and "little tombs,"[351] and called their residences "palace gates" or "gates of imperial residence." They called their children "imperial princes," set up a fortified palace with an armory as their home, and entered and left the palace with fifty guards of honor.[352] They would then, as if true members of the imperial family, impose labor on naturalized mixed-blood peoples and other chiefs' subjects who were not members of the same clan. These actions are more evidence that the emperor possessed all the privileges of the time than the fact of Emperor Sushun's assassination. We don't think it's enough to merely cite facts which even national polity theorists know of, but we do think it's important to show that, since the very beginning of recorded history, these supposed "exceptions" of rebellious subjects existed as powerful people attempting to resist the imperial family's strength from the very first page.

What came next was the era of Fujiwara tyranny, which emerged after the failure of the Taika Revolution to create an ideal state. The reason Emperor Tenji dreamed of building a sovereign civic state through Confucian political

---

[351] In *Nihon Shoki*, volume 24, Emperor Kogyoku Chronicles, Soga no Emishi has two tombs built in Konrai (near present-day Oyodo in the Yoshino District, Nara Prefecture). One was named Dairyo, and was Emishi's tomb, and the other was called Shoryo, and was Iruka's tomb.

[352] The term "guards of honor" refers to soldiers attached to the emperor, royal family, ministers, and dignitaries for ceremonial and security purposes.

science, at a time when the ancestors of the civilized Germanic peoples were still only in the early stages of their Dark Ages, was because he saw that the clan system and ancestral religion could not be a stable foundation for the imperial family at a time of social evolution and the arrival of new religion, as they were being suppressed and forced to follow the Buddhist-dominated Soga clan.

Here, the emperor crowned his triumph with the overthrow of the Soga clan and expressed his ideal of the emperor as the supreme authority of the nation, standing above and ruling over all people and land (for more on the realization of the ideals of the Taika Revolution, read the later section where we discuss the Meiji Revolution). Confucianism is not what is commonly referred to as a democracy (look at *The Enlightenment of Socialism*). Thus, it was exactly eight or nine decades during which the imperial household, through the wisdom of Emperor Tenji, embraced the ideal of standing as a national institution above all the people.

However, without a foundation, a building cannot be built. Ideals were set forth long ago, as in Plato's *Republic*,[353] but their realization came only after a long evolutionary process. At that time, the national sovereignty of the state and the emperor as the supreme institution of the state were ideals only within such a wise and far-sighted man as Emperor Tenji. Later, Buddhism was adopted as the state religion in place of the patriarchal religion, completely flouting the ideals of Confucianism. Thus, the ideal of state institutions was first destroyed by the imperial court, and the Taika ideal of a state was buried with the death of that idealist, as Buddhist prayers and chants were elevated to the political arena. The construction of Buddhist temples, the proliferation of monks, bishops, nuns,[354] and other people who merely played around, grew to such an extent that taxes and the private property of the imperial family

---

[353] Referring to Plato's ideal state.

[354] Female priests.

became insufficient to finance the government. The emperor, who exercised the right to rule for the benefit of the imperial family and became an institution of the state by buying and selling government positions, became a patriarchal monarch who asserted that the state existed for his own purposes. The provincial officials, who were institutions of the state through this system of buying and selling government positions, were reappointed to the same land and became indigenous,[355] owning many lands and peoples in addition to the native tribes. These were the beginnings of the patriarchal state that would later lead to the feudal system.

With the passing away of the mastermind of the Taika Revolution, the imperial family began to consider the right to rule as a right of ownership for its own purposes and benefits, and transferred the benefits gained from governing the land and people under the name of donations to those people. The provincial officials, made up of the previous land chiefs, used the right to govern, which they had bought through donations, to do as they pleased with the people and land, who they owned for their own purpose and benefit. Thus, the literal meaning of the word "emperor" at that time was a powerful patriarch with the greatest number of lands and peoples. This was a time when the ruler did not exist for the purpose and benefit of the state, but exercised his right to rule as an exercise of his property rights, and the Fujiwara Clan vied for the position of guardian to exercise their right to rule for their own benefit, giving rise to the era of Fujiwara tyranny. The era that Mr. Hozumi and other restorative revolutionaries dream of, in which the emperor was the owner of the land and people and the right to rule was his property right, was

---

[355] By the mid-Heian period, the Fujiwara clan had come to control the central political world, and middle-ranking nobles began to look to the provincial governors for places to perform their activities. As a result, there was competition for the position of provincial governors, and they competed to secure a stable position by paying more taxes to the central government, leading to severe deprivation in the provinces.

a patriarchal state in which the despotism of the guardians prevailed as a common practice, as when they had their guardian Michinaga sing, "I think this world is my world . . ."[356]

The emperor at that time was the product of the Fujiwara clan, and he and his mother, a Fujiwara woman, were taken to the home of his grandfather, who was to become the future regent, to be brought up by him. While still understanding little of the past or future, he inherited the property of the state and became the head of the state. Over the generations, the blood of the Fujiwara clan made up more of the blood of the emperor than did the blood of the distant Emperor Jinmu. In this way, he naturally loved his mother, the Fujiwara Clan, and adored his grandfather, the regent. The regent, as the emperor's grandfather, also wished for the succession of his beloved grandson, the emperor, due to the intense love between grandfather and beloved grandson, and was made guardian of the family head because the true family head was still very young. The guardian's exclusive authority over a legally incompetent individual with the right to rule was not at all illegal at a time when the right to rule was a right of property.[357]

Those who go back in time and criticize the rights and authority of the emperor and regent of later generations imagine an ancient time a thousand years ago and hate it, naming it "the age of the Fujiwara's tyranny," but in fact, it was only the grandfather's love and right to dispose of his property

---

[356] A famous waka (classic Japanese poem) by Fujiwara no Michinaga. It's a partial quote from the line, "This world, I think, is indeed my world. Like the full moon, I shine, and am uncovered by any cloud." This waka appears in Fujiwara no Sanesuke's *Shoyuki*.

[357] "Legally incompetent individual" means someone who, due to insanity or other circumstances, is considered incompetent to perform any act on property. The person is assigned a guardian, and the guardian performs property acts on behalf of the person. The term was used in the Civil Code until 1999, but is now referred to as "adult ward" or "minor ward."

against the will of the extremely young head of his household. No one in the world has ever prospered by unlawful means and persisted by unlawful means. The fact that the period called Fujiwara tyranny lasted until the local patriarchs in other lands, the Genpei clan, came to power, is because there was nothing illegal about their guardianship in the patriarchal state. The Fujiwara loved the emperor as a grandson, and the emperor loved the Fujiwara as a grandfather. It would be extremely unjust to say generations later that the grandfather was a rebel because he followed the orders of his ignorant young grandson, or that the young grandson was a rebel because he did not reject his grandfather's plans. It can be said that due to the mixture of blood, this family came to be called both the imperial family and the Fujiwara family, as if they were one family of masters and servants, and the imperial family and the Fujiwara family could be interpreted as equal kinship, as master-servant family theorists say. So, just as the beloved grandchildren of relatives are sacred, the chancellor of the realm, who was a grandfather and relative, enjoyed the inalienable right of non-responsibility, which means the Imperial Prosecuting and Investigating Office couldn't enquire into his responsibility.[358]

Therefore, Mototsune was able to easily abolish Emperor Seiwa, who belonged to his family,[359] as if he were simply removing the infant head of the

---

[358] The Imperial Prosecuting and Investigating Office was a government office in the Ritsuryo system that was in charge of enforcing the discipline of officials.

According to Kita's argument, the period that should be called the Fujiwara's tyranny was nothing illegal, because it was a period when the right to rule was treated as property (when one could buy and sell government positions). Therefore, the relationship between the emperor and the Fujiwara was similar to that of ward and guardian, and could be called "equal kinship." Because it wasn't illegal, the chancellor of the realm could accept the emperor's "inalienable right of non-responsibility."

[359] The original has a misspelling. In light of this error, it should be "Emperor Yozei" rather than "Emperor Seiwa." Both Emperor Seiwa and Emperor Yozei are related to

family. So Prince Sadami, who had descended to the vassalage with the surname of Minamoto, was retained by Mototsune as Emperor Uda,[360] and he gave Mototsune control and supreme authority, and was probably afraid of his wrath.[361] When Mototsune's son Tokihira received his position, his mother, seeing that the Imperial Edict was not in the emperor's own handwriting, tore it up, saying, "as a Genji who ascended the throne by the grace of this child's father,[362] he lacks proper manners." The emperor was so horrified that he took up the pen himself in order to quell her anger. The sword of Tsubokiri indicated that the succession to the imperial throne was in the mixed blood of the

---

Mototsune, and both were abolished at the will of the Fujiwara clan, but Mototsune was only involved directly in the abolition of Emperor Yozei.

[360] "Sadami" was Emperor Uda's name. In the original text, it's "Emperor Kogen," not "Emperor Uda." We're not sure what he's referring to here, but just for clarity, we've changed it to "Emperor Uda."

[361] When Emperor Uda acceded to the throne, he had written in his Imperial Edict appointing Mototsune Fujiwara to the post of chief advisor to the emperor. However, he issued a second edict, "Let you be in control and appointed as the position of Ako," but Mototsune accused Ako of being a "do-nothing position" with no real duties (known as the Ako controversy). The case was settled by disposing of Tachibana no Hiromi, the author of the Imperial Edict, but Emperor Uda was apparently very dissatisfied and wrote angrily in his diary.

[362] The original text has a compound which means "one's own father" or "someone else's father," and is marked with a (sic). However, the one saying complaining about "lacking manners" is Tokihira's mother—in other words, Mototsune's wife. From the wife's point of view, Mototsune is neither someone else's father nor her own. Looking at it from this point of view, the (sic) is correct. However, looking at it from Tokihira's point of view, "father" wouldn't be all that strange. The "Genji" she's referring to in the quote itself is Emperor Uda.

Fujiwara and the emperor,[363] and Emperor Go-Sanjo, whose blood contained little of the Fujiwara clan, tried to take advantage of the decline of the Fujiwara clan to fight against them. Upon attempting this, the Fujiwara, under an order that all Fujiwara should leave the capital, caused a massive strike of all cabinet members against the emperor, but the emperor won out.

The passive Dokyo, who sought to inherit the sovereignty of the nation through the favor of the empress,[364] was not the only exception. The period of the continuous tyranny of the Fujiwara clan, which monopolized the right of succession to the imperial throne by replacing the blood of the imperial ancestors with its own blood, the blood of citizens, and ejecting much of the imperial family's blood which had been inherited from the imperial ancestors, lasted hundreds of years, far too long to be called an "exception" of rebellious subjects.

The era of tyranny by the Fujiwara clan came to a close with the appearance of Kiyomori. To be precise, however, there was a very brief farce in between. It was the period of the battle monks' mikoshi-carrying forceful appeals, in which the imperial throne was indeed subjected to a great deal of intimidation. Of course, in the decades before and after the Shirakawa

---

[363] "Tsubokiri no tsurugi" or "sword of Tsubokiri" is a longsword handed down from the emperor to the crown prince during the investiture of said crown prince. It's said that Emperor Uda gave it to Emperor Daigo after it was consecrated by Fujiwara no Mototsune.

[364] "Empress" refers to Empress Koken (renamed Empress Shotoku after ascending to the throne). Dokyo was a monk of the Nara period who gained the trust of Empress Shotoku after he prayed for her when she was ill, eventually growing to wield massive power. Empress Shotoku attempted to install him as the emperor, saying it was a divine message from Usa Hachimangu Shrine, but was prevented from doing so by Wake no Kiyomaru, Fujiwara no Momokawa, and others.

Cloistered Rule,[365] the patriarchs and monarchs of powerful families, who had no basis for power and were only just beginning to compete for it, dreamed of a life of power on an equal footing, but it was the mikoshi of the battle monks that first dashed their dreams.

Today, the despised Temple of Baldies wags its tail in the face of power and follows in the footsteps of National Polity Temple.[366] The "traitors that trouble His Majesty's mind" is a declaration that is always used whenever a new idea is introduced, but the sigh of Cloistered Emperor Shirakawa,[367] which was likened to a game of sugoroku going poorly, came about precisely because the Buddhists simply did whatever they wanted. It is the public opinion of today's National Polity Temple monks and others that Mahayana Buddhism and the Imperial Rescript on Education do not conflict, but did the battle monks of that time not tear up Emperor Ichijo's edict, commanding "Monk Yokei to be the head of Tendai-ji Temple,"[368] and turn the imperial messenger

---

[365] It was Emperor Shirakawa who initiated the Cloistered Rule.

[366] "Baldies" referring to a monk's shaved head. By using this as the name of a temple, Kita is poking fun at the monks who follow the theory of national polity.

[367] The original said "cloistered royalty" or a similar meaning, but since "cloistered emperor" is more common, we've changed it to that. It says in *Heikei Monogatari* volume 1, "Gandate," "'The water of Kamo River, the dice of sugoroku, and the battle monks of Enryaku-ji Temple; these are the things my heart wishes not for,' said Sovereign Shirakawa." (*Heike Monogatari [Jo]*, 52)

[368] Head of the Tendai-ji Temple during the Heian period (919-?). "The chief of the mountain (note: this is Mt. Hiei) is Kendaisozu Yokei, also called Kendaiin Sozu. Succeeded [. . .] the lineage of Mitsui. Gifted the name Chiben. He became the head monk at age seventy-one on September 29th, in the first year of the Eiso era, and retired the same year on December 26th due to opposition from the monks of Mt. Heizan. (Chikafusa Kitabatake Jien, "Gukansho," in *Literary Masterpieces of Japan (9)* [Tokyo: Chuokoron-Shinsha, 1971], 109) The story referenced in the text probably refers to the fierce

away in shame? People today know nothing more of these monks than those who gather at the outer moat of the imperial palace to chant "Banzai," but in those days they broke through the moat, smashed down the gate, entered the garden of the palace, prayed with prayer beads, and threatened to cast the people into hell if their assertions were not heeded. Such a threat of damnation is not an effective threat today, but with the knowledge of those days, it was no less effective than the pope's excommunication. No, the banishment from one's clan, which could even occur to the most powerful people at the time, the Fujiwara clan,[369] was an obvious excommunication. There is no example of excommunicating an emperor before, but this is not because there was no monk equivalent to Gregory VII,[370] but because the emperor himself had descended to the ground and worshipped the mikoshi.

---

opposition of the Mt. Hiei monks. The book referenced above elaborates further: "The Ennin (mountain-style) and Enchin (temple-style) schools became the two major factions on Mt. Hiei, and the struggle for power between the two schools grew more and more intense as time went by. The 29th head of the temple, Yukei of the Enchin lineage, was appointed as the head of the temple in the first year of Eiso (989), but the priests of the Ennin lineage opposed the appointment and repeatedly prevented the imperial envoy from climbing up the mountain. Yokei, who had to take position as the head monk in a situation where the Imperial Edict had to be read aloud during their climb up the mountain due to all the fierce resistance, could not practically perform the duties of the head monk, and was forced to resign a mere three months later." (pp. 408–409)

"Tendai-ji Temple" refers to Enryaku-ji Temple.

[369] The battle monks of Kofuku-ji Temple probably threatened to expel the Fujiwara clan from Kofuku-ji Temple (Kofuku-ji Temple is a clan temple of the Fujiwara).

[370] Gregory VII was the pope who excommunicated Holy Roman Emperor Heinrich IV. Heinrich IV visited Gregory VII while he was staying in Canossa, did penance, and had his excommunication revoked (Humiliation of Canossa).

What audacity to have the emperor descend to the ground and worship you. The shameless monks of today would say, "Those were precept-breaking monks. They didn't know the loyal Mahayana sutras like we do." However, when we see them placing Kusunoki Masahige, who was neither a Buddhist nor a monk, above the Buddha and taking pride in him, while at the same time taking no responsibility for the activities of their battle monks, we are very much tempted to laugh in their faces. In response to the blow of the battle monks, the imperial family was forced to bring the two clans, the Genji and Heike, closer together to protect themselves, and at last the imperial family found itself in the bloody battles of the Hogen and Heiji eras. Much as an oil painting "looks uglier the closer you get," the rude Kiyomori discovered the disdainful aspects of Cloistered Emperor Go-Shirakawa and blatantly began to persecute him. The priests of today refer to one of these priests, Taira-no-Kiyomori, by the name of "Atrocious Monk," but many other priests, the battle monks, were even worse. It was these battle monks, who were committing evil outside the palace, which drove their "Atrocious Monk" to commit evil in the court. And to say that these are "exceptions" when counted as rebellious subjects, it would mean that nearly all monks on earth are "exceptions," aside from those few hermits training in the mountains or forests, or those monks which are as transcendent as the floating clouds.

Then, after the time of the Taira clan, a thousand years of long, long medieval history began, which even so-called national polity theorists call exceptions. That is, rule by the Minamoto clan, the Hojo clan, and the Ashikaga clan, into the Warring States period, and rule by the Tokugawa clan. The history of the Japanese people is the thousand years since the writing of the *Kojiki* and *Nihon Shoki*, just as the history of the Germanic peoples began with the medieval period—at the very least, the period of time after we imported the written word, minus the one thousand years of primitive time in which we had neither any method for recording history nor any consciousness of history, is around 1,500 years. What undeveloped-Oriental-village savagery it would be to bury the period of time starting with the Genpei era, which constitutes the majority of our history in terms of time, with the single word "exception." There are no savages which have history so inverted. Not the Australian savages,[371] nor the American Indians.

Let the facts speak for themselves. Aside from the pitiable bookworm who cried, stuck between loyalty and filial piety,[372] we daresay all of the Taira clan, not just Kiyomori alone, were dedicated to the orders of their chiefs. There's no point in even specifically referring to how they attacked the imperial palace and often imprisoned the emperor. Nor would the national textbooks tell us that the Minamoto clan destroyed the Taira clan by the decree of Prince Mochihito or by request of an imperial decree,[373] not for the sake of their own revival, but for the purpose of serving the emperor. We dare not compare the efficacy of the Imperial Edict with that of the imperial proclamation, as those who preach the principles of royalty with the principles of military, or say that the army of the Tohoku region, which sank the emperor with the three sacred treasures in the West Sea.[374] Yoritomo, who used the machinations of Oe-no-Hiromoto to seize control of all the legislative and judicial sovereignty,[375] was

---

[371] Referring to the Aboriginal Australians.

[372] The previously mentioned Taira no Shigemori.

[373] Prince Mochihito was the third son of Emperor Go-Shirakawa. He conspired with Minamoto no Yorimasa to send a decree to overthrow the Taira clan, but was discovered by the Taira clan and killed in battle.

[374] It's said that the Heike, together with Emperor Antoku, entered the water with the Ame-no-Murakumo sword and the Yasakani no Magatama. It's also said that the Genji never found the sword after all.

[375] Oe-no-Hiromoto was a nobleman active in the early Kamakura period. He served Yoritomo and continued to serve the shogunate after Yoritomo's death. It was Oe-no-Hiromoto who proposed the establishment of the famous Shugo and Jito. He's said to be an ancestor of the Mori clan.

a man revered by Hideyoshi,[376] but one can imagine that he was no more of a loyal retainer or a righteous man than the bronze statue of Mr. Ito Hirobumi erected on the Minatogawa River. Compared to many of today's patrons who gradually buy up titles in various names and flaunt their titles of "count" or what have you to the world, Yoritomo's wife Masako, who scoffed at the audience and refused the formal conferral of a title with the sarcastic response of, "This old Kanto nun does not know manners," may be guessed to be less of a loyalist than the present noble ladies, by her own ungracious diplomatic declarations. As for the Hojo clan, even the so-called national polity theorists were forced to consider them exceptions after facing them with extreme difficulty. However, this "exception" as a rebel was not limited to Yoshitoki alone, as they seem to think. To count as loyal subjects and righteous men the 190,000 other underlings who, as accomplices or accessories to Yoshitoki,[377]

---

[376] It's "Hideyoshi," but might be a mistake for "Ieyasu." Ieyasu is famous for his idealization of Yoritomo. In *Hotaiko*, Aizan Yamaji wrote the following anecdote about Ieyasu: "Tokugawa Ieyasu was once conversing with another family, asking them what kind of person they thought Lord Yoritomo was. They replied that it is said he was a black-hearted man who had killed his uncle and brother. The Tokugawa replied that he was not, and such a description could only be made by an ignorant fanatic of the magistrate. There is a certain standard for someone who rules the land. If they are lacking, they will be discarded, even if they be of the same family. This a requirement for the rule of the nation and the peace of the land, and to say that Lord Yoritomo is a heartless person is to say one knows not of what he speaks. This is an analysis of the hero's heart by the hero himself, he who endures countless mockeries for his heroism, past and present." (*Hideyoshi Toyotomi (Ge)* [Tokyo: Iwanami Bunko, 1996] 332–333. In addition, though the original title for the book is *Hotaiko*, the Iwanami Bunko version uses the title *Hideyoshi Toyotomi*).

[377] An "accessory" to a crime refers to someone who aides and abets in the committing of a crime. This term is still used in criminal law today.

had the three emperors banished to a distant island where no birds flew, and the 200,000 conspirators who were waiting to advance later,[378] does not help to sanctify the theory of national polity.

While retrospective critics say that the three emperors were "condemned to exile," we use the word "banish." This is because "condemned to exile" is a term which expresses an act of humble reverence rather reflecting the extreme persecution and distress suffered by Emperor Go-Toba, who lived for thirty-nine years in Oki islands, leaning his hut against a rock pit, and Emperor Juntoku, still called "Juntoku-bonsama" today on Sado Island,[379] who spent that time as mere beggars.[380] Using military force to bring in a man who is spread out underneath a pine tree, sleeves wet with dew, is to "capture" him. Is not the deprivation of freedom of residence and the exile of someone who basked in urban prosperity to uninhabited islands a clear case of banishment? If anyone were to say that the priests humbly and respectfully captured the

---

[378] At the time of the Jokyu Rebellion, the Shogunate forces numbered approximately one hundred ninety thousand.

[379] Since Sado Island is Kita's birthplace, this statement is based on his own experience. When Kita was a second-year student at Sado Junior High School, his class went on a field trip to visit the tomb of Emperor Juntoku's son, Hikonari-Ou (but Kita was too ill to join the trip). He was then assigned to write a "record of your visit to Hikonari-Ou's tomb," in which he wrote the following. "Ah, violent Hojo clan. Ah, wicked Hojo clan. There is no Hojo before Hojo, nor any Hojo after." Yukichi wrote that this was written after a visit to Mano Goryo, the resting place of Emperor Juntoku ("Fuunji Kita Ikki," in *Kita Ikki no Ningenzo* [Tokyo: Yuhikaku, 1976], 232), but it was actually the tomb of Hikonari-Ou. His wife Suzuko later had an experience in which Emperor Juntoku's spirit appeared to her after she visited the mausoleum of Emperor Juntoku.

[380] Basically, he's saying "the language of the national polity theorists makes it impossible to understand that Emperor Go-Toba and others lived miserable lives in their later years."

Daijingu from the old shrine and moved her into the new shrine, [381] he would be seen to have gone mad. Likewise, the use of such words as "Yoshitoki used military force to move the three emperors to Oki and Sado,"[382] would be an outrageous and retroactive statement.

---

[381] When the term "Daijingu" is used, it usually refers to the combined name of the Inner and Outer Shrines of Ise Jingu. Here, it refers to "Amaterasu." The expression "to be moved from the old hall to the new hall" refers to Sengu. Ise Jingu is built in the Shinmei-zukuri style (a construction method in which the pillars are buried in the ground), and the shrine is rebuilt once every twenty years in an event called "Sengu." Torii gates and other structures are moved to other shrines and reused. Even ancient architectural techniques could have been used to build a solid wooden structure, such as Horyu-ji Temple, but the Ise Jingu has continued to relocate its shrines, daring not to use such construction techniques. There are two possible reasons for this. One is based on the Shinto belief that gods always prefer a clean place, and that purity has been maintained through constant rebuilding. This is especially true of Ise Jingu Shrine, where the supreme deity, Amaterasu, resides. The other is a respect for precedent, in which the simplicity of the ancient architectural style was considered appropriate as the dwelling place of the gods. As to the reason for the twenty-year period, it's been pointed out that it has something to do with the way the ancient calendar was calculated. In the lunisolar calendar, one solar year consists of 365 days and one quarter, and because it has synodic months of twenty-nine and a half days, it's necessary to adjust the calendar by inserting seven intercalary months every nineteen years. So after nineteen years, the solar year and the synodic month coincide. The idea of returning to the starting point in twenty years was born from this, and was reflected in the concept of the relocation of the shrine. Given the fact that Amaterasu is an imitation of the sun, this idea seems to be the closest to the truth. For more information on Sengu, see Isao Tokoro, *Ise Jingu* (Tokyo: Kodansha Gakujutsu Bunko, 1993).

[382] Incidentally, Emperor Tsuchimikado was exiled to Sanuki. Emperor Tsuchimikado was reluctant to overthrow the shogunate and did not originally need to be exiled, but

Many historians cite an article that appears in *Masukagami*.[383] It is as follows:

> Yasutoki turned to his father Yoshitoki and asked, "What would you do if the emperor's palanquin were to advance toward you?" Yoshitoki replied, "At that time, break your arrows and surrender."[384]

Despite its lack of credibility, historians have used this article to say, "Even a rebel like Yoshitoki has the conscience of the Japanese people inside him, and all Japanese people are like this," which is used to ignore these so-called "exceptions." But Yoshitoki inflicted far worse suffering on the three emperors than death. When his son Yasutoki was later asked by Adachi Yoshikage, "What shall we do if Juntoku's prince stood in opposition?" he did not answer, "Fall on your knees and surrender." He ordered, "Abolish him."[385] The imperial

---

he requested to be exiled himself because he could not remain in Kyoto while his father and brother were exiled. Later, he was moved to Awa.

[383] This is a historical tale that describes the period from the birth of Emperor Go-Toba to the return of Emperor Go-Daigo to Oki. The most popular theory is that Yoshimoto Nijo was the author. The style of writing is said to be graceful.

[384] Article found in "Niishimamori," volume 2 of *Masukagami*.

[385] In 1242, Emperor Shijo died suddenly, and there was talk of enthronement of Emperor Shuntoku's son as emperor (this happened because Emperor Shuntoku's son, Prince Tadanari, was a relative of Kujo Michiie). However, since Emperor Juntoku was one of the emperors who attempted to overthrow the shogunate, Hojo Yasutoki strongly opposed the idea. Yasutoki dispatched Adachi Yoshikage as an envoy to Kyoto and was prepared to use force. In response to Yasutoki's fierce opposition, the imperial court reversed its policy and enthroned Emperor Go-Saga. In his *Nihon Seiji* (*Records of Japanese Politics*), Rai San'yo wrote, "Yasutoki sent Adachi Yoshikage to provoke the emperor. When Yoshikage returned from his journey, he asked what he should do if the

household itself had brought such disasters as the simultaneous alternate succession to the throne,[386] but Yasutoki, Tokimune, and others had been wise and bold enough to suppress them and not allow these things to make much of a splash. The heroic model of Emperor Go-Daigo against Takatoki's arrogance led to Takatoki being defeated, but he was once captured and thrown into Oki. When Takatoki died, there were more than 870 martyrs in addition to more than six thousand martyrs in Kamakura alone, families and relatives, priests, men, and women, who all heard about this and tried to repay their favor to Takatoki in the afterlife. And this is a far greater number than the remaining soldiers of Emperor Go-Daigo, who fell with a stroke of his sword. Ah, are all the people from the reign of the Taira to the reign of the Minamoto clan, and all the way up to the Hojo clan, which achieved peace for another hundred years, "exceptions?" Are they all rebels?

This was even more extreme under the Ashikaga clan. Emperor Go-Daigo's efforts merely replaced the Hojo clan with the Ashikaga clan, which replaced the rivalry between Kamakura and Kyoto by taking Kyoto from them

---

prince of Sadoin had risen. Yasutoki said, 'abolish him.'" (Rai San'yo, *Nihon Shiso Taikei (49)* [Iwanami Shoten, 1977], 314). Also referenced: Arai Hakuseki, *Tokushi Yoron* (Tokyo: Iwanami Buko, 1936), 91–92. Also, the phrase "fall on your knees" is a play on "break your arrows" in Japanese. This incident may have agitated Chikafusa Kitabatake, but he said, "Yasutoki has done his duty to his sovereign. (Note: Emperor Go-Saga) He honored his father and his devotion and filial piety were so great that it is only fitting that he should be considered as a proxy for Amaterasu's divine providence." (Chikafusa Kitabatake, *Jinno Shotoki*, [Tokyo: Iwanami Bunko, 1975], 156) So in fact, he didn't criticize Yasutoki, but rather praised him.

[386] This "simultaneous alternate succession to the throne" was an agreement by Hojo Tokimune to have the emperors of both lineages take turns in order to resolve the conflict between the Daikakuji lineage and the Jimyoin lineage. Often not honored, it became a source of conflict.

entirely. Ah, Emperor Go-Daigo and his loyal martyrs! This is one of only a few exceptions throughout Japanese history. This tragic and pathetic story became the very subject of poetry and literature during the era of the theory of national polity at the end of the Edo period, thereby giving poetic luster to the revolutionary theory (the significance of the theory of national polity in relation to the Meiji Revolution will be discussed later).

However, it cannot be said that the seventy ships and two hundred thousand troops that Takauji led to the front were not mere "exceptions" compared to the three hundred men at Minatogawa who were defeated in the battle.[387] Takauji, who won the war and took over the country over the defunct Nitta clan, was able to accomplish this because he had more "rebels." Even if the three sacred weapons were handed over as a courtesy between father and son in diplomatic relations, the fact that the Northern Court finally surrendered to the Southern Court cannot be said to be the defeat of a few rebels, a few "exceptions," since the majority were so-called loyal subjects and righteous warriors.[388] Ko-no-Moronao,[389] for example, said the following:

---

[387] Ashikaga Takauji was defeated in a battle in Kyoto, which he had been fighting since January 1336, and fell to Kyoto. The "seventy ships and two hundred thousand men" mentioned in the text refers to the forces that Takauji regained after his fall to Kyushu (though the "two hundred thousand" figure is an exaggeration from the *Taiheiki*).

[388] The original text reads, "Even though the three sacred treasures were handed over as a courtesy between father and son in diplomatic negotiations, it is not to be said that when the Northern Court, at its end, surrendered to the Southern Court, that the majority of loyal retainers were defeated by a few exceptional rebellious subjects." The phrase "the Northern Court, at its end, surrendered to the Southern Court" may refer to Takauji's request for a truce so that he could concentrate on the war against his younger brother Tadayoshi. However, we're not sure how to interpret the phrase, "The majority of loyal retainers were defeated by a few exceptional rebellious subjects." How could "a few exceptional rebellious subjects" defeat the majority of "loyal retainers"? Perhaps it's a mistake of "the few exceptions of rebellious subjects were defeated." So that's what we translated it as. The meaning of "courtesy between father and son" is also unclear.

[389] Ko-no-Moronao was a steward of the Ashikaga family and a close associate of Takauji.

There is a king in the capital, and he defends some territory, and there are places such as the inner palace, the imperial palace, and the old imperial palace, and they are all in the way of getting down from one's horse. If there is a truth that cannot be fulfilled without a king, simply build it out of wood or cast it from gold. The living imperial palace, the king, and all others like them should be cast away somewhere else.

This is from an article in *Taiheiki*,[390] and the author was familiar with the tone of his words,[391] so it was likely that Moronao let loose even more blunt, unreserved words that fit perfectly with egalitarianism.

Today, many political parties and other people assert, much as the loyal retainers such as Mr. Hozumi fear, what is in all effect a republican system of government—or at least a party cabinet or responsible cabinet based on an unwritten constitution that would realize a de facto republican form of government. The argument for a party cabinet or a responsible cabinet is, as loyal retainer Mr. Hozumi and others fear, an extremely frank and blunt assertion when compared to the slyness of the people who know that such a thing would result in a very large change in the significance of the emperor, yet pretend that they don't understand what democracy is. However, it can be said that the reason why the whole nation did not ostracize Ko-no-Moronao as if he had struck a blow like a certain minister who made a republican speech,[392]

He was a bold man and was renowned as an eccentric Daimyo along with Sasaki Takauji.

[390] This is found in the *Taiheiki*, volume 26, "Ko-no-Moronaotaishashi-no-koto." However, the quotation in *The Theory of Japanese National Polity* and the actual text in *Taiheiki* are quite different. Kita probably misremembered.

[391] This refers to using honorific words despite the content of his words actually being disrespectful to the emperor.

[392] Yukio Ozaki. "Republican speech" refers to a speech in which Ozaki stated, "If Japan

but followed him as the second in power after Takauji, is because the people then were rebels extreme enough that they wouldn't shame their party-cabinet theorist descendants who exist today.

Ashikaga Yoshimitsu, for example, created emperors of the Northern Court as he pleased and forced the emperor of the Southern Court to surrender.[393] When he wanted the position of Grand Minister of State and could not be given it, he tried to become emperor not by duress or demonstration, but by his own determination, and when he retired, he sought the title of Daijo Tenno from the emperor.[394] The Ashikaga clan, much as Emperor Go-Shirakawa dreamed of prosperity through the equal power of the Minamoto and Heike clans, merely built the Golden Pavilion as a prelude to the great battle of patriarchs and monarchs that later became known as the Warring States period, and learned the manners and customs of the tenjobito for no reason at all.[395] Therefore, it goes without saying that the imperial family alone cannot be held responsible for the downfall and impoverishment of the Ashikaga clan and later eras.

However, the so-called national polity theorists must be instructed as to who is responsible for the disastrous downfall of the imperial family during the Warring States period. When Emperor Go-Tsuchimikado died, he could not be buried due to lack of funds for a funeral, so he was left in his coffin at the back

---

were a republic..." when criticizing the distortion of parliamentary politics by capitalists through their financial power. It became a political issue when Emperor Meiji sent his entourage to express his dissatisfaction.

[393] The emperor of the Southern Court at this time was Emperor Go-Kameyama.

[394] "Daijo Tenno" means retired emperor. His son Yoshimochi refused, and this was never realized. Note that Kinkaku-ji (Rokuon-ji) treats Yoshimitsu as having been granted the title of Daijo Tenno.

[395] "Tenjobito" were people who were allowed entry into the imperial court.

door of the Seiryoden Palace for about forty days.[396] The vassals and court ladies were on night shifts in order to protect him, but the crown prince came and cried,[397] saying that it was not true what Bai Juyi had sung, "There is no misfortune to one who observes the ten good deeds."[398] Unable to hold a coronation ceremony for the emperor Go-Kashiwabara, Masamoto Hosokawa,[399] the then governor, was asked for the expenses, but Masamoto refused, saying, "The shogun alone is enough. There's no need for additional ceremony."[400] Because of this, the coronation ceremony couldn't be held for

---

[396] Masaie Konoe, the former chief advisor to the emperor at the time, wrote the following in his diary: "Tonight is the funeral of the former lord (note: Emperor Go-Tsuchimikado). At the time of the boar's hour, we will move from the Imperial Palace to Sennyu-ji Temple. The attendants of the chariot were on both sides of the chariot, and the court nobles and dignitaries were behind the chariot. I shall inquire about this at a later date. As of today, it has been forty-three days since his death. Such delay should not be allowed to further delay the proceedings." (*Go-Hokoin-Ki*, November 11th, 1501) However, the actual quotation used comes from Akira Imatani's *Nobles of the Warring States Era* (Tokyo: Kodansha Gakujutsu Bunko, 2002), 240.

[397] Prince Katsuhito. Later Emperor Go-Kashiwabara.

[398] Bai Juyi was a Tang Dynasty poet. He's best known for his "Chang Hen Ge," in which he criticized Xuanzong's favoritism toward Yang Guifei. The collection of poems by Bai Juyi, *The Collected Works of Bai*, was widely read among aristocrats in the Heian period.

[399] Son of Katsumoto Hosokawa. After the Onin War, he ousted the 10th shogun, Yoshtane, in a coup d'état and installed Ashikaga Yoshizumi to take real power.

[400] "In 1502, when the imperial court hurried to appoint Shogun Yoshizumi to the post of lieutenant general in the council of war, in order to hasten the accession of Emperor Go-Kashiwabara, Masamoto Hoshikawa said, 'Such a position is useless, and even if he were to be promoted, it would be worthless if he did not respond to the order.' He added, 'Even in the inner court, the ceremony of accession to the throne is worthless. Even if we perform such a ceremony, a person without a proper body cannot be considered a king,'

twenty years. The ceremony was finally completed with the borrowing of ten thousand pieces of gold from Kouken Honganji.[401] During the reign of Emperor Go-Nara, poverty reached such an extreme that Sanetaka Sanjonishi went around to various wealthy families to ask for donations of much rice and currency,[402] and finally obtained basic food and clothing. However, the fruit of Sanjonishi's hard work was limited, so the emperor himself sold the books he had written to supplement his food expenses.[403] It is even said that Sanjonishi was forced to live in the fallen imperial palace with his wife and children in tow, because some brigands who had formed a band had set fire to and robbed the place. There was no enclosure, no moat, and the fire in the inner court could be seen from Sanjo Bridge. Common people sold tea and sweets under the

---

as he refuted the court's policy, and the nobles and military were unanimous in their agreement." (Imatani, *Nobles of the Warring States Era*, 240–241). This was recorded by Jinson (son of Ichijo Kaneyoshi, a monk in the Daijo-in of Kofuku-ji) in *Daijo-in Jinsha Zojiki*, June 16th, 1502.

[401] Kouken Honganji was the son of Rennyo (whose Buddhist name was "Jitsunyo"), and the leader of the Honganji power. Aizan Yamaji also wrote, "Although the country has been in turmoil since Onin, and the accession of emperors has been difficult, in 1521, Saint Jitsuyo of Honganji donated money to complete the rites for Emperor Go-Kashiwabara, and in 1560, Mori Motonari donated one thousand koku of rice and some gold to complete the rites for Emperor Ogimachi." (Aizan Yamaji, *Toyotomi Hideyoshi*, [Tokyo: Iwanami Bunko, 1996], 96–97). Kita is referencing this.

[402] Sanetaka Sanjonishi was a poet of the late Muromachi period. He excelled in calligraphy and earned his living by copying books while being active as a cultural figure. He is also said to have had a close relationship with Sogi. The historian Hara Katsuro's account of his life is well known.

[403] Emperor Go-Nara was famous for making a living by making his own writing brushes and selling his own calligraphy.

bridge in front of the Shishinden.[404] Whenever there was a poetry party, red beans were served atop the three burnt, blackened imperial treasures.

Those who have no sense of reason exaggerate the "loyalty of Nobunaga," but what he did was only a small repair. Until then, the imperial palace was so poor that it was said,

> It is no different from a private house in the countryside, with thorns tied to a bamboo fence. When I was a child, I would go to the house and play at the edge of the house, kneading dirt, and whatnot. I would sometimes lift up the torn bamboo screen, but I would never see anybody.[405]

Of course, visionaries like Nobunaga did see the later benefits in having an emperor, but the majority of citizens were just like Masamoto. What is this poverty if not caused by a lack of regard for the emperor? And such poverty is the same deprivation that ordinary people fall into, with the only exception being that the emperors did not destroy their homes because of poverty or become unaware of their lineage, as ordinary people do. The vast majority of people did not unite their spirits as one and serve the one eternal lineage of the imperial line, so if you want to say these rebels are the few "exceptions," then you'd need to claim this vast majority of people are all exceptions.

---

[404] Shishinden is the place where the emperor performs his official duties.

[405] An article from Sensai Emura's *Rojin Zatsuwa* (Sensai Emura was a physician in Kyoto during the Azuchi-Momoyama period, and *Rojin Zatsuwa* were notes he actually took when looking at patients). Aizan Yamaji also quotes this passage in *Toyotami Hideyoshi (Jo)*, 137, but Kita's citations and Yamaji's citations are slightly different. Kita's quotation probably relies on memory, since many of his quotations differ from the original.

Hideyoshi's unification enabled the emperor to escape this lack of food and clothing—a type of poverty that did not exist in the royal families of foreign countries. However, to praise Hideyoshi as a loyal subject and a righteous warrior because of this is like saying that a philanthropist who donates a portion of the blood of the poor is a sovereign. How proud he, who held all the wealth of the nation, would be of the theory of national polity as he offers the imperial family a stipend of rice that was worth less to him than a single hair on the body of nine oxen. His theatrical temperament led him to try and impress the people of the capital at the time by saying, "The emperor's vehicles, oxcarts, and other such items had long been out of use, and even I, who know many things, did not know them for certain."[406] But how could he know the historical significance of the imperial family when there was so little education at the time that even the grand minister of state and the imperial regent didn't know these things? Many of his careless remarks reveal his true intentions.

Behold the words he uttered in fury when he received the taunting sovereign message from a Ming envoy.[407] He retorted, "I took over the world with my own power. If I wish to become king, I can. If I desire to become emperor, I can. Why must I wait for your approval?"[408] That's enough for

---

[406] In the text, the part we've translated as "I" was actually "old man." We believe it's an article from *Rojin Zatsuwa*.

[407] During the first Imjin War (the Japanese invasion of Korea), after the arrival of Ming troops as reinforcements the war reached a stalemate. Therefore, Japan began peace negotiations with the Ming, and an envoy came to Japan from the Ming. During the peace negotiations held on September 1st, 1596, the Ming read out a letter of state that read, "Hideyoshi (Taira) is hereby sealed and appointed King of Japan." It's said that Hideyoshi was furious at this. To be precise, however, he was not enraged by the wording of the letter, but by the fact that the Ming response did not reflect the Japanese side's intentions at all.

[408] This anecdote is recorded in Razan Hayashi's *Hideyoshifu*.

reciting history in capital letters. Instead, think about what would happen if this statement were said today. When the cunning Li Hongzhang said to Mr. Ito Hirobumi during negotiations that he would prevent the latter from becoming king of Japan,[409] Mr. Hirobumi did not get angry and respond with, "I organized the ministry with my own power. If I wish to become king, I can. If I desire to become emperor, I can. Why must I wait for the approval of someone with hair like a pig's tail?"[410] This is why he had a statue erected in Minatogawa.

Hideyoshi's position was indeed a right earned by mighty power. In ancient and medieval times, when mighty power determined all rights, if the imperial family had insulted those rights instead of the Chinese emissary, Hideyoshi would have become a king or emperor, enforcing his immense power via the rights he took by that power. One shouldn't underestimate the effect of a single phrase. Today, even when uttering a single phrase, one must often preface with "I beg your pardon," or add words such as "please" and "thank you" to the end. As long as such care is taken, no matter how furious the words may be, they are not words that will resonate in one's mouth. In other words, Hideyoshi was also one of these people with supposedly "exceptional" rebellious thoughts, and was a person who commanded the entire nation.

---

[409] Li Hongzhang was a politician in the late Qing Dynasty. After following Zen Guofan to pacify the Taiping Rebellion, he became active in central politics. He was responsible for numerous negotiations as a diplomat. At the peace conference of the Sino-Japanese War, he negotiated as the ambassador plenipotentiary of the Qing side. Munemitsu Mutsu's account of the Shimonoseki peace conference is very detailed in his book *Kenkenroku*.

[410] Literally "pig-tailed han" in the original text. Most likely poking fun at the queue hairstyle.

The Tokugawa clan's only measures against the imperial family were constant confinement and the unceasing forced abdication of the throne.[411] We have already mentioned that Mr. Nagao Aruga is a historian who engages in retroactive criticism, but we will explain this in detail once again. We can't help but laugh when he argues that Ieyasu's refusal to assassinate Hideyoshi when he visited the imperial palace, despite the fact that Ieyasu's retainers heavily advised the assassination, shows "proof that both warlords were allied with each other in their devotion to the emperor." This perverse view is probably the result of his opinion that sovereignty is divided into the main body and the function or operation of sovereignty, and that the imperial family had the main body of sovereignty for 2,500 years and had not lost it, while the shogunate was merely delegated the function of the main body of sovereignty.

However, the gravestone at Toshogu Shrine would tremble with emotion if Ieyasu, who was expressing Hideyoshi's ideas in reality, were interpreted as a loyal subject and a righteous warrior. Behold:

> The three princes, the regents, and even the nobles and lords are to be ruled by the appointment of the Shogun of the Kanto Region and the special government offices of the Junnain and Shokugakuin.[412] It is not necessary to inform the sovereign of the method of administration in order to inform him of all the affairs of state.

---

[411] Incidentally, the Edo period shogunate enacted the "Laws of the Imperial Family and Court," which stipulated that the emperor must put learning first.

[412] The Junnain was a detached palace built by Emperor Junna during his reign, while the Shokugakuin was a private school built by Ariwara no Yukihira. The directors of these places were called "betto," and since Ashikaga Yoshimitsu later served as one, it became customary for the Minamoto clan to hold two betto positions.

These regulations show a responsible cabinet that is unparalleled in other countries, befitting a national polity which is apparently unparalleled as well.

> One must not neglect his studies. . . . It is of the highest importance to protect the three sacred treasures.

This is the exact point in which the imperial household becomes one of poets, and the emperor's duty ends at protecting the three sacred treasures, which are nothing but false titles. We are still unaware of any constitutional history in which a person who claims to have been delegated the functions of sovereignty enforces such a law on the body of sovereignty.

In the first place, the root of the fallacy is to try to explain the relationship between the emperor and the shogun at that time by tracing back the meaning and significance of the word "appoint" today. Mr. Aruga always retroactively argues this way. Look again.

> The lords of the provinces are not allowed to visit the interior palace even by imperial order. When the lords of the western provinces correspond, they are to stop at Kyoto. If it is discovered that they have corresponded in secret, they will be cut off from their family name, no matter how much value their family may possess. If one wishes to see the sights of Kyoto we must be notified of the desire to do so, and one can only do so when permission is granted. If permission is granted, it will be granted only within the Sanjo Bridge.

What name should even be given for the Toshogu Cabinet, which had the authority to dispense with both court orders and rulings, and which strictly forbade anyone from approaching the main body of sovereignty with the most serious offense of severing ties with one's family? The prime minister of the cabinet was not called "His Excellency," but was revered as a "divine sovereign," his seat was hereditary, and there were no other ministers, nor was there anyone else to be held accountable. Finally, the prime minister of the cabinet allocated for imperial household expenses a mere twenty thousand koku from the imperial treasury, five thousand koku from the new imperial stock, and another five thousand koku from the true imperial stock.[413] Comparatively, the annual salary of Prime Minister Tokugawa was an incredible eight million koku,[414] a Magna Carta which makes one want to burst out laughing.[415]

Mr. Aruga's rebuke, "To assume that all Japanese citizens are descendants of Amaterasu and to use this fact alone as the basis for the sovereignty of the emperor over the people of Japan is nothing more than a common myth for one who doesn't know history", is not only an insult towards the Shinto faith of Mr. Hozumi and others, which is part of the foundation of the emperor sovereignty theory, but also an insult to the historical interpretation that Mr. Aruga himself has adopted as the basis of his own theory. If one is going to argue for the emperor's sovereignty based on history, one must not deceive history. The ownership of eight million koku by the Tokugawa clan, while the emperor had a mere twenty thousand koku, was a stranglehold on the imperial family from an economic point of view, which is the source of political activity. His decree,

---

[413] The "imperial household treasury" here refers to the domain of the emperor's family. When there are two or more retired emperors, the most recent one is called the "new emperor," while the previous ones are called the "true emperors."

[414] It was originally described as "eight million koku," but it was actually about four million.

[415] The Magna Carta is a document written in 1215 in which the English feudal nobles demanded that King John recognize their rights. Although it only stipulated the rights of the feudal lords, the interpretation of its provisions was extended, and it became a powerful basis for the civil revolution.

though technically peaceful, harshly severed the economic ties between Kyoto and the other lords:

> One must refrain from making offers of money to the surrounding samurai families from Kyoto. Even if the so-called stipend is heavy and the lord knows how to handle money as he pleases, a daimyo worth ten thousand koku should serve the nation and the people with ten thousand koku. A court noble has a small stipend, but he has no role to serve the nation or to care for and nurture his people. Therefore, all they need to do is to work at court and earn enough money to support their families. If they work without extravagance, life is easy even if the stipend is small...

Such words were designed specifically to bleed dry the emperor's coffers and economically isolate him:

> When a court noble enters into a samurai family, he must notify the Kanto region of this fact, and only after the Shogun's judgement has been made should the marriage be consummated. If the marriage is consummated without such a notification, he shall be met with a grave punishment.

These sorts of decrees were made with the aim to eliminate any sort of social forces which tried to join hands with the emperor. Because of this, the emperor was like a prisoner under surveillance. When Emperor Go-Mizunoo tried to travel around the Kinki region,[416] the shogunate did not allow him to do so.

---

[416] Emperor of the early Edo period, third prince of Emperor Go-Yozei. He welcomed Masako, daughter of the second Shogun Hidetada, but she rebelled against the oppression of the court nobles and gave up the throne to her daughter (Empress Meisho).

When he tried to go anyway, the shogunate forced him to stop by military power. Because he put much effort into practicing and engaging in swordsmanship, when the chief magistrate of Kyoto, Shigemune Itakura,[417] tried to stop him, his reasoning was, "If they hear about this in Edo, I don't think it will end peacefully."

Even father and son had to obtain permission from the shogunate to meet. Emperor Yomei's wisdom and intelligence was his demise, and because of it he was confined to the Sento Imperial Palace from ages twenty-one to fifty-four for no reason at all.[418] Except for one time during the beginning of the year, he was not allowed to meet his family at all, and he was never allowed a single face-to-face meeting with the princes, the regent, or the head priests.[419] He was strictly forbidden any personal excursions. This was the same method used by the clever and wise Yoshitoki, merely using Kyoto in place of Sado or Oki.

Incidentally, there is no record of an emperor named just "Mizunoo," but it was another name of Emperor Seiwa.

[417] A military commander in the early Edo period. He was praised for his decisiveness.

[418] "Emperor Yomei" is the father of Prince Shotoku. In view of the fact that he came from the Tokugawa clan, this is likely an error, and it should be Empress Meisho, daughter of Tokugawa Masako. However, since she abdicated at the age of twenty (technically twenty-one), this point makes sense, but it isn't consistent with the statement that she stayed on the throne until the age of fifty-four. It's probably an error of "fifty-four years after becoming ex-empress." The abdication of Empress Meisho and her subsequent treatment by the Tokugawa family is not necessarily an appropriate example of oppression by the Tokugawa family, since it's largely due to the manipulations of the imperial court, beginning with Emperor Go-Mizunoo.

[419] The word here refers to a temple where a prince resides, and the monks that live there. In the imperial family during the Edo period, it was customary for the prince who could not join the court family to be ordained.

Such a responsible cabinet can be found nowhere else but our national polity, which is unparalleled in the world. Just as Mr. Aruga divided sovereignty into action and main body, he also divides sovereignty into a ludicrous, infinite number of categories, reserving the honor rights for the emperor.[420] Nevertheless, Emperor Go-Mizunoo had even that right trampled upon, as the shogunate stole the purple robe he had given to a priest, exiled the priest who had been given it,[421] and finally sent Lady Kasuga to visit the palace, placing pressure on him to abdicate the throne. Forcing emperors to abdicate was a consistent policy during the Tokugawa's rule. Not only the outstanding Emperor Go-Mizunoo, but also the wise Emperor Yomei,[422] Emperor Go-Sai, Emperor Higashiyama, Emperor Nakamikado, and Emperor Sakuramachi—in other words, all the emperors during the Tokugawa shogunate were forced to abdicate for no reason other than the fact that they had grown from children into adults. In Emperor Go-Sai's case, they couldn't find a single excuse for abdication, so they used "the four seasons, his yin and yang do not harmonize well,"[423] as a reason to force him to abdicate, the kind

---

[420] These "honor rights" refers to the authority to grant official positions.

[421] The famous purple robe incident. The shogunate had restricted the granting of the purple robe in the "Laws of the Court and Courtly Families." However, Emperor Go-Mizunoo disobeyed this rule and gave purple robes to the monks of Daitoku-ji and Myoshin-ji temples. The shogunate confiscated the purple robes and exiled Takuan and the others who protested against the confiscation.

[422] See note 433 for the error about Empress Meisho.

[423] In the past, it was understood that the harmony of the world is maintained when the yin and yang that make up the world are in harmony, and this phrase expresses the fact that the harmony of the world is not well maintained. During the reign of Emperor Go-sai, there was a series of natural disasters such as the Great Fire of Meireki and earthquakes, and it is said that some people blamed the emperor for his immorality. Therefore, it is likely that this logic was forced upon him in order to force him to abdicate

of pretext a wolf would use against a sheep. Is there someone more apt to be called a rebellious subject than this?

Since there is some responsibility on the part of the emperor, considering that Emperor Go-Toba challenged Yoshitoki for the sake of frivolity and one of his favored princesses, we would never say, as the national polity theorists do, that Yoshitoki alone is a rebellious subject.[424] However, the fact that the Tokugawa clan persecuted the imperial family with evil actions which must now be kept out of the public eye is an abhorrent thought for those of us who try to observe history impartially. Yoshitoki employed passive self-defense against the emperor's challenge to overthrow him. However, the third shogun, Iemitsu, and others insulted Emperor Go-Mizunoo as much as possible and tried to exile him to Oki, as Yoshitoki had done, until he could no longer bear his anger and abdicated. The fact that he led an army of 350,000 men, spearheaded by Masamune Date, into the capital was a demonstration of the utmost pride.

Also, look at the bold policies of Hakuseki Arai,[425] who was called the talk of the high and low roads, and who predicted the theory of sovereignty that

---

his throne.

[424] Even Chikafusa Kitabatake, who was well-known for his dislike of the samurai class, was quoted as saying, "Yoshitoki became regent, but he was not guilty of any crime, not even defying popular opinion. It is the crime of the Emperor Go-Toba to pursue Yoshitoki on the grounds that the Minamoto clan was broken off after three generations." (*Jinno Shotoki*) It should be noted that even he thought Emperor Go-Toba wasn't in the right here.

[425] Confucian scholar of the mid-Edo period. He studied Confucianism under Junan Kinoshita and served Tokugawa Ienobu, who became the sixth shogun. After Ienobu became shogun, Hakuseki Arai participated in the shogunate administration and proposed various reforms known as the "Shotoku Reign." He's particularly famous for establishing the Kaninnomiya family and changing the sovereign message to Korea to

would later arise. He planned to strip the emperor of what Dr. Aruga called his honor rights and to make the shogunate the pure sovereign, or supreme governing power. Of course, his successors took the opposite and regressive course, and with his death, this was never carried out. However, he was a far greater conspirator than Yoritomo's accomplice, Oe-no-Hiromoto.

The *Tokushi Yoron* attributes to him the following:

> The dynasty had already fallen, and the warrior class ruled the nation, with the emperor as the common lord of the world. In name the warriors are the people, but in substance they are not. We have already received government positions from the emperor, but we do not follow his operations. If we in government positions command, "Those who serve us should follow our operations," how can the subordinates agree to it? And what we receive is also the emperor's office, and what our subjects receive is also the emperor's office. When both sovereigns and vassals receive the emperor's office, they are in reality vassals of the shogun, but in name they are both vassals in the service of the emperor. How can these vassals respect us in substance? The constant rebellion during Yoshimitsu's reign was the result of his immorality, but it was also due to the people's lack of substance in respecting their lord. That lord was already a vassal of the people. How could they forever avoid the crime of the inferior stealing from the superior when they had taken in a dynastic subject, named him their own subject, and made him their

---

"King of Japan" (these are written about in detail in his auto-biography, *Oritaku Shiba no Ki*). As a student of the Cheng-Zhu school of Confucianism, he took the position of the theory of reverence for the king, but he considered the foundation of the shogunate's power to be based on natural fate, and did not adopt the theory of the imperial court's mandate, as was the case with the theory of reverence for the king at the end of the Edo period.

vassal? Since the state of the world has already changed, we should determine the current courtesy according to that change. In other words, to respond flexibly. If one is unaware and uneducated, he should study the ancient and modern examples of China and Japan in order to make a name for himself. And if there were a system in which the emperor were to descend as the highest rank, and all the people of the sixty or so provinces, except the dynastic lords and daju,[426] were to be his subjects, it could be successfully applied even in this day and age..."

In other words, this is the point at which the revolutionaries of the Meiji Revolution, who denied the rights of the lords of the shogunate based on the emperor's sovereignty theory of the so-called theory of national polity at the end of the Edo period, composed their revolutionary theory, and it is also the attitude that naturally goes with the sovereignty theory of the shogunate, which completes Ieyasu's legacy.

Hakuseki didn't stop at speech, either, but ventured to put it into action. Educators love to tell elementary school students about his diplomatic negotiations with the Korean envoys, claiming that they were an achievement that enhanced national prestige, but in fact this was merely a controversy that arose because the shogunate itself broke with conventional practice by calling itself king of Japan and lowering the rank of the envoys,[427] placing them after the three imperial families. It is truly ludicrous to praise such a rebellious and atrocious rebel subject as having reverence for the king and loyalty to the monarch.

---

[426] In Hakuseki Arai's language, this refers to "5th ranked samurai."

[427] Hakuseki Arai gave a positive impression of "ruler of Japan" to the term "king of Japan."

He also tried to mix the blood of the imperial family with that of the shogunate, as the Fujiwara had done, by arranging a marriage between an imperial princess and a shogun.[428] In the shogunate system, the kimono and ancient head-dress was made the same degree in all cases, and the reply to an imperial edict was changed to be given on an equal footing. This historical evidence does not indicate the existence of a shogunate, especially not of a barbarian shogunate, as might be inferred from the form and pronunciation of the characters and words. Rather, it was a responsible cabinet. Of course, as historical research occurred, the theory of the sovereignty of the emperor came to power in the academic world under the name of the so-called theory of national polity, as the oldest records of this theory coincided with the Confucian dialectic of the low and high road. Although there are examples of the superiority of the shogunate sovereignty theory, such as the work of Sorai Ogyu, it is true that the feudal system was overthrown because it could not compete with the evolution of a society in which a view of equality developed. Moreover, as this became an actual movement, one can only imagine how the powerful class of the time, that is, the aristocracy of the shogunate lords, persecuted the revolutionary party of lower-ranked warriors.

The hardships of the loyalists as described in poems and recited in songs today are precisely the hardships of being persecuted by all Japanese people at the time. Needless to say, the loyalists before the overthrow of the shogunate were the true "exceptions," few as they were. Persecution of speech, for example, was carried out to an astonishing extreme. Shikibu Takenouchi,[429]

---

[428] This was arranged with the young seventh Shogun Ietsugu. However, this engagement was annulled when Ietsugu died of illness.

[429] Shinto man of the mid-Edo period. He preached the idea of the reverence for the emperor in Kyoto, and his students, including Tokudaiji Kinmura, gave lectures to Emperor Momozono and court nobles.

who lectured on *Seiken Igen*,[430] was exiled for disturbing the Imperial Constitution,[431] and the chief councilor of the state, Mitsutane Karasumaru,[432] along with seven others who heard his lecture,[433] were stripped of their official positions and imprisoned. The few honor rights reserved for the emperor which Mr. Aruga mentioned were, as Hakuseki worried, the only reason left to argue for the sovereignty of the emperor. As such, the shogunate tried its best to violently suppress them.

Emperor Kokaku, whose father was only a chief cabinet minister,[434] tried to make his father a Daijo Tenno in accordance with his own honor. Although this was a natural request of human emotion, Sadanobu Matsudaira ruthlessly and firmly rejected it. Instead, he summoned to Edo the two court nobles who had been serving as the samurai family advisors,[435] rebutted the argument,

---

[430] A book by the Confucian scholar Keisai Asami.

[431] The regents were concerned that having Takenouchi Shikibu and others lecture on the theory of the reverence for the emperor within the imperial court would damage relations with the shogunate. Despite the emperor's protests, chief advisor Konoe Uchisaki cancelled the lectures, punished twenty people, including Oogimachisanjo Kintsumu, who was seen as a representative of the Tokudaiji group, and filed charges against them with the Kyoto Office. In response, the Kyoto Office banished Takenouchi Shikibu from Kyoto. This incident is commonly referred to as the "Horeki Incident."

[432] Mitsutane Karasumaru was a nobleman (1723–1780) of the mid-Edo period. The original text has a spelling error, suggesting Kita spelled the name out from memory.

[433] In the Horeki Incident, a total of twenty-seven officials were punished, but since twenty had already been punished by the imperial court, the "seven" referred to here are thought to refer to those newly punished by the Kyoto Office.

[434] This rank is the third rank of subordinate. With this level of official rank, he is inferior to the Fujiwara and Seiga families.

[435] The "court nobles" here specifically refers to a position in the Edo period that served as an intermediary between the emperor and the samurai. They were Kinaki Ogimachi

and ordered the court nobles who agreed with Emperor Kokaku to refrain from doing anything.[436] His father, Sukehito-shinno, was only granted an additional two thousand koku in compensation for both his blessing and prestige.[437] The three hundred years of the Tokugawa Shogunate were, indeed, an era of rebellious subjects, more so than that of Yoshitoki and Takauji, from beginning to end. After all this, could one still say that these three hundred years are a mere "exception"?

We will not simply enumerate countless facts. With the exception of the primitive period of legends before the introduction of writing, which lasted about one thousand years, the subsequent 1,500 years of written history have connected the hands and feet of rebellious subjects like a coot monkey in order to create the history of Japan. Of course, the imperial family, as the primary power, was powerful and had the right to rule until the earliest historical records were compiled. During this period, along with idealistic monarchs such as Emperor Nintoku and tyrannical despots such as emperors Yuryaku and

---

and Naruchika Nakayama. However, Naruchika Nakayama wasn't, strictly speaking, a samurai missionary, but held the position of councilor.

[436] The so-called Songo Ikken. The course of the incident is generally the same as described in this text. However, it's thought that the severe attitude on the part of the shogunate in this case may have been caused by the earlier problem of rebuilding the Imperial Palace. The shogunate, which was struggling with financial difficulties over the reconstruction of the palace destroyed by the Great Fire of Tenmei (1788), proposed a modest palace, but the imperial court, which was in the midst of a mood of restoration, strongly demanded that the palace be rebuilt in a grand style. As a result, the shogunate was forced to build the palace at a cost of over two hundred thousand ryo. The shogunate, shouldering a heavy burden at a time of financial hardship, may have felt that it could no longer comply with the imperial court's demands.

[437] The original text reads "two thousand tsuto." "Tsuto" refers to "something wrapped in straw." It's very likely these were bags of rice, so we translated it as such.

Buretsu, the development of society and the growth of the population had already made the Soga clan powerful, producing idealistic, rebellious subjects, and turning them into despotic rebels who wielded tyrannical power. Then, a bold idealist emerged from the royal family and finally defeated the rebellious subjects,[438] but this lasted only one hundred years. As soon as history began being recorded, rebellious subjects known as the Fujiwara clan were born to replace the Soga clan. And after the departure of the Fujiwara, who dreamed of a moment of prosperity in the arrogant and conceited government of Emperor Shirakawa, the violence of the rebellious subjects known as battle monks soon appeared, who were then dealt a blow by Kiyomori, another rebellious subject, until Yoshinaka Kiso swept them away, becoming a rebellious subject himself. The rivalry between Yoshinaka and the cloistered emperor was so blatant that it was a comedy.[439] Yoshinaka bragged,

> I have already defeated the cloistered emperor. Will I become an abdicated emperor? If I become an abdicated emperor, a child ('s hairstyle) would not be good.[440] However, if I wish to become a cloistered emperor, a Buddhist priest ('s bald head)[441] would look strange as well.[442]

---

[438] Emperor Tenji.

[439] Kiso Yoshinaka imprisoned Cloistered Emperor Go-Shirakawa and had him approve of the title Great Shogun.

[440] Emperor Go-Toba was very young at the time, so he wore his hair in a child's hairstyle. From this, it is said that Yoshinaka misunderstood that emperors were supposed to wear their hair in the same way as children's hairstyles.

[441] It's said that he was under the mistaken impression that he had to have a shaved head in order to call himself cloistered emperor, since Cloistered Emperor Go-Shirakawa had been ordained as a monk.

[442] In *Heike Monogatari*, volume 8, "Hojuji Kassen," there is a line that goes as follows.

And Minamoto-no-Yoritomo, who defeated this rebellious subject, was (according to the laughable Mr. Aruga) a man who had been entrusted with the exercise of sovereignty through fraud, not to mention a rebellious subject himself. Yoshitoki, who appeared next, was (again according to the laughable Mr. Aruga) one who was entrusted with the sovereignty by appealing to the sword, and was, of course, a rebellious subject as well. Then came the era of the rebellious subjects known as Yasutoki and Tokimune, until finally entering the era of the rebellious subject known as Takatoki.

The Hojo clan was finally defeated by the imperial party of the time and the rebellious subjects disappeared, but another rebellious subject, Ashikaga Takauji, was born and defeated the imperial party. When Yoshimitsu came to power, the dance of the rebellious subjects was fully performed. The Ashikaga clan took this bloody stage, but the world eventually moved on to the Warring States and the rivalries of local warlords, filling the entire nation with

---

"To begin with, I, Yoshinaka, said I would stand against the cloistered emperor, and I was victorious in battle. Shall I become emperor, or cloistered emperor? Choose I to be emperor, a child's form would not suit me. I ponder becoming cloistered emperor, but a monk's form is not fitting either. Very well, I shall become chief advisor." (*Heike Monogatari (Ge)*, [Tokyo: Iwanami Shoten, 1993], 110). Kita's original text reads, "I defeated the cloistered emperor. Perhaps I shall become cloistered emperor, but those are monks. That would look strange, but an emperor is a child's, and a child is also not something fitting." It's quite different from the one in *Heike Monogatari*, so we've translated it using more from *Heike Monogatari* instead. Additionally, historian Hiroyuki Miura has stated the following regarding the above passage: "I can't even bring myself to translate the words that are written in this book that Yoshinaka is purported to have said. . . . There isn't a single person who reads it that wouldn't feel like they're reading a bad comedy." (*New Edition of History and People*, [Toyko: Iwanami Bunko, 1990], 99–100). As historical fact, it's likely to be as Miura says. Yoshinaka probably never made such wild statements.

rebellious subjects. The imperial family falling into poverty, even lacking basic food and clothing, did nothing to deter the flow, and upon finally arriving at what was thought to be peace, a monkey-faced rebellious subject appeared and boasted, "If I wish to become king, I can. If I desire to become emperor, I can."

Next came the Tokugawa clan, a period of consistent rebellious subjects, which began a three-hundred-year-long period of imperial persecution and ended by impoverishing the patriots of the Imperialist Party—we are going to stand before the history of Japan alongside the very national polity theorists and ask for a verdict.

Oh, the forty-five million people of today are almost all descendants of rebels and their accomplices. How can we assert that the people of Japan unite their spirits as one and serve the one eternal lineage of the imperial line when we only need turn to any page in Japanese history to see the facts which disprove this?

However, for those whose intelligence has been beaten into a pulp by the phrase "one eternal lineage," seeing these facts will only stimulate a few doubts. So we must not only show the "deeds" of these rebellious subjects, but also explain their "ideology." Political history and ethical history must go hand in hand to interpret historical phenomena.

CHAPTER 12

The history of Japan is as described previously. If we remove from political history the primitive period, which is said to have lasted a thousand years but which essentially exists as a legend, as well as the period of Takamagahara, the Japanese people have attacked and persecuted the imperial family for almost the entire 1,500 years since written history began, almost as if they were nothing but a bunch of rebellious subjects united only in the spirit of attacking the imperial family. What kind of ideology is this based on? We are not merely looking at the surface of political history and attempting to reverse what has become an established theory in the past and present. Instead, by examining the deeds described in political history and by inductions obtained from the history of ethics, which examines ideas, we have discovered that the historical interpretation of the theory of national polity is totally inverted, like the geocentric model. The history of all peoples, who originally branched off from one another, share a common path of social evolution as human beings. Therefore, political history and ethical history are narratives and explanations of the facts and reasons for the evolution of a particular people, while the philosophy of social evolution, which is applicable to all peoples, is the basis for the political and ethical history of all peoples (we hope you have finished reading the previous volume, *The Theory of Biological Evolution and Social Philosophy*).

And just as the history of all peoples, ancient and medieval, should be interpreted with the principles of lineage and loyalty and filial piety as the framework, the history of the Japanese people, ancient and medieval, should also be interpreted with the principles of lineage and loyalty and filial piety as the fundamental ideas, as a natural course of social evolution. Previously, we said,

The assumption of this principle of lineage of a pedigreed people has been true for all peoples of the world throughout antiquity and the Middle Ages. However, it is a total fallacy to conclude that Japan's history is dedicated to the imperial family of one eternal lineage. The assumption that Japan was a nation of loyalty and filial piety is true, but it is also true throughout the ancient and medieval periods of all peoples of the world. However, it is obviously false to conclude the history of Japan by assuming that the Japanese people had been nothing but loyal to the imperial family for over 2,500 years.[443]

We also said,

[I]n fact, because the Japanese people honor family lineage through this principle of lineage, they actually persecuted the imperial family. They have also attacked the imperial family because they considered loyalty and filial piety as the ultimate good.[444]

This tone of rejection is the same as the heliocentric theory against the geocentric theory, and is merely an attempt to break down the pope-like inverted superstition of the theory of national polity, but the very principles of lineage and loyalty and filial piety that are common to all peoples were the reason why the Japanese people attacked and persecuted the imperial family throughout history as rebellious subjects.

We have been saying for some time that all Japanese people are rebellious subjects in emulation of those who criticize retroactively. Such retroactive criticism, however, is a falsehood that comes from taking the side of the imperial family instead of critiquing morality as it evolved. In other words,

---

[443] See page 426

[444] See page 426

what was a rebellious subject from the imperial side was instead a very loyal and righteous subject from the other side, that of the rivals of the imperial family. The Japanese people, in their attempt to fulfill the moral duty of loyalty and filial piety to the nobles whom they serve, have become accessories and accomplices to their master, while from the perspective of the imperial family, they have become rebellious subjects. To reiterate, the Japanese people, like all peoples, were so devoted to the principle of loyalty and filial piety that they made it their moral duty to attack the enemies of the patriarchs they served at the cost of their own lives, and thus became rebellious subjects. At the time when the imperial family appeared in opposition to the patriarchal monarchs, the Japanese people, as moralists with great loyalty and filial piety to said patriarchal monarchs which they served, emerged as bold rebels against the imperial family, overpowering it.

Today's national polity theorists open their mouths to condemn Yoshitoki and curse Takauji. They know that Nogi did not capture Port Arthur alone,[445] and that Togo did not sink the Baltic Fleet alone,[446] but they think that rebellious subjects do work alone. What a pitiful savage village of the Orient! Do they not know that the reason why Yoshitoki was able to establish a secure position in Kamakura, and moreover to exile the three emperors to Oki and

---

[445] Refers to Maresuke Nogi, an army general during the Russo-Japanese War who led the invasion of Port Arthur. The Russian fortifications were sturdy, so he had a rather difficult time. (Akiko Yosano's younger brother was in the unit that carried out this operation.) Maresuke Nogi is also famous for his martyrdom upon the death of Emperor Meiji.

[446] Refers to Heihachiro Togo. He was appointed commander-in-chief of the Combined Fleet during the Russo-Japanese War and fought against the Baltic Fleet in the Sea of Japan. The Baltic Fleet was the main fleet of Russia, which was said to be the strongest in the world at that time. The sinking of the Baltic Fleet was truly shocking news that spread around the world.

Sado, was because 190,000 people defeated the imperial army, captured the emperor, and disposed of him in compliance with Yoshitoki's orders? Do they not understand that Takauji was able to drive Emperor Go-Daigo out of Kyoto because his ancestors, organized with a navy of seventy ships and an army of 200,000 men, defeated Masanari at Minatogawa? We demand reflection and introspection from a great number of Japanese people. Anyone who says that the Russo-Japanese War was won by the patriotism of Mr. Nogi and Mr. Togo alone, and all the Japanese people were loyal subjects of the Russian emperor, either Russian spies or traitors to our country, are simply madmen. Similarly, how could anyone but a village of savages come up with such nonsense as to say that only Yoshitoki and Takauji were rebels and that the rest of the Japanese people were loyal subjects of the imperial family and righteous warriors who had served their country well and helped the one eternal lineage of the imperial family?

History is not shaped by the whims of two or three people. They merely represent and stamp the actions of the nation in history as a sign that expresses the thought of the nation as a whole. Therefore, if we do not regard the history of the Japanese people as the history of Yoshitoki or Takauji, and if we do not regard the narrative of the imperial family as the history of Japan, as historians do today, Japanese history as the history of the people is indeed the story of rebellious subjects against the imperial family. The recorded representatives, the signs which are stamped in history, are not the only rebellious subjects. The "Japanese people" who lurk behind the well-known personages are indeed the rebellious subjects towards the imperial family. And from this imperial point of view, being a rebellious subject was a natural consequence of the ancient and medieval history of the principles of lineage and loyalty and filial piety, as it was for all peoples.

First, we must say one thing about the primitive period of legends which lasted for one thousand years. For all peoples, the principles of lineage and loyalty and filial piety existed as buds before history began being written down.

The Latin peoples, who were the earliest to achieve democracy in antiquity, initially had nothing but absolute and unlimited patriarchal power and the accompanying morality of filial piety, even after their migration to Greece and Rome, let alone during the period before. The Germanic peoples who form the European democracies of today passed through a primitive, republican, and egalitarian period, and like the Latin peoples, were subjected to monarchical rule and family systems throughout the long period of medieval history. Therefore, the principle of loyalty and filial piety was the only supreme morality at that time. Similarly, even though it was an era without writing, and the intervening years are of course only a period of trivial legend, if we do not regard the earliest historical records as meaningless, and if we can at least roughly estimate the time several hundred years before our written history (and in our historical records, unlike with the records of other Germanic peoples, records of the primitive, republican, and egalitarian period were not told to the rest of the world by the observations of other peoples,)[447] we can imagine that the period when the history of the Japanese people came to be written began with the inheritance of the principle of lineage and the principle of loyalty and filial piety. In that "matrilineal age," when there is no permanent matrimonial relationship, or even no awareness of matrilineal lineage, as in a more primitive society, the primitive village exists only as an equal republican group, with an instinctive social nature. They live peacefully, sometimes fighting, with no or a very weak sense of paternity, which is forgotten as they grow up. There is no moral imperative of filial piety, no complex relationship of domination and submission other than the simple beliefs and a few customs that form the basis of public law. As a republican organization based on primitive equality, there was no reason to demand the class morality of loyalty—this is why we said earlier that the patriarchal system was not a primitive stage of mankind, nor was it the final form.

---

[447] We assume he's thinking about something like *Germania* by Tacitus.

In the same way, the loyalty and filial piety associated with the patriarchal system is not a morality that humanity has had from the beginning, nor is it the final authority in life. In other words, filial piety is a morality that arises when a people reach a certain level of evolution and the patriarchal system arises; it is a class morality that arises when a people evolve to the point of conscious unity under the patriarch. First, the relationship that awakens social consciousness is that between the mother and the child, as the child begins nursing on the mother's breast, and the social consciousness awakened only between mother and child gives birth to a matrilineal lineage, which is further extended to the father and becomes a patrilineal lineage. This lineage in turn extends to the siblings, their wives and children, and their siblings, and thus three or four family lineages exist together in one family. The population gradually increases and the distinction between the main family and the branch families is born, and when the branch families are linked to the main family by a sense of lineage, it becomes the patriarchal system and the process of social evolution based on the principles of lineage and loyalty and filial piety begins. In the patriarchal system linked by lineage and loyalty and filial piety, the primitive religion of the time, ancestral religion, espoused the immortality of the ancestral spirits, and unified rituals were performed under the patriarch of the head family. The patriarch of the head family, as the head of the rituals, also had absolute control over his family and branch families as the spokesman of the ancestors, thus forming a monarchy that was united in its political and religious beliefs.

One can imagine that the Japanese people, perhaps having experienced primitive, republican, and egalitarian times in other lands, and having formed a unified political and religious patriarchal system under Shintoism, began to write the first part of their history in an era when history was written according to the principles of lineage and loyalty and filial piety.

In other words, the patriarch demands filial piety because he is the father of the children, and at the same time he demands loyalty because he is the ruler of a family. Loyalty and filial piety are public morals that are awakened in the competition for survival between villages (see our discussion of parochial socialism in *The Theory of Biological Evolution and Social Philosophy*), and they are also the most primitive of personal morals that sprout under the patriarchal system. In these most primitive times, the patriarch was the one who demanded loyalty and filial piety, so the idea of loyalty and filial piety coincidence was not a fabrication in the slightest, and phrases such as "the sovereign is the mother and father of the people" and "the people are the children of the sovereign" were not meaningless historically-derived expressions as they are today.

However, the idea of being the living object of loyalty and filial piety could only be said of a single family. When a family is gradually divided into dozens of branches from the main family, each family has its own patriarch, who becomes both the father to whom each family should look up to and the sovereign whom each family should obey. As the relationship between the main family and branch families gradually becomes less and less related by blood, it becomes necessary for all the members of the main family and branch families to look toward the spirits of their distant ancestors, who they look up to as their common fathers, as the link between the branches. In other words, they worshiped the spirits of distant ancestors not only to fulfill filial duty to them, but also to be faithful to them by obeying what was believed to be the commands of these ancestors. When the legendary ancestor of the imperial family, who was later gifted the name Emperor Jinmu, led his family group to conquer Japan, he said,

> The spirit of my ancestors descended from the heavens to illuminate and save me. Now that the numerous schemes have been put

to rest and there is no unsettling movement, let us worship the heavenly deity and express our great filial piety.[448]

This is, of course, a retrospective account from *Nihon Shoki*, a collection of supposed legends from later generations, as well as something spoken in the manner of Chinese literature, and so should be read with great caution. However, the phrase, "Let us worship the heavenly deity and express our great filial piety," is there because Amaterasu was the target of great loyalty and filial piety, and the national system of patriarchal government was based on the belief in the immortality of the ancestral spirits, making the ideas of the master-servant family and loyalty and filial piety coincidence absolute facts.

However, this should not be misunderstood. The fact that there was a single family of masters, and servants of extended families to honor them, merely indicates that the conquerors from the Jinmu family became sovereigns under the patriarchal system, and formed a family of servants under Amaterasu. The conquered slaves and lowly people were, of course, the property of the patriarch just as the family was, but they were not members of the family. Of course, they were not related to the countless family groups that had migrated to the area before and after the conquest. The coincidence of loyalty and filial piety, as in Emperor Jinmu's words, means that loyalty and filial piety coincided only toward the joint ancestor of the main and branching families, Amaterasu, in that they obeyed the commands of Amaterasu herself and expressed great filial piety to Amaterasu. It was not about expressing coincided loyalty and filial piety toward Emperor Jinmu himself, as the branch families, some members of which must have had hair even whiter than Emperor Jinmu, did after they split off from a common ancestor with the main

---

[448] This decree is found in Emperor Jinmu Chronicles in *Nihon Shoki*. It is said to have been issued on the twenty-third day of the second month of the first year of Kanototori, when Emperor Jinmu ascended to the throne at the palace of Kashihara.

family. Emperor Jinmu was only supposed to be the representative of their common ancestor, Amaterasu.

The way Mr. Hozumi describes today's Japan as a patriarchal nation, using an explanation such as an extension of the life of an individual, is the way of science after the invention of the microscope. To falsely claim that the present emperor is a living embodiment of Amaterasu because he is an extension of Amaterasu's body, and that the present emperor himself is fulfilling the same coinciding loyalty and filial duty, not only ignores the classical texts, but also defies Shinto beliefs. How can it be interpreted that a relationship of loyalty and filial piety forms between the equal extension of Amaterasu's life—that is, the branch families known as the Japanese citizens, and the emperor, who is also an extension of Amaterasu's life—in other words, a relationship between the molecules of one large individual, Amaterasu? Indeed, the so-called national polity theorists are heretics in the eyes of Shinto and traitors toward the classic texts.

In any case, during the time of the ancestral religion, it was believed that Amaterasu, the ancestor of the imperial family who was the most powerful being in the Kinki region, actually existed as a spirit and gave orders through the mouth of the head of the family, the patriarch. Therefore, since loyalty and filial piety were in coincidence with each other toward Amaterasu (and also toward the patriarchs of each family), loyalty and filial piety were practiced without the slightest contradiction, and the spirits of the patriarchs of each family and the distant patriarchs connecting them became the highest authority as the focal point of loyalty and filial piety coinciding. Of course, prior to the time when history was written and recorded, there were only legends, and we use them only as material for scientific reasoning. But the commands of the emperor (and the patriarch family groups of a certain land, who were gifted prestigious titles) were obeyed without question by members of these family groups as the voice of the body of both loyalty and filial piety, Amaterasu (and the distant ancestral patriarchs of the various families, as spoken of in the legends).

Even if we take the most solemn scientific attitude and place all emperors in the era of *Kojiki* and *Nihon Shoki* outside of recorded history, it can be sufficiently deduced that the patriarchs and their distant ancestors were the source of power as the main body of loyalty and filial piety, which occurred through the primitive religion of ancestor worship, which in turn was a process of both social evolution and the patriarchal system that was created when social consciousness was awakened through tracing lineage. And this is what it means that the ancestors of the imperial family came to the family groups of these various regions as either the patriarch, which is the main body of coincided loyalty and filial piety, or as the representative of the distant ancestral patriarchs. The majority of the family groups scattered throughout most of the other regions each had a patriarch or patriarch representing a distant ancestor who was their own main body of coincided loyalty and filial piety, and they used this to resist the imperial patriarch. As the saying goes, "The rough people far away still do not submit to my rule." The ancestors of the majority of the people in the one thousand years known as the primitive period, spoken of as legends, were independent and outside the theory of national polity. In the villages of the primitive people, each village existed as a different family unit united under a different patriarchal spirit, with no communication with each other, competing independently because of their different patriarchal spirits. In any case, the Japanese people, like all other peoples, gradually evolved from primitive times through the principles of lineage and loyalty and filial piety, and finally came to have historical awareness, which required them to record their history in order to pass it on to future generations. Thus, Chinese characters were imported and history began to be written.

The period in which history began to be written was a time of expansion and development of various large clans, which interchanged with each other as rebellious subjects. The Soga clan, mentioned earlier, is most notable because of its remarkable power—and this was likewise due to the principles of lineage and loyalty and filial piety.

Of course, the principles of lineage and loyalty and filial piety that emerged after the arrival of Confucianism and Buddhism differed greatly from the belief in the immortality of the patriarchal spirits held by the ancestral religion, and was not loyalty in the sense of great filial piety toward the common ancestors of the main family and branch families. The social consciousness that awakened in a family or a clan by tracing its lineage united that family or clan under the patriarch as a social group, and turned the definition of loyalty and filial piety into working for the benefit and purpose of the patriarch. The social consciousness was most active among close relatives, but gradually faded as they became estranged from each other. Thus, the powerful classes such as the omi and muraji,[449] who were originally branches of the same ancestral lineage as the imperial family, saw their respective patriarchs and immediate family members take precedence by a much more active social consciousness of loyalty, as compared to the much less active social consciousness of loyalty to their distant, original family. Finally, when the main imperial family and the patriarchs of the branch families—based on the equality of being of the same bloodline and the same branch—came into conflict with each other, the social consciousness of kinship led the families and branch families to serve their own patriarchs or those of their immediate families with loyalty and filial devotion. This made them submit to the moral obligation to attack the imperial family (we have already indicated the difficulties of the theory of loyalty and filial piety coincidence, which is now

---

[449] "Omi" (臣) and "muraji" (連) were titles in the ancient Yamato Imperial Court. Omi refers to a powerful family with a foundation in a certain region. Muraji refers to a powerful family with specific duties. The Soga clan were omi and the Nakatomi clan were muraji.

based on the order of moral fulfillment accompanying the degree of love, as taught by the Imperial Rescript on Education, and we are certain the reader understands that this was not done for no reason).

In these times, social consciousness was limited to a very narrow range, and the family or clan was the unit of competition for survival. The fact that the Soga clan defeated the ancient great clans of Mononobe and Nakatomi in this competition, and then began competing with another great clan, the imperial family, is one example of this. Social consciousness does not expand all at once. It awakens gradually, following one's own bloodline, and that bloodline begins to ostracize those of other bloodlines (see the section in *The Theory of Biological Evolution and Social Philosophy* in which we argue that the unit of competition for survival gradually expands from a narrow one).

Therefore, only the families of the emperor's immediate relatives were patriarchs who were loyal to the emperor, while other competing families, such as the omi and muraji, simply followed the principles of loyalty and filial piety under their own patriarchs and clan chiefs. Because of their sense of equality with the emperor as members of the same bloodline and their weakened social consciousness, they acted as estranged members of the same family when their interests differed from those of the emperor, and their relationship with the emperor became one of irrelevant bystanders during times when they had nothing to do with the emperor. When they had a conflict, they led their own families and clans and became rebellious subjects. There was never a time when only one single person was a rebellious subject. The fact that various large clans became rebellious subjects in turn is not simply because their patriarchs were inclined to do so alone, but because the family groups united by the closest bloodlines to those groups were loyal to their patriarchs and family heads. The fact that the imperial family was oppressed by the Soga clan for a long time before it took the initiative and stood up for itself is also due to the fact that many family and clan patriarchs led their family groups via loyalty and filial piety, and simply stood by and watched.

Because of this, the exemplary hero, Emperor Tenji, sought to transcend the patriarchal system and create an ideal state of national sovereignty with a single emperor as the supreme authority. Such an ideal state, however, could only be realized at a much later time. It was then something that could only be dreamed of in ancient societies, where society had not yet evolved and social consciousness was only slightly awakened through lineage. It's similar to how socialism could only be realized after the full development of the capitalist system, yet many idealists tried to build ideal states in newly emerging countries. The civic state idealized by Emperor Tenji could not be realized by interrupting the historical progress of the patriarchal state, but would require a widespread awakening of social consciousness in all the molecules of the state after a long evolutionary process, just like the patriarchal state required before it. And so, it is clear that Emperor Tenji's plan was merely his idealist utopia, which disappeared with his death, and that the imperial family itself existed as the patriarch according to the patriarchal state of the time, thus giving rise to the era of Fujiwara tyranny. The era of Fujiwara tyranny was indeed one in which the family or clan, a lineage of close kinship, was the unit of competition, and under the patriarch or clan leader, the members of that family were united by the principle of loyalty and filial piety, standing above the emperor for hundreds of years and making the patriarch or clan leader a rebellious subject.

The principles of lineage and loyalty and filial piety advocated by the so-called national polity theorists produced rebellious subjects, who attacked and persecuted the imperial family from the first page of Japanese history, when the ancestors of the imperial family existed as patriarchs.

From then on, it was the medieval history of the Taira, Minamoto, Hojo, Ashikaga, and Tokugawa clans. The patriarchal state of these clans was formed by a succession of rebellious subjects, and as a natural consequence, the vassals under these patriarchs attacked and persecuted the imperial family out of loyalty toward their patriarchs. Obviously, the ancient and medieval histories are very different in that society was organized solely on the basis of bloodlines, even if this shows the same patriarchal trend. It is understandable from the above explanation that only one family from the Minamoto clan lineage and one family from the Heike family lineage worked as rebellious subjects due to the patriarchal system and the principle of loyalty and filial piety, but the fact that many ancestors outside of these lineages were equally rebellious must be attributed to special reasons in accordance with social evolution. Let us begin by discussing the principle of lineage.

This explanation will be easily understood by those who have studied, in some detail, scientific ethics, such as the origins of morality and the formation of conscience. The essence of morality is sociality, which exists as instinct. However, in order for the form of morality to become an act, sociality must first be created by external compulsion in a way that is adapted to the times and the locality. Morality is the sociality thus formed, and to speak of it simply as morality is to speak of it only in terms of ideas, as if it were an atom in physics. It appears in action only as a local morality, as a period morality, as something formed by a society of a specific region and specific time. Today's barbaric village custom of enforcing even the most trivial of punishments with the utmost severity is a form of sociality that is shaped by external coercive forces. The ancient religion of ancestor worship and polytheism regarded everything from the sun, moon, and stars to dogs, horses, trees, and stones as deities, and there were countless deities everywhere that acted as external observers and enforced morality.

As society evolves, however, this external compulsion is gradually transferred internally, becoming the coercive force of conscience, which itself becomes a supreme order, without cruel punishment or supervision by a myriad of gods. Thus, we enter the age of autonomous morality. The evolutionary process of moral autonomy and moral heteronomy is an evolutionary process that takes place throughout a person's life, from childhood to adulthood. Similarly, society, as one large life, evolves from the age of moral heteronomy to the age of moral autonomy as it grows and develops.

Even the sequence of the moral development of the Japanese people is not exempt from this principle. The legendary one thousand years of time until the reign of emperors Ojin and Nintoku, before the importation of foreign civilizations, even if we accept these years as mere legends, are a repetition of barbaric acts like those of the savages of the South Pacific, who today have a history of tens of thousands of years. The natural consequence of primitive times was an age of moral heteronomy in which society was maintained by a myriad of external forces ranging from the sun, moon, wind, and lightning to serpents, birds, fish, and stone gods, not to mention all the spirits of our ancestors.

However, with the advent of Confucianism, Buddhism, and other autonomous moral systems of more advanced societies, those who had previously been united under the patriarchs by a heteronomy of the principle of lineage were now taught a clear sense of autonomy. The people came to regard lineage-based unity as the highest moral good, and began to willingly perform all acts under the guidance of their own conscience, without waiting for external coercive forces such as the spirits of ancestors or physical punishment.

Conscience, however, is merely the body of moral judgment, and the content of how one judges moral conduct is entirely created by the social environment after birth (see *The Ethical Ideal of Socialism*, where we explain the reasons for the formation of conscience). And since morality is created by the existing society before it evolves, there is nothing else for that morality to do but to maintain society as it is, and that is made into its very first duty. Therefore, even if we speak of an autonomous morality based equally on conscience, it did not transcend over existing morality, question existing morality, or set forth a more evolved moral ideal, not to mention that we speak of a time when society was less evolved than it is today. Plus, in the medieval period of the Japanese people, who were sealed off by the sea, there was no opportunity to compare and contrast one's own morality with the morality of other societies with different degrees or directions of social evolution in order to obtain a more evolved moral ideal and to criticize the existing morality, as is the case today.

Thus, the formation of conscience was entirely projective and imitative, limited to the acceptance of the moral customs and ethical precepts that existed in society. In this moral age of unquestioned imitation, it is not surprising that in the Middle Ages the value of lineage, once revered by all peoples, was greeted like a thirsty man seeking water. Through the breeding of the same bloodline due to population growth and the development of social consciousness due to social conflicts and upheavals—in other words, by following or transcending bloodlines—the view of human equality was gradually extended, yet from whom exactly descendants came was considered very precious and passively created the content of moral judgment as those to whom absolute obedience should be given.

Such lineage worship is not limited to the Japanese people. In ancient and medieval times, when social consciousness developed along the lines of lineage, it dominated the conscience of society for a long time, even among the European peoples of today. This is exemplified today by the attempt of the Holy German Emperor, who still defecates while putting on airs of being a member of his insignificant Hohenzollern family, to resist social democracy. And this worship of lineage was especially strong in medieval Japan, where their isolation due to the seas prevented rapid development, and any rebellious subject could act as a rebel because of the respect for his lineage and the adoration of that lineage that the people had.

The Fujiwara, who claimed to be descended from Amanokoyane-no-Mikoto,[450] excluded other classes of people through pride in their lineage and

---

[450] A deity that appears in mythology. It is said that when Amaterasu hid in Ame-no-Ihayato, Amanokoyane-no-Mikoto prayed for her to come out by reciting a prayer of congratulation. As pointed out in the text, he is considered the ancestor of the Fujiwara

concentrated the people's worship on themselves, thus overthrowing the ideals of the Taika Revolution set forth by the imperial court. The descendants of countless princes, who are spoken of in legends to have gone to the various provinces from the time of Emperor Sujin, settled in those provinces. They held pride in their lineage as being of the same branch as the emperor, and this became the bud of the aristocratic states that would later flourish and then perish as the feudal lords of the country.[451]

The Taira clan, always proud of their descent from Emperor Kanmu, and the Minamoto clan, equally proud of their descent from Emperor Seiwa, were able to act as rebellious subjects to the fullest extent, thanks to their ancestral conscience that regarded their lineage as the noblest in the world. The facts recorded in history clearly prove this. Taira-no-Masakado, of the first local clan to awaken to political power, and who became a bud of the later aristocratic state, granted himself the right to steal political power via his pride in his lineage. He said, "I am the grandson of Emperor Kanmu,"[452] in order to appeal to and control the conscience of lineage worship. There is no recorded evidence one way or another on whether Kiyomori, of the same lineage, did whatever he pleased in later years because of the same general ideas, but everyone knows that the plunder of the Minamoto clan was justified via concentration on the conscience of lineage worship using a single phrase, which showed the pride in their lineage: "descendant of Hachimantaro, otherwise known as Minamoto-no-Yoshiie,[453] who was in turn a descendent of Emperor Seiwa." The imperial

---

clan and is worshipped at Kasuga Taisha Shrine.

[451] Strictly speaking, almost no Warring States daimyo held this lineage. Most of them are forcefully linked to "Genpei Tokitsu."

[452] Not actually his grandson. He's about five generations after Emperor Kanmu.

[453] He went to Mutsu and pacified the Former Nine Years' War and Gosannen War, and established the Minamoto clan's power base in the East. The name "Hachimantaro" is another name for Yoshiie, and comes from the fact that Yoshiie had coming-of-age-

decrees that were often issued, forbidding warriors from belonging to the either of the two clans of Minamoto and Taira, serve as an example of the intensity of lineage worship.

The local nobles and provincial governors, in whose lands the Minamoto and Taira clans simply spent the night while passing through, became vassals of the Minamoto clan and the Taira clan. Of course, many of them were happy with being independent and unbounded during the period of what is called the Genpei War, which temporarily divided the country in two, and many of them followed whoever they pleased in accordance with their own freedom. Without the slightest connection of lineage, some simply followed the noble lineage of Tametomo because he was in Kyushu for a while.[454] Others say that they considered it an honor to their family name that they surrendered to the Taira clan when they came, and they consider that as belonging to an honorable lineage. All of this is evidence of just how the most minor of occurrences could result in people becoming vassals or subjects. The more fiercely loyal they were, the more fearless they became of being considered rebellious subjects when the imperial family appeared as an enemy before the Minamoto or Taira clans.

The Hojo clan was so inferior in lineage that it sought to compensate for its weakness through improvements to government, and always humbled itself to the point of being forced to settle for a lowly sub-fifth class rank. Nevertheless, the words of the nun general who raised a bamboo screen and cried out in indignation made one hundred thousand generals swear to die with tears dripping down their faces,[455] and the ascendants themselves, satisfied with being unified under Hojo's decree, finally became such rebellious subjects that the three emperors were banished.

---

ceremony at Iwashimizu Hachimangu Shrine.

[454] Eighth son of Minamoto no Tameyoshi. He was powerful in Kyushu.

[455] The "nun general" or "nun shogun" was Hojo Masako.

Takauji Ashikaga easily defeated Takatoki Hojo because he was a descendant of the Minamoto clan, which was far superior in terms of bloodline honor. When Takauji rebelled against Emperor Go-Daigo, the people again followed the noble descendants of the Minamoto clan and remained loyal to him. The enthusiasm toward Takauji was so great that a popular saying spread that "the descendants of Hachimantaro Yoshiie will surely take over the country."[456]

And when Yoshimitsu wanted the position of chancellor of the realm and could not obtain it, he said the following:

> Yes, yes. Yoshimitsu shall be king of the land, and I will appoint Shiba, Hosokawa, Hatakeyama, Rokkaku, and Yamana as the five regent houses, and Toki, Akamatsu, Niki,[457] Kyogoku, Yamauchi, Isshiki, and Takeda as the seven regent houses, and the other daimyo as other surnames. Following the form of the Sugawara and Oe families, the families shall be established under the surnames of Tachibana and Kiyohara, and those who are vassals of the lords and are renowned shall be designated as warrior families. Let Ujimitsu,[458] the lord of Kamakura,

---

[456] Yoshiie predicted, "The seventh generation of the Yoshiie will take the nation." However, Ietoki, the seventh generation of the Yoshiie family, could not bear the heavy pressure and committed suicide, leaving a "will" stating that he would leave his legacy to the third generation after him (e.g., his grandson). That grandson is said to be Takauji. This is written by Sadayo Imagawa in *Nantaiheiki*.

[457] Guardian of Iga from the Nanbokucho Period to the early Muromachi Period. A member of the Ashikaga family.

[458] Ashikaga Ujimitsu. Deputy Shogun of Kamakura at the time of Yoshimitsu (note that the quoted text refers to him as the "lord of Kamakura," but this is a misnomer for deputy shogun, since the lord of Kamakura was an assistant position, and the Uesugi clan was appointed to this position too). He had an ambition to supplant Yoshimitsu, but was

be the shogun, and if he should follow the correct path of Bushido and conduct his affairs in a civil manner, he would be called the Holy Emperor.[459]

When he confiscated the estates of the various lords and set about expropriating them, he claimed the right to do so on the honor of his lineage, saying, "I am a descendent of Emperor Seiwa, so I never behave irrationally."

The Japanese people persecuted the imperial family because they worshiped family lines based on the principle of lineage. The premise that the Japanese people were a people who followed the principle of lineage is something that's true of all ancient and medieval peoples. However, to conclude that Japanese history was one of helping the imperial family of one eternal lineage because of this principle of lineage is an obvious fallacy. This point is precisely why we have said all this.

While the principle of lineage was a form of lineage worship for the lower classes, for the nobility, which were the worshipped lineage, it was an explanation for the implementation of a bleak egalitarianism, on the grounds that the emperor and oneself were of the same lineage. Masakado, of the Taira clan, tried to be independent, saying, "I am a descendent of Emperor Kanmu."

---

admonished by Uesugi Noriharu, the Kanto lord, to cancel the plan.

[459] In an anecdote recorded in the military chronicle *Ashikaga Chiranki*, Yoshimitsu is said to have said this to a court noble who told him that it would be difficult for him to become Chancellor of the Realm. In *Two Thousand Five Hundred Years of History*, it's written, "He became the son of the emperor himself, confiscated the domains of a hundred lords and princes, made the Hosokawa clan and others his regents, and desired to make Hatakeyama and others the Seika rank. The Emperor Go-Komatsu was astonished and dismayed to hear this, and ordered Yoshimitsu to become Chancellor of the Realm." (Yosaburo, [1896 ed.], 459). The imperial court submitted to Yoshimitsu's strong stance and granted him the title of Chancellor of the Realm.

Yoshimitsu Ashikaga, of the Minamoto clan, tried to expropriate land, saying, "I am a descendent of Emperor Seiwa, so I never behave irrationally." Such actions as these are nothing more than following bloodlines in order to gradually develop the idea of equality. (The reader will see that we did not unnecessarily ignore history in our reasoning when we said earlier that the theory of master-servant coincidence was actually a bold egalitarianism which would end up as a suicidal theory that cancels itself out.)

Next, we will discuss the principle of loyalty and filial piety. Unlike the ancient morality of loyalty, which also meant the same thing as filial piety toward the spirits of distant patriarchs that linked the patriarchs of the time, loyalty itself eventually developed as a fully autonomous morality, and the people attacked and persecuted the imperial family as rebellious subjects in fulfillment of their moral obligation of loyalty. All morality is for the survival and evolution of society. Moral judgments are made in response to the survival and evolution of society. And the forms of society are organized differently according to their different economic relations. This is something we all know today: savages in an environment that cannot meet their economic needs do not consider eating human flesh evil, nor do they consider the killing or abandonment of infants immoral. They have different morals for different economic conditions. The Brazilian savages consider it a moral right to beat an old man to death with a stick as big as one's head when they migrate, and the Eskimos consider it their moral duty in times of famine for old men themselves to initiate a village meeting and decide to commit suicide. These are both unusual moralities that accompany social organization in times of economic scarcity. China, however, with its economic needs fully met, has a completely different moral code, and since ancient times has regarded respecting and nurturing the elderly as the highest good. In today's civilized world, killing a child is considered a horrendous crime. These are, of course, only extreme examples, but it can be inferred that the morality intended to maintain the survival of a society differs drastically depending on the economic environment of the society in which it is situated.

If we understand the fact that the organization and morality of a society differ depending on its economic condition, and realize that this is not cynically limited to only land or gold, but also encompasses the material resources that sustain life, it is only natural that a society, a large individual organism, would change its organization and the morality that connects it according to its purpose in order to sustain life in different economic conditions. Society is indeed an organism, and organisms take on forms adapted to their environment for the purpose of evolution and survival (see *The Theory of Biological Evolution and Social Philosophy*). Therefore, the evolution of morality comes from the evolution of society, and the evolution of society comes from the evolution of economic conditions. Thus, ethical history, which looks at moral evolution, and political history, which looks at social transition, can all be understood by examining economic conditions over time.

In slavery, where some human beings were property under the ownership of others, there was a morality of submission to their status as property. That is, a morality that recognized the right of other human beings to gift, buy, sell, or kill slaves, where one's own body did not belong to oneself, but to the person who owned it as property. This is the most primitive slave morality known as loyalty, in which the family under patriarchal ownership and the descendants of subjugated slaves are first required by external coercion to submit to their status as property because of the social construction of the morality we just described.

However, as the era evolved from this period of moral heteronomy through external coercion to an era of autonomous morality through internal coercion, a morality called "loyalty" arose, in which one considers the lord's disposal of one's own body as property as the supreme command of one's conscience—in other words, one's moral obligation to destroy one's own life for the sake of the lord's interests.

In the era of moral heteronomy based on slavery, the most primitive form of loyalty, the enforcement of morality had to be demanded by chains and whips in Europe, and perhaps even more brutally in Japan, by external coercion in the form of punishment. In Japan, however, the situation was not the same as in Europe, where slavery was maintained by chains and whips until recently. This was because European nations had always enslaved newly-independent foreign equals through foreign wars or through the capture of Negroes, and had needed chains and whips to suppress their independent spirit. Slaves in the period of Emperor Jinmu's emigration, and later ancient Korean and Emishi slaves, appear on record to have been independent-minded rebels in the first or second generation of slaves, but their slave descendants were socially created with consciences that, via heteronomy (and later autonomy), approved absolute submission to their status as possessions. (See *The Ethical Ideal of Socialism* for how the creation of conscience is freely and quickly shaped by the social environment.)

The extreme version of this slave morality, which submits to the disposition of property, is dying as a martyr. Just as Plato included human slaves and women in his socialist public ownership of property because they both had no status of human personality and were property, so it is because they were property that the lords buried their subjects, wives, and concubines in the ground as martyrs, along with gold, silver, jewels, stones, and other possessions. And as the most extreme fulfillment of loyalty, martyrdom[460] was said to cause constant crying day and night, so in the primitive period leading up to the Suinin dynasty, slavery was a complete heteronomy in Japan as well, as a natural consequence of primitive morality.

This slavery, which viewed mankind as property, continued in Japan until much later in history. While this economic condition and its accompanying

---

[460] "Martyrdom" here in the original Japanese is referring to a specific type of ritual suicide called *junshi* (殉死), wherein a vassal commits suicide upon their lord's death.

social organization existed, only martyrdom, as the disposition of property, could not be eradicated from society. Because society had evolved to a great extent and social consciousness had been sharpened by the influence of Confucianism in this evolving society, Emperor Suinin replaced martyrdom with the use of dogū clay figures.[461] However, pure slavery still existed under the name of "lowly people," and the buying and selling of slaves was done by notification to the government office. Just as how the calf of a cow would become the property of the farmer who owned that cow, if the slave who bore a child tried to sell that child themselves, they were punished as if they had committed theft. Similarly, one can see just how widespread the practice of martyrdom was at the time by looking at how, after the Taika Revolution, martyrdom was forbidden under the gravest punishment of triple-line execution.[462]

Slavery, in which human beings were treated as property, continued even in the Middle Ages; during the period of Japanese imperialism, there were slave traders and slave trading ships which sold and traded them. When slaves became sick, as in Rome, they were left in the corner of a hut or on the side of the road, or, as in the story of Obasuteyama, when they were old and no longer useful, they were thrown into the mountains or forests. The morality of loyalty is indeed a slave morality that strips humanity of its status as a human personality and submits it to the disposal of its owners as property. So it is not surprising that the disposal of property, such as martyrdom, continued to exist under various forms in the name of loyalty during the existence of slavery. As the age of autonomous morality entered, slaves gradually came to have personalities of their own, and when a lord was killed in battle, his family children and roto died as martyrs by the side of his corpse.[463] This is

---

[461] Referring specifically to haniwa.

[462] The "triple-line" refers to parents, siblings, and wives and children.

[463] A "family child" is a member of a warrior family who is related by blood to the head

exemplified by the fact that, despite the strict punishments imposed by the shogunate on the lords of the Tokugawa period,[464] there were always two or three samurai who became martyrs upon the death of their lords, as if they were offering themselves to the dead. The phrase "A chaste woman must never remarry. A loyal subject must never serve another lord,"[465] is thought to have taught women and subjects to recognize in autonomous morality that they were the property of their husbands and sovereigns, thus mitigating martyrdom to a small degree.

Indeed, Bushido in Japanese medieval history is quite beautiful in that it advanced to an autonomous morality. However, it meant the inheritance of a slave morality that approved of the gift and slaughter of humans, which were supposed to have their own personality, as the property of the monarch—that is, as a physical object under the monarch's ownership. This is an evolutionary step that all peoples must go through at least once in the process of social evolution and moral development, and it is not limited to Japan. Another example would be that, in the medieval history of Europe, because they were aristocratic nations like Japan, they gave birth to the concept of "chivalry," which placed the most emphasis on loyalty, the same as in Japan.

It is important to note, however, the **gradual** evolution of society. The patriarchs of the aristocracies of the Middle Ages, who owned the land and the people as objects for their own purposes and interests, had gradually evolved

---

family. A "roto" is a follower who is not related by blood to the head family.

[464] It was during the reign of the fourth shogun, Ietsuna, that martyrdom was prohibited for the first time. In 1663, the newly promulgated Samurai Laws, which accompanied the change of shogun, stated, "Although there have been many people who have been killed in the line of duty in recent years, and there are many more who will be executed in the line of duty in the future, it must always be insisted that they not be killed in martyrdom to their own Lords."

[465] Words from "Dentanden" in *Shiji (Records of the Grand Historian)*.

from the ancient patriarchal system, and the people, who were property, were to some extent recognized as persons in this system rather than the slaves they were under the ancient patriarchs. In other words, humanity itself was no longer treated as property directly under the ownership of the nobility, but since the land that nourished humanity was the property of the nobility, the economic subordination to the land led to the consideration of humanity itself, which was nourished by the land, as subordinate to the landowner, the nobility. It was, as one would say, an indirect relationship. This is why the common people, as serfs, were inherited, given as gifts, or slaughtered as if they were the property of the nobility. In particular, the fact that the warriors could not of their own volition reject a gift given to them by the nobles they served, and that they could not independently defend themselves even if the nobles executed them at will, was precisely because of the slave-like servitude that resulted from this economic subordination to the land.

And just as today's scientific ethics divides the evolution of morality into an instinctive moral age, an imitative moral age, and a critical moral age, the process of moral evolution in any nation, until the Middle Ages, was an imitative moral age in which it was not possible to critique existing morality and to set up a transcendent moral ideal based on this critique. Therefore, even though society had already evolved and entered an age of autonomous moral forms, it had no choice but to imitate and accept the moral teachings of slave obedience that had existed in society since ancient times. In this respect, the Bushido of medieval history came to regard slave obedience to one's sovereign as the highest good.

Bushido, with its majestic and splendid autonomous form, was a very noble moral form, yet the content of its moral judgment was filled with slave-like obedience. This is because of two reasons: economic subordination that resulted from the aristocratic class's occupation of the land, and the imitative moral age, a standard of the medieval period. It was the same with chivalry in Europe, both in its medieval history and in the later class state.

This is what we mean when we say that political and ethical history can be understood by examining economic conditions over time. Those who are independent in their economic foundations have independent political and moral rights, and those who are subordinate in their economic foundations are obligated to obey both politically and morally. Thus, in ancient times, when the emperor was powerful and owned all the land (which, however, was effectively limited to the Kinki region and was later divided among the various great families), all the people were political and moral subjects under him.

However, in the aristocratic period following the Genpei War, the aristocracy, which also gained economic independence through the plunder of land by its powerful forces, rejected their political obligations as subjects and moral obligations of slave-like servitude to the emperor thanks to their new position of political and moral freedom. The family children and roto samurai or serfs were subordinated to these rebellious subject with the political obligation to serve the nobles as their masters and the moral obligation of slave-like servitude under said nobles, based on their economic subordination to the aristocratic class. Thus, when the aristocrats, to whom the people were subordinate, asserted their political and moral freedom and independence in the form of so-called rebellion, the Japanese people in the Middle Ages became the ones to exercise their loyalty due to their economic subordination. In doing so, they became complicit with the rebellious subjects, attacking and persecuting the imperial family.

Yoritomo's teachings during the infancy of Bushido, "the lord and the subject should be mutually indebted to each other," can be seen as an explanation of this economic subordinate relationship, in which the lord grants land and a stipend from economic benefits, and requires the subject who receives the land and stipend to be subordinate to the beneficiary in return for the benefits. The Bushido that developed thereafter said, "I offer my life to my lord for my reward. Consider that my life is not my own." The reason for this commandment is that the subjects' families are sustained by the economic benefits of the lord. It implies the recognition of political and moral obedience arising from the relationship of economic subordination, that the life maintained by the lord's favor is a life to be discarded as a reward for the lord's benefit. Obviously, this Bushido, in its noble and autonomous form of making this loyalty the supreme command of conscience, made the thousand years of the medieval aristocracy a time of pervasive rebellious subjects toward the imperial family. In other words, they persecuted the imperial family because of their "Bushido conscience." This is exactly why we have said such things as, "the Japanese people attacked the imperial family because they regarded loyalty and filial piety as the highest good," and "the premise that the Japanese people were a people who followed the principle of loyalty and filial piety is something that's true of all ancient and medieval peoples. However, to conclude that all 2,500 years of Japanese history were years of dedication to the imperial family because of it is an obvious fallacy."

Today's national polity theorists are angered by the warrior class that arose along with Bushido, and they lament the decline of the imperial family because of the warrior class. Yet, they are struck in the skull with the hammer of the "one eternal lineage," and cry out "long live the emperor!" Behold this evidence of such a savage village. (The president of Daito Bunka Academy and professor of literature, Professor Tetsujiro Inoue, could be considered the chieftain of this savage village.[466] Read any of his works.)

The above explanation of the principles of lineage and loyalty and filial piety leads one to take a step further and consider the few exceptions of the so-called loyal imperial subjects and righteous warriors.

First, if we follow the national polity theorists in counting the loyal subjects and righteous warriors from the beginning of history, we can point to

---

[466] A philosopher who led the world of thought from the Meiji era to the early Showa era. He invited Koeber to Japan and promoted the introduction of Western thought, but later leaned toward nationalism.

the shogun of the four provinces and Takenouchi-no-Sukune, but such things are of primitive times, which we have eliminated from the scope of our discussions.[467] Those who would call Dokyo's actions, which were driven by love for the empress, treacherous and outrageous, would praise Wake-no-Kyomaro as a great loyal subject.[468] However, such things, too, are outside the scope of our discussion, and are merely the subject of a picture book. We dare not say that they were disloyal, but note that a large clan was lurking in the background and allowed for more daring actions to be taken. That large clan was the Fujiwara clan. There was no loyal retainer who could break even one finger until the decline of that clan.

Those who possess laughably poor intelligence would count Ariwara-no-Narihira among loyal subjects due to his poems, but he was such an egalitarian that he even communicated with the supposed empress, to the point where romance-focused poets later worshiped him. The Taira overpowered the Fujiwaras, but they could not be considered loyal subjects, and Yoshinaka overpowered the Taira, but he was still not a righteous warrior. Some would say that Tsuzumi-no-Hogan and his army of twenty thousand men,[469] who protected Emperor Go-Shirakawa against a wild samurai like Yoshinaka, were not disqualified from being loyal subjects. But what about the fact that these twenty thousand men were only half-samurai, half-thieves, made up of vagrants and bad priests who haunted the streets inside and around Kyoto?

---

[467] The four shogun who were sent out to conquer all four cardinal directions during the reign of Emperor Sujin.

[468] A nobleman of the Nara period. He was sent as an imperial envoy to confirm the authenticity of the divine message of Usa Hachiman Shrine. Upon his return, Wake-no-Kyomaro stated at court that no such message had been given, which angered Dokyo, and he was exiled. He returned to the center after Dokyo's downfall.

[469] Another name for Taira no Tomoyasu (a hokumen samurai of noble birth). He served as an envoy to Cloistered Emperor Shirakawa to negotiate with Yoshinaka.

Yoritomo, who defeated Yoshinaka and was entrusted with the execution of sovereignty, is an ideal loyalist to Mr. Nagao Aruga, but it is certain that the 17,500 battle monks who defended the three emperors against 190,000 rebels, all of whom attacked after being moved by a single widow's words, were not loyal subjects or righteous warriors. This is because the battle monks often threatened the emperor with a sentence to hell and followed him only out of self-interest. In fact, Shigetada was such a disrespectful man that he knocked on the gates of the inner palace and cursed, "It is a shame that I have been recruited into the company of an incredibly cowardly sovereign."[470] So, until the Hojo clan's defeat, there were no loyal subjects.

However, the Nitta and Kusunoki clans had loyal subjects. Of course, Nitta's initial attitude was one of freedom and economic independence, as the record attests. However, we don't believe that he acted around his own power, as we can infer from his blunt and unpretentious character. Nor do we fully

---

[470] Yamada Shigetada served Emperor Go-Toba and distinguished himself during the Jokyu War. According to the second half of *Jokyuki*, he fought hard against the shogunate forces, but was defeated, and afterward rushed to the Imperial Palace for the final decisive battle. Miura Taneyoshi said, "You have already lost the battle. Please open the gate . . ." but the decree of the emperor simply responded, "If you come hide in the palace, the Kamakura warriors will simply surround us and attack me, which I do not wish, so please flee somewhere else immediately." In response, Shigetada said that he felt sorry for Taneyoshi. (Yoshitada Tochigi, *Jokyuki, Hogen Monogatari, Heiji Monogatari*, [Tokyo: Iwanami Shoten, 1992], 349–350).

There's nothing about Shigetada's cursing in *Jokyuki*, but it does write, "According to an old printed text, Yamada Shigetada shouted in a shrill voice, 'I have been deceived by the emperor of utmost cowardice, and must die a dog's death!'" (Ibid., 350). The phrase used here for "deceived" can also be used to mean "to get convinced to join one's ranks" or "to be pulled into a group," It's likely that Kita's quotation was based on a different old book, as it's a little different.

agree with the view that the rivalry between the northern and southern dynasties was a war between Nitta and Ashikaga. The northern and southern dynasties were divided under the banner of Yamana and Hosokawa, and the Onin War was fought between them. It was merely the prelude to the coming war between the rival warlords, which was temporarily represented by the symbols "Nitta" and "Ashikaga." In the aristocratic periods of medieval history, each noble family was a ruler, even if some were united by coalition and others by oppression. In other words, we can well imagine Yoshisada as a man who first acted freely and independently as an aristocrat, who, as a simple, naive man, inherited without question the principles of lineage and of loyalty and filial piety of the imitative moral age, and who, by discovering the emperor with the most noble lineage, became the actual performer of loyalty, which was considered the highest good of the time. Otherwise, we would not be able to understand how he only shed tears and left after Emperor Go-Daigo's awful treatment of selling him off to make peace with Takauji,[471] or that he still had an imperial edict in the bag hanging around his neck when he was struck by a stray arrow and died. However, this should not be misunderstood. This was only about Yoshisada himself. His family children and roto were loyal to him because of their economic subordination. Whether the imperial family was an enemy or an ally of Yoshisada was irrelevant.

Masanari and Masayuki were the most outstanding exceptions. So, we don't believe, as the national polity theorists do, that he held ambition in his

---

[471] After Masashige Kusunoki was defeated at the Minatogawa River, the imperial court could no longer support Takauji's army. Emperor Go-Daigo then retreated to Mount Hiei. Nitta Yoshisada requested him not to make peace because they could regain their forces and position, but Emperor Go-Daigo did not listen to him and made peace. The point made in the text refers to this. Incidentally, Nitta was killed by a stray arrow while fighting against the army of Shiba Takatsune at Fujishima.

heart when,[472] under Takatoki's orders, he conquered Watanabe Jiemon of Settsu, Yasuda Shoji of Kii, or Ochi Shiro of Yamato,[473] all of whom were the first step in defeating the Hojo clan, who were against Takatoki. Nor do we think that Masanari should be singled out for special praise by likening his response to three summonses to Kongming's threefold visits.[474] Though it is also reckless to liken his death, like dancing flower petals, to a gonsuke's loincloth.[475] It is also easy to imagine that, at the time of his death at

---

[472] The original text says "one who questions the weight of the ding." This "ding" refers to an ancient Chinese pot, and the phrase means "to make light of the ruler and try to become one in his place." In other words, he's saying, "To follow Takatoki at first, but to lean toward the overthrow of the shogunate when the forces who wanted to overthrow the shogunate gained momentum, can be evaluated as a manifestation of ambition to replace the ruler, but this is not the case with Masanari."

[473] The Watanabe, Yasuda, Ochi, and others were powerful clans in the Kinki region who rebelled in the late Kamakura period. In *Koyashiyunju Hennenshuroku* and Razan Hayashi's *Kamakura Shogun Kafu* there is a record of Kusunoki Masashige's defeat of these powerful clans under the orders of the shogunate.

[474] Kongming refers to Zhuge Liang, who served Liu Bei and Liu Shan as vizier in Shu during the Three Kingdoms period. According to *Records of the Three Kingdoms*, when Liu Bei visited Zhuge Liang, he was away the first two times, and the two finally met the third time and Zhuge Liang accepted Liu Bei's invitation. Incidentally, the phrase "threefold visits" is derived from what Kongming himself wrote in the "Chu Shi Biao" presented to Liu Shan.

[475] "Gonsuke" refers to a servant man. In the Edo period, servants in general were sometimes referred to as "gonsuke" because many servants were named "Gonsuke." In Fukuzawa Yukichi's *An Encouragement of Learning*, volume 7, he argues the following: "It is not uncommon for a gonsuke to go on an errand for his master, lose one ryo of gold and, at a loss, decide to apologize to his master, hang his loincloth on a tree branch and hang himself. . . . Whether it is the death of a loyal retainer who kills ten thousand

Minatogawa, as a natural consequence of the imitative moral age, he died for the highest good at the time, loyalty, by serving the imperial lineage through the principles of lineage and loyalty and filial piety. This is something that cannot be interpreted as the economic independence of the aristocratic class, for in the age of imitative morality, unless one had an outstanding philosophical mind or otherwise stood outside the old morality and behaved as one pleased, such as Ko-no-Moronao, people fulfilled conventional morality without question. Even though Masanari alone can be said to be a loyal subject and righteous warrior of the emperor, the other three hundred men, as followers of Masanari, were loyal to Masanari himself and did not die for the emperor.

The story of Masayuki is truly a tale like a flower. Following his graceful, sober, and courageous character, as well as the strict moral teachings of his family during his early years, he did not fight for political ambition or economic power, but rather for the most dedicated of causes. However, the members of his own family who were named along with him in the halls of Nyoirinji Frog Temple were not willing to die for the emperor, in direct defiance to his attitude.[476] In particular, those who fought to the bitter end were those who

---

enemies, or the hanging of a gonsuke who loses one ryo of gold, the fact that these deaths do not benefit civilization in any way is the same for both.... These actions I have mentioned should not be considered 'martyrdom' in any way." (Fukuzawa Yukichi, "Masao Ito Proofreading and Annotations," in *An Encouragement of Learning*, [Toyko: Kodansha Gakujutsu Bunko, 2006], 114–115). Although Fukuzawa does not directly mention Kusunoki Masashige, he states in the first half of the book, "Many of them are related to the masters who fought for the two main governments" (Ibid., 113), which clearly implies Kusunoki Masashige. At the time *An Encouragement of Learning* was published, this was perceived as the "Kusunoki Gonsuke Argument," and caused a strong backlash. Kita must've been aware of this ridicule by Fukuzawa.

[476] Nyoirinji Temple is a temple of the Jodo sect in Yoshino, Nara. The temple was built

became his followers because they were so impressed by the shogun's character. They were greatly moved by his actions, such as his rescue of five hundred enemy troops who had fallen from the Watanabe bridge and were drowning in the bitter cold on November 26th,[477] during the Battle of Abeno,[478] and the fact that he even gave them new horse tacks.[479] Even the loyal souls of Minatogawa and Shijonawate were no different.[480] We would like to hear just how many of the ancestors of the forty-five million people of today, removing these two or three examples of true loyalists, were in fact loyal to the imperial family.

How it seems is how it was. Neither those who stood on the side of the imperial family to defend it nor those who willingly attacked it did so in order to become loyal subjects of the imperial family, righteous warriors for the imperial family, or rebellious subjects against the imperial family. They were all loyal to their respective masters, and this was a manifestation of their loyalty to what was closest to them. This point is most clearly expressed in the words of Nariaki Mito, a member of the aristocracy at the end of the Edo period, when the theory of national polity was increasingly advocated. He said the following:

> If people mistakenly think that they are repaying a favor to Amaterasu, and immediately think that they are going to serve the

---

at the behest of Emperor Go-Daigo.

[477] Watanabe is the name of a place around the mouth of the Yodo River in Settsu. It was often a battlefield during the Nanbokucho period.

[478] In the Battle of Abeno, Kusunoki Masatsura defeated the Northern Court forces.

[479] This is recorded in *Taiheiki*, volume 25, "Yamana Tokiuji Sumiyoshi Gassen-no-koto."

[480] Minatogawa is where Kusunoki Masashige died in battle, and Shijonawate is where Kuzunoki Masatsura died in battle.

imperial court and the emperor, instead of the lord and father before them, they will not be able to escape the charges of insolent rebellion.[481]

As an aristocratic class, it is natural to make this demand. The monarchs of the ancient and medieval class states, up to the Meiji Revolution, were consistent in this very idea of the lord and father who was before one's eyes. Without this "lord and father before one's eyes," there was no true loyalty and filial piety. The morality of filial piety does not exist between people who are not related to each other by blood or by any other special relationship that is comparably close. Likewise, the morality of loyalty can't arise without being the property possessed by another, or without economic subordination. So, for example, the forty-seven ronin, the most praiseworthy and idealistic example of loyal subjects and righteous warriors, were loyal subjects and righteous warriors because of their economic subordination to, as Nariaki said, the aristocratic lord and father in front of them. The idea of welcoming the shogunate's soldiers and using the castle as a pillow for their deaths had once been the subject of much discussion among the forty-seven ronin, but to become a loyal retainer of the shogunate and a vassal of the emperor, setting aside their immediate lord and father would, as Nariaki said, be a crime of insolent rebellion to them. Therefore, the three hundred men of Minatogawa who died as martyrs for their lord and father, Masanari, and the eight hundred men of Minatogawa who died as martyrs for their lord and father, Takatoki, and the thousands who followed them, did so because of their economic subordination to their lord and father, the aristocratic class. To these martyrs, who had sworn

---

[481] When Nariaki Tokugawa first returned to Mito in 1871, he presented his vassals with an eye toward reform, and these words are found at the beginning of his *Mitoke Uchiju e no Kyuyu* (Licensed Teacher Toward Those Members of the Mito Family). The "charges" here refer to "the crime of overstepping one's status or position and thus disturbing order."

an oath of allegiance, the insolent rebellion of becoming loyal subjects of the shogunate and righteous servants of the emperor over their immediate lord and father was unthinkable—this loyalty and filial piety to the lord and father before one's eyes is the key to the age of the class state, which is a time period that is common to all peoples.

In the period of the imperial family's immigration, the emperor and Amaterasu were the main bodies of loyalty and filial piety as the lord and father before the eyes of a limited family group and in a limited region. However, as society evolved and the population grew, various branch families of the same lineage as the imperial family spread their branches in the imperial court, and various powerful families spread their roots throughout the provinces. They then became aware that they were of the same bloodline as the emperor and developed a view that they were his equals, which led their loyal and filial followers to work as rebellious subjects towards the emperor. Another possibility is that, because of the principles of lineage and loyalty and filial piety of the imitative moral age, they belonged to the Genpei, to the Hojo, to the Ashikaga, to the imperial family, and then to nothing, as independents, and then to an independent group of men, and then to Toyotomi or Tokugawa, and then under those who belonged to the previously mentioned groups, and so on. This is how they organized a class state in the medieval aristocratic age. The people who followed the aristocracy had no choice but to follow the attitude of their immediate lord and father, the aristocrats, and to rotate around them like moons. Thus, they became consistent rebels against the imperial family, which possessed little land and little power.

Thus we affirm: the only people who were loyal subjects and righteous warriors with the imperial family as their lord and father in front of them were the nobles who were in economic subordination to the imperial family (the ancestors of today's court nobles and peers). All the rest of the Japanese people were enslaved under the aristocracy and were rebellious subjects and rebels of the imperial family. As the bud of the aristocracy existed since before history was first being written, the Japanese nation has been a rebellious subject of the imperial family for almost all of its history—this could be said to be the theory of heliocentrism as opposed to the pope's theory of geocentrism. Let us reaffirm: the Japanese people persecuted the imperial family because they revered lineage through the principle of lineage, and attacked the imperial family because they held loyalty and filial piety to be the highest good through the principle of loyalty and filial piety. The premise that the Japanese people were a people who followed the principle of lineage is something that is true of all ancient and medieval peoples. However, to conclude that Japanese history was one of helping the imperial family of one eternal lineage because of this principle of lineage is an obvious fallacy. The premise that the Japanese people were a people who followed the principle of loyalty and filial piety is also something that is true of all ancient and medieval peoples. However, to conclude that all 2,500 years of Japanese history were years of dedication to the imperial family because of it is an obvious fallacy. We must very quickly awaken from the pope's geocentrism.

Anyway, there still exists the problem which we have dubbed a hammer; a hammer which strikes the skulls of the Japanese people, reducing their intelligence—if all Japanese people were rebellious subjects toward the imperial family, how can the imperial line be one of one eternal lineage?

CHAPTER 13

What we have explained is all true, but in that case, why is the imperial line one eternal lineage? If the geocentric theory that the Japanese people are very loyal and dedicated to—the one eternal lineage of the imperial line—has been defeated, and our previous interpretation of the majority throughout history being rebellious subjects, with only a few exceptions who were actually loyal subjects and righteous warriors toward the imperial family, is correct, then there is reason to ask why the imperial line is one eternal lineage at all.

This interpretation of one eternal lineage is not only important as a historical interpretation, but it is also very important to the study of constitutional law, which studies modern national polity and systems of government. Of course, this is not to say that one can immediately interpret the modern Japanese Constitution merely by knowing the history of Japan, just as the British Constitution can't be understood simply by knowing its constitutional history. Even if the present Constitution was created by coming into contact with Western civilization and adopting a Western constitution, a nation does not change its framework just because it has put on a garment. The reason why those who uphold the theory of sovereignty today hold the emperor as the main body of sovereignty, and those who uphold the theory of state sovereignty hold the emperor as the sole supreme authority, is that both equally believe in the superstition of the geocentric model in Japanese history, and that is the basis for their interpretation of the Constitution.

Why is the imperial lineage unbroken? The explanation is still based on the principles of lineage and loyalty and filial piety. Also, the imperial family, unlike other aristocratic monarchs, was driven by the forces of the Shinto faith, although this became less pronounced in later generations. We must note the evolution of the content of the word "emperor," as discussed in the previous section on constitutional law. In other words, in primitive times, before the era of written history, there were countless family groups scattered over the land of Japan, and the imperial family stood as the patriarch of these family groups in the Kinki region, based on Shinto beliefs. This was the period described in detail previously, a legendary period of a thousand years when there was no writing, the concept of numbers was vague, and life was not much different from that of today's savages. During the legendary thousand years before we acquired script through exchange with ancient Korea, the population was extremely small, and not only the imperial family, but other omi, muraji, and other clans were not as large as later generations imagine. (The author of *Two Thousand Five Hundred Years of History*, the greatest historian since the beginning of Japanese history,[482] explained that the various great clans of that time gradually became powerful in order to show that they were merely the seeds of the monarchical aristocracy of later generations. He also showed with abundant facts that life in those days was purely primitive. However, it is regrettable that he named the history of Japan *Two Thousand Five Hundred Years of History*.) Many of the migrants from the three Koreas were independent or belonged to independent villages in the Kyushu and Chugoku regions, and had not yet entered the Kinki region to become naturalized citizens. Kyushu, Tohoku, and some of the Chinese provinces, through which Jinmu passed as the legends have it, were all independent primitive villages, united under the ancestral religion of a robust imperial family with ancestors of pure blood, and thus stood as powerful within the Kinki region as its conquerors.

The meaning of "emperor" in those days was completely different from the meaning of "emperor" in the period when the title was gifted, or from the meaning of "emperor" today. Back then, it signified the patriarch of a head family who acted as the head priest during ancestral rites—this was the first

---

[482] Takekoshi Yosaburo.

period of the word "emperor," when the content of the word had yet to evolve at all. We can look at the political and social status of the emperor in that period from the marriage of Emperor Jinmu (if we do not consider the whole legend to be completely meaningless), which we already mentioned earlier. The fact that Emperor Sojin collected bearskin and deer horns for his rituals is not enough to suggest that he was a Shinto priest, which would be much different from the significance of the emperor today. The ancestral doctrine, which says the spirit of Amaterasu never dies, united loyalty and filial piety, and the social consciousness, which was awakened by lineage, was based on the simple unity of one family group as the society and the exclusion of other family groups, thus creating the "main family" (be careful, as this meant the main family only within that family group), which consisted of the imperial family. This imperial family was the main body of supreme authority, so obviously the others obeyed it.

Essentially, the religion of ancestor worship, the master-servant family theory, and the theory of loyalty and filial piety coincidence are the first stage of social evolution common to all peoples, and there is no doubt that the Japanese people were equally linked by them to the social organization of primitive times. Even though the status of the imperial family can never be compared to its place in today's evolved period, it is clearly a fact that it was worshipped by the primitive religions of the time. (Dr. Hozumi's theistic constitutional theory is a revolutionary theory that is only possible when we reverse the laws of evolution, degenerate the emperor, who has evolved into what he is today, into the emperor of the primitive religious age, seal off the Japanese nation, reject the naturalization of foreigners, and replace the alien blood flowing in the veins of the people.)

However, the laws of evolution transformed the content of the word "emperor" from its previous meaning of head priest of the primitive religion, thus ushering in the second era. Japanese society itself evolved, and, after additional interactions with an even more advanced society and cultural exchange with ancient Korea, the emperor inherited all this advancement, evolving to a stage where he was the most powerful person and supreme authority in a time when all rights were determined by strength. We will hereafter refer to this system throughout the ancient and medieval periods as the "patriarchal national polity," and the period of monarchy leading up to the fall of the Fujiwara clan as the period in which the emperor legally evolved to the point where he was the supreme ruler as the owner of all Japan and its people.

Indeed, the Japanese people accomplished their first revolution while interacting with ancient Korea. Naturally, there is no basis to imagine whether the revolution was accomplished rapidly or gradually, since the period of contact with ancient Korea was several hundred years before classic texts appeared, but there would have at least been foreign interaction at any rate. This anthill of love then caused us to mix blood with the various naturalized races, and also caused the discrepancy in class between the conquered slaves and the conquerors.

In addition, the increase in the population caused a disruption of bloodlines and family lines, so that the social organization of the family unit could no longer maintain the purity of the primitive period. This upheaval was compounded by Confucianism and Buddhism, which were far more advanced than the primitive religions—especially Buddhism, which was the most highly evolved at the time, whether the people truly believed in it or it was merely idolatry. (Of course, it was the latter. Evolution is not a leap, and there is no reason why so many disparate, high-level beliefs should be understood at a time when people were only just beginning to break away from their primitive roots.) Buddhism, beginning with the upper class, completely eradicated the still-undeveloped Shintoism. The significance of the word "emperor" as a Shinto priest had to be completely changed.

Thus, the religious struggle took place under the banner of Soga vs. Mononobe. We believe that the religious struggle divided the imperial household itself into two armies. The Soga, who stood for Buddhism, assassinated the Shinto emperor Sushun because they differed in belief, which is something that should have been respected, while Prince Shotoku, who also stood for Buddhism, forced tears of compassion into the laws of cause and effect, and so allowed no reason to forcefully question the victory of the Buddhist party. See how society had evolved to the point where the "emperor" could not stand as a united patriarch under the ancestral religion, as his underlings were Han Chinese who were not members of the master-servant family and not related by blood to him at all! The two religions decided their clash of conscience by means of strength and power.

Mighty power itself is not good, but merely power. However, there is no power in that which is not good. Shinto was good in primitive times, but the good of the past is made evil by the good of the present, and the good of the present is made evil by the good of the future. In the same way, good and evil are only a process of evolution (see our discussion on class conscience and class struggle in *The Ethical Ideal of Socialism* and *The Enlightenment of Socialism*). The reason why social democracy lacks strength today is because there is still little in it that is recognized as good in the conscience of society. Similarly, the Buddhist Soga clan had more power than the imperial family not because they were a political force based on the economic power of their private lands and people, but because the people's ancestral faith had declined to the point where Buddhist goodness could overcome Shinto goodness.

However, a decision by immense power can be made on a plain with gunpowder smoke wafting up,[483] on the podium of a congress, or in a university lecture hall, but it can equally be made by the dagger of an assassin or the bomb of a revolutionary party member. The heroic Emperor Tenji chose the latter path, voluntarily attacking with the dagger and immediately proclaiming his theory of national sovereignty based on Confucianism.

---

[483] The expression "plain with gunpowder smoke" signifies a plain where a battle occurs.

Perhaps he was too much of a high-minded idealist. He did not believe in primitive religions and did not place the emperor as the chief priest. Nor was he like the later Fujiwara court, which had transformed Buddhism into an idolatrous religion where one should clasp hands together in prayer in front of bronze or gold Buddhist statues instead of clay or wood idols. Emperor Tenji sought to realize his ultimate goal, the Confucian ideal of the state with the emperor as the supreme authority for the good of the state (as opposed to the good of the people, which is a different subject entirely). However, this was of course impossible, and with his death, in accordance with the principles of social evolution, the nation became a patriarchal state of monarchical sovereignty in which the state was treated as a benefit for the emperor. With the overthrow of the Soga clan, the imperial family, along with their vassals of high merit, the Fujiwara, came to see the "emperor" as the owner of all peoples and lands by the right of the powerful. This was the second phase of the evolution of the meaning of "emperor" and marked the entry into the age of monarchy.

In such a patriarchal state, the emperor does not exist for the benefit of the state, but rather the state is a national entity treated as a means to fulfill the emperor's purpose (see the previous legal theory), and thus dividing, inheriting, and gifting the state are the free disposition of property by the owner, the emperor. While Queen Victoria could not inherit or donate the throne as her own property even after marriage, the former Empress Koken tried to make Dokyo inherit the state, which was her property. This is a clear indication of what we've described. This is an action that is incomprehensible regarding both emperors if we criticize them according to today's thought,[484] but Empress Koken's act was not illegal, it was within the rights of emperors

---

[484] Regarding "both," we assume one would be Emperor Koken's attempt to transfer the throne to Dokyo, but we wonder what the other refers to. Judging by "incomprehensible actions," it's difficult to interpret this as Queen Victoria.

at that time. For Dokyo, too, it was not as reckless as we might think (if, as later historians have said, it was an act of love). Especially since Empress Koken was a descendant of Emperor Tenji's younger brother and Dokyo was a descendant of Emperor Tenji's fourth son, we can infer that their love was not immoral in an age when both emperors were lineage-driven.

We said earlier that those who attacked and persecuted the imperial family did so via the principle of lineage. Dokyo was the first to awaken to this idea of equality, based on being of the same bloodline and same branch, and he did so via the honor of lineage and the chains of love. (This is the reason why he is known by later historians as "treacherous." And why Mr. Hozumi's theory of the master-servant family is the same as the treacherous Dokyo's logic as well.) The most remarkable manifestation of this lineage-based view of equality was the later appearance of Masakado of the Taira clan, who said, "I am a descendant of Emperor Kanmu," and Yoshimitsu Ashikaga of the Minamoto clan, who said, "I am a descendant of Emperor Seiwa."

However, it's obvious that, while this principle of lineage was, on the one hand, a source of equality for those of the same bloodline, it was also classist toward those of inferior or superior bloodline. Which is why we believe that lineage was both the reason for the attack and persecution of the imperial family and the reason for its preservation. And just as Shinto beliefs remain a force of inertia among the less reasonable men and women today (even among university professors, if Mr. Hozumi's worship of wooden genitalia is to be believed), so the evolution of society is not so clearly distinguishable.

Despite the great revolution of Emperor Tenji, which greatly reduced the power of Shintoism through Confucianism and Buddhism, there is no doubt that Shintoism remained a dominant force throughout the ancient and medieval periods. For the Japanese people, who had long been sealed off by the sea, Shinto beliefs were regarded as a theory of national origins, almost as if they were equivalent to Judaism, especially in that they were an exclusionary faith. Just as the belief that our people were the children of a special god and the rest were barbaric aliens was a belief that all of Japan had maintained until recently, the Japanese were equally unable to break free of their belief in Shinto until the end of the Edo period. This then became the idea of "reverence for the emperor, expulsion of the barbarians," and the idea that, while foreigners did evolve from monkeys, Japanese people were children of a god. This in turn caused a rejection of the theory of evolution and led to Mr. Hozumi's constitutional theory, whose after-effects still make waves even today.

Just as the exclusionist theory of Shintoism merged with the theory of reverence for the emperor through religious scripture, it is easy to imagine that egalitarianism would be restricted to the imperial family, which is believed to exist since the origin of the nation, as long as such a theory of national origins existed. In addition, it is easy to imagine that the elegant imperial family would have been in a position not to be invaded without reason in the ancient and medieval periods, when the principle of lineage was prevalent, in which the hierarchy of society was determined by the nobility of bloodlines.

In the Fujiwara clan, the family members under the chief, who were devoted to him by the principle of loyalty and filial piety, were not afraid to perform an entire cabinet strike if he gave the order, yet he did not lead his united and powerful forces to usurp the throne. This was precisely because the great imperial family was considered the direct descendant of the noblest lineage. It is true that the Fujiwara stood as guardians over the heads of this noble family and acted however they pleased as rebellious subjects, but this was a natural consequence of the chain of kinship and patronage. When the Fujiwara clan prospered and the various branches began to compete with each other for guardianship, the only way to obtain said guardianship was to bear an empress of one's own blood, and then to bring into one's own house the emperor-to-be, also born of one's own blood and raised by that empress, thereby establishing a stronger blood relationship than that of the other competitors. The fact that Dokyo represented his own bloodline with a sword and made it an element of his right to the throne is, to some extent, a confirmation of his actions, but in the age of the bloodline-oriented class state, the bloodline, of which he was proud and reverent, could not and should not have been violated by others. Therefore, the honor of the Fujiwara lineage retained privilege above all other lower classes, and the clan did not seek to supplant the honor of the imperial lineage, provided that privilege was not ignored and its demands were not rejected. But privilege has no limits, and demands that are satisfied give way to new demands. Thus, the principle of lineage provided a reason for the Fujiwara to act as rebellious subjects, and that same principle of lineage equally spared the imperial family, which had conceded everything, from turning the entire Fujiwara lineage into another Dokyo.

The same occurred yet again. The Taira imprisoned the emperor and ex-emperors, but did not harm them. The reason that Yoshinaka could not become a monk or a child, despite his boastful words, was that his bloodline-oriented conscience, which honored the lineage of the Taira and Minamoto clans, made him proud of himself in relation to them, but at the same time, he had a certain amount of hesitation toward lineages that had more royal blood than his own.

When their vassals, the family children, roto, and other local lords entered the imperial army in accordance with their loyalty and filial piety toward them, it was during a time when the medieval concept existed where one would first yell their names and long history proudly, then, for their honor, run into battle before the archers could even fire their arrows.[485] In addition, after noble Buddhism became entrenched in the ideology of seclusion of the Middle Ages and came to regard the many deities of the primitive religion as a temporary

---

[485] In the Kamakura period, generals first appeared to each other in battle and began to talk to each other, saying, "Yes, yes, I am the one ..." stating their military history to date. Only after that were they supposed to enter the battle. It is said that there were several generals who honestly did this when raided and were killed.

manifestation of the Buddha, they dared not persecute anyone without cause, unless it was a pure nonbeliever such as Ko-no-Moronao.

We believe the following—that the emperor of medieval history was not only the patriarch over his land and people, but also the "pope of Shinto," above all the patriarchs of the nation. Any historical researcher should be most careful not to assume that the word "emperor" means the same thing in both ancient and modern times, simply based on the form and pronunciation of the characters. Mr. Aruga, for example, thinks that the word "emperor" is the same in all ages, as if its content has not evolved, and he interprets the word "great shogun" to mean something like today's army general. In those days, a great shogun had the right to rule over all lands and peoples he possessed, just as the emperor and other feudal lords reigned as patriarchs over their respective lands and peoples, and each was a ruler in his own right. The only difference was that he was the "Holy Roman Emperor of Kamakura," crowned by the emperor, who was the pope of Shintoism.

Although this is not a perfect metaphor, we are not saying that Japanese history and European history aren't different in some ways. After all, different countries cannot match each other's history perfectly. For example, the European pope stood purely on the basis of Christianity, whereas the Shinto pope wielded the same authority over his lands and people as other patriarchs, even aside from his Shinto beliefs.[486] This is also well illustrated when remembering that, during the monarchical era, when all people and land were his property, he was constantly in conflict with the other patriarchs. However,

---

[486] The purpose of this sentence isn't clear. In terms of having patriarchal characters, they may have been different, but the pope also had a territory and wielded secular power in the Middle Ages (Alexander VI, Julius II, etc.), so we don't see any difference in the fact that they exercised the right to rule. Rather, one difference from the Western pope that should be noted is that the "Shinto pope" believed not only in Shintoism but also in Buddhism.

unless we compile a history of medieval Japan based on the framework of the "Shinto pope," the "Holy Roman Emperor of Kamakura," and the many other daimyo, known as the "kings of various countries," we will be forced to hide the period of Japan's history during the aristocratic era as an unsolvable puzzle in the closet of the theory of national polity.

However, all historians, both ancient and modern, have always traced back the history of the nation to the theory of national polity and described it retroactively, positioned the great shogun as vassals of the emperor, named the military leaders and lords as "rear vassals,"[487] and angrily denounced the thriving military rulers as tyrants. What kind of ideology could have been the basis for the continuation of such an absurd practice for one thousand years? Because they continue to maintain such a savage mentality, they treat the medieval history of the aristocratic period, which all peoples experienced at least once, as a battle of wars and defeats, and are completely unable to understand modern Japan, which has inherited this history.

Just as the Roman pope, while belief in Roman Catholicism was still strong, had the Holy Roman Emperor stand outside his gates in the snow in order to humiliate him,[488] the "Shinto pope," during the time when primitive religion was still strong, wielded vulgar power from atop his sacred platform, controlling the great shogun such as the Yoshie, the ancestors of the Minamoto clan.[489] (Of course, this can also be seen from the fact that, until the fall of the Fujiwara,[490] the emperor was the strongest person, which is fitting for what we have named the monarchical period.) However, as Roman Catholicism

---

[487] A vassal held by a vassal.

[488] The Humiliation of Canossa.

[489] The highest position ever achieved by Yoshie was only "mitsunokami," and he never became a great shogun.

[490] Not the literal downfall, as the Fujiwara weren't destroyed, but rather meaning "lost power."

waned, the power of the Holy Roman Emperors grew stronger, along with that of the various kings, and finally political power violated the papal crown. Similarly, the "Holy Roman Emperor of Kamakura" freely revised and abolished the "Shinto pope" when the Shinto faith ceased to flourish.

Just as the Holy Roman Emperor could not maintain his dignity unless the pope crowned him, so it was true that the "Holy Roman Emperor of Kamakura" was decorated by being crowned a great shogun by the "pope of Shinto" while the power of Shinto faith was still strong. In fact, it's true that shogun and daimyo were still happy to be crowned and knighted by the imperial court even after the Shinto faith had lost much of its power, just as the German emperor still desires to be crowned emperor of the Holy Roman Empire for his own vain glory, even today. However, the imperial court was not like Gregory VII's—it was much more graceful. Then, during the Warring States period, it was impoverished, and grew even more so during the Tokugawa period, when the Tokugawa constantly imprisoned the emperor. Thus, the vanity of the "Holy Roman Emperor of Kamakura" or the "kings of the nations" were never attacked, and thus the emperors were never exposed to their mighty power. Even when rejecting Yoshimitsu Ashikaga's attempt to become chancellor of the realm, the "pope of Shinto" made a concession and did not refuse to appoint even Hideyoshi, who himself was titled a descendant of Amanoyane-no-Mikoto and had sought his lineage in the divine era, as regent and imperial advisor, even though he was of lowly birth.[491] (This is why the master-slave family theorist must approve of the right to say, "If I wish to become king, I can. If I desire to become emperor, I can," after taking over the nation.)

If the medieval emperor was the same as the ancient emperor in terms of ownership of the nation, then Hideyoshi's declaration that "I have taken the

---

[491] Hideyoshi initially claimed to be a descendant of the Minamoto clan, but later claimed to be a descendant of the Fujiwara clan.

realm by my own power" would be a repudiation of the emperor himself in an age in which power was the rightful ruler of all. Historical fact, however, says otherwise. Even though the emperors of the time had lost their lands and people to the point of scarcely having enough food and clothing, they continued to exist in their own separate world, independent of the powerful, because their honor as the "pope of Shinto" was not impaired.

Naturally, as society evolved, belief in primitive religions gradually declined. There is no foundation to believe that the Hojo clan's last resort of the simultaneous alternating succession to the throne is evidence of a decline in reverence toward the Shinto pope due to Zen Buddhism, or that the Tokugawa clan's cruel imprisonment and forced abdication of the imperial family was justified by Confucianism. However, despite the decline of their power, the Ashikaga clan did not set up the Northern Court and become the pope of Shintoism themselves, nor did the nobles of the Warring States call themselves emperors. This is because the content of "emperor" had become "pope of Shintoism," completely different from the "emperor" of medieval history, which was a powerful man who owned the country.

Just as the Christian pope came to be replaced by the Holy Roman Emperors of Europe, so the Shinto pope came to be replaced by the Holy Roman Emperor of Kamakura on the basis of extreme freedom during the thousand years of medieval history. However, the Holy Roman Emperors of Europe never willingly usurped the throne of the Christian pope, nor did they need to do so. Similarly, the reason that the Shinto pope didn't have his position stolen by the Holy Roman Emperor of Kamakura, whose goal was to take over the nation and become the strongest person within it, was because the significance and meaning of their existences were different from each other, and thus there was no need for such a thing. If the content of the word "emperor" is not determined according to the evolution of history, it would be incomprehensible that an emperor, holding the ancient meaning of "owner of the nation," and a shogun who proclaimed, "I have taken the nation by my own power," who was called "Tenka-sama"[492] by all in the nation, could coexist.

Of course, we do not say that the emperor has never, in hope of being something other than the Shinto pope, endeavored to be the possessor of the nation as in ancient times. However, hope and historical fact are two different things. Taira-no-Masakado, by virtue of being a descendant of the emperor, had the hope of replacing another emperor, who was descended from a different line. Historical fact, though, shows that such a thing never happened. He couldn't replace the emperor, but only served the same duty as Chen Sheng and Wu Guang before the later aristocratic state, being named a traitor.[493]

In ancient and medieval times, when power determined all rights, great power was necessary to acquire great rights. Look at the ancient emperors. Emperor Tenji, with his fearful and trembling vassals at his heels, leaped out and cut down the strongest man with his sword. The age of the monarchies of great rights was based on such great power. Jinmu conquered from Kyushu to the edge of the Kinai region. Yamatotakeru-no-Mikoto ran between the tiger and dragon with only a single sword. The idea of rights evolves with the passage of time. If we deny that the aristocracy's plunder by force was a medieval right, as we did during the French Revolution and the Meiji Revolution, we are forced to go back further into ancient history and draw terrible conclusions about the emperors of those times.

Because we understand history only through such retroactive criticism, we ignore the natural rights of Emperor Yuryaku, calling him tyrannical and outrageous, and consider Empress Koken's attempt to exercise her rights

---

[492] Another name for the shogun during the Edo period. They were also called "Kubo" (公方).

[493] Chen Sheng and Wu Guang were the leaders of a rebellion during the Qin Dynasty. This rebellion was suppressed, but it led to the destruction of the Qin Dynasty. The term "Chen Sheng, Wu Guang" is therefore used to describe the pioneer of something.

nothing more than irrational love because she was a woman. We insist that the absolute and unlimited power of the ancient emperors was an absolute right that came with great power. And we argue more forcefully than anyone else that the medieval emperors, as the popes of Shintoism, maintained one eternal lineage by virtue of the fact that the aristocracy were rebellious subjects.

Ah, national polity theorists! In this sense, one eternal lineage is a hammer to the face of those national polity theorists who shamelessly and arrogantly boast that our citizens express incredible loyalty. The emperor demanded to stand as a ruler over all peoples and lands with deep and profound virtue. It was a demand that he would not forget even in the midst of extreme persecution, even in the midst of deprivation for lack of food and clothing, even when he was asleep. The hammer we mentioned, however, is that the people always rejected this demand by appealing to some other mighty power.

What even is the theory of national polity? If we say that our people, who possess such a history, have been loyal to the nation and have dedicated themselves to the imperial family of one eternal lineage, then both Yoshitoki and Takauji were great loyalists and great righteous warriors, and what honor would there be for the father and son of Kusunoki?[494] Some would say the following: "Yet they didn't turn their blades toward the imperial line's one eternal lineage, did they?" We will say it again. What even is the theory of national polity? Because all of the people were, at every possible turn, complicit with the rebellious subjects, or even aided them, it made the emperor hopelessly unable to fulfill the demands of the people. If even this can be said to be a sworn oath of allegiance and dedication to the imperial family, then both the Hojo clan's simultaneous alternate succession to the throne and the

---

[494] Kusunoki Masashite is called "Big Kusunoki" while Kuzunoki Masatsura is called "Little Kusunoki."

Tokugawa clan's constant forced abdication of the emperor can also be said to be a sworn oath of allegiance and dedication to the one eternal lineage. After all, how could the lineage be severed when safety was ensured by imprisonment?[495]

The problem is not the continuity of the one eternal lineage, but the reason why the one eternal lineage continued. The one eternal lineage that continued for this reason merely represents the continued and unending succession of rebellious subjects. Those national polity theorists who defend it by saying it's an oath of allegiance should stand before the gates of the imperial palace, apologize, and wait for the death penalty! How could one say they were dedicated to or served? It is said that the character of the Japanese people is the same as that of the French, who slaughtered Louis XVI. However, during the time when the imperial family was the most powerful presence in Japan, most of the family, with only a few exceptions, were not like Louis XIV, largely because they followed the Confucian theory of state sovereignty as their political morality with conscience as their supreme command. They stood on the sidelines, outside the struggle for power, as elegant poets when their rights were oppressed by the rights of other powerful people. The phrase "one eternal lineage" is a clear expression of the high morality of the imperial family, and no one else in Japan can be honored by it. For the Japanese people, it's an expression of the fact that they've been rebellious subjects.

Suppose the emperor had opposed Yoshitoki by his desire for power, as King Charles did.[496] Who can say with certainty that Yoshitoki would not

---

[495] Kita is essentially saying, "Because his hopes of reigning again as ruler had been completely cut off, the emperor was not considered dangerous enough to be attacked. Therefore, nobody turned their blades against him." In other words, the reason the emperor was able to continue as one eternal lineage is because he had no choice but to live a life where he wasn't exposed to such danger in the first place.

[496] Since Cromwell is mentioned, it's safe to assume that this is about King Charles I of

become Cromwell? Despite the fact that he greeted the Eastern Army with an attitude of apparent surrender, not one person in the entire nation was willing to protect the three emperors from an exile that was more painful than death. This is a far more brutal retaliation than that of the French people, who by a single vote decided on the death penalty, even though it was an unavoidable measure to eliminate any claims of foreign interference. (I still weep every time I visit Emperor Juntoku's grave in my hometown, thinking of the poet's agony.)[497]

In the days when strength determined ownership, so-called cut-throat robbery, where the warrior would kill someone and take their gold, was a custom of the samurai, so we will be using robbery as an example. A robber wields a blade for the purpose of taking a wallet. Only a homicidal maniac would wield a blade after obtaining the wallet. The offspring of a cut-throat robber who already has a well-stuffed wallet does not become a homicidal maniac toward those who lost their wallets long ago. Yoritomo was a robber who made clever threats, and Yoshitoki was a robber with a devious weapon. The shogun of the Hojo, Ashikaga, and Tokugawa clans, who staunchly defended their founder's business, were wealthy chiefs who had inherited wallets swollen with money stolen by their ancestors. They were all successful robbers. But for what reason should a robber simultaneously become a homicidal maniac, or a wealthy chief do the same?

Indeed, once the robber obtained the wallet, it was passed down to the robber's descendants as hereditary property, and hundreds of years later, even under today's law, the statute of limitations made the stolen property a sacred right, clearly forbidden to be violated even by the people of today. The previous owner of the property, in this case the emperor, had no memory of it, just as

---

England. Charles I was at odds with parliament, so he clashed with the parliamentarians, was defeated by them, and was executed.

[497] Emperor Juntoku excelled in waka poetry.

the owner of a field hundreds of years ago is not remembered today. This is why the phrase "rebellion of the emperor" exists. The hereditary purse is then robbed again by yet another robber's blade, and the robber immediately sets up his rights by his own mighty power. Hence Hideyoshi's declaration of "I have taken the nation by my own power."

In a society of robbers, just as other robbers recognize their rights from the night they rob another robber's wallet, in an age when strength determined ownership, all robbers in the nation, except those who were already plundered, recognized their rights from the time of the first generation of plunderers. That is why Ieyasu was revered as "peerless" by all the people. While purses were constantly changing hands from robber to robber, and robbers were killing each other to take them, the imperial family, having lost its mighty power, had no choice but to act as a bystander to this bloodshed. This is why the one eternal lineage was never stained with blood.

The reason that the shogun's end was always a grievous seppuku was because he held the purse and gripped it tightly, and the fingers that pen songs over poetry paper cannot even bear to hold the purse string. The Japanese people, the rebellious subjects, committed robbery beginning as far back as a thousand years and continued that whole time, forgetting, until history was compiled at the end of the Edo period, that the imperial family was the initial owner of that property. The poor don't have to worry about being robbed. The Shinto pope, deprived of his significance as the owner of the state by a nation of rebellious subjects, did not have the wealth to invite robbery. The strong men of the time could not become a Shinto pope, nor did they need to, just as the German emperor could not become a Christian pope, nor does he need to.

In Kiso, that monkey king said,[498] "I have already defeated the cloistered emperor. Will I become an abdicated emperor? If I become an abdicated emperor, a child ('s hairstyle) would not be good. However, if I wish to become

---

[498] Kiso Yoshinaka.

a cloistered emperor, a Buddhist priest ('s bald head) would look strange as well." We are not sure if this was bragging or not. We can see that the robbers were thorough in their act of casting the emperor out of his own purse using their mighty power by looking at the fact that even Emperor Go-Daigo, a heroic figure who was unmatched in the Middle Ages, was imprisoned on the distant island of Oki, as there was no need for the robbers to paint their blades with his blood. Such was the attitude of the Minamoto clan. The Hojo clan also had this attitude. The Ashikaga clan too had the same attitude. During the hundred years of Warring States and the three hundred years of the Tokugawa clan's rule, everyone had this attitude. The genuine national polity theorists of the last days of the Tokugawa shogunate repudiated these plunderers with the modern idea of rights, thereby advocating the revolutionary theory. Why is it that those today, inheriting that theory of national polity and advocating reverence for the lord and loyalty to the sovereign, are not outraged by the plunder, as the revolutionary party members were at the end of the Edo period, but rather defend the plunderers known as modern rebellious subjects, and make it seem as if the one eternal lineage is a result of these plunderer's own good graces, of their devotion and loyalty? Our end-of-Edo-period lord reverence theorists are not contradictory lunatics who advocate overthrowing the aristocracy while also chanting reverence for their lords, which would be the aristocracy. Look at *Explanation of Constitutional Law* by elder statesman of the Meiji Revolution, Mr. Hirobumi Ito. He clearly and unambiguously argues that the Meiji Revolution was the restoration of sovereignty. Restoration presupposed loss.

It should be understood that, from our previous explanations, the imperial family has continued as one eternal lineage because of the principle of lineage, the principle of loyalty and filial piety, and Shinto beliefs. In primitive times, Shinto, lineage, and loyalty and filial piety were all practiced in the regions where they had power. (Since this means that all other villages served their chiefs from all three of these points, it means that the so-called rebellious subjects that historians speak of actually predate written history.)

In the early monarchical period, when history first began to be written down, the Fujiwara reigned over all of Japan by the force of pure power alone. Despite the later tyranny of the great clans, the one eternal lineage was not violated due to the conscience of lineage worship, and the Fujiwaras ruled legally as a monarchy until the end of their reign (however, this was due to an egalitarian principle of lineage, which honored the Fujiwara clan's bloodline. Because of this, many rebellious subjects opposed this throughout the entirety of the monarchical period).

In the aristocratic period of medieval history, the emperor was revered by the dwindling Shinto faith as a "Shinto pope" who had nothing to do with the struggles of the powerful. This was during the long period of one thousand years, from the time of Yoritomo to the Tokugawa clan. One thousand years is the history up until we finally reached the current state. During the evolution of society over this long period, the imperial family was no longer worshipped only by bloodline, but was vastly extended by powerful forces with a view of equality, known as the age of the rear vassal. The words of the Meiji Revolution, "How can the status of a king, a prince, or a general be based on lineage or bloodline?"[499] first came to be realized by the hands of a lowly man, Hideyoshi. Thus, the imperial family lost its significance as a monarchy due to a view of equality. This equality extended only to the aristocracy at first, until the overthrow of the aristocracy, when it was extended further, eventually causing any significance from the monarchical era to wane and the emperor to become little more than a "Shinto pope" with religious honor.

Of course, we do not deny that the organization of society was based on the principles of lineage and loyalty and filial piety, since it was a class state before

---

[499] Words from *Records of the Grand Historian*. It indicates that a person attains a position such as a king by merit or luck.

the revolution. However, the principle of lineage was used as either an indication of the rights of the powerful, a view of equality via honorable lineage, which said that a group were masters of the country because of their ancestors, or to say that one came from the same branch as the emperor. It was nothing more than a vehicle for the rebellious subjects known as the aristocratic class, and a justification of their actions toward the imperial family. It epitomized the phrase, "Yeo's dogs barked at even Yao."[500] Loyalty and filial piety have no meaning at all for the aristocracy, which derives its political freedom from economic independence. The aristocracy can merely turn to the economically subordinate lower classes and demand the duty of those classes to attack the aristocracy's opponents when they come into conflict with other aristocrats or the imperial family. The reason for the continuance of the one eternal lineage after the Middle Ages was not because of the worship of the imperial family's lineage, nor was it based on loyalty and filial piety toward the emperor. It is due to the success of the rebellious subjects over the emperor. These rebels had the principle of loyalty and filial piety, based on economic subordination, toward the "lord and father before one's eyes" and lineage worship toward the aristocratic classes—in other words, it is a commemoration of the rebellious subjects.

This continuity of lineage is also present in the current priest of Izumo. He is not a sovereign of the people, but it is said that he is a continuation of a lineage that has existed since the time of the gods. The purest true lineage in this sense is that of the Indian Rana.[501] This line is not a political power, and in the three thousand years since the gods came into the world,[502] it has only

---

[500] This is a Chinese proverb. It comes from the idea of the dogs kept by an evil lord, Yeo, would even bark at a good lord, Yao. It's used to mean that underlings express the utmost loyalty to their master, even if said master is evil.

[501] Rana is a historical Indian title referring to an absolute Hindu king.

[502] This appears to be referencing a Hindu deity, but we couldn't find any deity with such

once adopted a collateral line to carry on its lineage. The only family that could intermarry was the great Indian imperial family of the Derubi.[503] Japan can't even compare to this, as the country has had countless collateral lines, immigration, emigration, and mixed blood, especially in the Fujiwara clan, where we can't even calculate how much blood has been mixed.

One eternal lineage has little to do with the people's devotion. Hideyoshi considered himself to be of the same one eternal lineage as Amanoyane-no-Mikoto, which was transmitted through the blood of many collateral lineages, but his ancestors were, of course, lowly women of the countryside. Mr. Hozumi and others like him believe that the imperial family and the people share the same blood, and so they consider themselves descendants of Amaterasu (what inferior intelligence!). This means that, even if the Hozumi family ancestors didn't serve the Tokugawa shogun, they're still, in a sense, one eternal lineage too. But they are not!

Is it enough to merely say that the one eternal lineage has little to do with the people's devotion? The Japanese people are far too rebellious, and one eternal lineage is the product of collective disdain. The national polity theorists of the Meiji Revolution, who resent the plunderers, have been succeed by the lowly national polity theorists of today, who defend the plunderers and consider themselves to be of the same one eternal lineage of Amaterasu! After Christ was nailed to the cross for truth, we have a pope who is nailing Christ to the cross under false pretenses of truth. Today, when the theory of national polity has become the pope, we cannot help but shed tears for the very national

---

a name. Seen in relation to the context, it may be Vishnu.

[503] It's unknown what family this refers to. Since there are many unclear parts in the text surrounding it, this was difficult to narrow down. However, Krishna, the demigod hero of the *Bhagavad Gita*, is said to be an incarnation of Vishnu and the son of Vasudeva, and "the Derubi family" may be intended as "the family of Vasudeva."

polity theorist of the past who ascended to the cross. The dead surely weep in their graves.

Therefore, we assert that the reason for the continuation of the imperial line's one eternal lineage is that the people have always been bold and cruel rebels, and that the emperor was plundered of most of his property long ago, despairing as the pope of Shinto. Yes, the one eternal lineage is certainly a commemoration of the rebellious subjects.

For the sake of those national polity theorists who truly have ascended to the cross, let us continue to discuss the pope who is nailing them to it.

In *National Jurisprudence*, Mr. Aruga says the following: "The action of sovereignty was delegated to the shogunate, but the main body of sovereignty was vested in the emperor of one eternal lineage."

We have not read, and probably will not have the honor of reading, *Historical Outline of the Empire,* which made Mr. Aruga famous as one of Japan's leading historians. However, we were surprised to find that in his *National Jurisprudence,* he uses jurisprudential terms such as "sovereignty" and "ruler" instead of more traditional Japanese language,[504] as well as describing things retroactively. It isn't surprising that historians, back when the country was secluded, did not consider history to be an evolutionary line, as societies had not yet evolved to the extent that we have today. In the same way, it's not surprising that historians in Europe, before the emergence of Darwin and Comte,[505] interpreted history as something that repeats itself, as

---

[504] This refers to an old form of grammar in ancient Japanese which one would use to avoid making conclusive statements—similar to saying "or so it seems." Kita is poking fun at Nagao Aruga for using the definitive word "sovereign" in his text despite classics like *Kojiki* and *Nihon Shoki* often using the previously mentioned ancient Japanese in order to make a passage less conclusive and definitive.

[505] Auguste Comte was a French philosopher famous for his positivist philosophy and for founding sociology.

it was a society that had not yet broken out of the framework of the cosmological cycle theory and was still in the process of evolution. However, a person who stands at the forefront of the nation and pens *The Theory of Social Evolution* (we have not read this either), historically studies modern national law, and bases his ideas on the theory of imperial sovereignty, yet does not understand that political history is a study of the order in which political power awakens, develops, and extends itself, can be called nothing other than a savage.

We believe that not only Mr. Aruga, but all Japanese historians have rarely approached Japanese history with a post-evolutionary mindset. That is not historical research. Nor is it a dynamic explanation. According to the Christian theory of creation or the Shinto theory of the origin of the universe, every animal, bird, tree, and stone was created individually. Following this, they believe that, from the very beginning—that is, the creation of earth in Christianity or the beginning of the universe is Shintoism—Adam and Eve's western nation was a democratic republic, and that Izanagi and Izanami's Japan was created as a monarchy. They then forget to categorize national polity and government systems according to the times in which they existed. Is there even such a thing as "our Japan's national polity" in the first place?

Rather than that, we admire the consistent attitude of the adorable Mr. Hozumi, who does not understand the theory of evolution and talks of constitutional law while believing in this Shinto theory of the origin of the universe. Mr. Aruga, like Mr. Hozumi, holds the Shinto belief in the origin of the universe as the core of his thought. Yet, to ridicule Mr. Hozumi's theory of sovereignty in the name of historical research, and to dismiss it as "a popular theory that does not consider history in defining the basis of the emperor's sovereignty on his being a descendant of Amaterasu," is outrageous. Mr. Aruga is not an advocate of imperial sovereignty based on history. Like Mr. Hozumi, he is a man who plays around with history based around his Shinto beliefs. His insults are him spitting up toward heaven and sullying his own face when that spit lands.

As long as the laws of cause and effect exist, there is no reason for Mr. Aruga's theory of governing action delegation to apply to the Tokugawa clan's eighteen articles of the laws of the warrior clans and the seventeen articles of the laws of the emperor and court nobles.[506] We will not describe the shogunate's countermeasures against the imperial family using these laws as examples, nor will we incessantly list the facts of constant imprisonment and forced abdication, which surpassed even Yoshitoki and Ujitaka in severity. However, if one has the attitude of a historical researcher, there is no reason to fall into the madness of trying to explain the existence of a delegate relationship between the imperial family and the shogunate by reversing these legal texts, which were used to oppress the imperial family.

Mr. Aruga says the following:

Since the Genpei period, the Tokugawa were the first to gain the right to rule without being victorious in war. Therefore, they had to look for other reasons to maintain their rule aside from military strength. Ieyasu was well versed in the classic texts and in national polity. Once he temporarily returned power to the emperor, he adopted the principle of organizing the shogunate by the emperor's delegation, and then enacted the laws of the warrior clans by imperial decree.

---

[506] The laws of the warrior clans, or Samurai Laws, were established by Tokugawa Ieyasu in 1615 for the purpose of controlling the feudal lords. Initially, there were thirteen articles, but they were later added to, resulting in nineteen articles. Kita refers to the law as "eighteen articles," but "nineteen articles" is correct.

The laws of the emperor and court nobles were established by Tokugawa Ieyasu in 1615, and consisted of seventeen articles.

What logic! To "temporarily return power to the emperor" in order to receive a delegation from the emperor means, obviously, to return the power that had been held at some point before that delegation, which assumes that the Tokugawa were in political power before the delegation was given.

Surely Mr. Aruga would say, "Hideyoshi took the delegated political power by military force, then gave it back to the emperor in order to accept his delegation." We will not ask how the Tokugawa, who had not been delegated the acting sovereignty of the emperor by the emperor (who did have that acting sovereignty), and therefore did not have supreme military authority, could take it away. If we assume that the Tokugawa, who were well versed in the classics and in national polity, were the "first" to obtain the right to rule by delegation, then it would be a clear statement that the political powers "from the Genpei period onward, as a result of victory in war" were not those to whom the exercise of sovereignty was delegated, and the theory of delegation of authority would be a suicidal theory which destroys itself.

To reiterate, Mr. Aruga's theory of delegation of governing power is as follows: "After returning political power to the emperor, the Tokugawa were the first to receive the right to rule by the emperor's delegation." Because of this, not all of the shogunate "since the Genpei period, as a result of victories in war," have been delegated the right to rule. Even if the first shogunate was delegated the actionable right to rule, the Tokugawa weren't—which means they didn't have supreme military authority. This means that even if the Tokugawa "temporarily returned political power to the emperor," they were never delegated actionable sovereignty to return in the first place.

However, Mr. Aruga continues:

> The emperor still theoretically had authority over the military affairs of the country. This is evidenced by the fact that Yoritomo was appointed to the post of "sotsui bushi" and great shogun by direct imperial command, and his military pursuits were always carried out

by the ex-emperor's imperial decree.... In addition, the emperor theoretically had the power in diplomacy. This is evidenced by the fact that, in the ninth year of Bun'ei, a letter was offered from Goryeo requesting friendly relations, and Tokimune presented the letter to the imperial court.

This erases the previous assertion that "the shogunate was organized by delegation," and that "the Tokugawa clan was the first to receive the right to rule," and instead asserts that those "after the Genpei period, as a result of victories in war," were equally delegated the function and action of the right to rule. This is certainly a theory of delegation of governing power which is unparalleled in other countries! We don't deny that Yoritomo was appointed to the post "sotsui bushi"[507] and great shogun, nor that his military pursuits were carried out by imperial decree. However, that doesn't mean the same thing as the emperor appointing a general of the army and issuing an imperial edict of declaration of war today, as Mr. Aruga believes it does just from looking at the shape and pronunciation of the words. It revolves around the relationship between the pope of Shinto and the Holy Roman Emperor of Kamakura. Mr. Aruga should naturally reflect on this. Who delegated to him the supreme military power necessary to defeat the Taira clan, which had received an imperial decree to come there, when he had not yet been appointed as a "sotsui bushi" or a great shogun? What right does an imperial decree have to order military action against the Taira clan, who are serving the emperor? Is the body of sovereignty in the ex-emperor's imperial decree or the direct imperial command? If Mr. Aruga considers both the ex-emperor's imperial decree and the direct imperial command valid according to the facts of the time, then this is the attitude of a historian who respects the facts, and it proves that Yoritomo

---

[507] "Sotsui bushi" is technically another name for a guard, but since Toritomo was also named "sotsui bushi of all Japan," it meant that he had practical power over all of Japan.

had de facto military authority from long before that time. This is not so! Not only did Yoritomo obey the imperial decree by killing all those who had received the direct imperial command, he didn't have any care for the imperial decree in the first place.

For example, even though he hadn't been granted permission, Yoritomo said, "I am going to conquer my vassals. Why should a lord wait for the ex-emperor's imperial decree in order to conquer his vassals?" He then boldly took his sovereign anger out on Ou, killing him. Again, we don't deny that Tokimune presented the letter from Goryeo to the imperial court back when communication with them opened up, during the ninth year of Bun'ei. However, this also does not have the same meaning as the emperor listening to reports of the minister of foreign affairs today, as one may think from the form and pronunciation of the words alone. The reason is that he was the Shinto pope, whose foundations stood on Shintoism to the extent that it was believed that a divine wind, a typhoon, occurred and wiped out the Mongol invasion, all because Emperor Kameyama abandoned his own safety and prayed at the Ise Shrine. Naturally, Mr. Aruga should reflect on this. Tokimune defied the direct imperial command by his despotic power, the declaration of war was made by the valiant roar of Sagamitaro,[508] and all Japan fought accordingly. These actions were based on acceptance of his diplomatic authority.

Did Yoshimitsu Ashikaga exercise his diplomatic power by executing sovereignty via delegation of the emperor, and was thus recognized by China as the King of Japan? Did Hideyoshi Toyotomi conquer Korea by the supreme military authority delegated by the emperor? Did he destroy the council of peace's letter by the sovereignty of diplomacy delegated by the emperor, saying "I took over the nation by my own power. If I wish to become king, I can. If I desire to become emperor, I can"? Were Ieyasu's policy of opening the country

---

[508] Refers to Tokimune. He was called "Sagamitaro" after his coming-of-age ceremony.

to foreign trade, and Iemitsu's strict policy of national seclusion, all exercises of diplomatic power delegated by the emperor? This is truly a theory of delegated right to rule that is unparalleled in any other country.

Delegation is an element of a consensual contract, and there is no freedom to terminate the contract on grounds other than the terms set forth at the time both parties agree to the contract.[509] There are languages and characters that say "stole another's wallet by fraud" or "stole another's wallet by extortion," but "stole another's wallet by delegation" seems to be a unique usage by Mr. Aruga. Property stolen with a blade was named "a thief's stolen goods," but "delegated property" is a phrase that doesn't currently exist in Japanese law. And what a strange delegation contract it was when the delegator canceled the contract or desired a refund. They would end up, in Yoshitoki's case, exiled to a deserted island, or, as in Iemitsu Tokugawa's case, threatened by an army of 350,000 men. Oh Mr. Aruga, you say that the body of sovereignty and the execution of sovereignty can be separated, and that the execution was delegated to the shogunate! The fact that the emperor, the body of sovereignty, ordered seclusion and exclusion of foreigners as the body of diplomatic power, while the shogunate, which was delegated to act in this capacity, signed the treaty opening ports to the outside world, suggests that this was a contract of delegation with the condition that the body and the execution were free to cancel each other out! Did the emperor, who theoretically possessed supreme military authority as the main body of sovereignty, delegate the execution of that supreme military power to Yoshitoki Hojo, thus forming a contract where that execution attacks the main body? Is sovereignty something whose main body can be overpowered by execution of that sovereignty itself? This is why

---

[509] We believe this statement was made in consideration of the mandate under the Civil Code. However, under the Japanese Civil Code, since the contract is based on a relationship of trust, it is no longer meaningful to bind a person if the relationship of trust no longer exists, and the contract can be terminated at any time (Article 651).

we have compared Japanese medieval history to European medieval history, and why we have named the emperor "the pope of Shinto" and the shogun the "Holy Roman Emperor of Kamakura."

This truly is a theory of delegation of authority that is unparalleled in other countries! If the Holy Roman Emperor of Kamakura was entrusted with the execution of the power to rule by being appointed a great general by the Shinto pope, then did the pope who crowned the Holy Roman Emperor of Europe have the main body of the right to rule? And, as a matter of logic, were the lords of that time further delegated the execution of the power to rule by the shogunate, which had been delegated the execution of the power to rule by the emperor? If so, are the monarchs of today's European countries delegated by the Holy Roman Emperor, who was delegated by the pope to exercise sovereignty, and today's European countries are empty floating islands without a main body of sovereignty? If one were to think in terms of such an execution of sovereignty delegation, France and America could all be "nations unparalleled by any other nations." A Japanese university professor might attribute Yoshimitsu Ashikaga's independent title of "King of Japan" to the independence that came from him being delegated diplomatic power. However, American university professors would not say that the American Revolutionary War was a delegation of independence from the main body of sovereignty, the King of England. A Japanese jurist might argue that Yoshitoki's exile of the three emperors was a rebellion after being delegated execution of supreme military authority. However, the French jurist would not say that the revolutionary party was entrusted with the exercise of sovereign power to decapitate the king by King Louis himself, the main body of sovereign power. In any situation that is unparalleled in other nations, there is an argument that is unparalleled in other nations.

Let us now have Mr. Hozumi take his revenge against Mr. Aruga's insults.

We can think of nothing else to call this but the comedy of a backwards village. Mr. Hozumi, along with Mr. Aruga, is a monarchist who bases his arguments on the history of Japan as well as his belief in primitive religion. Despite Mr. Aruga's abuse toward Mr. Hozumi's primitive religion, Mr. Hozumi himself treats history statically, based on the primitive religion's theory of the origin of the universe. Mr. Hozumi, who claims to believe in primitive religions, says that only the Japanese people sit still outside the laws of evolution and that the national polity of Japan has never changed in the past, nor does it change now. In this respect, he shares the same historical philosophy as Mr. Aruga. Yet, in spite of this happy agreement, Mr. Hozumi's enthusiasm for his view of the nature of sovereignty also fundamentally undermines Mr. Aruga's interpretation, just as Mr. Aruga's enthusiasm happens to be abusive toward Mr. Hozumi. At this point, one can't help but laugh. Of course, the two of them aren't enemies under the large umbrella of monarchical sovereignty theory; just as Mr. Aruga's enthusiasm isn't spouted toward Mr. Hozumi, Mr. Hozumi's spirit does not target Mr. Aruga. We dare not guide these two blind men into a clash with each other, nor do we intend to sit on the sidelines and laugh at them. In fact, we must express our deepest gratitude toward them both. Mr. Hozumi's theory of the nature of sovereignty is not an exposition of the doctrine of sovereignty spoken toward other monarchists, but an argument against the attempt by so-called party-cabinet democrats to establish a de facto republican government under a customary constitution.[510] He says the following:

---

[510] Minobe and others emphasize the importance of the non-enacted legal element of "reason and law" and insist that the Constitution be interpreted in accordance with "reason and law." When "reason and law" evolve, the interpretation of the Constitution must change, and it seems that they emphasized the importance of customary constitutions.

The words of Thiers, "the sovereign reigns, but does not rule,"[511] are not enough to even form a theory. All authority is authority because it is active. Inactive authority goes against the concept of authority. If a monarch is sovereign, he must have the power to exercise authority. He who does not have the power to exercise authority is not a sovereign.

This is an affirmation that the emperor was not a sovereign during the thousand years of the Middle Ages, since he didn't have the power to execute his authority. He continues:

> A person with authority who is incapable of exercising said authority is a self-contradiction. Authority is an act of will, and it is authority because of action. A sovereign with no authority is theoretically meaningless. This is not even worth attacking as a legal theory. Furthermore, even as a practical argument, it is impossible to distinguish between the subject of authority and the execution of authority. Although they can be separated in terms of language and explanation, such a distinction is meaningless because the body and action of authority in fact belong to the same person. A person who executes authority is called an authority.

This is an assertion that the present-day emperor, who exercises power, is considered to be an authority, and that the shogunate is an authority as well. He continues once again:

> Sovereignty in society is established by social forces. It is not established logically. Therefore, when reading history, the location of

---

[511] Adolphe Thiers was a liberal politician in the July Revolution of 1830 in France. He is known as a theorist of constitutional monarchy.

sovereignty is often unclear. In some cases, the monarch is the sovereign, but even the monarch is sometimes supported by aristocrats or powerful families, and the real power is in the hands of the powerful families. At other times, the monarch and the Diet are considered to be sovereigns in combination. In many cases, it is not clear whether sovereignty actually rests with the monarch or with the Diet. This is because of the nature of sovereignty. Sovereignty is a social force. The establishment of a society is determined by various causes. Therefore, we can only assume that sovereignty resides where the people are convinced that, as a result of history, sovereignty resides, and willingly submit to power.

Of course, this view has no other meaning aside from understanding the three main periods of evolution: monarchies, aristocracies, and democracies. However, from words such as "sovereignty actually . . ." it's clear that this interpretation of history shows that the sovereignty of Japan was never fixed in one eternal lineage, but was always in flux.

Is this not an acknowledgement of the authority of the rebellious subjects? Is this not a gift of the title of sovereignty to the tomb of Yoshitoki, and to the mausoleum of the Tokugawa clan? Ah, the grave of loyal retainer Mr. Hozumi!

Such a theory of the nature of sovereignty would be valid in the era of the Hojo clan, which happily submitted to the power of Yoshitoki, calling it the "emperor's rebellion." It would be valid in the era of the Tokugawa shogunate, who called Ieyasu "God-ruler" and all the shogun "exalted leaders," and were willing to submit to their power. What a wonder that the words of a man who is widely known throughout the world as one who works tirelessly to revere the emperor and be loyal to the lord, Yatsuka Hozumi, would be used to endorse the actions of a rebellious subject. I, for one, would describe Mr. Hozumi as a restorative revolutionary who wishes to transform the current national polity, changed the system of government, and thus overthrow one of the most important institutions of the state, the emperor. The public, however, misinterprets Mr. Hozumi's constitutional studies and calls him a loyalist jurist. After his death, he will surely be stood next to Hirobumi Ito, erected as a slightly smaller and humbler statue, dedicated to that yellow substance, keeping his honorable name as long as Minatogawa Shrine continues to exist. Yet, what a rebellious subject, to say that a sovereign without power is theoretically meaningless, and that sovereignty resides where the people are willing to submit. Furthermore, he says, "The sovereignty of the nation is vested in the throne of the one eternal lineage, which has not been transferred to anyone else, and thus forms our national polity." If a statue is to be erected, it must have two heads, and each head must be embellished with yellow excrement.

We are not insulting and messing with a law professor and president of a law school without reason. If, like the national polity theorists of the late Edo period who struggled against the aristocracy, he would admit that the aristocrats, the rebels, had plundered the sovereignty of the emperor and that the imperial family was deprived of its sovereignty because of this plunder, we would be inclined to sympathize with him in general, his argument notwithstanding. And if he were to use the fact that Mr. Hirobumi Ito was a meritorious retainer of the Meiji Revolution, and so claim that "the Meiji Revolution restored sovereignty," all it would do is suggest that he is satisfied with that achievement. He would still need a theory that explains what foundation a strong person's authority is built on. Of course, the *Explanation of Constitutional Law* that Mr. Ito asserts here is wrong.

However, when Mr. Hozumi walks up to the university lectern with his *Explanation of Constitutional Law* and nose held high, it is not an expression of honor for a strong man like him, but an expression of his slavery. A national polity theorist of the last days of the Tokugawa shogunate would have been outraged at the plunderers of sovereignty and would not have forgiven them. And yet, if he were a shogunate sovereignty theorist, he would say, "A sovereign without power is theoretically meaningless," or "Sovereignty resides in the place where the people are willing to submit." This is an insult to the patriot's loyal spirit. The national polity theorists of the late Edo period recognized that the shogunate was a powerful authority. However, this was a recognition meant to overthrow it, not a defense of it meant to prostrate oneself in front of it with a theory of the essence of sovereignty like Hozumi's. How could such a theory of the nature of sovereignty give rise to the historical interpretation that "the sovereignty of the nation rests with the throne of one eternal lineage, and it has not been transferred to any other, thus forming our national polity"?

Go goes on to say the following:

> The foundations of modern Europe were formed from the breakup and independence of the feudal system. In Japan, the feudal system declined, the lords lost power, and the central court regained power and unified the country. This is the great achievement of the Meiji Revolution. The feudal system in Europe had the opposite effect. As the feudal system declined, the central emperor completely lost his power, and at last the local lords swallowed up the smaller lords and established independent states. In the Middle Ages, the European countries of today were lords under the Holy Roman Emperor. Yet, the central government fell and the lords became independent. If one were to explain this using Japan, it would be similar to if places like Satsuma and Choshu were divided into independent states after the Meiji Revolution.

Everything is contradictory. The "lords losing power" presupposes that the lords had power, and "the central court regaining power" presupposes that the emperor had lost power. If "the sovereignty of the nation resides in the throne of the emperor of one eternal lineage, and our national polity is of a sovereignty that has never been transferred anywhere else," then "restoring sovereignty" via the Meiji Revolution doesn't make sense in any known human language, as the sovereignty was apparently "never transferred" in the first place. Would he advocate the sovereignty of the emperor or the sovereignty of the shogunate? Let him see the nightmare of Europe, where the central Holy Roman Emperor was destroyed and the vassal states became independent. He will abandon the theory of the master-servant family, the theory of a family of loyalty and filial piety, his belief in Shintoism, and everything else, and will join the sovereigns of Satsuma and Choshu, as he states with his "Sovereignty resides in the place where the people are willing to submit," and repudiate the sovereignty of the emperor as the head of the rebellious subjects. In other words, such a theory of sovereignty is purely about strength, based on a foundation other than religious morality, which is what theories such as the sovereignty theory of Shinto constitutionalism is based on. Indeed, in considering Mr. Hozumi, one can only imagine a two-headed monster.

Ah, Mr. Yatsuka Hozumi, the two-headed monster! The two heads on his shoulders affirm and deny, respectively. If the head on the right says he believes in Shinto as a religion, the head on the left says he is engaged in the scientific study of mythology. If the head on the left says he espouses the theory of the sovereignty of the shogunate, the head on the right says he preaches the theory of the sovereignty of the emperor. No! The head on his left believes in the sovereignty of the state, while the head on his right preaches the sovereignty of the emperor. See his theory of the nature of sovereignty quoted previously and his explanation of sovereignty given in the previous legal theory. The proposition that "sovereignty is a social force" is the very idea of the theory of state sovereignty, and it cancels the proposition that "sovereignty is the inherent power of the sovereign," which is the explanation of the theory of monarchical sovereignty. If sovereignty is a social force, society must be the subject of sovereignty, and if it is the sovereign's inherent power, it will die out with the death of the sovereign. We must not wonder how it is possible to spout these two mutually opposing ideas of jurisprudence at the same time. We can only understand it by imagining a two-headed monster. The phrase, "the most brilliant wisdom and the most foolish folly do not shift,"[512] means that the most brilliant has the knowledge to know that he is wise, but the most foolish doesn't even have the knowledge to know that he is stupid. Mr. Hozumi, of course, does not have the knowledge to know that he is stupid, but he does have the knowledge to know that he is wise, so we cannot say to which category he truly belongs.

However, these two-headed monsters monopolize the pulpit of the Imperial University (and nowadays wax poetic about the sanctity of university, which makes one almost want to laugh), making university graduates the stuff of ridicule. Furthermore, since the university stands at the gateway to the government's judiciary and administrative systems, the most important institutions for expressing the will of the Great Empire of Japan, young scholars who consider independence of thought to be the highest authority have no choice but to spend their days passing through the legs of people like him, a feat requiring the very patience of Han Xin.[513] Only in a village of savages would there be such a two-headed monster.

We must express our thanks once again. We did not set Mr. Aruga and Mr. Hozumi against each other, leading the blind to clash and ridiculing them from

---

[512] Words from *The Analects*, 17:3. It means that the wisest and the most foolish can never switch positions, regardless of how they're cultivated or trained.

[513] A general in the early Han Dynasty. He followed Liu Bang and rose to the rank of general, destroying the forces of various provinces and further isolating Xiang Yu to pacify the country. According to legend, he was humiliated in his youth by being forced to grope his own crotch in front of a crowd of people at the bidding of a rogue, but he persevered through it.

the sidelines, as if we were troublesome children playing a prank. How could they have guessed the painstaking efforts of Rai San'yo in his *Nihon Gaishi*?[514]

Did the emperor, then, in medieval Japan, meaning nothing other than "Shinto pope"? No. We believe that the emperor had the same right to rule as the shogunate and the lords, and was only inferior in terms of power. In other words, the reason why the shogunate and the lords had the right to rule over the land and the people was not because they were delegated the right to rule by the emperor, as in Mr. Aruga's theory of the delegated right to rule, but because they had the right to rule over their own lands. Even if, as in Mr. Hozumi's theory of the nature of sovereignty, there were times when the emperor was oppressed by other powerful forces, this does not mean that the shogunate had stolen everything from the emperor before the Meiji Revolution, and was thus the only ruler in Japan. All shogun, all lords, all emperors, all of them were rulers.

It's on this point that we insist on classifying national polity according to its evolution. In other words, states prior to the Meiji Revolution were a different kind of state, the "patriarchal state," and didn't necessarily have a single sovereign per state. This is because many rulers disposed of the land and people, which they owned as private property for their own benefit and purposes. The subject of this property right is called the ruler, and the exercise of the property right is called governing. This was a state of monarchical sovereignty, which is very different from today, where the state itself is the governing body for the purpose and benefit of the state. At first, the land and people of the Kinki region were under the sovereignty of the emperor alone. However, as branches of the emperor's lineage gradually invaded the countryside, they became local warlords, and then became rival chiefs who owned the land and its people, giving rise to countless sovereigns over the

---

[514] Confucian scholar of the late Edo period. He's famous for his *Nihon Gaishi*, written from the standpoint of the theory of the emperor's sovereignty in the Cheng-Zhu school.

entire nation. This was the era of aristocracy after Yoritomo. The period from the birth of historical records to the Meiji Revolution was a "patriarchal state" that lasted for more than one thousand years. What was initially a small area gradually expanded into a large area, and what was initially a single patriarchal monarch gradually became many patriarchal monarchs who came into conflict with each other. And, as mentioned before, throughout antiquity and the Middle Ages, rights were determined by one's strength.

So, the imperial family was the first powerful body to be the patriarchal monarch over a small amount of local land and people. Eventually, the Genpei, Ashikaga, Tokugawa, etc., of the imperial lineage became patriarchal monarchs over the local land and people, their authority determined by the strength of their power. In other words, despite the various names they were given, such as shogun, local chief, and lord, the nobles of the aristocratic period were all the same in that they were patriarchs who had absolute and unlimited rights over their lands and people. There's no doubt that the emperor, in addition to being the Shinto pope in the Middle Ages, also had unlimited and absolute rights over the land and people he owned.

Of course, in the latter half of medieval history—from the hundred years of the Warring States period to the three hundred years of the Tokugawa clan—it seems as if he had no rights left other than that of a Shinto pope, but even while he was poor and destitute, he still had the pitiable court nobles as vassals and was given a little land, even though he was under incredible pressure from the Tokugawa clan. So it is true that, legally, he had absolute rights as the patriarch over the land and its people (read the section in *The Theory of Biological Evolution and Social Philosophy* where we discussed the evolution of monarchies, aristocracies, and democracies from the perspective of social philosophy). The aristocrats of the aristocratic period were not citizens with the same privileges as the "nobility" of today. They were "monarchs" who had absolute rights over the land and people they owned. The period of the aristocracy was a time when there were many such "monarchs," who both fought each other and sometimes joined together.

What started as the honor of the emperor's lineage being extended to a small number of social classes eventually progressed to them standing on the same ground as monarchs during the monarchical period. However, while this reason rejects Mr. Aruga's theory of delegated authority, it does not affirm Mr. Hozumi's theory of the nature of sovereignty, which argues that the emperor is not a ruler. Both lords and shogun were sovereigns. Yet, it is a historical fact that the emperor was also a sovereign. However, if we understand the word "sovereign" in its original meaning—"supreme ruler," "ruler over rulers," "lord above lords"—this is precisely the reason for the disputes over the idea of the low and high roads in Confucianism, and a problem in general.

Mr. Hozumi's zero-point answer to this question is that, "When the whereabouts of sovereignty are unknown, that is when the nation is in unrest." As he defines it in *Summary of the Constitution,* state power is the sovereignty to govern the nation. If we forget the original meaning of sovereignty like this and consider medieval history within the framework of the modern state, in which only one has the right to rule in each nation, then all medieval history, which is the only way to understand modernity, would fall outside the scope of studies of the state, since not only Japanese medieval history but also European history would be considered this way as well.[515] And since the state is ceaselessly evolving, it will always be in unrest, and Mr. Hozumi will have no choice but to abandon constitutional studies.

The word "sovereign" was used to indicate who was "lord above lords" and "ruler over rulers," since there were many monarchs and rulers during the Middle Ages—it means "supreme authority." In today's nation, whether one

---

[515] Kita is saying that looking at medieval history within a modern framework makes it impossible to understand who the sovereign was, not only in Japanese medieval history, but also in European medieval history.

adopts the theory of monarchical sovereignty or the sovereignty of the state, there is no "supreme authority" because there is no other subject of rights than the sovereign or the state. The existence of a "supreme authority" means that there also exist one or more subjects of rights that is not supreme, and that applies to the medieval patriarchal state. If so, was the emperor of one eternal lineage a sovereign during the medieval history of Japan—that is, a ruler over rulers, with supreme authority, a lord over lords?

The low and high road of Confucianism must be understood as a determination of where sovereignty resides. It's a dispute as to whether the high ruler has supreme authority as a ruler over the other rulers, those known as daimyo, or whether the low ruler has supreme authority as a monarch over other monarchs, those known as the various lords. Even if we were to take the view of shogunate sovereignty theorists such as Sorai Ogyu, the shogunate of the Ashikaga period was not a sovereign that wielded supreme ruling power over the feudal lords since the time of Takauji. The Tokugawa clan could not be called sovereign either because, near the end of their rule, they were unable to exercise supreme power over the rulers of Choshu and Satsuma, and the imperial family had grown too powerful to be oppressed as they had been in the past.

Moreover, even if one were to advocate the theory of emperor sovereignty, as scholars of ancient Japanese culture do, on the grounds that the emperor was the source of honor and reserved this right of honor, the exercise of the right of honor was always inhibited by right of supreme military authority, and the emperor, the body of the right of honor, was subject to revision or abolition at the will of those with said right of supreme military authority. This argument, then, doesn't hold during certain periods. In addition, there was the term "emperor's rebellion" in the days when mighty power determined everything. Even today, international relations are still determined by the rights of the strongest, and from the perspective of the idea that the right of supreme military authority is the first element in classifying sovereign versus non-sovereign nations, it is difficult to maintain the theory of emperor sovereignty for that period of one thousand years. We assert that sovereignty is the rise and fall of power during the struggle of numerous patriarchs and monarchs, and the sovereign is determined by the time and age, and is by no means immutable.

We would like to assert that, irrespective of the sovereignty theory in this sense, the various lords and the shogunate were rules who became sovereigns, and the emperor never lost his nature as a ruler. In other words, the emperor, as emperor, was a sovereign. The evolution of society was an extension of equality, and the aristocracy strove to reach it by imitating the emperor. Then all the lords and princes evolved in their own way and became sovereigns within their own sphere. Therefore, we do not believe, as the national polity theorists did at the end of the Edo period, that the shogunate and the lords plundered the emperor's right to rule, turning his title into an empty name with no substance. However, they advocated that the people respected and showed loyalty toward the emperor. This is unlike the modern-day national polity theorists, who defend the plundering done by the shogunate and various lords, praising them as respectful and loyal subjects. They insist that the people were devoted to the one eternal lineage. However, they never cried tears of sadness when the one eternal lineage fell, and, eventually, reached an extremely pitiful state, since the one eternal lineage was served because of respect for and loyalty to the emperor. We can't know whether, when they looked down respectfully from the bridge at the fallen, miserable continuation of the one eternal lineage, they realized that this entire nation was one of nothing but rebellious subjects, and so felt complete despair, knowing that it was a commemoration of their sins. However, we do know for certain that the one eternal lineage is an honor reserved for the imperial family, and not an effect of dedication by the people. Ah, the theory of national polity has finally become the pope. And now it wants to crucify the true national polity theorists, who want to convey the true spirit of the theory of national polity!

We reject the doctrine of the pope in the name of the theory of national polity, and clearly proclaim it to refer to the one eternal lineage. It is a historical pyramid which the great benevolence of the imperial line has built, which in turn feeds into the imperial line's honor, but for the people, it's the work of all those generations of rebellious subjects, whose many spirits were united as one.

Chapter 14

We interpreted the theory of national polity earlier as if it were an expression of resentment against the aristocracy for its lack of loyalty and obedience to the emperor. However, from the standpoint of historical philosophy, it also rejects the duty of loyalty to the aristocratic class, thus indicating that the aristocratic class itself rejected their duty of loyalty. In other words, following the evolution of history, in which the view of equality extended to the aristocracy, it seeks to extend it further to the commoner classes—to realize the democracy of the Meiji Revolution!

It looked to Confucianism and the classic texts for an explanation, but ended up only as a revolutionary theory created to argue the following: "The nobles demanded the slave-like morality of loyalty and obedience from us. However, are they not rebellious subjects, the first to transgress their duty of loyalty? Rather, let us attack them for their rebellious actions as we become rebellious subjects ourselves." This is a denial of "loyalty" itself. In this way, the aristocrats persecuted the national polity theorists in order to maintain their position and land, which they obtained as rebellious subjects, and the national polity democrats, in order to evolve to the same position as the aristocrats, acted as rebellious subjects against their "lord and father before them." They were thus killed by rebellious subjects as rebellious subjects—the true significance of the Meiji Revolution was democracy. Yet, still without philosophical study of Japanese history, these people are misled by the fact that the revolutionaries were forced, under an astonishing persecution of free speech, to play with flowery language and write distorted facts, and interpret all Japanese citizens to have been loyal subjects of the imperial family and righteous warriors. They don't consider the class struggle with the national polity theorists, who are equally loyal subjects and righteous warriors, as bizarre, but simply turn to the next page without pause.

They are proud of the fact that the Japanese people, thanks to their history, were well equipped to absorb foreign civilizations. However, the proclamation of "deciding based on public opinion" at the time of the Meiji Revolution, and the movement to demand a constitution less than a decade later, were completely literal ideas taken directly from foreign cultures. Such radical changes seem to have come in a matter of years, and nobody even questions the bizarre ethnic psychology. Woe to the savage village of the Orient! By calling the Meiji Revolution a restoration of the monarchy, you have already revealed yourselves to be savages.

If we aren't barbarians, could we truly think that humans have the power to turn back 1,300 years of evolution through history, and restore the ancient civilization that existed there? History is not a cycle, nor is it something that should be restored. History is the traces of social evolution. To say that the Meiji Revolution is a restoration of the Taika monarchy is unimaginable without tracing back and regressing everything in society—lifestyle, human emotions, customs, ideas, written words, and even language—to a period that is nothing but legend, to the point that it doesn't even require recording its history. The Meiji Revolution was not a restoration of the monarchy of the Taika era. The Confucian "civic state," which was the ideal of the Taika Revolution, was finally realized after a long evolution of 1,300 years. The civic state was not built by cutting off the flowing currents of the patriarchal state. It is a new form of state that was realized only after the patriarchal state had fully developed and evolved. In this new state, the patriarchs (one patriarch in the case of a monarchy or many patriarchs in the case of an aristocracy) do not dispose of land and people as their property for the benefit of their owners, as they do in the patriarchal state. Nor do the patriarchs stand outside the state and treat the state as property and a means to their own ends. This state is a completely different form of evolution, in which the state grants its molecules their own privileges and makes them agents of the state, for its own purposes and interests.

Again, in the patriarchal period, society had not yet evolved to the point where it was aware of its own goals and interests and did not know that the state was a permanent entity, and a segment or a minority of society had no choice but to act in their own individual (rather than social) self-interest. The lower molecules are treated as sacrifices under the self-interest of the higher ones, and this is how society has been maintained (see where we explain the maintenance of survival via loss of individuals in *The Theory of Biological Evolution and Social Philosophy*).

This is not the case when it comes to the modern civic state. Society has evolved so much that it has come to understand itself as having a purpose of survival and evolution, and the interests and purposes of the state are made conscious to all its molecules. And even the molecules, the agents that express the will of the state, act with the social self-interest of being part of society (not the personal self-interest of the agents when they are conscious of themselves only as individuals). In other words, even when a molecule of society is sacrificed, it is not sacrificed to satisfy the personal self-interest of another individual, as in the patriarchal state. It's about becoming a lost individual, as part of a larger individual, for the sake of the other parts of society, whether in the present or future, due to one's recognition of themselves as part of society and that social self-interest.[516]

From the viewpoint of social philosophy, both outcomes are the same method of social survival. However, from the stance of jurisprudence, which examines from the point of view of will rather than of result, it must be clarified that even though they are the same method of sacrificing for the sake of social

---

[516] In other words, "they are not being sacrificed in the way they once were, but for the sake of such goals as the defense of the homeland; they are being sacrificed for the sake of society's goals."

survival, they have clearly evolved into different categories. The morality and law of the patriarchal period were those of the "loyal subject," leading to sacrifices for the personal interests of the monarch. The morality and law of the civic state is "patriotic," wherein sacrifices are made for the social self-interest of the society. Clearly, morality and law, which consider the will, must classify this national polity according to its evolution.

The Taika Revolution was an attempt during ancient times, when we may or may not have just broken out of our primitive lifestyle, to realize the grand Confucian dream of an ideal civic state. However, this was merely the dream of the great Emperor Tenji, and what actually emerged was a patriarchal state of monarchical sovereignty. It goes without saying that Emperor Tenji did not consider the land and people as his private property that existed for his benefit. The land nationalization system that emerged in the early years of the reign of Emperor Tenji is evidence of the strict political morality of the Confucian theory of national sovereignty. The fact that the Taika Revolution, which dreamed of realizing Confucian socialism, maintained the political direction of socialism as the emperor's political morality, and, at the same time, implemented the economic basis of national ownership of land, known as Seiden's Law,[517] is a true reflection of Emperor Tenji as a great emperor.

If the economic basis of the state—here being land, the only basis at that time—is privately owned by the aristocracy, as was the case in the patriarchal system until the overthrow of the Soga clan, each molecule of the state is not directly opposed to the state, and the state becomes a class stratified system. Thus, the members of the lower classes, who are economically subordinate to the upper classes, act in the interest of the members they are directly subordinate to, without the state as their purpose. Thus, when self-interests clash among the members of the upper class, it leads to a division of the state,

---

[517] A system said to have been implemented in the Xia, Shang, and Zhou dynasties. It is said that cultivated land was divided and distributed in the shape of a number sign (#).

as in the "rivalry of the warlords" of later times. Even when the state escapes division under a certain coalition or oppression, it loses its own purpose and is merely treated as an object under the self-interest of the upper class, the monarchs.

The Taika Revolution came close to realizing this ideal in the economic sphere. However, Confucian statecraft itself was too lofty an ideal even for the Han Chinese of the Confucius and Meng dynasties, and even Seiden's Law was not a theory of land nationalization in the sense that is advocated by socialism today. It was merely a retrospective look back at the periods of emperors Yao and Shun, who had adopted a communal village system when they settled in the nomadic or agricultural period, going against the historical progression of the private ownership of land system in patriarchal countries at that time. Therefore, the system of private ownership of land had to progress as far as it needed to go as a natural result of historical progression. It would be the same if the government today, with only the knowledge of a direct, literal translation, drafted laws in English. In fact, it was even more difficult to understand when it was made public back then, because Chinese was more difficult to understand at the time compared to English today, since there was no written language then. Of course, this means the whole thing was never properly implemented.

Because of this, the idealists of the imperial family worked to overthrow the Soga clan and spread the theory of land ownership, and for a while they tried to nip the germ of aristocracy in the bud. However, in the provinces where English law did not reach, the private ownership of land was vigorously promoted, with some provincial governors and landowners breaking the law and others evading it, cultivating the seeds of what would become the aristocratic state of medieval history. In the third year of Enryaku,[518] the following is written:

---

[518] The original text says "second year," but it's likely a mistake and should be "third

570 | The Theory of Japan's National Polity and Pure Socialism

The people are the foundation of the nation, and when the foundation is strong, the nation is secure.[519] The people depend on agriculture. At this time, there are many unjust rules in various provinces. They are not ashamed to defy reason, but are only afraid that they cannot skillfully steal what belongs to others. Some occupy large areas of forests and fields and deprive the people of their benefits, while others manage many rice fields and hinder the people's agriculture. Therefore, from now on, the governors must not cultivate any rice fields other than the "kugeden" public rice fields.[520] They must not secretly devour and cultivate the land, and they must not violate the peasants' farmland.[521]

---

year." What's written following it was a decree by Emperor Kanmu in an official Department of State document on November 3rd, Enryaku year 3, as recorded in the *Shoku Nihongi*. The emperor prohibited the cultivation of land by the provincial governors unless it was government land.

[519] These words appear in the *Book of Documents*, in the book of Xia, Songs of the Five Sons.

[520] The term "kugeden" refers to "rice paddy field used to pay for the various expenses of government offices," and in this case refers to the rice paddy allocated to the provincial governor's office. The number of rice paddies granted to the major provincial governors and below is stipulated in Denryo 31.

[521] In *Shoku Nihongi*, the following is written: "The people are the true essence of the land. If the essence is firm, the nation will be secure. The people's resources are agriculture and sericulture. The rulers of the land are not ashamed of the fact that their government is often backward, only that they are not yet skillful enough at poaching from others. Some occupy large tracts of forests and deprive the people (note: the public) of the conveniences of life, while others cultivate many fields and hinder the people (note: the masses) cultivating the land. This is the reason for the peasants' malpractice. The government must punish and reform greed and corruption by imposing prohibitions.

Again, in the third year of Konin,[522] the following is written:

> The provincial governors were especially restricted from cultivating rice fields on land or water other than the kugeden.[523] Yet, the provincial governors did not obey the laws of the imperial court, but instead sought only their own personal gain, engaging in all sorts of plots and intrigue for which they showed little repentance. Some bought many cultivated fields under someone else's name, while others have fought to take possession of fertile lands under the pretense of being royal vassals.[524] Without this, the people would not be out of work.[525]

From this time forward, the provincial governors must not allow any more rice fields outside of the kugeden (note: "rikuden" were added to the document on the 20th day as well). And do not allow devouring of the land of the peasants' hoes in self-interest." (Aoki Kazuo, *Shin Nippon Kotenbungaku Taikei 16*, *"Shoku Nihongi"* [Tokyo: Iwanami Shoten, 1998], 307). There are differences in how the kanji are read, but there are also quite a few abbreviations and word changes in Kita's quotation.

[522] Imperial decree by Emperor Saga in an official Department of State document on May 3rd, Konin year 3, as recorded in the *Shoku Nihongi*.

[523] The "restriction" referred to here is the official Department of State document dated November 3rd, Enryaku year 3.

[524] The "royal vassals" referred to here are nobles of the fifth rank or above.

[525] In *Nihon Koki*, t's written as follows: "Toward the provincial governors they were very strict about cultivating land outside the kugeden. However, the provincial governors did not obey the sovereign but instead their own self-interests. They have committed a hundred kinds of deception, and not a single one of them has ever been punished. They may buy a large number of cultivated fields under the pretense of another's name, or they may wear the guise of the king's vassals and compete to occupy the fertile lands. The people would not lose their jobs if not for this." (Nobuo Kruoita, *Nihon Koki*, ed. Tei Morita [Tokyo: Shueisha, 2003], 607). There are many omissions or abbreviations in

572 | The Theory of Japan's National Polity and Pure Socialism

Look at these examples. In this way, the provincial governors gradually came to own large private estates, and the economic source on which the civic state depended dried up. When the great monarchs of the Engi and Tenryaku periods looked down from their idealistic dreams and inquired about the condition of the people below,[526] there were no more taxes to be collected, and the fields in front of the Ministry of Finance were barren and filled with only weeds.

Thus, the imperial family failed in its dream of an ideal state, and because of economic demands—or because, with the death of Emperor Tenji, many monarchs who did not understand such lofty ideals were misled by Buddhism—they were forced to sell or reappoint the position of provincial governor to local clans, who became wealthy through gold, silver, and rice grain. This is how the imperial family itself curtailed the ideal of a civic state. The death of Emperor Tenji meant the death of an emperor who worked for the benefit and purpose of the state, and the nation then became a patriarchal state in which the land and people were treated as property for the emperor's self-interest.

At first, the emperor was the supreme ruler, standing as patriarch over the land and people of the region, and the emperor alone was the owner of the nation. However, the local governors, who became powerful as described previously, increased their power as society evolved, becoming the Minamoto and Taira clans, the rival warlords, and lords of later generations. The tide of patriarchal power flowed vigorously, forming an era of aristocratic states that culminated in the Meiji Revolution. The Fujiwara clan privately owned most of the country from the middle of that monarchical period. When several

---

Kita's quote, just like the previous one.

[526] Emperor Daigo (around the time of Engi) and Emperor Murakami (around the time of Tenryaku). Together, their achievements are referred to as the "Engi-Tenryaku Reign."

imperial princes went hungry and were given rice grain by the emperor, it becomes clear just how the imperial family had lost the economic basis to contend with the later patriarchal monarchs. Thus, it is no surprise in the evolution of society that the emperor, who dreamed of standing as the sole supreme authority over an ideal state, was so impoverished and constantly oppressed that his ideals were simply that: ideals.

No! The civic state of the Taika was not only a temporary, dreamlike project with an economic basis. When it came to political organization, it was a pure class state. Emperor Tenmu mixed many titles together, and instead gave out eight hereditary titles.[527] Chiefs of large clans were given large blades, and chiefs of small clans were given small ones. This clearly shows him inheriting the patriarchal system. The establishment of how noble and respectable one must be for each particular clan, for example, is still based on the principle of lineage of the class-based era. In the Taiho Code,[528] the appointment of officials was also restricted by lineage and clans, and it can be seen how this was an idea that went against the plan of the civic state. The fact that all government offices, which were the institutions of the state, were decided by family name and lineage, meaning all of the most important positions were privately owned by the Fujiwara family, that the law was the private property of the Oe and Nakahara clans, and that Sinology was the private property of the Sugawara and Miyoshi clans,[529] shows that this was

---

[527] The eight hereditary titles were organized and redone by Emperor Temmu in 684, and were, from highest to lowest rank, Mahito, Asaomi, Shukune, Imiki, Michinoshi, Omi, Muraji, and Inagi. They were ranked according to how close their ancestral lineage was to the imperial family.

[528] This expression is used because the decree stipulated matters related to appointments in the Taiho Ritsuryo Code.

[529] The above four clans are well-known as scholar families. The Kiyohara clan is also in this lineage. Incidentally, among the Sugawara and Miyoshi clans, Sugawara no

undoubtedly a patriarchal state rather than a civic state. The civic state of the Taika Revolution was the ideal of the wise and lucid Emperor Tenji alone, and obviously the ancient society of 1,300 years ago had not yet become aware that the state had its own evolutionary purpose and ideal for its own existence. It was merely an attempt by philosopher-monarchs of ancient times to become mankind's ideal politicians, as Plato had hoped for in his ideal state. What became a reality after the Taika Revolution was the overthrow of the theocracy based on primitive religions. The rest of these ideals were finally realized through the Meiji Revolution after a long evolutionary process of 1,300 years.

For a nation's national polity to become that of a civic state, a society must evolve to the point where the molecules of the state are aware that the state itself has a purpose and ideal for its own survival and evolution. That is, there must be a moral and legal evolution to the point where the molecules of the state think of themselves as parts of the state, never treating other molecules as means to their own ends, with their own interests as the ultimate goal. Legally speaking, we've arrived at the current nationalism, which is based off state sovereignty, after a very long evolutionary process since the days of monarchical sovereignty. On the one hand, we are still individualist in that, due to the self-interest of the monarchs and nobles (in other words, many of the lords), all other molecules become sacrifices for them. On the other hand, we are socialist in that all state institutions act as a part of society for the purpose of society's survival. Nationalism is socialism on a local basis, which will eventually lead to global nationalism of one grand nation. (Because of this, we do not take the views of individualists who call themselves socialists while

---

Michizane and Miyoshi Kiyotsura are famous persons from the same period. However, when Miyoshi Kiyotsura took an examination for promotion to a government official, he was rejected by the examiner, Sugawara no Michizane, and it is said that Miyoshi Kiyotsura was at odds with Sugawara no Michizane on every occasion after that.

professing to deny the state, as that is a suicidal argument which refutes the state itself.)

In order to reach nationalism from monarchism, it is necessary to extend the national consciousness not only to one or a few members of society, but to all members. The words of Louis XIV, "I am the State," are surprisingly barbaric from today's perspective, when the national consciousness has been extended to all members of society. However, it's still quite obviously further evolved than saying, "I am myself." This is because he recognized himself as part of society. However, since the lower classes didn't have any sort of consciousness as part of society, he was, legally, all of society. In those times, loyalty and patriotism went hand in hand. For Louis, since he himself was the whole nation, his own self-interest was patriotism, as loving the nation meant loving him, and the loyalty of the lower classes, which were not part of the nation, toward the self-interest of the sovereign, who had awakened a sense of nationhood, was patriotism, since it was equally an action toward the whole nation. In order for the theory of loyalty and patriotism coincidence to be valid, we must live in an age where the molecules of the state, aside from the monarch, are not considered part of the state. (There are cases where the relationship between the monarch and his subjects in this patriarchal period is as explained in the previous legal theory. In these cases, the monarch is placed outside the state, and the people and land are named the state. The monarch's patriotism then comes from his own love toward the state as his possession, and the people are loyal to him, but they aren't patriotic.)

Great Emperor Tenji, according to the Confucian ideal of the state, was not like Louis XIV, but was aware that the emperor was part of the state and that the state itself had a purpose for its own survival and evolution. However, not all are Emperor Tenji. Since ancient times, social evolution gave rise to incredible individuality in certain people, almost as if telling humanity to work toward the future until it could be attained. Much like Christ and Buddha, who spoke of ideals far head of their time, Emperor Tenji was born in a much earlier period, but none of the emperors after him managed to understand the obvious result of social evolution: that they were part of the state. Many of them considered themselves to be the whole of the state and regarded their sense of personal self-interest as the will of the state at the same time. This was the era of the patriarchal monarchy.

The patriarchal state age gave way to an aristocratic period in which many patriarchs, acting with the individual as the ultimate goal, fought each other, and the national consciousness extended to the minority classes. Of course, during the Warring States period, when the patriarchs fought each other in various regions, a situation was created wherein "I am the state" was true within that lord's area of ownership. However, when the aristocracy united upon entering the feudal system era, they did not interpret themselves as the whole of the state, but extended their sense of equality to all within their class, and became part of the state with the other aristocrats.

The evolution of the state is the development of a sense of equality. Conflicts, upheavals, turmoil, and personal contact within a society gradually expand the sense of oneself and others as fellow human beings. Slaves and low-ranked people became children and roto to families, those then became warriors. The descendant of one who was mocked as "Ise Heiji" became chancellor of the realm,[530] and the child of one who was elevated to being part of this world's memories became a great shogun.[531] The Hojo clan of the feudal

---

[530] In *Heike Monogatari* 1, "Tenjo no Yamiuchi," it's written that Taira no Tadamori (Taira no Kiyomori's father) was mocked, saying, "The Ise Taira clan is cross-eyed." The "Ise heiji" is normally a type of bottle produced in the Ise region, but since the Taira clan was based in Ise as well, it's a pun on "Taira clan," which could be read "Heiji," and the bottles, also read "heiji."

[531] Minamoto no Yoshitomo. In *Hogen Monogatari*, "Imperial Visit to the Emperor's Sanjo Palace," when he was summoned before the emperor and told by Shinzen to subdue the rebels and relieve their superior's anger, Yoshitomo said, "How can I live the rest of my

lords and the Toyotomi clan of the commoners became lords of the country, and vagrant samurai roamed the country with only a sword, becoming lords and daimyo. Just as the view of equality was extended to the aristocracy, who became aware that they were part of the nation, the same view of equality was extended to the general class of warriors and commoners as society evolved, leading to the evolution of national sovereignty and nationalism, in which all molecules of the nation consider themselves part of the nation. In other words, as Plato said, "Society is the sum of the individuals, and the individuals are the parts of society." We have come to a social democracy in which all the members of the state are the state itself.

The Meiji Revolution was the overthrow of the aristocracy of the old society by a democracy formed in the development and expansion of national consciousness throughout the nation. Perry's arrival awakened the national consciousness of the Japanese people (even the lower class) as living in one society, one nation, via the voice of "expulsion of the barbarians." The socialism of Imperial Japan's existence was shouted through the eardrums to their brains like an electric shock. A nation has a purpose of survival. A nation has an ideal of evolution. And we are all molecules of the nation, with no inferiors or superiors. As molecules of the state, we are the parts of the state that must strive to realize the state's purpose and ideal of survival and evolution.

Indeed, the revolution was socialist in that it clearly recognized the purpose and ideals of the state in terms of law and morality. It was also a democracy in that it clearly extended this awareness to all elements of the nation as moral and legal ideals. This is why the low-ranking samurai, sword in hand, roamed the land. The peasants abandoned the meaning of the title

---

life without going off into the garden of warfare?" Yoshitomo tried to force his way into the palace, saying, "I will ascend to the palace now, wish me well before I die," but was stopped by Shinzen. (Kishitane Seiichi, *Hogen Monogatari*, [Tokyo: Iwanami Bunko, 1934], 42.)

"commoners" and assumed the authority of monarchs, complete with bamboo spears and banners made of straw mats. Many of them were killed under the name "rebellious subjects." All of them were crushed in a peasant revolt. We should not say that this was a counterattack against the severe money collections. In terms of harsh collection, there is nothing worse than the ancient system of slavery, in which the body itself was treated as property. However, because of the social construction of conscience, they considered themselves lower creatures than their slave owners and never cried out in loud rebellion even if they were buried in the ground as martyrs. In the Tokugawa era, peasants and townspeople were no longer slaves or lowly citizens. There weren't serfs, nor were they commoners. They were a democratic people who were in the midst of swallowing their cries for a constitution that had been raised immediately after the Meiji Revolution.

The "theory of the national polity" was democracy, but cloaked in the garb of the classic tests and Confucianism. No matter how the garment was torn, the fine man of democracy walked leisurely down the boulevard with his chest hair uncovered. Loyalty to the emperor itself was not the purpose that had put the aspirants in such difficulty. The purpose was to repudiate their loyalty to the aristocracy. The aristocracy had already repudiated its loyalty and become independent. The general class, then, must also repudiate its allegiance and become free. History is evolutionary, not cyclical. Aristotle's three categories of government systems are a linear order according to the evolution of the three ages, not a cycle from democracies to monarchies, as was thought to be the case in his time. How could there be a restoration from aristocracy to monarchy in ancient times? Three hundred years of peace have completely changed our thoughts on rights. The samurai, who had a custom of cut-throat robbery, using their strength against townspeople who had borrowed money, almost as if merely enforcing their own property rights, could no longer perform these barbaric acts. This evolution of the idea of rights, in which might is not considered a right, was like a tidal wave against the very foundations of the medieval patriarchal monarchs who had gained their power through might, and thus it began to destroy them. Three hundred years of peace brought about an enormous economic evolution, and thus all property rights came to be determined by physical and mental labor. Yet, the nobles and warriors did not perform any labor, but simply remained calm and played with their authority. Three hundred years of culture have also given the people a simple historical awareness.

To be fair, they still did not enter the labyrinth of Takamagahara to wonder how the nation of Japan was founded and how the imperial family has existed to this day. However, the whispers of the ancient texts could clearly be heard, and they said that the rulers and shogun they served as their lords were, in fact, cut-throat robbers. Ah, cut-throats! They didn't realize that to deny the rights gained by the massive power of the aristocracy was to further deny the massive power of ancient history. They were faced with a situation where they had to hold a burning torch with their left hand and theorize with their right. The torch would go out in a cloud of flame. The undistinguished Shosetsu Yui appeared and fell. The theory of the revolution demanded more haste than fire—so even if the beliefs of primitive religions were to cease altogether, what time would there be during that period for useless scholarly research into primitive times?

The black ships of barbaric foreigners were billowing smoke over the sea, and emperors, like Emperor Kameyama, were no longer dependent on primitive religions for the security of the nation. The red-haired and blue-eyed men weren't yet considered fellow brothers, but the belief in the Shinto Adan and Eve was no longer strong enough to create a sacred typhoon to blow away their crowns. The situation was simply urgent. Revolutionary historiography left antiquity on a high shelf for the most part, and focused on the Middle Ages and later. Rai San'yo's *Nihon Gaishi* (Unofficial History of Japan), which would mislead today's national polity theorists into believing that the lords and even the shogun were noble and loyal, emerged amidst persecution for its surprisingly flamboyant style of writing and its bending of the facts. Mito's *Dai Nihonshi* (Great History of Japan) described in a detailed manner the aristocracy's plunder by power, just as Marx's *Capital* described the plunder of the capitalists. The three hundred years of medieval history caused as much social evolution as the three thousand years of ancient history. The rights that our ancestors had gained three hundred years before, while arrows and stones were flying through the sky at Sekigahara, were now, three hundred years later, being described by historians as a crime. The tide of the revolution was only too quick to repudiate. Just as they had once attacked and persecuted the imperial family for its loyalty to the aristocracy, they planned to overthrow the aristocracy in the name of loyalty to the imperial family.

The ancient and medieval loyalty to the aristocracy was genuine. The current loyalty is simply masquerading a democracy and trying to wash blood with more blood. They have drawn their revolutionary theories like threads, not using reason and logic, but from the old theories of the classics' Takamagahara and the Confucian idea of the low and high road. They will say that the shogunate, the lords, became rulers over the land and the people only because of the strength of their low road rulers. They assume, on the other hand, that the imperial family were virtuous, high road rulers. The people were not obligated to be loyal to the shogunate and the lords, who were merely cut-throat robbers. But the imperial family, on the other hand, was assumed to be the ruler of all Japan, having received orders from the heavens.

The Meiji Revolution was an explosion of the national consciousness, which was awakened by contact between nations, and the spread of the view of equality, which resulted from social evolution over the past 1,300 years, before the nation and nationalism (i.e., social democracy) were even discussed. It is by no means a miracle dating back 1,300 years.

Clearly understand the original meaning of the Meiji Revolution.

Because they do not understand that the fundamental meaning of the Meiji Revolution is democracy, the Japanese people have little awareness of their own history, and they make arbitrary assumptions and dogmatic statements about the restoration of the monarchy, and about the restoration of the regime and the domain of the feudal lords. Therefore, we ourselves are unaware of the significance of our existence today. If the aristocracy was so ardent that it was willing to restore the government and lands out of respect for the lord and loyalty to the sovereign, how could it have looted the country to the extent that firepower was required to take that plunder back? How could they slice and strangle to death the very national polity theorists to whom they were supposed to return the loot? Was the blood that stained the snow outside Sakuradamon the result of mutual vengeance for both sides' attempts to be loyal to the imperial family?[532] Was the Boshin War the result of Japan's national attempts to be loyal and reverent to the imperial family? Was the fleeing of the seven lords the result of the Tokugawa clan's reverence to the ruler and loyalty to the lord?[533] Were the arrows and bullets flying toward the lord's banner treason for the purpose of reverence and loyalty toward the imperial family?

Clearly understand the original meaning of the Meiji Revolution. Because it fails to note that the evolution of history is the development of the view of equality, even *Two Thousand Five Hundred Years of History*, which in parts is

---

[532] The Sakuradamon Incident was the assassination of Chief Minister Ii Naosuke by a group of ronin who had escaped from Mito. The reason why the Mito ronin targeted Ii is because the feudal lord Tokugawa Nariaki and his son, Yoshinobu, were ordered to stay under house arrests in the so-called Ansei Purge, which Ii led. Incidentally, the incident occurred on a snowy morning on March 3rd, hence the expression "blood that stained the snow," but March at that time corresponded to April now, so it was unusual for snow to fall.

[533] The fleeing of the seven lords to the capital was the expulsion of radicals due to a political upheaval (a coup d'état within the imperial court by the Kobutgattai faction) that occurred on August 18th, 1863.

a work of great beauty, dismisses aristocrats such as Yoshitoki and Takauji as democrats, and thus neglects the democratic principle of national polity theory. Yoshisada and Takauji were clearly egalitarians toward the sovereign, but they were aristocrats who stood as strict monarchs toward the lower class of samurai and peasants. The national polity theory of the Meiji Revolution resembled monarchism in that it shook hands with the emperor and overthrew the aristocracy, but it was a bold democracy in that it was an absolute egalitarianism in which both the emperor and the people acted as members of the state. Even if the aristocrats of Choshu and Satsuma were motivated by a desire to avenge the humiliation of Sekigahara, and an ambitious samurai made a pact to become an aristocrat after the overthrow of the shogunate, once the curtains closed on the Sekigahara stage, it would never again be performed before a historical audience. The personal strides of the ambitious are an inevitable phenomenon that accompanies revolutionary upheaval.

Even though the revolutionary theory of national polity had a Shinto hue and was a byproduct of imperialist theories, the true color of the aspirants of the time was democracy, which sought to overthrow the aristocracy. The jingasaren of Hikokuro Takayama and others were nothing more than a useless and harmful political frenzy,[534] similar to the way the Social Democrats shot the late German emperor as they were being founded. Just as the overthrow of the emperor was not the goal of the Social Democrats, the goal of the national polity theory was to overthrow the aristocratic government. The patriarchal state of more than a thousand years ago was an uncivilized age in which only a philosopher-monarch could be aware of the purpose and ideals of the state itself. The Meiji Revolution was not a restoration of that ancient patriarchal state. It was a new development toward a civic state, inheriting the

---

[534] An advocate for the reverence for the emperor in the late Edo period. Together with Hayashi Shihei and Gamo Kumpei, he is known as one of the three eccentric figures of Kansei. Incidentally, "jingasaren" refers to those at the lower ranks.

long evolution of the patriarchal state. A savage village of the Orient might call it restoration of the monarchy, but history is something that evolves.

Indeed, history is an evolutionary process. The evolution of society means the expansion of social consciousness, and political history is therefore the expansion of the consciousness toward government. In Western antiquity, the Latin peoples experienced periods of monarchy and aristocracy before evolving into the republican democracies of Greece and Rome. Similarly, the Germanic peoples also went through the evolution of monarchies and aristocracies before the English and Germans arrived at the democratic regimes of today. The same is true of Japan, which evolved from a monarchy in ancient times to an aristocracy in medieval times, and then to a democratic state after the Meiji Revolution. The present emperor is a heroic leader of the Meiji Revolution's democrats. The "theory of national polity" shook hands with the emperor in order to overthrow the aristocracy, but that emperor did not have the ancient meaning of a patriarch as the owner of the nation, but rather the meaning of a molecule with special privileges of the state—a citizen in Mr. Minobe's so-called broad sense of the word. In other words, the emperor himself, as a citizen of a democracy on an equal footing with the people, realized the ideals of Emperor Tenji and became the state institution of an ideal state for the first time. This is what the word "emperor" evolved to mean after the Meiji Revolution.

However, it is a clear fact that the democracy of the revolution was an unplanned explosion. They awakened to the egalitarianism that asked why one should be a prince, a general, or a minister based on family or lineage. They became aware of the liberalism that said they did not have to fulfill some slave-like duty of loyalty to the nobility, just as the nobles rebelled against the emperor. However, there was almost no constructive plan for what to do after overthrowing the aristocracies with this liberalism and egalitarianism.

For this reason, the Satsuma nobles dreamed of switching positions with the Tokugawa clan. Ambitious men hoped to become marquises in the process.

They dreamed of a debate among a confederation of lords, declaring that they would choose the best among them via public opinion. Even so, the basis for the upheaval was in the development of equality, in the demand for freedom, and in democracy. The revolution had already ended in destruction without a plan of construction. This was very different from the European revolutions.

In Europe, the ideals of the new societies were clearly defined after long deliberations, and in addition to that, the democratic government already realized by the Latin peoples in ancient times provided an historical example, allowing an attempt to restore those ideals. The European revolution was clearly planned. Therefore, we think that the Meiji Revolution succeeded only in its destructive aspect against the aristocracy, and the true essence of democratic construction was the "Constitution of the Empire of Japan" of 1893, which was obtained through the great movement demanding the establishment of a constitution, the declaration "to govern by public opinion," and the Saga Rebellion and the Civil War. The Meiji Revolution only destroyed the aristocracy in the Boshin War, while the construction of democracy was a movement that continued for twenty-three years and was brought to a conclusion by the Imperial Constitution.

Clearly understand the original meaning of the Meiji Revolution. In the name of "clan favoritism" and "parties," aristocracy and democracy fought to gain more power during said construction. Even the elder statesmen who supported clan favoritism were once fine and bold democrats during their youth, back when they wandered the nation, brandishing their swords as young warriors. The government of the land should be decided according to public opinion. Who are the lords and daimyo? We are not their subjects, and we are not obliged to be loyal to them. Yet, according to the principle of social evolution, in which all progressive forces become conservative as soon as they gain power, they overthrew the aristocracy and replaced it with themselves as lords, generals, and ministers.

Of course, it goes without saying that today's "nobility" are merely postoperative scars, a people who have completely lost their significance as monarchs and owners of public debt, as if the economic realization of socialism were imagined to place entrepreneurs and landowners in a special economic well-being for a while through public debt. (This is why there is no reason for today's socialists to equate these powerless individuals with today's economic aristocracy in the sense of the patriarchal era, and to attack the former.) However, when their flowery faces are covered with silver beards and their resourceful, adventurous eyes, glinting with light, eager to push things forward, are filled with the signs of deep thinking and grandiosity, it's clear that those today have become completely different personalities from who they once were. We don't believe the public's evaluation of them as people who use their names to engage in mere indulgence. They are brimming with ambition. Rather than having surrendered themselves to their former enemies, the aristocracy, they are fighting a fierce battle. As the cynicism of the upstarts fades, the declaration of "deciding based on public opinion" has been completely forgotten too—thus, the heirs to the Meiji Revolution became the so-called political opposition. The clannists were once the elder statesmen of the destructive facet of the Meiji Revolution. However, when it came to the main, constructive aspect of the revolution, they became the cause of oppression toward the democrats.

The elder statesmen of the Meiji Revolution were themselves divided into two factions, and the decisive and intelligent aristocrats were victorious. Against the absolute tyranny of Toshimichi Okubo, the democrats of the Seinan and Saga ended up disemboweled or imprisoned. Aritomo Yamagata's security ordinance rounded up the wildly enthusiastic Danton and Robespierre and banished them to three ri away from Tokyo.[535] Hirobumi Ito's Imperial

---

[535] This "security ordinance" was a decree enacted in 1887 to suppress the freedom and civil rights movement. Nakae Chomin, Ozaki Yukio, and others were banished. Article

Constitution added yet another layer of tyranny to the translation of German tyranny, and they roared toward the clouds above the defeated and disorganized remains of the democratic party's soldiers. Ah, what is it that one feels when one looks back on the Democratic Party? Under the threat of dissolution and the temptation of gold, they only call themselves things like the political friends, or the progressive party.

Let us repeat. Clearly understand the original meaning of the Meiji Revolution. Understand that the clannists are rightly regarded as the elder statesmen in the destructive aspects of the revolution, but also understand that they are clearly the source of oppression in the constructive aspects of the revolution. Finally, understand our Japanese history with a solemn historical philosophy.

Social democracy is the historical continuum of the Meiji Revolution, and it strives for the full realization of its ideals.

We must erase our previously-used phrase "rebellious subjects." They are something that only a savage village of the Orient would have. We merely had no choice but to use those words to break the geocentric theory known as "national polity theory." It would be barbaric, of course, to criticize thousands of years of political action and ethical will using the yardsticks and compasses of a single era. Those who don't understand the evolution of political and ethical history, observe and apply rules to ancient times based on their own

---

IV states, "When it is recognized that a person within three ri of the Imperial Palace or the destination to which the emperor has gone is plotting or plans to instigate a civil war or disturb public order, the Superintendent General or the District Director may, with the approval of the Minister of the Interior, order the person to leave for a limited period and prohibit entry to the area within three ri for a period of three years."

Danton and Robespierre were French politicians and radicals of the French Revolution, famous for their decisive use of fear tactics in politics. Used as an analogy for the militants of the civil rights movement.

time period, calling people rebellious subjects. This is also why there are people who interpret the political and ethical history of past emperors, such as Emperor Yuryaku and Emperor Buretsu massacring the people, whom they owned as possessions, since they owned the nation, as cruel and inhumane. They imagine the current emperor committing these acts of the past. Obviously the emperor was free to take away all the people's property, even if he said, "I will not ask what you do with your property."[536] Since the people themselves were the emperor's property, it was not politically illegal or a moral crime to take the wives and concubines of his subjects, unlike today. All right and wrong are right and wrong according to evolution (read the section in *The Enlightenment of Socialism* where we explain the class struggle). Therefore, being executed by the monarchs and others whom the revolutionary party served under the name of "rebellious subjects" no longer occurs, and the stigma attached to the name is gone too. Similarly, the names of the aristocrats who

---

[536] This line comes from part of a waka poem titled "Imperial order cannot be helped, but what answer shall be given the warbler who returns home?" The following article can be found in *Okagami*, volume 6, under "Michinaga." "During the reign of Emperor Murakami, the plum tree in Seiryouden Palace had withered, and when he was looking for a suitable plum tree as a replacement, he found a magnificent red plum tree at a certain house. When the emperor dug up this plum tree and was about to take it with him, the owner of the tree entrusted him with a letter, saying, 'Tie this to the tree and take it with you.' When the emperor read the letter in the palace, he found that it read, 'Imperial order cannot be helped, but what answer shall be given the warbler who returns home?' (Since this is a direct order from the emperor, I dare not disobey. However, please instruct me on how to answer the bush warbler who was nesting in this tree when he returns and asks 'Where is my home?') After reading the poem, the emperor, who thought it was suspicious, investigated the house and found out it was the home of Ki no Tsurayuki's daughter, and felt bad at what he'd done." (*Okagami* trans. Hiroshi Hosaka, [Toyko: Kodansha Gakujustu Bunko, 1981]).

named the revolutionary party "rebellious subjects" (not today's nobles, but their ancestors) must be completely revoked now that the revolution has succeeded. From the viewpoint of scientific ethics, just as the successful democrats today have been exonerated from the name of "rebellious subjects" by the aristocracy, the aristocracy never bore the title "rebellious subjects" by the society of the time, back when they were successful in defeating the emperor. Not only is this true in theory, but also in fact. All right and wrong are right and wrong according to evolution. The evolution of society is a class struggle, progressively moving upward, so all right and wrong must be decided by social forces. How can a rebellious subject, who is said to be the most unprincipled person in human ethics, be installed as a shogun or a lord by social forces? Some will defile the Imperial Rescript on Education for their own protection and, in an attempt to show that it says this, will declare the following: "This has been true throughout the ages, and it is not contrary to reason even if it is widely spread both domestically and internationally."

However, as discussed earlier, since the Imperial Rescript on Education does not have the authority to establish official ethics and doctrines, it does not have the authority to establish official historical philosophy either. Although the emperor, together with the Imperial Diet, organizes the legislative body, orders laws, and can issue orders with independent authority, he is not a state institution that prescribes official doctrines. Even though the emperor praises all the people for their "loyalty and filial piety," it is not dishonorable for so-called national polity theorists to denounce Yoshitoki and Takauji as rebellious subjects. In the same way, we can transcend all obstructions from the standpoint of scientific ethics, since we follow the moral standards of the time in our interpretation of our ancestors' deeds and criticize them according to their evolution. In the first place, the current scholars—especially, Mr. Tetsujiro Inoue, a professor of literature who walks around the academic world with the Imperial Rescript on Education as his only shield—are not afraid to blame their inferior brains on the emperor, and we are not going to give the following title to them, but it would be justified to give them the title of "disrespectful men."

Speaking calmly as a scientific researcher (since we speak of historical studies, and are not scholars rattling off weasel words like drummers at an event), it's clear that the present emperor is a preeminent, great emperor who can only be ranked with Emperor Tenji among the best of the emperors of one eternal lineage. The one who was always purely a poet had inherited in his sorrow and resentment the qualities of excellence and wisdom in order to eliminate the oppression of the Tokugawa clan. He was honed by the turmoil of the revolution from a young age, almost as if history itself, riddled with difficulties, was telling him "I will hone you into a gem." Much like how Mencius admired the son of King Qi from afar, saying, "people are inspired by the place where they live and the environment they live in,"[537] the imposing appearance of the Oriental model, created using the heroes of the Meiji Revolution, brought about an outstanding monarch right before our very eyes. (We think that today's cries of respect for the lord and loyalty to the sovereign signify hero worship of the personal excellence of the present emperor).

For this reason, however, it is the height of outrage to pull the emperor within the scope of academic research and demand his omnipotence as a scientific ethicist. From the infantile world of thought of the twenty-third year of Meiji, no one, regardless of their eminence, could possibly have understood the socially created conscience and its critique according to the evolution of right and wrong. Those of later generations who write Meiji history should absolutely never insult the emperor's wisdom because of that. The emperor has an important mission to the nation which goes beyond academic research. Even if the Imperial Rescript on Education incorporates old ethical doctrines, it is the negligence of a scholar, who exists in a highly advanced world of thought, that prevents him from shedding his old knowledge, not the Imperial Rescript

---

[537] Refer to chapters five and sixteen of *Mencius*.

on Education. To be more precise, the fact that Mr. Tetsujiro Inoue and others still adhere to dogmatic old theories of ethics today is due to the wisdom of Mr. Tetsujiro as a professor of literature. The Imperial Rescript on Education is not responsible for his foolishness. To be even more precise, the fact that the people of Japan have not been able to rise above a static, unchanging ethic even today is not the fault of the Imperial Rescript on Education.

Clearly understand the significance of the emperor to the nation. In scholarly debate, there must be no crude, self-serving use of the Imperial Rescript on Education, nor must there be any suggestion that the Imperial Rescript on Education is doing academia wrong because academics took a position which contradicts it. This is a sin of the people. It is the sin of the people themselves, as they don't understand the significance of the people and the emperor. As explained earlier, the emperor destroyed "the theory of national polity" a long time ago. Dogū clay figures may be safely set upon the battle-monks' mikoshi to become the guardian deity of the theory of national polity, but the Japanese emperor is strictly the Japanese emperor. The Japanese emperor did not give the Imperial Rescript on Education as a matter for scholars to confirm the ethics of Mr. Tetsujiro Inoue and others.

However, one mustn't misunderstand. The fact that we say that the medieval aristocracy were not rebellious subjects according to the moral standards of the time is irrelevant to the view of other dogmatists who say that the aristocrats were moralists who excluded the imperial family in the interest of the state and the well-being of the people. Yoshitoki Hojo was merely a representative of the interests of the aristocracy of his time, and did not realize any theory at all which could label him a democrat, and it should be obvious that no matter how rich the adjectives may be, enough to steal one's heart, Takauji Ashikaga was a man who occupied a large seat as a major patriarch over countless other patriarchal monarchs. He is not to be compared to Oliver Cromwell and others. In the ancient and medieval times of patriarchal states with no sense of national purpose or ideal, many patriarchal emperors acted out of their own personal self-interest. In the same way, it's out of the question to say that Yoshitoki and Takauji fought against the imperial family for the sake of the nation's interests and the happiness of the people. Furthermore, to say that they did their best for the people while enduring the stigma of being rebellious subjects is more dogmatic than even the dogmatism of the loyalists.

We say that they were not rebels according to the moral standards of the time because their freedom and independence were approved by their subjects or people they owned, along with the other aristocrats. It's true, of course, that the emperor's party didn't approve of their exertion of power outside the sphere of their possessions, nor did they recognize their conflict with the demands of the emperor's supreme authority, and so regarded them as rebellious subjects. However, in the struggle of the lower classes to evolve to the same plane as the upper classes, the rejection of the supreme authority of the upper classes in the form of rebellious subjects is not limited to the evolution from monarchy to aristocracy—it was also the name that the revolutionary party lords bore during the Meiji Revolution, which was an attempt to evolve from an aristocratic to a democratic state.

However, when the revolutionary party rejected the duty of loyalty to the nobility, it had the eloquence to launch a logical counterattack against them, that very nobility that had earlier rejected their duty of loyalty, whereas when the nobles gained political and moral independence, they had no claim but that of brute force. They used their mighty power to plunder the land and secure economic independence, thereby freeing themselves from all political and moral obligations. Not to mention, this all happened during an uncivilized period, the Middle Ages. Like Ko-no-Moronao, they had no choice but to exercise their freedom as they pleased. It's a fact throughout the history of the Middle Ages that the imperial party called them rebellious subjects, but they were recognized by the majority of society as monarchs in their own provinces, ones who had absolute freedom, and even if they clashed with the freedom of other monarchs as a result of this freedom, they were never regarded as rebellious subjects. The imperial family also clashed with them regarding both being monarchs.

So, let us affirm. As all acts of sovereigns with absolute and unlimited rights are beyond evaluation of right and wrong; they were sovereigns within their respective spheres and therefore had absolute freedom, which means all of them were morally void (this does not equate to immorality). The fact that the emperor failed to oppose Yoshitoki and Takauji was because he was not powerful enough, which is different from the question of whether or not he harmed the government. The reason why Takauji defeated the emperor was because he was superior in terms of his power, which has nothing to do with the noble concept of democracy. Democracy is a concept that came into the world under the old form of "national polity theory," around the time of the Meiji Revolution.

We must further rescind our earlier use of the term "rebellious subjects." We're referring to our assertion that all Japanese citizens were either accessories or accomplices to the rebellious subjects who attacked and persecuted the imperial family. As we have shown in the previous section, those in the warrior class were loyal and filial moralists who followed the path of their "lord and father before them" and circled around him like satellite bodies. Instead of being like the three hundred who died at Minatogawa following Masanari, they were more like the seven hundred who died in Kamakura following Takatoki throughout the whole of medieval history. Because of this, Bushido was perceived as (the teachings of) the bold and daring rebellious subjects against the imperial court, whose noble and autonomous morality expressed loyalty to the "lord and father before them," whom each served. We take back what we said about all being rebellious subjects.

The revolutionary party of the Meiji Revolution, the civil rights party that succeeded it in the constructive aspect, and we social democrats have all, at one time or another, been called rebellious subjects by the upper classes.

However, economic independence is the source of all independence. Just as ancient lords achieved political and moral freedom through economic independence, so too did medieval aristocrats achieve political and moral freedom through economic independence. Similarly, the evolution of economic history simultaneously became the evolution of political and ethical history, further liberating the lower classes of warriors and commoners from the aristocracy and extending the realization of political and moral freedom through economic independence to all molecules of the state. This became the Meiji Revolution, the movement for civil rights, and then the great demand for social democracy.

No, social democracy is not an attempt to rupture the unity of the state for the benefit of the individual, as was the case in the revolutions of the individualist era. Individual independence exists conditionally under the economic subordination of "supreme ownership of the state." The consciousness of society and the state is not a competition for survival among social units as it was around the time of the Meiji Revolution, but the expression of socialist ideals in moral and legal terms. The ideal of political power for all citizens (in the broadest sense), and the belief that any member of the population was part of the state and should not be sacrificed except to the ends of the state, became widespread. This is democracy—we absolutely don't think, like some socialists do, that social democracy will be realized by overthrowing the current national polity and system of government. It is with infinite joy that we see that the Meiji Revolution itself was of strict social democracy! (To cite just one example, Kaishu Katsu placed himself outside of the duty of loyalty toward the emperor or the shogun, and did not yield on acting as a unit of the nation).[538]

However, today's social democracy is characterized by this union of small societies, posing the questions of how their idealistic independence will further

---

[538] It's not completely clear, but Kita may be trying to say that he acted for the benefit of Japan as a whole by protecting Edo from war, rather than protecting the Shogunate.

evolve society at large and how to make the legal ideals of democracy a reality through a revolution of economic content.

Indeed, in its legal ideals and moral convictions, the morality and law of modern Japan is a bold social democracy. Let us now use the previously mentioned point of view to interpret constitutional law.

In other words, the phrase "one eternal lineage" found in "the Empire of Japan shall be ruled by an emperor of one eternal lineage" in Article 1 of the Constitution can be abandoned in favor of the Imperial House Law of Succession to the Throne in the Imperial House Law. This is because, even if it's a fact of history that the one eternal lineage isn't a literal direct line, but moves around here and there from countless collateral lines to collateral lines, and even if it is a fact of history that an emperor of one eternal lineage doesn't continually reign as ruler over all Japan at every turn, the right of emperors after the present emperor to serve as the most important institution of the state is clearly maintained by the Empire of Japan via the present Constitution. Furthermore, the term "one lineage" does not refer to a direct line, but rather to a provision in the Imperial Household Law that allows, in unavoidable cases, the right of succession to be extended to distant collateral lineages, each in a specific order. Also, the word "emperor" has evolved in meaning along with the evolution of the times, and no other "emperor" in the future of this "eternal" lineage will mean the same thing as the current emperor. Therefore, the Constitution's so-called "emperor of one eternal lineage" refers to the present emperor as the first emperor and to the future provision that the throne shall be handed down from the present emperor to all generations through direct or collateral descent. The words of the Constitution have no right to decide historical truth. It would then be a serious error to interpret the words "one eternal lineage" to mean that all emperors since the beginning of recorded history have been in one direct lineage, with no collateral lineages, and that all emperors for all generations have been manifestations of national authority like the present emperor is. So, there are only two paths to take with respect to the phrase "one eternal lineage." Either it should be discarded, as many constitutional scholars insist on doing with the word "sacred," or it should be interpreted, as we do, as meaning a future rule that says the throne should be transferred down the imperial lineage eternally, rather than attaching some historical significance to the words used in the law, according to the spirit of the Constitution. If the latter path is taken, it means that "lineage" should be extended based on the Imperial Household Law.

In our earlier discussion of the Constitution, we also noted that modern Japan's national polity is one of state sovereignty, and that the emperor and the people do not have a contractual, adversarial relationship as in the age of the class state. (In the constitutions of the European medieval class states, the monarch and the people were in direct conflict of rights and duties through contractual constitutions, but the various lords of the class state era in Japan became vestiges of the nobles due to the Meiji Revolution.) Therefore, the modern Japanese Constitution does not define the rights and duties of the emperor and the people, but expresses the relationship of the people to the state in a broad sense.

Of course, even in European countries that experienced contractual constitutions, monarchs and aristocrats are not a legal hierarchy, but rather state institutions that exercise the sovereignty of the state, so their evolution is completely different from the era of contracts. In Japan, however, no one would say that the present Constitution is a contractual constitution, since its enactment was under the exclusive authority of the emperor. Instead, in the name of Constitution granted by the emperor (which, of course, many scholars in fact interpret as a contractual conflict according to individualist jurisprudence, as explained earlier), the monarchical sovereignty theorists propagate a horrendous fallacy.

This fallacy has already been cleared of doubt by the previously mentioned historical interpretation. Post-Revolutionary Japan has a national polity of state sovereignty in that nationalism made the people discover that they exist as a social entity. It's a democracy in that its nationalism says all the people are part of the state, and all parts put forth their own representatives, who together with a privileged member (the emperor), organize the supreme authority. From the Meiji Revolution to the twenty-third year of Meiji, the country had a national polity of state sovereignty and its system of government was a monarchy, with the supreme authority being one single, privileged person (see the previously explained three categories of government systems relating to legal theory).

The term "monarchy" in both in terms of how it's written and pronounced should not be equated with that of the patriarchal state, in which the patriarch is in charge of the entire nation. The "monarch" or "emperor" after the Meiji Revolution was a citizen who, for the benefit of the nation as a whole, represented society's will as part of that society, rather than as an individual. He did these things out of a noble social self-interested, rather than individual self-interest like the rulers of the patriarchal state era. Such a monarchy was truly one of pure political morality. So, there have been times when the personality of the monarch, the single supreme authority, begins thinking that all parts of the country aside from himself aren't really parts of the country, and ignores all purpose and benefits of the state in favor of their own self-interest, or they begin to think of themselves as outside the state, and the state as their possession, and this turns the national into a patriarchal state. The competition for survival of the social unit was so intense and the heroes of the revolution were so preoccupied with the goals and interests of the state that there was no room left in their minds for inferior self-interest. In other words, the will of the emperor of Japan was legally the will of the Great Empire of Japan from the Meiji Revolution until Meiji year twenty-three. (Therefore, it bears repeating that we must not equate the emperor with the state. In such a monarchy, the emperor, as a part of the state, cannot be said to be the entire state just because he is motivated by the interests and purposes of the state, just as, in a republic, the parliament, as a part of the state, is not at the same time the entire republic.) As in a sovereign patriarchal state, all laws made for the interests and purposes of the sovereign are valid, so in a state sovereignty, the state has, in the very nature of its sovereignty, complete freedom to alter, abolish, or create state institutions for its own purposes and interests.

The Imperial Constitution of Meiji year twenty-three was a change in the supreme authority of the state, by the state, in the exercise of its full sovereignty for the purposes and benefits of the state. And the change in the institutions of the state was expressed by a single supreme authority showing the will of the state. The Imperial Constitution of Meiji year twenty-three was an announcement of the sovereignty of the state from the mouth of one supreme authority, and the present emperor is a completely different legal entity from the emperor before the Meiji Revolution. Before the Meiji Revolution, the emperor had the same legal status as the various lords, shogun, and other sovereigns, and was the patriarchal sovereign within his domain. However, after the Meiji Revolution until the twenty-third year of the Meiji era, he was a single, supreme authority who expressed the will of the state for the purposes and benefits of all of Japan. Therefore, while the state, by its very nature as the body of sovereignty, has absolute freedom to alter, abolish, or create state institutions, the emperor, who was the sole supreme authority in terms of simply expressing sovereignty, passed away after Meiji year twenty-three.

From now on, there will be no other state institution that will revise, abolish, or create state institutions in the name of state sovereignty aside from the supreme authority organized by the emperor and the Imperial Diet. This is evidenced by the fact that the current Constitution clearly prescribes the method of constitutional revision. Mr. Hozumi's assertion that the emperor has absolute freedom to amend or repeal the Constitution, in the name of the "constitution set by the emperor," is without a doubt an attempt to change the political system, which could be said to be crime of constitutional disorder. Let us ask Mr. Hozumi himself.

Mr. Hozumi's brain is worthless, and he's not even worthy of being a topic of discussion, yet, due to his important positions as president of a law university and professor at an imperial university, he has been the greatest target of abuse from our pen. We are deeply grateful to you, Mr. Hozumi, and we ask for your continued patience. If you say that, from the dogmatic idea that one who expresses will is the subject of that right, the present Constitution is a "constitution set by the emperor," and can thus be given and taken away by the emperor's right, we must ask you something. Would you call emperors such as Emperor Keitai, who hid in the countryside and only took the throne due to the will of Otomo-no-Kanamura, or Emperor Uda,[539] who received a title from the Minamoto clan and only took the throne by the will of Fujiwara-no-Mototsune, the "set emperors" of Kanamura or Mototsune?

Of the two heads possessed by Mr. Hozumi, the one who asserts loyalty to the sovereign and reverence to the lord would surely cry out in shock and deny this. "No! Since that was during the monarchy, they were merely expressing their will as institutions of their lord, for the benefit and purpose of their lord." However, his two heads can't live in peace. The other head, the one which espouses rebellious subjects, will strike the first head as it preaches loyalty to the sovereign and reverence for the lord, and will then yell loudly, "If we say that the Constitution is a 'constitution set by the emperor,' which can be freely revised or reorganized by the emperor according to his will, which is expressed as an institution of the state for the purpose and benefit of the state, then we must say that emperors Keitai and Koko[540] are 'set emperors' of Kanamura and Mototsune, who can freely abolish or change them at any time." The Constitution of the Great Empire of Japan is, of course, a constitution set by the emperor. However, "set" didn't mean this. Rather, it's an expression of the sovereignty of the state, through its sole supreme authority, to change the

---

[539] We again believe this is an error and should be Emperor Uda.

[540] See the previous annotation regarding Emperor Uda

supreme authority and to be organized by a privileged single person and an equal majority.

Mr. Hozumi is now at the limit of his patience. We express sympathy toward someone as worthless as he is, and we must now put away the arms we aimed at him. However, let us say one thing. Our previous explanation renders meaningless his argument over whether the emperor has the right to interpret the Constitution. This would be true for ancient laws in which the emperor was the main body of sovereignty, and it would be true when the emperor alone was the supreme authority. It would not be a problem if, as in some countries,[541] the power of interpretation were assigned to a judicial body independent of the legislative body. However, since the emperor and the Imperial Diet form the supreme authority together, but there is no provision for determining their wills in the event of a conflict, there is no way to resolve the conflict—it's an inadequacy in the law which we must accept. It's like when the House of Representatives and the House of Peers in the Imperial Diet support their own views, disagreeing with each other, there is no way to deal with the situation.[542] The absence of a legal provision is outside the scope of our authority as jurists to discuss.

---

[541] The fact that the judicial power is vested with the power of interpretation would mean that the courts have the power of unconstitutional review. In other words, the country mentioned here specifically is America. In America, it was established after Marbury v. Madison in 1803 that the courts were granted the right to review unconstitutionality. The fact that the right to review unconstitutionality is currently recognized in Japan is due to the influence of this American law.

[542] During the time of the Imperial Constitution, the House of Representatives and the House of Peers had equal powers. As a result, any laws that they disagreed with each other on couldn't be passed. For this reason, it was often the case that a proposal passed by the House of Representatives was rejected by the House of Peers. Incidentally, the postwar Constitution of Japan recognized the supremacy of the House of

It's all as mentioned previously. Oh, later historians! Do not misrepresent the protagonists of Meiji history by covering up the great leaders of democracy, who are, in all their actions, solemnly conscious of the purpose and ideal of the nation's survival and evolution, using the bad-mouthing performed by Mr. Hozumi and others.

Lastly, we'd like to describe the relationship between the emperor and the citizens.

Morality is both an external provision of law and an internal discipline. So, since the law realized nationalism, the national polity of state sovereignty, and national democracy—a government system in which all the people (in the broadest sense of the word) are in political power—it's true that we became a social democracy, which travels side-by-side with the internal law of morality, and has as its objective the survival and evolution of society and the ideal that all molecules of society should strive for that objective. It's unfortunate that the voice of "patriotism" has within it the echoes and odors of blood, of a medieval and barbaric custom. However, it is also true that this is what caused the people to gradually become aware of their social existence and take the first steps toward social democracy. It's a disgrace that the cries for "civil rights" still failed to shake people out of the enslaved conscience of the serfs and warriors, but it's also true that this awakening of the whole people to the fact that they are part of the nation has enabled them to understand the fundamental meaning of democracy. How, then, should we understand the moral relationship between the emperor and the people?

It's obvious from all the previous explanations that the relationship isn't one of a master-servant family, nor is it one of loyalty and filial piety coincidence. If we say, as in the "theory of national polity," that the current emperor is not emperor because he is a state institution, rather that he's emperor due to the beliefs of the primitive religion, it would essentially give

---

Representatives.

today's scientists, who don't believe in Buddhism, Christianity, or any other religions, the right to become Soga-no-Umako. It exposes all foreigners naturalized by law to a state of moral neglect in which they become pawns of the Han clan. Loyalty and filial piety can only coincide as a process of evolution back during the family group era, a primitive time when the population was small. If one were to say that, unlike today, such a thing would be impossible during an age of ethnic groups, when the sense of kinship of the family had been completely severed, then we would simply insist that we have no obligation to assert anything based on the lineages of three thousand years ago, which we can't know. Moreover, since the main and branch families are now pure equals, and the relationship between patriarch and family no longer conflicts in terms of the right to (give and take) life and death and the duty to slave, making the emperor the patriarch would lead to a situation in which the meaning of "emperor" couldn't be understood, and the emperor himself would be repudiated. Furthermore, loyalty was required only in the ancient times of slavery, when one's body was the property of the sovereign, or in the medieval days of Bushido, when slave morality was inherited through economic subordination. Knowing this, advocating it today would equally call into question the existence of the emperor himself, and also harm the interests of the nation through economic independence, which was established by the private property system. The premise which leads to this conclusion is one that the Great Empire of Japan would never allow. The emperor is the emperor because he is an institution maintained by the state for the benefit of the state. Ignoring the existence of this vital institution of the state, no matter if the perpetrator happens to be a foreigner, a branch family, or any other family for that matter, is a crime that the Great Empire of Japan will not tolerate, regardless of how many unrelated citizens participate.

Others will try to explain the moral relationship between the emperor and the people through lineage worship of the one eternal lineage. Of course, the progression of history is not clearly demarcated, and it is a common practice in social evolution that some lower classes, lacking in knowledge, still inherit medieval ideas even after the general class of society has entered into the evolution of the modern era. This, of course, means that, just as the German emperor still holds medieval ideas, many of the lower, less knowledgeable classes of Japan do not understand the meaning of the Japanese emperor and look up to him as if it were the Middle Ages. However, to compare the conscience of an uncivilized country like the Rana's India, which we mentioned earlier, with that of the people of Japan today is not only disrespectful to the people, it is an insult to the imperial family itself, assuming that they stand upon such an inert foundation.

Not true! Because the medieval conscience was controlled by lineage worship, the shogun and lords who split off from imperial blood became rebellious subjects, which has caused insane people like Mr. Hozumi to appear, defending the rebellious subjects by saying they were loyal to their sovereign and reverent to their lord, and even saying that the lowly Hozumi family is some sort of branch family of the imperial line with his use of the master-servant family theory. If, as Dr. Hozumi asserts, we clearly know that the Hozumi family is a collateral lineage split from Amaterasu, and that the imperial lineage is a broad one interwoven with innumerable collateral lineages—the emperor's blood also flows in the people and the pulse of the people can be heard in the emperor's veins—then it's likely the "rebellious subjects" head would call himself, Yatsuka Hozumi, sacred and inviolable, making the same arrogant demands towards the citizens as he would toward a chauffeur. (Despite the fact that his brain is no more valuable than a chauffeur's, who only needs to let people on his carriage and drive them to their destination, he says that speaking with a chauffeur somehow damages his honor. We express our hatred and disdain for him, even outside the realm of denouncing him as a scholar.)

Even if we aren't such rebellious subjects as he, if the human race is not born from the root of the plum tree, or from the fruit of the peach tree, or created by God, then we all have a lineage that has continued from apes, a bloodline that has existed for one hundred thousand years. Sincere people such as Professor Oka are tempted away from the theory of biological evolution by the rebellious words and acts of Mr. Hozumi. These very conclusions and premises leading to these conclusions would never be tolerated by the Great Empire of Japan, and the emperor represents the interests of the nation above and beyond those who have lost their sober judgment. The blood of the people enters the emperor, and the blood of the emperor enters the people, so that the emperor and the people are completely intermingled in blood, and no barriers can be built between the two because of this. However, that is only a fact, and it should not be a reason to endorse or even repudiate the emperor. The emperor is recognized by the sovereignty of the nation, and to deny the emperor is a violation of the sovereignty of the nation.

However, the restorative revolutionary spirit was so prevalent that it ostracized the emperor to the back lines and created dogū from a shockingly undeveloped village. The barbarians gave these dogū indescribable horns, fangs, enormous mouths, and huge noses; have painted their faces with red and white powder; and have sewed and dressed them with the rags of a false, lost, and disturbed mind. Then, holding one up, they cry out, "O brotherhood of forty-five million savages, bow down before this great god, and worship it." Forty-five million savages are on their knees before this barbaric idol of a god, and forgetting the existence of the emperor of Japan.

Before this barbaric god, Buddha was denounced as an offender of the state, Christ was denounced as the son of a carpenter of Nazareth, the original meaning of Shinto was trampled on at every turn, and the scientific study of mythology was once threatened. The barbaric priests of this god were wont to praise virtues and perform rituals in laughable pseudo-classical language, with little regard for the solemn relationship maintained between the Great Empire of Japan and the emperor. Since the current emperor has especially shown great talent at poetry, everything he expresses aside from that of a state institution is quickly stolen by the savages, defiled, then used to decorate their barbaric god. Scholars, politicians, journalists, and everyone else cower in fear with their tails between their legs in submission to the wrath of this barbaric god. How disrespectful! This one word is truly a sentence of social death in the savage villages of the Orient. Even the despotic modern Germany merely has an arrogant emperor. Why, then, does only Japan have a barbaric god? Basically, all they say is, "You're a disrespectful person who is in violation of the Imperial Rescript on Education, which says, 'You subjects must well demonstrate the virtue of loyalty.'"

We must reject the declarations of the barbaric god, in the name of national polity and the emperor himself. The national polity of "the theory of national polity" is the national polity of a savage village, not one of modern Japan. The emperor in "the theory of national polity" is a dogū in a savage village, not the emperor of modern Japan. We must take back the Imperial Rescript on Education from the very savages who stole it from us.

The Imperial Rescript on Education has been discussed several times earlier. In savage villages, where even the slightest violation of faith would result in an immediate massacre, the barbaric idols of the gods have an absolute right over the world of ideas. However, in a state that regulates external living, the emperor's actions cannot exceed these external boundaries. The dogū of the barbarian god would have the right to enforce the primitive religion and primitive morality of the savage village on its savage people through the power of demons, snakes, birds, and the like. However, it is a principle of the modern state that no major part of the state or the upper class should overstep the ideas and beliefs of individuals who are part of the state. Today, even if the emperor holds Buddhist beliefs or Christian morals, he cannot force them on the rest of the nation. Just as the emperor can't command medical theories or enforce the principles of astronomy, he cannot encourage a particular school of ethics or force a particular historical philosophy—the state can't enter the internal life of the conscience. Thus, the emperor, as an institution, cannot enforce morality. When morality takes the form of coercion, it becomes law.

The Imperial Rescript on Education, as the "education" in its name suggests, is within the scope of morality and has no legal power. Place enough trust in the clarity of the current emperor to balance out his effect on history! We declare the following: the meaning of the phrase "well demonstrate the virtue of loyalty" is absolutely not what Mr. Tetsujiro Inoue and the other interpreters of the Imperial Rescript on Education have been discussing in their hodgepodge of unorganized explanations. If interpreted as they see it, it becomes an expression of ill will toward the emperor who, as a second Emperor Tenji, realized the ideal of a civic nation.

Also, consider the moral beliefs of the general public. Isn't it true that the Russo-Japanese War wasn't fought for the benefit of the emperor, but was "for the state," based on the state sovereignty theory of socialism? Did the emperor not wipe tears from the eyes of his sons on their departure from the country? If the warriors had been slaves and subordinates under many different sovereigns, as was the case in the pre-revolutionary era of the class state, they would not have said "for the nation" but "for the lord," whom they each served. To say "for the nation," however, indicates that the state is recognized by the general public, not only in the text of law but also in moral conviction, as a personality with a purpose of survival and evolution, and that the people are "well loyal" to the state and fight for the purposes of this limited society itself, the "state," and that this loyalty is never for the self-interest of any other individual person. As long as one doesn't say, "I am the entire state, and the people are not part of the state," (even Mr. Hozumi does not say this), as long as one doesn't say, "the people alone are the entire state, and the sovereign is legally outside the state," (no Japanese monarchical sovereignty theorist says this), as long as one doesn't say that medieval history and modernity have combined and stopped moving (even Japanese scholars realize that history evolves), as long as one doesn't say that monarchical sovereignty theory and state sovereignty theory are one and the same (they fight each other precisely because they're different in Japan), there isn't a single reason to be found for the "ruler loyalty and patriotism coincidence theory."

If we say that the survival and evolution of the nation is its purpose, and that all parts of the nation—all the people—are the nation, then the loyalty of the people in striving for the nation's purpose and ideals, is to the nation. The joy of the emperor, who is part of the nation, is equally the joy of the people, who are a large part of the nation. It is the satisfaction of a large individual as a part of that large individual, and has nothing to do with the purpose itself. Therefore, if the emperor is a patriarchal monarch and the purpose of loyalty is to strive toward the satisfaction of his selfish desires, just as in the patriarchal class-state era, when the people were slavishly subordinate to their lords and shogun, and the personal interests of those lords and shogun were the goal of the peoples' loyalty, the following conclusion can be drawn. When the individuality of the emperor works to oppress his sociality (essentially, oppressing the will of the state as an institution of the state), as was the case with past lords, shogun, and the like, the people do not protect the oppressed sociality of the emperor, but must become rebels against the state, which has the emperor as an individual who has strayed from his status as an institution of the state. In such a hypothetical case, it goes without saying that the emperor has no legal responsibilities other than political morality, but the state, through the mouth of its solemn judicial body, has laws to punish the people. Isn't this when the theory of lord loyalty and patriotism coincidence contradicts itself?

If the emperor, by his very nature of being an emperor, is free from such contradictions, and if a barbaric dogū idol of a god exterminates him and commands loyalty to the subjects of the nation for the personal benefit of the barbaric god, then the emperor and the people, who form the whole nation for the purpose of its survival and evolution, must completely crush that idol. Mr. Inoue, for example, who does not study the state scientifically, may advocate such contradictions as the above. However, when Mr. Hozumi, a scholar who specializes in the legal theory of the nation, and others like him, preach the theory of lord loyalty and patriotism coincidence, what words could we use to properly evaluate him? How would this be any different from saying that his own monarchical theory and the state sovereignty theory he has put so much energy into defeating, actually coincide? The two heads of this monster will finally stop attacking one another and embrace each other instead. However, when they embrace, the two skulls explode and die. Ah, tomb of the loyal retainer, Mr. Hozumi! (We've examined his remains while building his tomb, but the stone we used to rebuild is strong. We hope his vengeful spirit is contained there, and doesn't come after our heads as they rest on our pillows at night.)

The content of the word "loyalty" in the expression "You subjects have expressed much loyalty" is quite different from the content of "loyalty" in ancient and medieval times, which was to respect the political prerogatives of the emperor for the benefit of the nation. If we focus on the form and pronunciation of the characters and ignore the historical evolution of their content, it would be like Dr. Aruga's argument that a sacred relationship of reverence for the sovereign and loyalty to the lord was established between the kakubo and the maroon shikibu just because they said "no formalities between friends."[543] We actually feel insulted to be put on the same level as the educated, scholarly class. The heroes of the democratic revolution are too great to be appreciated by the blind.

Let us organize the previous conclusions together again.

The historical philosophy that looks at the evolution of the Japanese people is naturally of a different nature from the biography of the imperial family, and the imperial family is not the spinal cord of Japanese history. All

---

[543] Kakubo and maroon shikibu were the attire of male and female students of the time.

peoples, having originally reproduced from a single human race, have a historical philosophy of social evolution that is common to all human beings.

Viewing Japan today as a patriarchal nation ends up in a suicidal argument that releases those of different religion and foreign races in Japan from their national duties, and also insists that the parents of the people are equal to their babies by virtue of the equal relationship of kinship laws.

The one eternal lineage is an expression of the Japanese people's loyalty toward the aristocrats, where they persecuted and attacked the imperial family at every opportunity, until said imperial family were utterly crushed by despair. Thus, the one eternal lineage is a historical pyramid for the rebellious subjects.

The history of Japan excludes the one thousand years of the primitive, legendary period, or possibly even the 1,400 years of time after entering recorded history, but before *Kojiki* and *Nihon Shoki* were written. The ancient period was a period of monarchies, since a single patriarch was the ruler of all Japan, and the medieval period was a period of aristocracies, since many patriarchs were rulers in their own right. During this long period, there was no awareness of the purpose of the nation's survival and evolution, so it was driven by a separate national polity called a patriarchal state.

Modern national polity is a civic state of state sovereignty; it has a democratic system of government, because all parts of the state are institutions that act with the purpose of the survival and evolution of the state as a whole. This means that both monarchical sovereignty theorists and state sovereignty theorists are fighting blindly in the dark, based on nothing but worthless speculation. In legal terms alone, Japan after the Meiji Revolution can be said to be a social democracy.

The meaning of the word "emperor" has evolved historically, and emperor of the primitive age, who was only gifted that title later, was the patriarch of a primitive religion, standing over a small region and a small population and fighting against other small family groups. Until the Fujiwara period, the word "emperor" meant that he was the supreme ruler who owned all the land and people of Japan. During the period of the aristocracy after Kamakura, the "emperor," like other patriarchal monarchs, was not only a patriarchal monarch within the limits of his power, but also a Shinto pope who was constantly at war with the Holy Roman Emperor in Kamakura. After the Meiji Revolution, "emperor" came to mean the supreme authority to declare the sovereignty of the nation as part of the democratic citizens acting for the ultimate goal of the state. Twenty-three years after the revolution, the title had evolved considerably, and together with the Imperial Diet, it took on the significance of an element of organization of the supreme authority.

To put it plainly, the emperor in the "theory of national polity" is a dogū idol crafted by a village of savages, and is, in fact, an enemy to the current emperor.

VOLUME 5: THE ENLIGHTENMENT MOVEMENT OF SOCIALISM

伍

The following explanation will show that the "theory of national polity" is rather clearly a restorative revolutionary theory that seeks to overthrow the modern state and political system. Social democracy acknowledges that the Japanese nation after the Meiji Revolution is, legally, a social democracy, and strives to maintain and further develop said social democracy. However, in the study of the state, the legal state and the political state naturally do not follow the same path of consideration. The state examined from the perspective of jurisprudence is a theoretical one, seen from the perspective of how the state, as manifested in law, is organized, and the extent to which the state's goals and ideals are expressed as goals and ideals of law. The state examined from the perspective of political science is a practical, factual theory that discusses the purposes and ideals of the state beyond the law and looks at how the organization of the state is in reality as well as legally, and how the purposes and ideals of the state as expressed in law are being realized.

Chapter 15

Law is an expression of the ideals of the state. Politics is the practical activities of the state. Because all do not make this clear distinction, the upper classes seek to persecute socialists who advocate the interests of society, and do so in the name of society itself. The socialists, who should also repudiate the upper class in the name of the state, are themselves on the logical gallows, professing, on the contrary, to wipe out the state itself. Obviously, any socialists who insist on public ownership of land and all productive institutions for the benefit of society are simply faithful, law-abiding citizens who seek to realize the ideal of the law, which stipulates that society is the supreme owner, and can never be persecuted for disobeying the law. Socialists, assuming they aren't as ignorant as Mr. Hozumi in claiming that the emperor alone is the state, or American Burgess in saying that Congress alone is the state,[544] will say the following. The workers must take Marx's declaration that "the workers have no state" as their article of faith, and on that basis, they must profess their rejection of the state itself, deny themselves as parts of the state, and deny the ideal state, which will come about through the future evolution of the state. Scientific socialism is a river flowing from the source of Plato's ideal state, which was laid out two thousand years ago. Plato said, "the state is a sum of individual persons, and individual persons are part of the state."

Now, look at modern law. Where is the rule defining the emperor or the upper class only as being the state? And where does it say that the laborer is not a part of the state, and the peasant is not a part of the state? Some would say, "The state must be denied because the upper class occupies all the

---

[544] John William Burgess (1844–1931). American constitutional scholar and author of several books, including *Political Science and Comparative Constitutional Law*.

institutions of the state, and the will of the upper class is the will of the state." Then the children of the upper class, who do not form the will of the upper class, are outside the state. Even after all parts of the state have come to express their will as political authorities, are all the children of society not part of the state because they do not form the will of the state? Are only elders the state? The demand for universal suffrage is being made for the purpose of making socialism the will of the state, and to deny the state while crying out for universal suffrage is the behavior of an unidealistic blind man who does not understand socialism at all.[545] If they deny the state, why do they not deny their own insistence that the state, which should be denied, owns the land? A denied state is an empty state, and an empty state can't own the public productive institutions. Even if the upper classes think they alone are the state, socialists should not fight back against their tyranny with the insolence of, "then we deny the state."

They are, of course, the evolved (materially or spiritually) part of the state within the state. The state, however, is a state that includes other still less evolved parts of the state, the lower classes. The state is not to be conceived, as it was during the individualism of the French Revolutionary era, as a dismantling of the old society and organization of a new one at the will of the individual through the assumption of a more primitive idea of the individual person. Even during primitive times, the individual person never existed as an individual person. Even when entering their graves, they formed a society.

---

[545] This isn't necessarily an overstatement. The early Marxists, who had faithfully embraced Marx's ideas, saw the Congress as an instrument of class domination, and therefore thought it was nonsense to join it. Therefore, they believed that they should only appeal to direct action. In reality, however, even a strict appeal to direct action would have resulted in difficulties in changing the status quo, so they sought a way to enter the parliamentary arena. This was the background to the advocacy of gradual socialism by Bernstein and others.

Individualist revolutionary theory sought to dissolve the state and organize it on the basis of freedom and equality. Therefore, the negation of the state can be logically maintained as long as it presupposes the construction of a new state. From the solemn scientific basis of socialism, however, the state is never a mechanical construct that can be dissolved or organized at will by individuals. Revolution means that the will of the state evolves with the social forces of the times. Therefore, in today's nation, the will of today's upper class is the will of the state because the upper class stands atop today's social forces. If today's nation is denied on this basis, then by the same logic, socialism, which is supposed to be the will of the nation based on modern social forces, must be denied as not being the will of the nation. Almost all socialists today, and I dare say not only in Japan, are pure individualists who seem to understand socialism as simply another French Revolution.

Clearly understand the difference between the state from a legal versus political perspective. The legal state is socialism with state sovereignty. However, since all political power is based on economic power, the economic class state of today represents the emergence of a practical class state in politics. This is why social democracy has embarked on a revolution in the economic sphere, while that revolution endorses the current law and decides its victories through wars fought with laws.

If the law itself represents a class state and sovereignty resides with the upper classes, then the socialists' efforts are merely to defend the interests of the upper classes. If one then considers the upper class as going against its purpose, it would mean that all their effort would be undone, and this must be stopped before it even gets to the Diet. At this point, the actions of the French Revolution, Meiji Revolution, and even today's anarchists are, theoretically, less contradictory than that of socialists. We believe that the social-democratic revolution is an economic revolution within the bounds of the law, in order to make the ideals of a legal revolution, such as the French Revolution or the Meiji Revolution, a complete reality. When Bebel said, "If France is challenged by Germany, it has the right of self-defense to respond to this challenge in the name of the state,"[546] it was an expression of what we're claiming—that the present age is an age of national sovereignty in which we've become aware that the state has its own objectives and ideals. There is a contradiction at the International, which overcame the views of Jaurès and resolved to repudiate the state itself,[547] claiming that the present state is a class state. We again declare: the socialist revolution is not a revolution like the French Revolution or the Meiji Revolution, which seeks to move the location of sovereignty. That is, it is not a revolution that appeals to forces greater than law, forces which renew the very basis of law. It is only a legal declaration of the social forces that are the will of society, on the basis of the established sovereignty of that society. Therefore, the economic revolution of socialism does not stain the pages of history with blood, as the previous legal revolutions did. Nor is it so spectacular for the revolutionaries themselves. It is enough, so to speak, to put in order the current economic organization that contradicts the legal ideals of the first revolution, and to make those ideals a reality. So, following our earlier description of the Meiji Revolution as social-democratic in law, we name the nationalization of land and capital, the economic aspects of socialism, the "Economic Meiji Revolution."

The full realization of the Meiji Revolution depends on public ownership of the legal resources that allow the state to act freely for the purpose and ideal of survival and evolution. For this purpose, it's necessary to further make public the economic resources, namely land and capital, and to make the

---

[546] August Bebel was a German socialist. He joined the labor movement as a young man and opposed Germany's militarist policies from beginning to end. He was a leader of the Social Democratic Party.

[547] Jean Jaurès was a French politician and leader of the Socialist Party (1859–1914). He was an advocate of pacifism, but was assassinated by nationalists on the eve of World War I.

purpose and ideal of the nation's survival and evolution a reality. From an aristocratic state, in which many monarchs exercised the legal sources as their own property rights for their own benefit as the main body of sovereignty, the Meiji Revolution transferred the ownership of the legal sources to the state and legally expressed the socialism of state sovereignty. In the same way, the sovereignty of the state expressed in law was intended to establish an economic civic state, and to overthrow the economic aristocracies, in which many economic patriarchs and monarchs privately owned the economic sources and considered themselves the subjects to whom profits belonged. The Meiji Revolution was, of course, a revolution from an economic foundation. Whereas before only the aristocracy had private property and the lower classes merely had the right to use it, the state then granted rights and established a system of private property, the basis of democracy. The Meiji Revolution was clearly social-democratic in the very foundation of its laws. But what is the state of affairs now?

When we look at the legal state obtained by the Meiji Revolution, then shift our eyes politically to the reality of the actual state, we feel as if we've been cast down from heaven to hell. We have legal ideals and ethical convictions to act in the name of "patriotism," with the interests and goals of the nation at the center. However, in terms of economic reality, we are treated to a patriarchal, class-state era, in which the people are sacrifices to countless golden aristocrats and economic daimyo so that this upper class may survive and evolve. While jurisprudence and ethics treat us as persons, direct economics treats us as objects that can be freely bought and sold by the golden lords. We are part of the Japanese empire in legal terms, and we have a survival and evolutionary purpose in that we are part of the state. From an economic standpoint, however, we exist as a means to the end of the landowner and must die as a sacrifice for the benefit of the mill owner—in other words, we are not part of the state. We are serfs bought and sold with the land, slaves bound by wages. The golden aristocrat, the landowner, privately owns the land

and makes us serfs. The economic lords known as capitalists, based in the feudal castles of their factories, treat us as lower humans. Just as the warrior class of old was enslaved under the nobility and exerted its power over the lower classes via martial arts, so the wretched gentlemen play on authority with their academic and business talents (a contrast that leaves one fuming!)

All things are done in the name of the emperor and the sovereignty of the nation. In reality, however, Japan is neither in the age of the emperor's sovereignty nor in the age of national sovereignty, but in the age of the capitalist's all-powerful state, as if the capitalists have sovereignty. The ministers stand under the patronage of the capitalists, as do the legislators. Thus, what the state institutions declare to be the will of the state is not truly the will of the state, at least in terms of the state's own purpose and ideals. It is, in fact, a class state, because these institutions express their will only in the interest of themselves or their own class. In other words, today's state is a nation divided into economic classes, such as capitalists, landlords, peasants, and workers, while the emperor and the nobility are institutions of the state that exist in a different world from the social-democratic revolution, and are, today, not classes in the same sense as in the medieval definition.[548]

The aristocracy, which had plundered the economic sources of power by military force, was swept out of the law by the Meiji Revolution. Now, however, the economic patriarchs, using capital, have swallowed up other capitalists and small and medium-sized tenant farmers, replaced the former monarchs, and are controlling the institutions of the state as they see fit. The state has taken arms out of the hands of the medieval monarchs, and while plundering and merging via armaments have stopped domestically, the even sharper sword of

---

[548] Although the meaning of this sentence isn't clear, it may mean that the present era is not the same as the sovereignty of the emperor in the pre-modern era, but a transitional state that has not yet reached the era of modern state sovereignty, and in this respect, the meaning of class is different from the medieval meaning of the term.

capital has forced shrewd or lucky men to merge capital and plunder the land. This is how a strict medieval class state was established under the cloak of the beautiful laws of freedom and equality. Aristocratic politics clearly exist. Where is the Meiji Revolution? Where is the nation gained by the Meiji Revolution—a revolution so ardently demanded in the name of the nation itself? Just like how the American people are drunk on the name "land of the free," not realizing that the economic lords are occupying that "land of the free," the social democracy of the Meiji Revolution remains only in law, while the actual country is returning to the Middle Ages.

It is precisely because purpose resides in the state that we make demands in the name of the state and may die in the name of the state. Today's social democracy is not limited to Greece, as Plato's social democracy was. Nor is it limited to the Japanese nation, as the Meiji Revolution was. It transcends the practical state in that it asserts that the state is a society of political units, and that the ideal independence of the state and the absolute freedom of the individual can be realized through the union of nations as units (read *The Theory of Biological Evolution and Social Philosophy*), but it contains its purpose and ideals at every turn. What is incompatible with nationalism, which strives for the purpose of the state, is the medieval aristocracy and monarchism, in which everything was sacrificed to the self-interest of the monarchs. The aristocracies, which were treated as sacrifices for their respective monarchs under the banner of monarchism, were overthrown by the Meiji Revolution in the name of nationalism and for the benefit of the state— but what to do with the economic class state, which is now being killed by these economic monarchs in the name of the state?

If we say that the aristocracy was overthrown for the sake of the nation, using the simple egalitarianism of "why should lineage or pedigree be a factor in becoming a king, a general, or a minister?" wrapped in the garb of the theory of national polity, then how can this economic aristocracy, which is in gross violation of the purpose of the nation, have gone unnoticed by egalitarians? If the aristocracy of the past was such an affront to the human rights that it had to be overthrown, how can the current developments of this economic aristocracy, which is so insulting to human rights, not stimulate any feelings in those who praise the Meiji Revolution?

The lords of the current economic class state have stolen the phrase "for the state" and are using it to defend all the sins they commit for and the benefits they give to the aristocracy. Everything that is done with the intention of attributing benefits to the economic aristocracy is falsified as if, on the contrary, it were for the benefit of the state or intended to benefit the state. This is monarchism, individualism centered on the interests of a few individuals, not nationalism—no, this isn't nationalism at all. Didn't Socrates drink his poison before such a "nation"? Oh, true patriots! How can you not see that the current golden aristocracy is using the same nationalism that overthrew the aristocracy to maintain the economic patriarchy? Nationalism and monarchism! In nationalism, the state is the purpose. In monarchism, the monarch is the main body of benefits. Thus, everyone else becomes a sacrifice, a means to an end. How strange that these two contradictions—two contradictions with no equal in all of history—glide right beneath the noses of the patriots. Nationalism should not allow the interests of the state to be trampled upon by economic patriarchs. If the nation is disposed of by the economic patriarchs as they please, it means that the nation's personality has been destroyed, and the "Great Empire of Japan" will be restored to the medieval age of the patriarchal state, leaving only its name on the useless paper of the Constitution. Oh, nation, please open your eyes and see—see an economic monarchism that serves the interests of two or three individuals, beautifully adorned by garments it stole from the state!

The patriarchal monarchs of the medieval aristocracy were more explicit than this economic aristocracy. In their time, the purpose of the state was not understood, so they demanded death "for the sake of the lord" from their economically dependent slaves. Today's economic monarchs, however, claim that production, which they do solely for their own benefit, is also for the benefit of society. Whether it's trying to monopolize sugar in Cuba or fighting for gold mines in South Africa,[549] they claim to be doing so under a nationalist agenda and for the good of the nation. The authority of the individual person has evolved markedly. In the past, the slave class warrior, despite the tiger-like intimidation and power he held over the lower classes, had little doubt of his moral obligation to get down on his knees like a kitten to the aristocrats he served. However, today's economic warrior class, known as "gentlemen," while still playing around with their authority over the lower classes, are ashamed to be seen in front of the economic aristocrats they serve, preferring to hide away like an *Uroctea* spider—it's like watching a comedy.[550] This is a sign of the development of the view of equality, not to mention the evolution of the idea of rights. The words "for the lord" are not words that King Carnegie, His Majesty Morgan,[551] Mitsui, or Iwasaki could utter. Thus, they are left saying "for the state" instead.

Oh, for the sake of the state! When the image of freedom was recognized as a wolf in sheep's clothing, appalling oppression and abuse were committed in the name of freedom. In the same way, since the state gained by the Meiji Revolution became occupied by a second economic aristocracy, all patriots would actually rather be persecuted in the name of the state (we say patriots, but individualist revolutionaries always laugh when they hear us say it). Socialism is a patriotism that respects the freedom and independence of other

---

[549] Refers to the Boer Wars. In 1899, the British launched a war to take control of the Transvaal Republic of South Africa, which was founded by the Boers. In 1992, the Transvaal surrendered to the British and became a British colony.

[550] These spiders are about one centimeter long. They live in houses and build round, flat webs on walls and other surfaces, in which they hide to catch food.

[551] J. P. Morgan was an American industrialist. He established an extensive network of control in the steel trust, railroads, shipping, and mining industries.

nations, extending to other nations the same patriotism that has finally awakened in modern times from the older loyalty to the lord. For what reason does the state, which is supposed to have "supreme ownership" itself, persecute social democracy (which seeks to make land and capital the property of the state), calling it a disturbance of order and harmful to peace and happiness? No! That's absolutely not the state's persecution. Let us remove the gloves of the state, and the muscles of the capitalist's iron fist will be fully visible. As Madame Roland once said, pointing to the statue of liberty as she ascended the gallows, "Oh, freedom! Oh, freedom! How many crimes have been committed in your name?" The ministers, the patriarchs of the economic monarchy, also said it was for the good of the nation. The senator, a warrior of the golden aristocracy, also speaks for the nation. The village chief and the police also preach for the sake of the state. Even in the kappore of the prostitutes,[552] the phrase "for the nation" appears, and so too during the evening parties of the noble ladies, themselves like prostitutes, the opening speech is made with the words "for the nation." Even the socialist party members are persecuted under the name of "for the nation," as the nation prepares its guillotine. When drunk with the name of freedom, tyranny appears, strangling true freedom; when maddened by the voice of nationalism, monarchism lurks in the shadows, attacking the most idealistic patriots.

We neither reject the modern Japanese people, who cry nationalism without understanding the nation, nor do we praise the modern Japanese Socialist Party, which equally does not understand the nation, and is also persecuted by the Japanese people, who do not understand the nation. However, why is it that the latter are so willing to solemnly resist the persecution they are subjected to everywhere, and why is it that they are so similar to the revolutionary party of the Meiji Revolution?

---

[552] "Kappore" is a type of Kabuki dance.

The social democrats of today are the economic revolutionary party that seeks to perfect the social democracy of the Meiji Revolution through economic revolution. The persecution of revolutionary parties is a normal part of the evolution of a society before it concentrates its social forces. Just as the revolutionary party of the Meiji Revolution broke free from the yoke of the aristocrats and were thus out of work, their refined minds could not become officials or company employees, they first had to become vagabonds under economic duress. And just as the guards of the shogunate and the lords persecuted the propagandists of the Meiji Revolution wherever they went, so too are the dignified scholars threatened and deprived of their freedom of speech, assembly, publication, and even their own personal bodies by a police force that has no power to pass judgement, no true power to pass anything other than their own urine. The party cabinet led by Hirobumi Ito, the former leader of the Meiji Revolution—a party cabinet, as the loyal retainer Mr. Hozumi and others clearly stated, was the establishment of a republican government under a customary constitution, even though the Meiji revolutionary party overthrew the aristocracy and democracy was established—prohibited the association of the "Social Democratic Party" under the banner of their being rebellious subjects. The current bureaucrats, all of whom are descendants of or complicit with the rebellious subjects, whose minds are filled with completely independent thought, are lazily guessing the meaning of "social democracy," thinking of it as a code, and are lying in wait to one day rope the party in. Just as the former Meiji revolutionary party had nowhere to run, nowhere to hide (oh, how many heroes have been buried in the ground because they were needlessly mistaken for monarchists, not earning the gratitude of the world like the French revolutionaries did!), so too does a human-faced dog trail behind the economic Meiji revolutionary party, fed and paid for by the state. They are told to "stop your speeches,"[553] and are hauled

---

[553] It's said that before the war, speeches and other events were monitored by the Special

off to the police station and thrown in jail. The reason? "It's for the sake of the nation."

Oh, for the sake of the nation! The people who died in the fields of Manchuria and Korea, believing it to be for the good of the nation, are not the same people who found social democrats suffering for the good of the nation and began persecuting them. The Russian people always retreated in the war in the Far East, not because of cowardice, but because they clearly understood that fighting the war was not for the good of the nation. But, for the sake of the nation, one would be chosen to join an assassination squad, and would become a member of the executive committee of the revolutionary party. The Japanese people who fought to join the death squads in the blockade of Port Arthur for the sake of the nation were not the people who fled from the violence of their economic masters and declined to be members of the executive committee for the sake of the nation. One mustn't misunderstand. We know that bombs will not solve anything. The explosions we sometimes hear are merely the sound of spray from the main current of evolution and history hitting the rocks set in front of it. But regardless of the question of what harm the bomb does to the nation, the fact is that terrorist bombings are a constant phenomenon.[554] The most obvious explanation for these terrorist bombings comes from Igor Sazonov,[555] who is firing artillery in the revolutionary war now becoming a

---

Higher Police, and if a speech was made in which there was a violent attack on the government, the speeches were stopped. The order to "stop your speeches" was an order to literally "stop the speech." This was particularly severe during the wartime government elections.

[554] The original text just said "bombings" but we've supplemented it to make the meaning clearer.

[555] Igor Sergeevich Sazonov was a Russian revolutionary who belonged to the Socialist Revolutionary Party. He belonged to the radical faction of the party ("People's Will" faction) and assassinated Plehve. Vyacheslav von Plehve served as Minister of the

reality in Russia. He describes himself as the user of the bomb that assassinated Plehve:[556]

The Russian government has banned our freedom of speech. Do they think that without speech, we cannot communicate? Humanity has a spirit that can communicate without speech.

Our Socialist Revolutionary Party is not cowardly in its choice of weapons. If the government comes at us by the sword, we will only use the sword against it. The killing of Plehve, who committed a great crime, was merely a demonstration to the Russian officials that the guilty cannot escape punishment. Our party, even reserve officers, is on active duty to do this, and I am honored to carry out that duty.

The revolution began with my submission, and for the first time the government found itself dancing on top of an erupting volcano. In fact, one could say that the government had received an irreparable wound forty years ago.[557] The reason it hasn't yet collapsed is because it has

---

Interior in Imperial Russia and suppressed the revolutionary movement of the 1870s–80s.

[556] "In 1903, Azef, Savinkov, and others planned to assassinate Plehve in Geneva, while Dulebov and Matzejewski disguised themselves as streetcar refuters and Kalyanev as peddlers to spy on Plehve's movements, while Dora Brilliant was given the task of storing and loading the bombs. After about a year of waiting, the opportunity finally arrived. At ten o'clock in the morning of July 15th, 1904, just as Plehve's carriage, escorted by officers of the secret police who were dressed up as normal policemen, was approaching Ismailovsky Prospekt in St. Petersburg, Igor Sergeevich Sazonov's twelve-pound bomb slaughtered this authoritative tyrant." (Kanson Arahata, *The Dawn of the Russian Revolutionary Movement* [Tokyo: Iwanami Shinsho, 1960], 146).

[557] This probably refers to the promulgation of the decree for the emancipation of serfs.

fallen into the alcoholism known as tyranny, and is barely bracing itself up. How can this be called normal life?

It may have seemed like the curtains closed when the serfs were emancipated at the time, but that's a cynical point of view. The emancipation of the serfs clearly made people aware of their freedom and independence. The reforms of Alexander II were the alpha of the Russian Revolution, and the Russian people have worked hard ever since. If that's true, it could be said that the omega of the revolution is today.Essentially, the question today is who will be the agents of revolution? I am not so foolish as to think that a bomb will carry out the revolution. We must not forget that tens of thousands of Russian people are standing behind one bomb. I, myself, cry when I feel this. We aren't inciting the people. The people already have the intelligence to think independently. The present system will be overthrown by the suffering of the people, with a few bombs merely being the signals for it. The suffering and grievances of the people will not abate as long as the present system is maintained. I have spent three years in pursuit of this goal, and one and a half of those years was spent in prison. This thoroughly considered punishment from heaven would not go unrewarded. How often I dreamed of defeating Grand Duke Vladimir and Plehve in one fell swoop when I was in Siberia![558] What else could turning men such as me into warriors be, but a sin of the government? When I saw that I'd defeated Plehve, I was happy that I'd obeyed my conscience.[559]

---

[558] Grand Duke Vladimir usually refers to the monarch of the medieval Kievan Rus' (Grand Duke of Kiev), but since Kievan Rus' is considered the first Russian state, the term here is thought to refer to the Russian emperor.

[559] However, it's said that, in reality, he did feel guilty and it never went away.

We cannot calmly dismiss these phenomena as mere resources for academia. This is something to be shuddered at by the unconstitutional persecutors of speech, as well as by ourselves. The Japanese character has been compared to that of the French or the Italians, and it's an unmistakable fact that we are a people who lack patience. In the past, when overthrowing the aristocracy, we had the political maniac Hikokuro, and in the time of the democratic movement, we had Kadota who trampled on a picture of the emperor in Osaka.[560] The people of Japan are a people who show little respect for the lives of themselves and others, and whose amount of murderers far exceed Italians, who statistically have the highest number of murderers. Just look at the many laborers who get mad for no reason, shouting "Beranme!" Yes, the phrase "beranme." When the present workers understand the reason for their condition, and when they are persecuted regardless, the very medicine Sazonov used will be in their iron fists as they raise those fists in the air with the cry of "beranme!" What will we do when this time comes? We read Igor Sazonov's words and shudder to see that the class currently in power dares to be an instigator of assassination.

Indeed, the barbaric practice of persecuting speech should never again be permitted in a civilized country. However, what is just as strange is that the persecutors, while banning socialism, are conversely trying to spread education. If we do not forget that Ieyasu Tokugawa's encouragement of education hastened the revolution against the aristocratic state,[561] what a

---

[560] Among the people who started a magazine in Osaka during the liberal civil rights movement was a man named "Saburobei Kadota," and he's probably the one being referred to here.

[561] Under the Edo shogunate regime, the shogunate used the Cheng-Zhu school of philosophy to maintain the hierarchical order, but it is said that Cheng-Zhu schools' philosophy of gaining a perfect knowledge of natural laws fostered no small amount of critical mentality and thus became the driving force behind the movement to overthrow

contradiction it would be not to realize that the Economic Meiji Revolution, which will sweep away the economic aristocracy, will arrive when the entire population, through the education they are given, "already have the intelligence to think independently," as Sazonov said. It is precisely the Russian government whose persecution is so pervasive in this respect. In that country, the government decreed the theories university professors were allowed to hold and forbade the comparative study of the national laws of different countries. Dr. Hozumi's independent lecturing of Hirobumi Ito's "Constitutional Law," though his own constitutional studies are not necessarily in agreement with the main points, is nothing compared to that. In Russia, if a student at a university owns a book with liberal tendencies, he or she will be expelled from the university. This is far more restrictive than the dismay and laughter directed toward the Muirhead ethics.[562] When lecturing on world history, they forbid teaching the republican government of Greece and Rome, Luther's Reformation, and the French Revolution, and allow only the rest, which has lost its meaning. Even an impudent country that rudely places the blame for the failure of the Kenmu Restoration solely on Emperor Go-Daigo's doting, and allows historical philosophers, who praise Yoritomo and Ieyasu as men who loved and nurtured the people with compassion, to lecture on the Imperial Rescript on Education, can't compare to this.

The enlightenment precedes all revolutions and becomes the basis for those revolutions. Social democracy awaits the awakening of the people so that it can be realized. We should be grateful that the people are gradually awakening from their long night's sleep and are ready and willing to independently judge the true value of social democracy, precisely because of the education they have received to date. There is no room to ask in Takamagahara or in the Land of the Rising Sun. There is no need to reflect on

the shogunate.

[562] John Hentry Muirhead.

Mr. Aruga's theory of treasonous delegation or Mr. Hozumi's theory of Yoshitoki's sovereignty. The spread of the written word of knowledge to almost the entire population—while the Russian Revolution has its difficulties in this respect, all the Japanese people hold in their hands the key to social democracy—means that the powerful class has been encircled by the entire population. Even if the cultivated fields are overgrown with weeds for a while, if socialism is actually the truth, each seed will blossom and bear fruit ten thousand times over (contrast this with the many scholars we have defeated who denounce social democracy, and see which is the truth). Everything is a competition for survival. When social democracy overcomes the struggle for the survival of truth and occupies the minds of the entire nation, the will of the state will manifest new social forces and an Economic Meiji Revolution will be accomplished through legal warfare.

Therefore, the social democratic movement is purely an enlightenment movement. Since the separation of Marx and Proudhon,[563] it is social democracy that has been the first to stand and fight back against those who resort to violence. Of course, in times and nations where there is no legal form to fight a legal war, fighting by "sword against sword," as Sazonov put it, is the only way, and is legally sound as well. In Russia, for example, just as the actions of the emperor cannot be said to be legal acts because they are not regulated by law, so the actions of the people cannot be said to be legal acts because they have no laws to follow. The relationship between the people and the emperor is not a legal relationship from the beginning, but one of morality or power. Specifically, they either submit to a slave-like morality and obey, or they appeal to their superior power and refuse. Therefore, if it is not unjustified to call the public killing of an emperor the death penalty, it is also justified for the revolutionary party to name the assassination of an emperor as executing the death penalty.

---

[563] Pierre-Joseph Proudhon was a French socialist and one of the founders of anarchism.

The death penalty in the modern state is the state killing of those who defy the state's purpose, and there is no distinction to be made between open and covert methods of execution. If the Russian emperor names the people who are against his personal interests as criminals, the people are free to call the emperor, whom they recognize as being against their interests, a criminal as well. One is named a criminal by the state because he is detrimental to the interests of the state, regardless of whether he is an emperor or a citizen. Look at the words uttered by the Russian emperor. He says things such as "my subjects" and "my nation." If, as before the emancipation of the serfs, the land and the people were property belonging to many patriarchs (like the emperor and the nobility), this claim would not be unreasonable, since it would be based on the patriarchs' rights as subjects of property rights. However, modern Russia, a monarchy in which one man organizes the supreme authority, is not a patriarchal state in which the emperor stands outside the state and treats the state as a means to his own benefit. He forgets, however, that any supreme authority, regardless of how much freedom he is given, when acting as a sovereign, must manifest the will of the state (not act in its own self-interest) as part of the state in order to have legal effect, otherwise his words and deeds will have no legal effect at all. If the Russian emperor, as an institution of the state, is a manifestation of the will of the state, anything contrary to the state is a crime under the law, not to mention that his killing of anyone would be considered the death penalty performed by the state. But he considers the people and the land as his property, which he can dispose of as he pleases, for his own benefit. Due to this, the people stand in legal self-defense from the very beginning. Things are then decided by the strength of their power. There is no punishment, no crime, no treason, only the gallows and dynamite.

We affirm that the Russian revolutionary party's use of forceful self-defense in the slaughter of state agents, however it may be evaluated from the standpoint of political interests, is at least not against the law (although "assassination is illegal, but permissible in the interests of the state" is not necessarily true in all cases). Of course, even Russia has some form of law. However, these laws aren't the expressed will of the emperor as a part of the state, but invalid laws that seek to sacrifice other parts of the state in order to satisfy personal interests. In fact, they aren't even laws. This is why many tyrannical monarchies fail to differentiate themselves from a patriarchal state. Since the sole supreme authority of the state is maintained not by legal provisions, but solely by the conscience of the emperor as a political morality, sovereigns of low conscience often destroy the state institutions themselves out of personal self-interest, plunder the state, and become nothing more than traitors with golden crowns on their heads.

If the Russian emperor, even if he is not legally bound to do so, acts with the interests of the state in mind—as if he were the Japanese emperor from the time of the Meiji Revolution until twenty-three years after it, who held Confucian political morality and was the only state institution that did not act in a disorderly manner—then even a single word or deed is an invocation of state sovereignty, and any disobedience to this is illegal behavior toward the state. But what about Russia? The emperor is a plunderer of the state, not an institution of it. He's a rebel against the state, not a sovereign executing state sovereignty. He is a plunderer and a traitor to the nation when he proclaims, "my subjects" and "my nation." The revolutionary party, which is trying to exterminate the plunderers, is of course not a state institution either, so its declaration of the assassination of the emperor as the death penalty has no legal significance, but the gallows built by the emperor, a traitor of the state, has no more legal force than their bombs.

Treason is to go against the sovereign. In patriarchal states, where the emperor considered the land and the people as property and treated everyone as a sacrifice, the emperor was the body of sovereignty, and treason was punished in his name. In the modern civic state, the main body of sovereignty is the state, and it has the purpose of survival and evolution. The principle of jurisprudence holds that even the Russian emperor is no more than a rebel if he acts with intent to ignore that purpose. Therefore, self-defense against a traitor is legitimate in law, and the state, having lost the way to declare its purpose, has no choice but to wait for the time when a new institution is established. (Mr. Hozumi's vengeful spirit would surely say, "A nation is in turmoil when the location of sovereignty is uncertain." He is, like us, one who asserts that Russia is currently in turmoil, and the emperor is not the sovereign.)

From this principle of jurisprudence, Sazonov's words are clearly true in contemporary Russia. It is for this reason that we fear that the current persecutors have deviated from their status as state institutions and are becoming rowdy servants. The Japanese government to date has often taken this form! If the prime minister orders a member of the Diet to be put to death, is he a national institution to which we should submit? If a police officer issues an edict to convene the Imperial Diet before a police box, is he a national institution to which we should submit? A state institution is only such within the powers granted to it. When the government deviates from its given authority when dealing with the Socialist Party, and does so with violence, it is the behavior of a violent servant, a subversive of state institutions. Social democrats can take any means necessary against violations of their rights.

The reason why the current Socialist Party overlooks this and doesn't wield the right to defend itself is not because it doesn't respect rights, but because it's based on the theory of interest, and much of the bloodshed is not in its interest. (All people of Japan should praise them for enduring such humiliation. They, who will not submit their conscience to anyone, are having all their rights trampled on by the mud-caked shoes of the police only for the benefit of spreading their message.) So, all the ridicule and abuse heaped on social democracy by anarchists who disregard interest theory is focused on this point. Anarchists say, "Socialists say that the lawful way is the way to go, but since the very laws to be obeyed were not made by any right that should be obeyed, no effective law can be made by following those laws into a crime-ridden Diet. The socialists are relying on a parliamentary utopia." However, it is no disgrace for a social democrat not to be able to answer such reasoned arguments. Reality is a stairway to the ideal, and it is absolutely impossible to reach the ideal without a footing on the real social state. If the legal war of social democracy is denied its effectiveness because it takes as its starting point the irrational laws of reality, where in the world can anything rational exist? Even an anarchist would not say that it is rational to deny everything. Then why not deny the frequent use of dynamite as irrational?

However, society evolves. Evolution depends on class struggle. Society has evolved to the present day and has come to express the result of the class struggle in the form of the ballot. The ballot is the revolutionary path that best expresses the social forces, the soundest and surest path up the ladder to the ideal, better than the bomb or the strike. In the absence of this path, the other paths of insurgency and bombings are opened. Those who have passed this path of insurgency and bombings and entered the avenue of legal warfare are the many nations now called civilized, and it is precisely the Russian people who are still on the path of insurgency and bombings. Suppose we were born in Russia. We would laugh and scoff at the mouths and tongues of the social democrats, and advocate terrorist bombings! Oh, you nihilists who fall with the emperor in the fumes of the explosions thrown to the ground from your very own hands! The doors of heaven will be opened by a priest's hand, surely. The revolutionary stage can be reached by a blood-stained path. The democrats of the Meiji Revolution hid a blood-stained blade on their persons for this very purpose. Today, though, we have the stroke of good fortune to be placed in a country that has evolved to the extent that legislation is now the method of choice, and we are never encouraged to assert our right to self-defense against thugs, however they may flout and deviate from the authority of the state institution. Social democrats, as the name implies, are often found to be more amenable to respecting the interests of society than those of individual authority (we again commend the current Japan Socialist Party for its moderation).

The demand for universal suffrage is made for this legal war.

Indeed, an economic revolution that seeks to realize the ideals of the Meiji Revolution can be achieved almost entirely with universal suffrage. When the state was not the body of sovereignty, revolutions were always carried out with blood and iron under the title of "rebels." Revolutions involving the content of the state are carried out solely by vote under the title "state sovereignty." The "vote" is the bullet of the Economic Meiji Revolution, and the acquisition of universal suffrage is the occupation of an ammunition warehouse. Before the legal wars, revolutions were always lubricated by the oil of blood. Revolutions with the bullet of the ballot open the stage with a round of applause.

Thus, the inclusion of bloodshed as an essential element in the definition of revolution is not even worthy of consideration. If bloodshed were a revolution, then the struggles within the imperial court would be countless revolutions, and the wars and defeats of the Warring States period must be considered as hundreds or thousands of revolutions that were fought and settled. Revolution means to completely change the way thoughts are organized, and bloodshed is not the issue. No matter how much blood is shed and how many corpses are piled up, if the same organization of thought is inherited, it's called a war, not a revolution. For example, the reason why the Jinshin War is not called a revolution,[564] the Taika legislation is called a revolution, the Genpei War is not called a revolution, the establishment of the Kamakura shogunate by Yoritomo is called a revolution, the Siege of Osaka is not called a revolution, and the Boshin War is called a revolution, is because each monarchy, aristocracy, and democracy has a different organization of thought. The revolution of social democracy is a revolution because it is about

---

[564] The Jinshin war was fought after the death of Emperor Tenchi between his son, Prince Otomo, and Emperor Tenji's younger brother, Prince Oama (later Emperor Tenmu).

fundamentally wiping out the current system of private property by a small class (not the system of private property by all parts of society that individualism idealized) and changing it to a different organization of thought. This is done in order to create a communist system in which the individual person is a part of society, and society, as a collection of these parts, is the subject of property rights. Revolution, therefore, is the death of the old society and the birth of a new one.

Of course, just as a child inherits much from his or her mother, a new society inherits and exhibits much from the old society. However, we don't live in a world devoid of intelligence, where one would say, "If a newborn is not born of a difficult birth, if it is not teetering on the brink between life and death, it is not a newborn baby." We merely say that the obstetrician/gynecologist called "voting," discovered by the principles of social physiology, has allowed new societies to be born easily and safely. What can't be helped is that the barbaric, childless mothers of the old society try to abort the fetuses they carry in their bellies, to stifle the babies that are about to be born. Ignorant and barbaric, the bad woman always refuses the help of the obstetrician, the right to vote, and suffers painful bloodshed as she alone falls. However, once a child is conceived, it must be born. Even if it is aborted or crushed, it will be born again as long as the mother herself is strong (hence the absence of any revolutionary climate in a declining country). Societies with historical experience, however ignorant they may be, know that bloodshed causes the mother herself to suffer. The evolution of love teaches us that the new society survives as a second self, replacing the old self, and also the fact that the power of the obstetrician/gynecologist makes childbirth surprisingly easy. So long as she knows that there is no possibility of destroying the self with the fetus, and since she is not debilitated by her own external pressures or internal malaise to the point of being unable to bear pregnancy, the fierce demand for universal suffrage can't be harshly rejected. She is already unable to bear the weight of the fetus—but how did this fetus come to be? Needless to say, the maturation of the mother has fertilized the social-democratic egg of social development. The fetus is completely created as an ideal to be realized. The fetus moves around inside the mother. It can almost feel the forthcoming birth. It is about to burst from the belly. It is just waiting for the obstetrician to come—and this is how the right of universal suffrage comes to be demanded.

Therefore, the universal suffrage demanded by social democracy is not for a false promise. A single vote as a slave, following the golden emperors' demands, like in the United States, is worthless. A single vote is the roar of the cannon that broke through the walls of feudalism. It shouldn't be, as it is in modern Japan, a ballot touched by dirty hands which exchange it for paper money. It's the blood dripping from the hands of the voter as he or she throws a piece of ballot paper into the box. Who can resist this ready and demanding campaign for universal suffrage? All will simply be kicked to the curb. We don't expect to hear the roar of explosions in Japan like the bold and splendorous patriots who are single-handedly blowing up the castle gates. Ah, but when the loyal and earnest Manchurian laborers, who consider unity as power and place great importance on rules governing every action, return—oh, they're coming home even now. One welcomes their triumph, but they are not (mere) triumphant warriors, they are a marching army to fight a legal war. They are not losers in Russia, but are marching to overthrow the rebels who wear the crown of kings. (I sometimes shed tears like rain when I open the window of my study and hear the cries of "Banzai!"—just like the voices of the people who lived in the area where Jie of Xia and Zhou of Shang ruled—welcoming the army of the king.)

Unity is a force. Social forces have sovereignty. In the face of this unifying power, can we still look with contempt at the ludicrous amount of taxes paid? If the amount of taxes someone pays being too little is a reason to refuse someone the right to vote, what explanation is there for having a serious administration that is incompetent in terms of the blood tax? Oh, patriots! As you lay on the stretcher and were carried to the back of the camp in a haze, the fresh blood that leaked and dripped from the bandages, wrapped around your body like a belt, only fertilized the withered winter grass and didn't produce even a single grain of rights. At dusk, just as the moon was beginning to brighten, while you stood at the front in the rainy darkness, thinking of your beloved wives and children back home, the minister of state was leisurely going around the world scavenging for prostitutes in the name of the Red Cross. Do you not know that when you were wiping your parting tears with your valiant hands, and tucking wild flowers in front of the small gravestone where only bones remain, the seven professors (they weren't the seven spears of Shizugatake,[565] despite what they may think!) used their rigid honor to get a leg up,[566] and your countrymen were guarding the front gate of a brothel where a single prostitute, Okoi, was located? Were the tears that welled up in the hollow eyes of your comrades-in-arms, as they stepped out onto the wharf and watched the smoke from your ship disappear to the east, merely from the cries of a child of your homeland?[567] Rather than becoming a slave without rights

---

[565] Warlords who served under Hideyoshi at the Battle of Shizugatake. The seven of them are Kato Kiyomasa, Fukushima Masanori, Kato Yoshiaki, Hirano Nagayasu, Wakisaka Yasuharu, Kasuya Takenori, and Katagiri Katsumoto.

[566] Before the outbreak of the Russo-Japanese War, seven professors of the Faculty of Law at Tokyo Imperial University (Hirondo Tomizu, Masaaki Tomii, Noboru Kanai, Toru Terao, Sakuye Takahashi, Kiheiji Onozuka, and Shingo Nakamura) submitted a letter of opinion on the main argument for war (June of 1903). Because these seven professors opposed the drafted treaty during the negotiation of the peace treaty, the government placed the head of the group, Professor Tomizu, on administrative leave.

[567] This is thought to refer to the poetic scene of the ghosts of soldiers who lost their lives in the fierce battles at Port Arthur and elsewhere seeing off the surviving soldiers as they return home.

and adorning your chest with a piece of gold,[568] like a child's plaything, you should become a demon and get lost in the fields of Manchuria.

Answer this, patriots! You have willingly sacrificed yourselves as part of the nation for the survival and evolution of the rest of the nation. Is this sacrifice of yours a permanent and unceasing one, in which you die as slaves for the lecherous pleasures and games of the upper class, even when there is no other national competition? Does "for the nation" not mean not only for the upper classes of the nation, but also for your wives and children, who are equally part of the nation? It's true that some parts of the state are threatened by Russian aggression. But isn't it also true that your class, which is equally a part of the state, is constantly and unceasingly massacred by the upper classes of the state, and that there is no way to deal with this other than writing it off as "for the nation"? When "Oh forty million countrymen, this is for the nation!" is shouted, it means all forty million of those countrymen are the state. It wasn't yelled out thinking that only a handful of people, or perhaps a few social classes, are the entire state. And yet, the benefits of the acts done on behalf of the nation were completely confined to the upper classes—widows, orphans, and those who starved to death in the fields received none of it! Are they not part of the nation, but rather counted as oxen and horses? Today's nation is not a monarchy in which one person, a part of the nation, monopolizes the whole of the nation. Nor is it an aristocracy, where a minority class monopolizes the whole of the state. A democracy is a nation that calls on all its fellow citizens to sacrifice in the name of patriotism, because the whole of the nation is the nation. Every sacrificial duty means an all-encompassing right. "For the nation" is a solemn cry that must be heard not only in the case of nation against nation, but also in the case of the overthrow of the current economic aristocracy that is slaughtering large parts of the nation.

---

[568] At the time, those who distinguished themselves in battle were awarded the Order of the Golden Kite.

Today, when we call the shared crimes of a capitalist government and a landowner's council a national unity; when we call the quarrels that occur in the distribution of stolen goods a clash between the public and private sectors; when the people, awakened by the voice of "the nation," march from the fields of Manchuria in blood-stained clothing; and when people welcome the marching army and prepare to join its ranks, can we still argue that universal suffrage is premature? May the gates of the foreign enemy be broken down with a charge, and the mansion of the monster that is the Diet be invaded with open arms by universal suffrage. Oh, they who have been standing upside down with their premature argument for the Diet are now turning around and advocating the argument of universal suffrage being premature. Thus, both the Seiyukai and the Progressive Party have completely lost their former Democratic Party spirit and are enslaved by the conscience of the economic aristocracy, who are in the service of the clans and the aristocracy of the Senate.

We declare: the acquisition of universal suffrage should not be obtained by the intermittent petitions of hundreds or thousands of people. It will be obtained precisely by the awakening of the whole people through a fundamental enlightenment movement, by intimidating and subjugating the powerful groups. All rights are determined by the strength of power. When we awaken to unity, great power is born. No matter how many children you have, zero multiplied by thousands is still zero. In the same way, there is no force behind demanding rights until the lower classes of a nation realize that unity is powerful. In this respect we defy the resolutions of the International Congress and celebrate in the name of natural law the effects of the Russo-Japanese War. The people have been united. The people are now clearly aware that unity is a mighty force. The banner of "patriotism" that had flown in the smoke is now held high by the ranks of the marching armies of the legal war. They are not willing to remain as a shouting, backward mob, but are rallying to the front line of the charge—this spirit is the same in the war of the ballot.

People have awakened to the point where they are no longer voices without the right to vote, but are willing to become warriors themselves. Immediately after the flag of the French Revolution first flew, the ammunition storehouses of the Bastille were taken, just as the bloodthirsty men of the Civil War first raided the ammunition storehouses. In legal battles, the acquisition of universal suffrage is what allows occupation of the ammunition storehouses, which are the ballots, and must precede any declaration of war.

What is truly hilarious is that the current government and capitalists actually greet the marching army bent on their destruction with joyous hollering and cheers. Do the governments and capitalists who praise and gain all the honors for these (victorious) assaults, death squads, and night raids, not understand that they will be overthrown at once by the assaults, death squads, and raids of the same people? Turn your heads and look back. The fire of the revolution is about to burn fiercely. If today we mistakenly understand the Socialist Party of Japan as a few moderate "writers" and "Christians," we are forgetting that these are just the scouts of an army that is gathering like a great thunder cloud.[569] This great army is known as the awakened general class.

Indeed, when the popular classes gain universal suffrage and send their warriors to the Diet, the class struggle will be fought not in the fields of smoke, but on the stage of the Diet chambers. The Meiji Revolution roused the general class to wage a class struggle, smoke billowing up from the ground, wresting land and power from the hands of the aristocracy. Likewise, the economic revolution will use the class struggle of voting to force the state to absorb the capital and land of the golden aristocracy, effectively breaking its monopoly on power. The class struggle of social democracy is not just a struggle to replace the (existing) ruling class. Any and all class struggles mean that the main body of the movement is in the lower classes, and the result of the struggle is both

---

[569] "Scouts" in the sense of soldiers sent to scout enemy conditions, terrain, etc.

the evolution of the lower classes into the upper classes, and the expansion of the upper classes through imitation and assimilation. This means that the lower classes are wiped out by their own evolution, it is not a return to primitive equality in which the status of the upper classes is transformed and they become the lower classes, or in which the upper classes, which evolved within a segment of society, are reduced to the lower classes. (Some in the current Socialist Party, Tolstoy followers, and others are absolutely not social democrats because they assert the latter.) In other words, it's the result of the compartmentalization and gradual evolution of parts of society in society's own evolution, so that all parts of society finally evolve into today's upper classes—or, rather, evolve even further than that. In the Meiji Revolution, all people legally became the state, all patriarchal monarchies were swept away, and the class state disappeared as social democracy, with the state as the goal, was held up as the ideal. Similarly, in the course of economic history, the economic patriarchs, to whom the benefits of production belong, will be absorbed into the state, and the entire nation will become an economic group. This economic group will be the goal of production, thereby fully realizing social democracy in terms of the economic content of the state. In other words, the goal is to overthrow economic monarchism and build an economic nationalism.

Oh, cry out for state nationalism on a strict Platonic formulation—and save the nationalism that is currently being used as a method for the economic monarchs' plundering. Monarchism is so named in the sense that the interests of one part of the state, the monarchs, receive sacrifices from the other parts of the state, to the point where the former decide whether the latter live or die, and that all interests and ultimate goals are the monarch's. This was swept away by the law of the Meiji Revolution. The capitalists and landlords, however, exist in the economic world as monarchs who can do as they please, using other workers and peasants, who are part of the state, as the means to their own interests and ends. Thus, their economic power has emerged as a political power, and nationalism is being driven out of the legal text and out of sight completely.

Look at the law. The Great Empire of Japan is a nation that exists with a purpose of survival and evolution. How can it be, then, that the Socialist Party and the people of the entire Japanese empire are unaware that economic monarchism is hiding under the guise of nationalism? Socialism is socialism, and it shouldn't even need to be said that it idealizes a nation one step higher than the one currently based on a geographical society. It is not, however, so non-nationalistic as to be calm and collected with the plundering of the state by economic monarchism. Socialism is a grand nationalism that solemnly recognizes this nation and seeks to develop it into an ideal independent state through the union of many such nations. Nationalism is an evolutionary process of socialism, and the economic monarchs are, of course, traitors to the state. How can the Socialist Party be a traitor? Also, why is there such confusion in the Socialist Party, saying that it denies the state? Luther said that the state is an ethical institution, and Mencius demanded that the state satisfy all ethical demands. We endorse the state together with them, contrary to the resolutions of the First International, and we do it in the name of social democracy.

Look at today's law. The Great Empire of Japan is a strictly ethical system. The ideal of it is to satisfy all ethical demands. But, under the laws of the state, an economic aristocracy exists, and since the individualism of the economic aristocracy has corrupted the ethical brilliance by stealing nationalism, the Japanese empire itself has been defiled and disfigured. Oh, the coming second Meiji Revolution! We must once again begin the class struggle against the second aristocracy and second lords. This will be done through the legal ideal of a state that transcends class. Everything depends on class struggle. Atop the head of the victor of these struggles shines a golden crown of rights. The goddess of justice holds a sword along with her scales. Justice idealizes law, and the goddess holding a sword shows that justice is a balance that can be obtained by overthrowing corrupt institutions that lie before the ideal. The determination of rights was entirely by force of arms throughout antiquity and the Middle Ages. As well, the first procedural laws summoned plaintiffs and defendants to court to duke it out. "I took over the world with my own power. If I wish to become king, I can. If I desire to become emperor, I can." Hideyoshi didn't say this because this method of obtaining rights was limited to him alone. The scales tip according to the weight of the sword, and the goddess of justice passes judgment according to that tilt.

Today's law is the justice determined by the capitalist class as they organize state institutions and express the will of the state. Capitalist governments and landowner assemblies tip the scales in the favor of the capitalist class with the weight of gold. The sword decides the scales, and the victor makes the right. Just as the victors of wars waged with physical power once established monarchies and aristocracies, so too, in today's chaotic economic wars, the victorious ones are the source of all rights. So we affirm: while the socialist party is weak, and while the workers accept their slavery, social democracy might not be a crime legally, but in practice, it holds no rights.

However, the winners are not always winners, and the losers are not always and forever losers. With the development of the equality principle and the countless peasant revolts, the lower classes of society broke away from the slave class of warriors and serfs and became powerful. The sword of the Meiji Revolution overthrew the aristocracy, thereby maintaining the scales with equal rights. Likewise, when peasants and wage slaves under the existing laws of social democracy are awed by the sharp sparkle of the sword and unite to form a powerful force, the economic aristocracy will be overthrown and the goddess of justice will emerge on the basis of economic equality. Oh, government and Diet, gambling and scattering gold on the constitutional rug woven in the blood of Democratic Party patriots! Behold the vast class that surrounds that gambling house, awakening from its long slumber and listening to the alarm bells of social democracy ringing in the darkness of the night.

When this great unity walks on that rug, like a worthy man, the gold you stole will no longer be considered a toy, an accessory to a game of cards. A sleeping lion is more foolish than a dog. A million or even ten million slaves are terrified of one nobleman. When the slaves, known as peasants and wage laborers, see that they could have an authority similar to the aristocracy, and they join hands to gain the might of a million or even ten million, the lion will rise to the top of the political scene, tossing his mane. Governments and parliaments will look like mice fleeing!

What is laughable, however, is that there are those who rudely throw bread crumbs in front of these million and ten million nobles with their hoes and hammers, whispering sweet nothings like foxes in the ears of the king of beasts.

Bread crumbs! This is praised as "charity." Oh, how the authority of mankind is insulted in the name of charity! We aren't so foolish and devious as to tell a man who is dying of hunger, "Push away the hand that is offering you these things out of good grace." However, many of the pit bulls who call themselves philanthropists, even the best of them, treat the poor as sacrifices for their own moral pleasure. The lowest of these philanthropists consider these people as nothing more than a sideshow during an evening ball. Should we swallow the scraps thrown at us out of the back gates of these plunderers' mansions, even if we had a pistol to our throat? When those who value their dignity and prestige fall into poverty, they commit suicide because they cannot bear the thought of entering a poorhouse.

The body is saved, but the spirit is slain. The philanthropist's view of life is one that completely reverses Christ's teachings, thinking that "Man can live by bread alone." The philanthropists who most grieve in indigence will say the following: "The laborer is a man of noble poverty, and the rich are beggars on the throne, because they are fed and clothed by the labor of the laborers." The fact is, however, that they are not beggars, but open plunderers. Let us expose our immorality. If we were born into poverty, whether as beggars on the street or beggars on the throne, we would rather be bandits and plunder than suck up to the sympathy of others. The social democrats are different from the worm-like moralists who are called "virtuous." The beggar is despised and the plunderer is revered. Greek poets admired piracy as a noble enterprise, and until recently their bravery was so revered that it was included in Byron's work.[570] In the Middle Ages, all Japanese warriors made a habit of cutthroat robbery, and it was an object of admiration. Beggars were never praised throughout history, and gold crowns were always placed on the heads of plunderers. No matter how much they may compare the capitalist landlords to beggars on the throne, or how much they may covet their own pleasures, their contempt for the plundered beggars of this land will never disappear, at least until there are no more ants on their knees before them, praising how the powerful plunder.

There is an arrogant smile on the lips of those who offer the hand of grace, and a cold sweat of humiliation drips from the neck of those who receive it. However, if this charity is done, as it was in the past, by a person sharing the result of their labor, tears in his hands, with other unfortunate souls, dividing his food and eating together, we would bow our heads in worship of this noble, precious person. In reality, however, the entire social work of steam and electricity is plundered by the upper class, a small minority, and a large portion of society, condemned to misery because of this plunder, is shoved into the prison of the "charity system" and thrown breadcrumbs through those iron bars. How cruel—even demons couldn't beat that. Wild dogs and podium socialists will be deceived by "charity." Humans aren't like dogs, satisfied as long as they're fed. The working class, having awakened to social democracy and gained personal authority like the aristocracy, does not have such a shameless conscience as the podium socialists, who get down on their knees

---

[570] Lord Byron was an English poet and a representative of Romanticism. After wandering around various countries, he participated in the Greek War of Independence.

beside roadside horse dung and worship their golden daimyo. See what happens if one throws some coins before someone espousing charity, and call that charity to them. Will they not become furious? All of society has become ashamed to receive charity because it has broken away from the servility of the slave and dyed its heart with the conscience of the nobleman. Everything is a power relationship. The era that plundered by force will be plundered by force, and those who plunder by current laws will be plundered by new laws. Might makes right. As long as the golden aristocrats are in power, today's plunder will be just, and we will approve their plunder as just even as we stand beside those starving to death. When the king of beasts makes all bow down, and his fangs are stained with blood, that will be when "just" means "social democracy." We're not bolstering our arguments with tears. We are appealing to a theory of rights that is colder than iron, and we are advocating social democracy. It isn't a question of bread crumbs. It's about the crumbs themselves. It isn't a moral argument to give crumbs to the hungry. It's a strict question of rights; it's about nobody questioning the act of starving for the sake of one's right to bread. Even if a warrior's belly is empty, he still flashes his toothpick.[571] How could social democracy exist if everyone in society doesn't possess such aristocratic authority?

No! Just as the people, who have awakened to authority, are humiliated by having crumbs thrown at them now, during their hungriest moments, the religious would point to the scripture and taunt them:

> Then Jesus was led by the Spirit into the wilderness to be tempted by the devil. After fasting forty days and forty nights, he was hungry. The tempter came to him and said, "If you are the Son of God, tell these stones to become bread." Jesus answered, "It is written: 'Man shall not

---

[571] A phrase meaning to show as if you're not hungry even when you haven't eaten. It used to show an example of living an elegant lifestyle even if poor.

live on bread alone, but on every word that comes from the mouth of God.'"[572]

Ah, these people are not Christ, so who led them to stand by the side of the road and beg for food? They are the ones being tested by the devil as to whether they're children of God or not by the hunger that comes after forty days and nights of fasting. Just as the hungry son of God was mocked and told to merely turn stones to bread, these people, who aren't sons of God, are put in front of a piece of paper that does not produce even a grain of bread, and taunted, "If you can work miracles, make this Bible your bread." The devil has made his attempt—yet, what is going on? The devil again begins to taunt them as they strive to gain bread for their economic evolution and divine authority for themselves. They say, "Have you not lived a long, good life? You mustn't seek material happiness." Worm-like religious theories have little understanding of personal authority.

Again, in the face of this solemn question of rights, the vile podium socialists insist on the harmony of capital and labor. Oh, yes, harmony of capital and labor—why does this sound like the idea of uniting the court and the shogunate? If it were not understood from Japanese history that the lands of the nobles and lords were plundered, and if it's not understood from reading *Capital* that capital plundered labor, this idea would still exist today. The harmony of capital and labor will be a system that will last forever on this earth. If today's podium socialists argued, much like how Mr. Hozumi asserts that the right to rule is attached to the emperor's skin, that, in economics, bank notes are attached to the umbilical cords when capitalists are born, then at least their argument would be consistent. Laughably, however, the podium socialists admit that capital arises from labor, and that capital gives birth to

---

[572] Matthew 4:1–4. The translation is based on the Japanese Bible Society's translation (same for all following).

more capital. Capital, then, is the material expression of labor—and thus they come to speak of the harmony of capital and labor.

This explanation is like an answer to the question, "what is the sound of one hand clapping?"[573] (See the section in volume 1: *The Economic Justice of Socialism*, where we argue that they're mixing up capital and capitalists.) Thus, in the name of harmony between capital and labor, they argue that the interest and profits of the capitalist class and the wages of the workers is proper distribution of production. As we've already said, it is beyond clear that the wage-fund doctrine of the old school of economics is a worthless hypothesis,[574] and that Lassalle's "iron law of wages," on which it stands, should not be advocated without modification. As long as the dictionary doesn't have any entries for "distribute" that include a farmer and a cow equally distributing their grass feed among each other, then the word "distribute" can't be used in this way. Capital and labor are a relationship of command and obedience. This is a ruling relationship. It is a relationship of sovereignty in which the monarchs of the economic aristocracies have the right to do as they please with the serfs and slaves according to the former's pleasure and interest. If one had said to the Meiji revolutionary party that it should abandon the theory of national polity because the senior samurai, who consisted of nobles and their retainers, would get more stipend, they would have been laughed at. Today's podium socialists, as if they were foxes or tanuki, think that they can suppress the rising of the working class, who have risen to repudiate the

---

[573] A famous koan from Zen Buddhism. (A Zen koan is a task to be presented to the Zen practitioner to help him or her devise a Zen meditation technique.) Another famous koan would be "If a tree falls in the forest, and there's no one there to hear it, does it make a sound?"

[574] A doctrine of the classical school in England, advocated by J. S. Mill. This theory holds that the fund earmarked for workers' wages is fixed and that the total amount received by workers is fixed.

economic feudal lords, by throwing the sweet words of "higher wages" at them. The workers are not hungry dogs barking. Social democracy is not satisfied by the working class simply escaping poverty. It is truly the awakened fury of the king of beasts.

In *Socioeconomics*, Mr. Kanai says the following:

> The Social Democrats, the most powerful party in Germany today, and a party that has many sympathizers in the rest of Europe, are, after all, nothing more than a variant of the old alliance that often existed between political revolutionary ideology and economic scarcity. The best way to deal with the disturbances instigated by these parties is to improve society. The recent economic studies, the social policy which the German Reich has practiced somewhat under the power of the Kaiser and Bismarck since 1877, are nothing else but this.[575] In carrying out this social policy, it is, of course, most necessary to prohibit violations of the law or incitement to disturbances, and if anyone violates these, to punish him severely.[576] In other words, on the one hand, laws and enforcement against the Socialist Party should be strictly enforced, and on the other hand, the causes of their emergence should be investigated, social improvements should be steadily made, and their harmful effects should be gradually eliminated. In the past, some of the means and methods adopted by governments to deal with the political and moral dangers of the Social Democrats have been justified, though some of them failed.... n retrospect, coercive measures against the party's violent behavior and education of the people will never be enough to completely wipe out the scourge. At the

---

[575] This political policy of Bismarck is famously known as the "carrot and the stick."

[576] It should be remembered that when universal suffrage was enacted in Japan, the Peace Preservation Law was also enacted.

same time, the poverty of the lower classes must be alleviated, the gap between the rich and the poor must be lessened, and what can be called aversion to this must be eliminated . . .[577]

In *Recent Economic Theory*, Professor Tajima says the following:

> The Socialist Party was originally created to interpret social problems, but now the Socialist Party itself has become an object of social problems. How to dispose of the Socialist Party is indeed one of the difficult questions of social policy.

From these examples, one can easily see how the idiotic daimyos and their retainers are banging their empty heads, wondering "what should we do about the citizens' arbitrary arguments?"

To those who don't hold the ideal of socialists, how can those who seek to revolutionize a fundamental idea and those who seek to preserve that same fundamental organization harmonize and cooperate? Oh, the flock of blind men who flounder wildly and merely sully the name of socialism. If you say that wage increases, eight-hour workdays, compulsory insurance laws, and the like are socialism, then we must strip these ideal-less blind men of the name of social democracy and force them to run back to the theory of uniting the court and the shogunate. The Meiji Revolution is by no means the same as the peasant revolts that complained about the pain of paying taxes and raised banners made of bamboo spears and straw mats.[578] Similarly, we must never

---

[577] The original text didn't finish the sentence here, possibly because Kanai's writings continued, but that made it difficult to understand, so we've made it a fully concluded sentence.

[578] In 1876, peasant revolts broke out frequently in Ibaraki, Mie, Aichi, Gifu, Sakai, and other regions, demanding a reduction in land taxes. In response, the government lowered

equate the factory revolts with socialism, in which people complain about the high price of rice and go on strike, shouting about low wages. The evolution of society is the evolution of the classes toward the upper class. In accordance with this, the Meiji Revolution, in which the aristocratic class evolved to the point of having absolute freedom as monarchs and reigned as monarchs in various regions, further advanced the entire nation. The nation went from the warrior and serf classes to an aristocratic class that evolved to monarchs, thus achieving freedom and independence for the entire nation and absolute authority for individuals, and became "democratic." Likewise, social democracy, which, in its economic content, strives to make the social democracy realized legally by the Meiji Revolution a full, practical reality, is a society-wide advancement that seeks to give the peasants and wage laborers of today an economic aristocracy or even better, and to include all the political and moral evolution that goes with it.

So (we repeat), such a name as "egalitarian democracy" is not much different from a podium socialist in its lack of ideals, and is the language of one who is nothing more than the head of a random factory revolt. Social democracy must be advocated in the name of society as a whole, that is, in the name of the authority of all individual persons. If poverty is eliminated by higher wages, the eight-hour workday, compulsory insurance laws, etc., this is when the so-called social policy of the podium socialists will succeed, and the ideal of "egalitarian democracy," equality of the lower classes, will be realized. Social democracy has as its immediate demands social evolution's world of religious ideals and individual authority, and these are higher ideals than "poverty" and "crime." Wouldn't it be bizarre if we were to suggest that social democratic ideals could be satisfied in any way by higher wages, eight-hour workdays, compulsory insurance laws, and the like? Because they achieved them, the German Social Democrats have leaped even higher, and their wings of

---

the land tax from 3 percent to 2.5 percent the following year.

conquest cover the whole world like a cloud spreading over the heavens. A sleeping lion is more pitiful than a dog, but even an awakened lion cannot break free of its iron chain on an empty stomach. When stupidity comes this far, historians should take note—does the podium socialist think he can throw a lump of raw meat at a hungry lion and make it fall back asleep? The peasant revolts of feudal times were often repeated, causing the lions to become full, and the Meiji Revolution broke the iron chain. The lion of the Socialist Party of Japan is one whose powerless body is lying in the iron cage, one who doesn't possess the strength to wake up from the slumber of cheap wages, excessively long working hours, and the fear of sickness and old age.

Oh, Social Democrats, who by three million votes and eighty-two Reichstag members have insulted and toyed with the German emperor! Does this not mean that they are chewing on the iron fence, growling violently because a lump of meat was thrown in by a fearful person? Of course, the lion cannot be starved to death. The lion has fangs that tear and eat everything. However, even workers cannot boldly continue a strike if they are starving. Creating a grand coalition of labor unions, and having those unions build up currency for use in war, is not something that can be done by workers whose wages are always so low that they can't even feed their wives and children. Excessively long working hours rob rational beings of time to think and deplete their ability to embrace social democracy. The lions of Japan are today still docile before their owners, the capitalists and landlords, only because their hunger leaves them powerless.

Ah, the ferocity of the German Social Democratic Party. Behold the fact that the lion manifests his authority upon having a full belly, discarding like a torn shoe the vice-chairman's seat that he occupies as a natural consequence of being the majority party, simply to avoid the indignity of having to salute one man, the German emperor, and increasing his number of votes and members at the rate of a geometric sequence with each election. (In this respect, the present-day patriots of the Socialist Party of Japan have a keen eye that tells them where the meat is, and they have the honor of being printed in the largest typeface on the first page of the *History of the Socialist Party of Japan*.) As long as Japanese history exists, it will not tolerate even the remnants of the plundering lords and nobles, and as long as the *Capital* is not burned, with its explicit history of capitalist plunder, even if only minor concessions are made via the idea of uniting the court and the shogunate, one concession will force another—nay, even without concessions, the "social policy conundrum" will never disappear unless the economic aristocracy is crushed under the sword of legal warfare. A revolution is always preceded by cowardly and ill-reasoned debates that use such nice-sounding terms as "harmony" and "compromise." Just as the idiot daimyos and their retainers were banging their empty heads over what to do about the self-serving arguments of the civilians—the civilians of that time were banging their bald heads as genro[579]—the revolution will kick these cohesion theorists to the curb, no matter how difficult the question of what to do about this Socialist Party might be to the podium socialists, with their law degrees and professorial dignity. Once conceived, a child must be born. Plastering a pregnant woman's belly does not take away her suffering.

We affirm—the so-called social policy concessions before the social-democratic revolution are like sending nourishing food before childbirth. The social democrats demand it strongly for the benefit of the newborn and for a safe delivery by the old mother, and when there are no concessions, they obtain them by sheer force. To think of social policy as reaping the rewards of social democracy is reminiscent of the quack doctors who tell mothers to use milk soup to abort their unborn babies. Mr. Kanai and Professor Tajima are too clever to be relegated to a corner of the Meiji Biographical Dictionary, but their discussion shows how interestingly organized the brains of the private

---

[579] This was a former elder statesmen position, assisting the emperor regarding a candidate for prime minister. Of course, it is not a state institution.

property era were, and their magnum opuses will be a museum curiosity for future generations of historical researchers. (No, they are merely interpreters, so they may not be able to obtain this honor. Those responsible are elsewhere.)

Therefore, we profess to transcend class interests. That is, the only way to deal with the Social Democrats is through the policy of repression that Bismarck dared to pursue, which is to slaughter all unborn babies through physical force alone. Without Bismarck's policy of repression, the emperor would have been ousted from his throne ten years earlier, and the abhorrent cry of "long live the Kaiser" would not be heard in Germany today. In Russia, a constitution was demanded almost simultaneously with Japan's, and yet the tsar still defends his palace on the battlefield of oppression, and the mother of despotism continues to live as she pleases—anywhere and everywhere, the powerful are more wicked than the professors, but also much cleverer than those who take pride in their university positions. Just as Russia has kept its people too stupid to understand the revolutionary movement, so the present government is very wise to persecute first the enlightenment movement, and then speech as well. Lo and behold, with the whole foot of oppression, it's trampling on the so-called social policies of those who theorize the idea of uniting the court and shogunate—persecution at this point is fine, bold, and unhidden. Bismarck's social policy is not what any podium socialist could have anticipated.

History commands us to declare: Bismarck's social policies succeeded only to the extent that he was able to suppress the opposition with his own mighty power. And the part that made concessions to the Social Democrats' power failed. The compulsory insurance laws, for example, which the podium socialists present as his social policy, are not exactly of his hand, nor his intention. The might of the Socialist Party won that from his own hands. Only, having been so defeated, he still wielded the hammer of repressive policies in war against the Social Democrats—which was also defeated. It was a sympathetic "lamb" that led Louis XVI to the guillotine, surrounded by children and crowds of people. Look at the current Russia. Surrounded by the great revolution that has swept across its entire territory, it is defending itself as if it were a solitary island standing alone in the midst of the great waves of the sea. Napoleon looked at the crowd that was storming the castle of Louis XVI and whispered: "How is it that you have never fought a single battle to drive out these crowds?" The only course for the powerful classes is persecution, even if it is ultimately unsustainable, and it is an affront to their rights to kneel before them and preach the interests of society and the state. We affirm, in the name of scientific research, that persecution is in the interest and a right of the powerful.

In other words, this affirmation shows the falsity of the Socialist Party's claim that the persecution of socialism actually leads to its increased prosperity, as well as the worthlessness of the so-called social reform measures advocated by the podium socialists and their idea of uniting the court and shogunate. Social reform measures are those that force the will of the upper classes to consider the interests of society as a whole. We know that the social policies of the upper classes are based on class sentiments that ignore the facts, since they're guilty of acting only in the interests of the upper classes. However, the upper classes, unless they are exceptional—Tolstoy or the anarchist Kropotkin, for example—can't escape the fact that all knowledge and feelings are class-created, just as physical appearance is a sign of class-based beauty. Acting according to one's conscience does not necessarily ensure that social improvements will benefit the lower classes.

So we declare: it isn't worthwhile to impose social policy from above by order of the monarch on a people who don't understand social democracy. A civic state which possesses true personality wasn't born from the imperial court's dreams during the Taika period. It was only with the development and expansion of national consciousness, to the point where all citizens became aware of the state's purpose of survival and evolution—in other words, permanent existence of the state—that the Meiji Revolution occurred and the civic state arose. Likewise, it goes without saying that social democracy can't be built by a single direct order from the emperor. No, just as social democracy can never be realized by a clan cabinet or a party cabinet, it can never be implemented at the level of the Japanese people today, even if a cabinet is organized by a couple of visionaries in today's Socialist Party. Of course, a slight inclination toward socialism versus a strong rejection of socialism by the powerful class would have a great impact on the speed of its realization, but nothing in history has ever been done by the powerful class willingly if it advocates their extinction. Nor can we find any reason that, through ethics, which says conscience is class-created, would confirm such a thing. Each class has different class interests, class knowledge, class feelings, and class conscience (see the previous explanation in *The Ethical Ideal of Socialism* and *The Theory of Biological Evolution and Social Philosophy*).

As such, the clash between class consciences is what would happen if the different nations of different religious and moral eras had no choice but to settle the clash of local conscience by war. There is no other way to resolve the class struggle than by a decision of great power based on legal warfare. Because they do not understand the historiography and ethics of this class struggle, they think that the Meiji Revolution was the restoration of power and land by feudal lords out of respect for and loyalty to the sovereign. And by the same logic, we find podium socialists arguing toward today's economic feudal lords for the restoration of the right of production, the land, and the productive institutions to the state—or sometimes to the emperor. (The State Socialist Party leader, Aizan Yamaji,[580] is a remarkable representative of this debate in that he is an uncivilized historian.) Whether it was excessively lecturing the patriots at the end of the Edo period on morality, or opposing the aristocrats

---

[580] Journalist and author of the Meiji and Taisho periods. Joined Minyu-sha and published excellent historical and literary essays as a reporter for the Kokumin Shinbun, especially in his critique of personalities.

who were constantly imprisoning the emperor and oppressively forcing him to abdicate the throne, the nobles, with their lands and power obtained by the right of the powerful, would consider those who advocated "restoration to the emperor" as violating their rights, and the Tokugawa would continue their suppressive policies to the present day. Natural law has never done anything useless or erroneous. Just as nations and states with different religious and moral beliefs resolve their local consciences by war, the democratic conscience of the revolutionaries sought to assassinate and wage war against the conscience of the aristocracy, and the latter won. The Economic Meiji Revolution will be a decision made by mighty power via a legal battle.

You can't preach Buddhist principles to cannibals and replace their conscience overnight. In the same way, if we let the state socialists, who think it is enough to constantly dictate to the conscience of the capitalists and landowners, who have been created as the current economic aristocracy, that they must return their production to the people, the realization of social democracy will only take place after the earth collides with a comet. In other words, after everyone in the nation has been enlightened. The democratic revolution of the Meiji Revolution looked to the classic texts and Confucianism to explain the economic evolution of the lower classes, and also the evolving idea of rights after three hundred years of peace, and overthrew the aristocracy as plunderers after a long enlightenment movement. They were the rightful owners at the beginning of the Middle Ages and only became plunderers because of the evolution of society. This social evolution is solely the enlightenment of society through an evolved idea of rights. Up to this day, individual ownership of capital and land as a right of labor based on individualism is not a plunder at all, but a natural right. However, when "capital" becomes steam and electrical power, swallowing up other small capitalists and smallholder farmers who cannot compete with loan sharks, it is clearly contrary to today's ideal of individualism and justice. If the social-democratic enlightenment movement awakens society as a whole to an evolved idea of rights, the economic aristocracy will bear the name of plunderers and will have to be overthrown.

Because they don't understand the logic of social evolution, some, such as Aizan Yamaji's faction, advocate the use of the powerful social class as in the Meiji Revolution. Others argue that socialism is premature because the economic evolution of modern Japan is still very low. Everything in heaven and earth depends on "power." Societies are driven by mighty power. If you win, you're the loyalist army, and if you lose, you're a band of bandits. All right and wrong is determined by the class struggle. Those who truly understand social democracy should clearly be prepared—in today's world, social democrats are criminals, and the upper classes have the right and duty to punish them according to their class conscience![581] Evolutionary thought does not allow for the assumption of a binary axis of opposition, in which there is absolute good and absolute evil in the world. In philosophy, the assumption of absolute nothingness has become an unsustainable principle. Good and evil are evolutionary, and they only arise from different degrees of evolution. What was good in antiquity became evil in the more evolved Middle Ages, and what was good in the Middle Ages became evil in the even more evolved modern age. And the upper classes of society are the most evolved in terms of goodness because they are the very ideals that the lower classes strive to attain and imitate. Therefore, the upper class has the right and the duty to criminalize and punish, in the name of the state, the class-based good of the lower class, which has not yet evolved to the good of the upper class in accordance with the theory we just explained (and according to this, future criminal law studies must be organized; see *The Ethical Ideals of Socialism*).

However, the evolution of the conscience of any individual person is a matter of degree. Today's so-called socialists inherit the dogmatism of individualism and deny the state as the political organization of society, which

---

[581] Because the socialists are still losing in the class struggle.

has an immediate negative impact on social democracy, and contesting them with a conscience lacking regard for individual freedom would make it impossible to arrive at social democracy. In this age of state sovereignty, if a state institution acts out of personal self-interest in a manner inconsistent with the social self-interest that it perceives as part of the state, its actions are clearly invalid under the law. Still, even if said institution acts in accordance with its own conscience, though it is more evolved than that of the others, it's still a crime in both the unevolved conscience of the criminal class and in jurisprudence. However, this is only a concept of jurisprudence, and it goes without saying that there is no way to go into a person's inner mind to know whether state institutions followed the dictates of conscience or not, or whether they were unable to suppress an outburst of self-interest.

Social democrats especially have to think very hard, when everything they say and do has jurisprudential force, since many of them act with a class conscience. Look at everything calmly and dispassionately. There are very few bad people in the world, and they all act according to their conscience, which is all they have. We would absolutely never look at the upper classes, who are pursuing a policy of suppression against the Socialist Party, and think that they're acting against their conscience and on the basis of their own evil. They're acting according to the good of the present, and the social democrats are acting according to the good of the future. In this way, everything is determined by power, and that power depends on social forces. (We shouldn't be too quick to dismiss today's powerful forces as brute strength simply because the brute strength of the Middle Ages was a gathering of social forces.) Social forces are replaced by new life as society evolves. Therefore, persecution can be defined as "all the means by which the powerful class prevents the social forces from gaining power over words and deeds, which it recognizes as existing, and which it considers harmful to the evolution of society."

People are not inherently free, nor are they equal. They are free and equal because their conscience is created as one that respects freedom and equality because it is within a society that recognizes freedom and a nation that is based on the principle of equality. So even in the age of social democracy, individual freedom is not absolute, as individualism assumes. Suppose one walks naked down a boulevard. Society cannot respect that freedom. Dare to commit arson, or commit adultery openly. Try to plunder the land and productive institutions of the state, or attempt to restore the system of private property. Obviously, these freedoms will be oppressed by the might of social democracy (we only say that morality will become instinctive, individual and social self-interest will cease to conflict, and that freedom will therefore cease to conflict with other individuals or with society as a collective of individuals). Everything is determined by who has greater power. In ages when nations of different religious and moral persuasions have determined clashes of regional consciences by war, is there anyone unintelligent enough to say that a furious attack will rather strengthen the enemy's position? The fact that today's Socialist Party in Japan is so afraid of the might of those with authority that it argues that persecution actually strengthens the socialist momentum is nothing but ignorance of the military science of legal warfare. Everything is in the enlightenment movement. Everything is determined by power.

If the conscience of the powerful classes considers social democracy to be contrary to society's purpose of survival and evolution, then, from the point of view of jurisprudence, the persecution of social democracy is both a right and an obligation.

If we understand this clash of class conscience in the legal war, we can see that questions such as what to do with capitalists and landlords after the realization of social democracy are really only a side issue. Whether we are talking about confiscation or introducing public debt—about whether that debt be interest-free or with annual interest—we never want to discuss these things. This is not an argument based on principle, but on policy. The previous explanation should make this clear. However one tries to escape from the myriad conditions that the upper class impose in order to feel secure, and from the extreme and radical epithets that express a general dislike of social democracy, one cannot expect a high road act in which the economic lords offer to give back the right of production. Principles should be promoted as principles, and theory tolerates no exceptions. Extremism or radicalism is an expression of the character of the individual who embraces it, or of the strength or weakness of its social forces, and the principle itself, as a theory, must necessarily be directed through to the end, to the best of its reasoning power.

The first and last movement of social democracy is solely an enlightenment movement, and policy theory is a temporary phenomenon that depends on enlightened social forces. In other words, the question of how to dispose of capitalists and landlords is completely irrelevant to today's social democrats. Of course, policies vary from period to period and from region to region, and during the French Revolution, priests and aristocrats had their property confiscated. However, in the age of individualism, the loss of private property was a failure of policy, as it immediately reduced them to the lower classes of society and forced them to degenerate. Not only that, the theory of individualism cannot explain how a mechanistic state with no personality has the legitimate right to confiscate their property unjustly. Therefore, the substitution of aristocratic lands by public debt, as in Germany and Japan, was not only a convenient policy to avoid social upheaval, but was also justified by theory during the age of the private property system.

The social-democratic revolution, however, is the transfer of private property that exists in law, as divided among individuals (but which is in practice private property of the upper part of society, which is occupied by the economic aristocracy), into the common ownership of all parts of society. This is quite different from the individualist revolution, which in law divides the private property of the upper strata of society, which is occupied by the upper classes, into the private property of the whole of society, the individuals, with the ideal of equalizing the private property of the individuals. History doesn't repeat itself. To think of following the policies of the individualist era in an age when social democracy has been realized and all individuals are part of society and owners of common property is pure ignorance of political science. If social democracy lacks truth in some aspects, or if the era hasn't evolved enough and most people aren't enlightened, then, because it wouldn't have enough power in the class struggle, today's plundering class would leave traces behind, but this is a different subject from political policy. Today, when there is still no need for anything other than an enlightened movement, for the set of principles themselves, to argue whether or not repeating the policy theories of the individualist era in socialism is simply a blind move. (Indeed, those who call themselves socialists today are the individualists of the French Revolutionary era, through and through.) Look at the citizens being drawing into the battlefield. Even life itself is being confiscated by society's sovereignty "for the nation."

Of course, as the name socialist suggests, we do not consider the individual as the ultimate goal, as in the thought of the individualist era. We know that the life of an individual can't be calculated by any substitute, even by today's law, and yet right now, precious individual lives are confiscated as sacrifices for the benefit of the state. So what jurisprudence is it that prevents the sovereignty of society from managing the land and capital it already has under its "supreme ownership" for the benefit of the survival and evolution of society? McCulloch doesn't understand anything other than economics, and materialism tells him that the worker is a machine made by long hours and great toil.[582] The two are similar in that they provide for their parents, wives, and children every year through their operation. These living machines are used by society today via its sovereignty, during conscription, which is the time in which they operate best, for the benefit of society. The current laws of society, which express socialism, allow this usage, along with sending them off

---

[582] The original text spells the name wrong, but it's probably referring to John Ramsay McCulloch (1789–1864), an economist of the early nineteenth century.

to the battlefield, even if it means destroying the machines themselves. In this case, what right would refuse the state using lifeless production machines, which plundered capital, for the state's own benefit, considering the fact that all production institutions belong to the state?

In today's system of private property, the pitiful productive institutions are sacrificed with a smile on their faces, leaving behind women, who are inferior in terms of labor, or children, who cannot work at all, without a single vile word of compensation. Public ownership of land and capital is not a sacrifice for capitalists and landlords. It's about making them co-owners of public property along with the whole of society, who have sustained and elevated them to their current status. It is to bring about a great economic evolution and make those "machines" co-owners of social property by managing the public economy together, not by condemning their wives and children to a lower class with no access to labor, as is the case today. The only thing to be done is to create a social force through the enlightenment movement, with the purpose and ideal of the survival and evolution of society. Even if the nobility is legitimate in today's world of private property, when social communism is realized, the economic patriarchs will remain the owners of the public debt, like a human with a beast's tail attached, a completely different race. Christ once said, "Render unto Caesar the things that are Caesar's, and unto God the things that are God's."[583] All social-democratic movements are like this—nothing in the world belongs to Caesar. Render unto God the things that are God's, and unto society the things that are society's!

Social democracy is about defeating the economic aristocrats in order to make the economic content of the state achieve the ideal. This is done by the sovereignty of the state and the political power of the people, which is the legal ideal that has been preached since the Meiji Revolution, where all people are part of the state. It isn't to deny the state, as in the French Revolution during

---

[583] Mathew 22:15–22

the age of individualism, but only to express the social forces, united under truth, as the will of the state through its institutions. That class struggle is a legal war.

Chapter 16

In the previous chapters, we have examined social democracy from the perspectives of economics, ethics, jurisprudence, political science, sociology, history, biology, and philosophy. In particular, we have argued that the Japanese people have reached social democracy in terms of legal ideals and moral convictions as a result of the evolution of history. From the standpoint of historical philosophy, we explained that the Meiji Revolution was the legal realization of the ideals of the distant Taika era. We concluded that the public ownership of land and capital is only possible if the economic content of the state under the law is brought to the point where it is expressed in the law. In other words, we said that the social democratic revolution of the future would be an Economic Meiji Revolution based on a war of laws. In this war of laws, new social forces would become the will of the state and transform the economic class state into an economic civic state.

It is now necessary to say a few words about the ideal state theory of Confucianism, which was the ideal of the Taika Revolution. It is similar to the way Plato's *Republic* eventually became the source of viewing socialism as the ideal state in Europe. Confucianism is the ideal theory of the state that was held up as the source of socialism in ancient China and Japan.

In ancient Greece, where Plato lived, political science (not in the sense of today's political science, but a broader version including statecraft) and ethics were not yet separated. Likewise, in ancient Chinese Confucianism, political science and ethics were also not yet differentiated. This proves that the principles of human nature and the principles of social evolution are governed by the same natural laws, in that both the West and the East, completely cut off from each other during ancient times, were originally both grand states in which the people broke off from the same ancestor of the human race. In later times, as an evolutionary process, political science became so polarized and differentiated that it came to contradict ethics, but it wasn't like that in the past. Political science is the ethics of the larger organism, society, and ethics is the politics of the smaller organism, the individual person. Therefore, ethics and political science are not only based on the same principles, but they cannot both bring their demands to fruition unless they are studied in conjunction with each other. Just as socialism seeks to ethically construct a political organization suitable for the inhabitation of ethical organisms, since mankind is an ethical organism, during the period of the history of philosophy when intuitive considerations were being made, we had an ethical political organization by ethical political instinct—formed as instinctually as the honeybee forming its nest. The basis of their political science and ethics was to liberate mankind from economic temptations, as the results of rigorous scientific research has shown that economic demands must first be satisfied before ethical activities can be undertaken.

"The path taken by the earlier saint (Shun) and the later saint (King Wen) were the same, though different in time and place."[584] Mencius' words are true. Just as European socialism looked to Plato for its source, let us speak a bit of the idealistic nationalism of Mencius, the Plato of the East. He inherited and developed the learning of Confucius, the Socrates of the East. It's the same as Plato following in the footsteps of Socrates, the Confucius of the West, and setting forth, at the beginning of the history of philosophy, the ideal state of mankind. In the opening volume of the history of oriental thought, Mencius shows how the socialist ideal of the state has been the ideal of mankind since antiquity. The words you see below, of Mencius' instruction to King Xuan of Qi on the high road, clearly express the ethical basis of scientific socialism. He said the following:

---

[584] *Mencius*, 4B.1

Only a very limited number of learned and cultured people can maintain their constancy even if they do not have fixed assets. The commoner has no constancy without fixed assets. Once they lose their constancy, they are free to do whatever they want to do, whether it be selfishness, envy, cheating, extravagance, or any other evil thing they desire. If we know this and do nothing to stop them, and if we punish them harshly as soon as they commit a crime, we are totally disrespectful to the people. How can a monarch, who is supposed to be benevolent and virtuous, rule well by completely ignoring the people in his political position? This is why the enlightened monarchs of ancient times took care of the people's livelihoods, making sure that their parents would have enough to live on, their wives and children would have enough to live on, and that they would be able to live comfortably for the rest of their lives if the harvest was good, and that they would not have to worry about starving to death if there was a bad harvest. He also taught them the way of humanity, and led them to goodness, so that the people could easily follow him. The lords and princes of today, however, are trying to provide for the people's livelihood, but the upper class is unable to provide for their parents, and the lower class is unable to provide for their wives and children. Even if, luckily enough, the harvest is bountiful, it only leads to a lifetime of suffering under heavy taxes. If the harvest is poor, however, the people starve to death. The king was so busy trying to save his people from death that he had no time to practice courtesy. If the king truly desires to conduct a benevolent administration, why doesn't he go back to the basics of politics and start by stabilizing the lives of the people?[585]

---

[585] Ibid., 1A.7

He thus placed ethical demands on political organization, which he called the root of politics—the theory of land nationalism. Land, unlike today's land and capital, was the only economic source at the time, and, according to the socialism of the time, should be made public. (Plato's Greece had the slave class and women as actual slaves. They didn't have personality, and were merely property, and so those were an economic source as well as the land, and should be made public also.) Mencius said, "The common people neither starve nor freeze. This is the ultimate in high road government, and there has never been a man in history who has not become a king of the world through this kind of government."[586] He also said, "The people's lives will be stable and they will be able to provide for their parents, wives, and children, and mourn their dead without regret. This is the beginning of high road politics."[587] This shows that economic needs must be satisfied before any sort of ethical activity.

Mencius' belief that mankind is fundamentally good was an acknowledgement of the inherent existence of intuitive social instincts. He said,

> The five grains are the best and most delicious of all the seeds we eat, but even the five grains are inferior to the lowly millet if they are not sufficiently matured. In the same way, the value of benevolence also lies in its maturity, in other words, in its full perfection.[588]

This is an illustration of the fact that social instincts are slight, thus some people have them impaired and others fully develop them, depending solely on the surrounding social environment:

---

[586] Ibid., 1A.7

[587] Ibid., 1A.3

[588] Ibid., 6A.19

When Mencius went from the city of Fan in Qi to the capital city of Linzhi, he saw the prince of the State of Qi from afar and sighed in admiration. The old saying goes, "The position one is in changes one's temperament, and nutrition changes one's body," but goodness. One's position certainly is an important thing. Be it the prince, or any other person, aren't they all the same human beings? Yet, the prince is so different in dignity. The prince's carriage, the horses he rides, and the clothes he wears are not so different from those of other people, but the reason he has such an unmistakable elegance is because of the position he occupies. The attitude of a person who lives in the most prestigious mansion in the world, in such benevolence, must be vastly superior to that of an ordinary person. It is said that, when the sovereign of Lu went to the state of Song, he called the gatekeeper from the Song city gate to open the gate, and the gatekeeper wondered, 'this man is not our lord, but his voice is so similar to ours,' and this is not an exception. Since both the sovereign of Lu and the sovereign of Song held similar positions, their voices and behavior naturally resembled each other.[589]

This is the reason why all the ministers are down on their knees like slaves in front of the gallant figure of the present emperor, the great oriental emperor, and it is consistent with what we have said about physical appearances being created by class.

Mencius said to grand master Dai Busheng, a Song king, "if you wish to be a fine king of Song, let me draw an analogy and make something clear. If the grand master of Chu wanted his son to speak the refined language of Qi because the language of Chu is vulgar, would he choose a person from Qi as his guardian or a person from Chu as his

---

[589] Ibid., 7A.36

guardian? Which would it be?" Dai Busheng answered that it would, naturally, be a person from Qi. Mencius responded that he was correct. "However, even if a person from Qi were to be his sole guardian, if a large number of people from Chu were to speak to him in Chu, no matter how much they whipped him day after day to make him speak in the language of Qi, it would be impossible. However, if you take the child to a busy town such as Zhuang or Yue in the capital of Qi for a few years, he will become completely accustomed to the language of Qi, and no matter how hard you try to whip him into speaking in the language of Chu day after day, it will be just as difficult as the previous example."[590]

This is in line with what we have said about conscience being socially created. Just as foreigners who speak different languages have different consciences, so the medieval conscience of the modern German emperor is created in the court of the smug, eloquent emperor, and the slave conscience is created in the society of government officials, full of pride. In the general lower classes, with their language like that of a barbaric village, the same brutal, savage, and lecherous conscience of the barbarians is created. Mencius also says the following:

> The craftsman who makes arrows is not necessarily more inhumane than the craftsman who makes armor, but the craftsman who makes arrows is only concerned with whether or not his arrows are high quality enough to hurt people, and if they're not, that's a problem for him. On the other hand, the craftsman who makes armor is only concerned with whether or not his armor is not low quality enough that people get hurt, and if it is, that's a problem for him. The same is true of priestesses who try to heal the sick and coffin makers who make a lot

---
[590] Ibid., 3B.6

of money when people die. Therefore, one must be very careful in one's choice of profession, since it is the skill (profession) one acquires that separates the benevolent from the inhumane.[591]

This explains how the competition between the nations and the industrial maelstrom of the economic aristocracy, with its barbaric medieval customs, has kept the whole world at a low moral level.

Mencius clearly understood that a developed genius is completely socially nurtured. His argument is extremely poignant as well because it can defeat the dogmatic inequality theory of the podium socialists with a single blow.

Mencius said that, in years of good harvest, there are many good and dependable young people because they can live in peace, but in years of bad harvest, there are many young people who do evil because they lack food and clothing. However, this isn't because the heavenly beings discriminated so fiercely between good and bad harvest years when they bestowed qualities on people. But in bad harvest years, when people lack food and clothing, there is always something tempting them and they are drawn into evil. For example, suppose you sow barley seed and cover it with soil. If the land is the same size and the time of sowing is the same, the seed will sprout and mature around the time of the summer solstice. If the yields were not always the same, it was because of the difference between fertile and barren land, the difference in the amount of rain and dew, and the difference in the farmer's care, not because of the barley seed itself. All things of the same type, not just barley, are generally like this. Shouldn't we doubt that only human beings are different in this respect? Saints are the same type as us. Therefore, there is no doubt that we are as good as the saints. The

---

[591] Ibid., 2A.7

ancient sage Longzi said, "Even if you make a shoe without knowing the measurements of your feet, you still know you would not make something as large as a bucket." This is exactly true. The reason shoes are similar in shape and size is because the feet of people all over the world are similar. This doesn't only apply to feet, though. The relationship between one's mouth and taste is the same. Human flavor preference is generally similar between people. Yi Ya, the famous ancient chef who served under Duke Hwan of Qi, was the first person to discover the bones (outline) of taste that we all consider good. If people's palates were naturally different from each other, like dogs and horses are different from us, how could anyone in the world like Yi Ya's food?

In fact, when it comes to taste, the fact that everyone in the nation expects that Yi Ya's food is the only way to go is proof that human taste buds are similar to each other. Hearing is the same. When it comes to music, everyone in the nation desires only Shi Kuang because our sense of hearing is similar. Sight is the same. There is nobody in this nation who does not know the beauty of Zidu. Anyone who doesn't must not have eyes. So, I would say, "When we taste with our mouths, there is something that everyone finds delicious, when we listen to music with our ears, there is something that everyone finds wonderful, and when we look at a beautiful person with our eyes, there is something that everyone finds equally beautiful. How could it be that our hearts alone are different? What quality do we share in our hearts? It is the sense of what is proper and right. The one called a 'saint' was merely the first to grasp what our hearts all took pleasure in. And in this way, what is proper and right pleases my heart, not just the saint's, in just the way that meats please my mouth."[592]

---

[592] Ibid., 6A.7

His equating the saints with us is a fundamentalist egalitarianism, arguing that there is no way a saint can be understood by society if he is considered a completely different species from us, the same as a dog or horse. He was truly a magnificent sage of the ancient times!

He describes the current working class with the following:

> The hungry think whatever they eat tastes good, and the thirsty think whatever they drink tastes good. They do not yet know the true taste of food and drink, because their sense of taste is impaired by hunger and thirst, and they are unable to make correct judgments. By the way, is it only the mouth and stomach that are affected by hunger and thirst? The human heart, too, is affected by poverty and is unable to make correct judgments. If a person's righteousness is not impaired by poverty, he need not worry in the slightest if he is inferior to others in terms of wealth and nobility. For that alone makes him a noble person.[593]

He grasped the ideals and laws of social evolution with simple intuitive faith. One who recognizes the ideal ahead and discovers the law by which it will be realized can never become a theorist of the harmony of labor and capital or the idea of uniting the court and shogunate. He traveled the nation with the most radical and fundamental revolutionism. It is said that "Mencius preached his usual view of the goodness of human nature, and whenever he opened his mouth, he always referred to the ancient saints Yao and Shun, and urged the people of the world to strive hard and become enlightened rulers like Yao and Shun."[594] Given this, one can imagine how all the arguments came out of his mouth, like threads, from his fundamental idea of socialism. The "innate

---

[593] Ibid., 7A.28

[594] Ibid., 3A.1

goodness of people" and the "greatness of Yao and Shun" are the intuitive understanding of the conclusion of today's scientific socialism—that people have social instincts by their nature as social animals, and that as social animals during the primitive age of Yao and Shun, things were peaceful and all were equal.

In his ideas on human nature and society, he had abandoned from the beginning the reformism and principles of harmony that are the spirit of today's social democrats. He believed that "mere good intentions are not enough to make a good government, but a system that is merely formal without heart will not be effective in practice."[595] This is an outpouring of his conviction:

> When Zichan was the prime minister of Zheng,[596] taking pity on the people who had to cross the river on foot in the cold winter, he allowed the people to cross the Coushui (湊水) and Xiaoshui (洧水) in his own boats.[597] Zichan was a gracious man, but, unfortunately, he does not know how to play politics. If a temporary bridge is built in November, when the farmers are off-season, so that people can walk across the river, and the bridge is ready for vehicles and horses in December, the people should have no trouble crossing the river. If a politician were to be fair in his politics, there would be no problem even if he clears away the people when passing through, considering the separation between aristocrat and plebeian. Why would he give each and every person

---

[595] Ibid., 4A.1

[596] Zheng was a former Chinese state during the Zhou dynasty, and Zichan was the chief minister of Zheng.

[597] These are both rivers in Kaifeng, Henan Province. Also, the phase "his own boats" would more accurately be "the emperor's boats" in a literal translation, but that doesn't fit the rest of the grammar, so it was translated as it is here.

passage in his own vehicle? Therefore, those in politics must look at the big picture. If we tried to satisfy each and every single person, even if it took us all day, day after day, we would have too much work to do and too few days to do it.[598]

The class stench of entering a monarchical era is repugnant, but it also shows that the so-called "charity system" is completely worthless. He was radical and fundamental in his efforts to nationalize the source of the economy, like Christ, who said "Tear down this temple, and I will rebuild it in three days."[599] He would always say, "to begin with, there is only one way,"[600] and, "medicine is only effective if it's enough to make you dizzy when you take it, otherwise it won't cure any ailment."[601] These sorts of statements are direct expressions of

---

[598] *Mencius*, 4B.2

[599] John 2:19. The passage is as follows: "Now the Passover of the Jews was at hand, and Jesus went up to Jerusalem. And He found in the temple those who sold oxen and sheep and doves, and the money changers doing business. When He had made a whip of cords, He drove them all out of the temple, with the sheep and the oxen, and poured out the changers' money and overturned the tables. And He said to those who sold doves, 'Take these things away! Do not make My Father's house a house of merchandise!' Then His disciples remembered that it was written, 'Zeal for Your house has eaten Me up.' So the Jews answered and said to Him, 'What sign do You show to us, since You do these things?' Jesus answered and said to them, 'Destroy this temple, and in three days I will raise it up.' Then the Jews said, 'It has taken forty-six years to build this temple, and will You raise it up in three days?'

But He was speaking of the temple of His body. Therefore, when He had risen from the dead, His disciples remembered that He had said this to them; and they believed the Scripture and the word which Jesus had said." (John 2:13–22)

[600] *Mencius*, 3A.1

[601] Ibid., 3A.1

today's social democrats, who reject almost everything but the public ownership of land and capital. A man named Dai Yingzhi once said,

> We would like to take only one-tenth of the tax and abolish customs duties and commodity taxes in the market, but since that is not possible this year, we would like to reduce the taxes for now and abolish them completely next year.[602]

Oh—why did he sound so much like a podium socialist in that moment? It really is amusing—Mencius then decisively rejected it in the name of economic justice, through the fundamental ideas of socialism. Mencius said the following:

> Suppose there is a man who comes in from next door and steals chickens day in and day out. Someone advises him, "That is not proper behavior for a sovereign, so you should stop it," and he responds with, "Very well, I will reduce the amount I steal to one chicken per month, and by next year I will stop all together." What kind of response is this? If you think something is wrong, you should stop it immediately. There is no reason to wait until next year.[603]

It goes without saying, however, that not all of Mencius' words can be equated with today's social democracy. Mencius is significant simply because, in the history of Oriental thought, he dreamed up the most obviously idealistic theory of the state and strove throughout his life to realize it. His theory of national ownership of the land, for example, could be very easily transformed into a theory of the lord owning the land. "Seiden's Law" is merely a restoration to

---

[602] Ibid., 3B.8

[603] Ibid., 3B.8

the primitive days of village common ownership, and it is nothing more than a mere bud for the future. It's completely different from the state management of scientific socialism, where agriculture is done by machines. Private property and the absolute tyranny of the monarch are natural processes of social evolution in life. According to the special and superior conscience of Mencius and others like him, they were evil, but according to the standard conscience of societies throughout the ancient and medieval periods, they were rights that were acquired with the approval of society. Therefore, we assert that even the severe money collections were not immoral. The fact that the powerful class was supported by the social forces, despite how harsh they were in their collections, is proof of the moral standards of the time. The historical record shows that Mencius and others were treated as mere dreamers.[604]

In the time of early humans, in the Yao and Shun eras, when the population was small and people had finally settled the land, the freedom of the land was only a little scarcer than the air, and it was a paradise with abundant natural crops. As society evolved, the population increased and the competition for survival began to grow village by village, until finally Mencius himself said,

> Those who use their minds stand above and govern others, while those who use their bodies are below and governed by others. He who is governed feeds him who governs by paying taxes, and he who governs does not have time to cultivate, so he is fed by he who is governed.[605]

---

[604] Because Zhu Xi included *Mencius* in *Four Books and Five Classics*, it is now highly regarded, but up until the Tang dynasty, *Mencius* was barely considered at all. It was only after Han Yu praised the writings of Mencius that his reputation finally begin to rise.

[605] *Mencius*, 3A.3

And so a plundering class emerged. Of course, it was impossible to restore the system of village common ownership in this period. The system of private property first gave rise to monarchies, in which a single monarch became the subject of property rights, and then to aristocracies, in which a small number of aristocrats became the subject of property rights. Then came the democracies, in which the general classes, who had previously been regarded as slaves or peasants and the property of the monarchs and nobles, were finally given recognition of their personalities, and they became the subjects of property rights in all cases and were now entitled to tenant farming on land owned by the monarchs and nobles. Thus, individual freedom and individual authority expanded from one molecule to a few, and then to all. As a path of social evolution in ancient and modern times, the system of private property is not based on the evil of those in power, as was thought during the "fantasy socialist" period. However, Mencius clearly had a socialist utopia in mind when he left his idealistic theory of the state in the opening volume of the history of philosophy, on par with Plato's. He said the following:

> If the fields are well governed and taxes are collected sparingly, the people can be made wealthy. If we consider the time period when helping the people with their livelihoods, and use the people in a moderate manner, the wealth of the nation will accumulate to the point where it cannot be entirely used up. Without water and fire, human beings cannot survive a single day. However, if you knock on someone's door at nightfall and ask them for this precious water and fire, they will gladly give it to you because they have an abundance of it. If this is the case, then the ideal way for a saint to rule the nation would be to make sure that the food the people eat, such as beans and grains, are as plentiful as water and fire. When beans and grains are as plentiful as

water and fire, the people will naturally be civilized, and how can there be anyone who is inhumane?[606]

Of course, he called Yao and Shun saints because they were in the primitive age when there was peace and natural crops such as beans and grains were as abundant as water and fire. It wasn't because they ruled the world so skillfully, as might be implied from Mencius' respectful words when speaking of the past. Therefore, no matter how well the fields were governed and how little taxes were collected in those days, beans and grains could never be as abundant as water and fire. That was only the dream of an idealist.

Two thousand years of social evolution, though, have finally brought us to today's material civilization, where steam and electricity have replaced mankind's material labor. Thus, mankind has become almost exclusively a mental laborer. To use Mencius' words, those who use their mind would be all of mankind, while those who use their body would be steam and electricity. Those who nourish man are steam and electricity, and all mankind is nourished. He who is ruled by man is steam and electricity, with only philosophers recognizing them as having life,[607] and all mankind, as the saint who rules over this steam and electricity and made the universe peaceful, is the sovereign over all things in heaven and earth. The fountain of socialism, started by Plato and Mencius, passed between the precipices of monarchies, aristocracies, and democracies with private property systems, flowed into the plains of material civilization, and became for the first time "a lake overflowing with mercy." Just as the Meiji Revolution absorbed into the state the right to rule, which had belonged to numerous patriarchs, the economic revolution would absorb into the state the right to produce, which had belonged to numerous economic patriarchs. The state would then manage the land and

---

[606] Ibid., 7A.23

[607] Legal fiction, which acts as if they are alive.

productive institutions as the main body of sovereignty over all economic sources.

Most important to note, however, is that Mencius had no understanding of the "socialist enlightenment movement" we're talking about. This is unavoidable, since Mencius was a man of the past, however distinguished he may have been. Even in Europe, the principle of class struggle was only discovered by Karl Marx (though of course his explanation was not complete), and Mencius, two thousand years ago, had no choice but to teach its realization to the monarchs and other powerful classes. In other words, Mencius was technically an enlightenment activist in that he strove to create a socialist conscience for the monarchs, but as I explained earlier, the true enlightenment movement was aimed at the lower classes and was a prerequisite for the emergence of a powerful force in the class struggle. So, whereas Mencius's movement was a touring explanation to various monarchs, today's socialism takes as its sole method the development of the knowledge of the general class, especially the working class. Since this point touches on the most dreaded question of all, "whether social democracy and the Japanese emperor are compatible," we can't avoid a further word about Mencius' theory of statecraft principles.

A terrible fallacy commonly believed has been to think of Mencius' political science as vaguely democratic. Of course, from our point of view, Mencius's thought is a staunch democracy. As we have explained before, we classify states according to their evolution, and we define a sovereign patriarchal state as a state in an age when mankind is not conscious of its social existence and simply acts according to the personal interests of one or a few monarchs. The modern state, which has undergone a long evolutionary process, in which all parts of the state have finally become aware that the state has a purpose of survival and evolution, and in which all parts act in the interest of the state through legal and social self-interest, is the civic state of state sovereignty. Things depend on whether the monarch is a subject outside the state, possesses the state and treats it as an object, or a part of the state acting under the personality of the state. If we call the former a monarchy and the latter a democracy (we used the term democracy to mean this earlier as well), then naming Mencius' political science democracy is, of course, what we're trying to argue (read *The So-Called Theory of Japan's National Polity and its Restorative Principle of Revolution*).

However, many scholars, like the individualist jurisprudence that is still central to their thought, see monarchism as the sovereignty of the modern monarch, and democracy as the sovereignty of the individual people. The worst classify monarchism simply according to whether the number of rulers is one or many, and, like Aristotle, call it monarchism or democracy. Mencius' political science has never considered anything other than a single despotic body, so, from this standpoint, it is clearly erroneous to speak of his thought as democratic in this sense. Therefore, we view Mencius in the light of what we have said earlier in our legal theory: Mencius recognized the ethical purpose of the state and believed that the actions of political authorities must be ethical and centered on the interests of the state. When the state deviates from this status as an institution, Mencius argues, it becomes a mere man without the obligation of obedience.[608] In this point, Mencius is a state sovereignty theorist. It is the same regarding the first of our three categories of government, in that he advocates organizing the supreme authority around a single, privileged person, who would express the will of the nation in accordance with his inner political morality. The Taika Revolution was an attempt to realize this ideal, and the period from the Meiji Revolution to twenty-three years later was an

---

[608] King Xuan of Qi asked Mencius about the story of King Wu of Zhou's defeat of King Zou of Shang, and said, "Is it right for a retainer to kill his lord?" Mencius replied, "A lord who disobeys benevolence and righteousness is no longer a lord, but merely a man. Therefore, King Wu's defeat a mere man, he did not kill a sovereign." The famous idea of the dynastic cycle arose from this.

era in which all of Mencius' political ideals were realized. However, after the Imperial Constitution of Meiji year twenty-three, the organization of the supreme authority was changed as the state exercised its sovereignty, and the supreme authority was organized by the emperor and the Imperial Diet. The "rulers" were thus a group of one molecule who held the privileges of the state and many other molecules whose will all complied with each other. So it isn't enough to make only the emperor a social democrat, as Mencius did, even if, legally, he realized everything except the enlightenment movement. We must anticipate the legal possibility that the capitalists and landowners, relying on the upper and lower houses, would prevent the emperor from realizing social democracy.

Mencius' theory of state sovereignty seems to have been based on his intuitive knowledge of the existence and purpose of the state from his instincts as a political animal. From this view of the monarch, he drew his theory of institution sovereignty. Democracy in the sense of "the individual before the contract was the body of sovereignty," which was believed around the time of the French Revolution, or democratic systems of government in the sense of a majority government as the Greek philosophers put it, couldn't even have been dreamed of by a people unfortunate enough not to have discovered "majority rule by ballot"—the only way to fully express the will of the state which is completely compatible with its objectives. The means of expressing the will of the nation through the method of majority rule by ballot is the first step in mankind's entry into the utopia of political organization, similar to the invention of the lever in physics. This difference in the first step has greatly delayed political evolution in the East as compared to the West. Of course, the long thousand years of medieval history that it took for the Germanic peoples to inherit their culture after the fall of the Greek and Roman republics was not unlike that of the East: a period of patriarchal rule, a period of warfare, a period of deprivation. (The term "civilized" in the West refers only to the majority government after the French Revolution, and until then, the West was an aristocracy made up of warriors and serfs, just like Japan.)

We have already explained in detail that the state was a real personality, an organism with an evolutionary purpose and ideal, and that even though this personality was real, it was legally owned by the sovereign as an object, like the personality of a slave. Mencius, standing in the midst of this patriarchal rule, is the one who clearly articulated the theory of sovereignty of the state with his "theory of being a mere man," which we mentioned above. In other words, the sovereign has the right to demand obedience because he is a state institution that acts in the interest of the state, with the same social consciousness as the kings of the pen and sword (examples in Japan include Emperor Tenji and the emperor after the Meiji Revolution). Russian or German emperors, who disregarded the interests of the state based on their own petty individual self-interests, instead of acting in a socially responsible manner as state institutions, are, as he said, mere men in law, not monarchs, just like Jie and Zhou. Therefore, he deprived Jie and Zhou of the word "lord," which denoted state authority, in order to argue that killing a mere man who was not a sovereign was not treasonous, as it didn't disregard the purpose of the state. This is exactly in line with the current Russian revolutionary party, looking for an opening to slaughter the tsar, whom they don't regard as an emperor, but a traitor.

In the Japanese imperial family, the emperors have been deeply virtuous, even though the people have not been loyal to them since antiquity. With a few exceptions, such as Emperor Yuryaku and Emperor Buretsu, and during times when they weren't able to be virtuous due to the pressures of other powerful forces, history has shown that there's no doubt they were virtuous in general. However, not all monarchs in the world are the same as the Japanese imperial family. Even the Japanese imperial family didn't have the succession of philosopher monarchs that Plato expected. The Russian and German emperors, for example, have evolved in the modern era and have become clearly aware of the eternal purpose of the state, yet they are still "mere men," having lost their positions as monarchs for the sake of their petty egos. Therefore, in order to maintain a national polity of state sovereignty, the state must be a purely democratic system of government, or a democratic system organized by a privileged individual and an equal majority, otherwise national sovereignty becomes merely a matter of political morality.

In the Imperial Constitution of Meiji year twenty-three, the present emperor has developed this political morality into a legal provision, evolving the supreme authority, which expresses the supreme will of the nation, into an organization of one privileged person and an equal majority, with a noble social nature centering on the interests of the nation. Needless to say, a mere man like the German emperor would, in the presence of such a democratic system of government, act selfishly and without regard for the purpose of the state, as he is now doing. In such a case, it's possible for a revolution to erupt based on the "mere man" theory, in which someone who isn't considered the monarch, which should be a state institution, is regarded as a rebel wearing the crown of the emperor. However, there's no room to imagine that one could evaluate the present emperor, who has become the grand master of the democratic revolution, in light of the historical facts, and infer that future Japanese emperors would lose their noble patriotism, except in the event of psychosis, and in that event the Imperial House Law stipulates the appointment of a regent.

However, what cannot be helped is that today the sovereignty of the state cannot be expressed by the emperor alone. So, even if Emperor Tenji reappears and tries to decree public ownership of economic sources (land in the past, land and production institutions today), as long as the private property system is established, and land and other property of landlords and capitalists are not the property of the emperor, and as long as they are free to rely on the upper and lower houses to deny the emperor's will, he alone cannot wait for the time to realize social democracy as Mencius did. Therefore, the Economic Meiji

Revolution Party seeks to exterminate the economic aristocracy from the will of the nation through a massive enlightenment movement. This would be a completely different kind from the theory of reverence for the emperor, which calls for the restoration of the land and productive institutions to the emperor. What are incompatible with social democracy are the economic aristocrats who plunder the interests of the state and the rebels wearing the crown of the emperor, such as the German emperor, who subvert the purpose of the state. This enlightenment movement is based on a completely free exercise of sovereignty for the state via special privileges, in order to protect its vital institutions for the purpose of survival and evolution of the state itself.

To reiterate, Mencius' statecraft is Plato's counterpart in the East, as well as the source of the East's socialism.

Even if all his closest advisors on both sides praise him as a great man, he should not be promoted immediately. Even if all the chief vassals praise him as an extraordinary person, do not promote him immediately. Even if everyone in the country praises him as an extraordinary person, he should be promoted only when you investigate and judge him to be an extraordinary person. The same applies to dismissal. Even if the king's closest advisors on both sides of him say that he is no good, you should not listen to them immediately. Even if all the chief ministers say he is no good, do not listen to them immediately. Even if all the people in the country say he is no good, you should still carefully examine him for yourself, and only when you clearly see that he is no good should you dismiss that person from office. The same is true in the case of punishment. Even if all the close advisors on the left and right say that he should be put to death, do not listen to them immediately. Even if all the chief ministers say that he should be put to death, do not listen to them immediately. Even if all the people of the land say that he should be put to death, you must examine the matter for yourself and only once you can say, "It is unavoidable. He should be put to death," should you do so. Then you can say, "The monarch did not put him to death, everyone in the country did." Only by taking a prudent attitude, respecting the will of the people in appointments, dismissals, and punishments, is a monarch truly qualified to be the parent of the people.[609]

In an age without the political lever of the ballot, Mencius was not only approving the exercise of the clear social spirit of the "mere man" theory, but also expressing the ideal of a democratic government in which the monarch is the voice of the social will through his political morality. In his writings, too, there is what appears to be an explanation of the primitive state. He said the following:

In a nation, the people are the most precious, followed by the state, which is symbolized by the god of the nation,[610] and the sovereign is the lightest. Therefore, if a man receives the confidence of the people, he becomes a heavenly mandated ruler; if he receives the confidence of such a ruler, he becomes a lord; and if he receives the confidence of a lord, he becomes a high steward. Therefore, if a lord is immoral and endangers the nation, he must be removed from his position and a new wise ruler must be chosen to take his place. This is because the sovereign is less important than the nation. If the offerings for the state land rituals are well-fed, the grain is perfectly clean, and the rituals are held at the right time, but there are still droughts or floods, the tutelary

---

[609] *Mencius*, 1B.7

[610] The god of the five grains.

altar is to be destroyed and rebuilt. This is because the state land is less important than the people.⁶¹¹

The word for "state" they use refers to the national land. This land had evolved through the nomadic period, being settled through agriculture; a certain amount of the land was turned into territories and various gods were worshipped there. If the state land they settled on wasn't suitable for agriculture, it was regarded as being lighter than society, and they would leave. If a lord endangered the nation, they would abolish that sovereign, because the sovereign arose as a battle commander from the clash with other nomadic tribes, or with the original agricultural tribes that had settled on the land first during the nomadic struggle for that state land. The sovereign was thus considered lighter than the land, since the land was their goal. In other words, this was a primitive period of village common ownership, in which the monarch was not the owner of all land and people, as was the case in later periods of private property ownership, and the survival of the state was instinctively the goal. In order to achieve this goal, a temporary institution was created. In his writings, Mencius seems to have explained the reasons for the emergence of this institution, the monarch, and the succession to the throne. He said the following:

> Wan Zhang asked whether it is true that the heavenly emperor Yao gave the land to Shun.⁶¹² Mencius replied, "No, even the heavenly emperor cannot give the land to others without permission." Wan Zhang then asked who gave Shun the power to maintain the land. Mencius replied, "It was given by heaven." Wan Zhang asked if that meant it was given by polite words, a firm command, or some other manner of speech.

---

⁶¹¹ *Mencius*, 7B.14

⁶¹² Wan Zhang was one of Mencius' students.

Mencius replied, "No, heaven says nothing. It merely shows its will through the actions of that person and the results which accompany them." Wan Zhang asked what it means for heaven to show its will by actions and results. Mencius replied with the following. "In the first place, the heavenly emperor can recommend a suitable successor to heaven, but he cannot make heaven grant him the land. It is up to the heaven to decide whether or not to grant him the land. Just as a lord may recommend a suitable person to the emperor, but the emperor may not grant that person the rank of a lord, or a high steward may recommend a suitable person to the lords, but the lords may not grant that person the rank of a high steward. In the past, when Yao recommended Shun to the heavens, the heavens accepted him. Then, when he made him as the regent and clearly presented him to the people, the people accepted him willingly. Thus, Shun became the heavenly emperor.

Thus, I said, 'Heaven says nothing. It merely shows its will through the actions of that person and the results which accompany them.'" Wan Zhang then asked what Mencius meant specifically when he said, "In the past, when Yao recommended Shun to the heavens, the heavens accepted him. Then, when he made him as the regent and clearly presented him to the people, the people accepted him willingly." Mencius replied, "Yao ordered Shun to worship the gods of earth, mountains, rivers, and others, and all accepted him without any natural disasters or accidental deaths. This is fine evidence that the heavens accepted Shun. In addition, when the Shun was given the government, everything was well governed and the people were satisfied with the peace and tranquility. This is fine evidence that the people accepted Shun. This is why I said, 'Even the heavenly emperor cannot give the land to others without permission.' Think about it. Shun served as the regent of Yao for twenty-eight long years. This could not have been done by human power alone. This is truly the will of the heavens. After three years of mourning after the death of Yao, Shun retired to the South River to let Danzhu, the son of Yao, take over the position.[613] However, all the lords of the land who came to seek an audience did not go toward Danzhu, son of Yao, but to Shun. Those who wished for a trial did not go to Yao's son, but to Shun. Those who praised virtues did not praise Yao's son, but praised Shun instead. This is why I can say it was the will of the heavens. Because of this, Shun had no choice but to return to the capital and assume the position of the heavenly emperor for the first time. If he had remained in the palace of Yao after Yao's fall, and had threatened Yao's son so he could forcibly assume the position of heavenly emperor, it would have been considered as theft, not something the heavens had bestowed on him. This is what *The Tai Oath* within *The Classic of History* means when it says, 'Heaven has neither eyes nor ears, so it sees through my people's eyes and hears through my people's ears.'"[614]

Wan Zhang asked if it was true that declining virtue in the Yu era was due to the position of emperor not being given to sages but to the emperors' offspring instead. Mencius replied, "No, that is not true. The position of heavenly emperor could be given to a sage if heaven wishes, or it could be given to a son if heaven wishes. It all depends on the will of heaven. In the past, Shun knew that Yu was wise and recommended him as the heavenly emperor, and had him rule for seventeen years. Yu mourned Shun for three years after he fell, then Yu retreated to the distant Yangcheng in order to let Shun's son, Shangjun, take Shun's

---

[613] "South River" refers to the Yellow River. According to notes by Zhu Xi and others, the capital cities of ancient emperors were all located north of the Yellow River, and thus the Yellow River was called the "South River."

[614] *Mencius*, 5A.5

position. However, all the people followed Yu, much like how all the people followed Shun after Yao's fall. Later, Yu also recommended Yi to the heavens, and he was allowed to rule for seven years. After three years of morning after the fall of Yu, Yi then left for north of Mt. Ji to let Yi's son, Qi, assume his position. This time, however, it was the opposite of before. Those coming for audience or judgement did not follow Yi, but said, 'He is our Lord's son' and went to Qi instead. Those singing praises did not praise Yi, but instead praised Qi, saying, 'He is our Lord's exalted son.' This makes it obvious that Yu did not transfer his position to his son out of self-interest, but instead that it was the will of the heavens.

Now then, Yao's son Danzhu was not unworthy compared to his father, as was Shun's son Shangjun. Many years passed after Shun became Yao's regent and Yu became Shun's prime minister (twenty-eight years for Shun, and seventeen years for Yu), and the people had benefited during that long period, so the hearts of those people did not go to Yao or Shun's sons, but returned to Shun and Yu instead. Contrary to this, Yu's son Qi was a wise man who respectfully followed Yu's path. On the other hand, Yi was only Yu's prime minister for seven years, so there was not as much time for the people to benefit from him like Shun and Yu. Thus, there was no way for the sentiment of the people to go with him. The difference in time spent as prime minister between Yi and the others, and the difference in competency between the emperors' sons were all heaven's will. It is something beyond human power. It is heaven that makes things happen spontaneously, even when we do not want them to, and it is this will that comes spontaneously, even when we do not invite it. By the way, in order for a person to go from a commoner to a heavenly emperor, his virtue must be as high and excellent as Shun or Yu, and he must be recommended by the emperor of the time to heaven. Therefore, though Confucius was as virtuous as

Shun and Yu, because he did not have the recommendation of the heavenly emperor, he suffered the lifelong misfortune of never becoming a ruler of the land. Once the heavenly emperor's position becomes hereditary by the will of the heavens, heaven's will becomes predetermined, and it is only in the case of a malevolent and inhumane ruler like Jie or Zhou that the heavenly emperor, who succeeded his parents, is abandoned and abolished by the heavens. Thus, men like Yi, Yi Yin, and the Duke of Zhou could never become heavenly emperors, despite being of outstanding virtue. Therefore, Yi Yin became the prime minister of monarch Tang of Shang and helped him become the ruler of the land. When Tang collapsed, his son Tai Ding died before he could take the throne, so his younger brother Wai Bing took the throne, but he died after only two years, and his younger brother Zhong Ren took the throne, but he also died after four years.

Tai Ding's son, Tai Jia, took the throne, but he broke the common law established by Tang, so Yi Yin had no choice but to exile him for three years to a place called Tong, where the tomb of Tang was located. Tai Jia did regret his actions, blamed himself for his misdeeds, and devoted himself to cultivation and benevolence, and so the three years passed. He then listened carefully to what Yi Yin taught him and was able to return to the capital of Bo and assume the position of the heavenly emperor. In Yi Yin's case, he did not become a heavenly emperor of his own will. The reason the Duke of Zhou could not become the heavenly emperor is the same as for Yi and Yi Yin. As Confucius put it, 'Yao and Shun gave up their position to sages, while the Xia, Shang, and Zhou dynasties generally had the rulers give their positions to their offspring, but it was all the will of the heavens. The logic was the same for all.' It was absolutely not a decline in virtue."[615]

---

[615] Ibid., 5A.6

Let's take away the formal adjectives and the "honoring the past" type of speech from the previous two chapters. Such things as how many years he mourned, how many years he served as prime minister, where he retired to so that his children could succeed him, his recommendation to the heavens, and his handing down of his throne were, of course, created out of the idea of respecting the past during the Confucius and Mencius eras. The letters and words used were also based on the ideology of the time, so the superfluous branches and leaves can be discarded.

In the era of Yao and Shun, which they considered ideal, people could not descend to the fields until Yu fixed the flooding, and they still dug holes in the mountainsides to make their dwellings. It was such a purely primitive period that they made their beds in trees to avoid being attacked by animals at night. There's no need to discuss this. Moreover, in China at that time, food was especially plentiful, so life was peaceful, equal, and without the slightest struggle. Thus, in a primitive village based on happy primitive equality without such struggles, chiefs did not arise to seize the land as they did in later times. Rather, as Yao and Shun said, meek, baby-like persons held the position of village elders and handled simple incidents. (In the republican and egalitarian primitive times of the uncivilized Germanic peoples, who competed for the land through nomadism and agriculture, they had the strongest fighters as their chiefs.) This was the very earliest form of monarchy, and when the chief died, another competent person took care of the incidents without having to give up the throne or step down to allow his children to succeed him, as was done in later times. Therefore, the praise, visits for audience, and requests for trial were, of course, fictions of a later generation. Things such as ". . . had threatened Yao's son so he could forcibly assume the position of heavenly emperor, it would have been considered as theft," are nothing more than ideological blunders that arise from a respect for the past.

However, by the time of Yu, the population had grown so large and the mountainsides so narrow that the people had to move down to the plains and devote their energies to flood protection. By this time, society had evolved to the point where it had to have a solid political structure. Succession to the throne occurred as a result of this evolutionary stage. The larger organism known as society, like the smaller individual organisms, evolves or degenerates its institutions as is necessary for its evolution and survival according to Lamarck's theory of use and disuse. The social consciousness, which evolved from an instinctive and unconscious existence to a conscious one, gradually expanded its awareness by following lineage. Therefore, people began to define noble and plebeian by the closeness of one's bloodline (see the section in *The So-Called Theory of Japan's National Polity and its Restorative Principle of Revolution* where we discuss the principle of lineage), and this became the bloodline worship of "I am the son of my lord." The need for a constant monarch due to constant wars for the survival of the social unit (see *The Theory of Biological Evolution and Social Philosophy*), combined with the demand to avoid social chaos by constantly fighting for the throne whenever the monarch died, led to the age of dynastic succession. In the words of Confucius, quoted in Mencius' writings,

> Yao and Shun gave up their position to sages, while the Xia, Shang, and Zhou dynasties generally had the rulers give their positions to their offspring, but it was all the will of the heavens. The logic was the same for all.

This is a good recognition of the fact that justice evolves in accordance with the evolution of a society. The fact that the sovereignty of the state was hereditary in this patriarchal age of the lineage principle was based on the evolutionary needs of the society, and unless, as in the case of Jie and Zhou, it seriously violated the goals and ideals of the society, the personality of the state would not be invoked in accordance with the "mere man" theory. The sovereignty of the state was clearly and unequivocally expressed in the words, "No heavenly emperor can give the land to another without permission." This shows an elimination of the idea in monarchical sovereignty that the land and people are objects owned by the monarch for the benefit of the monarch.

Mencius endorsed everything based on the religious belief that "everything depends on heaven's will," in the same way that we believe that "natural law" drives everything under the heavens through the philosophy of cosmic teleology and the science of biological evolution. To understand the succession to the throne as if it were due to the injustice of the monarch is the argument of a dogmatic blind man, as shown when Wan Zhang asked Mencius if "it was true that declining virtue in the Yu era was due to the position of emperor not being given to sages but to the emperors' offspring instead." Like us, he was determined to see the laws of social evolution before his eyes, and he resolutely rejected the claims of such men. "The position of heavenly emperor could be given to a sage if heaven wishes, or it could be given to a son if heaven wishes."

"Heaven" grabbed the position of sovereign from the many nobles and gave it to the wise emperor we have now. "Heaven" further commands in the Imperial Constitution to give the throne to the emperor's children for the purpose of the nation's survival and evolution, even if their descendants are not as wise as the present emperor. To look at the present situation, in which the heavens have deprived the foolish Russian emperor and are refusing to give the son of the German emperor his kingdom (Germany would be a pure republic by the time the current prince could inherit it),[616] and to immediately think of social democracy as an enemy of the emperor, is to realize that Lamarck's theory of use and disuse is a principle that applies to the larger organism of society as well. Though, if heaven doesn't give rank to the wise and

---

[616] This may have seemed like a prophecy at the time, but it became reality. In Germany, their defeat in World War I was followed by a revolution and the abolition of the imperial regime.

not to a ruler's children, what was the purpose of the Meiji Revolution and the Imperial Constitution? Institutions arise because there is an evolution of society that requires their emergence, and when evolution requires their continuation, it creates continuing institutions. The Japanese emperor is an institution that arose and continues for the purpose of the nation's survival and evolution.

Indeed, Mencius' idealistic theory of the state is a magnificent one, and he lives up to his name as the Plato of the East. The Japanese, however, were an agricultural people who had already plundered the land through battles when they migrated to this land, so they had experienced the primitive, republican, and egalitarian times of the Yao and Shun dynasties while wandering in other lands. It can be imagined that they had evolved to the point when "the heavens bestow rank to their children." This succession to the throne, unlike Mencius' ideal, was not a system of institutions that exercised the right to rule the state as we know it today. The patriarchal state inherited the right to rule in the sense of ownership over the state, which was property (as explained earlier, the Spring and Autumn period and the Warring States period described by Mencius was also a patriarchal state). The historical record of the Japanese people was written from the patriarchal state, not from the primitive, republican, and egalitarian times of the uncivilized Germanic peoples as recorded and transmitted by the Romans. So, even when Confucianism came to be taught in later generations, there was not enough history to understand Mencius' original theory of statecraft, and thus the idea of the revolution decreed by heaven when the incumbent emperor is found lacking in moral virtue was treated merely as a sanction for disobedience to the political morality of the monarch.[617]

---

[617] Kita interprets this to mean that the Japanese of the past didn't understand Mencius' ideas, but this isn't exactly the case. It is said that when Confucius' ideas were being spread around, Mencius' concept of dynastic cycles was dangerous, and so was removed

However, the ancestors of the present emperors, although they have long been emperors in the sense of patriarchal monarchs, have never, with only a few exceptions, ignored Mencius' political morality. In contrast, the patriarchs who emerged in medieval history, such as shogun and lords, were always solemnly sanctioned as they prospered or perished in accordance with the theory of "mere man." In this context, the "mere man theory" refers to the rebellion of a slave, the state, which, in the eyes of the patriarchal monarchs, still had no legal personality, against its cruel and violent slave owners, for its own biological purpose. The slave evolved gradually toward recognized legal personhood through repeated rebellions. In the same way, the nation evolved through the patriarchal period of medieval history by repeating the "mere man theory," and finally the purpose and ideal of the nation became the consciousness of all molecules of the nation, patriotism became the moral purpose, and the state became a legal personality and the source of all laws and commands.

However, what couldn't be helped was that when the patriarchal state of medieval Japan was swept away by the Meiji Revolution's social democracy, the classical texts *Kojiki* and *Nihon Shoki* began with the records of the patriarchal monarchy, so the ideal Confucian theory of state sovereignty was not understood. Therefore, even if only for a short while, discussions began of restoring the meaning of the word emperor as a patriarchal monarch, as it was understood in the time of Emperor Jinmu. In order to deny the aristocratic class the right of life and death over the land and the people, they were forced to extend the rights of the emperor over the entire nation, to import Western post-revolutionary jurisprudence and statecraft, and to insist on a restorative revolutionary theory that constantly defied nationalism and nationalist demands, until they finally put a stop to it in the Imperial Constitution of Meiji

---

from Confucian teachings. The fact that they thought of dynastic cycles as dangerous shows that they understood the concept very well.

year twenty-three. Those that struggled most against this "theory of national polity" were the current political parties, which stemmed from a system of private property that had gained economic independence and held up the demands of democracy as a direct translation of the bloody French Revolution. Social democracy thanks them for this time when they were not yet corrupt!

This gratitude expresses our infinite contempt for the present-day podium socialists. It should be clear from the explanation above that podium socialism has no theory, no organization, no claims, and no ideals in economics, ethics, or any philosophy of science. And although they advocate "state socialism," they are completely ignorant of the nature of the state and its legal principles, which is simply astonishing. See Mr. Kanjiro Higuchi's *State Socialism's New Pedagogy*. He says the following:

> It is a historical fact that Japan is prone to socialism. Our country as a whole forms a family. With all due respect, the imperial family is the patriarch of that family. The masses are all equal before the emperor, and when the emperor looks upon his people, he treats them all equally and with benevolence. If this is so, then the idea that the land belongs to the family of Japan has never changed. During the reign of the 37th emperor Kotoku, he confiscated the fiefs of powerful families and gave them a stipend instead,[618] but people did not think this was strange at all. The prohibition of the landowners from swallowing up the small farmers and allowing the general public to choose their favorite occupation was indeed a socialist revolution, carried out with the same benevolent spirit based on the idea of the whole country as one family. Read *Commentary on the Ryo*.[619] When a person turned five

---

[618] Called "jikifu." (食封).

[619] *Commentary on the Ryo* is a commentary on decrees made by direct imperial order. It was compiled to unify the interpretation of the "decree." The text of the *Yoro Code* can

years old, they were given an allotted rice field measuring two tan (1983.48 meters squared) if male, and two thirds of that size (1322.19 meters squared) if female.[620] When the person dies, that land is returned to the government. Later, things like the koden and manorialism were developed,[621] and we did enter into feudalism, but it was still the emperor who gave land. At the time of the Meiji Revolution, all feudal lords large and small throughout Japan renounced their ownership of their territories and said they would return them to the emperor. This was a beautiful concept that could not be found in any foreign country. Land and property belonged to the emperor. It is up to the patriarch to confiscate it from the children of the family for the sake of the great house of Japan. It is the virtue of the child to return it to the family. However, when confiscating sweets once given to a child, it is a mercy of the parents to give the child a toy or sugary treat. This is why a stipend was given to the large and small feudal lords. In our country, such reforms are relatively smooth and easy. There may be occasional disputes between children, but it would not be difficult for the patriarch to curb such disputes with a single roar . . .

Ah, anyone hearing such words feels the chill of embarrassment run down his spine!

---

be understood via this commentary.

[620] The quoted passage is from *Nation Socialism's New Pedagogy*, 364. "Turned five years old" is what the text in Higuchi's book says, but the actual Yoro Code (Denryo 9) says "Allotted rice fields shall be given of two tan to men. Women, two thirds of that size. Those five and under receive nothing." (*Nihon Shiso Taikei 3: Ritsuryo* [Tokyo: Iwanami Shoten, 1976], 240). This means "six years old" is correct.

[621] "Koden" refers to the rice paddies granted to persons of national merit under the Ritsuryo system.

Shame on you! Shame on you! If this is what "state socialism" is, it isn't nationalism, and it isn't socialism. It's absolute and unlimited monarchism! How can anyone save face when they boast "our state socialism is based on our history, our national identity, and our country's current situation, and not the literal socialism that is being spread in the world"? The Japanese people are a people who regret their small physical size, but they aren't "children" who stop fighting when the emperor gives them "toys" or "sugary treats." Children with mustaches and beards, children with bald heads, children with babies dwelling inside their bodies, decrepit senior children, children with grandchildren! Descendants of the "one eternal lineage" can become emperor, no matter how old they are. However, parents who are babies, parents who are ten years old didn't give birth to the modern state socialists as the parents of a family. Mr. Hirobumi Ito is a child of the current emperor's noble blood, not a compatriot of His Imperial Highness the Crown Prince. Taro Katsura is not an awesome person who would be the son of His Imperial Highness the Crown Prince and a brother to the emperor's grandchildren. This isn't "our nation's history" or "our nation's national polity." It isn't! No matter where you search in the world, there has never been such a history that tickles one's funny bone, such a national polity that makes one want to laugh so much. Clearly answer this. If you say, "The land assets are the property of the emperor," and "sweets once given," then tell us in what year, during the reign of which emperor were all the production institutions of steam and electricity "given" to the current capitalists? "This is a beautiful concept that could not be found in any foreign country," you say. "It's the patriarch's right to confiscate from their children, since Japan is one large family," you say. Well then, what right do you have to take the capital of foreign capitalists however you please and add it to the imperial budget, to advocate the extravagances of foreign aristocrats, and to then confiscate their treasures and decorate the emperor's crown with them? Answer us. Needless to say, this isn't limited to Mr. Higuchi alone. Living in a savage village in the Orient, people such as Mr. Aizan Yamaji, a "baby" with a figure-eight beard who created the principles and platform of the current "State Socialist Party," do not understand the social democracy of the Meiji Revolution, and so they selfishly advocate the economic principle of reverence for the emperor and expulsion of foreigners, which is to consecrate the right to production.

Social democracy is a nationalism and cosmopolitanism that inherits the full development of private property and individualism, leading to the ideal independence of the state and absolute freedom of the individual person. Without the process of the social evolution of individualism, in which all the members of a nation become the subjects of private property, nationalism and cosmopolitanism—which seek to evolve society into one comprising all people as molecules through free and equal competition, development, and mutual support—will remain only a pipe dream. This is why the Taika theory of land nationalization remained a pipe dream. If all the molecules of society had not awakened, no matter how lofty the ideals of a single molecule, Emperor Tenji, might have been, a society composed of sleeping elements would still have had no choice but to fall into that ancient sleep. When the emperor alone awakens like a "parent" and all forty-five million people have no self-consciousness but are only alive as "babies," then "I am the nation." Unless we say that the forty-five million are beasts existing outside the nation, the nation of unconscious babies will still be an unconscious nation, or else it will remain a primitive communist society. Remember, however, that the first process of evolution from a primitive communist society was precisely the sprout of a monarchy, in which all land and property were under the ownership of a chief. All are not the philosopher-kings that Plato envisioned. The only ones who realized Mencius' social democracy as an ideal, in high moral tone and without regret, even within the Japanese imperial line, were the heroes of the Taika Revolution and the Meiji Revolution.

After the heroes of the Taika Revolution, when mediocre monarchs who did not understand their heroic enterprise emerged, the socialism of the Taika was overthrown and the land that Emperor Tenji had made state property became the property of the monarch. The monarch then gave the land to his favored vassals, donated it to temples, and sold it as a transfer of the monarch's property rights to the local nobles and provincial governors, which had been set up as a state institution. There is no room to believe that Japan's emperors, who were at the forefront of social evolution, disobeyed social evolution and degenerated toward antiquity. The words and deeds of the state socialists are merely a kind of plaything, a scheme that many of the rebellious subjects also toyed with, distancing themselves from the emperor even though they respected him.

What must be clearly explained is whether public ownership of the land means either national ownership of the land or sovereignty of the land. Were the steam and electric-powered machines plundered by the capitalists a monopoly of society's production or a theft of the emperor's labor?

Slaves! Oh, gathering of slaves! We should rather work toward the relief of the rights of capitalists and landlords in the name of national sovereignty than enjoy ancient slavery with so-called "state socialism." They speak of "state" and "society" without understanding anything, lacking even the knowledge of the "babies" they call themselves. Socialism means that all parts of society are subject to property rights. Nationalism means that the whole of the state is the subject of the rights to which the benefits belong. Today's economic aristocracy is one where a small minority of society is the subject of property rights, and the vast majority has nothing other than the right to use their property—and the state socialists, instead of evolving from an economic aristocracy to an economic democracy, seek to revert to an economic monarchy in law. The current economic class state is one in which the small minority are the subject to which benefits are attributed, while the majority are victims of war and poverty. Does state socialism not try to evolve from an economic class state into an economic civic state, and instead attempt to legally establish absolute and unlimited patriarchal rights, like back during the time when the very bodies of the people were the property of the monarch?

Answer further. Do you, the members of the State Socialist Party, offer your wives into the ownership of Emperor Yuryaku? Do you offer your parents to be destroyed as property under the ownership of Emperor Buretsu? Surely you would say no. Then this is a despicable act that must be discarded: to toy with the emperor in order to benefit one's own claim. Not to mention that this is the very "disrespect" they shout all the time. Rather, they would use this arrow of "disrespect" to fire at the Social Democrats, making them nothing more than savages. Mr. Kuwata,[622] who always opposes social democracy with his "nationalism," is the most blatant example of this (he even reportedly sought membership in the State Socialist Party of Yamaji, but was rejected). He inferred the behavior of the Japanese Socialist Party from the struggle between the German emperor and the German Social Democrats, saying that the Social Democrats were dangerous to the national polity and were made up of those who behaved disrespectfully toward the emperor. These rebels wearing the imperial crown, who have deviated from the status of a state institution like the German emperor and have become "mere men," do not allow the Social Democrats the honor of sharing the same meal as them (which is said would be an enviable position for Social Democrats). The Social Democrats also never once gave these rebels the utmost respect, and in fact they proposed to abolish impunity in the criminal code, which was defeated because they had been a minority for some time (this is where the Social Democrats cannot help but be discouraged). However, the emperor of Japan is not an ordinary man to be placed on the same level as the likes of the German emperor. The position of emperor is an important state institution, which the "heavens" granted to the "wise" current emperor through the Meiji Revolution, and to his "son" of one eternal lineage through the Imperial Constitution.

---

[622] Kumazo Kuwata. See note 66 in volume one, chapter three.

Anything that goes against the state institution is treason against the state. Social democracy can't be treason against the state, but only an effort for the survival and evolution of the state through the full and free exercise of its sovereignty. It's always important to remember that, though the word "emperor" may be the same form and pronunciation in this language, the content and meaning of the word is different throughout different regions and time periods (read *The So-Called Theory of Japan's National Polity and its Restorative Principle of Revolution*).

The previous explanation shows that so-called "state socialism" not only does not have any fundamental ideas that can be called socialism, but also has no understanding of the "state," which it uses as a crown before socialism. And this assertion expresses that what is now called "socialism" is in fact a purely utopian cosmopolitanism—in other words, an individualist position, flailing blindly in its attempt to refute the state without even understanding the "state."

The current so-called "non-war theory of the Japanese Socialist Party" is, as some call it, a religious theory of nonresistance. However, this religious theory of nonresistance, like Tolstoy's nonresistance, repudiates even the class struggle of the lower classes against the upper classes and leads to the rejection of socialism. It's a cosmopolitanism that posits the atomic individual and immediately seeks to unite the billions of people of today—yet this world unification principle endorses Napoleon's dream of an individualist French Revolution. It would force Japan to give up its independence in the face of Russian aggression and to become a soldier under Napoleon in the event of Japanese aggression against China and Korea. Utopian cosmopolitanism rests on the assumptions of individualism. Individualism becomes Napoleon when it ignores other nations, and the Jewish people when it forgets its own nation.

For this reason, we affirm that social democracy cannot find a single reason to approve of those who deny the state, even in the most vehement terms (and Marx did so in vehement terms). This affirmation leads us to a further affirmation—the First International's repudiation of the Russo-Japanese War, which took as its preconception the fiery words of Marx's Communist Manifesto, and resolved on the basis of the words spoken and actions taken by the individualists of the Japanese Socialist Party, is simply not enough to be worth adopting.

We, the weak, don't believe that we can oppose with a single stroke of the pen the resolutions of all the socialist parties of the world. However, it would be a terrible mistake for all the socialist parties of the world today to be enamored of Marx's greatness. His greatness is only in the field of economics, where he gave a historical account of the capital of the early modern machine industry, and in the field of history, where he discovered that the evolution of society was due to the class struggle. The theory of value is false, and the theory of class struggle is not a spiritual consideration. Social democracy is not an invention of the nineteenth century. It is a great idea that has flowed from the sources of philosophical history since man began civilization. Plato's *Republic* is its source. In ancient times, the great idea of social democracy was land nationalism, since land was the only economic source, but in modern times, since capital became the most common economic source, it has come to refer to public ownership of land and capital together.

There is class competition as well as state competition in the evolution of society. Did Plato advocate the theory of land nationalism only for the state to be repudiated? Socialists of all nations! Plato said, "Those outside the state are either God or beasts."[623] If one doesn't deny that Plato's words are consistent with today's scientific socialism, which holds that all ideas, morals, races, and peoples are socially created at all times, then how could one deny the state, or deny national competition? Every member of the Universal Socialist Party must be a god or else a beast. Tolstoy, who, on the basis of his utopian

---

[623] This same quote is attributed to Aristotle in volume 3, chapter 5, which is in fact correct, as it is from his *Politics*.

cosmopolitanism, sees the primitive, republican, and egalitarian world as the home of God, does not seem to be God, since he had sexual intercourse, and has never sworn to God to stop, even today. Like the German emperor, Bebel is not a god because he has no choice but to perform excretion through bodily functions. In order to reach God, who does not have sex nor excrete, mankind cannot exist individually like animals, but must exist in the state, as Plato said (see *The Theory of Biological Evolution and Social Philosophy*, in which we discuss the utopia that mankind will reach through evolution). Is it possible for there to be no state competition, even though we already exist in the state? Of course, national competition is something we must try and escape as quickly as possible. However, we have yet to do so in reality, just as we can't stop excreting or having sex. Everything is socially created. Therefore, just as class struggles are fought today on the basis of class morality, class knowledge, and class appearance, so today's national competition for national morality, national knowledge, and national appearance can't be avoided among nations, where class segregation has become more severe and assimilation is more difficult.

Social democracy is idealized as the extinction of national competition along with class competition. In reality, however, the absence of equality of material protection and the lack of diffusion of spiritual development in the state has led to class warfare in the name of socialism. In the same way (see *The Ethical Ideals of Socialism* and *The Theory of Biological Evolution and Social Philosophy*), national competition can't be ignored in the name of socialism until the great differences in economic conditions and the enormous variations in spiritual activity are wiped out by the realization of a world federation and a world language (such as Esperanto).[624] Just as no one can

---

[624] Esperanto is a constructed language developed by a Polish-Jewish linguist named L. L. Zamenhof, who wanted it to be a universal language for international communication. The same year this book was written, the Esperanto Association was established in

transcend class truth, goodness, and beauty aside from the very best, so too is it impossible for an ordinary citizen who has little contact with foreign races and peoples, and who does not understand foreign languages and ideas, to transcend national morality, knowledge, or appearance. In other words, the individual's relationship to the world must be through class and nation. Just as class struggle is caused by class segregation, so national competition is caused by this very national conflict.

However, the Socialist Party of Japan members who stood in the midst of the intense victory fever and advocated non-war, and the First International, which used their words and deeds to repudiate the Russo-Japanese War, are in fact grossly ignorant of the facts. They understand the Russo-Japanese War as if it was simply the result of capitalists with interests in Manchuria and Korea doing as they pleased. It is a direct lament to think that Japan's relatively small Mitsui and Iwasaki could have such power today. It's true that the South African War was highly motivated by British capitalist interests, and the Spanish-American War was motivated by American capitalist interests. However, very little of the Russo-Japanese War was motivated by Japanese capitalist interests. We assert that the main motive of the Russo-Japanese War was the clash of national authorities, and that the underlying ideology that demanded the war was precisely the continuation of the theory of reverence for the emperor and expulsion of foreigners.

We cannot bear the pain of the coldness and cruelty that is invoked in the name of scientific research in this case. Indeed, such an affirmation goes so violently against the sentiments of admiration held for the non-war theorists, who struggled against the whole of Japan—but this assertion comes from another, from the assertion that all socialist movements must stem from an

---

Japan. The insistence on Esperanto as the world language was maintained in the later *Outline of Principles of the Japanese Reform Law* and *Outline of the Japanese Reform Law*.

enlightened foundation. The war was not fought for the honor of soldiers. Nor was it fought for the benefit of capitalists. It was fought for the very spirit of the Japanese people, who believed in the principle of reverence for the king and exclusion of foreigners. Unless ethno-psychology teaches that the national spirit can be transformed in a couple of decades, it goes without saying that the Japanese people have inherited the principle of reverence for the emperor and expulsion of foreigners. If it was a matter of capitalist interest, all they had to do was simply open up Manchuria. The explosion in Hibiya Park was a clear manifestation of the demands of the Russo-Japanese War.[625] It was indeed a call for "reverence for the emperor and expulsion of foreigners," as one European critic put it, "a Tatar nation dressed in civilized clothes." Humiliating diplomacy! This single sentence was more than the interest of the capitalist class. They shouted, "The fact that Japan is still on equal terms with Russia and have not been able to bring her to her knees completely is due to poor diplomacy, for which the authority of the nation has been insulted."[626] "The fact that the color of the map merely changed by half of Sakhalin was not enough to avenge their former grudge and did not show that Russia was made to submit."[627] Since the lower classes remained in a low evolutionary state

---

[625] The failure to obtain reparations at the peace conference in the Russo-Japanese War led to an outburst of dissatisfaction among the citizens, who had endured the burden of war, and riots broke out. In Hibiya, a convention was held to oppose the Treaty of Portsmouth, which led to a riot (Hibiya incendiary incident).

[626] Given Japan's capabilities at the time, it's impossible to deny that the people's assertions at the time were excessive demands. This is because Foreign Minister Jutaro Komura was skillful in his negotiations regarding the peace conference in Portsmouth. However, it's unavoidable that the people, who had little information available to them, felt this way.

[627] This "former grudge" probably refers to the return of the Liaodong Peninsula, which was forcibly returned due to the Tripartite Intervention during the Sino-Japanese War.

regarding all knowledge and morals, and had little contact with foreign thought, language, and races and peoples outside of Japan, they most sincerely died for this theory of reverence for the emperor and expulsion of foreigners. To the so-called socialists who blame the Russo-Japanese War on the capitalists, who were still in their infancy, I say the following. Just as the "theory of national polity" makes the laughable claim that only Yoshitoki and Takauji were rebellious subjects, and that the hundreds of thousands who defeated the emperor's army were his loyal subjects and righteous warriors, the same "theory of national polity" logic remains when claiming that the Russo-Japanese War was fought for Mitsui, Iwasaki, Nogi, and Togo, that forty-five million people were compelled to start a war and became assault troops and suicide squads for this reason.

There is no uselessness or fallacy in natural law. The theory of reverence for the emperor and expulsion of foreigners is precisely the barbaric assertion of a nation's authority by its own personality. When an individual person awakens to his authority, he becomes a warrior and tries to assert his authority over other individuals. In the same way, a nation that has escaped from under the ownership of its monarchs, having awakened to the authority of its real personality, ignores the authority of other nations and seeks to exert its own authority over them—this is imperialism. There is no uselessness or fallacy in natural law. Socialism clearly inherits the evolution of imperialism in its assertion of the authority of the state. Just as there would be no economic freedom and equality in socialism without the evolution of private property systems, which assert the authority of the individual, there would be no socialism of a world federation based on freedom and equality for all nations without the evolution of nationalism, which asserts the authority of the state.

The term "imperialism" was first called out in response to Napoleon's individualistic cosmopolitanism asserting the authority of the state—and yet, what's happening now? The social democrats, who advocate a cosmopolitanism made up of units based on nations are today, on the contrary, rejecting the state and adopting Napoleon's cosmopolitanism, which is supported by the individualism of the French Revolution. Incredible that capitalist and landowner classes, which are individualists, stand for an imperialism that asserts the authority of the state! Ah, because of the great confusion in the world of ideas, enemies and allies are standing under the same banner.

Without individualism, there would be no socialism built on the authority of all individuals. Without imperialism, there would be no world federation built on the authority of all nations. Therefore, social democracy was a pipe dream for the "commoners," all of whom were slave-like subjects of aristocrats and monarchs and had no personal authority. Similarly, in a set of nations that serve only a mighty power and do not understand their own national authority, there can be a Roman Empire, but not a world federation. In this respect, Isoo Abe, in his book *Switzerland,* is, of course, mistaken when he describes Switzerland as the ideal country on earth and regrets that it has a military. Such a country, independent and propped up between the bayonets of other countries, is not an ideal state. What makes Switzerland ideal is its national authority, which disappears once it falls due to its meager armaments. When all personalities awaken to authority and assert their freedom, they don't first respect the freedom of others, but ignore those freedoms for the sake of their own freedom. Thus, before exercising the freedom to respect other freedoms in one's own freedom, as in the freedom of democracies, one must first attack and defeat the nobility, a freedom that oppresses other freedoms. Today, the "state" has been freed from the hands of monarchs and has evolved slightly in freedom—and it has still been less than two hundred years since the cry of "patriotism" in Europe. In Japan today, only five or six decades have passed since the Meiji Revolution—we are currently a small aristocracy known as Japan. However, we praise our shaking off of the oppression of the larger aristocrats known as the Slavs, as well as our assertion of our freedom, contrary to the decision of the First International. Freedom, however, must not only be freedom to respect one's own freedom, but freedom which recognizes the freedom of others as well. We must firmly stop the freedom of the Japanese nation to practice its aristocratic and barbaric customs from further evolving into the democratic freedom of civilization and trampling on the freedom of China and Korea. The social-democratic doctrine of non-war shall be attributed to future efforts.

Therefore, without national freedom caused by foreign oppression, socialism cannot be realized. A savage village of the Orient, living under the threat of "the theory of national polity," with no authority of the state, is no different from a savage village of the South Pacific and has no more right to demand a position in the world federation.

www.ingramcontent.com/pod-product-compliance
Lightning Source LLC
Chambersburg PA
CBHW030244010526
44107CB00030B/1325/J